Retailing

TONY KENT AND OGENYI OMAR

palgrave
macmillan

First published 2003 by
PALGRAVE MACMILLAN
Houndmills, Basingstoke, Hampshire RG21 6XS and 175 Fifth Avenue, New York, N.Y. 10010
Companies and representatives throughout the world

PALGRAVE MACMILLAN is the global academic imprint of the Palgrave Macmillan division of St. Martin's Press, LLC and of Palgrave Macmillan Ltd. Macmillan® is a registered trademark in the United States, United Kingdom and other countries. Palgrave is a registered trademark in the European Union and other countries.

ISBN 0–333–99768–9 hardback
ISBN 0–333–99769–7 paperback

This book is printed on paper suitable for recycling and made from fully managed and sustained forest sources.

A catalogue record for this book is available from the British Library.

10   9   8   7   6   5   4   3   2   1
12 11 10 09 08 07 06 05 04 03

Printed and bound in Great Britain by
J. W. Arrowsmith Ltd, Bristol

Contents

Acknowledgements

The authors and publishers wish to acknowledge the following for permission to reproduce copyright material:

Simon & Schuster Inc. for material from Michael E. Porter, *Competitive Strategy* (© The Free Press 1980, 1998); John Wiley & Sons for material from G. Johnson (ed.) *Business Strategy in Retailing*, and also from S. McKie, *E-business Best Practices: Leveraging*; Henry Stewart Publications for material from Keith Dugmore in *Journal of Targeting, Measurement and Analysis for Marketing*; The World Advertising Research Centre for material from *The Retail Pocket Book 2001*; Roland Berger Strategy Consultants for material from *Category Management Best Practices Report*; Emerald Publishing for material from its journals, *International Journal of Retail and Distribution Management*, *International Marketing Review* and *Fashion Marketing and Management*; Blackwells for the diagram on page 250 from *Developments in the Management of Human Resources* by J. Storey; *Financial Times* for excerpts on pages 245, 246, 344, 265; J. Sainsbury for the layout of their Greenwich store; Ashgate Publishing Limited for the diagram on page 346 from P.G. Eibl, *Computerised Vehicle Routing and Scheduling and Road Transport*, published by Avebury; Kogan Page for diagrams from M. Stone and B. Foss, *Successful Customer Relationship Marketing* and A. Ruston and J. Oxley, *A Handbook of Logistics and Distribution Management*; Palgrave Macmillan for a diagram from *Retail Power Plays* by A. Wileman and M. Jary.

Every effort has been made to contact all the copyright-holders, but if any have been inadvertently omitted the publishers will be pleased to make the necessary arrangement at the earliest opportunity.

Preface

The retail industry is increasingly imposing itself in a number of fields. In the economy it is a major employer and creator of wealth; it provides many opportunities for consumption, not only of products but also of experiences. Shopping is a leisure activity for many, an agreeably social way to spend time (although families may disagree on this). In a changing world, retailers are a reassuringly familiar part of our everyday landscape, and retail brands provide consistent, if sometimes disappointing, reference points. If anything retailers at least partly shape these changes, driven by the energy of competition to offer new products and services in enjoyable and occasionally entertaining shopping environments. And with the Internet, these physical environments can now virtually extend into our homes. The industry is nothing if not relevant.

For these reasons the retail industry has come more specifically to the attention of academics. At its most prosaic, where primary and manufacturing industries have declined and fallen, distribution has remained in place and the focus simply shifts. However the industry has become more complex offering extensions to existing fields of study as well as inviting enquiry into new ones. Some highlights stand out; the development and application of information technology has been a key driver of change in critical areas of customer service and in the management of suppliers and merchandise; and brand management has become an altogether more sophisticated activity as has locational planning.

Given this context the purpose of this book is to provide a study of retailing from a Eurocentric perspective. As emphasis is placed on independent student learning, so the need has emerged for an accessible textbook that embraces the main issues facing the retail industry. In part, then, the book is designed to meet the needs of student learners, providing both underpinning knowledge and analytical and conceptual tools. In this respect, a specific feature is the relation of theory to practice in the retail industry. For the same reasons, it aims to shine some light into some of the more obscure corners of the industry so that students are made aware of the linkages and relationships between different functions and activities. Where appropriate, examples have been drawn from countries outside the UK to emphasise the differences both in retail practice and the application of underlying principles.

The other objective of the book has been to support the traditional management pedagogical approach of lectures and seminars. The book is structured to move from higher level and external issues to more detailed internal and developmental ones:

Part 1 begins with an overview of retailing and continues into an analysis of the macro environment. Chapter 3 introduces the process of distribution, and Chapters 4 and 5 deal in more detail with competitive retail strategies and the internationalisation of retailing.

Part 2 develops the key functions of marketing, financial planning and control, location and human resources and their relationship to strategic-level decisions.

Part 3 deals with the issues concerning merchandise management in more detail. This is an area that deserves close attention, and the authors draw on their retail management experience to define the *sequence* of management activities as it takes place in the industry. The section opens with a chapter on *product planning and selection*, progresses logically into *supply-chain management*. Decisions about which products and from where they are to be sourced relate closely to the next chapter on *inventory management and control*: the movement of products through the company's internal distribution chain and into the store. The final chapter assesses *pricing* policies and merchandise pricing practices available to retailers. Therefore this section deals with the process of merchandise management from planning to in-store availability.

Part 4 concerns the store, or operational environment. Chapter 13 distinguishes the design process from management approaches before moving to discuss operational functions. Chapters on communication and service develop customer-focused issues that have a bearing on the store itself.

Part 5 introduces information technology and non-store retailig including e-commerce, and new developments. This needing recognises the constantly changing and dynamic nature of these functions.

Each chapter is supported by a case study, with specific questions for classroom discussion, as well as more general questions on the substance of the chapter to stimulate further thinking about an exciting and dynamic industry.

Many people have contributed their time, views and suggestions in the course of preparing and writing this book. Colleagues and students at the London Institute have provided numerous insights into the retail industry over the past six years. In particular we should like to thank Jonathan Baker, Helen Beswick, Alan Hirst and Dawn Lavelle for their comments. Professor Barry Davies and Dr Charles Blankson have contributed valuable advice. We have benefited from considerable help and advice, too, from the retail industry in meetings with long-suffering training managers in London, we extend our particular thanks to Alexandra Logan. Other experts have contributed generously in different fields, and here David Zinkin, John Serocold, Emma Brown and Richard Kent have been most helpful. Most of all we should thank Elizabeth-Anne and Victoria for their forebearance over the time taken to prepare the book.

TONY KENT
OGENYI OMAR

PART ONE

The Retail Environment

Part 1 introduces the retail industry and its environment. In Chapter 1 the purpose of the retail industry is explained, with its role in the economy and ways in which it can be classified and understood. Chapter 2 progresses to examine the external elements that form the retail environment and the dynamics of change in the industry. Chapter 3 focuses more closely on the industry itself and its channels of distribution, which leads to Chapter 4 in which the competitive environment is examined and, together with issues arising from earlier chapters, explores the implications of these for retail strategies. The final chapter in this section extends the theme of competitive strategy by assessing the appeal of international retail markets and the process of internationalisation.

CHAPTER ONE

Retailing in the Economy

LEARNING OBJECTIVES

After studying this chapter, the reader will be able to:

■ Understand the historical development of the UK retail industry.

■ Appreciate the importance of retailing and its contribution to the economy.

■ Understand how retailers create value for consumers.

■ Describe the structure of retailing in the United Kingdom and the criteria by which retail stores are classified.

INTRODUCTION

This first chapter provides an overview of the retail management process, explains the functions of retailing, and discusses its importance in the UK economy. Specifically, it identifies the significance of retail institutions and industry classifications by which the development of the retail industry can be reviewed.

Retailing has become a significant force during the past century. In the UK it employs around 10 per cent of the workforce in over 200000 businesses, and contributes around 14 per cent of the country's wealth (Broadbridge, 1998). It is the primary point at which most people have contact with the world of business, and consequently it is such a common part of people's daily lives that its institutions are taken for granted (Omar, 1999). The scope of the industry has steadily extended. Retailers have grown, first at home and then increasingly abroad, into some of the world's largest companies, rivalling and in some cases exceeding manufacturers in terms of global reach (*The Economist*, 1995).

Each of Europe's top half-dozen food retailers, for example, has bigger sales than any of the continent's food manufacturers except for Nestle and Unilever (Mintel, 1999). The range of products and services offered by retailers is continually extending; Metro, one of Europe's largest retail groups, operates cash-and-carry outlets not only in Germany but also in another 20 countries, as well as retailing through hypermarkets and food stores, non-food specialists and department stores. The growth of Wal-Mart from obscurity into the world's largest retailer during the 1990s has focused

---

Exhibit 1.1   A discount chain turned world's top retailer

The meteoric rise of Wal-Mart to the position of the world's largest retailer occurred in a relatively short time frame. Sam Walton, the founder, opened his first Wal-Mart Discount City store in 1962 (see Walton with Huey, 1993). The company became a public company in 1970, SAM's Clubs were rolled out in the 1980s and supercentres in the 1990s. Wal-Mart's sales from all of these formats totalled $US138 billion for the fiscal year ending 31 January 1999 (Wal-Mart, 1999). This volume not only makes Wal-Mart the world's largest retailer but considerably larger than its nearest global competitors. However, the growth of Wal-Mart was not as straightforward as its history may read.

Following the successful geographical expansion of its discount stores during the 1980s, Wal-Mart started to diversify into other formats in 1983, opening its first warehouse club. In 1988 it launched into food retailing with its first supercentre, a combination of supermarket and a discount store. It had a struggle to adapt to fresh-food distribution, but readjusted to open many supermarkets offering one-stop, low-price shopping. With retail marketing perseverance and continuous readjustment of retail strategy, Wal-Mart discount chain has become the world's top retailer and achieves higher sales than any of its main suppliers. Its turnover of $89.8 billion in the year to 31 January 1998 was the third largest of any American company. It is Procter & Gamble's largest single customer, buying as much as Procter & Gamble sells to the whole of Japan.

---

attention on the sheer size and dynamics of the leading companies in the industry (see Exhibit 1.1).

But as Ghosh (1994) has emphasised, in spite of its enormous economic success those outside the industry often see retailing as an unsophisticated business requiring limited management skill. This is no longer the case, however, as retailing has undergone a many-sided revolution from which it has emerged as a leader in business innovation and the management of complexity. Too frequently the challenges and demands of retail management are underestimated; every year thousands of new retail ventures start up, many of them failing because of inadequate management and understanding of the special demands of retailing. Success in the industry not only requires hard work and dedication, but also places increasing demands on managerial ability.

THE HISTORICAL DEVELOPMENT OF RETAILING

The earliest forms of exchange took place in markets, drawing local produce from the surrounding area and providing food, clothing and goods for consumption in the home and workplace. Simple as these were, markets from early medieval times were recognised for their contribution to the economy. A royal charter was required to authorise the market, allowing traders certain freedoms from the local lords in exchange for duties to be collected for the royal treasury. Less regularly but on a larger scale, fairs provided local people with the opportunity to buy hardware and luxuries from outside the local region. As trade in towns grew, so markets became larger and more specialised, and were often extended by the construction of permanent covered markets. The precise number fluctuated over the centuries but by 1600 around 800 markets existed in England and Wales (Braudel, 1982), with some 300 confined to single trades including grain, fruit and leather.

However, this represented a high point in market trading, as both an increasing population and economic growth stimulated the development of private trading by travelling merchants, and pedlars, but particularly shops. The first workshops were to be found in towns at a much earlier time, when artisans such as cobblers, bakers and tailors sold their products from their own premises. Selling took place from the window of the workshop directly onto the street, initially only on the days between markets. In the course of time the production of goods became detached from the selling function of the shop, goods were bought and traded by the shopkeeper. By the eighteenth century, the retail shop and retailing methods had been transformed, with many stocking indiscriminate assortments of goods and thus transforming themselves into a general store.

In reviewing the trends in retailing, Samli (1989) concluded that the provision of basic needs that caused the general store to develop also ultimately reduced its role. Since general stores attempted to satisfy the needs of customers for all types of goods, they carried a small assortment of each good; but with economic development new stores opened that concentrated on specific product lines. Howe, following a similar line of argument, suggested that the general stores were not able to compete and their owners converted them into more specialised stores (Howe, 1992).

Such specialisation distinguished shops selling by *weight*, such as grocers, from those by *measure*, drapers, and those who sold *objects* such as ironmongers (Braudel, 1982). More specifically, McNair in tracing elements of modern retailing to the middle of the eighteenth century identifies three different types of shop:

1 The fashion business developed out of the mercer's shop concerned with the silk trade. It sold not only the material, but also anything belonging to fashionable clothing.

2 The furnishing business from the shop of the tapestry maker. It grew to a large supply business able to furnish an apartment or salon with a range of goods including mirrors candelabras, sofas, carpets, paintings and etchings.

3 The luxury item business providing costly and superfluous objects, exotic curiosities and gifts. Its clientele consisted of browsers and people of leisure (McNair, 1958).

Developments in the Nineteenth Century

The *department store* evolved from the specialised types of shops described above (Tse, 1985). Initially the departments were limited to clothing; in England, Kendal Milne and Faulkner launched 'The Bazaar' as an extension of their clothing shop in 1831, and shortly after in 1845 Bainbridge extended his range of clothing to create 'departments' in his Newcastle shop. Harrods, on the other hand, started out as a grocery shop. But regardless of their origins, the stores rapidly extended their merchandise to offer a comprehensive choice in clearly defined departments, saving time and effort in shopping. The department store became a popular destination for the middle classes, taking on a social function through a format that offered convenience, comfort and a visibly high-quality environment. These were places for ladies to shop or order for home delivery, as well as meet for luncheon, and take tea in gracious, socially acceptable surroundings. With the growth of their middle-class clientele, the UK came to support over 200 department stores by 1900 (Winstanley, 1983).

Serving a quite different sector of the population, the *co-operative movement* began with the opening of its first shop in 1844 providing quality groceries at a fair price to working-class people. The movement spread rapidly through the north of England and Scotland, leading to the formation in 1864 of the Co-operative Wholesale Society in Manchester, and by 1889 the co-operatives had acquired over 800 000 members. The distinctive feature of the co-operative wholesale and subsequently retail societies was that their ownership lay with their members, the shoppers themselves, to whom surplus profits were distributed through dividends.

Multiple retailers, those retailers trading from over 10 stores, emerged in the second half of the nineteenth century. Early multiple retailers included W.H. Smith, which started selling newspapers from railway stations in the 1850s and the Boots Company. The rate of growth was such that by 1877 Singer sewing machines were sold from 160 stores (Philpott, 1977). By 1914 there were many established multiple retailers trading both regionally and nationally in a broad range of sectors including footwear, groceries and books. Some of these had created substantial distribution networks by this time; the Boots Company and shoe retailer Freeman, Hardy and Willis each traded from over 500 stores, and another 14 companies traded from over 200 branches.

Between 1920–50, multiple retailing gained further momentum due to a number of amalgamations between smaller store groups, such as the United Dairies. This later stage of development saw the spread of multiples into new trades, and also the integration of production and distribution.

Developments in the Twentieth Century

The *variety store* appeared in the UK with the arrival of Woolworth in 1909 from the United States. There was a modest growth in the format initially, but from 1920–39 with the development of British Home Stores (subsequently BhS), Littlewoods and Marks and Spencer, the number of such outlets increased from 300 to 1200 (Jefferys, 1954). The variety store was differentiated from other shops in three ways that contributed to its popularity virtually to the end of the century:

- Display – customers were invited to look around.

- Low prices – these were clearly indicated at the point of sale.

- High level of self-service – customers were not expected to be served but left to shop by themselves among the rows of merchandise.

As consumers demanded different products and services from retailers, new institutions emerged to meet this demand. *Supermarkets* appeared in the early 1930s in

> **Exhibit 1.2   The development of retail services**
>
> UK retailers are involved in developing specific retailing mixes designed to satisfy selected groups of customers. Shopping centers provide a balanced array of consumer goods and services and include parking facilities for their customers. In extending their services and making shopping more convenient for their shoppers, major high street retailers including Sainsbury, Marks & Spencer, Safeway and Tesco have installed automatic teller machines (ATM) for the banking convenience of their customers.
>
> The development of financial services within the retail sector has offered retailers the opportunity to build closer relationships with their customers. This development has occurred within an increasingly competitive environment where retailers faced with limited growth opportunities in their core markets have sought to secure existing customer loyalty with schemes that establish a relationship built on retailers' better understanding of the customer and customers' greater involvement with the retailer.

response to a consumer desire for lower prices and supported by self-service, introduced from the United States in 1952. More recently *convenience food stores* and *mass merchandisers* have met consumers' desires for convenience in purchasing and late-hour availability (Davies and Brooks, 1998). *Discount retailers* and *catalogue stores* such as Argos and Index reflect consumer demand for lower prices in a trade-off for services, while shopping centres meet demands for a wide variety of products and services. Vending machines, door-to-door retailing and Mail Order offered higher levels of shopper convenience (McGoldrick, 1989) extended still further by the arrival of the Internet.

After the Second World War, the geographic scope of retailers themselves increased significantly (Gist, 1968). Multiple retailers continued the process of consolidating their national networks of outlets, but increasingly turned to foreign markets by opening their own outlets, through joint ventures and acquisitions or by granting franchises. Retailers such as Carrefour and Benetton have become significant global operators, competing in many national markets and earning a significant portion of their sales and profits from foreign outlets.

The rate of change accelerated during this period with the importation of new formats to Europe from the United States. American innovations include the *shopping centre*, firstly as a town centre development but from the 1960s onwards appearing as an out-of-town location. *Category killers*, wide-assortment low-price retailing out of large 'sheds', typified by Toys R Us, have come from the same direction. More recently still, *factory outlet centres* crossed the Atlantic to create a major competitive element in the 1990s. The process has not been entirely in one direction; the French hypermarket format has also crossed continental borders, finding an acceptance in Asia and South America. Figure 1.1 summarises the periods of introduction of these various retail formats.

THE CONTRIBUTION OF RETAILING TO THE ECONOMY

The retail system plays an important role in our lives because retailing involves all of the business activities that are concerned with selling goods and services directly to

Figure 1.1   *The Introduction of Major Retail Formats in the UK, 1875–2000*

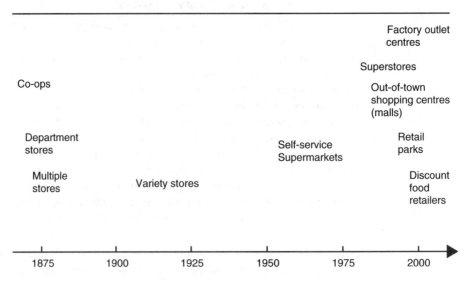

Figure 1.2   *The Traditional Process of Distribution of Goods and Services*

ultimate consumers. Thus our definition of retailing consists of all the processes in selling goods and services to the ultimate consumer, including direct-to-consumer sales activities made through store outlets, door-to-door selling, home shopping, mail order and the Internet. Retail firms are, therefore, business organisations that sell goods and services to customers for their personal or household use. Since retailers sell goods and services only in single units, the retailers' customers are the ultimate or final consumers who buy products or services for their own use and not for resale to others; this differentiates retailers from manufacturers and wholesalers.

Manufacturers and wholesalers sell goods to other businesses that resell them in the same or in different forms. It is the retailers who provide the final link, selling products to the ultimate consumers as shown in Figure 1.2. However, it is necessary to understand that not all retailing takes place in store environments. During the latter half of the nineteenth and the early part of the twentieth century, the mail-order industry evolved to satisfy the needs of rural communities and to provide goods on credit to them. The 1980s and 1990s saw the increasing importance of specialised catalogues and other types of non-store retailing such as computer shopping, television shopping programmes, telemarketing, and vending machines (*The Economist*, 1995).

The UK economy relies upon mass production and specialisation of labour to achieve economies of scale or lower unit costs in the production process, which increases the standard of living. Such specialisation within the production process tends to separate production from the distribution activities that take place outside the factory. As shown in Figure 1.3, this results in large quantities of

Figure 1.3   *A Macro-Economic View of UK Retailing*

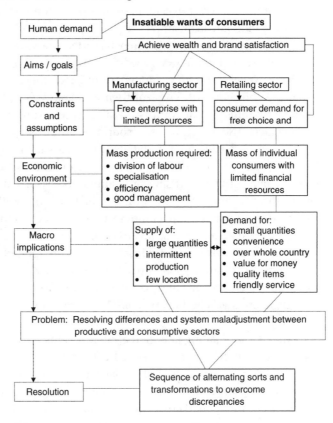

goods being produced by few firms on non-standardised time-scales and at a few locations.

As Johnson (1988) noted, manufacturers normally turn to distribution specialists (wholesalers and retailers) to sell their goods and services to end users, and they continue to use such specialists until they are no longer the most efficient means for reaching the ultimate consumer. Similarly, Davies and Brooks (1989) observed that changes in the distribution system are usually necessitated because the ultimate consumer, who is highly mobile, continuously demands small quantities of goods near the place of consumption.

The retailer partially justifies its existence by providing the consumer with the opportunity to make transactions conveniently. Retail outlets provide transaction convenience by collecting together many different items that consumers can purchase in one place and in one transaction. They also provide consumers with place convenience (Ghosh, 1994); although manufacturers may be located many miles from the consumer's residence, retailers and other middlemen help bridge this geographical gap by providing outlets that are near to consumers' homes.

The retailer performs a useful function in creating access to goods by helping other middlemen break the large-volume shipments from specialized manufacturers and producers into smaller units that consumers can use more efficiently. McGoldrick

(1990) has emphasised the necessity for breaking up bulk deliveries, as illustrated by the supermarket which receives case lots of fresh produce but sells small quantities to meet the individual consumer's needs. Typically a sorting and transformation process is carried out; the raw material may be sorted before manufacturing, transformed into a consumer product and shipped to a warehouse where stored until needed. After different styles, sizes and colours are ordered, they are displayed by the retailer so that the consumer will know of their availability (see Chapter 14) and can purchase the merchandise in the form and at the place and time they desire.

Retailers also function as a source of information to both manufacturers and consumers (see Chapter 17). Retailers, the mass media and fellow consumers are the main sources of product and/or service information available to consumers. In many cases, cooperative advertising programmes between a manufacturer and retailers are used to provide consumers with information. In addition, the trend towards consumerism has placed more emphasis upon the presentation of factual information by retail sales staff and retail advertisements. Since retailers are closer to consumers, they are able to provide a feedback of consumer preferences and reactions to manufacturers. This information is needed if manufacturers are to respond to changes in consumer demand. Retailers communicate consumer information to manufacturers by their order levels, buyers' comments, refunds on inferior merchandise, and so forth.

All of these retailing and marketing functions must be performed if goods and services are to reach the consumer at a convenient place and time and in the quantities demanded by consumers. Individual retailers are likely to compete effectively and survive in a hostile business environment if they perform these functions efficiently. In terms of direct marketing, manufacturers can eliminate all middlemen, including retailers, and sell directly to consumers, but in this case the manufacturer also functions as a retailer.

The Size of the UK Retail Industry

In spite of daunting challenges, Britain's retailers also face dynamic opportunities for further expansion as one of the most advanced retail industries in the world. The retail industry in Britain is worth an estimated £208 billion a year, and according to the market analyst Mintel accounted for almost 40 per cent of all consumer expenditure in 2000 (see Table 1.1). The economic importance of retailing can also be gauged from the activities of the leading retailers in the country. It is important to note the strength of the leading grocery retailers among the top firms (Table 1.2). Nevertheless, there is a diversity about in the way these retailers operate. Some, such as the supermarkets, concentrate predominantly on a single type of retail sector, others such as Kingfisher trade from a diversity of formats and fascias.

Retail Employment

The employment potential of the retail industry is important to the economy. The Office of National Statistics (ONS) estimates that retail firms employ around 2.2

Table 1.1   *Retail Sales by Sector (£m)*

Year	1997	1998	% Change
Food, Drink and Tobacco	63,990	67,800	+6.0
Food retailing	57,205	61,055	+6.7
Off-licenses and Ctn.	6,785	6,745	–0.6
Non-food and mixed goods	74,000	75,640	+2.2
Mixed goods and mail order retail	14,900	15,065	–1.1
Clothing and footwear retailing	19,095	19,745	+3.4
Household goods retailing	16,155	16,635	+3.0
Other non-food retailing	23,850	24,195	+1.4
Total	137,990	143,440	+3.9

Source: ONS/OECD/Mintel.

Table 1.2   *Leading Retailers in the UK (ranked by sales in £m, 1999–2001)*

Retailer	Nature of Business	2001 sales £ (millions)	2000 sales £ (millions)	1999 sales £ (millions)
Tesco	grocery retailers	20 988	18 796	17 158
Sainsbury	grocery retailers	17 244	16 271	16 433
Kingfisher	multi-sector	12 134	10 885	7 458
Asda	grocery retailers	9 680	6 398	8 178
Safeway	grocery retailers	8 151	7 659	7 511
Marks and Spencer	variety stores	8 076	8 196	8 224
GUS	multi-sector	6 041	5 658	5 467
The Boots Co.	multi-sector	5 221	5 187	5 045
Somerfield	grocery retailers	4 612	5 465	3 218

Source: Company reports.

million people in the UK, comparable to Germany in terms of the size of the labour force although less in absolute numbers than Italy, Spain and France. Moreover, official figures tend to underestimate the number of people employed by small family-run stores and the employment of seasonal and part-time workers during busy periods.

As a service industry, retailing particularly relies on its employees to represent the store to the customer and provide essential points of contact, consequently the cost of staff forms one of the most important elements of overhead expense. In general, however, the retail trade has had a poor image in the past as an employer. Retailers must provide services for the public at times when they can use them, which increasingly involves working long hours and weekend working. These conditions, together with low pay have tended to make retailing an unpopular source of employment for young people. Nevertheless, nearly a quarter of all school leavers in the UK enter the distributive trades each year, and nearly 12 per cent of all employees in distribution are under the age of 20 (*The Economist*, 1995).

Despite its poor image and conditions of employment, retailing can offer an interesting range of careers, particularly in working with people. There are good prospects for skills and career development in the management structures of larger retail organisations, and as the industry becomes more complex it offers a wider diversity of responsible jobs than many other industries. Opportunities for buyers to travel and handle aspirational merchandise are attractive features throughout the industry, but particularly in the fashion sector.

Retail Profitability and the Exchange Process

At the heart of every business transaction is an exchange. Simply stated, an exchange is the act of obtaining a desired object from somebody by offering something in return. An exchange, therefore, requires two parties (see Figure 1.4), each of whom has something to offer that the other values. Retailing is no exception; retailers must offer to sell products and services that are valued by customers and for which customers are willing to pay.

The creation of value through the exchange process is part of the retailer's strategy to satisfy customers. But as Sivadas and Baker-Prewitt (2000) have suggested, retailers must be careful in pursuing such a strategy because of the differences in customer perceptions of value and utility (see also Exhibit 1.3).

Exhibit 1.3   Creating utility for consumers

A student shopping for a pair of jeans is unlikely to find use in a formal suit, however high its quality. The suit simply does not match the student's need at the time, so it does not create any value for him or her. Similarly, a consumer's perception of utility also depends on the manner in which the retailer offers its products and services. Knowledgeable, helpful sales personnel and shopping services such as delivery and gift-wrapping, for instance, can enhance the value of the retailer's offering. A convenient location that saves the customer from travelling far to patronise the store may enhance utility. If two stores sell the same brand of jeans at the same price, the student is more likely to choose the more conveniently located one.

Figure 1.4   *Retail Exchange Process*

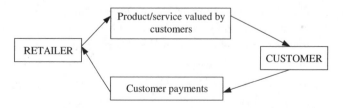

Figure 1.5   *Derived Value from the Retail Exchange Process*

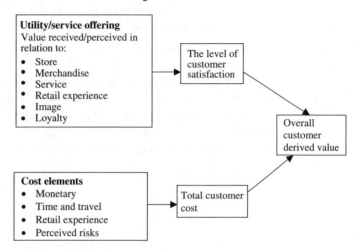

Greenley and Shipley (1992) found that the value created by retailers for their customers depends on two factors:

1 the utility of the retailer's products and services, as perceived by the customer; and

2 the price the customer has to pay for those goods and services.

In Figure 1.5, the price paid by the customer is viewed in the form of cost elements in terms of time taken, travelling expense, the risk involved in shopping and so forth. Although the notion of price (see Chapter 13) is quite clear, the concept of utility requires discussion. Utility, according to Kotler (1997), is the benefit or worth of the retailer's offering as perceived by the customer. Figure 1.5 describes the components of retail offering and the overall level of customer derived value, (satisfaction), being an outcome after the deduction of the total cost elements.

The higher the utility the greater the level of perceived benefit and satisfaction the customer receives (see Gilbert, 1999). Since utility depends on customer perceptions, different customers may have different levels of utility for the same set of goods and services. Individual needs, tastes and preferences determine the level of utility each consumer perceives. A customer who gets more satisfaction from a retailer's offering perceives a greater level of utility. Thus, as indicated in Exhibit 1.3, one way to increase utility is to offer goods and services that closely match the customer's needs. By stocking products and services desired by customers, the retailer creates utility, and with it the potential for exchange.

The utility of the retailer's offering and price jointly determine the value the retailer creates for its customers. Since the perceived utility of an offering determines how much a customer will be willing to pay for it, the greater the utility relative to price, the higher the value of that offering to the customer. Higher value, in turn, makes the consumer more willing to purchase from the retailer, completing the exchange process. When the asked price exceeds utility, the perceived value for the retailer's offering becomes negative and there is no potential for exchange. The customer may forego the purchase or patronise a different retailer who offers better value. The customer will have no demand for the retailer's offering if perceived utility is less than the asked price.

Consumers have access to many competing retail stores but they will shop only at those that create value for them. One major goal of retail strategy is to find new, innovative ways to enhance value to potential customers. Retail managers must continuously strive to increase utility and at the same time monitor their costs in an effort to reduce the prices they have to charge. Implemented in tandem, these actions will enhance value and attract customers to the store.

The Creation of Value

Retailers usually continue to search for ways to create value for their customers, as in the following five categories:

- create utility by offering the right merchandise;
- create utility by creating a good shopping atmosphere;
- create utility by decreasing the risk of shopping;
- create utility by making shopping convenient;
- reduce price by controlling costs.

These are now discussed in more detail.

The right merchandise

A retailer's merchandise (products and services) offered for sale fundamentally determines the utility of the retailer's offer. Consumers expect retailers to provide products and services that satisfy their needs and wants; and in quantities and packages that are convenient for them.

Although a retailer does not manufacture products, it creates utility for consumers, by bringing together at a single location a combination of products and services that are varied but related. A department store, for example, sells a wide variety of merchandise that at least includes cosmetics, clothing and household goods, but often furniture, toys and electrical goods. Within each of these different merchandise lines it also carries various brands, styles, colours, sizes and so on. This range of choice within a merchandise line is referred to as the level of assortment, which in a large department store can exceed a hundred thousand. The merchandise offered for sale is one of the major factors influencing the consumer's decisions to shop at a particular store. Although other factors also influence the ultimate purchase decision, the potential for exchange will never be created if the retailer does not carry the products and services consumers need. The retailer must anticipate what products and services its customers will want and procure them from manufacturers or wholesalers, thus acting as the consumer's purchasing agent.

The retailer's role as a purchasing agent significantly benefits consumers since it increases the efficiency of shopping. Consider consumers' difficulties if they had to deal with many different food producers separately instead of buying all the groceries they required at a supermarket. This would be so inconvenient and time consuming that it would be practically impossible. To fulfill its role as a purchasing agent properly, the retailer must carry merchandise that meets the different needs and expectations of its varied customer groups. Each retailer must match the items it carries to the needs and expectations of the customers it wants to attract. To satisfy diverse consumer needs, a variety of retail institutions such as department stores, discount stores, supermarkets, chemists, specialty apparel stores and so forth has emerged, each satisfying a different set of consumer needs. Consumers have expectations about the kinds of goods and services sold by each type of store and the variety and assortment of its merchandise offering.

The merchandise offering is the most important vehicle through which retailers create utility for their customers, and, to be successful, it must be matched to customer expectations. A well-defined merchandise offering creates a clear image about the store in the consumer's mind. When each store carries a well-defined and consistent merchandise assortment, the consumer can limit the search for goods to a small number of stores likely to carry what he or she wants to buy.

The shopping environment

Although the merchandise is a key element in determining utility, as discussed earlier, it is not the only one. As Kotler (1997) put it, supporting the merchandise with a good shopping atmosphere can further enhance utility. In making a purchase decision, consumers respond to more than the tangible product or service that is being offered (Omar, 1999).

The physical environment in which the product or service is sold is also an integral part of the exchange process. The aesthetics of the store influences the customer's perceived utility and therefore the value of the exchange. This is often described as psychic utility, since it derives from the psychological feeling generated by the physical environment. By creating a shopping atmosphere that evokes pleasant feelings, retailers can enhance the perceived value of what they sell. The store's decor, colour, layout, merchandise displays and even its piped music are important in creating a proper shopping atmosphere. In its design the retailer must also consider the type of customers it wants to attract. Just as the merchandise must match the needs of customers, the shopping atmosphere, too, must be consistent with customer expectations to fortify the attitudes and emotional feeling customers have towards the store (see Exhibit 1.4).

Reducing shopping risk

Buying products and services carries levels of risk to consumers. Too many products and brands are available for a consumer to know much about all of them, but as Gilbert (1999) noted, retailers can enhance their perceived value by reducing the risk of imperfect knowledge to shoppers. Retailers provide consumers with merchandise

---

Exhibit 1.4 Airport entertainment

The past ten years have witnessed the increasing involvement of retailers in airports in general, and in departure lounges in particular (see Rowley and Slack, 1999); retailers have found waiting passengers to be a lucrative source of revenue. Thus, goods and services available at airports range from sunglasses, jewellery, luxury food items and clothing to gifts, souvenirs and books. The retail outlets, coupled with the other facilities and general ambience of the airport, together conspire to create a service environment. This environment has been specifically designed to entice, occupy and entertain passengers who are in transit or waiting to board a flight and is a significant component of both the customers' travel experience and their experience of the country.

Indeed, many large airports now offer a variety of entertainment and leisure facilities in addition to retail and restaurant areas, and even business and conference centres, with a view to maximising revenue from air passengers and airport visitors. Thus, in order to create a good atmosphere for airport shoppers, in the UK the British Airport Authority (BAA) developed the landside facilities at London Gatwick airport as an extension to the Gatwick Village; at the same time offering a variety of entertainment and leisure facilities in addition to retail and restaurant areas with a view to maximising revenue from air passengers and airport visitors. BAA is thus using the airport shopping atmosphere as a marketing tool for gaining competitive advantage.

---

information as one way to decrease the risks. Consumers learn a great deal about products and services from retail sales assistants and by providing this merchandise information, sales assistants can greatly enhance the value of the retailer's offering to consumers (Hurley, 1998).

Retailers' policies for accepting returned merchandise and warranties play a complementary role. This is especially important for mail-order firms and other direct retailers who must overcome consumer resistance to buying products sight-unseen. Most mail-order firms, therefore, have generous returns policies to reduce the risk of shopping by mail. For example, the Company Store, which sells coats by mail, will not only fully refund the price of any item that a customer wants to return, but will also arrange for free pick-up by United Parcel Service. This policy has attracted many consumers who might otherwise have found mail order shopping too risky.

Shopping convenience

Making shopping more convenient for potential customers is another important way to increase utility and value. Dual-career households in today's time-pressed society make shopping convenience very important. Retailers can increase shopping convenience in many ways:

- Location techniques increase shopping convenience by reducing the time customers have to spend travelling to the store.

- Access by keeping stores open longer hours, especially late at night.

■ Many consumers find it more convenient to shop from their own homes than to travel to retail stores.

■ Adequate customer service can also enhance shopping convenience. Acceptance of credit cards, for example, makes shopping easier for consumers by eliminating the need to carry large amounts of cash. Gift-wrapping and alterations are two other examples. Many department stores even offer personalised shopping assistance to help customers complete their shopping quickly and conveniently.

Controlling costs

As mentioned earlier, utility and price jointly determine value. Therefore, in addition to increasing utility, retailers must continuously control their costs so that they can price their merchandise competitively. Four major types of costs in retail operations are cost of land and buildings; labour costs; cost of goods; and inventory carrying costs (see Chapter 7).

Efficiently controlling these costs gives the firm the ability to keep prices lower than competitors and yet earn adequate profits. The determinant of successful retailing is the ability to create value for customers through careful merchandise selection, supporting the merchandise with a good shopping atmosphere, reducing shopping risk, increasing shopping convenience and controlling costs. Astute retailers continuously search for new and innovative ways to increase customer utility, giving consumers reasons to shop at their stores as opposed to those of their competitors.

CLASSIFICATIONS OF RETAILING

Retailing is extremely diverse. Many different types of retail stores compete for shares of the market and, although they all share the common focus of selling to the ultimate consumer, they have different formats, sizes, policies and marketing strategies. Diverse types of organisations operate these different retail outlets. Some large retailers operate hundreds of outlets, while others are small independent businesses with one or two outlets. Also, franchised stores and voluntary chains, although independently owned, belong to larger networks of wholesalers or retailers. Several classification schemes (Figure 1.6) have been proposed to categorise retail stores into groups based on similarities in strategies and operational procedures:

■ Service versus product retailing;

■ Size by number of employees, sales area, number of enterprises, turnover;

■ Type of activity, for example retail sale of food, beverages and tobacco in specialised stores;

■ Product strategy;

■ By margin and turnover;

Figure 1.6   *Types and Classification of Retailing*

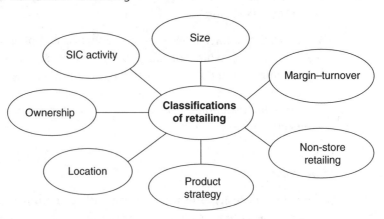

- By location: town centre, and out of town;
- By type of ownership;
- Store versus non-store retailing.

Service versus Product Retailing

The boundaries of retailing are not precisely drawn, and a distinction can be made between retailers of goods – stores – and those that sell services. These are retailers that do not sell *tangible* products to their customers, but rather provide them with *intangible* services. The strategies adopted by service retailers vary considerably depending on the type of service they provide and the degree of contact with the customer. Hotels, airlines, hospitals and banks have high degrees of customer contact, and with these types of service customers' satisfaction with the service depends critically on their perception of the quality of the service personnel.

Like non-store retailing, services themselves are becoming more significant to product-based retailers, who can use their product and customer relations skills to offer a broad range of products and services to all or selected groups of customers.

Size

Official national and European industrial classifications use measures of enterprise (business) size including total sales, number of enterprises and number of people employed (Eurostat, 1999). These can be used to characterise the structure of distribution and its contribution to the economy, and inform government policy – for example on employment and entrepreneurship. The reduction in the number of enterprises in northern and increasingly southern Europe as store size increases and ownership becomes concentrated into fewer hands has been an important feature of European retail structure. These trends have impacted on levels and type of employment recorded in the industry, and distinguish problems in the small and medium-sized enterprises (SME) sector that include very small (micro) enterprises (0–9 employees), small (10–49) and medium-sized (50–249) enterprises from large enter-prises with over 250 employees.

The size of sales areas can also be used to define retail formats. Some formats fit a general size profile so it is possible to discuss a typical high street solus site trading from 1000–3000 square feet, a convenience store from around 3000 square feet and a department store from upwards of 30 000 square feet. However, other formats are precisely defined by their size:

- *Supermarkets* trade from 400–2500 square metres;

- *Superstore*s trade from 25 000–50 000 square feet (over 2500 square metres), in food as well as non-food sectors; and

- *Hypermarkets* trade from over 50 000 square feet (over 5000 square metres) with at least 35 per cent of selling space given to non-food merchandise (Broadbridge, 1998; Euromonitor).

These measures provide a further indication of the structure of the retail industry, and over many years there has been clear evidence that store sizes are increasing whilst smaller sized stores with sales areas of less than 400 square feet (380 square metres) are in decline.

Type of Activity

The Standard Industrial Classifications of economic activities (SIC) used in official government statistics classify retail outlets based on the type of merchandise predominantly sold by the store. Since most government statistics on retailing are organised in this fashion, the classification is useful for comparing historical trends and sales for different types of stores. (The more general categories or trading sectors were shown in Figure 1.1.) Official categorisation also has some serious drawbacks:

- Since retail stores often sell a variety of products, it is not always possible to assign them precisely to any specific product group. Mixed goods – or non-specialist – retailers including Woolworth, Boots and Marks and Spencer form a significant force in UK retailing.

- Such a broad classification masks changing sales patterns and categories. While total sales at stores that sell food exclusively, for example, have grown only modestly, food stores that have expanded into non-food areas have grown markedly. Such changes in sales patterns within the merchandise and retail category go unnoticed in the broad classifications of retailers.

- This classification scheme does not provide an insight into stores' strategic or operational differences.

Further problems arise in distinguishing distributive trades themselves; the statistical classification of economic activities in the European Community defines them as 'wholesale and retail trade; repair of motor vehicles, motorcycles and personal and household goods' (Eurostat, 1999), which broadly relate to SIC codes 50–52 in the UK. However, some care needs to be taken in disaggregating the classes for more specific industrial analysis.

Product Strategy

Stores can also be classified according to their levels of merchandise specialisation. A key distinction separates stores that concentrate on limited merchandise assortments and those that sell a wide variety of products.

Specialty stores sell a limited variety of products, but offer more choice or depth within their assortment. Specialisation gives each of these retailers the opportunity to offer a *large selection of brands, models, styles and sizes*. Tie Rack and Sock Shop compete in this way by focusing on a narrow range of products from very small retail units. It can be combined with other competitive elements, such as low price, to create discount formats: for example the *category killer* reflects an extensive, deep selection at low prices.

Very different merchandise strategies characterise retail formats with broader product mixes. In the food sector, broad product strategies differentiate *hypermarkets* and *superstores* from *supermarkets* and still smaller *convenience* outlets (C-stores) through their food and non-food product assortments. The European *'hard discount'* food retailers, such as Aldi, stock an even narrower selection of product categories at heavily discounted prices.

Department stores and *variety stores* typically use the broadest product strategies. Instead of specialising on narrow product assortments these stores sell a wide variety of merchandise covering different types of products and services. Department stores are typically organised around a number of separate merchandise operations such as cosmetics, clothing, household goods and furnishings. The physical organisation of these stores, their merchandise displays and even their management hierarchies reflect this departmental structure. In this way, department stores derive a major competitive strength by facilitating one-stop shopping (see Table 1.3). Their advantage is that consumers can shop in one visit rather than make separate trips to different specialty stores. Where department stores seek to limit their risk to selling fast-moving or complex products, and to offer more choice, they can allocate space to *concessions*. A concession pays for the space through rent or commission based on turnover, usually provides their own staff, but otherwise fits in with the host store's operational strategy. Typical department store concessions include cosmetics and perfumery, and high fashion clothing brands. Variety stores, such as Woolworth and W.H. Smith are generally much smaller, and therefore offer a more limited choice of products within a narrower range than department stores.

Margin–Turnover Classification

The strategic positioning of different types of retailing can be classified by the two fundamental dimensions of gross margin and inventory turnover (Ghosh, 1994). Due

Table 1.3   *Store Operational Differences*

Retailing mix instruments	Operations		
	Discount store	**Department store**	**Supermarket**
Retail location	Low-cost rental location	Expensive location in shopping centre with high level of shopping traffic	Larger stores located out-of-town where parking area is available
Store fixtures	Simple and basic	Elegant fixtures and fittings with good window display	Excellent fixtures and fittings to enhance good store environment
Stock level	Limited and cheap discounted brands	Full selection of branded goods to facilitate one-stop shopping	Full selection of own-label and national brands
Store services	Very basic and little flexibility	Flexibility in services including home delivery, good relationship marketing	Adequate car parking, long opening hours, seven days a days a week opening
In-store sales	Reliance on self-service	Use of sales assistants, attractive display of merchandise	Use both self-service and sales assistants. Quick service, easy-to-find goods
Store promotion	Based upon price leadership	Aimed at developing brand image	Television ads, money-off vouchers to generate sales
Store pricing	Continual use of price offers	Special end-of-season clearance or special occasion	Use of attractive prices and everyday low prices (EDLP) to increase store traffic
Store facilities	Very basic	Changing rooms, coffee shops, and cafés/gift wrap. Personal shopping services	Wide range of facilities including ATMs. café, cash back etc.

Table 1.4   *Margin/Turnover Classification*

Gross margin	Stock turnover	
	High	**Low**
High	Convenience stores; stores with high turnover and high margins	Jewelry store; stores with high margin, low turnover
Low	Supermarkets; stores with rapid turnover but low margins	Stores with low margins and low turnover (not likely to succeed)

Source: Ghosh (1994).

to their fundamental importance in retailing, the concepts of gross margin and stock turnover are discussed in more detail in Chapter 7, only a brief explanation is provided here. To measure gross margin, the amount the retailer paid the supplier is subtracted from its sales revenue; and so a retailer with higher margins makes more money from each sale. Stock turnover measures the number of times the retailer sells its average inventory during the year (see Table 1.4) and reflects how quickly the merchandise sells once it is offered for sale.

These two concepts determine store classification. Based on their margins and turnovers, all stores fall into one of the classifications discussed above. Jewelry stores, especially those selling high-priced merchandise, are typical of stores with high margins and low turnovers. The store's inventory does not turn over very quickly, but the margin on each item of jewelry sold is high. A supermarket, on the other hand, trades off margin for turnover: their stock turns over very quickly, but sells at very low margins.

Marketing strategies of most stores stress either margin or turnover, although some stores achieve both high margins and high turnovers by creating local monopolies. One example is a convenience store, which due to its access to customers can charge comparatively high prices (thereby maintaining high margin) and still turn its merchandise over quickly.

Location

A hierarchy of retail locations has been observed that relates the range of goods sold in a centre to the size of the population it serves (see Chapter 7 for more on location). The 'town centre' forms a core shopping area in towns, cities and suburban centres, providing the widest and deepest selection of facilities and shops; whilst district and local centres provide less choice but are more convenient to local communities (Parliamentary Planning Guidance (PPG6), 1996).

Many changes in the high street reflect some of the more general long-term trends in retailing (BCSC Report, 1996). There has been a long-term decline in the representation of independent clothing and footwear retailers and space-intensive goods such as bulky electrical goods and home furnishings across most British high streets. This has been due to a greater dependence on multiple chains, the rationalisation of multiple stores themselves and the growth of out-of-town retailing.

On the one hand, retail development has been pushed from inner cities to out-of-town locations by congestion and the lack of space for further development (Markham, 1998). On the other, a number of factors including strong economic growth, increasing levels of consumer spending and a less restrictive regulatory environment in the 1980s led to a surge in the number of out-of-town shopping opportunities. In the UK, non-central locations are defined still further by their relationship to the centre. *Edge-of-centre* is within easy walking distance of the main shopping area, *out-of-centre* and *out-of-town* developments are found on greenfield sites outside the main urban area (see Chapter 8 for a more detailed discussion of these store types). Out-of-centre retail formats include:

■ retail warehouses; single storey, low-cost structures, also referred to as 'sheds'.

■ retail parks, an agglomeration of at least three retail warehouses totalling at least 50 000 sq.ft (5000 sq.m.);

■ warehouse clubs; and

■ factory outlet centres.

On a larger scale, out-of-town shopping centres are defined at two levels, regional and sub-regional, and need large areas of land and a good road system, but also access by other forms of transport. Shopping centres usually include at least one department store or other large store to 'anchor' the site, and a good mix of variety and speciality stores with a limited food retail representation.

Type of Ownership

Retailers can be classified by ownership in *independent, multiple retail, franchise, co-operative* and *government* categories.

The Independent Retailer

The independent retailer can be defined as a single owner trading from up to 10 shops, and includes a broad group of shopkeepers amongst whom every commodity is represented in varying degrees. Although McGoldrick (1990) observed that the number of independent retail businesses had remained fairly stable despite the multiples' market growth, other surveys show that the independents' share of retail trade is declining in all sectors (see Mintel, 2001).

Some products are by their nature and tradition almost the prerogative of the independent shop. Confectionery, tobacco and newspaper (CTN) retailers are typical of this group, but many other traditional independent businesses in the food sector have been less successful, with fruit and vegetable shops, butchers and bakeries in particular placed under considerable price pressure by multiple food retailers. Nevertheless, a privately-owned shop can seem an attractive proposition to an entrepreneur, or an independently minded manager as well as a highly valued occupation by some cultures.

To compete more effectively, an increasing number of independent retailers enter into an agreement with a voluntary symbol group, which are mostly owned by wholesalers and buying groups. Typically retailers pay a membership fee and contract to take an agreed quantity of goods each week. In return they receive a range of benefits, including lower costs passed on from bulk buying, assistance with store formats, own-label products, advertising and promotion, and centralised accounts processing. The symbol groups also encourage investment by their retailers in shop fitting and instore information systems.

Ownership in voluntary associations and buying groups is variable and can be complex, as demonstrated in some of the largest groups:

- SPAR is a wholesaler buying group and symbol retail chain. The SPAR organisation is owned by 6 wholesaler members and central office operations are funded by contributions from wholesalers and retail members. Some SPAR wholesalers also operate wholly owned stores. The SPAR organisation trades from around 2600 stores.

- Londis is a symbol retail chain that primarily buys groceries and provisions in bulk for its group members. It is owned by its members who buy a share in the company based on the number of stores they own.

- Costcutter is a symbol retail group founded by a number of local independent retailers in the north of England. It is an important member of the Nisa-Today buying group.

- Booker, a wholesaler, operates both Cash and Carry depots, and jointly with other wholesalers, the Mace symbol group. Independent retailers can also choose to trade under other fascias provided by its wholesale business, Booker Belmont Wholesale.

Many of these outlets can be described as Convenience store (C-store) formats, some of which are independent but others are part of larger multiple chains and associations. There is no official definition of C-stores, but they generally include self-service, 1000–3000 sq.ft sales areas, 7-day trading over long hours, and a wide range but limited brand choice. The types of store are indicated below:

Major C-store retailers	*Independent/specialist C-stores*
Specialist convenience store multiples	Bakers; smaller grocers
Symbol group stores owned by buying groups and wholesalers	Confectionery, tobacco and newsagents (CTN)
Co-operatives	Chemists
Petrol station forecourts	Hospital, factory and office shops
Off-licence stores selling liqour	Fast-food outlets; leisure centres, mobile shops

Multiple retailers

Multiples have been defined as stores belonging to a retail company with 10 or more branches all selling a similar type of merchandise, having similar appearance and following similar business procedures (Ghosh, 1994).

One of the most significant changes in the retailing structure has been the long-term trend towards an increased proportion of trade taken by multiple retailers at the expense of other types of retail organisations, in particular independent retailers (Johnson, 1988). Multiple stores offer major advantages over independent outlets:

- The opportunity to standardise retail operation and gain economies of scale.

- Since all outlets belonging to the same chain have the same or very similar merchandise, a common advertising and promotional campaign can be developed for the entire group of multiple stores. Pooling these resources reduces the amount of money that each outlet spends on advertising.

■ Compared to independent stores, multiples also have access to more varied advertising media and can advertise on national network television as well as by using the Internet.

■ Multiples can gain scale economies in distribution and information systems. A large chain, for example, can gain cost efficiencies by performing its own shipping, storing and order processing, thereby reducing its reliance on wholesalers.

■ Multiple stores have a significant bargaining power advantage in negotiating with their suppliers.

In the UK, most multiple retailers are publicly owned but there are a few, such as Clarks, that remain in private ownership. However, in Europe this ownership pattern has been less common; family control and cross-holdings between companies create stable platforms for development but may be restricted in terms of access to capital for investment. Manufacturers and wholesalers may also choose to exercise control over their channels of distribution by developing multiple retail businesses as part of a vertical marketing system (Berman and Evans, 1998).

Retail franchising

Franchising is a huge force in the UK economy providing many potential opportunities, and presenting several pitfalls as well, for existing and potential franchisors as well as franchisees (see Quinn, 1999). Franchising can be defined as a type of business arrangement in which one party, the *franchisor*, grants a licence to another individual, partnership or company, the *franchisee*, which gives the right to trade under the trademark and business name of the franchisor (Clarke, 1997); the arrangement is formalised through a legally binding contract (Boyle, 1999). Within this definition, however, there may be considerable variations in the precise nature of the arrangement. However, Lafontaine and Shaw (1998) classify franchises into traditional and business format franchising. Traditional franchising involves using franchisees to distribute a product under a franchisor's trademark commonly found among petrol stations, car dealerships (Omar, 1998), and soft drinks bottlers (Hoffman and Prebles, 1993). Forward and Fulop (1993) have argued that this type of franchise is little more than a licensing arrangement.

In contrast to traditional franchising, business format franchising may be seen as a form of 'business cloning'. Through the business format, franchisors seek to have franchisees replicate in their locality an entire business concept, including a product or service, tradename and methods of operation (Hoffmann and Prebles, 1993). According to Clarke (1997), this involves providing the franchisee with:

■ the knowledge and use of the franchisor's trade secrets;

■ all the elements necessary to establish a previous untrained person in their own legally separate business;

■ method of running it with continuing advice; and

■ method of supporting it on a predetermined basis for a specified period of time.

To ensure success for this type of franchise system, the terms of business format franchise contracts are particularly stringent. Rubin (1978) explains that through the contract control by the franchisor may extend over products sold, price, hours of operation, condition of the plant, inventory, insurance, personnel and accounting and auditing. The stringency of the typical business format franchise contract led Rubin to argue that the definition of the franchisee as a separate firm, rather than part of the franchisor, is a legal and not an economic distinction. The franchisor also provides franchisees with information systems, thorough training programmes and a detailed operations manual. Thus each franchisee operates with the franchisor's corporate image, offering customers consistency in product and/or service from every location in the network (Clarke, 1997). This explains the success of organisations such as McDonald's and, on a smaller scale, Body Shop, which operate the same design of shop and operating systems throughout the world.

The requirement for capital investment by the franchisor is low, but know-how must be formalised in sufficient detail that it can easily be transferred to a franchisee. Through franchising, retailers can control the format and the product and obtain economies of scale by additional volume in domestic and foreign markets without incurring large-scale investments or risks.

Co-operatives

An important distinguishing feature of the UK Co-operative is that is belongs to its members, numbering over eight million in the UK who join on payment of £1 to open a share account. In 2000, the UK Co-operative Retail Services Ltd (CRS) merged with the Co-operative Wholesale Society (CWS) to create a £4.5 billion buying group supporting over 1900 shops. Somewhat confusingly, both the CRS and CWS had traded from retail outlets, a situation that has contributed to the lack of business focus evident in the organisation. The co-operatives have declined under the competitive pressures of multiple retailers, particularly supermarkets over the past 20 years.

Government

State ownership of retail outlets has been evident in a limited number of formats, notably Post Offices. However, state involvement in retailing has diminished in the UK with the privatisation of utilities, such as electricity and gas, that supported showrooms for their products. The sale of telephones and personal communication products and services in particular has been transformed since the relaxation of government ownership.

Non-store retailing

A challenge for retailers in the twenty-first century will be to combine both 'real' and 'virtual' shopping to maximise opportunities for reaching customers while competing effectively with the numerous new entrants that electronic media is already attracting. At the broadest level, retail institutions can be distinguished by whether the selling takes place at a store or not (see Chapter 18). Vending machines, door-to-door sales and direct retailing are some of the major forms of non-store retailing. Freemans, Kays and Marshall Ward are some of the prominent non-store mail order catalogue businesses which have traditionally relied on agents to sell directly at the consumer's home or workplace, although telephone ordering from a mailed catalogue has become more usual. Many insurance agents and other salespeople who call on customers at their homes or workplaces are referred to as direct-selling retailers.

Direct retailers such as The Home Shopping Network are currently developing their business by reaching consumers through mail, telephone, television, radio, magazines or Internet. These provide opportunities for consumers to learn about the retailer's offerings, and subsequently to order by mail, telephone or through electronic media. In addition, some of the large multiple retailers such as Next sell merchandise through catalogues mailed to consumers' homes, often in the form of 'specialogues' or more precisely targeted smaller product offers. Non-store and Internet retailing are considered in more detail in Chapter 18.

SUMMARY

Retailers normally perform two major functions. One is the satisfaction of consumer needs and wants; the other is providing an outlet for production. It was observed earlier that these functions are complementary. Goods produced have no value in themselves; and it is only when they are made available to consumers who want them and are able and willing to buy them that they assume any value.

In tracing the history of retailing, it was observed that early retailing started with markets and workshops. Today, the retail trade comprises a wide and varied collection of outlets for goods and services which can be classified in several ways. This first chapter has identified that retail firms are those businesses that sell goods and services to customers for their personal or household use. Retailing is the primary institution through which most people come in contact with the world of business, and retailers exist wherever people need products or services. Retail organisations take a number of forms; they can be comprised of large chains with hundreds of outlets as well as small, local outlets operated by individual entrepreneurs. Less obviously, non-store and service retailing also form an important part of the UK retail economy.

In order that retail exchange can take place, the retailer must offer to sell products and services that are valued by customers. Retailers create value for customers by offering the right merchandise, creating a pleasant shopping atmosphere, decreasing shopping risks, increasing shopping convenience, and reducing price by controlling costs.

QUESTIONS

1 Why is retailing important in the UK economy and what are its main contributory factors?

2 What are the primary factors that determine the success or failure of a retailer in its attempt to providing value for the consumer?

3 Historically, supermarkets appeared in response to consumer desire for lower prices. Do you think such desire is being satisfied?

4 The installation of automatic teller machines in stores assists banking convenience. Discuss.

5 Out-of-town shopping facilities may have accelerated the trend of city-centre shopping decline; it did not initiate it. Explain this statement.

6 Some retailers operate hundreds of outlets, while others are simply very small. How could you account for the co-existence of these two types of retailing groups?

7 What do you consider to be the most appropriate way of classifying retailers and why?

8 Identify and briefly discuss the factors that a retailer uses to create value for its customers.

Case Study

Wal-Mart's Retailing Style: The Right Way to Retail

The takeover of ASDA by Wal-Mart has sent a ripple of fear through UK stores, although Comet has already adopted Wal-Mart's retailing style in the United Kingdom. For a retailer based over 5000 miles away from London, Wal-Mart is having amazing success in scaring UK retailers out of their domestic market. Since its acquisition of ASDA, every retailer from the cornershop to the largest hypermarket has been preparing for a new retailing revolution and intensive competition. Each sector has its own theory of what Wal-Mart is likely to mean for the retailing industry – ranging from category-killing low prices, to wacky songs to motivate staff.

In 1995, Kingfisher recruited Joe Riordon, a former vice-president of Wal-Mart's people division to inject some American retailing know-how into the Woolworth's, Comet and B&Q chain. By June 1998 he was made managing director of Comet, and following his promotion, he opened a £2 million, 30 000 sq.ft Comet store in Paisley, near Glasgow – regarded as the blueprint to transform the industry. In terms of competition, Kingfisher is attempting to beat Wal-Mart using its retailing style regarded in the industry as the right way to retail. Kingfisher is adopting American retailing tactics in the electrical field before the new Wal-Mart/ASDA has a chance to turn its competitive retail marketing weapons on Comet's sector. Thus, the operation tactics of Riordon's new Comet store in Paisley is a carbon copy of Wal-Mart's retail operational strategy. Every morning, the staff recites the 'Paisley chant' before work. There are people-greeters deployed on the door, working under the same 'every day low pricing' (EDLP) motto used by Wal-Mart. Newly-recruited employees are trained in new retailing operations (that is, American styles) at the University of Glasgow. Riordon has justified the cost of such training as a necessity because he thinks that 'the British have almost no understanding of US-style customer service'. He was quoted as saying that 'people here wear badges saying customer is everything, but they do not smile, they do not look after you, they ignore you' (*The Times*, 5 July 1999). Wal-Mart's principle is that if they look after the customer, the customer will look after them – that is what Comet is encouraging, and that is what 'the right way to retail' is all about.

The Paisley store is the largest of its kind in Scotland and could be described as a retail theatre – a new way to sell electrical goods. Retail theatre allows the customers to touch, feel and experience the product. The aim is that when customers walk about in the Paisley store they should feel as if in Disneyland. They should have the 'wow' factor, and shopping should be fun. Being able to touch and feel rules out having products locked away in the traditional glass cases still the norm in much of the electrical retailing industry. Customers, for example, are able to play with printers, pick up cameras and fiddle with toasters without asking the staff. Entering the Paisley store, customers may find up to 24 camcorders in front of them, for instance, and are able to pick them up and try them out.

It seems as if the store is very relaxed about these products being stolen, when not protected by glass cases. The fear of theft has always being an excuse used by retailers to lock things up, but these camcorders and other electrical items in the Paisley store are in fact alarmed and tied down. Theft would not be easy, and the sales staff are also about keeping as eye on the various products. In general, Comet's new store in Paisley offers retail theatre and a taste of what is to come from the retail revolution expected to follow Wal-Mart's ASDA acquisition. In Britain, people talk about customer focus as the Wal-Mart way of retailing; it is not, it is simply the correct way to retail. Stores need to motivate their staff, with a cheer, a song, or whatever they enjoy. The cultural changes of, for example, chanting, people-greeting and celebration of the customer are no longer restricted to Kingfisher and Comet, the British supermarkets Marks & Spencer, J. Sainsbury, Iceland and Safeway are all claiming conversion to the customer-focus theory.

SEMINAR QUESTION FOR DISCUSSION

Mr Riordon has introduced an American retailing style into the British retail system. Argue for and against the introduction of this style into Britain.

References

Alexander, N. and Colgate, M. (2000) 'Retail Financial Services: Transaction to Relationship Marketing', *European Journal of Marketing*, vol. 34, no. 8, pp. 938–53.

BCSC (1996) 'Town Centres Futures: The Long-term Impact of New Development'. The British Council of Shopping Centres Report (November), p. 5.

Berman, B. and Evans, J.R. (1998) *Retail Management: A Strategic Approach* (New Jersey: Prentice Hall International).

Boyle, E. (1999) 'A Study of the Impact of Environmental Uncertainty on Franchise Systems: The Case of Petrol Retailing in the UK', *Journal of Consumer Marketing*, vol. 16, no. 2, pp. 181–95.

Braudel, F. (1982) *Civilisation and Capitalism, 15th–18th Century, Volume II: The Wheels of Commerce* (London: Collins).

Broadbridge, A. (1998) *Distributive Trades Profile 1997. A Statistical Digest.* Institute for Retail Studies, University of Stirling.

Clarke, G. (1997) *Buying Your First Franchise*, 2nd edn (London: Kogan Page).

Davies, G. and Brooks, J. (1989) *Positioning Strategy in Retailing* (London: Paul Chapman).

The Economist (1995) 'Change at the Check-Out'. A Survey of Retailing', *The Economist*, March, pp. 3–18.

Financial Times (1998) 'News and Analysis of the European Retail Sector', FT European Retail Analyst, issue 1, August, pp. 3–21.

Forward, J. and Fulop, C. (1993) *Large Firms' Entry in Franchising: Strategic and Operational Issues* (London: City University Business School).

Ghosh, A. (1994) *Retail Management*, 2nd edn (New York: The Dryden Press).

Gilbert, D. (1999) *Retail Marketing Management* (London: *Financial Times*/Prentice Hall).

Gist, R.R. (1968) *Management Perspectives in Retailing* (London: John Wiley).

Greenley, G.E. and Shipley, D. (1992) 'A Comparative Study of Operational Marketing Practices among British Department Stores and Supermarkets', *European Journal of Marketing*, vol. 26, no. 5, pp. 22–35.

Hoffmann, R.C. and Prebles, J.F. (1993) 'Franchising into the Twenty-first Century'. *Business Horizons*, vol. 36, no. 6, pp. 34–44.

Howe, S.W. (1992) *Retailing Management* (London: Macmillan – now Palgrave Macmillan).

Jefferys, J.B. (1954) *Retail Trading in Britain 1850–1950* (Cambridge: Cambridge University Press).

Johnson, G. (1988) *Business Strategy and Retailing* (London: Routledge).

Kotler, P. (1997) *Marketing Management: Analysis, Planning, Implementation, and Control*, 9th edn (New Jersey: Prentice Hall International).

Lafontaine, F. and Shaw, K.L. (1998) 'Franchising Growth and Franchisor Entry and Exit in the US Market: Myth and Reality', *Journal of Business Venturing*, vol. 13, no. 1, pp. 95–112.

Markham, J.E. (1998) *The Future of Shopping: Traditional Patterns and Net Effects* (London: Macmillan Business – now Palgrave Macmillan).

McGoldrick, P. (1989) 'Departmental Store Concession – Strategic Decisions and Consumer Reactions', in L. Pellegrini and S.K. Reddy (eds), *Retail and Marketing Channels* (London: Routledge), pp. 287–310.

McGoldrick, P. (1990) *Retail Marketing* (London: McGraw Hill).

McNair, M.P. (1958) 'Significant Trends and Developments in the Post War Period', in A.B. Smith (ed.), *Competitive Distribution in a Free High Level Economy and its Implications for the University* (Pittsburg: University of Pittsburg Press), pp. 79–88.

Mintel (1999) *Wholesaling*, Retail Intelligence.

Mintel (2001) *Retailing: Annual Review*, Retail Intelligence.

Omar, O. (1999) *Retail Marketing* (London: *Financial Times*/Pitman).

Omar, O.E. (1998) 'Franchising Agreements in New Car Retailing: An Empirical Investigation', *The Service Industries Journal*, vol. 18 (2), pp. 144–60.

Philpott, W.J. (1977) *Retailing Made Simple*. Made Simple Books (London: W.H. Allen).

Quinn, B.(1999) 'Control and Support in an International Franchise Network', *International Marketing Review*, vol. 16, no. 4/5, pp. 345–62.

Rowley, J. and Slack, F. (1999) 'The Retail Experience in Airport Departure Lounges: Reaching for Timelessness and Placelessness', *International Marketing Review*, vol. 16, no. 4/5, pp. 363–75.

Samli, C.A. (1989) *Retail Marketing Strategy: Planning, Implementation and Control* (New York: Quorum Books).

Sivadas, E. and Baker-Prewitt, J.L. (2000) 'An Examination of the Relationship between Service Quality, Customer Satisfaction, and Sore Lyalty', *International Journal of Retail and Distribution Management*, vol. 28, no. 2, pp. 73–82.

Tse, K.K. (1985) *Marks & Spencer: Anatomy of Britain's Most Efficiently Managed Company* (Oxford: Pergamon).

Walton, S. and Huey, J. (1993) *Sam Walton: Made in America – My Story* (New York: Bantam).

Winstanley, M.J. (1983) *The Shopkeeper's World 1830–1914* (Manchester: Manchester University Press).

CHAPTER TWO

The Changing Retail Environment

LEARNING OBJECTIVES

After studying this chapter the reader will be able to:

- Define the influence of the changing retail environment on an organisation's strategic and operational capabilities.
- Understand the broader environmental forces that shape the retail industry.
- Distinguish from the microenvironment, primarily concerning competitive forces that are discussed in detail in later chapters.
- Assess theories of change for the retail industry.

INTRODUCTION

The business environment provides the arena in which retailers operate. In every industry the future of organisations is determined by an ability to acquire information about the environment and analyse its influence on their development. Therefore, it is essential to have a clear understanding of the major elements and trends within the retail environment that enable companies to detect significant opportunities and threats to the company before they undermine its position (McGoldrick, 1990). Indeed, external factors have been shown to account for around one-third of causes of organisational decline (McKiernan, 1992). The emphasis in this process has less to do with information about the future, which can be broadly recognised, but how such trends will transform industries and create new opportunities (Prahalad, 1999).

This chapter examines the broader, or macro-environmental forces shaping the retail industry, returning to an analysis of the more immediate competitive forces in Chapter 4. It continues onto an assessment of the dynamics of the environment and the theories of change that have been applied to the industry.

THE RETAIL ENVIRONMENT

The external environment is relevant to retailers in terms of the type and significance of various influences on the growth or maintenance of their businesses, and also in terms of their stability and predictability. It is the dynamic nature of these fluctuating environmental forces that cause uncertainties (Dibb *et al.*, 1994), and which will ultimately influence an organisation's transactions with its customers (Kotler, 1997). The influences are significant at different levels, whether the organisation is concerned with longer-term direction and profitability decisions, business unit strategies, or managing its store operations. In other words, monitoring current events underpins an organisation's ability to anticipate and plan ahead.

Identifying and assessing environmental factors forms the initial stage in the process of deciding the retailer's ability to compete, and ultimately its strategic position (Wilson and Gilligan, 1997). However, the very complexity of the environment has been reflected in complex but often unsatisfactory scanning processes, and, as a result, a simpler approach has gained ground in recent years. Mercer (1998) suggests that practical guidance is achieved from

> a deep on-going curiosity about the external world, coupled with the ability to recognise which signals from the mass of data which every new day brings are relevant – and important – to the future of the organisation.

In their analysis of the environment, retailers need to be able to distinguish the types of external forces (Figure 2.1):

■ The *macroenvironment* that describes the wider or contextual environment in which industries operate. This typically includes economic, social and demographic, political, legal and technological forces.

■ The *microenvironment* includes aspects of the external environment that are more directly influential on the organisation than others, due to their close interaction with the internal workings of the organisation. This operational environment defines the competitors, suppliers, customers, labour markets and financial institutions that immediately shape the organisation's planning and operations.

Within the retail organisation, an internal environment is sustained by its strategy, culture and structure. How retailers manage themselves is largely dependent on how they adapt to the environment, and their ability to align themselves with significant external actions. Consequently, a rational approach typified by 'one best way of doing things' may be an inadequate response to the complexity of environmental influences. Organisations put boundaries around areas which require rational decisions and attempt to reduce uncertainty with rules; therefore, individuals tend to search for answers in familiar areas and limit the scope of their enquiry to routine processes. Within the retail environment, organisations behave in different ways according to senior managers' perceptions of what is happening outside their business, in order to bring it into conformity with what the organisation is already doing.

Figure 2.1   *Environmental Forces*

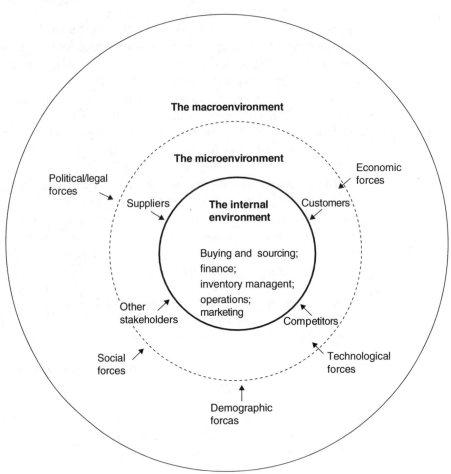

There are further dimensions to the role of the environment in determining organisational responses. The environment can be perceived to be more or less significant in determining an organisation's growth, depending on its stage of development. Mature businesses will be characterised by slower growth rates and many competitors, and a more risk-adverse and possibly less responsive management. In these circumstances, managers tend to interpret the environment as more pressured and threatening (Baden-Fuller and Stopford, 1992).

Younger and more dynamic businesses, on the other hand, tend to think about the same environment in different and more positive ways. Typically, they invest in building up detailed knowledge about how their technology, customers and environment work. The view taken by dynamic businesses suggests that industry factors are not so important in determining business success; choosing the right strategy to succeed is. This challenges the view of a universal approach to understanding the business environment, and obliges us to consider whether the same environment can be interpreted in different ways depending on market conditions and managerial leadership and

Figure 2.2   *PEST Factors*

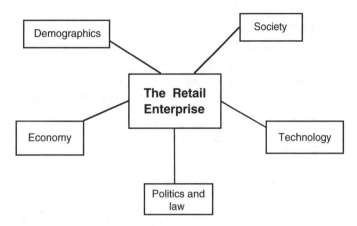

style. From this perspective, the industry environment is filtered through the lenses of its management.

THE EXTERNAL ENVIRONMENT: POLITICAL, ECONOMIC, SOCIAL AND TECHNOLOGICAL FACTORS

The macroenvironment concerns the broadest national trends and policies in the population and society, in the economy, and political and legal governance. It has an overarching effect on the performance not only of industries but also on national growth. The importance of each environmental force is relative to individual industries. The political environment created by government policy may be vitally important to the oil industry, for example, if regulations over the control of pollution are tightened. For the retail industry, on the other hand, other influences such as social changes may be more important in defining their environment by providing new opportunities to develop leisure goods and services.

Analysis of the external environment is often defined in terms of political, economic, social and technological (PEST) factors (Figure 2.2). These form the principle fields for analysis of the environment, but they can be extended in other models to include further relevant areas. For the retail industry, global and natural environmental (in the 'green' sense) issues have become increasingly significant.

The Political and Legal Environment

There are a number of dimensions to political influence on business activity. In the broadest sense the nature of the political system, its institutions and processes raises issues of stability and consistency; of decision-making and executive responsibilities. More specifically the way the government manages the economy has considerable bearing on business planning and strategic management. Governments may seek to influence market structures and behaviour, taking views on monopolies and acquisitive behaviour by organisations. They may restrict growth by constraining out-of-town development, whilst on the other hand they may provide new opportunities by extending trading hours, a topical issue in some European countries, during the week or through Sunday trading.

Government itself is the largest employer in the UK, which enables it to articulate its policy, for example, through pay restraint in the public sector. In the international environment, the globalisation of both retailers and their sources of supply are subject to intergovernmental action both within the EU and in global arenas. The government also has a role in creating and maintaining effective trading frameworks such as the World Trade Organisation (WTO). Under its predecessor, international textile trade controls through the Multi-Fibre Agreement (MFA) have had a significant impact on the competitive practices of clothing retailers.

The influence of the EU continues to be felt in a number of areas. For retail employers the implementation of a minimum wage has had a direct effect on the industry, which in 1997 employed over 700 000 people at rates of less than £3.50 per hour. Working-week legislation provides individuals with some greater control over their working hours and restricts, if only marginally, the employer's demands. The European Monetary Union, with its integration of 'Euroland' economies and the implementation of a single currency, provides a major trading opportunity. The EU is active, too, in consumer protection and brand-management rulings against unauthorised trading of products, both of which carry implications for retailers.

Specific instances of regulation concerning the retail industry can be found in the following areas of policy:

■ *Competition*. Competition laws can impact directly on retailers' strategies, as Wal-Mart experienced in Germany with its pricing policy. When the company promised to compensate customers if they found better prices for the same products in competing retailers' stores, the German competition authorities banned the practice (*Financial Times*, 1999). Alleged uncompetitive practices by retailers, such as those in car dealerships and supermarkets, and issues of consumer protection can be investigated in the UK by the Competition Commission and Office of Fair Trading.

■ *Planning*. Governments throughout Western Europe have intervened to a greater or lesser extent with the development of retail outlets. In the UK, planning guidelines (PPG6) have restricted out-of-town development since 1993; in one ministerial pronouncement '. . . promoting investment in existing shopping centres is central to government policy . . . Out of Town development is the last resort' (*Retail Week*, 1997). In France and Spain legal regulations, rather than guidelines, determine new store development and location.

■ *Health and safety*. In addition to Health and Safety regulations concerning the safe handling of food and working practices in the food industry, the UK government has had to create policy on more fundamental food-chain issues concerning animal health and genetically-modified foods. With food safety concerning both public and government, retailers will have to examine their supply chains, sourcing and product management policies through to the accuracy of their labelling and packaging.

Exhibit 2.1 Government investigation of supermarket pricing

After a nine-month investigation into supermarket pricing, the Office of Fair Trading (OFT) concluded that consumers are paying more for their groceries than they should. Amongst their findings, the OFT established that the pricing behaviour and other strategies adopted by major food retailers were unconstrained where there was only a modest threat of new competition.

In April 1999, the Director General of Fair Trading referred the supply in Great Britain of groceries from multiple stores to the Competition Commission for investigation under the monopoly provisions of the Fair Trading Act 1973 (FTA). The origins of the investigation lay in a public perception that the price of groceries in the UK tended to be higher than in other comparable European countries and the USA. Secondly, that there appeared to be a disparity between farm-gate and retail prices, which was thought to contribute to grocery multiples profiteering from the crisis in the farming industry. Thirdly, there was a continuing concern that large out-of-town supermarkets were contributing to the decline of the high street in many towns.

However whilst the Commission's report criticised a number of aspects of supermarket pricing, it stopped short of regulation; instead it concluded that a code of practice should be adopted.

■ *Environmental responsibility*. Several European countries, in particular the Scandinavian countries and Germany, have been active in passing highly restrictive enviromental legislation that will place greater responsibilities on manufacturers to raise the level of environmental protection with implications for both logistics and distribution companies and retailers themselves. The EU has legislated on recycling practices since 1997, designed to force companies to recover or recycle at least half their packaging waste.

In summary, government legislation and intervention may impact on the nature of the organisation, its relationship with customers and suppliers, certain internal procedures and activities, market structures and international trade.

The Economic Environment

It is useful to be able to assess the position of the retail industry within the structure of relative strengths and weaknesses of the productive sectors:

1 The *primary sector* – concerned with the extraction and production of basic raw materials, for example agriculture, fisheries and mining.

2 The *secondary sector* – transforms the outputs of the primary sector into products ready for consumer use through manufacturing, construction and so on.

3 The *tertiary sector* – comprises services including retailing.

The relative importance of these sectors is subject to change, and is recorded by the proportion of the labour force employed by the sector, the contribution of the sector to the nation's balance of payments – the share of gross domestic product (GDP) accounted for by each sector. In the UK the long-term trend has seen a decline in the importance of agriculture and mining from the primary sector, due largely to competition from lower-cost overseas competitors, for example imported coal from Australia. Manufacturing in the secondary sector has declined too; however, the UK has seen growth in tertiary-sector activities, in particular financial services, retailing, leisure and tourism. These developments have been seen in many economically developed countries, if not as pronounced as in the UK, and have given rise to the concept of post-industrialisation (Worthington and Britton, 1997). The effect of these changes is seen in economic policy where increasing attention has been given to the wealth-generating characteristics of service industries, and acknowledgement of the retail industry as an important source of employment.

Organisations need to be able to assess how the economy will affect their investment decisions in particular. The range of decisions is both strategic, to do with longer-term profitability, and operational. Strategic decisions involve, for example, considerations of the source and cost of capital, the deployment of resources, including people, and mergers and acquisitions. Operational ones concern the management of stock levels and product assortments in response to more immediate economic conditions. Some important measures of the economy are detailed below:

Economic growth

National economies are seldom stable, and the business cycle describes fluctuating levels of activity in the economy. An important measure of how fast the economy is growing is the gross domestic product (GDP), broadly defined as the total value of goods and services produced within the economy. Typically, GDP growth in the UK has been 2–3 per cent per annum since 1945, rather lower than other developed Western economies. If GDP grows more quickly than the population, people will become wealthier; but government taxation decisions and the distribution of wealth may reduce the effect on particular groups, and some groups may experience a reduction in their income or wealth, as a result of changes in demand for their services. Output levels indicate changes in different sectors of the economy and provide opportunities to forecast future business trends. As a generalisation, a growing economy should underpin decisions about retailer growth.

Unemployment rates

In the past 50 years, governments have accepted different rates of unemployment. During the 1950s–70s a national objective was to create full employment, whilst from 1979 economic flexibility competitiveness and the fight against inflation took higher priority and unemployment was allowed to reach a new postwar high of 3 million. In the UK cycles of approximately five-year periods may be observed as unemployment rises with recession and declines in periods of economic growth. It can be argued that it may not be desirable to reduce unemployment substantially below 1 million, because of the effects fuller employment has on wage inflation at about this level.

The influence of unemployment on retailing can be understood in terms of supply of employees to the industry and demand for retailers' goods and services. Areas of high unemployment create poorer communities, which may be unattractive to retail investment; at the same time recruitment of staff should be easier than it is in areas of full employment.

Earnings, spending and savings

The value of measuring earnings lies in the measurement of inflationary trends. Government interpretation of rising average wages may be to direct policy towards restraining economic growth to manageable levels. Disposable income is individual income available after tax.

Consumer spending which takes account of spending by individuals on goods and services is clearly an important measure for retailers. The source of spending can arise from income, savings or borrowings and depends on disposable income less other financial outgoings, such as mortgage payments and insurance. Savings derive from income that is set aside in anticipation of higher financial benefit in the future, rather than spent immediately. A policy objective in the UK is to increase individual savings, particularly for pensions, that may reduce disposable income available for shopping.

The inflation rate

Inflation concerns the measurement of prices in the economy, measured by the retail price index (RPI). Since 1945 prices have only moved upwards, and from the mid-1970s in particular, sometimes quite spectacularly. The 2000s, however, have seen more control over inflation as a key economic target, with inflation running between 1.5 per cent and 3.5 per cent. Commentators have suggested that economic deflation, brought about by a global decline in prices, may prove a new threat to economic development.

Success in controlling inflation in the 1990s in the UK resulted in part from widespread acceptance of the idea that the effect of changes in the amount of money in the economy was primarily seen in changes in the level of prices. It was previously thought that inflation could only be caused in two ways: demand-pull inflation from excessive demand for goods and services, resulting in an increase in their market level price; or cost-push inflation on the supply side where increases in production costs push up prices for supply into the market unless offset by increases in productivity.

One effect of inflation is its erosive effect on the value of money and savings, but price *deflation* on the other hand will affect sales and profit growth in the retail industry unless costs can be contained elsewhere. Retailers' solutions to this problem include the sourcing of merchandise in lower-cost countries, reducing numbers of employees and disposing of unprofitable stores.

Interest rates

Since 1979, economic policy in the UK has been informed by a desire to reduce taxation and government spending. Reduced influence over the economy through the Budget (fiscal) process meant that more importance was given to the money supply and the price of money, expressed through interest rates. Economic management, through a monetarist approach, requires control of money supply and interest rates. Raising and lowering interest rates eventually influences the cost of borrowing, whether for investment or consumption by organisations or individuals, and results in higher or lower levels of output than would otherwise be the case.

Interest rates directly affect business decisions, as more expensive money limits expansion plans; and indirectly through effects on business and consumer confidence. The business cycle affects interest rates. Rates rise during the upswing in the cycle as demand for borrowed money rises, and is in turn affected by them. Lower interest rates enable institutions to borrow for investment more cheaply, and increase distributions from profits to investors. With the election of the Labour government in 1997, the Bank of England has been given the responsibility for setting interest rates independently of the government in an attempt to make to economic policy goals more consistent, particularly the control of inflation.

The balance of trade: imports and exports

Historically, the UK government has sought to influence the trade balance through a range of policies directed at the domestic economy. The government paid for its adverse balance of trade in goods through export of capital and business services, 'invisible exports'. When governments target the overseas trade balance as a policy objective, they use a mixture of direct controls, such as exchange controls and quotas, and price-based controls. Both types of control can have a direct impact on the retail sector by restricting the supply of imported goods and reducing consumption. However, free-trade policies, under which government impact on trade flows is reduced, are now widely accepted by industrialised countries.

Exchange rates

The exchange rate between sterling and other currencies is a measure of the relative value to business investors of each currency. Outside agreed exchange frameworks such as the European Monetary Union (EMU) or national controls, for example as found in Taiwan, and the UK itself from 1939–79, currencies are traded freely and find their own level as international businesses, banks and speculators establish current and future prices at which to buy and sell currency.

Floating rates have major implications for the retail industry, in particular those importing large quantities of own-brand merchandise. With delivery schedules and supplier payments running some months into the future, currency can be bought at a rate agreed at the present time for future delivery. With large fluctuations in rates, delivered prices and selling prices can be difficult to manage consistently. However, the euro is expected to provide significant savings in trading costs between partners in the EU through more efficient banking practices. These are offset by the initial conversion costs of tills, accounting systems and packaging and labelling from national currencies to the euro.

> **Exhibit 2.2   Impact of exchange rates on tourist spending**
>
> Harrods Holdings, the group that owns the luxury department store in London's Knights-bridge, experienced a downturn in retail sales of over £24 million accompanied by a 22 per cent decline in profits during 1998. The company attributed the decline to tourists staying away from the UK because of the strong pound and the financial crisis in Asia, and pointed out that similar trading patterns were reported by other department store groups in London. However, from the start of the summer in 1999, the tourist element of the retailer's trade had strengthened, and although it had not returned to previous levels was having a positive effect on sales.

The Social and Demographic Environment

Retailers need to define their customers in such a way as to provide a competitive assortment of products and services. George Davies saw an opportunity for Next in the early 1980s to design and sell formal clothing to businesswomen to wear at the office. For the woman in her late twenties and thirties at that time the only choice lay between chain stores, and expensive designer brands. As the retailer became associated with affordable fashionable clothing, so the company extended their products to attract men and children sharing the same lifestyle characteristics. Understanding the location and structure of the population and society enables retailers to take decisions about existing and new market opportunities. As Next's development illustrates, environmental scanning for opportunities with an identifiable group, or groups of customers, should not be an occasional or one-off process. It is easy for organisations to overlook major social changes over a period of time, especially when they enjoy a successful trading format. The difficulties lie in assessing exactly which changes are significant to their business, and how they will impact on them.

Social changes

A society is composed of individuals, identified by common social interests and cultural values. The term can be used broadly to define national groups, and more narrowly to define much smaller groups with specific aims and values. The defining differences lie in beliefs, family structures and the pattern of interaction between individuals. The ways in which individuals share characteristics and form recognisable groupings enable organisations to develop products and services with a meaningful identity and application.

   The methods of defining groups are themselves changing. Official censuses and surveys deal with classification by using occupation as the basis for measurement. The socio-economic group (SEG) 'brings together people with jobs of similar social and economic status. The allocation of occupied persons to socio-economic groups is determined by considering their employment status and occupation'. A commonly-used classification for marketers is found in the A–E socio-economic groups (Table 2.1), although these are limited by their broad association of occupation, income and common interest. For example, the income of a minister of religion today would

Table 2.1   Socio-Economic Classifications

Class category	Occupation
A	Higher managerial, administrative or professional
B	Intermediate managerial, administrative, or professional
C1	Supervisory or clerical, and junior managerial
C2	Skilled manual workers
D	Semi- and unskilled manual workers
E	State pensioners or widows, casual or lower grade workers or long-term unemployed

be considerably less than a train driver, yet the former will be classed as B and the latter as D. Occupation alone does not produce common perceived interests; it fails to reflect differing values, attitudes and loyalties shared by a group of people, and it cannot reflect the interests of 'non-working' people. Therefore market researchers have attempted to find more meaningful descriptions of consumer groups. In this undertaking, lifestyle measurement has become more important in the past 20 years as a means of usefully classifying the population.

The continuous decline in manufacturing industries has resulted in the disappearance of traditional large-scale employers of skilled and manual male labour. These changes have found expression in cultural and social attitudes and behaviour, evident in the decline of traditional working-class values and, increasingly, the decline of mass consumer markets. As people's identities are bound up with consumption as well as work roles (Mackay, 1990), they carry implications for both retail and product brands as people seek identities in what they consume. Ethnic social groups provide a further dimension of identity as a multiracial society becomes a reality in many urban areas, creating opportunities for specialised retail products and services. Other emerging areas include the 'pink pound', targeting the gay population, which has been recognised by marketers as a significant and distinctive sector.

Lifestyles

Lifestyle segmentation groups individuals according to how they spend their time, the importance of items in their surroundings, their beliefs about themselves and broader issues, together with characteristics such as education and income (Dibb *et al.*, 1994). From a sociological perspective, shopping can be understood as connecting commodity and identity to lifestyle:

> Lifestyles are routinised practices, the routines incorporated into habits of dress, entry, modes of acting and favoured milieus of encountering others, but the routines are reflexively open to change in the light of the mobile nature of self-identity. Each of the small decisions a person makes every day . . . contributes to such routines. (Giddens, 1991)

Lifestyle tends to stress powerful cultural patterns made up of signs, representations and media. It also highlights its inherent instability since it is an extension of consumer choice to mode of life, and as such lacks both sub-culture and obligations to the long term. Consequently, market segmentation is becoming more difficult as people join interest groups, or tribes, that reflect how they feel on different occasions, and adopt a personal portfolio of alternative identities according to time and place (Section D. 2000).

Lifestyles now reflect a greater individuality, unburdened by family and cultural ties and supported by greater mobility in work as the lifetime job becomes increasingly remote. Personal relationships, too, reflect this lack of continuity, and these trends will fuel greater individual independence and self-centred behaviour with implications for more individualised retail product design and selection.

Changes in employment

The main occupational changes in the past 20 years have seen an increase in the number of professional and managerial jobs for men and, in particular, women. As observed in the preceding section, a substantial decline has been recorded in the numbers involved in manual work, and in particular large numbers of jobs lost for men in general unskilled labour and transport work. Offices, too, have witnessed the loss of routine clerical jobs as information technology replaces these lower-level functions. Types of work have changed, to include an increasing number of service industry jobs, often in low-skilled positions such as in fast-food restaurants.

These changes in the workplace have meant that by 1997 more women were in employment than men. Over a longer period increased employment opportunities for women has resulted in them enjoying greater financial independence, accompanied by less time at home with implications for traditional homemaking roles such as food and meals preparation and housework. As more women take up the role of household breadwinner, and increasingly enter management and the professions, so there has been a more profound effect; raising the average age at which a family is started. However, long working hours are likely to be unsociable with severe effects for family and leisure patterns and personal lifestyles, with more than 32 per cent of men and 8 per cent of women in Britain 'sometimes' and 'usually' working nights (Scase, 1999).

The ways in which people work are characterised by an increase in part-time work and job flexibility. They are also more likely to work on Saturdays and Sundays, a trend that is set to continue as Britain moves towards a 24-hour society in which shops and services provide extended access. Retailing is a key driver in longer working hours, as seven-day shopping brings with it implications for transportation and distribution, delivery systems, communications, catering and entertainment.

Distribution of employment

Localities attract clusters of industries with specific characteristics providing employment and new market opportunities. Employment tends to be created in new industries in the service sector based on the use of information, for example in the high-technology industries of central Scotland, 'Silicon Fen' or the Thames Valley. This leads to areas of new wealth and lifestyle, distinct from older manufacturing regions, bringing with it the need for retailers to examine their location strategies. If regional inequalities continue, so too will diversities within and between large urban communities. Large urban areas continue to be divided on the basis of income, occupation and lifestyle. Greater diversity has now become evident, with the growth of new cultures associated with ethnic communities introducing greater variety in lifestyles, patterns of spending and consumption, that define modern urban living.

Households

The proportion of the male adult population who are married is predicted to fall from 56 per cent in 1996 to 48 per cent in 2011. In addition, the proportion of adults who have never married will increase from 32 per cent to 39 per cent for males and from 24 per cent to 31 per cent for females over the same period (Scase, 1999). This trend will become particularly pronounced in the 30–44 age group. More single people in society are likely to bring a greater preoccupation with personal appearance and social acceptability, and the demands of this growing sector of the population are likely to have a significant impact both on retailing, including healthcare and fitness centres, and corporate marketing strategies. Fashion and brands, for example, are likely to become even more important. The specific personalised needs of single people are likely to be a factor sustaining the growth of small retail and service businesses. The growing number of households suggests the need for between 4.4 and 5.5 million additional homes by 2015 (Scase, 1999). This increase will be driven by longer life expectancy, more people choosing to live alone and a greater frequency of divorce and breakups among those living together. There will be a large increase in the number of single-person households and of women who, because of their earning capacity, can choose to live alone. Both trends will affect the demand for services as well as patterns of leisure, consumption and lifestyle. This trend has implications for house builders to provide homes for smaller households, and potentially for retailers in home furnishings and electrical appliances as the internal space available declines. The return to the city centre will see demands for specialist food outlets as well as 24-hour stores where cosmopolitan and fashionable lifestyles will be focused.

Education

Fundamental structural changes in employment require more educated or skilled employees, typically in information and communication technology and finance. With the expansion of higher education and the promotion of lifelong learning and retraining opportunities, retailers will have to respond to the demands of a more educated society. This brings implications both for retail assortments, the type of products people want, as well as levels of service.

Demographic change

A key force for change over the next 10 years will occur in the demographic profiles of many developed countries. Demography concerns the study of population, and is valuable to the retail industry in a number of ways. It enables market sizes to be predicted for specific age groups in the population, an important characteristic for all commercial organisations. Retailers use age-based information as a measure of market segmentation to decide on corporate as well as marketing strategies.

As well as forecasting demand for products and services, demographic data enable employers to predict the supply of labour by age group. The decline in school leavers in the 1990s resulted in retailers rethinking their employment strategies. In the case of B&Q, the company ran a trial to recruit employees over 50 years of age, partly to provide higher levels of customer service but also to overcome a shortage of younger staff.

In the first decade of the twenty-first century, Britain's population, like that of many other European countries, will only grow slowly. Birthrates will fall which, combined with increasing life expectancy, will lead to an ageing population. Over the next 20 years these demographic trends will bring about a decline in the proportion of the population under 25 and a large increase in the middle-aged and the over-65s (Table 2.2).

Exhibit 2.3   The teenage clothing market

The early 1980s saw new opportunities for marketing teenage products. The baby boom of the mid-1960s inevitably increased the teen population by around one million at this time, supporting the growth of Top Shop, Miss Selfridge and Top Man clothing multiples. As this group matured, Next found a new market for its branded ranges of formal and leisure clothing, initially targeted at the career woman. The teen market has declined since this time. The lowest birthrate since 1945 was reached in 1977, and the result of a much reduced teenage population in the mid-1990s contributed to the reorganisation of at least two of the groups which had enjoyed earlier success.

Table 2.2   *Population Trends by Age, 1996–2006*

Age group	1996 (millions)	2001 (millions est.)	Change, 1996–01	2006 (millions est.)	Change, 2001–06
0–9	7.7	7.4	−0.3	7.1	−0.3
10–19	7.2	7.6	+0.4	7.7	+0.1
20–29	8.4	7.5	−0.9	7.5	0
30–44	12.9	13.7	+0.8	13.3	−0.4
45–59	10.6	11.2	+0.6	12.0	+0.8
60–74	7.8	7.8	0	8.2	+0.4
Over 75	4.2	4.4	+0.2	4.5	+0.1
Total UK	58.8	59.6	+0.8	60.3	+0.7

Source: ONS, *Annual Abstract of Statistics 2001*.

These demographic changes will create more free time for some groups of people, particularly the older and retired segments of the population. The idea of early retirement is likely to remain popular, but it is less clear whether early retirement schemes will be as easily attained as in the past. Nevertheless, it seems that a culture of early retirement or at least flexible part-time working may continue. Affluent groups will find personal freedom attractive after years of full-time employment, although for the less wealthy the need to work into old age will be a necessity.

Future growth opportunities for retailers are likely to arise from the lifestyles and spending preferences of the older middle-aged, the baby-boomers of the late 1940s. Growing numbers of time-rich and cash-rich older consumers will bring a reorientation of corporate marketing, selling and retailing strategies. With mortgages paid off and children leaving home, but provided with company pensions and possibly inherited wealth, this group will have the capacity to spend. However, it is likely to be split between retailers and other service providers including holidays, travel and entertainment, and healthcare. Within the retail sector, department stores may be best-placed to appeal to this group, by offering a wide assortment combined with a range of services and interesting experiences, convenience and accessibility. This group of time-rich consumers may also enjoy the search for value, using the Internet and off-peak travel to locate best-value retailers to the benefit of discount retailers.

Of particular interest to retailers is the size of the 20–29-year-old age group, high spenders in employment and whose disposable income has yet to be constrained by family and house-ownership commitments. The decline of over one million in this group between 1996–2001 alone will impact on retailers in fashion, music and household products (*Design Week*, 1999).

Demographic changes will also affect communities. Geographical areas will be defined by communities of interest, for example by their popularity for retirement, and will also account for diversity in the provision of facilities and services (Scase, 1999). The more privileged may segregate themselves in 'secure' housing developments in Britain or continental Europe. Trends for the retired to live in rural or seaside areas are unlikely to change, provided infrastructures remain in place for healthcare and social services. For these groups, shopping and socialising will be important activities, in part substituting for employment, bringing with them implications for retailers' store design and location strategies.

The Technological Environment

Investment in technology and innovation is often seen as a key to strategic success. In many industries, technological development is expressed in new products or augmentation of existing products in new ways. A critical base of technological skills and materials and access to compatible suppliers enables companies such as Sony, Honda or 3M to stay ahead of their competitors in selected product markets.

For most retailers, manufacturing-led development is distanced from the process of distribution to individual customers. The competitive edge of technology is found in the way retailers identify and configure their technology systems to increase their efficiency and effectiveness (Figure 2.3). Clearly these control and planning activities can be thought of in terms of information management. Through the design of

Figure 2.3   *Dimensions of Retail Technology*

- Capture information about sales
- Maximise selling opportunities

- Increase responsiveness to consumer demand

- Evaluate promotional activity

- Minimise stock holding
- Reduce human resource and distribution costs

- Control pricing policies

information systems (IS) retailers seek to create advantages in increasingly competitive markets. Whilst information technology has a clear role in creating efficiencies in planning and control, it also opens up new markets by providing new distribution opportunities through interactive television and the Internet. Developments in virtual selling environments enable retailers to provide information about their businesses and products, but also to make additional sales.

E commerce

Whilst there is considerable debate about the size of the Internet market, if the European market follows trends in US growth it will display 'massifying' characteristics (Reynolds, 1999). And with the potential to supplement or replace conventional retailers, there is little doubt that the retail industry is taking the opportunity seriously. The Internet is becoming a distribution channel for both *information on* and *access to* an increasing range of goods and services in both business-to-consumer (B2C) and business-to-business (B2B) activities.

In B2C, where traditional businesses were initially slow to react, dot.com operators moved rapidly into the market with the intention of developing experience and knowledge of customers, branding and fulfilment systems. Nevertheless, whilst numerous online start-ups competed head on with retailers for a limited number of potential customers (Mintel, 1999), 'bricks and clicks' retailers have tended to be more successful. With the slower than expected emergence of online markets, store-based retailers have used their brand and financial strengths to their advantage to develop new e-retailing operations.

In the context of rapid technological development, the e-commerce environment will emphasise the need for responsive and flexible management styles, as well as appropriate investment strategies in online site design and customer order fulfilment.

Other Environmental Factors

The four factors – political, economic, social and technological – described above provide the basis for evaluating the retail environment. However, two further aspects of the environment should be evaluated for their relevance to organisational planning.

Globalisation

Retailers need to assess developments in the international environment beyond those defined by political and legal frameworks. These issues concern the extent to which conditions in the domestic market hinder the development of a business or retail concept, and the identification of markets sharing acceptable characteristics for development. Thus, globalisation is shaped by the convergence of economic systems, for example the demise of communism, societies and cultures that create demand for new products and services.

The retail industry has become increasingly concentrated throughout northern Europe and North America, a trend becoming evident elsewhere in the developed world. One response by the largest organisations is to develop global businesses, demonstrated by the acquisition of Asda by Walmart, and the merger of Carrefour and Promodes. In the clothing sector, Zara and Esprit have enjoyed significant European or American success; and Disney, Nike and Borders in their different markets are expanding their retail initiatives in the UK. Size is not everything though; an alternative view suggests economies of scale will assume a diminishing importance as retailers become the 'coordinators' of products produced within global-based supply chains.

There are wide-ranging managerial issues arising from the globalisation of retail businesses. More sophisticated buying and merchandise management will be required as global suppliers and retailers work more closely together to reduce costs and improve responsiveness to consumer demand. There will also be profound effects on 'backroom' functions; there will be an increasing demand for employees with multilingual skills and the ability to adapt to and work with other national cultures. Supply chains will be characterised by co-operative relations between companies through joint ventures, strategic alliances and partnerships. These activities require skilled supply-chain and logistics managers and support staff to achieve accurate on-time deliveries. Retail-management information systems will need to be developed to service complex global supply, payment and banking requirements. The UK's acknowledged status as a leader in retail design will be enhanced by new global design opportunities.

The natural environment

Commitment to the natural environment may be expressed at a number of levels, ranging from passive support for care and protection policies, to practical approaches to sustainability. These attitudes can perhaps be seen at their most committed in Body Shop where they have formed the guiding principles of the organisation. Food quality and the management of responsible food chains has also become a significant issue, stimulated by highly publicised concerns about BSE in beef, salmonella and other dangerous biological contaminations. The testing of genetically modified foods has provoked widespread public concern which requires a strategic response. Interpreting the significance of these issues can prove distinctly advantageous; the food retailer Iceland took the issue up at an early stage to obtain favourable publicity. Retailers must match their product and sourcing policies to the critical requirements of increasingly informed and environmentally aware European consumers. Misjudging public opinion on the environment can be costly as oil companies frequently find with accidental spillages.

Two key issues concern the viability of 'green' as a retailing objective. One concerns the value of environmentally sound manufacturing and packaging and the price at which consumers will buy these products. In the USA one study showed that 75 per cent of consumers claim their buying decisions are influenced by a company's environmental reputation, and that 80 per cent would pay more for environmentally 'friendly' products (Lamming and Hampson, 1996). The second issue is how retailers can enforce environmental codes of practice on their suppliers. This may be facilitated by government action, for example in Germany and Canada to support changes in consumer behaviour, and through business coalitions and associations. The World Business Council for Sustainable Development is one such organisation, promoting sustainable development policies that include environmental protection, social equity and economic growth.

CHANGE AND THE RETAIL INDUSTRY

The analysis of the external environment provides a basis for decisions about the retailer's strategic direction, both by identifying relevant issues for a particular organisation and for determining the degree of uncertainty in which it operates. Some 30 years ago, Toffler (1970) warned against underestimating the impact of the rate and degree of technological change, and the retail industry is not alone in facing increasingly dynamic conditions.

Uncertainty and Change

Uncertainty can be determined by the extent to which the environment is stable or dynamic and its level of complexity. Types of uncertainty are discussed by Van der Heijden (1997) in terms of:

- *Risks* – from which historical evidence enables the organisation to assess the probabilities of future outcomes.

- *Structural uncertainties* – unique enough not to have evidence of probabilities.

- *Unknowables* – cannot even imagine the event.

These are reflected in different types of change (Table 2.3). Change may be profound due to fractures in the environment, and such discontinuities will determine the long-term future of the organisation (Morgan, 1988). Stacey (1990), too, identifies different types of change situations and their impact on an organisation's ability to achieve successful strategic outcomes. The closer organisations are to certainty the more likely they are to face repetitions and therefore make a useful forecast some time ahead. In any given situation, past experience provides useful links between cause and effect; however the further organisations move from certainty the more likely they will act in unique circumstances that have never before been encountered. There is no reli-

Table 2.3   *Types of Change Situation*

Closed change	Contained change	Open-ended change
■ Clarity and agreement on events and future course ■ Typically continuing operations of an existing business ■ Fairly clear-cut relationships	Less certainty about: ■ What happened ■ Why it happened ■ What the probable consequences are Market research helps to define what kinds of products will sell better in the future	No clarity about what caused the change, why it occurred to its future implications

Source: Stacey (1996).

Table 2.4   *Types of retail change*

Cyclical oscillation	Conflictual interinstitutional antagonism	Environmental socioeconomic change drivers
Wheel of Retailing; Retail Accordion; Life cycle	Dialectic	Ecology crisis

Source: from Brown (1987).

able cause and effect linkage and managers are unable to predict outcome in the long term.

It is important to distinguish between the features of the environment that can be predicted and planned for well in advance, and features that are less controllable but must still be taken into account. The paradox of forecasting is that forecasts are general in terms of events, and vague in terms of time, but to be useful they must be specific and precise (Toffler, 1970). However, the retailer's ability to manage the business environment will involve ways of understanding and modelling it to meet its requirements.

CHANGE THEORIES

A number of views have been put forward to explain changes in the retail industry structure. In part these theories have attempted to explain observable phenomena, such as the apparently cyclical association of price with increasing service and product assortment. In part, too, they have a prescriptive function, to suggest ways in which retailers can model future retailing developments. Brown (1987) defines the approaches to change in three categories, cyclical, conflictual and environmental (Table 2.4).

The Retail Lifecycle

The product lifecycle was first identified and analysed in the 1960s to describe a series of stages in sales and profit growth and decline for individual products. These can be thought of as an introductory phase, which if the product is successfully adopted by increasing numbers of consumers leads to a growth phase. As competitors are attracted to the opportunities demonstrated by the successful product, sales and profit growth mature, and ultimately the product may decline and be withdrawn (Figure 2.4).

The escape from maturity can be facilitated by strategic innovations on many fronts; from the build up of multiple combinations of advantages using variety, quality, fashion or speed as low-cost variables. Organisations need to innovate to escape from hierarchical thinking through strategic networks and new organisational structures, for example decentralisation or cross-departmental team-working. (Baden-Fuller and Stopford, 1992; Bennett and Cooper, 1984).

The life of a typical retail concept has been halved in the past 25 years as consumers have increasingly shopped for value and retailers use information to recognise and respond more rapidly to consumer needs (Burns *et al.*, 1997). With such shortening lifecycles it may be necessary to plan to extend the maturity phase, to develop continuous renewal policies, rather than attempt to escape from it; a situation that may

Figure 2.4   *The Retail Lifecycle*

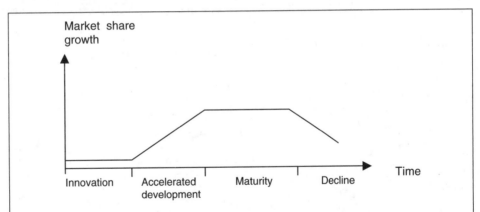

In a development if the product lifecycle, Davison et al. (1976) proposed an institutional lifecycle to explain changes in the retail industry through four phases:

■ *Innovation* New, entrepreneurial retail format. It holds advantages over its competitors due to its tight cost structure, distinctive product mix, location and ease of shopping. Sales increase rapidly, profits may lag.

■ *Accelerated development* Sales volumes and profits increase market share, conventional outlets get hurt. Retaliatory programmes start up from established companies. Profits growth is achieved through fixed expense leverage, creating economies of scale.

■ *Maturity* Market share levels off, resulting in (1) the entrepreneurial management culture facing an unfamiliar stable environment with a large organisation and limited skills; (2) over-capacity, with too much square footage; and (3) New forms of distribution are set up.

■ *Decline* Major loss of market share, marginal profits; inability to compete is obvious to shareholders.

require greater retailer flexibility, creativity and responsiveness (Davidson, Bates and Bass, 1976; Burns *et al.*, 1997).

Independent retailers, department stores, supermarkets, retail parks and regional shopping centres provide a range of retail formats at different lifecycle stages. Individual retailers and their competitors can be positioned on the lifecycle as a contribution to strategic analysis and planning. The history of the Next fashion clothing retailer provides an insight into the development, rapid growth and competitor responses of a retailer aiming at a new market, the younger career woman. Catching the underlying social trend, Next in many ways took over the fashion position held by Laura Ashley during the 1980s, a retailer that for well over a decade has appeared to struggle to avoid the final stages of its lifecycle.

The Wheel of Retailing

A variation of the Lifecycle, the Wheel of Retailing was originally proposed in 1958 from a study of the US retailing industry. The entry point for new retailing formats is through a low margin, low status and low price position, and as the business grows it becomes more elaborate incurring higher operating costs until it moves into a high-cost/high-price position (Figure 2.5). From here it is vulnerable to new low-cost entrants, and the cycle commences once again (McNair, 1958).

Despite its inadequacies the model remains a 'dominant concept . . . in retail' (Brown, 1991). The phases it describes are observable, and at the very least the Wheel

Figure 2.5   *The Wheel of Retailing (after McNair)*

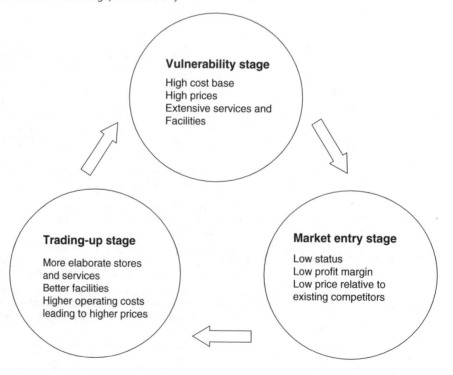

stimulates discussion through an accessible metaphor of time-bound development. However amongst its weaknesses are its lack of universal application to every retailing institution, and its focus on price–quality variables.

In an early review of the Wheel, Hollander (1960) suggests some reasons for this cyclical change: relaxation of entrepreneurial drive by retail leaders, misguidance in trading up due to superfluous modernisation, imperfect competition and secular trends. Other proposals have included excess capacity, where the available business has been spread more thinly; and illusion, the original low price offer is hidden by higher-priced product ranges. There are elements of the wheel in the evolution of multiple food retailing in the UK. Established food multiple retailers such as Sainsbury, but particularly Tesco and Asda, had started their supermarket operations with relatively limited product ranges and services but began to move into more value-added products and services, such as in-store bakeries and butchers. By the early 1990s they had created opportunities for food discounters to enter the market.

There has been considerable academic discussion about the merits of the Wheel, whether it can be tested and its applicability. It is perhaps most useful in explaining the pressures on retailers to expand innovative concepts into new products and store types.

Accordion Theory

The Accordion theory of change is based on the idea of retailers moving from generalist to specialist positioning in the long-term development of retailing. The growth of urban communities allowed profitable segmentation in consumer markets for which the old general store could not cater. As society became more complex and impersonal it provided a new social content to shopping resulting in a return to more general merchandise offers and leading to the growth of shopping centres that themselves resemble large general stores. In the USA at least, the Accordion appears to be contracting once again as consumers show signs of turning back to smaller store formats.

The Accordion theory can also be applied more specifically to the development of retail concepts. The Accordion expands from a compressed base as the retailer develops the successful core business. External stakeholders may exert pressure to maintain the initial high sales and profit growth, and so product ranges are developed to exploit the differential advantages of the business. As sales growth in each product range rapidly matures, so other ranges are added to maintain the momentum, and the width of the retail concept increases.

The process is typified by the development of Next plc: the innovative core business of women's formal wear extended into leisure and then mens wear; accessories, for example shoes, follow on; and childrenswear was a natural extension for mothers with very young children or for older children looking to buy into the fashion label of their older peers. The effect increased as the retailer added new outlets to capitalise on the brand name. The Accordion is fully stretched when selling space and product assortments reach their most productive limits. At this point the retailer is unable to continue its growth rate, disappoints its shareholders who rationally seek to invest for better returns elsewhere, and the retailer is left to refocus on the most productive outlets and competitive products.

Combining the Accordion with the Wheel, Brown has proposed a hybrid theory of change based on product assortment, and price and image dimensions (Brown, 1988).

This suggests that retailers start with a narrow assortment and low price and progress through broader assortments away from price to differentiate themselves by image before finally narrowing their range in a stage of organisational decline.

Non-Cyclical Change: Conflict Theories

The second change theme concerns non-cyclical, conflict theories. Conflict theory asserts that interinstitutional conflict is the main driving force of change, that vigorous competition between old and new maintains market economies' progress. Changes are invariably led by an innovative outsider, and forced onto existing players; non-respondents can survive but at a reduced level. Martenson (1981) defined seven categories of reaction, in two major groups:

1 Imitating the innovator in some or all of its characteristics.

2 Avoiding direct competition; for example discount stores in the USA encouraged traditional stores to move upmarket.

The imitators' main responses begin by recognising the problem, proposing possible solutions and testing them out, and the adoption of a new trading format. Alternatively, four stages can be described similar to typical change management processes; progressing from shock, to defensive retreat, acknowledgement and adaptation. It is suggested that the attacker's behaviour also changes during the hostilities. The challenge evolves in a dialectical process, one of *Action – Reaction – Resolution*, formalised by Gist (1968) into a series of stages each one rejecting the previous orthodoxy. According to this application of dialectic, an increasingly diverse retail structure is the inevitable outcome of interinstitutional conflict. However, it has only been applied to a limited area of research in the USA, and then only to the retail of formats of department stores (thesis), discount stores (antithesis), and discount department stores (synthesis).

Non-Cyclical Change: Environmental Evolution

Changes in retailing can be explained in ecological terms in that there is a sense of natural selection in the retail environmental 'jungle'. Such change is strongly supported by the underlying continuous processes at work in retail structures, and the adjustment of retailers to a wide variety of resources. This takes place over time with many of the features of retailing today evolving from earlier forms as far back as 1900 (Dawson, 2000). Businesses that best adapt to their environment are most likely to survive through identifying and adapting to changes in the demographic, social and economic characteristics of consumers, in the use of technologies and their response to retail competition. The rapid decline in the number of formal menswear retailers, with their core business in suits during the 1980s, and the drift away from variety retailing in the late 1990s can be explained in this way. More specifically, individual companies' ability to adapt strategically to the environment may ultimately decide their survival or extinction in the judgement of their shareholders (Whittington, 1993).

Exhibit 2.4   Evolutionary change

The power of economic recession to bring about sectoral change can be seen in the evolution of food retailing in Denmark. The food sector was formerly dominated by co-operatives, due to constraints on large store development and large companies. However, the late 1980s economic recession led to the rapid growth of limited line discounters, By 1992 discount stores took 15.4 per cent of food sales in Denmark, and have continued to grow significantly during the past decade.

A further perspective on evolutionary change is provided by the mediating role which retailers play in cultural and social preferences amongst consumers. Commodity forms – the values of products and their roles – influence the size and structures of retail sectors within the wider retail structural 'system' and environment. Consequently change occurs when these different spheres of activity interact (Pioch and Schmidt, 2000).

SUMMARY

This chapter has presented the business environment as an important determinant of retailer decision-making. It has proposed that the objective identification of key issues will provide a clearer understanding of environmental forces and the ways in which they may impact on the organisation. The macroenvironment formed by political, economic, social and technological areas, together with global and environmental developments, has been analysed to show its implications for the retail industry.

Decisions were also shown to be dependent on uncertainty in the environment. Retailers need to establish the extent to which this is stable or dynamic, and its level of complexity and their understanding can be assisted by examining a number of change models proposed over the past 40 years. These basically explain changes in the retail industry as either cyclical or non-cyclical. Certain characteristics of retail development can be observed in cyclical models as recurring; non-cyclical models look to environmental or competitive actions as forces for change.

QUESTIONS

1   To what extent does the economy determine retail success?

2   In what ways have retailers adapted to changing socio-demographics trends?

3   Explain how a retailer might monitor changes in the external environment.

4   Assess the theories of change and their application to the retail industry.

5   How might change theories be used to predict the future development of the retail industry?

Case Study

Retail Opportunities with an Older Population

Service-sector industries are failing to target an increasingly affluent 'grey market' of 23 million consumers aged over 45. The number of older people is increasing as a percentage of the population, not only in the UK but also in Western Europe. Between 1995 and 2015 the number of 20 to 29-year-olds will drop by as much as 20 per cent to around 11 million, and over the same period the numbers aged 50 to 64 will grow by more than a quarter to 16.5 million people.

In the UK the older age groups have also managed to increase their income faster than those in younger lifestage categories. The over-65s can attribute their increased affluence partly to occupational and personal pensions and a history of continuous employment, often with just one employer, and partly to home-ownership. With mortgages long since paid off, income can be set aside for other purposes and the equity in the home itself can be realised after many years of growth in property values. This affluence is reflected in the USA too, where the typical household's wealth peaks between the ages of 55 and 74.6.

However, there is a need to subdivide the older population age groups, rather than treat them as a single market. The social and cultural meaning of age is being redefined, partly because of rising life expectancy as age itself is becoming an increasingly unreliable predictor of lifestyles. Consequently organisations need to avoid stereotyping older consumers and develop policies that account for the grey pound.

Working 'greys', the over-45s numbering around 13 million, represent the wealthiest section of the market today, and will be part of the newly retired market in 10 years. The very nature of their work may change as they seek shorter hours or fewer working days. The number of mature entrepreneurs, 'generation M' will increase as more older individuals work for themselves, and in general the older work-force's aspirations are also likely to be more entrepreneurial than previous generations. Moreover, this group will consist of both single-earner and two-earner households, as more women continue to work. Not only will households enjoy a reasonable income, but they will have more time for leisure activities. There is a lifestyle factor in the spending patterns of the over-45s that reflects the priorities of more youthful groups, in increased spending on leisure goods and services typified by holidays, sports and social activities.

For newly-retired greys, spending on leisure has been described as 'spectacular' averaging around £39 per week, only slightly below the £42 for all households. Once children have left home, types of holiday can change offering greater flexibility and, at least for the retired, more time to try out different types of holiday. Keeping fit and healthy are important as older consumers aim to enjoy life more fully. Leisure time is spent in going out each week to restaurants and other forms of entertainment. However, older consumers already have much of what is on offer in shops; household goods are relatively unimportant as many older people have already furnished their homes. Of more interest to retailers is an openness of greys to try out new electronic goods, audio-visual products, computer hardware and software, and online connectivity. There is evidence, too, that personal appearance will take a higher priority in accessing more fashionable clothing, footwear and beauty products.

Elderly greys, too, have doubled their weekly spending on leisure services in the past decade. This group spends 25 per cent more on motoring than the average household, accounting for a higher share of weekly spending than any other single product or services. They also spend 15 per cent more on household services than the average household. And for frail or disabled older people retailers may find potential markets for services and products to provide a better quality of life.

However, the older population will not be entirely affluent, and pensioner poverty is likely to continue to affect significant numbers living on basic state pensions or social benefits. For this group, lack of spending power and mobility may restrict access even to appropriate nutritious foods as food retail multiples relocate to larger superstores and affluent areas creating 'food deserts' in poorer inner-city and rural areas.

What is clear is that consumer demand of the future will be increasingly driven by the tastes and needs of a growing number of older people, customers who will prove to be more exacting than their younger counterparts. The service sector, including retailing, leisure, travel and tourism has yet to fully understand the older market and to respond to its needs and potential spending power.

SEMINAR QUESTIONS FOR DISCUSSION

1 To what extent do older age groups present realistic retail opportunities?

2 Why does the service sector ignore the 45+ population?

References

Baden-Fuller, C. and Stopford, J.M. (1992) *The Mature Business: The Competitive Challenge*, (London: Routledge).

Bennett, R.C. and Cooper, R. (1984) 'The Product Lifecycle Trap', *Business Horizons* no. 5 pp. 7–16.

Brown, S. (1987) 'Institutional Change in Retailing: A Review and Synthesis', *European Journal of Marketing*, vol. 21, no. 6, pp. 5–36.

Brown, S. (1988) *Quarterly Review of Marketing* Spring pp. 8–11.

Brown, S. (1991) 'Variations on a Marketing Enigma: The Wheel of Retailing Theory', *Journal of Marketing Management*, vol. 7, no. 2, April, pp. 131–55.

Burns, K.B., Enright, H., Hayes, J.F., McLaughlin, K. and Shi, C. (1997) 'The Art and Science of Retail Renewal', *The McKinsey Quarterly* no. 2, pp. 100–13.

Davison, W.R., Bates, A.D. and Bass, S.J. (1976) 'The Retail Lifecycle', *Harvard Business Review*, vol. 54, no. 6, pp. 89–96.

Dawson, J. (2000) 'Retailing at Century End: Some Challenges for Management and Research', *The International Review of Retail, Distribution and Consumer Research* vol. 10, no. 2, April, pp. 119–48.

Design Week (1999) 'The Big Picture Retail,' June (London: Design Week).

Dibb, S., Simkin, L., Pride, W.M., Ferrell, O.C. (1997) *Marketing: Concepts and Strategies*, 3rd European edn (Boston, Mass.: Houghton Mifflin).

Financial Times (1999) *Wal-Mart Shakes up Germany's Food Shopping Sector: US Retailer May Struggle to Expand Further in Europe*, 23 June.

Giddens, A. (1991) *Modernity and Self-Identity: Self and Society in the Late-Modern Age* (Cambridge: Polity Press).

Gist, R.R. (1968) *Retailing: Concepts and Decisions* (New York: John Wiley and Sons).

Hollander, S. (1960) 'The Wheel of Retailing', *Journal of Marketing*, vol. 25, pp. 37–42.

Johnson, G. and Scholes, K. (1999) *Exploring Corporate Strategy*, 5th edn (London: Prentice Hall Europe).

Kotler, P. (1997) *Marketing Management: Analysis, Planning, Implementation, and Control*, 9th edn (London: Prentice Hall International).

Lamming, R. and Hampson, J. (1996) 'The Environment as a Supply Chain Management Issue', *British Journal of Management*, vol. 7, special issue S45–S62, March.

Mackay, H. ed. (1997) '*Consumption and Everyday Life*' (London: Sage).

Martenson, R. (1981) *Innovations in Multi-National Retailing: Ikea on the Swiss, Greman and Austrian Furniture Markets,* Department of Business Administration (Gothenburg: University of Gothenburg).

McNair, M.P. (1958) 'Significant Trends and Developments in the Postwar Period', in A.B. Smith (ed.) *Competitive Distribution in a Free High Level Economy and its Implications for the University* (Pittsburgh: University of Pittsburgh Press), pp. 17–18.

McKiernan, P. (1992) *Strategies of Growth: Maturity, Recovery, and Internationalisation,* (London: Routledge).

Mercer, D. (1998) *Marketing Strategy: The Challenge of the External Environment* (London: Sage).

Mintel (1999) *Online Shopping* (London: Mintel International Group).

Mintel (2000) *British Lifestyles 2000* (London: Mintel International Group).

Morgan, G. (1988) *Riding the Cutting Edge of Change* (San Fancisco: Jossey-Bass).

Palmer, A. and Hartley, B. (1996) *The Business and Marketing Environment*, 2nd edn (Maidenhead: McGraw Hill).

Pioch, E.A. and Schmidt, R. (2000) 'Consumption and the Retail Change Process: A Comparative Analysis of Toy Retailing in Italy and France', *The International Review of Retail, Distribution and Consumer Research*, vol. 10, no. 2, pp. 183–203.

Prahalad, C.K. (1999) '*Mastering Strategy 2: Changes in the Competitive Battlefield*', 4 October, (London: Financial Times).

Reynolds, J.R. (1999) 'Who will Dominate European E-commerce? Threats and Opportunities for European Retailers?', Paper presented at the 10th International Conference on Research in the Distributive Trades, University of Stirling.

Scase, R. (1999) *Britain Towards 2010 The Changing Business Environment* (London: Economic and Social Research Council).

Section, D. (1999) *Janet and John Go Shopping: and Discover Real Life Amongst the Rails* (London: Section D.).

Stacey, R.D. (1996) Strategic Management and Organisational Dynamics 2nd edn (London: Pitman).

Toffler, A. (1970) *Future Shock,* (London: Bodley Head).

Van der Heijden, R. (1997) *Scenarios: The Art of Strategic Conversation* (New York: John Wiley and Sons).

Whittington, R. (1993) *What is Strategy and Does it Matter?* (London: Routledge).

Wilson, R.S. and Gilligan, C. (1997) *Strategic Marketing Management: Planning, Implementation and Control*, 2nd edn (Oxford: Butterworth-Heinemann).

Worthington, P. and Britton, M. (1997) *The Business Environment* (London: Pitman).

Channels of Distribution

INTRODUCTION

Distribution channels play a key role in retail management strategy. They provide the means by which goods and services are conveyed from producers to consumers and end users. Channel intermediaries exist at both the wholesale and retail levels, as specialists in distribution functions rather than production or manufacturing functions.

Distribution channel is the term used to refer to the various marketing institutions and interrelationships responsible for the physical and title flow of goods and services from producers to consumers or industrial users. Channels of distribution make products available at the right time, in the right place and in the right quantity by providing such product-enhancing functions as transport and storage (see Lambert and Stock, 1993). Conceptually, these middlemen are the marketing institutions in the distribution channel that link producer to other middlemen, or to those who ultimately use the products. As Kotler (1997) stated, a marketing intermediary is a business firm operating between the producer and the consumer or industrial purchaser.

The importance of distribution channels and marketing intermediaries can be explained in terms of their use and the functions they perform within the retail industry. Distribution strategy within the UK and European retailing is the focus of this third chapter. It covers such basic issues as the role and types of distribution channels, the process of moving goods and services from manufacturer to consumers, the role of brands and changes in distribution systems, retailer decisions with respect to parallel trading and grey markets. The chapter therefore starts with a review of what the channels of distribution are, in terms of retailing.

CHANNELS OF DISTRIBUTION: MANUFACTURING, WHOLESALE AND RETAIL

Lambert and Stock (1993) identify the main channels of distribution as:

■ Manufacturer–wholesaler–retailer–consumer;
■ Manufacturer–retailer–consumer;
■ Manufacturer–consumer.

Usually, the manufacturer distributes from a factory, the wholesaler from a warehouse and the retailer from a store. Each of these channels may be a customer of the previous one, and the final customer is the consumer. Kurtz and Boone (1987) warned that the structure of distribution is not always so well-defined. Some manufacturers operate wholesale warehouses and their own shops. Likewise, some retailers have their own warehouses and factories with products produced under their own brand names. This is known as vertical integration through the industry, as opposed to horizontal combination by firms in the same line of business. In practice, many distribution channels exist from manufacturer to consumer, without there being a single best distribution channel.

As stated in Chapter 1, since the industrial revolution and the subsequent development of mass production, specialisation and division of labour have created distributive activities as specialist entities in the flow of goods from producer to consumer (see Gilligan and Sutton, 1987). In the last 50 years the trend has reversed as both manufacturers and retailers have sought to 'go direct' and cut out others in the pipeline (see Davies and Brooks, 1989). By shortening the pipeline and eliminating intermediaries, economies were anticipated and extra profits gleaned with further advantages arising from trading directly with the customer's customer. But as Exhibit 3.1 demonstrates, some merchandise still requires specialised channels.

Exhibit 3.1   Merchandise requiring specialised channel decisions

Certain commodities such as meat and vegetables, newspapers, flowers and pharmaceutical products by their nature lend themselves to wholesale treatment by specialists. Other products such as furniture, and fashion merchandise, tend to be sold mainly by the manufacturer 'direct' to the retail trade, the responsibility of holding stocks, storing goods, providing delivery and credit usually falling on the supplier. In food, especially, wholesalers have undertaken an active role in the development of the voluntary group concept, with several wholesale warehouses combining to provide the smaller grocery shop with supplies. Wholesale companies have also developed the self-service approach for retailers visiting their warehouses with 'cash and carry' methods of business.

Bryce and Useem (1998) have highlighted the costs and risks involved in taking over other channels' functions. The manufacturer who cuts out the wholesaler and goes 'direct' to the retail trade sets up a wholesale selling system, necessarily performing functions previously carried out by the wholesaler on his behalf. Many manufacturers, for example, sell through agents, on commission terms, to the wholesale trade, who buy in bulk for storage and resale in smaller amounts to shops. The wholesaler in turn employs travelling sales representatives, who visit retailers with samples from which orders are taken for delivery.

Retail Distribution (1998) recorded that a large wholesale warehouse may have several million pounds of stock, and sell to anything up to 10000 shops through 20 to 100 representatives. The capital investment, risk and expenses involved can be enormous, but it does mean that the manufacturer and retailer can use the wholesaler as a 'reservoir' while they focus on their own activities of manufacturing and serving the public respectively (Hobbs, 1996). Smaller retailers and smaller manufacturers, and particularly those dealing in small items, may benefit most by using the services of such a warehouse. The factory can unload its products at suitable times in bulk consignments, yet reach thousands of outlets scattered all over the country. The retailer has a choice of many different factories' goods, which can be bought on demand without even leaving their shop (Popp, 2000).

The arrival of e-commerce has added a further dimension to the distribution process. In business-to-consumer (B2C) transactions, the consumer accesses information and services, including products, directly from the online supplier. Manufacturers may sell directly to the consumer, typically in the case of computers and software, excluding wholesaling and retailing intermediaries. This process of disintermediation provides opportunities to bypass the normal distribution system. With the failure of many early B2C businesses there is a prospect too of reintermediation, the insertion of new types of intermediary to undertake consolidation and distribution functions.

Manufacturing

For manufacturers the *marketing* function relies heavily on the presence of intermediaries between the themselves and the consumer. As well as serving as product conduits, intermediaries also serve as information conduits (Kurtz and Boone, 1987). Often, producers have little or no direct contact with end-user customers and must rely almost entirely on intermediaries for information about them. Likewise, intermediaries often carry information for end users from manufacturers. Some of the key issues in retailing from the manufacturer's perspective are:

■ A move towards 'hybrid' distribution systems in which a large number of short channels replace a small number of long channels;

■ The growing prominence of non-traditional retailers; and

■ The increased pressure producers are bringing to bear on retailers to adopt technologies such as electronic data interchange (EDI) and techniques such as Efficient Consumer Response (ECR).

As Omar (1999) has explained, many manufacturers in the past tended to *distribute* their products either indirectly through intermediaries, or directly to end users. However, there is a trend for manufacturers to move towards the simultaneous use of both direct and indirect distribution, with the aim of providing the greatest market coverage in the most cost-effective way. Thus, manufacturers such as IBM and Xerox that previously sold only through indirect channels are now adding direct channels. Similarly, travel companies such as British Airways and Virgin Trains are adding direct channel options for end users through their websites. Such moves are facilitated by the rising power and falling cost of information technology.

At the same time, many manufacturers are finding that it is uneconomical for them to serve smaller indirect accounts. This is resulting in the outsourcing of some of their retailer customers to other distributors with low-turnover retailer customers being supplied indirectly by larger distributors. In the future, some packaged goods manufacturers are very likely to ask some of their retailers to become 'master distributors' and take on smaller retailers as customers. In moving to such complex hybrid marketing channels, manufacturers are likely to face a number of areas of potential conflict with retailers, and preventing and managing such conflict will be an important factor in the success of these arrangements.

Owing to greater social and demographic diversity in the UK and many other European countries, coupled with a rising geographical mobility, manufacturers are finding that traditional retailers do not adequately cover many shopping locations. As, increasingly, shopping occurs in the home and in public places such as airports, non-traditional retailers are stepping into the breach and manufacturers need to include these in the mix in order to achieve greater market coverage (Omar and Kent, 2001). As discussed in Chapter 17 of this book, the search for efficiency and productivity is leading manufacturers to press retailers of all sizes to integrate information technology (IT) into their operations, especially for the sake of vertical information flows.

Wholesaling

Wholesalers make it possible to efficiently provide possession, time and place utility. The wholesale function is economically justified because it improves distribution efficiency: by 'breaking bulk' from manufacturers for typically small independent retailers, and provides financing for their retail or industrial customers. A further function is to create assortments of goods; in the clothing sector in particular, independent retailers rely on wholesalers for fast-moving fashion lines that need to be replenished swiftly.

Traditionally some products have had large enough unit prices or margins to enable the manufacturer to sell directly to retailers, even when the number of items sold to each retailer is small. However, manufacturers of low-value or low-margin items such as cigarettes and some food items may find it profitable to sell only through wholesalers, even though retailers may order in relatively large quantities. Although grocery products dominate the wholesale sector, newspapers and magazine distribution have been reliant on wholesalers, and significant distribution networks exist for the pharmacy and electrical trades. Manufacturers' generic and unbranded merchandise can also find a distribution channel through wholesalers: office supplies and seasonal clothing suppliers typically operate in this field.

Wholesalers' market power is greatest when retailers order a small amount of each manufacturer's products, or when the manufacturers involved have limited financial resources (Howe, 1992). Their financial strength determines the number of marketing functions they can perform, from product origination and packaging to advertising and promotional support. Each function represents a profit opportunity as well as an associated risk and cost, and the presence or absence of other firms offering comparable services influences the market power of individual wholesalers. In symbol groups, for example, the retailer is committed to buy a large proportion of their purchases, including own label, through the group using their order and payment procedures.

Two methods of wholesaling take place, delivered and cash and carry.

- *Delivered* wholesalers provided the original form of wholesale distribution, delivering goods to the retailer's trading location and charging them for the service. Delivered wholesalers work on low profit margins of less than 1 per cent and distribute a wide range of grocery, household and health and beauty products from depots covering catchment areas of some 80–100 miles. The majority of their customers are grocery retailers accounting for 60–70 per cent of sales with caterers taking between 30–40 per cent (Mintel, 1999). Newspaper wholesale distributors regularly supply newsagents and other stores with magazines and newspapers from many publishers. These are made available on a sale or return basis leading to a more complex process for redistribution and recycling.

- *Cash and carry* operations were primarily established to serve small food retailers with grocery products in the 1960s; retailers take away small quantities using their own transport. The product range is dominated by cigarettes and tobacco, general groceries and confectionery and soft drinks. As a member of a cash and carry wholesale organisation, the shopkeeper eliminates the need for wholesale representatives by selecting and finally paying at the wholesaler's checkout point. In practice, the difference between delivered wholesaling and cash and carry is becoming blurred as companies add value to their services. Many cash and carry retailers now deliver, particularly fresh, frozen and chilled items.

Wholesaling has declined as the number of multiple retailers sourcing directly from suppliers in large quantities has multiplied. In the food sector this has resulted in the consolidation and restructuring of the leading companies. However, new opportunities for delivered wholesaling businesses to offset the decline in traditional independent retail businesses have arisen during the 1990s with the increase in convenience food retailing, developed around symbol retailers and petrol forecourt shops. The increasing popularity of eating out and the consequent expansion of restaurants and takeaway businesses have provided further opportunities for expansion. It has been estimated that around 80 per cent of the UK catering market was supplied through wholesalers in 1998 (Mintels 2000).

Retailing

Retailers are one of the most significant types of intermediary, situated as they are at the point of direct contact with customers. As McGoldrick (1990) has demonstrated, the retailing function adds value in a number of ways, most of which are difficult for manufacturers to replace. These include:

- Breaking caseloads into smaller quantities;

- Providing an assortment of products so that customers can go 'one-stop' shopping;

- Creating an inventory buffer between producers and consumers so that products are available when desired; and

- Providing support services such as display, demonstration, credit, delivery, assembly, repair and return and warranty services.

These functions are summarised in Figure 3.1. The retailing sector has grown enormously (see Chapter 1 of this book), and over its long history the retailing function has changed in response to:

- Consumption patterns: for example, the rise in the proportion of expenditure allocated to services;

- Demographic shifts: for example, the migration from inner cities to suburbs; and

- Technological forces: for example, the widespread use of credit cards.

In terms of distribution, retailers are faced with a variety of other decisions, many of which ensure that adequate quantities of stock are available when consumers want to buy. Retailers exist in the channel of distribution to provide a convenient product assortment, availability, price and image within the geographic market served. The degree of customer preference, and loyalty due to customer service and price/value performance that a retailer enjoys in a specific area, directly affects its ability to

Figure 3.1   *Key Retailing Functions*

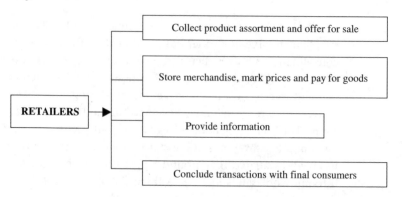

negotiate channel relationships. The retailer's financial capability and size also determine its degree of influence over other channel members.

Channel Selection

The choices of appropriate channel are based upon an analysis of market, product, producer and competitive factors as show in Table 3.1. Each factor can be of critical importance, and the factors are often interrelated in the creation of value for the final consumer. Stronger linkages through the chain of distribution will enable members to create more distinctive and enduring values than weaker ones. Increasingly, retailers and suppliers are faced with channel decisions, concerning relationships, that enable partnering to take place. This reduces traditional confrontational relationships in which channel members seek to gain advantages over each other.

As shown in the table, both retailers and manufacturers need to take a careful look at their organisation in making channel selection decisions. It may be necessary to examine all the factors cited and to add others that may be particular to the organisation. The discussion here is concerned with a brief review of the factors listed in Table 3.1.

Market factors

A major determinant of channel structure is whether the product is intended for the consumer or the industrial market. Industrial purchasers may prefer to deal directly with the manufacturer (except for supplies or small-accessory items). On the other

Table 3.1   *Factors Affecting the Selection of Distribution Channels*

Factors	Characteristics of few (short) channel members	Characteristics of extended (long) channel members
1 Market	■ Industrial user ■ Geographically concentrated ■ Technical knowledge and regular servicing is required ■ Large orders	■ Consumers ■ Geographically diverse ■ Technical knowledge and regular servicing is unnecessary ■ Small orders
2 Product	■ Perishable ■ Complex ■ Expensive	■ Durable ■ Standardised ■ Inexpensive
3 Manufacturer	■ Has adequate resources to perform channel functions ■ Broad product line ■ Channel control is important	■ Lacks adequate resources to perform channel functions ■ Limited product line ■ Channel control is not important
4 Competitive	■ Manufacturer feels that intermediaries are inadequately promoting products	■ Manufacturer feels that intermediaries are adequately promoting products

hand, most consumers purchase from retail stores. Often, products intended for both industrial users and consumers are sold through more than one channel.

The needs and geographic location of the company's market affect channel choice. Direct sales are possible, for example, where the company's potential market is concentrated geographically (Kotler, 1997). A small number of potential buyers also increases the feasibility of direct channels. Households everywhere purchase consumer goods, and since households are numerous and geographically dispersed, and purchase a small volume at a given time, intermediaries must be employed to market products to them.

A shift in consumer shopping patterns (see Fernie, 1997) may also influence channel decisions through:

- the desire for credit;
- the growth of self-service;
- the increased use of mail-order houses;
- shopping via the Internet; and
- the greater willingness to purchase from door-to-door salespeople

All these factors are likely to affect a firm's choice of distribution channels.

Product factor

Products play a role in determining optimal distribution channels. Perishable products such as fresh vegetables and fruit, and fashion products with short life-cycles, typically move through relatively short channels directly to the retailer or the ultimate consumer. On the other hand, the producer typically sells complex products such as custom-made installations or computer equipment direct to the buyer. As a general rule, the more standardised the product, the longer the channel. Wholesalers usually market standardised goods, whereas products that require regular service or a specialised repair service are not usually distributed through channels employing independent wholesalers. Cars, for example, are distributed through a franchised network of dealers whose employees receive training on how to properly service them. Another generalisation about distribution channels is that the lower the unit value of the product, the longer the channel. Convenience goods and industrial supplies with typically low unit prices are frequently distributed through relatively long channels. Installations and more expensive industrial and consumer goods employ shorter, more direct channels.

Producer factors

Companies with adequate financial, managerial and distributive resources are less compelled to use intermediaries in distributing their products. A financially strong manufacturer can employ its own sales force, warehouse its own products, and grant credit to retailers or consumers. A financially weaker producer must rely on intermediaries for these services (although some large retail chains purchase all of the manufacturer's output, thereby bypassing the independent wholesaler). Some producers may be forced to use the marketing expertise of intermediaries to replace the limited financial and managerial resources in their organisation.

A manufacturer such as Northern Foods in the UK with a broad product line is able to market its products directly to retailers, since its sales force can offer a variety of products. The manufacturer's need for control over the product may also influence channel selection. If aggressive promotion is desired at the retail level, the producer chooses the shortest available channel, but for new products the producer may be forced to implement an introductory advertising campaign before independent whole-salers will handle the items.

Competitive factors

Some firms are forced to develop unique distribution channels because of inadequate promotion of their products by independent marketing intermediaries. Avon's famous shift to house-to-house selling was prompted by intense competition from similar lines of cosmetics.

Evolution of Distribution

In discussing channels of distribution, it is essential to recognise the extent to which the conventional barriers between manufacturing, wholesaling and retailing described above have broken down. A glance at Figure 3.2 shows that many of the functions are duplicated and retailers are doing almost the same functions as the wholesalers. Thus, major retailers have increasingly subsumed the wholesaling role and many have also taken over the task of physical distribution, although areas of distribution such as logistics and transportation may also be subcontracted to specialist and professional agencies. Supply chain management is discussed in detail in Chapter 10.

In terms of product design and development, McGoldrick (1990) has highlighted the erosion of the manufacturer's exclusive hold over these functions. He noted that although few retailers have chosen to acquire manufacturing facilities directly, they could be very closely involved in the design specifications and the quality control process. This is one reason why Tse (1985) has described Marks & Spencer as a manufacturer without factories.

Figure 3.2   *Conventional Channel Members and their Functions*

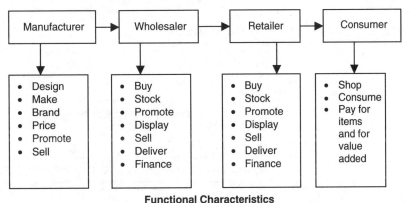

Functional Characteristics

THE PROCESS OF DISTRIBUTION

The process of managing the movement of goods from suppliers, through the retailer and on to customers is termed retail logistics (Omar, 1999). Logistics combines physical distribution management (PDM) with the concept of materials management into a single system. The management task in physical distribution can therefore be stated as the planning, coordinating and controlling of the physical movement of products. The aim is to provide a level of timely and spatial physical availability for customers, appropriate to the needs of the marketplace and the resources of the retailer (Howe, 1992).

This statement shows that physical distribution is concerned with a number of elements which can be described as the distribution mix. The distribution mix (Fernie and Sparks, 1997) is concerned with making decisions about:

■ the number, type and location of storage facilities;

■ the transport system to be used in moving goods;

■ the level of stockholding in terms of both quality and quantity;

■ packaging and unit sizes and how these are handled; and

■ communications both within the retail organisation and the external environment.

These elements of the distribution mix (storage facilities, inventory management, transportation, unitisation and communications) have to work together to ensure an efficient distribution process (see Figure 3.3). A retailer, for example, has to be aware of consumer demand for his or her merchandise in the store, knowledge which is translated both into product orders to suppliers and to resupplying shelves at the retail outlets. These communications trigger the setting of inventory levels at various storage points, and also force product movement through transportation. As shown in Figure 3.3, all the elements interact in providing distribution and in setting service levels and costs incurred.

The distribution function has to manage these elements of the distribution mix to provide the correct balance for the market and the company between the lowest

Figure 3.3   *The Elements of the Distribution Mix*

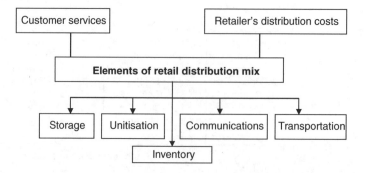

possible distribution costs on the one hand, and the highest possible customer satisfaction on the other. Distribution is explicitly concerned with costs and customer service and the elements of decision-making that influence these. Even though the provision of goods is an essential element of service, retailers cannot forecast precisely what the demand for goods is going to be. A balance has therefore to be struck. To some considerable extent a better awareness of the costs incurred in making this balance, and the potential service gains that are available have caused the emergence of a new direction in distribution processes.

In the past, manufacturers or wholesalers made most deliveries in Britain directly to retailers' premises. Today the norm is for delivery to be made to a retailer's own or controlled central warehouse. So, instead of a wholesaler delivering an assortment of merchandise to the retailer, the retailer has replaced this role with its own warehousing and transportation. It is unlikely that the multiples could have secured their market share growth without the economic and operational benefits of centralised distribution.

However the advantages to the retailer do not stem from replacing the manufacturer's delivery system so much as from reducing stock levels, as reducing the need for delivery procedures at store level, and freeing up storage space in retail outlets that can be converted to selling space. Other benefits stemming from better control may include fewer stockouts and lower shrinkage. This practically means that retailers are now able to innovate into retail logistics and to adopt strategies for centralising retail distribution.

In the UK there has been a significant move by multiple retailers towards centralisation of inventory through the use of integrated regional distribution centres (RDC) and integrated warehousing. This has had wide-ranging consequences in the development of responsive distribution channels:

1 Quantity purchase discounts achieved as a result of bulk purchasing mean that instead of store managers from each supermarket placing orders with suppliers, joint orders are placed through the RDC or a central purchasing office. This, in effect, means making larger orders and gaining improved discounts from suppliers.

2 Better control of levels of inventory. By this method there are advantages in centralisation since inventory held at an RDC can be released to supermarkets according to the changing levels of demand at each supermarket. As a result, there should be less risk of keeping too much inventory within the supply chain as a whole or, conversely, of running out of particular products at some supermarkets when faced with unexpectedly high demand. Furthermore, the centralisation of inventory can, in itself, reduce the inventory requirement for multiple retailing according to the square-root law. By eliminating storerooms at supermarkets and keeping all inventories at RDCs, there should be a reduced overall inventory requirement within the retail supply chain.

3 Reduced stock loss. By converting space from supermarket storerooms into sales space means that goods delivered to the supermarket are put straight on to the shelves. This reduction in handling means that there is less likelihood of breakage and less opportunity for theft.

Exhibit 3.2   UK retailers see benefits of centralisation

Clearly many UK retailers, including Sainsbury, Mothercare, Boots, Asda and Argos, have found the benefits of centralisation impossible to resist. Consciously or unconsciously, they have been using 'logistical competency to gain competitive advantage'. And, given the pivotal role of inventory in promoting the centralisation concept, retailers have also recognised the importance of inventory as the focal asset of business. The skill of UK retailers in logistics innovation is well-documented in the literature. Sainsbury, pioneer of the RDC concept, now has around 25 distribution centres strategically located throughout the UK and responsible for handling over seven million cases (85 per cent of the volume) each week to an estimated 296 supermarkets. Another innovator is Argos, whose efficient distribution enables it to achieve an approximately 95 per cent level of product availability on an almost 4000 product range throughout the year at all of its 250 catalogue showroom outlets.

---

4 Opportunities for mechanisation means that the large RDCs, by breaching throughput thresholds and exploiting economies of scale, make it economic to introduce more mechanisation to materials handling. This reduces the retailer's dependence upon labour and makes maximum use of storage volumes within RDCs, especially with respect to height (Omar, 1999).

Movement of Goods in Europe

In their quest for efficient movement of goods within the UK and Europe, how retailers organise and manage their own distribution systems varies considerably. Where retailers insist on organising the collection of stock from their suppliers, some own their transport and warehousing systems, whilst other retailers 'contract'-out to third parties. Such contracts vary in their scope but can be very comprehensive, to include custom-built premises, incorporation of the retailer's order processing, vehicles painted in the retailer's corporate colours, specialist racking and much more (Lambert and Stock, 1993).

Contracting-out may release a retailer's capital and allow it to focus on its core business of retailing. The third-party operator may achieve economies such as back-loading for other companies or combining entire operations to make best use of its transport. This method may, however, introduce another company and another organisation into the supply chain. Having absorbed the wholesaler's role many retailers are to some extent now recreating it in their third-party relationships.

Most sectors of retailing in Europe can provide at least an example of excellence in logistics. In clothing, Benetton has used innovative approaches to logistics to develop and sustain its position as a leading fashion retailer (Cooper *et al.*, 1994). In furniture retailing, Ikea would have been unable to expand from its Swedish home market without a strong logistics base.

One sector, which has consistently led with new ideas is grocery retailing (Fernie, 1995), particularly in European countries where retail multiples are dominant. France and the UK are now emerging as the leading innovators in grocery retail distribution (Harvey, 2000), although the development of grocery retailing in the UK has advanced along different lines from those in France. In the UK, grocery retailing is based on supermarkets, typically sited in urban high streets and out-of-town superstores with additional ranges of food and non-food products (Gilligan and Sutton, 1987). By contrast, the hypermarket format takes the largest share of food sales in France, and it must be recognised that innovations in distribution and storage will not necessarily transfer in an unmodified form between formats. In hypermarkets in provincial France, for example, storage space must often be adjacent to the sales space because there is less scope for serving several hypermarkets from a separate distribution centre.

Information Technology (IT)

Spectacular advances in computer technologies have made IT a key component of logistics planning in the retail industry (Skjoett-Larsen, 2000). According to Skjoett-Larsen, a major contribution of IT in logistics is that it increases transparency within the supply chain, replacing the uncertainties of physical stock counting (Moore, 1991).

The introduction of electronic point of sale (EPOS) systems has completely changed both how retailers check quantities at the store and reorder new supplies. As customers pass through checkouts at supermarkets, light pens or bar-coded readers are now widely used to identify the products purchased. Whereas once the checkout operator had to enter the price of an individual item into a cash register, the EPOS system is used to check the price of the item and automatically add it to the total of other goods purchased by the shopper. At the end of the transaction, the customer receipt is printed out to include descriptions of the goods bought, together with prices of individual items.

As Bamfield (1994) has argued, this is all very helpful for the customer, not least because the time through the checkout is reduced by the automatic identification of purchased items using the EPOS system. And for the retailer, there is an immediate registration within the EPOS system of goods sold. When this data is matched to data for goods delivered to the store, it is possible to have an immediate and up-to-date understanding of items held at the store for any given product line. As a result, this procedure reduces error and saves time; it can eliminate waste and reduces the risk of oversupply to outlets relative to demand.

A Controlled Transportation Environment

It is in grocery retailing that EPOS has its greatest impact in the selection and management of distribution channels. The growing demand for fresh food to contain fewer preservatives means that product life is shortened, and as a result there is pressure on retail logistics to maximise the life of fresh food on the shelves of supermarkets and in the customer's home. EPOS systems in association with controlled atmosphere packing (CAP) and controlled environments for the growing of fresh food will help in the realisation of this objective. This means that demand forecasting, linked with EPOS to monitor actual sales, can be used to inform growers of the short-term requirement. In this way, food production and demand can be better harmonised so that there is less product waste within the supply chain.

The freshness of food products such as meat and fish, as well as vegetables, can be prolonged during transit by the use of vehicles with controlled environments, again contributing to longer shelf life.

Maximising Sales Space

A major development in retail operations management is the release of more sales space in retail outlets by eliminating storage space. The opportunity cost of storage space will often be substantial in high-street locations, and converting this storage space into sales space has important implications for both retailers and the suppliers of logistics services.

Most retailers will be united in the belief that retail outlets are for sales rather than storage. But many retailers feel they are forced to retain stock rooms at retail outlets for fear of running out of essential product lines. However, storage space within the store has two important disadvantages. Most important of all is that it reduces the sales area and hence the revenue-earning potential of a given retail outlet. A second factor is that storing products in the shop's stockroom is an additional financial commitment, and this impacts on both cashflow and profitability.

The prospect of eliminating stockrooms at shops is better for an affiliated independent retailer if, say, the voluntary group to which he or she belongs is prepared to innovate in logistics. Essentially what is required is a frequent delivery service from the voluntary group acting as wholesaler. Daily deliveries may have to replace deliveries every two or three days. Furthermore, support will have to be forthcoming from other independent retailers affiliated to the same voluntary group to ensure sufficient volumes for economic delivery on a more frequent basis. Overall, multiple retailers have the best prospect of eliminating storage space at shops and, indeed, many of them have already done just that. In some cases, however, the opportunity to do so may have come about as a consequence of first following other priorities.

BRANDED DISTRIBUTION CHANNELS

The pressure on brands today is intense. Products are functionally equivalent in many categories and new product development cycles are shortening so that functional innovations can be quickly imitated. The squeeze on margins in many categories has led some companies to leap conventional product market boundaries, making it increasingly difficult to anticipate who future competitors will be and how they will play the game (*The Economist*, 1999). New channels of distribution are emerging and power within conventional ones has shifted from the manufacturer towards the retailer as a result of both industry consolidation and the growth of retailers' own labels which account for as much as 70 per cent of sales in some categories (see Table 3.2).

Against this backdrop, it is not surprising that even powerful brands such as Coca-Cola, McDonald's and Levi's are struggling to sustain leadership positions, but nevertheless many continue to thrive, as Exhibit 3.3 shows.

Own-label Distribution Channels

Products developed by retailers themselves are distinguished by a range of titles (discussed in more detail in Chapter 10), but in the context of distribution, own-label is

Table 3.2   *Own-Label Penetration by Country, 1997*

Country	Own-label share (% units)	Pop/km²	% large stores (≥3000 m²)	Top 3 retailers' market share (%)
Switzerland	41.2	155	36	80
UK	37.1	228	70	45
Germany	21.8	225	40	47
Canada	21.0	3	50	25
Belgium	19.8	325	56	58
USA	17.6	25	70	17
France	16.4	103	76	38
Netherlands	16.3	363	31	47
Denmark	15.1	118	37	77
Sweden	10.7	19	38	95
Finland	8.0	148	27	75
Spain	7.7	77	35	20
Italy	6.8	19	26	11
Austria	6.3	91	26	56
Norway	5.0	13	19	86
Ireland	3.6	50	53	43
Portugal	2.3	113	43	41

Source: S. Dhar and S.J. Hoch (1998), 'Why Store Brand Penetration Varies'.

Exhibit 3.3   Successful brands

Consider the Swiss watch manufacturers. Japanese corporations such as Seiko, Citizen and others offer highly accurate watches at ever-lower prices, yet buyers spend more globally on Swiss watches than on all other watches combined. Similarly, many good-quality inexpensive pens are available, yet Waterman's newest entry, the Edson line, includes a £250 ballpoint pen and a £450 fountain pen. Sales are brisk. Haagen Dazs continues to have a significant impact in the growing premium ice-cream segment. Toyota's Lexus sports car sells well despite its £37 500 price tag and the availability of many fine similar alternatives at lower prices. The success of these brands reflects a growing realisation that as consumers and competitors have changed in fundamental ways so must the nature of brands.

---

used to distinguish retailer-led from branded product development. The lesson from UK retailers is that own-label strategies can only achieve significant market share where the retailer controls the supply chain, particularly for fresh and chilled products. Heavy investment is needed in dedicated stockholding regional distribution centres (RDCs), frequent delivery to stores via integrated logistics and in information technology. In this way sales at store level can trigger demand upon the individual manufacturer. Decisions on range, promotion, pricing and space allocation must be communicated between the store, the retail management and the logistics function.

Information technology is the essential management tool requiring significant capital investment, around 2 and 6 per cent of sales value in the UK (Bell *et al.*, 1997). The necessary investment to drive supply chains can be facilitated through financial restructuring, a decision taken by one of Europe's largest retail companies, Metro, in Germany. Elsewhere in Europe there may well be the need for further retail concentration to achieve economies of scale. Efficiencies in the supply chain depend upon sharing information upstream and downstream, requiring supply-chain members to control store operations rather than being controlled by store operations. This is difficult to achieve in franchise operations or retailer co-operatives, commonly found in, for example, Italy and less-developed retail markets.

However, the local relevance of the product range is also an important source of competitive advantage. This may often be better achieved through competent store managers in touch with the needs of their consumers, rather than through retailing and logistics functions. This situation is most likely to arise in large countries which have significant regional cultural differences, as in Germany. The challenge for retailers is to determine the relative advantage of national supply-chain efficiencies which require retailing, versus local relevance of range and promotion, and to then organise accordingly.

Own-label Suppliers

Manufacturers have felt able to supply own-label products in addition to their brands, attracted by increasing volumes without incurring the level of marketing and product development costs associated with branded products. The changing structure of retailing may lead to a polarisation of manufacturers between those supplying branded and own-label products. Major branded manufacturers such as Procter & Gamble, Coca-Cola and Mars have refrained from producing own-label, whilst on the other hand we have witnessed the development of specialist own-label suppliers such as Northern Foods, Hazlewood and Hillsdown (*The Grocer*, 1998).

Changes in retailing pose unique challenges to manufacturers planning to supply own-label (Christopher, 1997). These challenges are quite different to those facing the branded supplier. The retailers' first requirement will be purchase price, often through some form of bidding process, and this situation will be exacerbated as the international perspective of retailers grows. Suppliers will find themselves in a global marketplace, creating both greater potential volumes and more intense competitive threats. Integration of the supply chain creates demands for increased production flexibility. Each own-label item is dedicated to an individual retailer who can thus influence production cycles as the route to minimising inventory levels. Production flexibility is as important as price in the selection of suppliers by retailers; as retailers become better organised they are able to increase their product development expertise. Marks and Spencer have pioneered this approach with their food products in the UK. The transfer of technical competence to the retailer will reduce differences in product specification between suppliers, increasing the emphasis on price competitiveness.

CHANGING PATTERNS OF DISTRIBUTION

Changes in the channels of distribution for both consumer and industrial goods can have far-reaching consequences for existing competitors and would-be entrants.

Changes take place in part because of product life-cycle phenomena as the market matures to more intensive distribution, increasing convenience, and often lower levels of channel service. Changes also frequently take place as a result of new institutional development in the channels themselves. Few sectors of American industry have changed as fast as retail and wholesale distribution, with the result that completely new types of outlets may be employed by suppliers seeking to develop competitive advantage. Whatever the origin of the change, the effect may be to provide an opportunity for a new entrant and to raise questions about the viability of existing competitors. Gillette's contemplated entry into the blank cassette-tape market is a case in point (Exhibit 3.4).

Choosing a distribution channel is thus a strategic decision with major investment implications for both manufacturers and retailers. In some retailing sectors such as airlines and travel, it is more profitable for the airline if customers order directly from the airline rather than going through travel agents. There are major drawbacks, however, if an airline promotes its direct channel so heavily that travel agents recommend other airlines in retaliation.

An analysis of the UK new-car retail market suggests that dramatic gains in distribution and retail marketing efficiency are realised when manufacturers and retailers work together through strategic collaboration (Omar, 1998). The partnership between these two groups is a major departure from their traditionally antagonistic relationship. Strategic collaboration between suppliers and retailers recognises that both are part of the distribution process, which can be greatly streamlined and simplified. These forms of channel partnerships have been adopted in such diverse categories as household goods, personal care products, personal computers and home furnishings. As Alba *et al.* (1997) have noted, inventory is pulled through the system rather than pushed down, allowing companies to provide greater product availability for customers with lower average levels of inventory. This is reflected in Black & Decker's distribution philosophy of 'sell one, ship one, and build one'. Strategic collaboration therefore provides the advantages of vertical integration without the attendant drawbacks.

Exhibit 3.4   Gillette's entry into blank cassette tapes

As the market for cassettes evolved due to increased penetration and new uses of equipment for cars, study, business, letter writing and home entertainment, so did distribution channels broaden into an increasing number of drug chains, variety stores and large discount stores. Presumably it was recognition of a possible 'strategic window' for Gillette that encouraged executives in the Safety Razor Division to look carefully at ways in which Gillette might exploit the cassette market at this particular stage in its evolution. The question was whether Gillette's skill in marketing low-priced, frequently purchased packaged goods, along with its distribution channel resources, could be applied to marketing blank cassettes. Was there a place for a competitor in this market to offer a quality branded product, broadly distributed and supported by heavy media advertising in much the same way that Gillette marketed razor blades?

Actually, Gillette decided against entry, apparently not because a 'strategic window' did not exist, but because profit prospects were not favourable. They did, however, enter the cigarette lighter business based on a similar analysis and have reportedly had considerable success with their Cricket brand.

These systems are likely to improve efficiency and customer service primarily by replacing physical assets with information. They may reduce the retailer's inventory while providing a supply of merchandise that closely matches consumers' actual buying patterns. Resources that were formerly tied up in inventory might also be directed elsewhere, for example to increase advertising. The result is a likely winning outcome. Consumers may consistently find the merchandise they want and often at lower prices; suppliers may increase sales, lower costs and cement ties with retailers; and retailers may gain increased sales and stock turnovers.

New methods of distributing products have also emerged, many of which are technology-driven. In financial services, the automated teller machine (ATM) has replaced the branch visit for many routine financial transactions. Building societies which never offered current accounts are now doing so, and customers can phone insurance companies for loans. All these changes have had a major impact on European banks causing a decline in the number of bank branches across Europe. In the UK, the major banks have been steadily rationalising throughout the 1990s, resulting in the disappearance of hundreds of branches from the high street.

Teleshopping

Countries such as the Netherlands, Ireland and the UK have been vying for the position as the most attractive call-centre location in Europe, not only for selling physical products such as personal computers (PCs), but also for hotel and travel reservations, customer-care operations and so on. These changes are the result of an increasing willingness on the part of customers to use the telephone for purchasing goods and services and improvements in payment mechanisms. Freephone numbers and the increasingly sophisticated use of telephone call-centre technology are changing the ways in which retailers and manufacturers go to market.

Virtual retail distribution

Beyond facilitating channel partnerships, technology is affecting the retail industry through the substitution of electronic shopping for store-based retailing. A normal shopping trip involves deciding what to purchase, travelling to the store, selecting items for purchase, taking them to the checkout, queuing, paying for the goods, putting them in bags and them taking them home. Virtual or e-retailing allows consumers to select the items they require, pay electronically and have the goods delivered when it is convenient. Selecting the goods can be done from work, a hotel, at home or even in the car. As a result the implications for retailers will be enormous, as location no longer becomes a barrier to entry.

Virtual retailing is being made possible by the proliferation of distribution networks and computing technology. It takes place through the supplier's unique website, but also through online shopping malls, hubs and auctions using home computers or interactive television. For many time-pressured customers, shopping online or via a catalogue for next-day delivery provide greater time value than a trip to the store. According to *The Economist* (1999), UK consumers spend £3 billion a year on items from TV shopping networks, £10 billion shopping over the Internet and £60 billion on purchases from mail-order companies such as Littlewoods and Marshall Ward. While this still represents a very small portion of the retailing sector, recent growth trends indicate that electronic retailing is poised to enter the mainstream.

The World Wide Web, even in its current narrow-band mode, demonstrates the vast potential of technology. Electronic shopping (Field, 1996) is typically more cost-effective than store-based retailing and can enable costs to be lowered by around 25 per cent. However, other factors must also be evaluated: these include the number of alternative products and services that can be made available; the social and recreational dimensions of shopping; the amount of information that customers need and the amount that can be readily provided; and the type of product – the 'total shopping experience' must be considered in order to assess the strengths of different retail formats.

Reynolds (2000) proposes that successful electronic retailers will usually seek competitive advantage in one or more of the following areas:

- distribution efficiency;
- assortments of complementary merchandise;
- collection and use of customer information;
- presentation of information through electronic formats; and
- unique merchandise.

Alba *et al.* (1997) suggested that catalogue retailers are the most vulnerable to electronic shopping. While it has some of the same limitations as catalogue retailing,

Mini Case Study

Dell's Application of a Full Integrative Value Chain

Dell computer's factory on the outskirts of Limerick, on the West Coast of Ireland, supplies custom-built PCs all over Europe. As orders come into the factory via Dell's website and call centres, the company relays to its suppliers details of which components it needs, how many and when. All the components are delivered by lorry to loading bays at the back of the building, and move off again as complete computers just a few hours later.

Dell creates considerable attention as a pioneering e-business because it sells $15m worth of computers from its website each day. Because Dell's suppliers have real-time access to information about its orders via its corporate extranet, they can organise their production and delivery to ensure that the company always has just enough of the right parts to keep the production line moving smoothly. By plugging its suppliers directly into its customer database, Dell enables them to track the progress of their order from the factory to their doorstep, thus saving on telephone or fax inquiries.

Dell was regarded as an efficient company before it started using the Internet, but now it is able to do even better by creating a 'fully integrated value chain'. The Internet has enabled it to create a three-way 'information partnership' with its suppliers and customers, treating them as collaborators who together find ways of improving efficiency across the entire chain of supply and demand, and sharing the benefits.

such as delivery times, electronic shopping can provide customers with much more information than catalogues. Electronic shopping can provide an ideal channel for retailers with strong reputations for high-quality and unique merchandise but incomplete market coverage, for example Harrods department store.

In order to succeed, store-based retailers will have to emphasise merchandise that has predominantly experiential attributes; that is, it must be seen directly, touched or has other sensual qualities to promote the non-informational benefits of shopping such as entertainment and socialising, and treat electronic shopping as a complement to their in-store business. Similarly, Alba *et al.* (*ibid.*) outline the conditions under which manufacturers would have an incentive to disintermediate, that is to bypass retailers and deal directly with customers. Manufacturers possessing both strong brand names and the ability to produce complementary merchandise such as Levi Strauss are most likely to consider this. However, they should carefully consider the impact on their relationships with intermediaries. In situations where the advantages of electronic shopping are very strong, store-based retailers would be ill-advised to try to counter the trend. Rather, they should devote their efforts to developing strategies to take advantage of the opportunities offered by electronic shopping.

PARALLEL TRADING AND 'GREY' MARKETS

Buying and selling discounted or counterfeit branded goods has its origins in the 'black' market, undertaken as an alternative, unofficial distribution channel to legitimate business operations. The practice of buying branded goods from cheaper markets, for sale at lower prices than those charged by authorised distributors, has come to be known as parallel, or 'grey' importing.

Manufacturers normally decide on the distribution channels for branded products. With international brands, distribution is organised in each country through sales teams, dealers or agents. The merchandise is sold at prices determined by the manufacture and, in most cases, the price paid by the consumer varies from country to country. Manufacturers argue for this level of control as a right, but also on the grounds of protecting their brand image and to support future investment in the brand. There is also the concern of authorised dealers and retailers about lost sales, as well as the loss of goodwill, when they refuse to honour the manufacturer's guarantees on grey-market purchases.

Retailers can bypass these authorised dealers and purchase goods from markets where the cost is lower. The goods are imported to sell in their domestic market in parallel to the goods sold by the manufacturer's distributor, and are marketed to their customers at cheaper prices. Parallel imports from America can be particularly profitable because of the higher costs charged by distributors in the EU; Calvin Klein products cost less there than in the EU but still manage to maintain an exclusive brand position. Branded clothing forms a significant area of grey importing, but opportunities arise with many other products from perfumes, to CDs and cars. Nor is America the sole country of origin; the Far East and even other parts of Europe provide opportunities to import products more cheaply such as lower cost Levi jeans imported into the UK from Greece. The differences in price can be stark with retailers selling

---

Exhibit 3.5   Supermarkets sourcing from the grey market

Supermarkets sourcing from unauthorised suppliers have outraged the world's high profile brands. Since suppliers have refused to sell their prestige brands through the supermarkets, the stores have been forced to source merchandise from unofficial trading channels. Supermarkets have attempted to establish their own niches in so-called 'grey market goods. Asda, for example, has been active in the market for perfumes and Safeway in children's clothing including Calvin Klein, Adidas and more recently official England football kits. Tesco, too has attempted to sell designer brands, including some of the best-known designer brands such as Levi, Calvin Klein, and Nike to its UK customers.

Among industry observers, opinion is divided over why the supermarkets are concerned with exclusive branded goods. In the past, supermarkets have gone out of their way to move on from discounting, yet this is opportunistic buying which cannot give them any continuity of supply. Even if the suppliers called their bluff and supermarkets are able to access stocks through regular distribution channels, they only have a limited space to provide a creditable range. But the 'when it's gone, it's gone' policy of special purchases appears to work well with a wider range of products, and high profile arguments with expensive brands does nothing to harm a supermarket's image as the shopper's champion.

---

grey market designer labels at prices 50 per cent less than those from the authorised distributor.

The issues surrounding the supermarkets' involvement in the grey market and clashes with designer-brand owners such as Adidas, Levi and Calvin Klein are complex but essentially come down to the ability of retailer to sell what they want, at the price they want. Exclusive brands refuse to let supermarkets sell their products because they claim the stores do not create the right image or sales environment, and so reduce their exclusivity. Retailers respond that the brands want to control the artificially high price of their goods to maintain their profits, and that customers are denied a range of branded products at fair prices. Following a ruling in 2001 at the European Court of Justice it appears that the brands have won the argument and that parallel importing of goods from outside the EU will have to cease.

SUMMARY

Historically, the primary emphasis of retailing was on transactions that resulted in the movement of merchandise. In the future, it will increasingly emphasise services, and transactions will only be part of the experiential elements of shopping and consumption. In the past retailing was based predominantly on a model in which store locations were the primary driver of customer shopping behaviour. Such a model placed clear constraints upon customers in terms of times and places since transactions could only occur at the store during specified hours. In the future, retailers must acquire the ability to allow transactions to occur at any time, in any place.

The trend towards the reduction of distribution channels between manufacturer and consumer is still in its early phases, but it will result in dislocations in current working practices. It will also cause major growth in support services for companies that deal directly with larger numbers of customers. For example, growth in small-package shipping will be likely to exceed by far that in bulk shipments or the building of warehouse space.

Another important consequence of this trend is likely to be the emergence of new types of intermediary that will capture the value-creating opportunities generated by the merging of new modes of consumer–producer interaction. Examples of such intermediaries may include rating services, automated ordering services, services based on consolidating small orders from numerous consumers into more economically viable quantities, and so on. Market specialists might emerge who will orchestrate the offerings of numerous suppliers around the specialised needs of a single customer. Wholesalers and other intermediaries between manufacturer and retailer are faced with a challenge: to adapt to the emerging realities in a way that ensures their continued relevance and thus prosperity. They must identify a value-adding role for themselves in the new landscape of producer–consumer relationships and create a blueprint for moving towards a new business model.

QUESTIONS

1   Explain with the aid of diagrams what you understand by the term 'channels of distribution'.

2   In channel selection, both suppliers and retailers usually take four key factors into consideration. Briefly explain the role of each of these factors.

3   What are the key elements of the distribution mix which retailers should consider in making distribution decisions?

4   Discuss briefly what you consider to be the role of information technology (IT) in the development of efficient distribution of goods in Europe.

5   What factors must brand manufacturers consider in deciding whether or not to supply own-label products?

6   Big-name labels are refusing to let supermarkets sell their goods because of supermarkets' lack of image for their upmarket products. Discuss this issue in the light of retailers' active participation in the grey market for designer goods.

7   Do you consider selective distribution satisfactory from the retailer's point of view?

8   In terms of non-standard distribution of goods, how will strategic collaboration help the relationship existing between suppliers and retailers?

9   Beyond facilitating channel partnerships, technology is affecting retailing through the distribution of electronic shopping for store-based retailing. Briefly discuss this statement.

10   What are the key features of virtual retail distribution that you consider may change how retail operations are conducted in the future?

The Internet as a Collaborative Supply-Chain Management Strategy at Safeway's Stores

Safeway, a supermarket chain, could be regarded as an efficient retailer even before the introduction of the Internet into its distribution system, but now it is able to achieve even more by creating a fully integrated value chain. The 'integrated value chain' is a process of collaboration that optimises all internal and external activities involved in delivering greater perceived value to the ultimate customer. The Internet's universal connectivity has enabled it to create a three-way information partnership with its suppliers and customers by treating them as collaborators who together find ways of improving efficiency across the entire chain of supply and demand, and share the benefits. The Internet gives customers unprecedented power to seek out the lowest prices, but it can also be used to deepen relationships and ultimately build far greater customer loyalty than before. Thus, for strategic retail management Safeway needs to create an integrated value chain to cope with the future.

It must be emphasised here that although Safeway was an efficient company before the Internet, it struggled to speed up and improve its supply-chain interactions. The most effective collaborative tool has been electronic data interchange (EDI), prevalent in industries where suppliers replenish in high volumes, such as food manufacturing. EDI, although effective, has several drawbacks. The first is that it is both limited and inherently inflexible. It provides basic information about transactions, but it is unable to adapt to rapidly changing market conditions. Secondly, it is very expensive to implement and so many retailers find it difficult to justify their investment. Thirdly, because it is based on proprietary technologies rather than open standards, it locks suppliers and customers together. Finally, the greatest drawback as far as retailing is concerned is that as a purely business-to-business tool it excludes the end-user (that is,

the main retail customers) from the value chain.

Internet technology is everything EDI is not. It is ubiquitous and open to everybody. The intuitive interface of the browser makes it easy to use; it is flexible enough to work either inside an organisation (Intranet) or outside in open (Internet) or secure (Extranet) form; it is cheaper to set up and run and it is global. Overall, it is the open standard of the Internet that gives it its extraordinary power to create new business models. Applications that used to sit in discrete data 'silos' within companies, such as logistics, manufacturing, financial information, procurement and human resources, are now able to talk to each other and to equivalent systems in other companies, pushing out information and retrieving it as needed. For Safeway and other similar retailers, this means that a quantum leap in collaboration with partners and customers is now possible.

Safeway, one of IBM's customers, has constructed a web-based integrated value chain that has revolutionised the way it does business. On the buying side of its operation it allows hundreds of its suppliers access to its data warehouse, giving them real-time information about how each of their products is selling in every one of Safeway's stores. That enables them to tailor production to demand and shifting tastes, as well as ensuring that Safeway never runs out of stock.

Since the cost of connecting to Safeway's intranet is only a few thousand pounds against several million pounds for EDI and the value-added network (VAN) needed to carry it, the supermarket can easily increase the number of its suppliers, giving it more choice and better prices. On the selling side, it uses its website for remote shopping and electronic cataloguing, as well as collecting and mining data on customers' preferences both from the site and from loyalty cards, so it can personalise promotions.

SEMINAR QUESTION FOR DISCUSSION

Discuss how the use of the Internet will help cement the collaboration that exists between Safeway's stores, its suppliers and customers, to deliver greater perceived value to the ultimate customers.

References

Alba, J., Lynch, J., Weitz, B., Janiszwski, C., Lutz, R., Sawyer, A. and Wood, S. (1997) 'Interactive Home Shopping: Consumer, Retailer and Manufacturer Incentives to Participate in Electronic Marketplaces', *Journal of Marketing*, vol. 61, no. 3, pp. 38–53.

Bamfield, J. (1994) 'Technological Management Learning: the Adoption of Electronic Data Interchange by Retailers', *International Journal of Retail and Distribution Management*, vol. 22, no. 2, pp. 3–12.

Bell, R., Davies, R. and Howard, E. (1997) 'The Changing Structure of Food Retailing in Europe: the Implications for Strategy', *Long Range Planning*, vol. 30, no. 6, pp. 853–61.

Bryce, D.J. and Useem, M. (1998) 'The Impact of Corporate Outsourcing on Company Value', *European Management Journal*, vol. 16, no. 6, pp. 635–43.

Christopher, M. (1997) *Marketing Logistics* (Oxford: Butterworth-Heinemann).

Cooper, J., Browne, M. and Peters, M. (1994) *European Logistics: Markets, Management, and Strategy*, 2nd edn (Oxford: Blackwell).

Davies, G. and Brooks, J.M. (1989) *Positioning Strategy in Retailing* (London: Paul Chapman).

Davies, G. (1993) 'Is Retailing What the Dictionaries Say It Is?', *International Journal of Retail and Distribution Management* vol. 21, no. 2, pp. 3–7.

Dhar, S. and Hoch, S.J. (1998) 'Why store Brand Penetration Varies by Retailer', *Marketing Science*, no. 16, pp. 208–27.

Fernie, J. (1995) 'International Comparisons of Supply Chain Management in Grocery Retailing', *The Service Industries Journal*, vol. 5, no. 4, pp. 135–47.

Fernie, J. (1997) 'Retail Change and Retail Logistics in the UK, Past Trends and Future Prospects', *The Service Industries Journal*, vol. 17, no. 3, pp. 383–96.

Fernie, J. and Sparks, L. (1997) *Logistics and Retail Management* (London: Kogan Page).

Field, C. (1996) *Retailing on the Internet*, Financial Times Report (London: Retail and Consumer Publishing).

Gattorna, J.L. and Walters, D.W. (1996) *Managing the Supply Chain: A Strategic Perspective* (Basingstoke: Macmillan).

Gilligan, C. and Sutton, C. (1987) 'Strategic Planning in Grocery and DIY Retailing', in G. Johnson (ed.), *Business Strategy and Retailing* (Chichester: John Wiley and Sons).

Harvey, M. (2000) 'Innovation and Competition in the UK Supermarkets', *Supply Chain Management: An International Journal*, vol. 5, no. 1, pp. 15–21.

Hobbs, J.E. (1996) 'A Transaction Cost Approach to Supply Chain Management', *Supply Chain Management*, vol. 1, no. 2, pp. 15–27.

Howe, S.W. (1992) *Retailing Management* (London: Macmillan).

Kotler, P. (1997) *Marketing Management: Analysis, Planning, Implementation, and Control*, 9th edn (New Jersey: Prentice Hall International, Inc).

Kurtz, D.L. and Boone, L.E. (1987) *Marketing*, 3rd edn (New York: The Dryden Press).

Lambert, D. and Stock, J. (1993) *Strategic Logistics Management*, 3rd edn (London: Irwin).

McGoldrick, P.J. (1990) *Retail Marketing* (Maidenhead: McGraw Hill).

Mintel (2000) *Food Wholesaling* (London: Mintel International Group).

Moore, E.J. (1991) 'Grocery Distribution in the UK', *International Journal of Retail & Distribution Management*, vol. 19, no. 7, p. 18.

Omar, O.E. (1999) *Retail Marketing* (London: Financial Times/Pitman).

Omar, O.E. (1998) 'Strategic Collaboration: a Beneficial Retail Marketing Strategy for Car Manufacturers and Dealers', *Journal of Strategic Marketing*, vol. 6, no. 1, pp. 65–78.

Omar, O. and Kent, A. (2001) 'International Airport Influences on Impulsive Shopping Trait and Normative Approach', *International Journal of Retail Distribution and Management*, vol. 29, no. 4/5, pp. 226–35.

Popp, A. (2000) 'Swamped in Information but Starved of Data: Information and Intermediaries in Clothing Supply Chains', *Supply Chain Management: An International Journal*, vol. 5, no. 3, pp. 151–61.

Retail Distribution (1998) The Institute for Grocery Distribution Annual Report.

Reynolds, J. (2000) 'E-Commerce: a Critical Review', *International Journal of Retail & Distribution Management*, vol. 28, no. 10, pp. 417–44.

Skjoett-Larsen, T. (2000) 'European Logistics Beyond *2000*', *International Journal of Physical Distribution & Logistics Management*, vol. 30, no. 5, pp. 377–87.

The Economist (1999) 'The Net Imperative: Business and the Internet Survey', *The Economist*, 26 June, pp. 5–44.

The Guardian (1999) 'Are our Supermarkets Out of Control', 4 January.

The Grocer (1998) 'Internet Retailers Should Try Harder', *The Grocer*, 31 January, p. 8.

Tse, K.K. (1985) *Marks & Spencer: Anatomy of Britain's Most Efficiently Managed Company* (Oxford: Pergamon).

Verdict (1999) *Verdict on Electronic Shopping* (London: Verdict Ltd).

CHAPTER FOUR

Competitive Strategies in the Retail Industry

INTRODUCTION

Chapter 2 examined the influence and importance of environmental factors on the retail industry and outlined the broad forces of change. The first part of this chapter continues that theme by turning in more detail to the impact of the competitive environment on strategic planning. The aim is to define competitors and the level of competitiveness within an industry, the opportunities and threats these bring, and their effect on the strategic process. The next section turns to definitions of strategy and ways in which retailers are 'strategic', before moving to the internal retail environment and its resource implications. These lead into an explanation of strategic choice, concerning growth and reorganisation strategies. The final section of the chapter examines cultural issues in the implementation of strategy.

DEFINING RETAIL COMPETITION

Identifying competitors can be a difficult task; some competitors appear to have a very direct impact on a retailer's activities, but with more detailed analysis many others compete for customers in different ways. The retail industry itself is becoming more competitive as economic liberalisation and globalisation create new forms of competition, and through the emergence of larger and more powerful retailers. New competitors in the form of Internet-based and international entrants, and the blurring of traditional trading formats, have created a much less predictable competitive environment. In this situation, managers will need to take an active role, rather than a passive one, to influence, shape and create the competitive dimensions to their advantage (Prahalad, 1999).

As a result of these trends, the identification of retail competitors will be a critical task. The aim should be to understand the competition by focusing intently on competitors to learn as much as possible about their intentions. Grant (1995) proposes that a company should attempt to predict competitors' choices of strategy and tactics, their likely reactions to environmental changes and responses to any competitive moves. The process of competitor analysis will require inputs on competitors' assumptions about the industry and their capabilities, in addition to assessments of strategy and objectives. The retailer must then decide upon the critical dimensions of their competitive strategy, and forecast how competitors might react. Sam Walton, founder of Wal-Mart, recommended companies to 'swim upstream', to find out what the competition is doing and do something different (Raphel, 1999).

The broad dimensions of competitive strategy can be understood through levels of:

■ *Interdependence*. The degree to which retailers are affected by other retailers' strategies, with important implications for each competitor, the more so as the industry concentrates and the behaviour of a few competitors increasingly defines the competitive environment.

■ *Direct competition, cooperation* or the *avoidance of competition* if possible (Ohmae, 1990). Some competitors may not be in direct competition; in segmented markets they may offer products that are not direct substitutes. Others may compete through activities that are peripheral to their core business, and may be open to collaborative initiatives (Hussey and Jenster, 1999).

■ *Mutually destructive behaviour*. Price wars in which customer expectations of a reasonable price are unrealistically low raise the stakes and consequently the cost of doing business. Clearly there is a danger that retailers may become involved in self-destructive behaviour, so they need to formulate strategies to minimise or prevent uncooperative responses and encourage cooperative ones. This is evident amongst retailers in a number of industry sectors: the leading multiple food retailers in the UK; clothing multiples whose end-of-season sales, as well as pricing and broad assortment strategies, can be generally predicted.

Strategic Groups

Competitive analysis is difficult until the retailer is clear about who its competitors are. Competitors can be defined as organisations selling to the same set of customers or market segments and who serve some of the same functions. At its simplest, retailers will be concerned with the number of competitors in their market, to distinguish their scale of business activity, and the strategic ambitions that may be achieved in each group. Clearly regional retail businesses trading from, say, 10 stores will have a

Table 4.1   *Criteria for Strategic Group Analysis of Grocery Retailers*

Scope of activities: the size and intensity of retail activity	Measurement	Resource commitment: investments made by the firm to serve customers	Measurement
■ Overall size of company's retail activities ■ Commercial offer, through the breadth of the product range ■ Importance of retail activities to the company ■ Spread (geographic coverage)	■ Total sales area ■ £000s stock at value: higher stock investment is taken as a proxy for broader assortments ■ Retail sales as a % of total company sales ■ Number of areas of operation (measurement of % of regional: national distribution)	■ Growth strategy ■ Type of outlet (hypermarket/supermarket) ■ Level of service ■ Fixed capital intensity ■ Relationship with suppliers	■ Annual growth rate (%) ■ Ratio of outlet type ■ Personnel as a % of total sales ■ Fixed assets as a % of total assets ■ Credit period in days: longer cerdit periods taken as expression of retailer power

The application of the analysis in Table 4.1 led to the identification of seven strategic groups in UK grocery retailing:

1 Major hypermarkets – includes Asda
2 Small mid-range supermarkets – E.H. Booth
3 Regional large supermarkets – Waitrose
4 Mixed wholesale/retail stores – Adminstore
5 Differentiators on facilities – Sainsbury
6 Discounters – Aldi
7 Mid-range nationals stores – Budgens

Sources: Flavian and Polo (1999), Flavian *et al.* (1999)

different configuration of resources and strategic opportunities to those global companies trading with many outlets in prime locations.

The process of identifying retailers that share characteristics can be undertaken through strategic group analysis (Table 4.1). The dimensions originally proposed by Porter (1980) distinguished businesses by the degree of specialisation and vertical integration, the extent to which they owned operations higher up or further down their distribution chains. However, key strategic dimensions will vary between industries and the analyst should draw out similarities between competitors and their strategies, for example by using the scope of the retailers' activities and their resource commitments (Flavian and Polo, 1999). The aim is to explain differences in profitability, identify barriers to mobility between groups, and to analyse initiatives and responses between competitors. As a result the company should locate competitive space that is unoccupied or weakly held by competitors.

The approach has its limitations, since it assumes that the diversity of the industry can be simplified by classification. More seriously in a rapidly changing environment are the assumptions that groups will remain stable due to mobility barriers that limit movement into strategic space, or imperfections in the market for resources that create difficulties in acquiring specific assets to implement a strategy (Flavian and Polo, 1999; Flavian *et al.*, 1999). Criteria for identifying groups with similar activities and resource commitments are outlined in Table 4.1.

Five-Force Analysis

Strategic groups define types of competitor by shared characteristics. However, the degree of competition in the retail industry will strongly influence strategic decisions; at its most extreme it may oblige retailers to withdraw from a market completely as in the case of C&A from the UK market. Assessment of the structural forces that create the competitive environment will enable retailers to understand their impact on industrial profitability, as well as company performance. A valuable model for this analysis was derived by Porter (1980) from five forces: the extent of competitor rivalry, the ease with which new entrants can enter the industry, the introduction of substitutes for products or services, and the relative power of buyers and sellers.

Threat of new entrants

New entrants to a retail sector require access to customers at an affordable cost, and above all to property in the right locations. In the USA, changes to industrial structure are leading to a polarisation of stores by size that have enabled new retail formats to open. The threat is reduced in conditions where there are barriers to entry that hinder easy access to retail markets, such as:

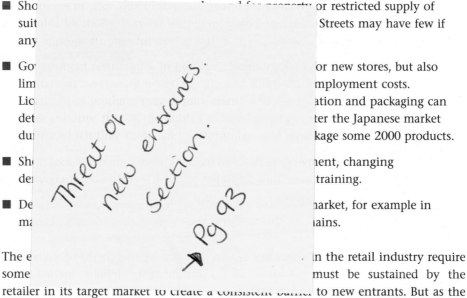

- Sho_____ges of ____ ___ to strong demand for property or restricted supply of suit____ ____ ____ ____ ____ ____ ____ ____ Streets may have few if any ____ ____ ____ ____ ____ ____ ____

- Go_____t r___l___ions ___ l___ ___ ___ or new stores, but also lim_____ ____ ____ ____ ____ ____ mployment costs. Lic____ ____ ____ ____ ____ ____ ation and packaging can det___ ____ ____ ____ ____ ter the Japanese market du___ ____ ____ ____ ____ kage some 2000 products.

- Sh_____ ____ ____ ____ ____ ____ ____ ____ ____ nent, changing de____ ____ ____ ____ ____ ____ ____ training.

- De____ ____ ____ ____ ____ ____ ____ ____ narket, for example in ma____ ____ ____ ____ ____ ____ ____ ___ains.

The e____ ____ ____ ____ ____ ____ ____ ____ _n the retail industry require some ____ ____ ____ ____ ____ ____ ____ must be sustained by the retailer in its target market to create a consistent barrier to new entrants. But as the decline of Marks and Spencer has shown, seemingly strong barriers created over many years can be rapidly breached by entrants who respond more closely to its customer needs.

The power of suppliers and buyers

The factors that create powerful suppliers and buyers are similar. Suppliers or buyers can exercise their power by dominating a market and aggressively negotiating price, quality and terms. If there are only a few alternative trading partners in the market there is little scope to negotiate a better deal. However where there are many suppliers or buyers competing for the same business, the market is more fragmented and opportunities to negotiate improve. As the retail industry concentrates into fewer businesses, so the balance of power has moved away from suppliers, and into their hands. The balance varies in each retail sector; multiple clothing retailers often source globally with low switching costs from one supplier to another. They buy from a diversity of suppliers for largely undifferentiated products, adding their own brand values through design and labelling; these create powerful bargaining positions. In the electrical sector retailers may have to source products exclusively from a narrow range of global branded suppliers who exert their power through pricing structures that limit retailer margins.

Power can be exercised in other ways. If the supplier has products or brands that are important or cannot be substituted then it gains more power over its retail customers who have little or no choice but to buy from them. Retail buyers' experience and market knowledge may provide a source of power, depending on the size and sophistication of their supplier. Porter highlights a specific retailer strength in their ability to influence consumers' purchasing decisions through their range selection and instore presentation. This bleak analysis for suppliers can be redressed through the provision of unique or distinctive products.

Threat of substitution

Substitution can be seen at different levels. The way we shop in physical stores may be substituted by an alternative, such as shopping through virtual stores on the

Figure 4.1   *A Model for Structural Analysis*

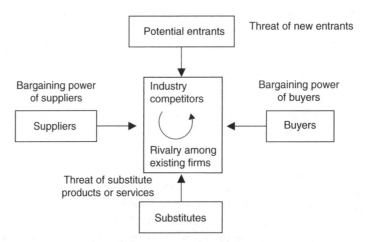

Internet. In turn, interactive TV could substitute for Internet connectivity through PCs, which could have a serious impact on PC manufacturers and retailers. Long-term substitution of lifestyles can result in the decline or complete eclipse of entire product categories: in menswear, sales of formal hats and gloves have almost disappeared over the past 50 years. The demand for suits has more gradually declined, to be substituted by casual clothing. The susceptibility of the industry to substitutes will make it less predictable and more competitive as businesses compete to hold on to market share of their current products and services.

Competitive rivalry

Fewer, predictable competitors reduce the level of rivalry, whereas, and the retail industry reflects this scenario, new entrants will increase competition by reducing the market share available to existing retailers. In the UK, discount retailer Kwik Save successfully dominated a low cost 'no frills' position in the grocery market until European competitors – Aldi, Netto and Lidl – entered their market to provide direct competition. On a larger scale, the arrival of Wal-Mart in the UK through its acquisition of Asda in 1999 demonstrates how the competitive equilibrium may be upset. Its high growth rate in the USA enabled the company to develop economies of scale and achieve successful consistency in low-price positioning and wide product assortment. The sheer size of the company gives it enormous financial leverage with global manufacturers and suppliers, and for investment into new businesses and physical resources. It can easily transfer its expertise with information systems and its operational style across borders. Competitors will be drawn into defensive mergers to enable them to compete as more equal rivals, effectively redefining the strategic groups once the scale and rate of change can be assessed.

Structural analysis of the competition assists retailers in taking strategic decisions about market entry or withdrawal, as well as defining competitive opportunities and threats. The ways in which they can be drawn into the strategic process depends at least in part on the retailer's approach to strategy itself, its objectives and management.

DEFINITIONS OF STRATEGY

Although parallels have been drawn between military and business strategy in the earlier part of the twentieth century, strategy's entry into management thinking only seriously began in the 1960s. As industries became more complex, taking them into new products (particularly consumer ones) and markets, so techniques were required to plan long-term business development. Organisational aims and objectives were subjected to a closer focus, strategic planning approaches were established, and growth strategies assessed in terms of the common thread between current and new business.

However, the objectives and processes of business strategy came to be understood in more diverse ways as business decision-making was studied. The very purpose of strategy, the ways decisions are taken about the direction of the business and the implementation of a course of action has taken on different characteristics. These have had fundamental implications for the organisation. Whittington (1994) provides a valuable summary of the characteristics of different approaches:

1 *Rational strategy* can be understood in terms of long-term profit maximisation. This approach is strongly analytical, leading to detailed plans and often providing direction for five years of company activity.

2 *Processual strategy* by contrast, assumes an internal shaping by resources, particularly human ones. The direction of the organisation is arrived at more by a consensus of 'what is achievable' and is planned in small steps.

3 *Evolutionary strategy.* Companies have to adapt themselves to economic and market circumstances, and the financial environment will determine survival or otherwise.

4 *Systemic strategy.* This approach relates strategies to sociological contexts and the cultures in which they operate. As such there is no single appropriate way of undertaking strategy, instead it is dependent on what is acceptable to national cultures, and companies choose to take decisions in ways that they feel most comfortable with.

These different approaches raise fundamental issues about strategy in the retail industry which need to be considered briefly from one further aspect, the dynamic environment in which it is located.

The Effect of Dynamic Environments on Strategic Planning

Strategic planning assumes some degree of predictability in both the wider retail environment as well as in retail markets. Clearly if we are dealing with distant time horizons and large-scale projects, we will be presented with a range of strategic opportunities that are not available to businesses with shorter and less predictable timespans.

However, time horizons are reducing and speed of reaction to adjust and adapt quickly within a given strategic direction will be essential (Prahalad, 1999). BAA has five, seven and half and ten-year plans for its conventional business, but only 12-month plans for its Internet business. The significance of increasing rates of change is to place the rational strategic planning approach in context, both in time and by industry. Formal financial planning techniques become increasingly constrained by unpredictability; in place of strategic *choice* it may be more appropriate to talk of strategic *change*, and with it a focus on the uncertainties of implementation (Whittington, 1995).

From this it is clear that retailers are rarely afforded the chance of strategy-making in a deliberate form; long-term plans and rational decision-making processes can be overturned by competitors, investor sentiment and fashionability, even the weather can prove unnerving. Instead strategies tend to emerge in response to opportunities and threats arising all around. For nearly all the leading UK retailers, profitable adaptation to prevailing conditions will reap stockmarket rewards and survival; failure is not long tolerated.

Exhibit 4.1   Unpredictable planning horizons at Next plc?

By the end of 1995, Next was in a buoyant position, sales had increased by 13% in the second half of the year and the company had been a star performer over the Christmas trading period. The key to success was the product range that offered 'value and quality'. The company continued to impress over the next two years, reporting annual growth of 38% in Directory home shopping sales during 1997 and improved trading densities in its stores as another aspect of its strong performance.

However by early 1998 the company was less confident. The womenswear range had experienced poor Christmas trading after the range had been repositioned at a too fashionable level for its market, and the company was unable to reverse the changes to its spring/summer season's merchandise. The company blamed a number of other factors on this reversal; a slowdown in economic growth, absence of price inflation and intensifying competition made the delivery of value more difficult. The chairman departed the company later that year.

Strategies are planned and implemented within an organisational context. Involvement mostly concerns people within the organisation, such as directors, employees or staff, but also provides guidance to external parties such as suppliers. These groups with varying levels of involvement in the organisation are frequently referred to as stakeholders. It's important that the organisation attempts at least to describe its range of stakeholders so that it can assess the power of each group and the demands and values each may place on its strategy. Without the acceptance of the managers and employees the strategy will founder in its implementation. There is a danger of 'ivory-tower' thinking, a plan produced by a strategic team that has little commitment from those not involved in the process. Implementing the strategy may then be slow, or even wilfully obstructed in managerial power plays.

External stakeholders are important too. The concept of the organisation as an 'open' or 'closed' system, directs our thinking away from the organisation as an internally contained, self-directed and regulating entity, towards one which is permeable to external influences. Individuals in the form of shoppers, and organisations including suppliers, logistics providers, financial institutions, politicians, trade unions and pressure groups such as Greenpeace may in varying ways influence and constrain the organisation's ability to act. Their attitude to the organisation will be formed both from their expectations and level of involvement.

In recent years the issue of how organisations should manage themselves has become prominent. For many companies this finds expression in the Mission statement – a brief summary of guiding principles that combines the qualitative values of the organisation with the more objective strategic aims. Ideally it should link the vision of the business to its working practices; in reality that may be a difficult process. If the style of the organisation leans predominantly towards a rational, planned approach to decision-making, constructing reflective value statements may be uncomfortable. However, as stakeholders become more informed about business activities and their impact on their investment, and business becomes more influential in society and the environment, so there is a need to state the ways in which the organisation will conduct itself.

Corporate governance is central to this thinking in its concern for the ways in which organisations should manage themselves. Boards of directors and shareholders need to agree on the extent of their self-regulation and their acceptance of external regulation, their responsibilities and moral obligations internally and to the wider society. These issues have become topical for a number of reasons. Most visibly, businesses have been in the spotlight over the ways in which they run themselves. British Airways and Virgin have been engaged in a public relations war over 'dirty tricks' for a number of years, whilst The Gap and Nike have been accused of allegedly employing underage workers in clothing production from Far Eastern factories.

More generally the public's perception of business behaviour has increased as environmental protection and human-rights standards take on a more prominent role in international trade negotiations. This was demonstrated in 1999, at the World Trade Organisation's meeting in Seattle where the concerns of pressure groups highlighted the developed world's corporate governance in its dealings with developing nations. The need to establish a comprehensive statement of governance issues had already been realised in the Cadbury report, whose effect has been to provide behavioural standards by which organisations can measure and change themselves. Importantly, it provides benchmarks for external stakeholders as well as stimulating further debate.

The ethical position of the business (Figure 4.2) concerns right and wrong conduct, and ethical principles provide guides to moral behaviour – what the company considers to be the right way it should behave. The type of ethical problems that an organisation should consider can be classified into four main areas:

1 Ethics of the economic system – competition, profit motive;

2 Ethical issues in the boardroom – product policy, marketing strategy, environmental issues and remuneration;

3 Ethical issues facing managers – implementing redundancy, hiding truth;

4 Ethical dilemmas of employees – honesty, whistleblowing, sexual harassment.

The company's corporate governance can be translated into an ethical policy which serves a number of purposes: to maintain the reputation of the company's integrity,

Figure 4.2   *The Place of Ethics in the Organisation's Strategy (after Webley)*

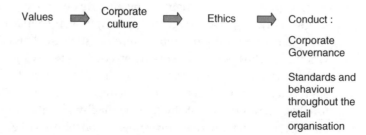

Exhibit 4.2   Ethical principles at Boots Co., plc

The Boots Company is working with other leading retailers and the British Retail Consortium to develop guidance and codes of practice. The company is a member of the Ethical Trading Initiative, comprising government, non-governmental organisations and retailers brought together to develop common standards and approaches to ethical issues. The company insists on only doing business with manufacturers in the Far East which meet certain standards in their employment of workers, including pay scales and facilities. Systems have been implemented to check that employers conform to local labour laws and that they comply with the legal age of employment. On the issue of animal testing, the company does not undertake any testing itself and only endorses test undertaken by other companies to meet government regulations in the interests of public safety.

---

to act as a safety ____ and because an organisation owes an ethical way of working to its employees. The effectiveness of the policy can be judged by its integrity and application in ____ because the failure to implement the policy may directly impact on the ____ of ____ there is the rising pressure on companies to formalise their eth____ ____ and written guidelines on how it obta____ its ____ ____ such standard served it well, until in April 2000 the company ____ ____ to ____ ____ group pressure to publish its pol____ ____ ____

[handwritten note: Ethical Trading. Pg 244]

INTERNAL RESOURCES A____ ____ ____ ____

Within the c____ ____ ____ ____ ____ and ____ uity, strategy is concerned with ____ ____ ____ ____ ____ ____ what it____ an do – with what it could do. An ____ ____ ____ ____ ____ ____ ____ sation's capability to undertake a strategy, and through the ____ ____ ____ e ways in which they are linked businesses can identify unique or distinctive sources of competitive advantage.

In practice the process of internal resource analysis has not been easy to manage objectively. It tends to be a static activity where it should be dynamic and ongoing, raising issues of strongly-held beliefs and confronting management with facts that may contradict existing opinions and ideas (Brownlie, 1989). Screening should assess resource characteristics for their inherent value, their rarity among competitors, their lack of substitutability, and imperfect imitability (Barney, 1991). Through this process organisations can identify the key drivers of strategy (Johnson and Scholes, 1999).

Resources can be both tangible and intangible. The tangible resources in the retail may include:

- *Property.* The location of retail properties, the type of shops and the terms on which they have been acquired as well as the size of the retailer's portfolio are a highly visible resource. A retailer with prime locations in shopping areas will command a strong marketing presence, and desirable customer service attributes such as accessibility and convenience. The acquisition of new shops, the wrong size of shops in the property portfolio for the stage of business development, or shops in the wrong area due to changes in commercial planning and property redevelopment can limit the retailer's strategic opportunities. In the UK the high cost of property in important shopping streets or centres may prove burdensome during flat periods of trading or economic recession. Similarly, warehouse and off-site stockroom space may be in place as a strategic resource to facilitate retail growth. A mismatch in size and location of warehousing with the retailer's strategy can be problematic as the French Intermarché group found when they moved from a bulk forward-buying policy requiring very large warehouses to a strategy that required more flexible consumer-driven responses from their supply chain (Pache, 1999).

■ *Financial resources.* Strategic capability will be determined by the financial resources that exist with, or are available to, retailers. Control of current assets, especially stocks, and its expenses, including staff costs, and management of debtors and creditors provide strong indicators to investors and banks of the financial soundness of the company. The cost of capital and the company's ability to raise funding, for acquisitions for example, contribute to the importance of this resource.

■ *Human resources.* The skills of its people, their organisation and coordination have an important role in service industries. Shop staff provide a physical point of contact between customers and the company, and their service skills and abilities will be critical in building new business and creating loyalty. At Head Office, buying and stock management expertise is decisive, too, in key marketing functions of product sourcing and selection and pricing.

■ *Information systems.* The successful design and implementation of information systems for sales and stock planning and control contributes to the retailer's responsiveness to market trends and ultimately customer satisfaction. Data capture for marketing, such as customer research and loyalty card schemes has become an increasingly valuable resource.

■ *Intangible resources* can include branding, reputation, culture, motivation and skills. For Kay (1993), the key measure of business success is added value based on the exploitation rather than creation of resources. Capabilities need to be lacking in others, and they need to be appropriate and sustainable. Innovation combines with organisational architecture, information and flexible relationships, adding to business reputation.

Resource analysis concerns the relevance of each resource to the organisation's capabilities without creating a list of generalised attributes. Individual resources may be easily replicable; IT hardware, retail sites, store and product design, amongst others, can be acquired or copied by competitors. Part of the sameness of many shopping locations is due to this factor. However, the configurations and linkages between resources provide a more enduring source of advantage. Two approaches to developing competitive advantage in these ways are the *value chain* and *core competences*.

Retail businesses can only sustain long-term growth by creating competitive advantage by successfully identifying customer values. Differential advantage itself should be *customer*-based and relate to *customer*-perceived advantages, in whatever target market the organisation is competing. Retailers should look for a matching of distinctive competences in the organisation with specific groups of customers. Moreover, the organisation should seek to implement a 'value-creating strategy not simultaneously being implemented by any current or potential competitors' (Barney, 1991). The creation of value-added packages, which may consist of tangible and intangible benefits and are economically viable, combined with precise identification of a market segment's needs, distinguishes successful organisations.

The Value Chain

Internal resource analysis will identify areas of strength within the organisation; however, these alone may not provide a particularly consistent and sustainable strategic capability because individual resources may not be integrated with each other to create sustained advantage across the company. The value chain relates the value of the organisation to the consumer and with its competitors, and identifies how competitive differences can be achieved through a chain of unique value activities connecting the company's supply side with its demand side. It is based on how consumers view an organisation's products or services in relation to its competitors (Porter, 1985). The significance of this concept lies in the chain of conversion processes of products or concepts that integrates the retailer with its suppliers through to the final consumer. It enables the retailer to understand how its activities are extended to other resource providers who contribute to its service and products. The integration and coordination of different functions and businesses in multi-business, diversified organisations will lead to greater synergy and enlarged scope for growth (Campbell and Luchs, 1992). Through the consistent management of linkages in the value chain, successful competitive advantage can be established and maintained.

The value chain has an important influence on strategic choice, and also the planning of resources during the implementation stage of the strategy. It highlights the fact that suppliers will perform many value activities outside the organisation that create competitive advantage for the retailer. The value chain for an exclusive department store retailer like Harrods will be linked though its exclusive merchandise, in turn made or processed from the highest quality materials and ultimately raw materials. For a discount retailer, competitive advantage is partly achieved through its linkages with suppliers to exploit efficiencies in production that bring lower costs. If the linkages between activities that form the basis of competitive advantage are difficult to copy they provide a more enduring source of advantage than if they was managed individually. Analysis of the stages in the chain back through suppliers enables companies to redesign internal and external processes to improve efficiency and effectiveness.

Figure 4.3   *Possible Sources of Differentiation through Internal Value Linkages*

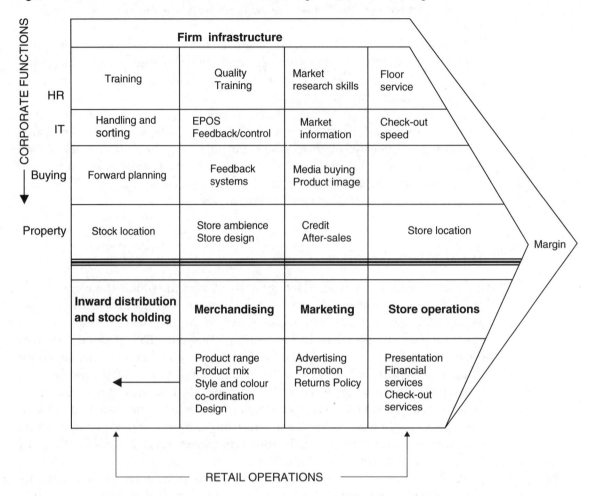

Source: McGee (1987) 'Retailer Strategies in the UK'.

Within the company, the internal value system (Figure 4.3) is divided into primary and support activities. Primary activities in retailing have been categorised by McGee (1987) as distinct operational areas and defined as:

■ *Inbound distribution and stock holding*: the receiving, storing and distributing of merchandise.

■ *Merchandising*: product design and selection to create competitive assortments.

■ *Marketing*: activities make the customer aware of the product and able to purchase it.

■ *Store operations*: the store design and facilities to enhance the shopping experience.

■ *Service*: to enhance and maintain the product.

Marketing in this context takes on the specific meaning of promotional activities, use of in-house credit cards and loyalty schemes, and the development of the retailer's image. The type of retailing activity will affect the boundaries of these functions too; for example, food and clothing retailers are organised differently and so create different types of linkages.

Primary activities are supported by the corporate functions of human resources, technology, buying, and property. The ways in which they are applied to the primary activities add value to the retailer and create its profit margins. The firm's infrastructure provides a framework in which all these activities can take place.

Value-chain analysis can be a useful diagnostic tool, the more so as it can be used at a corporate level to highlight broad structural linkages, and taken in greater detail to identify linkages at the divisional or business-unit level. Given the constraints on time and resources to complete strategic analysis by retailers, the model's qualitative approach and visual impact give it a practical value. As the objectives of delivering customer satisfaction are managed more systematically, the value chain has two considerable benefits to offer. Firstly, it points the way to the closer auditing of, and reduction in the number of suppliers, and the control of quality; it provides a framework for just-in-time deliveries and flexible manufacturing lead times. Secondly, the chain can satisfy the need to improve profit margins by creating or enhancing value adding linkages.

Core Competences

The concept of linkages rather than strengths located in individual activities finds a response in competence theory. Successful organisations compete with unique abilities or competences applied to their market, and core competences provide key organisational skills and technologies that enable a company to provide a particular benefit to customers (Hamel and Prahalad, 1994). Competition between firms is a race for competence mastery. Core rather than peripheral competence is defined by customer value, competitor differentiation being competitively unique, and extendibility of the competence to new applications, and it is these that give rise to real long-term prosperity. New competencies should be built to protect and extend existing business or to participate in the most exciting future markets. Better use of existing core competencies (Figure 4.4) will create the opportunity to improve the company's position in existing markets or to creatively develop new products or services.

For service industries it has been suggested that core competencies raise a number of specific questions about competitiveness. It may be important to consider how competencies might be developed when not based on technology, and, critically, to evaluate what core competencies services have at the heart of their businesses.

Critical Success Factors

External and internal resource evaluations provide a basis from which to assess strategic direction. The frameworks for comparing competitive positioning between

Figure 4.4   *Core Competences*

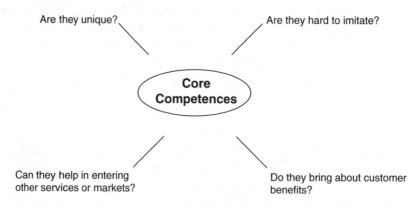

Table 4.2   *Potential Critical Success Factors (CSF) for a Clothing Retailer*

CSF	Importance to the industry (b)	How successful (scoring from 0 to 1) (c)	Weighted ranking (column b × c)
Range mix	5	0.7	3.5
Price	4	0.3	1.2
Lifestyle position	2	0.5	1
Supply-chain management	3	0.6	1.8
Location	1	0.8	0.8

organisations can include critical (or key) success factor (CSF) analysis. Resource evaluation leads to the identification of key internal relationships; for example, in the clothing sector these might concern retail market positioning and location, product range width, buying and merchandise forecasting skills and pricing. The relationships should be limited to no more than five, derived from two variables that define the characteristics of the industry and form the critical success factors. These were initially proposed as economic and technological variables, but need to reflect the competitive dimensions for retailing. The next stage requires decisions about the relative importance of each CSF in the industry sector, and then to give a weighted ranking to each competitor. This is more of a quantitative process as values are assigned to the most important competitive elements in the industry sector. The company's position in each of these is then separately assessed. The aim of the analysis is to define four or five absolutely critical factors to turn distinctive competences to competitive advantage in a market or market segment (Table 4.2).

SWOT Analysis

At this stage, SWOT analysis provides a valuable insight into strategic positioning by drawing together the internal strengths and weaknesses, with external opportunities

Figure 4.5   *Strengths, Weaknesses, Opportunities and Threats Analysis*

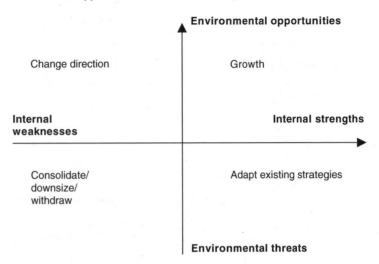

and threats (Figure 4.5). The advantages of creating an analytical framework from these factors are borne out by its popularity as a strategic planning technique. Although commonly used by companies it often tends to be undertaken indiscriminately (Glaister and Falshaw, 1999), and there is a danger that the analyst lists many relevant factors, sometimes at great length, without highlighting key issues. Defining an opportunity or threat can present its own problems; an environmental threat may carry the seeds of an opportunity, so the SWOT analysis must be seen as the basis for qualitative assessment of strategic choices. It has also been shown to reflect the knowledge and proximity of managers to different parts of the business: directors show a keener concern at financially-oriented SWOT issues, whilst middle managers create operationally-biased SWOT analyses.

STRATEGIC CHOICE

Strategic selection is concerned with the deployment of internal resources, to use strengths to the best advantage whilst minimising weaknesses. It should exploit opportunities whilst avoiding or negating threats as far as possible: both sets of activities are directed towards achieving objectives and creating strong competitive positions. The overall direction of the organisation is set out whereby the businesses of the organisation and allocation of resources are decided in the context of the demands of all the stakeholders.

A key issue is to select a strategy on the basis of competitive positioning, as it has been shown that at least 50 per cent of profitability variations may be put down to the choice of strategy (Baden-Fuller and Stopford, 1992). The retailer should aim to define the type of competitive advantage and methods to sustain its advantage. The dimensions of advantage (Figure 4.6) may be fundamentally determined by three generic strategies centred on *cost leadership*, *differentiation* and *focus* (Porter, 1980). The

Figure 4.6   *Three Generic Strategies*

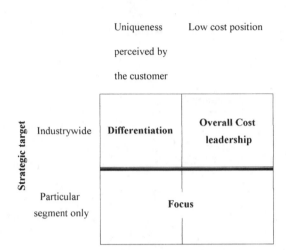

Strategic Advantage

Uniqueness   Low cost position

perceived by

the customer

	Uniqueness perceived by the customer	Low cost position
Industrywide	**Differentiation**	**Overall Cost leadership**
Particular segment only	**Focus**	

Strategic target

Reprinted with the permission of The Free Press, an imprint of Simon & Schuster Adult Publishing Group, from *Competitive Strategy: Techniques for Analyzing Industries and Competitors* by Michael E. Porter. Copyright © 1980, 1998 by The Free Press.

first part of this section will analyse retailers' positioning using this model, but also take a critical approach to its value in strategic management.

Cost Leadership

Porter states that the aim of cost leadership is to become the lowest cost producer through, for example, economies of scale, technology or access to the lowest cost goods. The producer must command prices at or near the industry average. Cost leadership will yield higher profits if the organisation can combine lower costs with proximity to average selling prices. To achieve lower costs, activities need to be maintained as appropriate through the value chain. For example the discount retail chain, Aldi, created a low-cost position that its UK competitor, Kwik Save, was unable to match. As a matter of definition cost-leadership characteristics should be related to competitors in the same market segment and not the total market (Bowman, 1992).

However, if we take the case of the clothing sector, successful cost leadership is emerging from the exploitation of discounted price–brand positions that closely relate cost to significantly lower prices than those achieved by established competitors. Cost-leadership users have been assumed to be companies who 'seek out customers who care more about price than image and novelty' and thus tend to be found in commodity markets (Miller, 1986). This definition adequately describes the variety retailers who have previously dominated the High Street, such as C&A and Littlewoods. However, regional retailers such as Hughes, and nationally Matalan, have used their low cost base to drive down discounted prices, often on branded merchandise.

Differentiation

With a differentiated strategy the organisation seeks to be unique in a 'dimension valued by buyers'. However, the price premium must exceed the extra costs incurred, and must aim for parity with competitors. Differentiation distinguishes an organisation from its competitors by discrete value activities and linkages which are recognised and valued by its customers. Porter argues that differentiated businesses achieve superior profits through their ability to achieve premium prices or increased market share from competitors in the same market segment. Nor is differentiation achieved independently from cost, as he observes 'a differentiator . . . aims at cost parity or proximity relative to its competitors' (Porter, 1980). The connection between cost and difference is most commonly seen in retailer statements such as Next's, discussed earlier in this chapter, that relate quality with value for money.

This definition of 'differentiation' has led to further assessments, between marketing and productivity-led dimensions, with demand and supply-side implications. The narrowness of the framework was highlighed by Mintzberg (1988) who argued for a wider typology of generic competitive strategies that more accurately reflect the complexity of the external environment. In general terms, though, marketing differentiation attempts to create a unique image for a product through sustained marketing practices. One way is to lead through configured value activities and linkages that are directed to specific target markets, the other through building competitive strength into and around evolving products (Kay, 1995).

In practice, differentiation strategies in the retail industry have reflected its dynamic and competitive characteristics. The notion of 'competitive price' is relative to time

---

Exhibit 4.3 Matalan: low cost–low price retailing

Matalan was founded in 1985, based on the American price-club concept. It uses membership to improve its understanding of customer profiles and spending habits as well as maintaining their loyalty. As a result it has typically targeted female customers who visit five times each year, spending an average of £23 during a 45-minute store visit. Its success comes in part from this strong customer relationship, but also its out-of-town store base and especially its ability to provide exceptional value for money; designer labels are sold at 50% below high street prices.

Savings are achieved through large low-cost locations that reduce operational costs. By the end of 2000 the company expected to operate around 117 stores, increasing to 200 by 2005, and the average trading area in the new stores will expand to 30 000 square feet. The company buys direct from suppliers and factories reducing distribution channel costs. The management structure is non-hierarchical; even the buyers report to the Chief Executive directly, and the culture is hands-on. The company has invested in EPOS systems to respond quickly to sales trends and closely control its stock investment. Automated warehouse systems create efficiencies in delivery, retrieval and despatch.

Its high growth rate has been achieved through geographical expansion, and more recently expansion of the product range to develop formalwear, suits and footwear ranges. The Home Store range is a significant new concept that extends the ranges of dinnerware, kitchenware, bedding and home furnishings.

and place: periods of economic growth and disposable income contrast with belt-tightening recessions; and post-industrial heartlands contrast with wealthy south-east England. Low switching costs between suppliers and underinvestment in value chains enable clothing retailers to change design and quality to match market characteristics. Over time retailers have bundled together two or more of the following strategic attributes:

- *Marketing image* – many design companies have turned to retail branding to project a consistent message from logos and fascia design, to store environment and packaging.

- *Product design* – a range of desirable product features is consistently developed to meet customer needs at competitive prices.

- *Innovative differentiation* creates the most up-to-date and attractive products, by leading competitors in quality, design innovations and style.

- *Product quality* – the retailer provides higher quality at comparable prices to the competition.

- *Locational differentiation*, provides opportunities to be the most accessible, the most exclusive or the most convenient.

- *Customer service differentiation* – through consistently unique standards of service to a particular market segment.

Differentiation can be achieved through productivity dimensions which provide higher service levels, faster stock turnovers or more responsive supply chains. Productivity-led differentiation includes effective cost management, distribution systems, supply-chain management and optimal store design for efficient delivery (Walters, 1988).

Focus

The narrow competitive scope of the *focus* dimension, enables companies to exploit a niche strategy. The aim is to avoid exposure to large (and powerful) organisations by dominating smaller markets, using either a lower cost base or greater differentiation. Niches can be exploited in a number of ways, by geographical area, customer type or product line. The scope of these strategies is deliberately narrow and success can depend on less obvious areas such as customer relations and the development of defined store cultures (Greco, 1997). Differentiated niches are attractive to retailers in several ways: operational efficiencies can be achieved in a locality or region and market segments can be better served; and national chains can be created by focusing on single product groups, such as Tie Rack or Claire's Accessories, where specialisation creates competitive advantage.

Failure to engage with a specific generic strategy may result in being 'stuck in the middle'. On the other hand, where several strategies are attempted it has been argued that the company has reduced its competitive advantage due to its inconsistent actions. Budgens grocery stores in the early 1990s established an alliance with REWE, one of Germany's largest food retailing and wholesaling groups, to develop the Penny discount format in the south of England. The failure of the format was due in part to the simultaneous pursuit of both differentiation and cost/price strategies (Hawkesworth, 1998). However, integrated low cost/differentiation strategies can succeed. Dell, the computer firm, for example, manages low cost and differentiated products through its integration of corporate culture, use of technology and commitment to high-quality products and services.

STRATEGIC DIRECTIONS

The generic strategy model provides a starting point in strategic selection to determine the fundamental direction for the business. Ansoff (1988), writing from a profit-maximising perspective, demonstrated how organisations need to define the strategic direction for their business. Businesses need to create a common thread from the present to their future directions through synergy – the combining of two activities for greater effect – and the development of distinctive competencies.

Strategies of Growth

Growth can be achieved in a number of ways and the product/market making (Figure 4.7) summarises the possibilities. A straightforward objective is to maximise market share. *Market penetration* can be achieved through the relatively low-risk development of existing products to existing markets. *Product development* takes place in an existing market segmented in different ways, geographically by area or country, or by demo-

Figure 4.7 *Product/Market Matrix*

		Products	
		Present	New
Markets	Present	Regeneration	Product Development – New product ranges – New assortments/ categories – New services
	New	Market development – Geographical – New market segments/ customers	Diversify – Related-within the retail industry – Unrelated-beyond the retail industry

Source: after Ansoff (1988).

graphic and social groupings. Where the organisation has a strong position in its market it can use its strength and expertise to develop new products. Alternatively the company could take a strong and successful product brand offering into new markets as a *market development* strategy; new products need not be developed because its low cost base or differentiation from its competitors are unique enough to allow it to compete in other markets. The acquisitions by Tesco of William Low in Scotland, or Carrefour's takeover of Cora in France, extended market share in this way through increased geographical distribution.

The product–market matrix has been developed into a number of more specific applications for the retail industry. Robinson and Clarke-Hill's (1990) matrix (Figure 4.8) defines three dimensions by adding related products and distinguishing existing markets from new domestic and international ones. Reflecting retail developments into new services, the matrix includes developments outside retailing such as financial services, in-store credit cards and catering.

The common theme in these directional matrices is to relate two or more fundamental dimensions for decision-making to the strategic direction of the company. Whilst they define a range of viable options, the choice of direction must be firmly grounded in the retailer's objectives and aversion to risk, with the alignment of its capabilities and opportunities. For publicly-owned retailers at least, new market and new product strategies can be relatively difficult to achieve within acceptable timescales to shareholders. The ability to extract higher profits through acquisitions has also become increasingly difficult. Multinational and global diversification present greater risks still; starting-up and sustaining this strategic option requires a distinc-

Figure 4.8 *Extended Product/Market Matrix Adapted for Retailers*

Market segments

		Existing	Related/domestic	New/overseas
Product mix and trading format	Existing	Market expansion Market share growth Store extensions/revamps	New stores	New stores
	Related	New stores with different product mix Shop in stores Product range extensions	New trading formats and stand-alone product mixes	New stores with new formats
	New	Financial services In-store credit cards In-store catering	Vertical integration	Vertical integration

Source: Robinson and Clarke-Hill (1990).

Exhibit 4.4 Market penetration strategy

Walmart initially grew by out-competing the small, family-owned general stores in small towns. Other US retailers have followed Wal-Mart's strategy and consolidated their industries including Home Depot, Office Depot, Best Buy, and Barnes & Noble, the US-based bookseller. Even in the mature funeral parlour industry, Service Corporation International has achieved high growth by pursuing a strategy of acquiring family-owned parlours and making them more efficient. It does so through purchasing power, sharing and financial leverage. The force of industry consolidation makes market penetration, and globalisation if it is a global industry, the only sensible growth option. Companies face the stark choice: get bigger or get out (Karmani, 1999).

---

tively differentiated format implemented through determined leadership and a supportive culture.

Diversification

Diversification strategies take the retailer into new market and new product development, and Walters (1988) suggests that longer-term strategic decisions develop existing advantages, or lead to new areas of development. Diversification concerns the development of interests outside existing retailing activities primarily by integrating new activities in vertical or horizontal directions

■ *Vertical integration.* Vertical integration expands the organisation's operations into other industries up or down their supply chain to exert greater control, and in some cases creates entry barriers to protect their unique design or technology skills. In this way Disney and Warner Brothers have extended into retailing to exploit character-merchandising opportunities from films and TV series. Many grocery retailers have taken over an upstream distribution role through investment in distribution centres that bypass wholesalers, and have used their buying power to influence production processes. These moves add value to the retail offer through greater control over primary activities between retailer and consumer.

However, a trend of vertical *disintegration* has been observed across a range of industries as businesses seek to avoid being locked into inappropriate technologies, and to increase their flexibility, from which the UK retail industry has not been immune (Harland, 1996). Retailers have reduced their exposure to low growth or inflexible vertical integration between manufacturing, distribution and retailing.

The trend has been particularly evident amongst clothing retail multiples, such as Arcadia and more recently Laura Ashley, but can be found in other sectors too, for example at Asda and Body Shop, companies that once owned extensive manufacturing facilities but consistently refocused their strategies on to their retailing activities. As the competitive environment changes, vertical integration may yet reappear in response to a new problem arising out of e-commerce. The need for home delivery as online sales develop may require a reassessment of forward integration into distribution services by retailers.

■ *Horizontal integration.* The organisation grows through combining operations in the same industry, enabling it to strengthen its position by increasing its market share. This direction has been far more evident in retailing, as growth strategies have frequently turned on geographical expansion by acquiring businesses either purely for their sites or as complementary fascias. Kingfisher's international development in DIY and electrical goods in France demonstrates this approach.

Diversification can also be considered in terms of the degree of relatedness to the existing business; the more distant the diversification, the higher the levels of risk.

■ *Related/concentric diversification* – the addition of a business related in terms of products, markets and so on with a high degree of compatibility between core and the new business. It occurs when combined company profits increase strengths and opportunities and help minimise risks. Relatedness might be defined by relating application of expertise to degrees of business interdependence. The degree to which the new industry is related to its core businesses and the degree to which the company operates at the same centre of gravity through its values, systems, organisation and paradigm, determines the proximity of existing and new businesses. In practice, types of relatedness include operational skills, customer use, product or technological similarities.

The growth strategy for Woolworth is typified by its relatedness to its existing business and the incremental way in which it is being developed. New formats are evaluated as they become operational, enabling flexible responses to customer demand. If any of the new formats fails to meet its strategic objectives, costs of withdrawal are minimised.

This approach can be contrasted to Cargo Club, a warehouse club format developed in the mid-1990s as a direct competitive response to Costco's arrival in the UK. Nurdin and Peacock, whose core business was in wholesaling, invested so heavily in this diversification that when it collapsed within one year the financial impact was so serious that the parent company was unable to continue independently. Research among managers in the failed operation identified a number of problems. These included excessive start-up and operating costs, a higher cost base from investment in a broader product assortment with greater emphasis on food, overstretched management, and excessive levels of advertising.

■ *Unrelated/conglomerate diversification* – undertaken for a profit opportunity primarily, but also inspired by personal ambition, the need to spread risk in cyclical businesses, and the need to expand beyond existing mature or declining markets (Kotler, 1998).

Exhibit 4.5   Growth through acquisition: Arcadia's acquisition of Sears Womenswear business

In 1999, the clothing retail multiple, Arcadia, decided to take over the Sears womenswear brands. This group of stores, with a turnover of £417 million, represented a significant opportunity to Arcadia to increase the profit of its fashion clothing retail business in the UK and overseas. The Miss Selfridge, Wallis and Warehouse facias complement Arcadia's portfolio of strong fashion brands and increased its market share from 8 per cent to 11.5 per cent of the UK womenswear market. Following acquisition the enlarged group will operate through a number of channels: 2629 UK outlets, 186 international outlets, and the home shopping and Internet retailing businesses. This multi-channel expertise will allow for greater development of all brands, and Arcadia sees considerable potential for brand development:

- Wallis will be expanded from 216 outlets to around 270 outlets in the UK.

- Warehouse is a strong brand with growth potential to expand in the UK from 95 outlets to around 150 outlets.

- Miss Selfridge is a well-known young fashion brand and operates from 96 stores and 18 concessions in the UK.

- Arcadia will use its expertise in this market to focus Miss Selfridge as a distinctive brand alongside Top Shop.

The integration of these businesses will create additional advantages for Arcadia. Arcadia's brand-oriented management structure will enable the new business management teams to focus exclusively on product and marketing objectives, and it will enable central and field management costs to be rationalised within two years by around £13 million. Store locations will be optimised to ensure an appropriate spread of brands and to maximise trading space, and margin improvements will be generated through increased buying power.

Strategies of Reorganisation

After the high growth of the 1980s, the retail industry turned to 'engineering' its strategy with the focus more on the productivity of existing businesses rather than investment in riskier initiatives. Where the organisation's resource and external environment analyses constrain growth through limited finances, site availability or personnel skills, strategies can be developed to hold or increase market share within the existing market. Figure 4.9 illustrates the dimensions of consolidation and rationalisation. The launch of new fascias by the clothing multiples was stopped in the early 1990s by economic recession that reduced consumer spending and affected investor sentiment towards the retail sector. It became clear that the ambitious expansion of property portfolios had resulted in too many unprofitable stores. This led to rationalisation of both fascias and individual stores wherever possible, a process evident throughout the 1990s and into the 2000s as many High Street multiples continue to reassess their property and brand portfolios.

Figure 4.9   *Strategies of Reorganisation*

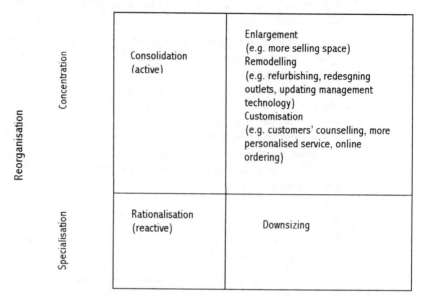

Source: Jones (2000).

In other retail sectors where growth had been achieved through out-of-town or edge-of-town retail parks, development has been increasingly constrained by government planning restrictions and site availability. In the food sector, strategic choices have arisen from trade-offs between price and product assortment. Traditional supermarkets are surrounded by innovators targeting customers demanding lower prices or more locational convenience. Within the saturated market conditions of UK grocery retailing, a two-dimensional decision matrix based on modified or new product or outlet type developments may be appropriate.

The least-risk approach for grocery retailers will arise from increasing the range of goods in larger stores and the refurbishment and extension of existing stores, broadening their appeal through wider ranges and a clearer marketing offer (Guy, 1996). The addition of new products to an existing market of customers is evident in a range of initiatives such as the launch of 'healthy food' ranged by Sainsburys and other grocery multiples.

The organisation may plan to withdraw from a market to concentrate its resources elsewhere. Withdrawal from local markets through store closures, and national markets, such as the UK in the case of C&A, reflects a focus on how retailers sustain profitability in highly competitive conditions. In these instances markets have become too unattractive for further financial and managerial investment.

THE FIT OF THE STRATEGY TO THE ORGANISATION

The ability of retailers to both plan and implement their strategies successfully will be determined by their organisational resources and structure. The central concern is

---

Exhibit 4.6   Woolworths: development of a retail format

Woolworths opened in Liverpool over 90 years ago, and became the focal point in many communities. In 1982 it was bought out, and by 2000 was once again the UK's leading family chain. Woolworths' retail formats for the twenty-first century include Big W, Woolworths General Store, and E-tailing. The new Woolworths, the Big W concept, was launched in 1999 and is designed to offer a fun day out for the family. Based on the edge of towns it offers very attractive pricing and extensive product ranges. The Woolworth's General Store offers products from Superdrug, another of the Kingfisher formats, from early in the morning to late at night. Customers can explore a friendly and convenient alternative shopping environment, Woolworth's Direct catalogue supports the store proposition and provides home shopping opportunities. It is also the interactive retailer, on Sky TV. Managing the change is essential to Woolworths' competitive position, formed around five dimensions

- Suppliers

- Customer Knowledge of their consumer is essential for Woolworths to compete

- Product. Product based differentiation is becoming more difficult to achieve, for example in computers, where the innovation of today becomes the commodity of tomorrow.

- Format. New retailing formats must be addressed that demonstrate a real understanding of customers, their needs, wants and aspirations.

- A new mindset. Woolworths lost customers in the 1970s and early 1980s to food and specialist retailers due to complacency, when traditional strengths turned to weaknesses.

The focus will be on customer needs, top management commitment, empowered format teams and central infrastructure, and the testing of the proposition's robustness during its roll-out, supported by a responsive infrastructure.

---

the role of organisational structure on the management of strategy; decisions about where the company' strategy is heading are closely related to assessments about who will put it into action. Growth strategies in particular demand careful assessment of different options, and the implications these hold for the organisation's structure, and the available human resources. Lack of specialist knowledge and skills, the cost of their acquisition or expensive restructuring may exclude some options. All strategies should aim to achieve internal consistency with the organisation's situation. Where simple organisations have a focus on function and product, complex ones will also be concerned with organisational structure. The size of the retail business, and the process of divisionalisation into manageable units will both contribute to issues of strategic control.

The retailer's approach to strategy, discussed earlier in the chapter, will depend on cultural influences too. These may be embedded in the national culture, so that ways of working may not be universally received but only be acceptable to some societies.

The organisation's own culture will influence the approach to strategy and methods of implementation. Market leadership companies have been observed to possess characteristics of greater foresight into the future of their market, willingness to unlearn past approaches, and a capacity to challenge conventions and create new competitive forms. These types of strategic approaches are exemplified in charismatic leaders, for whom rewriting of industry rules is more powerful than incremental gains in market share.

The underlying theme is the building of current practice and managerial beliefs about the organisation's competences within a political and historical context. The guidance that directs strategy will be influenced by cultural assumptions, beliefs and values within managerial experience and existing culture (Johnson, 1987); the overarching set of beliefs that are commonly held is the paradigm. Therefore, if we consider the cultural paradigm governing the business's response to the competitive environment, we can expect the problems and processes of change to differ depending on the organisation's position in its lifecycle (Schein, 1986). The connection between patterns of cultural beliefs and strategy is seen in the rationalisation of processes which may be accounted for in other ways. For example, decision-making processes may arise through the application of managerial experience filtering internal/external stimuli in a political setting (Johnson, 1988).

The paradigm evolves over time and creates a homogeneous approach to the interpretation of the complexity facing the organisation; the external signals facing the organisation are filtered in terms of the paradigm. It also provides a stock repertoire of responses for managers; that is, it becomes a device for interpretation and a framework for action. The paradigm configures strategy formulation, but is itself shaped by cultural elements: the routine of the member's rituals, control systems, and rewards that define activity.

One consequence is that it governs managers' views of strategic change, in that they are likely to deal with change in terms of the cultural, political and social norms of organisational life. But changes may be beyond the paradigm and the constraints of the cultural 'web', and in this situation managers will often respond with the familiar routines and actions that have worked well in the past, typically the implementation of existing strategies through greater centralisation and tightened controls.

SUMMARY

An important characteristic of competition in the retail industry is its increasing intensity and concentration into fewer companies. Accurate assessment of these factors will enable retailers to develop appropriate strategic responses. In order to understand competitors' characteristics retailers can group them using strategic group analysis and the five-force model, which focuses on the relationship between the main dimensions of competition. The outcome will be to identify direct competitors, the basis of their competitive position, and the ways they may influence the competitive environment in the future. This assessment contributes to the selection of growth strategies, or in more threatening environments strategies that best maintain the current position or, if necessary, allows withdrawal from markets.

Competition provides one important dimension on which to base strategic decisions. The process will need to balance assessments of other factors, too, to provide a realistic and viable direction to the retail business. These will include the wider external business environment trends discussed in Chapter 2, but equally importantly internal resources and organisational disposition to undertake a strategic option.

Internal resource analysis enables the company to establish its ability to differentiate itself from its competitors and to achieve competitive advantage. These factors could be found in some or perhaps many linkages between the skills and abilities of people in the organisation, locational and design advantages, product and branding, financial and information management. Identifying and listing is less valuable than linking or bundling together critical resources that together provide some distinctive ability to compete for customer attention and loyalty.

The combination of internal and external factors will provide the basis of strategic selection; in effect what could be possible with the available resource configurations given the opportunities and threats of markets and competitors. The strategy will have to meet organisational objectives which for most retailers are dominated by financial requirements, but increasingly influenced too by issues of corporate values and governance. The process of strategic selection and implementation will in part be determined by the organsiational culture and structure. As a service industry, retailing has a considerable investment in its people, around whom culture will be understood and enacted. In well-established cultures strategic change may be difficult to contemplate as well as implement, and those issues are more closely examined in Chapter 9.

QUESTIONS

1   Examine the internal value chains for retailers in two different sectors.

2   Do companies pay enough attention to their core competencies?

3   Write down an example of a retailer that meets the criteria for each of the cost, differentiation and niche strategies. Explain why each one demonstrates these characteristics.

4   Assess the relevance of product–market matrices to retailers' strategic choices.

5   Select a retail organisation and map its stakeholders in a way that clearly illustrates their involvement in the business. How close are they? How will they influence the organisation?

Strategic Direction at W.H. Smith plc

W.H. Smith opened its first bookstall in response to the growing demands of the railway travelling public. Its ability to meet the requirements of travellers was so successful that in just nine years it was operating over 1240 bookstalls. Within a short space of time it became the natural destination for buyers of newspapers, books, stationery and pens.

The company maintained its strength in these areas whilst expanding over the years into greetings cards, toys and games, and recorded music. It was respected as a well-managed, conservatively run business, which nevertheless continued to keep abreast of new products and merchandise range extensions as they were launched onto the markets. The stores, too, were professionally redesigned and replanned to match the aspirations of its target market. Its attempts to diversify outside the core business, for example into Travel Agencies, met with less success until increasing competition and new acquisitions changed the shape of the company.

Since the 1980s new competitors began to encroach onto Smith's territory. Specialist retailers expanded into towns where previously W.H. Smith had been the only multiple book retailer, and possibly the only book retailer of any description. During the 1990s generalist retailers, in particular the supermarket groups led by ASDA and Tesco, began to encroach into their newspaper and magazine businesses. In the face of this competition, Smith bought specialist retailers such as Our Price records and Waterstone's bookshops. They also developed new areas of business including specialist stationery retailers and DIY superstores.

The continuing decline in the core businesses' profitability required more drastic action, and in 1995 a new Chief Executive, Bill Coburn, set about identifying non-core opera-

tions. As a result, the company disposed of Do It All, Business Supplies and Paperchase, which were either loss-making or only marginally profitable to the organisation. The next step was to introduce a new strategy for the remaining core businesses. A key aim was to lift net margins from 5 per cent to the levels achieved by Boots (12%) or Marks and Spencer (14%). The top priority was to get to grips with 'rotten margins, high costs, inefficiency and flabby accountability' within W.H. Smith.

When Coburn himself left in 1997 his earlier pruning of the organisation had resulted in a more rational portfolio of six businesses: W.H. Smith Retail, Virgin/Our Price, Waterstone's, W.H. Smith USA, and The Wall, an American music chain. W.H. Smith News, the wholesale distributor of newspapers and magazines, remained because it was highly cash-generative and commanded a high market share. In the UK the group had a dominating shares of the books, stationery, music and video markets, too, attracting some 10 million customers.

The main problem area was W.H. Smith, which contributed about one-third of the £124m group profits (1996–97). By contrast, Waterstone's reported sales increasing by 11 per cent to £200m and profits up by a third to £20m. W.H. Smith's profits actually rose from £41m to £43m on sales up 1.5 per cent to £788m; but figures showed that a £6m provision had been made to clear unsold stock, £20m more than expected. The slow-moving stock occurred in videos, music and books, and the slowdown in music sales was in part supported by the £4m decline in profits (down to £14m) in the Virgin/Our Price business due to lack of big releases. The markdown provision was even more unsettling because two years previously Coburn had claimed that by focusing on a narrower range of stock the group was freeing up the equivalent of 50 new stores. The disappointing results caused one City analyst to comment 'we still do not feel there is a strong consumer proposition in the main retail chain'. However, the Chairman remained confident: 'people go to W.H. Smith because they like a middle of the road store where you can buy music, books, videos, magazines and stationery. They like the fact that it is a variety store.' These people add up to 7 million potential customers passing through the stores each week.

City analysts had calculated that the group could be worth £500m more than its current stockmarket value if W.H. Smith was demerged from the other parts of the group. During 1998 this began to take place as Waterstones was sold for £300m. W.H. Smith certainly had to concentrate its mind on the book side of its business, because since the mid-1990s new retailers including Borders and Ottakers had entered the market and Internet book retailing had taken off with the arrival of Amazon.com.

A new CEO, Richard Handover, who had many years experience of the business, supplied this focus. Firstly the 75 per cent stake in Our Price was sold to Richard Branson. Then during 1999 part of the cash from the sale of Waterstones was spent on the acquisition of John Menzies stationery shops for £65m with a further £9.4m going to buy the Internet Bookshop. Three publishers were acquired and the US store formats and buying procedures were changed to more closely model the traditional UK stores. The publishing and retailing strategic directions continued into 2000 with the announcement of plans for larger, 20 000 sq ft store formats as well as trials of a new type of convenience store. By the end of the year the company was able to announce an 8 per cent rise in profits due to 'excellent performance' from its stores and a 40 per cent increase in publishing profits. The only problem appeared to lie in the disappointing profitability of its Internet ventures.

The book retailing market 1998

Chain	Branches	Sales	Operating profit (£m)	Market share (%)
Waterstones (inc. Dillons)	184	200	20	20
W.H. Smith	547	837	50	17.9
Book Club Associates	M.O.	n/a	n/a	6.4
Ottakar's	49	38.6	2.2	2.1
Books Etc. (owned by Borders)	25	31.5	2.2	2.0

Source: Mintel.

SEMINAR QUESTIONS FOR DISCUSSION

1 Explain the changes in W.H. Smith's strategic direction.

2 Discuss the future of W.H. Smith as a concept.

3 To what extent is there a danger that W.H. Smith will be 'stuck in the middle' of the book market?

References

Ansoff, I.H. (1988) *Corporate Strategy* (London: Penguin).

Baden-Fuller, C. and Stopford, J.M. (1992) *The Mature Business: The Competitive Challenge* (London: Routledge).

Barney, J. (1991) Firm Resources and Sustained Competitive Advantage, *Journal of Management*, vol. 17, pp. 99–119.

Bowman, C. (1992) 'Interpreting Corporate Strategy', in D. Faulkner and G. Johnson (ed.), *The Challenge of Strategic Management* (London: Kogan Page).

Brownlie, D. (1989) 'Scanning the Internal Environment: Impossible Precept or Neglected Art?', *Journal of Marketing Management*, pp. 300–8.

Campbell, A. and Luchs, K.S. (1992) *Strategic Synergy* (Oxford: Butterworth/Heinemann).

Flavian, C., Haberberg, A. and Polo, Y. (1999) 'Subtle Strategic Insights from Strategic Groups Analysis', *Journal of Strategic Marketing*, June, vol. 7, no. 2, pp. 89–107.

Flavian, C. and Polo, Y. (1999) 'Strategic Groups Analysis (SGA) as a Tool for Strategic Marketing', *European Journal of Marketing*, vol. 33, no. 5/6, pp. 548–70.

Glaister, K.W. and Falshaw, J.R. (1999) 'Strategic Planning: Still Going Strong?' *Long Range Planning*, vol. 32, January, pp. 101–15.

Greco, J. (1997) 'Retailing's Rule Breakers', *The Journal of Business Strategy*, March, pp. 28–34.

Guy, C. (1996) 'Grocery Store Saturation in the UK – the Continuing Debate', *International Journal of Retail and Distribution Management*, vol. 24, no. 6, pp. 3–10.

Hamel, G. and Prahalad, C.K. (1994) *Competing for the Future* (Boston: Harvard Business School Press).

Harland, C. (1996) 'Supply Chain Management; Relationships, Chains and Networks', *British Journal of Management, Special Issue S63–S80*, vol. 7, March.

Hawkesworth, R.I. (1998) 'Budgens plc: Coping with Competition in UK Grocery Retailing', *International Journal of Retail and Distribution Management*, vol. 26, no. 1, pp. 38–48.

Hussey, D. and Jenster, P. (1999) *Competitor Intelligence* (Chichester: John Wiley).

Johnson G. and Scholes, K. (1999) *Exploring Corporate Strategy*, 5th edn (Hemel Hempstead: Prentice Hall Europe).

Johnson, G. (1988) Rethinking Incrementalism, *Strategic Management Journal*, vol. 8, pp. 75–91.

Johnson, G. (1987) *Strategic Change and the Management Process* (Oxford: Blackwell).

Jones, K. (2000) Key Note Presentation presented at the Contemporary Issues in Retail Marketing Conference, Manchester Metropolitan University.

Karmani, A.G. (1999) '*Five ways to grow the market and create value*', *Mastering Strategy*, 4, *Financial Times*, 18 October 1999.

Kay, J. (1995) *Foundations of Corporate Success* (Oxford: Oxford University Press).

Kotler, P. (1997) *Marketing Management: Analysis, Planning, Implementation, and Control*, 9th edn (London: Prentice Hall International).

McDonald, M. and Tideman, C. (1993) *Retail Marketing Plans* (Oxford: Butterworth-Heinemann).

McDowell Mudambi, S. (1994) 'A Topology of Strategic Choice in Retailing', *International Journal of Retail and Distribution Management*, vol. 22, no. 4, pp. 32–40.

McGee, J. (1987) 'Retailer Strategies in the UK', in G. Johnson (ed.), *Business Strategy and Retailing* (Chichester: John Wiley).

McGoldrick, P.J. (1990) *Retail Marketing*, McGraw Hill.

Miller, B. (1986) *Strategic Management Journal*, vol. 7, pp. 223–49.

Mintzberg, H. (1988) 'Thoughts on Strategy', *Californian Management Review*, pp. 11–24.

Pache, G. (1999) '*When Logistics Threaten to become a Source of Competitive Disadvantage: The Intermarché Co-operative Case*', in Dupuis M. and Dawson J. (eds) *European Cases in Retailing* (Oxford: Blackwell).

Porter, M.E. (1980) *Competitive Strategy: Techniques for Analyzing Industries and Competitors* (New York: The Free Press).

Porter, M.E. (1985) *Competitive Advantage* (New York: The Free Press).

Prahalad, C.K. (1999) *Changes in the Competitive Battlefield*, Mastering Strategy 2, *Financial Times* 4/10/99.

Raphel, M. (1999) 'Up against the Wal-Mart', *Direct Marketing*, April, vol. 61, no. 12, p. 2.

Robinson, T.M. and Clarke-Hill, C.M. (1990) 'Directional Growth by European Retailers', *International Journal of Retail & Distribution Management*, vol. 18, n. 5, pp. 3–14.

Schein, E. (1986) 'What you Need to Know About Organisational Culture', *Training and Development Journal*, January.

Tse, K.K. (1985) *Marks and Spencer: Anatomy of Britain's Most Efficiently Managed Company* (Oxford: Pergamon Press).

Walters, D.W. (1988) *Strategic Retail Marketing: A Case Study Approach* (Hemel Hempstead: Prentice Hall Europe).

Whittington, R. (1993) *What is Strategy and Does It Matter?* (London: Routledge).

International Retailing

INTRODUCTION

This chapter is concerned with the development of retail businesses across borders. It examines the motives for internationalisation before moving on to analyse differences in retail industry structures in selected geographical regions. Even within Europe, the types of retail formats, their relative strengths and the opportunities for new entrants are perhaps surprisingly diverse, and these are contrasted with two other important geographical areas of retail development: the USA and the developing countries of the Far East. The second part of the chapter assesses the types of market-entry strategy available to retailers and concludes with an overview of the issues arising from store operations in other countries.

THE DEVELOPMENT OF INTERNATIONAL AND GLOBAL MARKETS

In one sense retail internationalisation is well-developed. The sourcing and buying of merchandise has a long tradition for countries with well-established trade routes, and as a consequence 'customers have been provided with more and different goods at lower prices' (Muhlbacker *et al.*, 1999). The dispersion of retail trading formats and operations has a shorter history, arising from demographic, social and cultural forces that converge and shape global marketing policies (Hibbert, 1989) and open up new opportunities for store operations (Dawson, 2000).

The opportunity to internationalise is dependent on a number of factors, of which national cultures, and increasingly globalisation, play an important part. Marketeers find it useful to cluster countries where consumers share meaningful cultural characteristics. One method is to define cultural affinity zones and classes by shared criteria such as language, religion, family life patterns, work relations and consumption patterns (Usunier 1999). Cultural barriers, too, have a significant impact on retail internationalisation. Outsider impressions of homogeneity and cultural uniformity may be misinterpreted; a typical example arises from European conceptions of the USA and its perceived cultural uniformity. To overcome these sorts of problems in geographical and cultural distance, retailers initially prefer culturally proximate markets where the business distance is short, and consumers are more easily understood (Dupuis and Prime, 1996).

However establishing the notion of proximity is becoming more difficult. The blurring of cultural and, in the EU at least, national boundaries has implications for the demand for goods. In a broad sense, globalisation is defined by a number of dimensions not only by cultural and economic but also by political and technological ones (Giddens, 1999). Above all, proximity owes much to the spread of media and communications, most recently Internet-based. In terms of supply of goods these trends lead towards the standardisation of products and services by competitors, increasingly at a global level.

The markets of the developed world present many opportunities, but to achieve truly global scope retailers will require a wider reach into new and emerging markets. Emerging economies derive their appeal from their long-term growth rate, and the sheer size of some countries makes them very attractive with China, India and Indonesia alone accounting for 2.4 billion people and around 40 per cent of the world population. However, unequal income and wealth distribution may not necessarily create attractive markets; countries with a more even distribution of income or a large middle class represent more of a mass market and have greater appeal for retail development (Terpstra and Sarathy, 2000).

Table 5.1   *Alternative Global Scenarios*

Crisis in Asia	A collapse of globalisation as Asia stagnates
The West builds barriers to the rest of the world	Trade conflicts between the USA and Europe creates disagreement and animosity to the West
Evolutionary survival	A no-change scenario in which only the strongest and best-managed firms survive, thereby creating global winners and losers
Post-modern capitalism	Increased global responsibility results in higher cost bases for business
New World Order	Sustained economic growth: in former communist countries this is accompanied by political and economic liberalisation in Russia and China. Japan and emerging markets recover. Global regulation and responsibility is achieved

Source: based on Dawson (2000).

The path to globalisation itself may not be a straight one. Dawson (2000) proposes a number of alternative global scenarios (Table 5.1) that may yet determine retail growth opportunities. The research evidence for a global consumer is not yet conclusive as studies continue to show the significance of national, cultural and psychological differences and the ways they shape consumer tastes through local rather than international trends (Usunier, 1999).

THE INTERNATIONALISATION OF RETAILING: MOTIVES FOR RETAILER INTERNATIONALISATION

International marketing literature has identified a number of reasons for internationalisation in which economies of scale, the use of specialist capabilities, and the need to develop knowledge and skills are significant. Organisational needs too, may push the company in this direction, and internationalisation may be driven by satisfying the vision or ambition of the Chief Executive (Quelch and Bartlett, 1999). Whilst these are relevant to the retail industry, retail internationalisation requires a different focus, one that is also concerned with the transferability of *intangible* elements of the brand, the acceptability of the format and its marketing position in another country. More specifically, retailers seek to exploit competitive advantages they have developed in their domestic country into new markets, through their formats, branding, expertise and networks (Howard, 2000).

In the simplest terms, motives for retailer internationalisation can be understood in terms of 'push' factors out of the domestic country, and 'pull' factors into another country. There is evidence for both driving forces in the process of retailer internationalisation in the UK. Some company internationalisation has been shown to be triggered by the push of market concentration and maturity; for example economies of scale have been recognised by Kingfisher in their drive to create European electrical and DIY retailing businesses. Other companies have been attracted by market opportunities in which their distinctive competencies can succeed, through brand or cost positioning or product differentiation.

Push and pull characteristics (Table 5.2) provide a basic framework in which to understand retailer motives, and from these it has been argued that retailers demonstrate either reactive or proactive positions towards internationalisation. Reactive responses occur where the home market is saturated and opportunities are marginal, the retailer will respond by seeking opportunities in new markets. Proactive motives emphasise the importance of international opportunities and a willingness to exploit these before domestic saturation creates competitive and growth problems. These have been extended to four retailer groups by Williams (1992):

- Growth-oriented. Due to competitive pressures, retailers seek to identify new opportunities for sales and profits in underdeveloped markets.

- Limited domestic market growth opportunities. Domestic market typified by maturity perceptions of market saturation, high levels of competition, problems in diversification or excessive regulation.

Table 5.2   *Push and Pull Factors for Internationalisation*

Push factors to expand outside the domestic market	Pull factors into a new market
■ National conditions, including unstable political structure; unstable economy; poor economic conditions; negative social environment; unfavourable operating environment; operating costs ■ Mature domestic market ■ Format saturation ■ Competitive environment: oversupply of retail space for the population ■ Pressure on profit margins from competition ■ Technology for management. ■ Leading-edge formats/unique products ■ Shareholder pressure for earnings growth ■ Experience of international development	■ National conditions, including stable government and economy; favourable demographics and social groups; national infrastructure (communications, transport, quality of built environments); legal constraints on development; cultural and geographic proximity ■ Size of market ■ Retail industry structure and level of competition ■ Industry infrastructure (technologies, logistics, retail and distribution locations) ■ Ability to achieve higher profit margins ■ Economies of scale

■ Motives stemming from an internationally appealing and innovative retail concept. The opportunity arises here from 'the existence and convergence of certain international market segments'.

■ Passive and subjective motives. Retailers are led into internationalisation though offers from other retailers, to use surplus resources, to imitate competitors' moves.

From these it can be shown that retailer motivation to internationalise is not a strongly held reaction to limited domestic market opportunities. There is evidence, found for example in the development of Body Shop and Benetton, that growth-oriented motives and internationally appealing and innovative retail offerings may prove more important than domestic expansion. These retailers have been international from a relatively early stage of development if measured by the number of international markets and the contribution of international sales to turnover. By contrast, some large retailers have not developed fully internationally – their ownership structure can constrain activity, for example British investors are often cautious or prefer to see development within the UK (Alexander, 2001).

The themes of reactive and proactive motives are developed further by Alexander (1997). Using the dimensions of market saturation and global relevance of the retailer's operation, internationalisation can be shown to take place at any stage of the retailer's domestic market development. The issue of market saturation may not significantly motivate some retailers who proactively exploit international opportunities at an early stage in their development. The development of e-commerce may hasten this type of development for smaller, focused businesses.

RETAIL STRUCTURES

National retail structures influence both the push out of a domestic market and the attractiveness of the pull into a market. Above these there are international communities, alliances and organsisations that shape patterns of trade at global and regional levels. The core trading blocs of the world's economy, the European Union, the USA and Japan, are in the strongest position to stimulate economic growth. But international relations can also raise problems of trade barriers. These can be tariff-based, typically through import duties and non-tariff based, often found in complex import documentation and product-testing requirements. Trading or community agreements between countries aim to reduce these. At a global level the World Trade Organisation has an important role to play in the promotion and de-regulation of international commerce. More generally, the United Nations and its agencies, the International Monetary Fund (IMF) and other financial organisations, also have concerns in issues of governance and responsibility.

At a regional level the European Union (EU) negotiates trading and business agreements with many countries, as well as settling its own boundaries. In 1991 Poland, the Czech and Slovak republics and Hungary negotiated association agreements with the EU which have since been extended to other Eastern European states. The EU enables member states to compete more effectively by removing internal barriers such as import tariffs, VAT differences, and work permits, to create the Single European Market (SEM). The purpose of the Economic Monetary Union (EMU) is to simplify currency exchange processes and costs across most member states, and by so doing create new opportunities for business expansion. In theory, the SEM should provide greater cross border opportunities to retailers, with national borders playing a less significant role (Myers 1996).

Elsewhere, regional trade agreements exist on a less integrative scale. Within the Americas Free Trade Area (FTAA), the North American Free Trade Agreement (NAFTA) forms a bloc of some 360 million people in the USA, Canada and Mexico which has resulted in important cross-border activity. Mexico appears attractive to US retailers as it expands its retail space, and the most successful moves by Sears and Walmart have been into Mexico and Canada. However, the USA has proved a harder market to enter from other countries, and Canadian expansion into the USA has resulted in a 90 per cent failure rate (Sternquist, 1997). APEC and ASEAN established across the Pacific and Southeast Asia regions form Asian trading blocs, but with less significance for retailer expansion.

Europe

Within Europe, national retail markets and industry structures vary significantly, with the result that the shopping experience in France is different to that in say, Greece or Norway. Economic and social development, geography and urbanisation, government policy and regulation have all played their part in creating distinctive retail industries. However, a number of processes are at work to erode the regionally defined historical patterns of retail distribution (Figure 5.1). Internationalisation of formats, such as discount food retailing and hypermarkets, of retailers themselves from France,

Figure 5.1   *European Retail Structures*

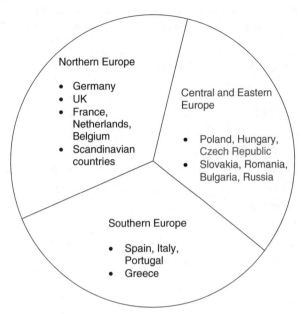

the UK and Germany in particular, combined with broader industrial themes of concentration, are leading to greater homogenisation. As a result national markets present opportunities according to the stage of development of their commercial structures which together with the intensity of retail formats (McGoldrick and Davies, 1994), enable the internationalising retailer to define its broad aims, and target more specific market-entry points.

Northern Europe

The wealth and size of northern European economies contribute to the concentration and segmentation of their retailing structures. Higher levels of market concentration are evident, as the largest retailers increase their market share through internal expansion and mergers. Some of the largest retailers in Europe are German, with retail activities in many industry sectors. Rewe, one of the market leaders, trades through a variety of outlets including corner shops, discount markets, supermarkets and hypermarkets, as well as a large number of specialised outlets and wholesaling. In Northern Europe there tend to be fewer, but larger stores employing fewer people with the result that there is a lower density of outlets per head of population compared to other parts, where smaller sized businesses are more evident. The diversity of highly-developed formats contrasts with southern Europe where the modern hypermarket, supermarket and discount store formats have predominated.

Marketing has been a particular strength of German and UK retail businesses through the use of differentiation strategies, and typically the development of own brands by many retailers in the UK and discounters in Germany has been the source of competitive advantage. More recently, French retail groups have turned to these marketing-led techniques to create sources of differentiation other than price.

Table 5.3   *Europe's Largest Retailers*

Company	Country	Sales 1997–98 (€ bn)	Retail activities
Metro	Germany	46.55	Hypermarkets, supermarkets, cash and carry, DIY, electronics, department stores
Intermarche	France	34.50	Food, various non-food
Rewe	Germany	32.32	Food, non-food
Promodes	France	32.31	Food, cash and carry
Edeka	Germany	30.29	Food, DIY
Tesco	UK	27.45	Food
Carrefour	France	27.41	Food
Tengelmann	Germany	27.07	Food, clothing, DIY, drugstores
Ahold	Netherlands	26.48	Food, drugstores, beauty
Aldi	Germany	23.72	Food

In these countries the retail industry displays a mature relationship between suppliers and retailers, with the balance of power moving towards the retailers (Table 5.3). The need for detailed stock management of own-brand merchandise has enabled British food retailers to develop sophisticated supply chains. New stock management technology is evident; for example the Dutch retailer, Ahold, uses new technology to create strong competitive advantage through the use of scanners to target customer needs, and more recently self-scanning and electronic shelf-edge labels. The trend to manage inventories and service quality more closely is beginning to follow the same pattern of development in France and Germany.

The varied retail structures in northern Europe can be seen in the dominance of different types of format in each country. In the food retailing sector, Germany has been distinctively defined by the strength of its 'hard discount' retailers. These self-service formats maintain their position through a sustained focus on costs. Trading from secondary locations with limited space of 300–1000 sq m, they retail less than 1000 lines with core product ranges in drinks, dry groceries and basic chilled and frozen foods. The concept is supported by few personnel, limited services and a functional ambience.

French food retailing is dominated by hypermarkets (Figure 5.2) with an average size of about 5000 sq m, nearly twice the size of their UK food retailing equivalents. Food sales in these stores account for around 55 per cent of total sales, with the balance in clothing, electrical goods and housewares. The growth of the hypermarkets has been achieved at the expense of the superettes (100–400 sq m) and independent stores, as they compete not only on assortment but accessibility and price with operating margins around 1 per cent. The hard discount store concept transferred from Germany has formed a second growth area seeing sales double in the mid-1990s, and the

Figure 5.2   *Superstore Distribution in the EU, 1996*

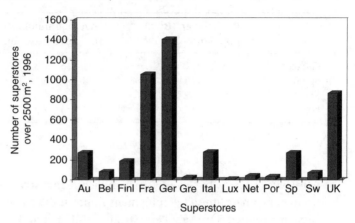

Source: Eurostat (1999).

number of outlets increase to 2171 by 1998. Distribution of sales in smaller super-markets are more influenced by hard discounters than in the UK.

The distribution of large, bulky goods has developed along comparable lines in northern Europe. DIY, home furnishings and to some extent electrical goods are conveniently accessed by car, and so large out-of-town warehouse stores prevail in this sector. Speciality clothing retailers achieve extensive national distribution, and in the case of variety stores such as C&A have created an international business of many years' standing. However, these retailers have come under increasing pressure from discounters leading to a polarisation between low-price mass merchandisers and higher fashion retail multiples.

The northern European retailers lead in the internationalisation of concepts and ideas finding growth opportunities within Europe but also in other continents. Ahold holds 36 per cent of the Dutch grocery market through 600 supermarkets, and trades through over 500 stores in the USA. It is also one of Portugal's leading retailers and has diversified into the Czech Republic. Carrefour, with its merger with Promodes, retails in South America and Asia as well as extensively across Europe.

National retail industries are further differentiated by their operating style and financial structures, with most UK retailers being publicly-owned whereas many French and German retailers are privately controlled often through complex cross-holdings between companies. This results in different strategic objectives, long-term profitability and growth being one main area of difference, along with cultural differences in mergers and acquisitions.

Southern Europe

Southern European retailing has been typified by the preponderance of small shops and family-owned businesses (Table 5.4), with less large-scale retail development and concentration of ownership. Independent retailers have been an important source of employment and services for rural areas in particular, as well as sustaining the

Table 5.4 *Density of Retail Outlets in Europe*

	Outlets per 10 000 population	Average number of employees per outlet	% self-employed
Greece	170	1.8	71.1
Spain	61	8.7	15.8
France	83	4.5	23.8
UK	61	8.7	15.8

Source: Bennison and Boutsouki (1995).

wholesale industry. In Greece, for example, the industry structure has been determined by low incomes, limited employment opportunities and low barriers to entry, with easy credit raised from suppliers. Strong family ties and individual entrepreneurialism distinguished social attitudes to work. Not least the retail environment was constrained by legislation concerning prices and profit margins, store openings and the use of part-time labour (Bennison and Boutsouki, 1996, 1998). Domestic deregulation and the arrival of foreign retailers has inevitably affected the small independent food retailer in major towns and cities, and the traditional wholesale system, which at least in Greece has been partly substituted for by cash-and-carry outlets.

However, during the 1990s retail structures began to rapidly transform and the picture is now less generalised. Both Spain and Portugal have seen extensive hypermarket development as French retailers, Carrefour, Promodes and Auchan expanded their formats into their southern neighbours. The impact has been radical, creating patterns of retail concentration similar to those in northern Europe. However, in Italy hypermarket progress has been slower largely due to complex planning restrictions on large stores in place since 1971. As a result, stores under 100 square metres accounted for 30 per cent of total food expenditure in Italy, compared to only 5 per cent in the UK and France with the Co-op Italia being the only national food retailer (Bell, 1998).

Food discounters have enjoyed a longer period of success in Spain, where the Dia operation was successfully introduced from France in the mid-1980s, than in Italy. Nevertheless, even here German retailers succeeded in entering the market and establishing some 2300 discount outlets by 1997. Of more importance in Italy have been buying groups formed by retailers prevented from large-scale development by legislation, who sought to take advantage of economies of scale.

Due largely to different approaches to planning permission, distinctions can now be more usefully made between Spain and Portugal together, and Italy and Greece; and even between northern and the more rural southern Italy. However, retail market structures are not static, and more recent deregulation of retailing in Italy and Greece has enabled large store developments to progress relatively unconstrained. At virtually the same time legislation was passed in Spain to effectively slow down large-scale development, further stimulating convergence in southern Europe in terms of the mix of supermarkets and hypermarkets.

Outside the food retailing sector, other distinctive elements of national retail structures are being eroded. In Spain, department stores have traditionally formed the focal point of Spanish urban shopping, and while they still occupy an important position in clothing and electrical retailing, they have lost ground to other formats. More recently the country has seen the rapid expansion of the Zara and Mango fashion clothing brands, a previously underdeveloped format, into multiple retailers. By contrast, department stores in Italy have never played a significant role in urban life; rather, Italian design has been applied to multiple retailing in fashion clothing and even more exclusive brands, typified by Benetton at one level and Gucci at the other. In both Italy and Spain, successful international formats lie in the clothing sector where design strengths are combined with flexible and high-quality manufacturing.

Eastern Europe

The retail structures of Eastern European countries present quite a different picture to those of the West. The centrally controlled economies of the postwar communist period did not favour distribution, and, typically, Polish industrial policy had concentrated on heavy industry and mining leaving the retail sector almost entirely undeveloped. State planning was unable to consistently balance demand with supply, and there was little awareness of the logistics capabilities required to move goods through the supply chain. Rationing, long channels of distribution, bureaucratic administrative processes through the 'obligatory intermediation' of trade agencies, and recirculation of materials created an inefficient industry (Waters, 1999). In the food sector, the state intervened through ownership of farms, farm produce and the purchasing, processing and wholesale as well as the retail trade of products.

Since 1989, Eastern European countries have been in a state of transition in which the retail sector, now a major economic force, has played a significant role. The former socialist states have turned to parliamentary democracies with varying degrees of conviction. In those that have reformed more successfully, shortages have been eliminated, the basic economic institutions of the market economy are in place and unemployment is controlled. These countries have generally developed market economies in which market prices and margins are no longer state-controlled. In practice, subsidies for farm products have been withdrawn, along with state controls on food distribution. Markets have been opened up to imports, with new distribution channels developed outside state or co-operative links.

Table 5.5   *Evolving Retail Structures in the Czech Republic and Poland, 1989–99*

Czech Republic		Poland	
1990–94	Fragmentation of the retail sector as a result of privatisation	1989–95	State-owned and co-operative ventures ceased trading, to be replaced by wholesale and trade centres. Open-air market and bazaars become important
1995	Re-concentration by multiples and foreign entrants		
1997	Independents form less than 50% of the turnover of the top 50 retailers	1991	Foreign entrants create a new level of competition
		1996	Retail chains begin to develop and small uneconomic businesses decline

The rate of retail development has not been even throughout the region. In addition to more rapid political reform, the central European states of Poland, Hungary and the Czech Republic border on Germany and Austria, enabling cross-border retail operations to be implemented. They share some of their cultural traditions and have generally higher standards of living than those further to the south and east. As a result these countries have drawn in new investment to create new retail industry structures. In the Czech Republic, retailing developed through smaller stores during the early years of post-communist government, but since then a second phase of development has seen an increase in large-scale stores such as supermarkets, food discounters and DIY, with hypermarkets growing the fastest with 25 constructed by the end of 1998.

The Czech Republic, Hungary and Poland have seen a high influx of foreign retailers attracted by high levels of consumer spending and demand for consumer products. Due to their proximity, German retailers have been the most dynamic entrants although many other northern European businesses have moved into the region to take advantage of the growth opportunities.

North America

Superficially North America appears to be an attractively large, single market sharing many common characteristics, most obviously language, and for UK retailers a shared ancestry of customs and institutions. However, its geographical size is deceptive and the country can be more usefully considered as a number of separate consumer markets. This fragmentation creates difficulties for European retail expansion, and failure to interpret geographical segmentation successfully has frequently caused problems for new entrants. The drivers of the North American retail economy can be defined by its demographic and social trends, the demand for innovative products and services, and development of management information systems.

Demographic and social trends

There is a diversity in the geographical location of the population and lifestyles which create broadly defined regions:

- Canada contains a diversity of cultures and social groups, with local retailers very much under pressure from competitors from the USA due to the NAFTA agreement.

- Eastern states are sophisticated, densely populated in many parts and commercially advanced.

- The Midwest is the flat plain bordered on the west by the Rocky Mountains and on the east by the Mississippi river. It is largely agricultural, and less commercially developed and typified by large distances between centres.

- The Southeast is agricultural. Although a less populated area, its mild winter climate encourages inward movement of population.

- The Southwest. Increasingly sunrise industries are investing in the region; for example Phoenix, Arizona is one of the fastest growing US cities.

- The Western States. California is the wealthiest state and the main consumer market in the USA; critically it has been opinion leading, its population open to adopting new ideas and products.

These areas themselves often contain a wide range of social groupings, and immigration has created multicultural societies of which the Mexicans have an increasing influence even as far north as Chicago. The differences between urban centres and vast rural spaces throughout the continent can hardly be understated.

Restless consumerism

American consumers appear to continually seek new goods, services and experiences, demanding more from retailers, which has resulted in the diversification and proliferation of retail outlets. In this dynamic market new formats have emerged in the past 20 years that have transformed the character of retailing, becoming more diverse and creating new patterns of competition (Figure 5.3).

Figure 5.3   *Evolution of Food Stores in the USA, 1940s–1990s*

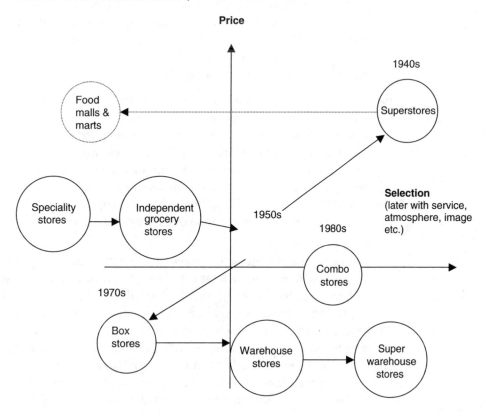

Source: Swinyard (1997).

Technological change

In response to increasingly demanding consumers, technology has been used in a number of ways to increase responsiveness and improve services. Supply-chain management techniques such as efficient consumer response (ECR) originated in the USA. An essential part of these systems is the use of information to plan and control the flow of merchandise into store; capturing sales, automating orders and tracking deliveries and stock levels are managed through IT. Access to the Internet has provided another channel for business-to-consumer distribution, with success in specialist sectors such as books and computers.

Enterprise

Entrepreneurial decisions concerning investment, consolidation and acquisitions, competition and globalisation shape the industry. Access to consumer markets is relatively open, at least for local and regional retailers, with land usage and retail development virtually unregulated by government.

The structure of American retailing has reflected consumer preferences in different ways:

■ City and metropolitan areas offer retail outlets in downtown, district centres and shopping malls. Downtown and local shopping areas have generally declined through the accessibility and convenience of shopping malls. However, the shopping mall itself is under threat from lower-cost formats; older and less attractive centres are being redeveloped to offer a more specialised shopping experience or for other uses altogether.

■ The increasing popularity of warehouse clubs and supercentres is beginning to make a competitive impact on many sectors including DIY and home furnishing, electrical goods and food. Warehouse clubs offer low-cost, low-price and low-ambience environments that are reflected in their pricing policy. Discount retailers have entered food retailing through 'supercentre' formats, representing one of the fastest growing sectors in US retailing. There is evidence, however, that supercentre locations are too remote to support regular shopping visits, because of their non-prime locations (Morganosky, 1997).

Consumer enthusiasm for low prices has resulted in the rapid growth of many other types of discount format, including discount department stores, outlet stores and off-price family clothing stores. Typically, low prices are combined with other components to create value: off-price stores combine lower prices and designer-name products, whilst discounters combine private brand and cost control. Category-killers, based on low price, and broad assortments have achieved their greatest success in radio, TV and computer sales, and to a lesser extent in DIY. Although variety stores have been largely ignored, and in the case of Woolworth transformed, the sector has proved remarkably resilient. Traditional retail formats including department stores and speciality clothing stores have been the most underperforming sectors during this period (Rogers, 2000). Increasingly it appears that retailers are sharing their customers across a wide range of formats (Morganosky, 1997) and that product assortments will broaden by combining food and general merchandise in supercentres and variety stores.

For the future, Griffith and Krampf (1997) identify four key trends in the US retail industry. Firstly, consumers will become more focused, value-oriented and diverse, and secondly that there will be growth in everyday low price and private labels. Thirdly, store sizes will polarise, and as a result new retail organisations will evolve to create new centres of power; and lastly technological innovations such as direct store deliveries will create competitive opportunities.

Exhibit 5.1   Body Shop USA

The company found that although entry and expansion costs were low, competition is vigorous and unrelenting; it entered the market in 1990, and by 1995 faced 12 direct competitors. Speed of competitor response created a strategic problem, it had to establish a physical presence quickly in the top 200 malls or be squeezed out by competitors. In the 'rush for 250 stores' it actually achieved a total of 247 stores, 77 of which were opened in just 14 months.

As a result a number of other problems occurred in the roll-out. The company suffered from a lack of people resources needed to establish the brand, and lost control over the details of its operational management. Consequently other measures were required to increase customer flow; the company responded by increasing its spend on promotions, marketing and merchandising. The aim was to introduce an innovative marketing programme, drawing on the Internet and CD ROM promotions, an in-store radio station, and setting-up a home sales business. The marketing strategy focused on Body Shop's 'authority', and environmental and social aspects of its range.

In 1996, like-for-like sales declined by 8 per cent, leading Gordon Roddick to comment somewhat ruefully 'American retailers have learnt the art of rapid change, and anyone who goes over there and trades learns rapid lessons'. By 1997 the US operation continued to cause concern. In an intensively competitive market Body Shop found itself under pressure from me-too retail copying, as well as price discounting, leading to a £2.7 million loss in just six months. It responded by taking over underperforming franchise stores, ending the year with ownership of some 210 out of a total of 280 stores. Management problems emerged, too, from the selection of key US managers, and the resiting of the US Head Office to rural North Carolina was not considered to be successful. Operationally the range needed to be tailored more to the local market in stores that were designed and fitted out to a higher standard.

With a further loss of £1.7million in the following year, Body Shop considered radical changes were required, and these resulted in the transfer of ownership to a joint venture operation controlled by an experienced American retailer, Adrian Bellamy. Major cost-cutting resulted in a turnaround in profitability, and announcements that the company was to focus on US expansion. But the ownership story took another twist when in 2001 the company received a takeover offer from Mexican nutritional supplements retailer, Grupo Omnilife. In an apparently unrelated move the Roddicks bought out their joint venture partner to once again take control of the operation.

Far East

In the Far East, market-oriented economies create significant opportunities for retail growth. Fundamentally these are determined both by the size of the total population, around 1.7 billion, and wealth, some $5.8 trillion GDP, which accompanied by high levels of overall economic growth and increasing industrialisation have led to significant social and demographic changes. Populations are becoming less rural as people move from country to city to seek higher paid employment. Growing personal affluence and education as well as access to international media raise local populations' aspirations and create demand for higher quality stores and products. The consumer-orientated societies of Japan, Hong Kong and Singapore are being joined by others, such as Malaysia, where the emergence of a mass middle market enables retailers to sell higher priced and more specialised merchandise.

Such an assessment highlights the diversity of retailing in the region, ranging from one of the world's most developed states, Japan, to some of the most inaccessible – for example North Korea and Myanmar. As a result, clusters of countries can be defined by their stage of development in order to position industry and retail-sector opportunities (Figure 5.4). Even so, research into the detailed characteristics of each market is important. Superficially Japan presents an attractively prosperous opportunity, yet a considerable slowdown in consumer spending that took place during the 1990s, combined with complex distribution channels and regulations has resulted in a heavily indebted industry. A slow process of change is taking place to create a more competitive environment. This seen at a number of levels; through relationships with suppliers, sectoral concentration, and competition at store level as well as in the relaxation of government protectionism (Dawson and Larke, 2001).

Figure 5.4   *East Asian National Characteristics*

Highly-developed ⟷ **Under-developed**

Japan	Hong Kong Singapore, Taiwan South Korea	Malaysia Thailand, Philippines, Indonesia	China	Vietnam, Laos, Kampuchia
Politically stable	Politically stable	Moderate–high political risk	Communist government embracing elements of market economy	Communist governments becoming more receptive to external investment
Economic stagnation during 1990s	Strong economic growth to late-1990s, subsequent moderate recovery	Volatile economic development, currently recovering after late 1990s recession	Uniquely large and diverse market	Early stages of economic development
Large middle class	Rapidly growing middle classes create demand for consumer goods	Developing middle classes	Marketing and logistics issues	Poor retail infrastructure
Cautious consumers				

Developing markets

Market entry into newly developing countries is limited by both national and retail structural weaknesses. Retail structures are more diverse and fragmented than in more developed countries; in Vietnam, for example, 60 per cent of retailing is undertaken in open markets, 38 per cent in small businesses and just 2 per cent in large stores. Distribution is complicated by the emergence of a parallel economy, with non-official channels taking up to 40 per cent of the market according to some estimates. Wholesaling takes place through compulsory government trading companies whose purpose is to administrate the process, and undertake only some retail distribution. Non-importer wholesalers are dominant in the south of the country, sorting stock and supplying markets. Weaknesses in the retail structure include short profit taking, the length of the distribution channel and lack of management knowledge. The country was closed to foreign investment until 1986 so that development has taken place over a relatively short time period (Vernard, 1996). Logistics are difficult with poor roads, low speed limits and a lack of specialised transport such as refrigerated trailers.

Specific geographic, demographic and economic factors affect shopping behaviour in developing countries and much of China. Behaviour is determined by the custom of regular buying trips and bargain hunting; men rather than women spend the most, and undertake the main shopping activity due to their higher incomes and opportunities to travel further. Small quantities typify the shopping visit, with 90 per cent of shoppers purchasing no more than four items because transport congestion, storage constraints in small dwelling spaces in urban areas and limited refrigeration capacity reduce the ability to shop less often for larger quantities. Time conflicts with the opportunity to buy as an important issue in these households. The more affluent, urban population already purchase a disproportionate share: consumers in the hundred biggest cities allocate more than 40 per cent of their spending to such goods, compared with about 23 per cent among rural consumers. Distinct consumer segments are already emerging as a result of the wide availability of consumer goods, massive increases in advertising, and steady exposure to new retail outlets (Chan *et al.*, 1997).

Although China's market is likely to remain dominated by independent shops – of which there are more than nine million with average annual sales of $20 000 – there is plenty of scope for modern retail formats. The early success of Carrefour, Makro and Wal-Mart indicates that the Chinese will accept modern, large-scale outlets. In Shanghai, a scaled-down version of a European hypermarket achieves returns of more than 50 per cent even though most customers can buy only what they can carry because they do not have cars (Chan *et al.*, 1997). Other major cities in Southeast Asia have also developed very large shopping centres, for example Bangkok's Seacon centre at 5 million square feet, enabling a greater diversity of Western-style retail formats to be accommodated.

Davies (1999) has summarised the expansion opportunities in the region as:

- Duplication of successful formats such as hypermarkets from other countries.

- The use of market-research techniques to determine customer wants and needs more effectively and responsively than local competitors.

Exhibit 5.2 Boots the Chemists entry into Thailand

Boots, the chemist's chain, took the opportunity to expand in the Far East following the collapse of asset values caused by the recession in 1997. Initial results from six pilot stores opened a year earlier had shown that the company's health and beauty format was popular. Although the pilot project had initially been run as part of a joint venture, the stores were now under Boots' sole control. The company cited a number of reasons why they chose to enter Thailand; these included higher economic growth prospects than in the UK, the ability of Thai managers to speak Cantonese enabling them to be trained as managers for future development in China; its growing middle class and the strength of the health and beauty market in the country, worth around £1 bn per annum. The recession provided the opportunity for retail space and greater flexibility on the part of landlords.

The country was believed to hold potential for 150 stores, primarily around Bangkok and the main tourist areas; Boots planned to open 40 pharmacy stores initially at a cost of £9.2 m, and these were expected to be profitable at the trading level within two years. The style of the stores was based on the Health and Beauty format, and around 200 square metres in size, large enough to differentiate themselves from competitors, to satisfy customer expectations and achieve optimum sales and profit densities. Some adaptation of ranges has been required, and government regulations have required that around 4000 Boots' brand lines needed to be registered for sale.

Losses of £43.9 m in 2000 for Boots Retail International and the arrival of a new Chief Executive contributed to an appraisal of the Far East operations which had seen openings in Japan and Taiwan as well as Thailand. By 2001, only 68 stores had been opened, and the whole strategy of developing stand-alone stores came to be questioned. Instead, existing stores will be downsized and further development lies in supply agreements with other retailers.

- The use of IT and management systems to control businesses efficiently.

- Larger retailers beginning to move the balance of power away from manufacturers.

- Use of market power to reduce prices.

- Innovative marketing to gain and reward customers.

- Extracting changes in government regulation of foreign businesses (in Thailand).

The challenge for retailers will be to understand the marketing environment and changes within the region. Economic factors such as GDP growth and inflation, and political and cultural factors such as religion, the role of the family and language and population changes must be related to the proactive development of appropriate products and marketing programmes (Dibb, 1996). The economic crisis affecting nearly every country in the area in 1997 highlights the need for this type of assessment. The total loss of purchasing power in the region between mid-1997 and mid-1998 alone amounted to some US$500 bn, and consumer spending is estimated to have fallen by 10–15 per cent and up to 70 per cent on luxury goods (Davies, 1999).

In addition to the direct economic impact on retailers, it has led to fundamental industrial changes in Korea and political instability in Indonesia. On the positive side, many Western retailers, from Europe in particular, have been able to take advantage of the opportunities afforded for investment and local alliances that have arisen.

THE PROCESS OF INTERNATIONALISATION

Organisational objectives as well as market opportunities will determine the method of retailers' international development. At the least ambitious, the retailer could join a trade association or retailer alliance to learn about new markets. Higher risks and rewards will clearly arise from more demanding approaches, from the strategic testing of a new market to the expansion of a multinational or global business. These bring with them strategic decisions about their distinctive competencies drawn from internal resources that enable them to compete, and their culture and organisational structure to enable them to implement their international strategy. These decisions stand alongside those concerning the proximity of their geographical and market characteristics to the domestic market. Again the aim is to reduce the risk of launching an unacceptable retail format.

The direction of international activity is determined by a complex interplay of influences and is essentially a dynamic process reflected in the development of international retailing (Myers and Alexander, 1996). Cross-border retailing began in Europe in the early 1900s, but it was not until the 1970s that geographical expansion took place more consistently. Typically it took place from domestic markets into adjacent ones sharing market characteristics, a phase described as 'border hopping'. Through the 1980s the number and diversity of cross-border moves increased, a trend that continued with 610 cross-border moves made by European retailers from 1990–94, the same number as achieved in the whole of the preceding 10 years.

Not only the number but the focus of international development is changing; from border hopping to more ambitious strategies, undertaken by the largest retailers as well as specialist ones (Howard, 2000). With increased confidence retailers have moved away from geographically and culturally similar markets to others that are more distinct and geographically distant. Distance may not be simply a geographical measurement, but a combination of geographical, psychological and structural factors. The more culturally and geographically distant the market, the more likely it is that the internationalisation process will be difficult (Dawson, 1993).

The geographical dimensions of international expansion are demonstrated by Treadgold's (1988) classification of international retailer development:

- *Cautious internationalists*: high control/high entry costs result in limited international presence in geographically/culturally proximate markets.

- *Emboldened internationalists*. Through the length of their international activity, retailers begin to move into more remote geographical or cultural markets.

- *Aggressive internationalists*. High control over operations but in a wider variety of markets.

■ *World powers*. Low-control methods, and presence in a very high number of markets around the world.

Within these dimensions, the ability to compete will be based on the critical dimensions of consumer profiles, the retail network and the retail environment in which the new entrant will operate (Dupuis and Prime, 1996). However, marketing–led theories of entry strategy can be also be usefully qualified through other theoretical approaches. Internationalisation and agency theories both concern realistic assumptions about behaviour; for example, that decisions are constrained by managerial knowledge, and that there is a potential for opportunism, but also goal conflict. Profit-maximisation objectives are often to be achieved by retailers in their use of knowledge, technology and goodwill; in other words intangible assets are recognised as significant sources of competitive advantage. To protect these intangible assets, market-entry strategies may be developed from internalisation factors, 'the issue of how company secrets are handled' and the level of control that the company must exercise to protect its valuable assets (Docherty, 1999).

Geographical market coverage and organisational integration, have been synthesised by Alexander and Myers (2000) in terms of internationalisation, change in market conditions, vision and organisation to create the dimensions of Figure 5.5. These terminologies relate a retailer's levels of internal commitment to their geographical scope. Ethnocentric describes a retailer's attachment to their domestic market ways of thinking and doing things whilst a geocentric retailer has a broader capability to adapt to and manage many international markets. The problematic definitions of multinational and global retailing are explained as:

■ *Multinational retailers* demonstrate an ability to use internal resources to create competitive advantages into many markets. However, the organisational

Figure 5.5   *Market and Operational Internationalisation*

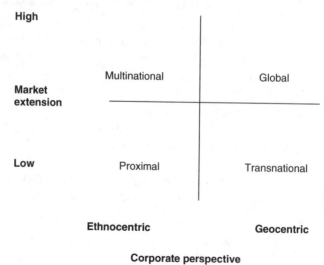

Source: Alexander and Myers (2000).

thinking and use of resources is firmly based on a domestic market approach; these retailers have not achieved an internal capability to fully exploit international opportunities. Their international businesses operate in ways comparable to the parent and maintain similarities across markets; and although they achieve high international exposure these retailers are less able to develop flexible responses to changes and to adapt successfully.

■ *Global retailers* are able to extend and exploit internal resources to competitive advantages in many markets. They have internal facilitating competences through the organisational integration of different functions, marketing and advertising strategies, distribution and operational management to reproduce the successful domestic formula outside their country of origin, and also to adapt and change to meet local market conditions. These retailers work hard to support their global strategy through learning from the markets in which they compete, and the use of capabilities as drivers of change. Certainly globalisation has attracted increasing attention, as the world's largest retailers, Wal-Mart and Carrefour, have demonstrated both the financial and organisational potential to shape new and truly global forms of retailing.

■ *Proximal and transnational international retailers* are defined by the smaller number of markets they have entered, but distinguished by their domestic market approach and broader geocentric capability in each case (Alexander and Myers, 2000).

MARKET ENTRY STRATEGIES

The mechanisms for internationalising, through market entry strategies, are typically found in:

■ Acquisition, or merger;
■ Franchise;
■ Internal, or organic expansion;
■ Joint venture or non-controlling interest (Dawson, 1993).

Acquisitions

Acquisitions enable a substantial market presence to be established quickly. The strategy provides an opportunity to extend into complementary or new markets, as seen in IKEA's motives to acquire Habitat with the intention of restoring it to Conran's original proposition of trading innovative design–led products at affordable prices (Warnaby, 1999). Since management and locations are already in place, financial planning becomes more predictable, particularly in terms of positive cash flows. In addition, it may provide the means to gain prime sites, especially out-of-town sites where government planning policy holds up future development. An organisation may be able to transfer learning and technology from its acquisition; product sourcing and use of information technologies may be expensive or require long-term investment.

Table 5.6   *Major International Grocery Retail Acquisitions, 1999*

Acquiring company	Target	Investment
Royal Ahold	ICA group, Scandinavia's leading food retailer	50 per cent holding
Royal Ahold	Pathmark, US food multiple retailer based in New York (abandoned)	$1.75 bn acquisition
Carrefour, French retail group	Promodes, French retail group	Merger
Wal-Mart	Asda, the third biggest UK food retailer	Acquisition
Delhaize, Belgian supermarket chain	Hannaford, US east-coast grocer	$3.6 bn offer for acquisition

E-retailing may emerge as a significant area of learning acquisition as the market develops beyond an introductory phase.

Problems may arise in the time taken to evaluate the takeover target, and suitable targets may not be available. Substantial senior management commitment may be required to achieve a successful conclusion to the acquisition, which, if it goes wrong, may be difficult to exit. There will be a need to find a suitable buyer, and to close all or part of the business may incur heavy redundancy and other employment or property-based costs.

Acquisitions are more commonly used in North America and the UK because larger retailers tend to be publicly rather than privately owned. Substantial shareholdings will be held through a limited number of institutions whose relationship with the retailer may be tradable depending on the retailer's strategy, performance and the objectives of shareholders. When the retail sector falls out of favour with the stockmarket, share prices fall and provide valuable acquisition opportunities for international market entrants. In Europe and Japan, ownership may be in private family hands, or in a more complex cross-holding with other companies. In Germany two-tier directorial board structures tend to favour longer-term investments and agreed rather than hostile mergers and acquisitions. Some major international retail acquisitions for the grocery sector in 1999 are summarised in Table 5.6.

International Franchising

Franchising can be used in many business activities, but the form in most common use is business-format franchising. It has been defined as,

> the granting of a license for a predetermined financial return by a franchising company (the franchisor) to its franchisees, entitling them to make use of a complete business package, including training, support and the corporate name, thus enabling them to operate their own businesses to exactly the same standards and format as the other units in the franchised chain. (Grant, 1985)

> **Exhibit 5.3 Managing the franchise: Kookai and Benetton**
>
> The fashion retailer, Kookai, entered the UK market by initially distributing through whole-salers. However, to strategically penetrate the market the company appointed one master franchiser who took responsibility for the development of the brand and distribution through stand-alone stores and department store concessions (Moore, 1997).
>
> At Benetton, the franchise system has enabled the company to focus on its product development activities; to avoid becoming directly involved in the selling side, in its early days it looked to external partners for financial support. By 1995 the company operated 8000 stores of which only 50 flagship stores were directly owned, and with independent retailers owning 5–6 stores each. When entering a new market, the site for a lead store is selected after which the agent attempts to blanket the area with several other shops. Shop owners are selected for their 'cultural fit' with Benetton and do not sign a franchise agreement, nor pay fees or royalties, and agents receive 4 per cent commission for orders placed with them and supervise retail operations.

With franchising, the strategic advantages to the retailer are rapid expansion, opportunities of entering new markets at low cost: the franchisee is expected to make some investment into the business so higher returns on investment may be achieved. Furthermore, it enables entry into marginal markets where the risks might preclude investment. Franchising is a relatively flexible method of market entry, as a wide range of forms of agreement are available. The costs associated with the learning curve in a new market are reduced through local management expertise, and at an operational level savings may be made from a reduced regional management structure and better service achieved from local management enabling smaller more remote units to become viable. The single-brand focus of fashion retailers enables them to realise economies of replication and to expand through international franchise strategies.

Disadvantages are based around selection of suitable franchisees and the control of the operation. Franchisees may become too independent and in training them the retailer is training future competitors. There is a need to establish channels of communication to maintain trust and motivation; franchisees may be tempted to under-declare their sales and profits. Operationally it may be difficult to persuade franchisees to update or refurbish their premises and to create effective communication and promotion strategies. The management style needs to be open and advisory, but in practice franchise management practices tend to be standardised; non-economic power sources such as expertise and reference are commonly used, whilst coercive and reward systems are relatively weak. Decision-making too has been found to be very formalised and participatory and tends to reflect low levels of conflict (Manresi and Uncles, 1995).

Organic Growth

Organic growth or internal expansion can be undertaken by any size of firm. Experimental openings are possible with modest risk and relatively low cost, allowing retailers to adapt operations with each subsequent opening and to rapidly prototype its format. The disadvantages of this form of expansion lie in the initial demands on senior management time and ability to research and assess the feasibility of new store locations. Once launched, the format may take a long time to establish a substantial presence in the new market, and consequently costs of investment and profitability may not be quickly achieved.

Strong consumer association of the brand with the country of origin has been an advantage for international retail branding. The ability to standardise the brand element of the retail offering has been seen to be restricted by the need for national coverage and by the long-term need to build a branded reputation (Usunier, 1999). Some standardisation can be made, for example from productivity, IT management standards and equipment. Economies of scale can also be gained from the branding of the retail offer. However, consideration needs to be given to the ambience, atmosphere, service and retail format, and the extent that these could be standardised.

Leadership in a new format development or distinctive marketing differentiation can be significant, and category-killer retailers like Toys' R' Us and Blockbuster have been able to take advantage of their expertise to gain access to new markets. Speciality formats, unique product retailers, and brand flagships like Levi travel well as do innovative specialists such as Gap and Footlocker.

Certain types of retail format seem to have the ability to cross borders more successfully than others. Hypermarket concepts developed in France have transferred successfully to southern Europe and into Latin America and the Far East. However, they have proved less successful in the USA and the UK. Category-killer, single-industry warehouse discount retailers have proved to be a particularly potent vehicle for organic growth. The twin advantages of a broad product range and low prices have been most successfully deployed in sectors where competition is fragmented, typically with independent retailers holding significant shares of the market. Sports retailing is one such sector in which Decathlon is emerging as a multiple category killer. DIY, too, has seen international development of this format with OBI of Germany entering the East European market.

At the other extreme in terms of store size, the European discount food format has demonstrated its ability to transfer its formula across borders. The sector includes extended range discounters, discount superstores, as well as limited line discounters that have a distinctive and focused style. Leading food discounter Aldi (Albrecht Discount) first opened in 1960, started international operations in Austria in 1967, and moved into other adjacent countries. In 1989 Aldi arrived in the UK and 10 years later was operating from over 1000 cross-border sites. The company's European market-entry strategy is based on organic growth, developing new geographical markets through a tightly managed business formula. Investment in new sites is low, development is based on small sites in urban neighbourhood locations occupied by relatively weak competitors, in which the stores themselves require low fitting-out costs.

Alliances

An alliance is a coalition of two or more organisations intended to achieve mutually beneficial goals. The nature of the alliance (Table 5.7) is determined by what the par-

Table 5.7   *A Taxonomy of Alliances*

Loose affiliations	A focal point for a number of members with the aim of researching and disseminating market data or political lobbying, for example the IGD
National Buying Club	Benefits members usually living in one country for the procurement and maximisation of purchasing power; typically found in wholesale and retail voluntary chains such as Paridoc and FNCC in France, and Nisa Today in the UK.
Co-marketing agreements	The function is to engage in some form of marketing activity, such as format franchising by Benetton or Tie Rack, or Marks and Spencer's shop in shops and licencing agreements with partners in Spain and Hungary
International alliances with central secretariats	International alliances of retail groups whose function is to coordinate operational activities in buying, branding expertise exchange and product marketing. A formal centre acts as a focus
Equity participation alliances	Each member has an equity stake in their partners such as the ERA alliance of Safeway, Ahold and Casino. This alliance is a majority shareholder in a looser buying alliance
Joint ventures	'Business agreements where two or more owners create a separate entity'; Sainsbury and G.I.B. managed Homebase until 1997 in this way
Partial acquisition	One retailer acquiring a minority stake in another retailer. Strategically there may be opportunities for technology transfer or as a precursor to a full acquisition
Controlling interest	Acquisition of a majority interest to take total control

Source: Clarke-Hill, Robinson and Bailey (1994).

ticipating organisations are prepared to put in and to take out of it, and these will depend on the strategic or operational objectives of the alliance. Closeness of the potential allies' perspectives on strategic positioning and resource commitment and retrieval is critical to a workable alliance (Lorange and Roos, 1997).

Measurements of success can depend on the business environment in which the partners operate. For some businesses, the partners may define success by achieving their initial strategic objectives and recovering their cost of capital. In this case, progress is measured through market share, sales volume or new product development. For Japanese and many European companies, longer-term and less financially-based measures may be more important (Bleeke and Ernst, 1993).

There are obvious advantages as well as hidden benefits in strategic alliances. There may be access to new technology, manufacturing capacity, markets and distribution and service capabilities. There will be an exchange of resources and competencies between partners, and to some extent an exchange of learning. Many of Europe's largest food retailers have already established purchasing centres to coordinate the purchase of leading brands at a European level; these are often based in Switzerland to avoid pricing regulations enforced nationally. Some of the hidden benefits include the need to present internal processes to partner organisations. Alliances can create challenges, and indicate possible areas for innovation and change. New ideas may arise from the detailed explanation of processes to other, demanding partners; the processes themselves may benefit from being tested in new conditions.

However, there is the danger of a learning race to extract the most first; Moss Kantor (1995) expresses it as a need to 'be open to romance but court carefully – partnerships are based on relationships'. Types of alliance range from the loosest levels of commitment and investment, where the retailer might affiliate themselves to a trade group in order to gain market information or to benefit from a trade pressure group, to highly developed alliances characteristic of joint ventures, partial acquisitions and controlling interests. Many joint ventures are acquired by one of the partners as a means of terminating the alliance, so managers need to monitor developments to secure their own strategic interests. The key decisions concern an assessment of business strengths and an understanding of their importance to the venture's success, but also levels of control in the partnership. Power will lie with the partner that invests most in the venture and places most of the senior managers in key functions (Bleeke and Ernst, 1995).

The types of benefits to be gained from retail alliances are typically seen in buying economies and product development. However, benefits often appear to develop slowly out of alliances, with larger groupings making particularly slow progress because of the time spent negotiating. The most effective achievements have been shown to take place in smaller alliances that have congruent objectives (Robinson *et al.*, 1997). Joint ventures, on the other hand, appear to achieve more in terms of increased profitability, joint buying power, skills attainments, market leadership and learning operational skills in another country. Size of business is less important than risk reduction and assessment of perceived gain; for example Wal-Mart entered into a joint venture with CIFRA, the most powerful retailer in Mexico, to gain access to the Mexican market.

Joint ventures are usually established between a foreign retailer and a domestic partner, an entry mode often adopted in Central Europe. Occasionally joint ventures may be set up by two foreign companies whose combined expertise provides the opportunity to operate in an independent market. Central Europe was targeted this way during the 1990s as the UK cash-and-carry wholesaler Booker and Portuguese retailer Jeronimo Martins worked together on a new food retailing venture.

ISSUES IN IMPLEMENTING INTERNATIONAL STRATEGIES

The implementation of market-entry strategies raises a number of human resource issues. For retailers requiring high levels of control and low levels of local experience, typically in organic growth strategies, these will be more serious than for low control ones or where local expertise is in place. Most fundamentally communication barriers will need to be overcome. As language is the means by which people communicate or even think, and as human interaction depends on shared language and language skills, the foreign language has to be acquired or otherwise accounted for by the retailer. The cultural relevance of non-verbal communication is important too;

even the ways people sit and stand, particularly in formal meetings, gestures, and their attitudes to personal space and time will vary and can cause serious misunderstanding (Schneider and Barsoux, 1998). Ethical values concerning what is 'right' or 'wrong' are deeply embedded in societies, and it should be recognised that such values are not easily changed by either marketeers or retail employers.

Operating in non-domestic markets will require local employees, and problems can arise out of incompatible cultural values with the internationalising company and the interpretation of the company's culture by the local workforce. Local suppliers, too, may have different interpretations of timescales, and the use of technological systems. In business-to-business situations, strategies, negotiations and working practices may be conducted according to local norms and traditions. Issues of control and conformity to strategic aims and operational practices often require non-local managers in the introductory phase of development, but local management brings with it domestic market expertise and business skills and may be better placed to develop the business. Exclusion of local employees from senior positions in the long term will be demotivating and lead to staff retention and performance problems.

Market-entry strategies should fully evaluate the costs of employment from the perspectives of operational management but also as barriers to exit the market. The average cost of employees varies widely through the EU alone, with costs per employee in Sweden being around four times those of Portugal. To payroll costs can be added tax and national insurance charges to the employer that are often substantially higher than in the UK or the USA. Although the European Social Chapter provides employment legislation across member states, many European countries still maintain their own pay and conditions structures. Holiday pay may be higher than in the UK, for example Dutch employees are entitled to a holiday allowance of 8 per cent of their salary over and above their paid leave. Similarly, obligations for sick pay vary and there may be heavy redundancy costs to bear too, which make market withdrawal a costly process. Less obvious are the restrictions on flexible working practices through government intervention demonstrated in Table 5.8.

SUMMARY

Retail internationalisation and the process of globalisation has become an important issue with implications not only for individuals retailers' growth strategies but also on the competitive environment in many retail sectors. Cultural convergence forms a broad theme behind the acceptance of new forms of retailing, whilst global trading blocs provide both opportunities and constraints in implementation.

Motives for retailer internationalisation are both externally and internally generated. Push and pull factors describe a range of environmental conditions that dispose a retailer to internationalise its business and attract it to one or more other countries. Internally the retailer may demonstrate a proactive or reactive approach to international growth, depending on its position and perception of domestic and external market opportunities and threats.

National retail structures share some characteristics, but even within Europe there are significant if diminishing differences that shape the opportunity to enter a

Table 5.8   *Labour Force and Employment Characteristics*

Employment characteristic	France	Germany	Spain	Sweden	UK
Average hourly gross earnings, women (ecu 1995)	6.4	10.7	4.5	8.8	5.0
Statutory notice period	1–2 months	Up to 6 months (after first 6 months of employment)	1–3 months according to length of service	1–6 months depending on age	1–12 weeks according to length of service
Statutory holiday entitlement	5 weeks	18 days	22 days	25 days	None
Statutory maternity leave	16 weeks (up to 32 exceptionally)	12 weeks	16 weeks	15 months for either parent. Up to 90 days sick leave for children under 12	18 weeks
Maximum overtime allowed	9 hours per week	No statutory restrictions	80 hours per year	Over 40 hours per week must be registered. Maximum of 200 hours per year	No statutory restrictions
Statutory career breaks	Up to 1 year full time. Part time varies	3 years parental leave for either parent	Up to 3 years for parents of either sex	Unlimited unpaid leave for educational purposes	None

Sources: Graham and Bennett (1998); Eurostat (1999).

particular market. Society and demography, economic growth and government intervention in retail planning and trading regulations have a fundamental role. The ownership and type of organisations in the distribution industry create the competitive environment for new entrants to assess.

The entry mechanisms present different growth options. Acquisition provides the fastest route to build market share in a target country, organic growth the greatest control, but these two strategies both attract higher risks and costs. Franchising and alliances reduce risks but at the loss of some degree of control. The levels of risk in entering, but also operating in and exiting from, a market are evident in the diversity of property and employment costs. Market attractiveness should be measured, too, by the ease with which it can be managed, and the proximity of national culture and local customs to the country of origin.

QUESTIONS

1   To what extent does Europe offer international growth opportunities for food retailers?

2   Evaluate the impact of market concentration on retailer internationalisation.

3   In what ways might US retailers influence the course of retail globalisation?

4   Assess the stages of internationalisation in the context of at least two retail sectors.

5   In what ways does the following case study explain market-entry strategy?

Case Study

Tesco's Experiences in Poland

The traditional retail sector in Poland is very unsophisticated. In 1998 there were around 425 000 stores under 5 square metres, one for every 100 people. But most of those were mobile street vendors, kiosks or small family-run shops which started up after the collapse of communism. In this transitional stage to a free economy, retailing was privatised and entrepreneurship legalised by the government as a means of providing a living for people. Western companies were quick to spot the opportunities and moved in to Poland in large numbers and began to revolutionise the market. Some 500 western-owned stores have opened in the past nine years and in 1998 alone the number doubled. In 1991 supermarkets and hypermarkets accounted for 6 per cent of food sales, a figure which had risen to 14 per cent by 1998 and is expected to reach 40–50 per cent by 2003.

Seven out of the top 10 European retailers are now in Poland, and Tesco is the sole British representative. On 18 November 1998 Tesco opened its first hypermarket in Poland, at Wroclaw in the south-west of the country. At 10 000 square metres it is far bigger than its UK outlets (excluding the hypermarket development at Pitsea which will be extended slowly). The hypermarket is situated on a 70 000 square metre retail park with IKEA, Vision Express and a number of other retailers including OBI, the German DIY retailer. The Mall will be the largest in Poland with 70 units in total.

Tesco first started in Eastern Europe in 1993 when it bought into a small supermarket chain, Globus, in Hungary. It developed this chain and gradually introduced the Tesco brand through the fascia, opening some larger supermarkets and over the past two years two hypermarkets. In the Czech Republic and Slovakia it bought the K Mart department stores which it rebranded as Tesco and subsequently opened hypermarkets there too.

The strategy in Poland has been similar; in 1995 it bought a chain of small supermarkets called Savia in the south of the country. It refitted and refurbished them, improved their operational standards, visual appeal and range of goods. It retained the Savia brand name and worked with the management to learn about the Polish market and understand Polish customers. Its strategy now is to focus on

(Continued)

hypermarkets, where it will implement what it has learnt over the past three years. The difference between the new hypermarket and existing Savia shops can be seen in terms of scale:

	Hypermarkets	Regional stores
Number of lines	40–50000	12000
Types of lines	Grocery and non-grocery including TVs, washing machines, lighting, DIY and clothes	Grocery only

Among the problems facing Tesco's initial development were:

- Lack of middle management. Tesco put in place a senior management team but were faced with inadequately trained middle managers and supervisors who had not been taught decision-making skills. Trying to change that culture has been a learning exercise, but one that is necessary to develop a tier of middle managers.

- Cultural differences. The Directors of Tesco Poland are trying to create a mix from the best of British, Tesco and Polish cultures. The Poles are quite formal in the ways they speak and interact, whilst Tesco wants to create more of a team culture. Values, too, are different: the Tesco brand is unknown in Poland and different approaches may be needed to develop the brand.

- Customer service has been an alien concept in Polish retailing. Typically information is power, is rarely volunteered and requires the customer to ask the right questions; an early challenge was to get staff to look customers in the eye and to say hello.

- Supplier relationships. In Poland, suppliers traditionally had more power than retailers and products were pushed through the supply chain: it was a case of 'here are my products, put them on your shelves'. Local suppliers had few modern techniques for growing, packing, cooling and so on, which Tesco had to assist with. 'The produce market is so fragmented here – you get a tractor turning up on your doorstep with a truckload of turnips – that it is difficult to help with a common production system or techniques' was an early comment. To start with, Tesco had to source 90–95% of food products from domestic suppliers partly because of shipping timescales from the UK but also because Polish tastes differ from British ones.

- Polish consumers are different from those in the UK. There is a divide between the old who continue to shop locally, and the young who are willing to try out the new hypermarkets. Many consumers have still to form shopping loyalties such as are found in the West. Price consciousness is dominant in purchase decision-making, although this is giving way increasingly to an awareness of value. Many Poles aspire to branded purchases and spend a high proportion of their income on branded goods, such as Adidas, Nike and CAT, although price still remains more important than brand. Increasingly Poles are interested in local products too, and now 40% of consumers claim to prefer local rather than high-profile western brands.

Tesco launched with a new media campaign focusing on price, service and product assortment, where most other retailers have competed on price. In doing this it believed that it was the first to create an aspirational image for a hypermarket, where service and environment added value. Two years later a storecard scheme was trialled to develop customer trust and loyalty to the brand, as well as providing low interest credit.

Tesco had opened 10 stores by the end of 2000, but the market in Poland had already begun to show signs of format saturation. Other food-based hypermarket retailers from Western Europe including Metro, Casino and Ahold, had made significant investments, resulting in intense competition in major Polish cities. By 2001 the company had moved from positive like-for-like growth in sales to a decline

of 1%, although it remained optimistic about longer-term sales growth. However, the new store-opening programme had also run into difficulties as local authorities took greater control over planning permission, and local retailers were provided legal support to influence the product range of any new hypermarket proposal. Nevertheless, Tesco remained confident about its expansion throughout Eastern Europe, including Poland, whilst predicting consolidation in the market and the withdrawal of some of its international competitors.

Source: Drawn from *Marketing Business*, October 1998, with updated material from a number of sources.

SEMINAR QUESTIONS FOR DISCUSSION

1 Discuss Tesco's priorities in the development of their Polish business.

2 To what extent is Tesco's food retailing expertise transferable to Poland?

References

Akehurst, G. and Alexander, N. (1996) *The Internationalisation of Retailing* (London: Frank Cass).

Alexander, N. (1997) *International Retailing* (Oxford: Blackwell).

Alexander, N. (2001) 'SMEs and Internationalisation of Retailing', Paper presented at the Contemporary Issues in Retail Management Conference, Manchester Metropolitan University.

Alexander, N. and Myers, H. (2000) 'The Retail Internationalisation Process', *International Marketing Review*, vol. 17, no. 4/5, pp. 334–53.

Bell, D. (1998) 'Food Retailing in Southern European Countries', *The European Retail Digest*, 18, pp. 17–21.

Bennison, D. and Boutsouki, C. (1995) 'Greek Retailing in Transition', *International Journal of Retail and Distribution Management*, vol. 23, no. 1, pp. 24–31.

Bleeke, J. and Ernst, D. (1993) *Collaborating to Compete: Using Strategic Alliances and Acquisitions in the Global Marketplace* (New York: John Wiley & Sons).

Bleeke, J. and Ernst, D. (1995) 'Is your Strategic Alliance Really a Sale?', *Harvard Business Review*, January–February.

Clarke-Hill, C.M., Robinson, T.M. and Bailey, J. (1994) 'European Retail Alliances – Towards a Taxonomy', Paper presented at the Marketing Education Group Conference, University of Ulster.

Chan, W.-K., Perez, J., Perkins, A. and Shu, M. (1997) 'China's Retail Markets are Evolving More Quickly than Companies Anticipate', *The McKinsey Quarterly*, no. 2, pp. 206–11.

Davies, K. (1999) 'The Asian Economic Recession and Retail Change: The Implications for Retailer Strategies in Asia', Paper presented at the 10th International Conference on Research In The Distributive Trades, University of Stirling.

Dawson, J.A. (1993) 'The Internationalisation of Retailing', in R.D. Bromley and C.J. Thomas (eds), *Retail Change* (London: UCL Press).

Dawson, J.A. (2000) 'Retailing at Century End: Some Challenges for Management and Research', *International Review of Retail Distribution and Consumer Research*, vol. 10, no. 2, pp. 119–48.

Dawson, J. and Larke, R. (2001) 'Japanese Retailing through the 1980s: Retailer Performance in a Decade of Slow Growth', Paper presented at the 11th International Conference on Research in the Distributive Trades, University of Tilburg.

Dibb, S. (1996) 'The Impact of the Changing Market Environment in the Pacific Rim', *International Journal of Retail and Distribution Management*, vol. 24, no. 11, pp. 16–29.

Docherty, A.-M. (1999) 'Explaining International Retailers' Market Entry Mode Strategy: Internationalisation Theory, Agency Theory and the Importance of Information Asymmetry', *International Review of Retail Distribution and Consumer Research*, vol. 9, no. 4, pp. 379–402.

Dupuis, M. and Prime, N. (1996) 'Business Distance and Global Retailing; a Model for Analysis of Key Success/Failure Factors', *International Journal of Retail and Distribution Management*, vol. 24, no. 11, pp. 30–8.

Giddens, A. (1999) *Runaway World: How Globalisation is Re-Shaping our Lives* (London: Profile Books).

Graham, H.T. and Bennett, R. (1998) *Human Resources Management*, 9th edn (London: Financial Times/Pitman Publishing).

Griffith, D.A. and Krampf, R.F. (1997) 'Emerging Trends in US Retailing', *Long Range Planning*, December, pp. 847–53.

Hibbert, E.P. (1989) *Marketing Strategy in International Business* (Maidenhead: McGraw-Hill).

Howard, E. (2000) 'Globalisation – Adaptation', *European Retail Digest*, Issue 25, March, pp. 6–9.

Karnani, A.G. (1999) 'Five Ways to Grow the Market and Create Value', *Mastering Strategy 4*, Financial Times, 18 October.

Lorange, P. and Roos, J. (1997) Strategic Alliances: Formation, Implementation and Evolution, (Oxford: Blackwell Business).

Manresi and Uncles, M. (1994) 'Retail Franchising in Britain and Italy', in P.J. McGoldrick and G. Davies, *International Retailing* (London: Pitman).

Morganosky, M.A. (1997) 'Retail Market Structure Change: Implications for Retailers and Consumers', *International Journal of Retail and Distribution Management*, vol. 25, no. 8, pp. 269–74.

Morganosky, M.A. (1997) 'Format Change in US Grocery Retailing,' International Journal of Retail and Distribution Management, vol. 25, no. 6, pp. 211–18.

Moss Kantor, R. (1995) *World Class: Thriving Locally in the Global Economy* (New York: Simon & Schuster).

Muhlbacker, H., Dahringer, L. and Leihs, H. (1999) *International Marketing – A Global Perspective* 2nd edn (London: International Thompson Business Press).

Myers, H. (1996) 'The Changing Process of Internationalisation in the European Union', in G. Akehurst and N. Alexander (eds), *Internationalisation of Retailing* (London: Frank Cass).

Myers, H. and Alexander, N. (1996) 'European Food Retailers' Evaluation of Global Markets', *International Journal of Retail and Distribution Management*, vol. 24, no. 6, pp. 34–43.

Quelch, J.A. and Bartlett, C.A. (1999) *Global Marketing Management* (Harlow: Addison-Wesley).

Robinson, T.M., Clarke-Hill, C.M. and Bailey, J. (1997) 'Skills and Competence Transfers in European Retail Alliances: Alliances vs Joint Ventures', Paper presented at the 9th International Conference on Research in The Distributive Trades, University of Leuven.

Schneider, S. and Barsoux, J.-L. (1997) *Managing Across Cultures* (Hemel Hempstead: Prentice Hall Europe).

Sternquist, B. (1997) 'International Expansion of U.S. Retailers', *International Journal of Retail and Distribution Management*, vol. 25, no. 8, pp. 262–8.

Swinyard, R. (1997) 'Retailing Trends in the USA: Competition, Consumers, Technology and the Economy', *International Journal of Retail and Distribution Management*, vol. 25, no. 8, pp. 244–55.

Terpstra, V. and Sarathy, R. (2000) *International Marketing*, 8th edn (New York: The Dryden Press).

Treadgold, A. (1988) 'Retailing without Frontiers', *Retailing and Distribution Management*, vol. 6, no. 6, pp. 8–12.

Usunier, J.-C. (1999) *Marketing Across Cultures* (Hemel Hempstead: Prentice Hall Europe).

Vernard, B. (1996) 'Vietnamese Distribution Channels', *International Journal of Retail and Distribution Management*, vol. 24, no. 4, pp. 29–40.

Warnaby, G. (1999) 'Strategic Consequences of Retail Acquisition: IKEA and Habitat', *International Marketing Review*, vol. 16, no. 4/5, pp. 406–16.

Water, C.D.J. (1999) 'Changing Role of the Retail Sector in Poland During a Period of Economic Transition', *International Journal of Retail and Distribution Management*, vol. 27, no. 8, pp. 319–27.

Williams, D.E. (1992) 'Motives for Retailer Internationalisation: Their Impact, Structure and Implications', *Journal of Marketing Management*, no. 8, pp. 269–85.

PART TWO

Strategic Retail Functions

The following four chapters focus on strategically important functions and activities in retailing. The retailer strategies identified in the previous part are demonstrated through the use of resources in marketing, finance, location planning and human resources. Chapter 5 introduces the marketing function and consumer behaviour in developing appropriate strategic positions. Chapter 6 introduces financial resources in order to explain how financial reporting, and investment decisions relate to the retailer's capability to achieve its strategy. Chapter 7 introduces the strategic dimensions of location planning, the types of retail location available to retailers, the ways in which locational decisions are made and briefly outlines the location planning process itself. The final chapter in this part examines Human Resource Management from the perspective of the structure of organisation and culture before moving on to assess the role of people as a retailing resource in more detail.

Marketing Functions in Retailing

INTRODUCTION

Retailing has changed radically over the past two or three decades. Even in the early 1980s, it was a relatively fragmented and unsophisticated business where retail flair appeared to be the key to success. Now, however, it is an industry in which flair remains important, but is no longer sufficient. According to Cook and Walters (1991), effective retailing demands a high level of skills in marketing, store operations, advanced logistics systems and in sophisticated sourcing.

In the past, even large multiple retailers spent little time engaged in marketing, which tended to be seen purely in terms of a selling function. This attitude is long gone as multiple retailers all over the world now recognise the need to integrate their overall marketing plans and develop marketing strategies for achieving their retailing objectives. This chapter deals with the process of developing and monitoring marketing functions in retailing. The marketing strategy must specify the retailer's target market, and show how a retail organisation will position the various elements within the marketing mix in order to satisfy the needs of the target market. The chapter starts with a review of various definitions of marketing and continues by placing it in the context of consumer behaviour. It looks at consumer classifications for the purpose of establishing marketing relationships between retailers and their customers. The ways in which people behave informs the market segmentation process and the retailer's position in the market. The chapter concludes with an overview of relationship marketing, and its impact on retailing.

DEFINITIONS OF MARKETING

The industrial era in the last century saw the manufacture of standardised goods that led in turn to mass marketing and mass distribution. However, as the flow of goods and services from producer to consumer or user became more complex and diverse, it gave rise to 'classical' marketing approaches. These were product- and sales-driven and were based on competitive business strategies. Marketing became the process by which the demand structure for economic goods and services was anticipated or enlarged and satisfied through the conception, promotion and physical distribution of such goods and services.

These classical definitions of marketing emphasise the physical movement of economic goods and services, revealing several weaknesses. The role of physical distribution and marketing channels tends to be overvalued, and government and non-profit institutions, which frequently engaged in marketing, are omitted from these definitions. A more useful definition of marketing should cover the broad activities of marketing-oriented organisations and be differentiated from selling.

Another aspect of marketing is its role as the arbiter between sales and production. The objectives of production are usually focused on manufacture at lowest cost, which means long, inflexible machine runs. On the other hand, the objectives of sales are often the very opposite: to keep customers happy by delivering exactly what they want, and when they want it, without regard to the additional internal costs. The function of marketing is to take both sets of objectives into account and to establish solutions that meet the objectives of the company as a whole.

In the past twenty years the focus of marketing has changed from the producer to the consumer, in the form of consumer-goods marketing or 'exchange' views of marketing (Fitchett and McDonagh, 2001). These take into account consumer transactions and satisfaction of customer needs and wants as well as recognising the significance of networks and interactions. The purpose of marketing is now about satisfying customers; what they value and what they buy is decisive and will ultimately determine the nature of the retailer's business (Sivadas and Baker-Prewitt, 2000). This refocusing on the customer has found expression in the development of relationships with the customer, formally defined as Relationship Marketing. Relationship Marketing is often contrasted with transaction marketing. Transaction marketing demonstrates a short-term focus on attracting and selling to the customer, a one-off process, whilst relationship marketing is concerned with attracting but also retaining the customer for multiple transactions with more far-reaching returns than single transactions (Gummersson, 1999). It develops 'mutually beneficial' themes, by assuming sophisticated customers, retaining rather than recruiting customers, embracing new technology for rapid transmission, storage and analysis of market data, and rewards companies from the trust and loyalty of their customers (Fitchett and McDonagh, 2001). It is also argued that relationship marketing brings about an internal company integration of quality management and customer service and marketing functions (Christopher *et al.*, 1991).

As observed above, many definitions of marketing arise which differ in their emphasis on its process, functional activities and orientation. However, the Chartered Institute of Marketing provides a further insight into marketing with its definition as *'the management process responsible for identifying, anticipating and satisfying customer requirements profitably'*. The focus is on customers and their impact on the success of the retail business. The American Marketing Association (AMA) provides a more extended definition as:

> the management function which organises and directs all those business activities involved in assessing and converting consumer purchasing power into effective demand for a specific product or service, and in moving the product or service to the final consumer or user so as to achieve the profit target or other objectives set by a company.

The analysis in Table 6.1 is based on the expanded definition by the AMA. The value of this definition is that it recognises that organisations may have objectives other than profit: some may be non-profit making, or even have the effect of reducing profits.

MARKETING IN RETAILING

A retailer's products and services must relate to their target markets and attract customers to buy on the basis of their performance and price. Competitors who are more aware of market needs outsell those retailers that give insufficient attention to customers' needs and offers them production-led rather than marketing-led products. This is the essence of retail marketing – developing products and services that will satisfy specific needs of customers, and supplying them at prices that will yield profits. It's essential, too, that retail marketing responds to, and changes with, the retail environment, for instance with the changes in British retailing arising as a result of the arrival of the Internet (Sauer and Burton, 1999).

Retail marketing has developed over the past 40 years as the balance of power in the distribution of goods and services has moved away from manufacturers and towards retailers. In the process, fundamental industry differences between retailing and manufacturing have been observed. Brown (1987) classified marketing practices in retailing into strategic and operational levels, noting that at the marketing strategy level, fundamental activities include environment search, strategy development, and building an appropriate organisation to implement strategies (see Figure 6.1).

At the operational level, complementary marketing activities are found in the collection for retail decision-making, the implementation of strategies through tactical decision-making, and the recruitment and management of operational resources at store level (see Piercy and Alexander, 1988). Although the activities specified in Figure 6.1 should in theory be universally applicable to all retail sectors, differences

Table 6.1   *Marketing Definition: Operational Functions and Analysis*

Operational function	Analytical explanation
It is a management function	It is part of that function concerned with the establishment and definition of objectives. It deals with the creation of the conditions under which it will be possible to achieve the objectives
It organises and directs	It is a function which determines what shall be done, how it shall be done and when. It is not purely concerned with, and may not actually be concerned with, the performance. It may pass on actual performance to others, e.g. salesmen, advertising contractors, transport contractors, etc. But being concerned with organising and directing, it must necessarily also be concerned with controlling, monitoring and evaluating what has been done
It has a function of assessing	It has a function of gathering and evaluating information in order to better be able to organise and direct. This function of assessment covers all the features of marketing research, i.e. market research, product research, distribution research and promotion research
It has a function of conversion	It has a function of creation and persuasion – it must create products or services, which will be demanded, and it must inform and persuade those with purchasing power to exercise it
It deals with consumer purchasing power	It must, therefore, analyse what this is in terms of the ability of the customer to purchase now by using purchasing power which he has either now from current earnings or from savings
It deals with consumers or users	It deals with real people in the real world. Unlike other academic disciplines such as economics, which must make assumptions in order to build models of the world, and which, in consequence, have to make unreal assumptions about the potential behaviour of humans, marketing must deal with people as they are. We cannot make the assumption that people will act rationally or objectively, but we can study the influences which will tend to make them act in a subjective or an irrational way. Behavioural sciences play, therefore, an important part in the study of marketing
It moving products to final consumer	It deals with the means by which, and the channels through which, the producer and consumer are brought together
It achieves the profit target or other objectives set	It recognises that marketing, or any other business activity, does not operate in a vacuum. Marketing is not an end in itself, but exists to achieve the overall objectives of the organisation, and it follows from this that the establishment of marketing objectives is dependent upon the establishment of overall organisation objectives. One cannot properly exist without the other and it is probably not too strong to suggest that, in the majority of cases, the overall organisational objectives must be stated in terms of a marketing objective

Source: Omar (1999) *Retail Marketing* (London: *Financial Times*/Pitman), p. 7.

in marketing practices are evident. For example the marketing strategies undertaken by department stores and supermarkets are different due to their distinctive product mixes, segmentation strategies, competitive rivalry and organisation structures (Greenley and Shipley, 1992).

Textbooks on marketing management, such as Kotler (1997), tend to explain retailing in terms of the mix elements: the dimensions in which marketeers put their plans into action. However, as Chisnall (1994) wrote, these descriptions fail to explain the

Figure 6.1   *Marketing Practices in Retailing*

differences between retail and manufacturing marketing mixes, but rather explain major differences between different types of mix. A number of distinctions between manufacturing and retailing have been made though:

- ■ *Buying motives.* The buying motives of shoppers are distinct from those associated with the business acquisition of goods and services (see also Samli, 1989).

- ■ *Product assortment.* The number and type of products required by consumers from retailers far exceeds individual manufacturers' product mixes (McGoldrick, 1990). The scope of the product assortment is much greater in retailing.

- ■ *Retail marketing mix.* Elements of the retail marketing mix differ from those of manufacturers. Greenley and Shipley (1987) identified four levels of the retail product offering including: the physical product, the store itself, the total ambience achieved in the store, and the services offered, and they advised that the other elements of the mix could have similar differences.

- ■ *Pricing.* Research into retail marketing departments noted that pricing was the key element of retail marketing competition, and was widely focused on value to customers as opposed to volume/profit margins (Piercy and Alexander, 1988). There was also an indication that attractive prices were the most important form of retail promotion.

CLASSIFYING CONSUMERS

The essence of retail marketing management is to identify in numerical terms a target market that is not being adequately served at present, and to which the retailer can respond with existing or potentially available resources. Traditionally this task of

---

Exhibit 6.1   Targeting hybrid consumers

In retailing, there are already signs that the retailer will face an increasingly complex world as some intriguing forces begin to shape the next era of retailing. The key element is the emerging technology that may allow retailers to communicate more directly with customers than has been possible in the past. But using it successfully will require retailers to be very clear about the basic questions: who the customer is; who the competition is; and what the retail offer is. In the past, rightly or wrongly, retailers thought in terms of a single target market. For example, in grocery it was largely the housewife with varying degrees of price consciousness or quality and range consciousness. Consequently, these factors were used to target the housewife during the 1980s. Yet the food stores confounded critics and became a huge success story by recognising the value of time to harassed working men and women. The success of selling a packaged and washed salad for £1.29 instead of the 20 pence of its basic ingredients has overcome initial suspicions that it would turn out to be an expensive extravagance.

---

identification has been thought of in terms of clear attributes or variables such as gender, age and socio-economic group.

The analytical role of the marketing manager is to identify the existence of such opportunities in retailing. This can be done by reference to economic and demographic data, which will reveal the size of the customer segment to indicate the spending patterns of the target market. In the past, retailers thought in terms of a single target market such as food-shopping habits of women homemakers. Modern retailers have changed such retailing strategy, and Exhibit 6.1 makes the point that the consumer is trading off more dimensions than quality, choice and convenience, because his/her life has become more complex. Hence the emergence of the hybrid customer (Figure 6.2) and the fragmentation of traditional customer market segments.

For retailers, the key points to consider are the dynamics of the market that result in demographic and social change and the impact that these changes have on their customers. It is critical to step back periodically and reassess the targeted consumer group.

Consumer Needs and Wants

According to Kotler (1997), marketing starts with the identification of human needs and wants. Drawing on Maslow's hierarchy of needs, he observed that people need food, air, water, clothing and shelter to survive. Beyond this, people have a strong desire for recreation, education and other services, and they have strong preferences for particular versions and brands of basic goods and services. At this point it is important to distinguish between needs and wants.

- A human *need* is a state of deprivation of some basic satisfaction. People require food, clothing, shelter, safety, belonging and esteem. These needs are not created by society, they exist in the very texture of human biology and the human condition.

Figure 6.2   *The Emergence of the Hybrid Consumer*

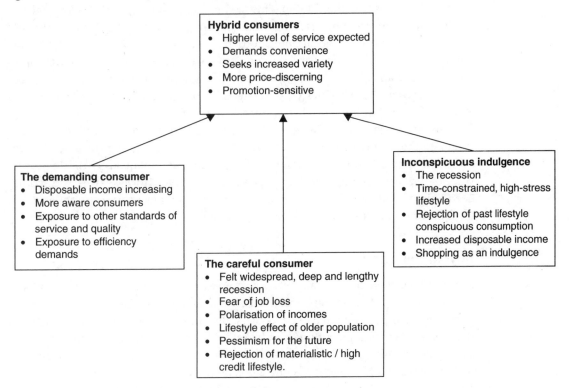

Hybrid consumers
- Higher level of service expected
- Demands convenience
- Seeks increased variety
- More price-discerning
- Promotion-sensitive

The demanding consumer
- Disposable income increasing
- More aware consumers
- Exposure to other standards of service and quality
- Exposure to efficiency demands

Inconspicuous indulgence
- The recession
- Time-constrained, high-stress lifestyle
- Rejection of past lifestyle conspicuous consumption
- Increased disposable income
- Shopping as an indulgence

The careful consumer
- Felt widespread, deep and lengthy recession
- Fear of job loss
- Polarisation of incomes
- Lifestyle effect of older population
- Pessimism for the future
- Rejection of materialistic / high credit lifestyle.

■ Human *wants* are desires for specific satisfiers of needs. In Britain, a person who needs food may want baked beans to eat and a Coke to drink depending on the eating habit and culture of the nation. On the other hand, in Nigeria for instance, or elsewhere in Africa, a hungry person may want pounded yams, fried yams or a mixture of rice and beans to satisfy his/her food needs because these are the types of food many Africans prefer to eat.

Although people's needs are generally few, their wants are many (see Plummer, 1974). Human wants are continually shaped and reshaped by social forces and institutions, including religion, education, technology, families and business corporations. Thus, customers' demands are wants for specific products that are backed by an ability and willingness to buy them. Wants are likely to become demands when supported by purchasing power. Retailers must therefore measure not only how many people want their product, but how many would actually be willing and able to buy it.

CONSUMER BEHAVIOUR

In order to increase their successful positioning in a market, retailers must understand consumer behaviour. Consumer behaviour has been defined as the process that underlies an individual's decision of what, when, where, how and from whom to purchase goods and services (Solomon, 1996). This section presents consumer behaviour models as they apply to retailing drawing from numerous consumer behaviour theories and research sources. The focal point in each model is the extraction of vital behavioural principles in the store selection and store patronage processes that are important for the retailer. In this context, some socio-economic and racial differences have been assumed, along with lifestyle characteristics and education and numerous other external factors that influence behaviour.

Consumer behaviour models and research that either support these models or contribute to their construction have enjoyed much popularity during the past 15 years. Increased emphasis on the marketing concept and, simultaneously, the increasing voice of dissatisfied consumers has helped to accelerate it. However, this research has been only partially extended into retailing and retailing-related areas to its detriment in terms of its application to retail consumer behaviour.

Buying Behaviour

Purchase behaviour at the retail level is a complex phenomenon with multiple phases and dimensions. Any attempt to systematise and organise information relating to purchase behaviour is desirable for retailers. By adjusting to different components of the market it enables practitioners to be selective and to concentrate on more feasible segments. Adopting the customer's viewpoint is the essence of good retail marketing. The focus of this section is, therefore, on the customer and the way the shopper behaves while shopping. In particular, it is about how shoppers make buying decisions and the processes (awareness, trial and repeat, for instance) and the factors, which influence them (traditional or cultural). These lead to the diffusion processes and related elements of brand loyalty, as well as specific models of consumer behaviour.

The section starts with a brief review of purchasing. Owing to the disparate nature of the differing retail outlets (see Table 6.2), relevant information on purchasing patterns has been adopted from International Target Group Index's (TGI) research as an example. Table 6.2 details the purchasing pattern of toys and games in the UK during 1997. As can be seen, 50.5 per cent of TGI respondents bought toys and games during

Table 6.2   Toys and Games Purchased by UK Adults in 1997

Expenditure (£)	Toys and games purchased for each age group listed (yrs)					
	Under 2	2–4	5–7	8–9	10–12	13+
Under £50	12.6	11.5	10.3	6.7	5.7	4.9
£51–99	3.7	4.9	4.7	3.0	2.9	2.3
£100–199	1.7	3.1	3.1	2.2	2.3	1.6
£200 and over	0.9	2.0	2.1	1.4	1.5	1.9

Total number of adults = 23 290 (i.e. 50.5% of all adults)

Source: Target Group Index (TGI), 1998.

that year. When analysed by expenditure, under £50 is the most regular amount for each of the age groups; purchase of over £200 would seem to be limited to special occasions, such as birthdays and Christmas. From the table, it can be seen that these occur most frequently for the five to seven years age bracket.

A key deduction from Table 6.2 is that each individual product or service evokes a specific, and possibly unique, response from its set of customers (see Howard, 1994). Indeed, each shopping situation is unique; a uniqueness which retailers can exploit through face-to-face contact with shoppers. However, in mass markets this uniqueness is not so achievable and the retailer will have to deal in terms of groups and averages. Nevertheless, or both levels retailers will need to recognise and understand their customers' specific needs and wants (McDougall and Levesque, 2000). Grouping customers and observation of the factors that influence them during their shopping process and how decisions to buy are made, despite some reservations about the artificiality of the distinctions, are useful to retailers (Greenley and Shipley, 1992). Their purpose is to serve as a 'reminder list' when the retailer is building the specific framework for own-label brands, although the dangers inherent in such simplistic classification must be recognised.

It is possible to vary the shopping decision-making process from an almost intuitive reaction to shopping for food through to an extended process in a case of a consumer durable (see Tauber, 1972). The shopping process is complex and the individual often makes complex shopping decisions depending upon their various circumstances; Figure 6.3 shows the basic influencing factors.

Figure 6.3   *Basic Influencing Factors in the Shopping Process*

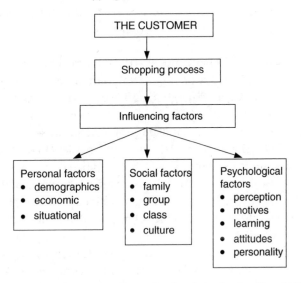

Source: Adapted from Omar (1999) *Retail Marketing* (London: Financial Times/Pitman), p. 52.

A MODEL OF BUYING BEHAVIOUR AND ITS APPLICATION TO THE RETAIL INDUSTRY

An understanding of how the theory and models of consumer behaviour and their application tools evolved will enable the validity of the theory and give guidance in its practical application to be appreciated. This section discusses the reasons, importance and application of consumer behaviour models to the retail industry.

Consumer behaviour theory is a simplified, abstract representation of reality; although such behaviour is complex, the more simplified picture provided by theory helps enormously in understanding it. In addition, theory provides a language to talk about consumers enabling retailers to gain acceptance from shoppers and manufacturers for their retail marketing plans and ideas. Theory guides retail managers in deciding what data on consumers to collect, and helps them in analysing that data. Above all, it helps in interpreting the results of the analysis in terms of the design of retail marketing strategies and market planning.

Previous sections have considered factors that may have an impact on consumer shopping behaviour, but it is important to recognise that these factors do not act in isolation; the effect is often the result of their combined influence and interactions. One of the best known of the explanatory models that have been developed to explain these interactions is that of Howard and Sheth (1969). Of it various components, inputs (stimuli) that the consumer receives from the environment are defined as:

1 *Significative* – the 'real' (physical) aspects of the product or service (which the consumer will make use of);

2 *Symbolic* – the ideas or images attached by the supplier (for example by advertising);

3 *Social* – the ideas or images attached to the product or service by 'society' (for example by reference groups).

Outputs are what happens – the consumer's actions as observable results of the input stimuli. Between the inputs and outputs are the constructs – the processes which the consumer goes through to decide upon the desirable actions. Howard and Sheth group these into perceptions (concerned with obtaining and handling information about the product or service) and learning (the processes of learning that lead to the decision itself). The Engel–Kollatt–Blackwell model (1978) follows a slightly more 'mechanistic' approach, but one which is also based on the same parameters.

Howard's Consumer Decision Model (CDM) is more relevant for retail management and is reproduced here in a simplified form. Originally developed for financial services, it has been modified for general supermarket shopping decisions. The CDM is defined as a model made up of interrelated components (Figure 6.4) including information (F), brand recognition (BR), attitude (A), confidence (C), intention (I), and purchase (P). Of these, the three central components – brand recognition (BR), attitude toward the brand (A) and confidence in judging the brand (C) – make up the buyer's brand image and can be thought of as the ABC's of consumer behaviour.

Figure 6.4   *Consumer Decision Model (CDM)*

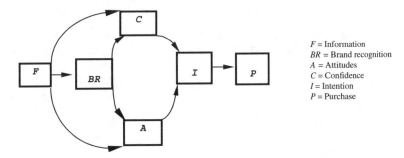

F = Information
BR = Brand recognition
A = Attitudes
C = Confidence
I = Intention
P = Purchase

Source: adapted from John Howard (1994).

Application of the Model

In applying the model, information or 'facts' (*F*) has to be defined with care, as a massive amount of research indicates (Table 6.3). First, as a stimulus it is some physical event that one or more of the shopper's five sense organs (seeing, hearing, smelling, touching and tasting) are exposed to, either voluntarily or involuntarily. Typically, brochures, newspapers, radio, television and word-of-mouth are sources of information for the shopper.

Once the retail manager acquires an understanding of the shopper provided by the theory, he/she has to relate that understanding to the company's needs. The vehicle to accomplish this is the marketing strategy as applied to retailing. In the past decade the role of marketing strategy in retailing has been a major development in management practice, by providing the thinking and organising framework through which the annual retailing plans for a brand are created. The retailer's task is the complex one of designing this strategy for a brand through the use of marketing management tools.

CONSUMER PROFILES AND MARKET SEGMENTATION IN RETAILING

In order to profile consumers accurately, retailers have to be aware of environmental features and their trends. Average levels and growth of income, and the distribution income in society by socio-economic group, gender and age are important. Demographic trends including the regional and urban/rural balance of the population and of course the age profile of customers are similarly important. Data on 'geodemographics' are particularly relevant for the new style of upmarket mail-order retailing. Increased accuracy in respect of customer profiles allows greater fit between catalogue merchandise and potential customers, and allows economies in the sending out of catalogues.

These factors are undoubtedly important characteristics and variables that can be used in retailing to identify potential consumer groups and their spending patterns.

Table 6.3   *Analysis of the Consumer Decision Model*

Terminology	Definition	Process / Action
1 Source of Information (F)	A stimulus or perception caused by the stimulus	Since the retailer's interest is in the perception, information (F) is defined as the perception that is caused by the stimulus. The standard measure of the consumer's perception (F) is recall. Facts from varied sources are often critically important to the consumer when making a purchase decision. Information (F) causes the shopper to recognise the brand (BR)
2 Brand recognition (F)	The extent to which the shopper knows enough about the criteria for categorising, but not for evaluating and distinguishing it from other brands in its product category	Recognition helps the shopper to build both an attitude (A) toward the brand and confidence (C) in his/her judgement of it. Recognition attributes of a brand tend to be physical: the colour, size, shape and texture of the box. A simple outline of the object with little data is adequate
3 Attitudes towards the brand (A)	The extent to which the shopper expects the brand to yield satisfaction of a particular need	The extent to which the shopper likes the brand prompts the intention to buy it. Dissatisfaction may prompt on intention not to buy
4 Confidence in judging the brand (C)	The shopper's degree of certainty that his or her evaluative judgement of the brand is correct	The shopper's confidence in a particular brand is increased when repeated reminders from retailers and peers clarify the thinking that other shoppers like it, that it is distinct from other brands, and that the information is consistent with what the shopper already knows about the brand. In turn, confidence causes intention to buy by removing the hesitancy to act caused by uncertainty
5 Intention to buy the brand (I)	A mental state that reflects the shopper's plan to buy some specified number of units of a particular brand in some specified time period	It is useful for the retailer to understand the shopper's intention. If the retailer surveys consumers, a feel for the typical consumer's current intentions may be assessed. Simultaneously, the retailer can tap other elements of the customer's thinking F, B, A and C
6 Brand purchase (P)	When the buyer has paid for a brand or has made some financial commitment to buy some specified amount during some specified time period	Represents the payoff or lack of it for retail management expenditures. It is caused by intention to buy. Measurement of purchase (P) is relatively simple: the shopper did or did not buy, or make a financial commitment to buy, during a certain time period

However, successful retailing involves more than demographic or socio-economic characteristics. Walters and White (1987), quote the managing director of Harvey Nichol's as saying: '... all this AB, C1, C2 stuff is meaningless. What matters is the style and attitude of a person, regardless of age. We are aiming at United Kingdom

Mini Case Study

Segmenting the Women's Clothing Market

The total market for all potential purchasers of women's clothing is vast. But not all of these customers have the same expectations when they shop for clothing. They differ in terms of the relative importance they give to fashion and price in the purchase decision. The clothing market can thus be divided into segments based on these criteria. Table 6.4, for example, shows a scheme for segmenting the women's clothing market based on a study done for WHICH magazine. The market is divided into four groups including fashion enthusiasts, style-seekers, classics, and the uninvolved.

Each group has different levels of fashion involvement. At one extreme, the fashion-enthusiasts are highly motivated by style, social status and high-quality clothing. At the other extreme is the uninvolved segment whose members do not enjoy shopping, give little or no importance to fashion, and are very price conscious. According to the study, the fashion-enthusiasts and style-seekers together comprise 18 per cent of all shoppers, but account for 68 per cent of all expenditures on women's clothing. Compared to that, the timid and uninvolved segment make up 62 per cent of all shoppers but account for only 22 per cent of expenditures.

It is unlikely that a single retailer can meet the expectations of all of these segments. To meet the expectations of fashion enthusiasts, a store must stock up-to-date fashionable clothes, otherwise these customers will not patronise the store even if its prices are low. The buying decisions of the uninvolved segment, on the other hand, are more influenced by price than fashion. They may be willing to accept a not-so-fashionable dress if the price is low. Their different attitudes towards fashion and price give the segments different preferences for shopping atmospheres. Customers of high-price, fashionable merchandise expect stores to employ salespeople who know the latest trends in fashion and designer names. On the other hand, members of the timid segment may prefer self-selection and self-service. Similarly, the ambience and decor that may suit one group may not please the other. Due to differences between the groups it is difficult, if not impossible, for a single store to meet the needs of all segments.

Table 6.4

Segmentation of the Women's Clothing Market

Segment	Per cent of consumers	Shopping behaviour
Fashion enthusiasts	8 per cent of consumers, but style-seekers account for 68 per cent of all expenditures on clothing	Confident, highly motivated by style, social status and high-quality clothing
Style-seekers	10 per cent of consumers; with fashion enthusiasts the account for 68 per cent of all expenditures on clothing	Keep a close eye on latest styles and are more oriented towards quantity than quality
Classics	20 per cent of consumers and expenditures on clothing	Look for traditional, good-quality styles that have stood the test of time
Uninvolved	60 per cent of consumers; but account for only 22 per cent of expenditures	Little or no interest in fashion; shop only when they have to and spend as little as possible

Source: based on a study conducted by WHICH Magazine, March 1996.

residents, of whatever nationality, who appreciate fine quality and good design, and take this as an illustration of a broader, "lifestyle approach to retail marketing".' This approach to identifying consumer groups concentrates not so much upon the age or socio-economic class of a group of consumers but upon a particular cluster of wants. In this contest, profiling variables can include:

1 Consumers' concepts of value for money (what customers are prepared to pay more for in a store in terms of service as they move away from purchasing on a price basis alone);

2 The type of merchandise in which they are interested in terms of 'fashionable' or 'class' styles and the degree of exclusivity;

3 The kind of shopping experience which they want in terms of level of services and store design or ambience;

4 Personal attitudes to shopping such as an enjoyment of choosing individual items in specialist outlets – for example Sock Shop, Tie Rack or Knickerbox;

5 Some variant of 'one-stop shopping' – for example a large ASDA superstore, or combined food and clothing purchases at Marks & Spencer;

6 The 'edited retailing' of Next where the customer is offered a careful coordinated range of clothing.

The result of such analysis is the identification of consumer market segments within the total universe of consumers. A segment may be defined as a set of consumers with common expectations and perceptions regarding particular combinations of merchandise and retailing styles based broadly upon possession of certain income levels and attitudes (Darden and Ashton, 1975). It should again be stressed that while some of these features may be susceptible to measurement, others can only be identified as a result of what may be described as retailing flair. But according to Solomon (1996), consumer market segments must possess three characteristics:

1 It must be possible to describe or identify them uniquely in terms of the parameters outlined above, and it must also be possible to measure the size of the segment in terms of the number of customers and the volume of expenditure.

2 While a segment of consumers may be unique, it has to be economically viable in terms of being of a size which makes it worthwhile catering for. This is really only to recognise that specialisation on the part of the retailer will be limited by the extent of the consumer market segment.

3 From a practical point of view, it must be possible for the retailer to communicate clearly with the chosen consumer segment.

The more clearly a consumer segment has been identified and the clearer the channel of communication, then the more specific and possibly more economical will be communication between retailer and potential customer.

Segmenting Consumer Markets

The essence of segmentation is to group together people who evaluate the benefits of a retail offering, and therefore retail stores, similarly. The total market can be viewed as containing a number of these segments. All consumers belonging to the same segment will respond similarly to the retailer's marketing strategy since they have similar expectations about their shopping experience. On the other hand, consumers from different segments have different expectations and, therefore, respond differently. A retailer must choose the segment it wants to serve, and design a marketing programme that most effectively meets the expectations of customers in that segment. As Fant (1998) observed, market segmentation is the means of relating retail strategy to differences in consumer needs and expectations. Fant made the following observations:

- Since it recognises differences among groups of customers instead of treating the entire market as homogeneous, segmentation makes the marketing programme more efficient.

- By understanding the differences among segments, a retailer can match its resources to consumers' needs most effectively.

- The retailer can combine the retail mix elements to gain the maximum response from the chosen target market.

- Segmentation also allows a better focus on competition, since not all firms compete for the same customer segments.

- By determining the firms that focus on the same customer segment, a retailer can determine the stores with which it will have the greatest competitive rivalry.

As illustrated in Exhibit 6.2, markets can be grouped into different segments based on differences among consumers in terms of their motivation for shopping, the benefits they seek, the types of merchandise and service they desire, and their sensitivity to price. These are the fundamental bases for market segmentation. Once these differences among segments are understood, each segment must then be described in terms of its observable consumer characteristics. This makes the segments identifiable and measurable. By describing segments in terms of these characteristics, retailers can easily differentiate the members of the segment from the rest of the population. It also makes it possible for the retailer to estimate the number of people or households that belong to the segment.

Exhibit 6.2 Customer segmentation

Consider the differences between customers who patronise full-service camera stores and those who buy from discount stores. Patrons of full-service stores are willing to pay higher prices because they derive considerable benefit from the services offered by these stores. These customers are typically uncertain about camera features and how to choose among alternative models and brands of cameras, and they therefore value the help they get from the sales personnel of full-service stores. Discount store shoppers, on the other hand, are willing to forego such help but seek lower prices. Thus, due to the differences in their shopping behaviour in terms of the type of service they require, customers of full-service and discount camera stores constitute different segments.

The furniture market provides yet another example. Although a wide spectrum of consumers buy furniture, there are distinct differences among them. Some are first-time homemakers who seek affordable yet attractive furniture that they can easily replace when they move or their families grow larger. The furniture they buy often comes in modular form which customers assemble on their own. Ikea is an example of such stores that cater to this segment. Other stores, such as DFS, cater to customers who view furniture as investments. They are willing to pay more for furniture they plan to keep for a long time. The two types of furniture buyers constitute different market segments.

Table 6.5   *Common Demographic Variables for Segmenting Retail Markets*

Variable	Typical breakdown
Age	Infants, toddlers, teens, adults under 35, adults 36–55, adults over 65
Sex	Male, female
Family size	1, 2, 3, 4, 5, more than 5
Income	Under £15 000, £15 000–£25 000, £25 000–35 000, £35 000–£50 000, more than £50 000
Occupation	Professional, managerial, clerical, agricultural
Stage in life cycle	Young single, young married with no children, married with pre-school-age children, married with school-age children, married with children living away from home, retired
Education	Secondary school or less, college, graduate degree
Housing	Own, rent

Source: based on UK consumer profiling.

Demographic Segmentation

Most retailers describe market segments in terms of consumer demographic and socio-economic characteristics such as age, sex, income, occupation and lifestyle (Table 6.5), since information on such variables is easily obtained from secondary sources and they are easy to measure and interpret. These characteristics are highly related to product preference and usage. For example, teenagers and young adults are more likely to patronise stores selling jeans than any other population group. Similarly, newly-married young couples are more likely to buy furniture and home appliances than older couples that have already furnished their homes.

Table 6.6   *Common Dimensions in AIO Surveys*

Activities	Interests	Opinions about
Work	Family	Themselves
Hobbies	Home	Social issues
Social events	Job	Politics
Vacations	Community	Business
Entertainment	Recreation	Economic issues
Club membership	Fashion	Education
Community	Food	Products
Shopping	Media	Future
Sports	Achievement	Culture

Source: Assael (1987) *Consumer Behavior and Marketing Action* (Boston: Kent Publishing), p. 261.

A vast amount of demographic and socio-economic information is available from secondary sources to help retailers describe market segments, and consumer markets can be segmented with reference to one or more of these variables. Age and income, for example, may help describe the market for clothing retailers. A retailer such as Miss Selfridge appeals to teenagers and young adults whilst, the typical customer of a Gap store is older and more affluent. Similarly, household appliance and furniture retailers can best segment their market by lifestyle. Homebase, for example, targets its do-it-yourself (DIY) home supply and kitchenware outlets towards people making their first major investment in home decoration. These customers are more likely to be young home-owners and more likely to live in urban areas.

Lifestyle Segmentation

Although demographic segmentation has traditionally been the most popular basis for describing segments, consumer lifestyle or psychographic characteristics can also be used to develop more detailed pictures of different consumer groups. A lifestyle is broadly defined as a mode of living identified by how people spend their time (activities, A), what they consider important in their environment (interests, I), and what they think of themselves and the world around them (opinions, O) (Table 6.6).

Retailers typically develop lifestyle or psychographic profiles of consumers through this AIO method. Such information, combined with basic demographic variables such as age, sex, income, occupation and stage of life-cycle, provides richer descriptions of consumer segments.

Once the retailer has analysed potential customers and identified a number of viable segments, it can choose the target market it wishes to serve. To accomplish this, the retailer must evaluate each segment in terms of its market potential and competitive environment. Based on these criteria, the retailer can judge the desirability of targeting a particular segment. A viable target market must generate a volume of sales and profits adequate enough to make the venture economically feasible. The segment's market potential is affected by the size of the segment and the expected growth rate.

Exhibit 6.3   Marketing strategy geared to consumer lifestyles

Many retailers focus their marketing strategy on serving consumers with particular lifestyles. Next has implemented this type of strategy with great success, specialising in selling mid-priced clothing to women between the ages of 24 and 45 with a distinctive lifestyle. The target consumer is well-educated, affluent, gregarious and fashion-oriented, and more often than not is a working woman who lives in or near a major metropolitan area. Next is her favourite place to shop because of its fashion and quality.

Exhibit 6.4   Theo Wang's plan for a coffee shop

Theo Wang, a young entrepreneur, has plans to open a coffee shop in a nearby town with a population of around 15 000. There is not a coffee shop in the town at present, although there are a number of restaurants and cafes. Based on his previous experience and discussions with coffee shop managers in other towns, Mr. Wang believes that single people in the 15–35 year old age groups and families with young children would be ideal targets for his venture. To measure the size of his potential market in the town Mr. Wang needs to estimate the number of people in both these categories. This information is available from the Census of Population undertaken every 10 years, copies of which can be found in many libraries. The census provides detailed information about the number of people residing in the town, including their ages and gender. The census is an example of a secondary data source, since the information in it is not collected specifically for Mr. Wang but is available to the public. The biggest advantage of the census is that the information is readily available for no cost.

The number and purchasing power of customers in a segment determine the level of sales the retailer can generate from that segment. This factor, called market size, is important in determining whether the segment is worth pursuing. The retailer usually estimates the size of the segment from secondary data sources, but sometimes that information is not available. Mr Wang, for example (Exhibit 6.4) might not find information on eating habits of people in his town from secondary sources; he will have to collect that information himself. Such primary data can be obtained either through direct observations of people's behaviour or by conducting a survey through personal interviews, mail or over the telephone.

A small segment may still be attractive if its size is expected to increase in the future; growing segments are typically better than stagnant ones. A number of retailers, for instance, entered the opticians' business in the 1980s to take advantage of the growing number of people reaching 40 years of age (Davies and Brooks, 1989) – who typically need some form of eye care. As the population ages, the size of the eye-care market will therefore continue to grow. Similarly, Body Shop, has grown rapidly by targeting its stores towards the increasing number of consumers who want personal care products made only of natural ingredients (Body Shop's *Annual Report*, 1999).

Positioning is the process of creating an image for a product or store in the minds of target customers. It may start with a product, a company or even a person. Positioning is not what is done to the product or the store, it is what is created in the minds of the target customers. The product must be perceived by the selected target customers to have a distinct image and position *vis-à-vis* its competitors. Product differentiation is widely viewed as the key to successful marketing; that is, the product must stand out and have a clearly defined position in its market sector.

Business and Product Positioning

Positioning is based on consumers' perceptions and is therefore only partly within the control of retailers. Positions are described by variables and are within parameters that are important to customers and are essentially selected by them. Price, for example, may be key in grocery shopping, service level in banking, quality and reliability in car purchase, and value for money in choosing a travelling agent from whom to buy a flight ticket.

Customers generally assign positions to a retail organisation that is a market leader, such as Tesco in the UK grocery market. Tesco probably has the highest profile and perceptions of other grocery retailers are orientated to Tesco as a market leader. Similarly, in the market for baked beans perceptions of brands are orientated towards the market leader Heinz. Occasionally the brand that consumers may have perceived as the market leader may not be the genuine market leader in terms of market share, but simply the one most visible at that time. This may possibly occur because of heavy promotional exposure. Customers respond to the attribute of a product and to its promotional imagery, but the product's position as perceived by its target customers is affected by the reputation and image of the company, coupled with its other products, and by the activities of its competitors. Bad publicity, such as that experienced by British Airways following allegations of dirty tricks against Virgin Atlantic, for example, can negatively affect British Airway's brand positioning. Retailers normally use their marketing mix to carefully eliminate negative effects.

RELATIONSHIP MARKETING IN RETAILING

The concept of relationship marketing (RM) has continued to receive support as a major trend in marketing (Mattsson, 1997). Although RM was originally conceived as an approach to industrial and service markets its domain has been extended more recently to incorporate innovative applications in mass consumer markets. Within consumer marketing, the development of relationship strategies has been most evident in retailing in its broadest sense. The widespread use of store loyalty cards provides clear evidence of the take-up of RM in retailing and it is perhaps unsurprising that retailers should be interested in its development. The closeness of the industry to consumers intuitively suggests that the nearer the retailer can get to the customer the better they will be able to provide the service that customer seeks. As it is the retailer who, most often, manages this face-to-face interaction and who, historically, has gone beyond the mere "service encounter" their potential interest in relationship marketing strategies becomes even more understandable.

Recent applications of RM in retail markets have been facilitated by developments in direct and database marketing and an increasingly competitive and fragmented retail marketplace. RM involves retail organisations gathering information about their customers and then deciding on those with whom they can develop a dialogue. It allows retailers and suppliers to work together in joint problem-solving, easing the pressure on the retailer in the process of satisfying customer needs. Thus, as Conway and Swift (2000) observed, rather than employing market share as a measure of retailing success, this approach uses customer retention (see also Gronroos, 1996).

Morgan and Hunt (1994) defined RM as referring to all marketing activities directed towards establishing, developing and maintaining successful relational exchanges. Levitt (1983) anticipated stages in the development of a relationship to include:

- awareness,
- exploration,

Table 6.7   *Factors in Successful Relationship Marketing in Retailing*

Variable	Importance
1 Commitment	Defined as the intention to continue a course of action or activity, or the desire to maintain a relationship. This is often indicated by an ongoing 'investment' into activities, which are expected to maintain the relationship. Commitment is likely to be stronger when levels of satisfaction are high, when the quality of alternatives is perceived to be poor, and when the investment size is large
2 Trust	Relationships in retailing must be based on mutual trust. Trust has the potential to influence the development of customer orientation and customer satisfaction. A high level of trust is likely to engender a more positive attitude, which in turn is likely to increase the level of customer orientation/empathy. Low trust can have the opposite effect
3 Customer orientation/ empathy	This factor links with the concept of social bonding. Empathy means the ability to see a situation from someone else's point of view. In the initial stages of retail relationship development, the onus is more on the retailer to empathise with the customer, but as the relationship develops mutual empathy becomes increasingly important. Customer orientation therefore means adopting a collaborative strategy to retail operation
4 Experience/ satisfaction	The decision to continue in a relationship can be seen as dependent on the level of congruity between relationship expectations and performance so far. Negative experience may hinder the relationship between the retailer and the customer, and may even lead to customer defection. Customers tend to best remember the last experience, so that one positive experience may be sufficient to alter perceptions of more than one preceding negative experience, and vice versa
5 Communication	This is a vital component in the establishment of retail marketing relationships, yet it is a variable that is often assumed or taken for granted and consequently overlooked. Effective collaboration between the retailer and the customer or supplier and retail marketing coordination depend on effective communication. Communication between the parties, therefore, remains the pivotal factor to establishing successful relationships in retail management

- expansion,
- commitment, and
- dissolution.

Levitt explained that once exploration has taken place, the degree of interdependence is increased during the expansion stage; the commitment stage is where individual concerns merge with collective interest. But in view of the number of potential variables in any relationship, it is necessary to concentrate on those variables that, according to the literature, are deemed relatively more important in most retail management relationships. These factors are:

- commitment,
- trust,
- customer orientation/empathy,
- experience/satisfaction, and
- communication.

Each of these is examined briefly in Table 6.7 indicating the importance of the element in the development of successful relationships in retail operations. In addition, in retail marketing relationships the customer's view of the desirability of entering into a relationship with the retailer will be affected by perceptions of the likely size of the transaction costs involved.

THE MARKETING MIX IN RETAILING

There is no single marketing strategy that suits all retailers. Each store has to formulate its own strategy and implement it by selecting the correct retail mix elements to achieve the desired differential advantage. This is an important task since the store's combination of retail mix elements will determine its overall image and its ability to differentiate itself from competitors.

The marketing mix elements in retailing are developed using the 4Ps:

1 *Product*: the merchandise assortment, including the number and different types of products and brands and own-label products.

2 *Price*: its pricing policy, including promotional pricing and discounts, and the retail prices it charges.

3 *Place*: location of its stores and, increasingly, other channels of distribution such as the Internet, but also the shopping experience of the store environment. Manageable elements will include store accessibility and convenience, store design and layout. As marketing becomes more integrated into the organisation it will need to assess the role of distribution centres, warehouses and stockrooms in creating customer value.

4 *Promotion*: the way in which it advertises and promotes itself through its brand image carried through the organisation from signage to packaging and labelling.

These 4Ps can be extended to include other Ps, people, process and physical evidence (Jackson and Shaw, 2000). Of these Jackson and Shaw observed that the most valuable is the people element because of its role in customer service and customer relationship management. Many service-related concepts rely on a total service approach from everyone in the retail organisation, together with their suppliers, to satisfy the product and experiential wants of the customers in the service encounter.

The marketing mix is the vehicle through which a retailer's marketing strategy is implemented and, in planning the mix, retailers should be guided by three basic principles (see Gilbert, 1999):

- the retail marketing mix must be consistent with the expectations of the target customers;

- the elements of the retail marketing mix must be consistent with each other to create synergy; and

- a store's retail marketing mix must be responsive to competitive strategy.

The first principle states that all retail marketing mix elements must be consistent with the expectations of the store's target market. This consistency with target market expectations is one of the main reasons for the success of supermarkets in Britain. In this way the marketing policies of discount chains such as Kwik Save, Aldi and Lidl meet the needs of and expectations of middle-income customers in small towns and rural areas (see McDougall and Levesque, 2000). In its location selection, for example, Lidl has concentrated on sites in rural areas and smaller urban markets and has mostly avoided the metropolitan areas typically targeted by market leaders such as Tesco and Sainsbury. Both Aldi and Lidl stress basic merchandise in a simple setting. The location, size, decor and merchandising policies of these stores are all consistent with the expectations of their target market. This successful strategy has produced one of the highest levels of profitability per square foot among discount store operators.

At the other end of the spectrum from discount stores are clothing stores such as Marks and Spencer, and Next, which are located in prime shopping locations. Customers patronise these stores depending on their lifestyles and their perceived self-images. Target markets, of course, vary from retailer to retailer, and whatever the characteristics of its target market no store can compete effectively without keeping all policies consistent with the expectations of its target customers. The second principle seeks to create synergy by making each component of the retail marketing mix consistent with the others (see Proctor, 1998). The store's merchandise, atmosphere, customer service, advertising and prices must evoke the same feeling in the customer. Each retailer keeps its location, merchandise, store design, service and pricing policies consistent with each other and in line with the expectations of the target market. The third principle also requires a consistent approach to managing the marketing mix within the retailer's strategy.

Retail Marketing Planning and Control

Planning is the process of anticipating the future and determining courses of action to achieve organisational objectives (McDonald and Tideman, 1993). As this defini-

Table 6.8   *Types of Plans Prepared by Different Levels of Retail Management*

Level of management	Type of plan	Purpose of plan
Senior management Board of directors, chief executives and divisional directors	Strategic planning (long-range plans)	Specifying objectives of organisations; determining fundamental strategies; setting total budget
Middle management Senior store managers, technical managers and operating managers	Tactical planning (short-term)	Annual and quarterly plans; divisional or store budgets; policies and procedures for each department or store
Supervisory management Store supervisors and sales managers	Tactical planning (short-term)	Monthly, weekly and daily plans; setting unit budgets; daily operating plans

tion indicates, planning is a continuous process that includes specifying objectives and the actions required to achieve them. The planning process creates a blueprint that not only specifies the means of achieving organisational objectives, but also includes checkpoints where actual performance can be compared with expectations to determine whether the organisational activities are moving the organisation towards its objectives (Meadows and Dibb, 1998).

Retail Marketing Planning

This involves the implementation of planning activities as they relate to the achievement of retail marketing objectives, and it is the basis for all marketing strategies in retailing. Retail management, retail operations, product lines, pricing decisions, selection of appropriate distribution channels and decisions relating to promotional campaigns all depend upon plans formulated within the retail organisation.

Planning is often classified on the basis of scope or breadth. Some plans are broad and long-range, focusing upon strategic objectives with a major impact on the organisation for a time period of five or more years. Other plans are short-term, have a more operational focus and require immediate action. The relative amounts of time spent in planning activities and the types of planning vary at different organisational levels (see Table 6.8). As the table shows, senior management is more likely to devote much of its planning activities to longer-range strategic planning, whereas middle-level managers tend to focus upon narrower tactical plans for their stores. Supervisory personnel are more likely to engage in developing specific programmes to meet the goals for their particular responsibility areas.

According to Omar (1999), the strategic objectives of the retailer provide the starting point for retail marketing planning. These serve as the guideposts from which retail marketing objectives and plans are derived. As Figure 6.5 shows, objectives provide direction for all phases of the retail organisation and serve as standards in evaluating performance. One result is the formulation of retail marketing objectives designed to achieve the retailer's objectives and the development of a retailing plan.

Figure 6.5   *Steps in the Retail Marketing Planning Process*

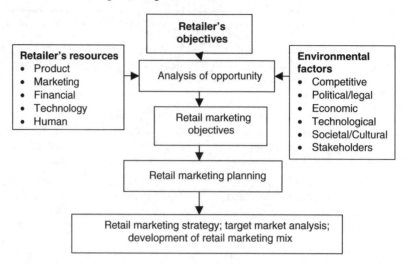

Retail planning efforts must be directed towards establishing marketing strategies that are resource-efficient, flexible and adaptable.

Implementing and Controlling the Plan

As Thomas (1998) identified, control is a vital aspect of implementation of retail marketing plans, whether the plan is long-term (strategic) or short-term (operational). It helps to ensure that retail activities happen as planned, with proper management. It also provides important feedback that enables retail managers to determine whether or not their decisions, actions and strategies are working according to plan. Thus retail marketing programme recommendations are the culmination of the various analyses and statements of strategies: exactly what needs to be done, how and why – a detailed presentation of the proposed retail marketing mixes to achieve the goals and implement the chosen strategies (McGoldrick, 1990). It is very likely that each market segment targeted by the retailer may require its own, unique marketing mix. This section of the retail marketing plan is of paramount importance, as it gives the specific details of the marketing activities required to implement the retail marketing plan and to achieve the retailer's strategic goals. Each element of the retail marketing mix should be discussed in turn, with specific recommendations explained in sufficient detail to enable managers to put them into action.

It is essential that controls be established along with measures to assess the ongoing implementation of the retail marketing plan (Samli, 1989). The control parameters detail how the results of the plan will be measured. In some cases, financial measures include sales volumes, profitability and market shares and the financial projections and budgets section outline the return on investment expected through implementation of the plan. The results of promotions designed to increase market share in terms of increases in sales volume or improved brand recognition and brand acceptance can also be measured. Senior management will establish the responsibilities for monitoring the implementation of the marketing plan and taking corrective action.

SUMMARY

This chapter has emphasised that each retailer must specify in a well-formulated marketing strategy how it will compete in the marketplace and attract customers to its outlets. The development of the marketing strategy takes place in five major steps: customer analysis to identify potential market segments; selecting the target market; identifying how the firm will create a sustainable differential advantage in the marketplace; planning retail mix elements; and assessing store image.

Consumers differ in terms of their tastes, preferences and the ways in which they perceive value from the shopping experience. These differences create the potential for dividing the market into several relatively homogenous customer groups. The total market can thus be viewed as comprising a number of smaller market segments. Retailers commonly describe segments based on consumer demographic, socio-economic and lifestyle characteristics. Research evidence suggests that consumption patterns and shopping behaviour have been found to be strongly related to these factors.

Once retailers have identified viable segments, they must choose one or more of them as the target market. To select the target market, each segment's market potential and competition level must be analysed. Market grids are often used to summarise this information and identify potential market opportunities. With the target market selected, the retailer must choose how it will compete in the marketplace; it must create a sustainable differential advantage over stores catering to the same target market. In order to differentiate itself, the retailer must create a retail marketing mix of location, merchandise, shopping atmosphere, price, advertising, customer service, personal selling and sales promotion. The elements of the retail marketing mix must be consistent with customer expectations, competitors' actions, and each other.

QUESTIONS

1   During the 1960s and early 1970s, even the large multiple retailers spent little time thinking about marketing in retailing, but now retailers have come to recognise the need to integrate their overall marketing plans and develop their marketing strategies to achieve their desired retailing objectives. What do you consider to be the major steps in developing marketing plans for retail operations?

2   The retail marketing plan incorporates all the components of retail operation. Discuss this statement stating clearly the steps in preparing the plan and how it should be controlled.

3   Consumers have different tastes, preferences and perceptions of value, yet retailers tend to group them together for the purpose of serving them. Basing your argument on the concept of market segmentation, are retailers justified?

(Continued)

4 Market segmentation is the means of relating retail strategy to differences in consumer needs and expectations. Discuss this statement with the aid of examples from the retail industry.

5 Once the retailer has analysed potential customers and identified a number of viable segments it can choose the target market to serve. Discuss how this process could be accomplished.

6 Consumer buying behaviour models could only be relevant in theory and are not practicable. What are the essential characteristics of a good theory?

7 What do you consider to be the usefulness of consumer decision models?

8 What are the major principles that guide all retail marketing mix planning activities that retailers must conside?

9 Why is relationship marketing necessary in retail management?

10 Retailers can only position themselves based on consumer perception. Comment.

Case Study

Gender Pricing: A Discriminatory Retail Marketing Strategy

In the theory and practice of retail marketing, women are not supposed to be charged more than men for services because 'gender pricing' is discriminatory. In Britain however, women can still pay more than men for some everyday services. Gender pricing means that retail organisations and others offering products and services charge consumers based on their gender, rather than the quality and value of the item on offer. This means that hairdressing salons, for example, may have prices that distinguish simply between men and women on the basis of gender instead of the time taken to undertake the work or its quality.

Sex and shopping have long been linked in most women's minds, but never quite so literally. Both New York City and California in the USA have outlawed gender pricing for being discriminatory. In Britain, despite Section 29 of the Sex Discrimination Act, which outlaws gender discrimination on goods and services, some women's items are priced higher than the men's equivalent. Retailers can achieve higher prices because it is difficult to prove that women are charged more than men on the basis of gender rather than the quality or value input. The justification for higher prices for women's items lies in the higher cost of labour overheads, different costs in manufacturing or provision of services and so the Sex Discrimination Act is unlikely to apply.

Although gender pricing is a discriminatory marketing strategy, it remains generally under-researched. The National Hairdressers' Federation counters that higher prices in the salon were justified, saying that it costs more to cut ladies' hair than men's. The justification is based on the visual evidence that most women's hair is longer than men's and needs more styling. The Federation was quick to support the notion that the introduction of

American measures in Britain may be disastrous, emphasising that some salons may get more men passing through each hour than women. So if a salon is only cutting women's hair it will have fewer customers and may lead to declining revenue and subsequently go out of business. The other side of the argument is that if these retailers could not bring the prices down for women, they would end up charging men as much as women and in the end penalising men.

Gender pricing is evident in the provision of a wide range of services from dry cleaning to car insurance. Although retailers and dry cleaners may not admit it, there have been circumstances when the price of cleaning a woman's shirt was greater than that of a man's shirt. But following complaints, most dry cleaners now charge the same price for cleaning similar items for both men and women. On the other hand, women tend to receive favourable premiums for their car insurance compared to men. Evidence from the motor insurance industry suggests that young women can receive quotes, which can be some £100 less than men of a comparable age. However, the issues are more complex, involving assessment of risks and costs; women are considered a lower risk because men under 40 years of age are twice as likely to drive without due or reasonable care and attention, and twice as likely to break the speed limit. Young men have a much higher number of driving convictions and claims per person, and when they do crash, the damage tends to be more severe, leading to higher claims than for accidents involving women drivers. Insurers justify their gender pricing as based on experience, saying that females in the younger age groups make fewer, less expensive claims.

There are other areas in which women may still be charged less than men: for example, 'ladies nights' in pubs and clubs where women get subsidised drinks and free entrance to attract their custom. Recent evidence from the Brewers and Licensed Retailers Association, however, suggests that this practice is dying out as women tend to become more independent and exercise greater choice about their social behaviour.

SEMINAR QUESTION FOR DISCUSSION

In light of the argument presented in the case study, do you agree with the author that gender-pricing strategy is discriminatory and could not be justified as a retailing tool for providing the customer with a fair service?

References

Brown, S. (1987) 'Institutional Change in Retailing: A Review and Synthesis', *European Journal of Marketing*, vol. 21, no. 6, pp. 5–36.

Chisnall, P.M. (1994) *Consumer Behaviour* (Maidenhead: McGraw-Hill).

Conway, T. and Swift, J.S. (2000) 'International Relationship Marketing: the Importance of Psychic Distance', *European Journal of Marketing Review*, vol. 34, no. 11/12, pp. 1391–413.

Cook, D. and Walters, D.W. (1991) *Retail Marketing: Theory and Practice* (Hemel Hempstead: Prentice Hall).

Darden, W.R. and Ashton, D. (1975) 'Psychographics' Profiles of Patronage Preference Groups', *Journal of Retailing*, vol. 50 (Winter), pp. 99–112.

Engel, J., Kollat, D. and Blackwell, R. (1978) *Consumer Behaviour* (New York: Drydon Press).

Fant, D. (1998) 'Understanding Customers. the Key to Retail Success', *Marketing News*, vol. 32, no. 4, p. 7.

Fitchett, J. and McDonagh, P. (2001) 'Relationship Marketing, E-commerce and the Emancipation of the Consumer', in A. Sturdy, I. Grugulis and H. Willmott (eds), *Customers Service, Empowerment and Entrapment* (Basingstoke: Palgrave).

Ganesh, J., Arnold, M.J. and Reynolds, K.E. (2000) 'Understanding the Customer Base of Service Providers: an Examination of the Differences Between Switchers and Stayers', *Journal of Marketing*, vol. 64, July, pp. 65–87.

Gilbert, D. (1999) *Retail Marketing Management* (Harlow: Financial Times/Prentice Hall).

Greenley, G.E. and Shipley, D. (1992) 'A Comparative Study of Operational Marketing Practices Among British Department Stores and Supermarkets', *European Journal of Marketing*, vol. 26, no. 5, pp. 22–35.

Greenley, G.E. and Shipley, D.D. (1987) 'Problems Confronting UK Retailing Organisations', *Service Industries Journal*, vol. 7, no. 3, pp. 353–64.

Gronroos, C. (1996) 'Relationship Marketing Strategic and Tactical Implications', *Management Decisions*, vol. 34, no. 3, pp. 5–15.

Gummersson, E. (1999) *Total Relationship Marketing: Re-thinking Marketing Management from 4Ps to 30 Rs* (Oxford: Butterworth Heinnemann).

Howard, J. (1994) *Consumer Behaviour in Marketing Strategy* (Englewood Cliffs, New Jersey: Prentice Hall).

Howard, J. and Sheth, J. (1969) *Theory of Buyer Behaviour* (New York: John Wiley).

Jackson, T. and Shaw, D. (eds) (2000) *Buying and Merchandising Management* (Basingstoke: Palgrave Macmillan).

Kotler, P. (1997) *Marketing Management: Analysis, Planning, Implementation, and Control*, 9th edn (Hemel Hempstead: Prentice Hall International).

Levitt, T. (1983) 'After the Sale is Over', *Harvard Business Review*, vol. 61, no. 5, pp. 87–93.

Mattsson, L.G. (1997) 'Relationship Marketing and the Markets as Networks Approach: a Comparative Analysis of two Evolving Streams of Research', *Journal of Marketing Management*, vol. 13, no. 5, pp. 447–61.

McDonald, M.H.B. and Tideman, C.C.S. (1993) *Retail Marketing Plans: How to Prepare Them; How to Use Them* (Oxford: Butterworth – Heinemann).

McDougall, G.H.G. and Levesque, T. (2000) 'Customer Satisfaction with Services: Putting Perceived Value into the Equation', *Journal of Services Marketing*, vol. 14, no. 5, pp. 392–410.

McGoldrick, P.J. (1990) *Retail Marketing* (Maidenhead: McGraw-Hill).

Meadows, M. and Dibb, S. (1998) 'Implementing Market Segmentation Strategies in the UK Personal Financial Services', *The Service Industries Journal*, vol. 18, no. 2, pp. 45–63.

Morgan, R.M. and Hunt, S.D. (1994) 'The Commitment – Trust Theory of Relationship Marketing', *Journal of Marketing*, vol. 58, no. 3, pp. 20–38.

O'Brien, L. and Jones, C. (1995) 'Do Rewards Really Create Loyalty?' *Harvard Business Review*, vol. 73, May/June, pp. 75–83.

Omar, O. (1999) *Retail Marketing* (London: Financial Times/Pitman).

Piercy, N. and Alexander, N. (1988) 'The Status Quo of the Marketing Organisation in the UK Retailing: a Neglected Phenomenon', *Service Industries Journal*, vol. 8, no. 2, pp. 155–75.

Plummer, J.J. (1974) 'The Concept and Applications of the Lifestyle Segmentations', *Journal of Marketing*, vol. 38, Winter, pp. 21–8.

Proctor, T. (1998) 'A Framework for Marketing Strategy Formulation', *Journal of Targeting, Measurement and Analysis for Marketing*, vol. 5, no. 3, pp. 280–91.

Reichheld, F.F. (1993) 'Loyalty-Based Management', *Harvard Business Review*, vol. 71, March/April, pp. 64–73.

Samli, A. (1989) *Retail Marketing Strategy: Planning, Implementation, and Control* (New York: Quorum Books).

Sauer, C. and Burton, S. (1999) 'Is There a Place for Department Stores on the Internet? Lessons from an Abandoned Pilot', *Journal of Information Technology*, vol. 14, pp. 387–98.

Sivades, E. and Baker-Prewitt, J.L. (2000) 'An Examination of the Relationship Between Service Quality, Customer Satisfaction and Store Loyalty', *International Journal of Retail & Distribution Management*, vol. 28, no. 2, pp. 73–82.

Solomon, M.R. (1996) *Consumer Behaviour: Buyer, Having, Being* (Englewood Cliffs, New Jersey: Prentice-Hall).

Tauber, E.M. (1972) 'Why do People Shop?', *Journal of Marketing*, vol. 36, no. 4, pp. 46–9.

Thomas, M.J. (1998) 'Measuring Marketing Performance', *Journal of Targeting, Measurement and Analysis for Marketing*, vol. 6, no. 3, pp. 233–46.

Walter, D. and White, D. (1987) *Retail Marketing Management* (London: Macmillan).

CHAPTER SEVEN

Financial Planning and Control

LEARNING OBJECTIVES

After studying this chapter, the reader will be able to:

- Understand the importance of financial planning and control in relation to retail operations.
- Know the financial objectives and financial implications of strategic planning in a retail organisation.
- Learn how to interpret income statements and balance sheets of a retail firm.
- Describe the major techniques of project appraisal and sources of finance for retail operations.
- Explain the measurement and cost of finance for retailers.
- Apply budgeting and financial control techniques to retail operations.

INTRODUCTION

This chapter demonstrates how financial planning and control affect retail management and the retailer's operational performance. It develops a framework for evaluating that performance and presents a systematic approach to financial planning for retailers.

Financial planning is one of the key pillars that support successful retail management operations, and like all businesses, retailers must be concerned about the financial well-being of their organisations. This is because even the most elaborate retail marketing strategy will fail without an adequate, well-conceived financial plan. Financial planning is important for all types of businesses, to ensure survival and enable growth to occur in an increasingly performance-driven environment. In the UK, statistics indicate that 48 per cent of retail business start-ups fail within three years. Although financial management in larger retail organisations is more formalised, the failure of multiple retail businesses illustrates its continuing importance and the need to integrate planning and control strategies to maintain a successful retail operation. For both multiple and independent retailers, these techniques are an essential ingredient of success.

FINANCE AND MANAGEMENT ACCOUNTING IN RETAILING

Retailing is a fast moving industry, typically involving many products, suppliers and volumes of daily sales through many outlets. All these combine to create many detailed transactions and demands on the financial management and control of the business. The financial and legal environment in which retailers operate is complex too. Retailers need to manage their operations within the banking systems, taxation, legal and regulatory frameworks governing business activities, both in the UK and overseas. Financial records need to be maintained for different stakeholders, shown in Figure 7.1. Public companies need to provide information for their shareholders, investors and market regulators, summarised in the Profit and Loss and Balance Sheets of its Trading Accounts and supplemented by updates on the state of their business. Both public and private limited companies need to prepare and submit annual accounts of their trading activities by law. Within the retail organisation, a key task is to evaluate current performance and set future targets using information concerning its use of resources, its sales and its costs. Therefore financial information in retailing is required to make sure that the retailer fulfils its legal obligations and to provide detailed information to internal and external stakeholders.

These processes require the collection of a considerable amount of financial information before they are summarised into a suitable form for publication. This data gathering and processing is the financial function of the retailer, which although increasingly specialised, falls into two areas, financial and management accounting.

Figure 7.1   *The Main Users of Retail Accounting Information*

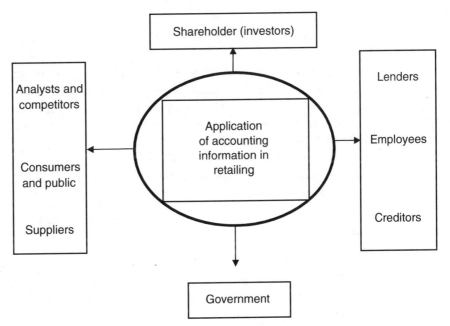

Financial Accounting

This form of accounting is defined by the Chartered Institute of Management Accountants (CIMA) as 'the classification and recording of monetary transactions of an entity in accordance with established concepts, principles, accounting standards and legal requirements and presentation of a view of the effect of those transactions during and at the end of an accounting period'. Based on this definition, financial accounting concerns the development and preparation of information relating to trading, profit and loss and the balance sheet. In a practical sense, the information enables retail managers to answer questions from their external stakeholders concerning the company's annual performance. From a strategic perspective, the financial overview informs senior managers' decision-making. Of fundamental concern is the profitability of the company and its ability to manage existing resources and if necessary, raise new capital to invest for future growth. Alternatively, decisions may be taken in more difficult circumstances to rationalise or reduce the activities in the company to maximise the value of its resources.

Management Accounting

Management accounting is an integral part of management concerned with identifying, presenting and interpreting information that relates to retail trading. As management accounting is a significant component of the retail management process it is important for non-financial specialists to understand its scope and significance. The main purposes of this function are:

■ The preparation of accounts and the management of budgets

■ The provision of timely and accurate financial information in management functions

■ The interpretation of financial and management information

Management accounting will reflect the financial activity of the retailer in planning, operational control and decision making at tactical and operational levels rather than at the strategic level, typically through budgeting, costing and variance analysis. Despite the different emphases of financial and management accounting the two functions share some common characteristics:

■ they reflect the retailer's operating activities in quantitative, and predominantly in financial terms;

■ they share certain data sources – for instance, personnel data may be used by both financial and management accounting – though in different ways and for different purposes;

■ there is a limited area of common ground between the two as regards users – for instance, operating budgets prepared for internal use may form the basis of annual profit forecasts; and

Figure 7.2   *Retail Financial Planning And Control Cycle*

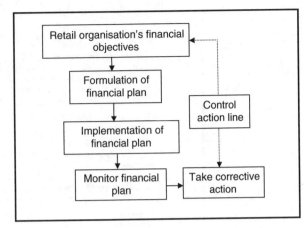

- they are key elements within the retail management information system, and a degree of integration between the two is often present, for example, budgetary control prepared by management accounting may require the input of actual costs and revenues which have been recorded in the financial accounts.

These similarities can obscure the different uses for financial information and the potential for their mis-application. However, they also point to the emergence of financial management as an increasingly commercial and active function, concerned with decision-making throughout the retail organisation.

Retail Financial Operational Planning and Control

It is not possible for a retail organisation to survive without some form of operational planning and control. The cycle of financial planning and control is shown in Figure 7.2 in which the retailer's objectives form the starting point for its financial plans. The relationship between objectives and financial planning and control need to be aligned, otherwise objectives may be over-ambitious and financially unachievable. Likewise, control of current activity and information about how the business is performing need to feed into planning for the future. However, it may not always be possible to exercise complete control over a plan due to changes in the industry or competitive environments.

Retail Management Decision-Making

Retail operational decision-making is an integral part of retail management as shown in Figure 7.3, illustrating the essential components of the operational decision process. Management accounting's main inputs to retailing decision-making occur at the evaluation and monitoring stages. The need to make a decision may become apparent from financial information available to retail management, and may arise from either internal or external sources to the retail organisation. A particular difficulty is that

Figure 7.3   *The Alternative Retail Financial Choice Decision Process*

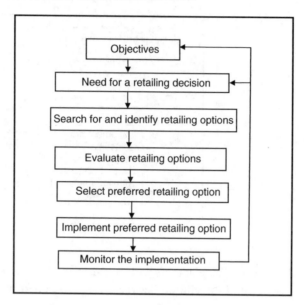

identification of all feasible options is unlikely because of the limitations of any single person or group to know everything.

Management accounting offers a range of financial criteria against which, the retailer may gauge tactical and operational decisions. The attraction of such criteria is the ability of the retailer to express complex retail operational realities concisely and comprehensibly. But there is the pitfall of overreliance on financial evaluation, to the detriment of other criteria; and, as with planning and control, quantified financial decision criteria may suggest a precision, which does not truly exist. There is also the possibility that certain financial criteria may be misunderstood, or that their limitations could be overlooked. It is therefore important that retail managers have an understanding of the nature, strengths and weaknesses of the financial information presented to them.

A key task in developing the retailer's financial strategy is to analyse current performance and set future targets. Since financial evaluation and analysis require information from the company's income statement and balance sheet, it is useful to first review these. The primary purposes of an accounting system are to inform the retailer of the profit or loss for a period, and of the financial position of the business at the end of the period. These two main objectives are reached by what are popularly known as the 'final accounts', that is the trading and profit and loss account and the balance sheet. It is important to bear in mind that the balance sheet is not strictly an account; it is rather a statement of assets, liabilities and capital accounts drawn up from balances in the ledger. These aspects are now reviewed.

The Trading Income Statement

Retailers, whether they are engaged in any formal financial planning or not, are all required to prepare income statements. The income statement summarises the

Table 7.1 *Trading and Profit and Loss Account of Ogenmar Ltd, for the Year ended 31 December 1998*

	£	£	£
Gross sales	572 200		
Less returns in	2 200		
Net sales			570 000
Opening stock	170 000		
Add purchases	340 000		
		510 000	
Less closing stock		148 800	
Cost of goods sold			361 200
Gross profit			**208 800**
Wages and salaries	76 400		
Rents and rates	26 000		
Selling expenses	10 000		
Electric and gas bills	6 000		
Sundry expenses	2 000		
Total expenses			120 400
Net profit			**88 400**

financial results of the company for a specific time period such as a quarter, six months or a year. It reports the revenues earned by the company and the sources and amounts of all expenses incurred during that time period. Based on these revenues and expenses, the profit or loss for the period is calculated. As such the income statement is a concise summary of the financial impact of the retailer's operations during the specified time period.

The trading account (income statement) of Ogenmar Ltd, for the year 1998, is shown in Table 7.1. Ogenmar is a fashion store opened in Manchester in 1993 that sells both ladies and children's clothing, including outdoor sportswear. It mainly serves the local female population as well as shoppers from other areas outside Manchester. Although the shop struggled for the first few years, it is now doing well with increasing sales and profits since 1995.

Using Ogenmar's trading and profit and loss account as an example, five elements of the income statement summarise key dimensions of Ogenmar's operations for the year including, sales, cost of goods sold, gross profit (margin), operating expenses and net profit. Each of these elements is now defined to indicate what they measure in terms of trading and profit and loss accounts.

Sales for Ogenmar's store for the year were £572 200 and net sales were £570 000. Gross sales states the total amount of money obtained from customers through the sales of merchandise and services. In practice, Ogenmar has to return some of the money to the customers who brought back defective items of clothing. The amount after accounting for such returns and other adjustments is the net sales figure.

To generate the net sales of £570 000, Ogenmar had purchased merchandise from various fashion suppliers. This merchandise cost Ogenmar £361 200, the cost of goods sold (COGS), which forms the largest expense item for Ogenmar and is usually the largest item for all retailers. The ratio of the cost of goods to sales, depends on the retail sector and the ability of the retailer to negotiate the cost. The range can extend from a high cost to sales in groceries and electricals, around 70–80%, to a low cost to sales in clothing, around 40% or less to fashion retailers. The cost of goods sold is the total expense the retailer incurred to put together the merchandise it sold to customers. In a typical supermarket, the COGS includes the cost of all packaged goods as well as the costs of items such as meat and produce (vegetables and fruits). For restaurants, the COGS includes all food supplies and cooking ingredients plus cost of disposable napkins, plates, tableware, and so forth.

The gross margin is the difference between sales revenue and the cost of goods sold. This is an important measure because it indicates the amount of money that is available to cover expenses. In 1998 when Ogenmar's data were revealed, the store's gross margin was £208 800. Gross margin is often expressed as a percentage of net sales using the formula:

$$\text{Gross margin percentage} = \frac{\text{Net sales} - \text{cost of goods sold}}{\text{Net sales}} \times 100$$

Ogenmar's gross margin percentage can be calculated as follows:

$$\text{Gross margin percentage} = \frac{£570\,000 - £361\,200}{£570\,000} \times 100 = 36.63\%$$

Which means in practice that for every £1 of sales, 63 pence is spent on the cost of merchandise, leaving the 37 pence to cover its operating expenses, including property, employees and general administration. For Ogenmar these expenses amount to a total of £120 400 in the 1998 financial year.

Net Profit is the final element of the income statement for Ogenmar. This reports the amount the firm earns (or lost – if the net profit is negative) during the period covered by the income statement. It is found by subtracting the cost of goods sold and total business expenses from the net sales.

Stock Loss

A less obvious factor affecting retail profitability is the level of stock loss. Stock loss is estimated to have cost UK retailers over £3.6bn. or 1.76 per cent of their turnover in 2001. Of this 46 per cent is thought to be due to customer theft, 28.5 per cent to staff or supplier theft and 8 per cent to supplier fraud (The European Retail Theft Barometer 2001). A typical supermarket can lose around 2.5 per and estimates in for clothing retailers vary between 2–5 percent cent of sales through reductions, disposals, theft, damage and wastage. The costs of 'shrinkage' can be high; the food retailer Iceland, reported that its shrinkage costs rose by over 15 per cent in a recent 15 month period causing a 20 per cent fall in its profit (The Grocer, 2001).

Balance Sheet

Whereas the trading and profit and loss accounts show how the profit or loss has been achieved during the financial year, the balance sheet (Table 7.2) shows the state of the operation on the last day of the financial year. The 'balance' is between what the

Table 7.2   *Balance Sheet of Ogenmar Ltd, as at 31 December 1998*

	£	£
Fixed assets		
Premises		78 000
Equipment		30 000
Vehicle		21 500
		129 500
Current assets		
Stock	25 300	
Debtors	23 850	
Bank	1 239	
Cash	125	
	50 514	
Less current liabilities		
Creditors	28 756	
Working Capital		21 758
Net assets		**151 258**
Financed by:		
Capital		
Opening capital		62 500
Add net profit		64 200
Less drawings		10 442
		116 258
Long-term liabilities		
Long-term loan		35 000
Capital employed		**151 258**

retailer owns (assets), and what the retailer owes (liabilities – what the money has been spent on).

- Assets are items owned or owed to the retailer, normally listed in order of performance; that is, fixed assets are assets held for the long term, while current assets are short-term. The balance sheet usually divides the company's assets into two categories: current and fixed assets. Current assets include items that can be converted into cash within the next twelve months such as cash in hand, stocks and trade debtors. Fixed assets are items that are used for the operation of the business and are not intended for resale or immediate conversion to cash.

- Liabilities are monies owed by the retailer for goods or services or for money borrowed. They are divided into short-term and long-term categories; short-term refers to debts payable within the next accounting period and include trade creditors and bank overdrafts. Long-term liabilities are payable outside this period and include bank loans and debenture stock.

- Capital is money invested in the business by the owner(s) and consists of initial investments plus retained profit less any profit withdrawn as drawings or dividends. Loan capital is provided to a company by banks or debenture holders for the medium to long-term. The value of the company can be derived from its Net Asset Value, expressed as assets (fixed and current) less external liabilities and is equal to its capital structure; in the case of Ogenmar this amounts to £151 258.

From these definitions it is possible to see that the balance sheet of a retailer (in our case, Ogenmar) shows how the retailer is financed in the long term. It is important to note that the balance sheet shows the assets and liabilities of the company at a particular point in time, in this case 31 December 1998. The balance sheet gives valid information to evaluate the retailer's performance for the year only if the year-end data represent the typical conditions during the year.

Both the balance sheet and profit and loss account are historic documents, Within themselves they yield a certain amount of financial information about the retailer's operations and retailing activities but, as will now be obvious, it is rather the way in which these documents are studied in drawing conclusions as to relationships between figures contained within them which holds the key to the maximum amount of useful information to be derived from them. The trading and profit and loss account and balance sheet provide information to analyse the financial state of the business through financial and operating ratios. One of the most important operating ratios is Return on capital employed (ROCE), which measures overall profitability. ROCE shows the percentage return on long-term capital (including debentures if any) invested in the retailer, and is calculated as:

$$\text{ROCE} = \frac{\text{net profit before interest and tax}}{\text{Capital employed}}$$

This enables comparisons to be made between the performance of different retailers for investment purposes, for capital investment decisions and also internally in the evaluation of different divisions or departments. In the retail industry, analysis of ROCE can be found in decisions concerning new properties, retail brand development or withdrawal, and acquisitions.

Cash Flow

The retailer's flow of current resources could be considered in terms of cash or working capital; these two items being effectively the different resources flowing through or circulating within the retail organisation. The main constituents of working capital are stock, debtors, creditors and cash. Thus, a cash flow is subordinate to a working capital flow. It is necessary to emphasise the distinction between cash flows which consider only cash transactions, and funds flows which take account of all movements in assets, liabilities and capital. Positive cash flow may be derived from profits or in other current assets or an increase in current liabilities. Our main focus here is on cash flows.

In retailing, cash enters the operation continuously. Financial transactions in the store are made in cash, including debit cards, and by credit card payments, but both are effectively immediate. But wherever possible, retailers delay payment to their suppliers through the use of settlement terms, which can extend up to 90 days. As a result, many multiple retailers are normally cash-rich and tend not to suffer from liquidity problems. Grocery multiples in particular may be able to turn their stock into sales so quickly that they have a very low working capital requirement. Where liquidity problems do arise, usually caused by slower-than-planned sales or overstocking, then price reductions, markdowns and discounting are used to increase sales to ensure a sufficient flow of cash into the business.

Financial Implications of Mergers and Acquisitions

In the last decade, the balance of power between manufacturers and retailers has gradually shifted towards retailers. Today, the typical retail firm wields considerably more power than it did 10 years ago, and some academics (McGoldrick, 1990; Omar, 1999) argue that retailers now have an upper hand over their suppliers. Mergers among supermarkets in particular have increased the power of these consolidated retailers over their suppliers. Indeed, greater bargaining power over suppliers is often cited as a major reason for retail mergers; by merging, retailers can consolidate their buying power and reduce administrative costs.

The main implication of mergers and/or acquisitions is that the companies available for purchase are often in financial difficulty, and considerable time and financial support is therefore required to restore such companies to profitability. The cost of buying into more successful companies with strong management teams can be extremely high: Wal-Mart's £6.7bn. acquisition of Asda is an indication of the magnitude of these bids.

Financial Start-ups and Entrepreneurial Businesses

Starting-up a successful retail business involves the combination of many elements: hard work, a willingness to live with uncertainty, staying power while the business gets going, and good business skills. The most important element is perhaps having a good idea – that is, for products and/or services that consumers want and need, and of course are willing to pay for. In planning to open a new retail business, a further challenge faced by the owner is how to secure financing. Funds are required to furnish the store, procure merchandise, advertise, and arrange for working capital to cover salaries, insurance, utilities and so forth. Most entrepreneurs are faced with the question of how to raise money. Some common sources of entrepreneurial capital include:

■ Personal sources – where entrepreneurs initially use some of their personal resources for start-up capital. Many entrepreneurs, for example, tap into their personal savings, obtain second mortgages on their houses, or cash-in life insurance policies to obtain start-up capital. Loans from family members and close friends are another popular source. Outside investors will typically insist on some equity participation from the entrepreneur before agreeing to invest in the new venture.

■ Private investors – where many wealthy individuals may want to invest in a new business in the hope of sharing future profits. This is often called informal risk capital. The retailer's ability to tap into this source depends on his/her personal contacts and ability to network. Typically, the entrepreneur will need a written business plan in order to obtain informal risk capital. 'Business Angels' are individuals prepared to invest significant sums in small businesses and accept high levels of risk that the venture fails in return for high financial rewards if it succeeds.

■ Debt capital – is another source of capital for new businesses. Commercial banks are the most popular source of debt capital. Banks lend against a company's assets such as it, inventory and store fixtures.

■ Venture capital – refers to a professionally managed pool of funds that are invested in new ventures. Venture capitalists will expect the owner to invest in the project too, in order to secure their commitment and seek high rates of return on their investment to balance the risk of the start-up and early-stage development. They will usually plan to sell on their investment in the business once it has reached a viable level of profitability, in order to realise their gains.

RISK ASSESSMENT AND PROJECT APPRAISAL TECHNIQUES

In many retailing situations, the most significant factor affecting the level of profitability is probably the quality of retail management decisions affecting the commitment of the retailer's resources to new investments. The reasons which render such strategic decisions so important may include:

■ The involvement of substantial sums of money;

■ The commitment is made for a long period of time, so the element of risk through uncertainty is therefore much greater than in the case of short-term decisions;

■ Many capital investment decisions are impossible to reverse should they appear in the future to have been wrongly made;

■ The success or failure of the retailer's operation may depend upon this single decision; and

■ The future profitability of the organisation may be affected by this investment decision.

According to Glautier and Underdown (1997), capital investment decisions encompass two aspects of long-range profitability: the estimation of future net increases

Figure 7.4   *Methods of Proposed Capital Investment Appraisal*

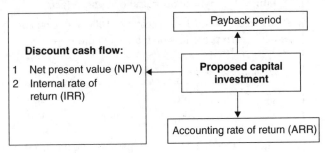

in cash inflows or net savings in cash outlays which will result from the investment; and the calculation of the total cash outlays that are required to effect the investment.

Project Appraisal Techniques

Retailing is centred on profit maximisation, and there is little point in investing in a project unless it is likely to make a profit. Two considerations for capital investment are; firstly, how long it will take to recoup the original cash outlay, and secondly, what return will be earned on the investment. These two fundamental ideas form the basis of the traditional methods of capital investment evaluation. The more commonly used methods of evaluating capital investment proposals are (Figure 7.4):

1 The payback period;
2 The accounting rate of return (ARR);
3 Discounted cash-flow (DCF) techniques, of which there are two main forms:

   ■ the net present value (NPV), and
   ■ the internal rate of returns (IRR);

The Payback Period

This is a basic guide to the desirability of a capital investment project. It measures the time period in which the original outlay on the project is recouped from the cash flows originating from it, and is normally represented as the number of years over which a project must operate before the total net cash flow matches the cash expended on the original investment.

By concentrating exclusively on the recovery of initial costs, however, certain difficulties are immediately apparent as Exhibit 7.1 shows where the payback system can be seen to be concerned solely with the time necessary for the cash flow generated to amount to the original investment, and is not concerned with subsequent earnings. Thus, Dyson (1997) has referred to this method as a crude attempt to assess risk or the possibility of losing all or part of the investment, but that it ignores profitability.

Exhibit 7.1   Payback appraisal of two projects

Two projects X and Y each costing £1000 are being considered, where the net cash flows (£) over each project's working life are given as:

Year	1	2	3	4	5
X	300	300	400	400	400
Y	500	500	100		

It can be seen that project X repays its original investment in three years, and project Y in two years. Under the payback technique whichever projects repays its initial cost soonest is regarded as the most favourable, and project Y would therefore be considered preferable. But this fails to take account of cash flows after the payback date and ignores the fact that X generates further cash flows of £800, while Y only generates a further £100.

The Accounting Rate of Return (ARR)

This method attempts to compare the profit of a project with the capital invested in it. It is usually expressed as a percentage:

$$ARR = \frac{Profit}{Capital\ employed} \times 100$$

Two important problems arising from this definition may be summarised as:

■ The definition of profit – the average annual net profit earned by the project is used. However, the accounting profit can be subject to a number of different assumptions and distortions, and so it is relatively easy to arrive at different profit levels depending upon the accounting policies adopted. In retailing, the most common definition is to take profit before interest and taxation. Thus, the profit included in this equation is a simple average of the profit the project earns over its entire life.

■ The definition of capital employed – this could be either the initial capital employed in the project or the average capital employed over its life.

Depending upon the definitions adopted, the ARR may be calculated in one of two ways as:

using the initial capital employed:

$$ARR = \frac{Average\ annual\ net\ profit\ before\ interest\ and\ taxation}{Initial\ capital\ employed\ on\ the\ project} \times 100$$

using the average capital employed:

$$ARR = \frac{\text{Average annual net profit before interest and taxation}}{\text{Average annual capital employed on the project}} \times 100$$

The accounting rate of return method has several advantages and disadvantages (Dyson, 1997), and the advantages include the following:

- the method is compatible with a similar accounting ratio used in financial accounting;

- it is not difficult to compute;

- it is relatively easy to understand; and

- it draws attention to the notion of overall profit.

Its disadvantages are:

- the net profit used can be subject to different definitions;

- it is not always clear whether the original cost of the investment should be used or whether it is more appropriate to substitute an average for the amount of capital invested in the project;

- the method gives no guidance on what is an acceptable rate of return; and

- it does not take into account the time value of money.

Discounted Cash Flow (DCF)

A point which has been referred to earlier is the timing of money received, and this is fundamental to an appraisal of the value of future cash flows. The 'time value of money' basically means that £1.00 received today can be invested to amount to (with interest) more than £1.00 in a year's time; or can be immediately employed within the business to generate trading growth during the year. It follows, therefore, that because cash received now can be invested in the business or invested outside the business to accumulate interest, early cash flows are preferable to later cash flows.

In DCF, all values are expressed at the same point of time; the present is often the most convenient, but some problems may be better dealt with by a terminal value. For our discussion the present time is considered best. In order to do this we must take the principles of simple and compound interest into consideration. Obviously as money grows with interest, future cash flows must be discounted in order to arrive at what their value would be were they received or paid now – that is, their present value.

The DCF techniques can be seen, therefore, to evaluate projects by recognising the timing concept. Using the rate the retailer pays to borrow capital, projected cash flows

Exhibit 7.2   Net cash flows of two different projects

The following are net cash flows which it is estimated will be produced by two different projects, the initial outlay in each case being £1000.

Year	X (£)	Y (£)
1	200	400
2	200	300
3	300	300
4	300	200
5	400	200
Total	1400	1400
Average	280	280

Since the overall and average net cash flows are the same in each case, each would appear to be equally financially desirable. An inspection of the distribution of the flows over the five years, however, reveals that the net cash flows on project Y are higher in the earlier years, while those of project X are higher in the later years, indicating that project Y may be preferable. What would improve our criterion for making such a decision, however, would be some way of reducing all the net cash flows to a value at the present time, that is effectively stating all cash flows as if they occurred immediately and not at some future date, making them instantly comparable.

can be converted to a present value at the start of the project. If the present value (PV) of the future net cash flows exceeds the capital outlay the project may be regarded favourably. Since all transactions must ultimately end in the movement of cash, it is desirable to express future activity in terms of the cash flow associated with that activity as opposed to the profit, as profit includes items allocated to a period independently of when such items are paid or received.

In operating the DCF technique the appropriate discount rate must be ascertained. We referred to this above as the rate the retailer pays to borrow capital, that is the cost of capital, and we shall return to this concept shortly. The two main methods of using the DCF techniques, the net present value (NPV) and the internal rate of return are now considered.

The Net Present Value (NPV)

This is the present value of the future net cash flows as duly discounted at the relevant interest rate. The selected rate of interest will vary from one retail organisation to another and various rates may be used within the same organisation for different projects where each may be expected to provide different rate of return. The NPV method deals with such problems as whether or not it is advisable to invest £100 for a return of £120 in a year's time if it costs 15 per cent per annum to borrow the capital for investment.

Mini Case Study

Investment Appraisal

Mr Chande, a grocery retailer, can borrow money at a cost of 10 per cent to finance only one of the two projects (computer C and photocopier P) he is considering. The minimum acceptable return of capital for his company is 12 per cent, the difference of 2 per cent representing the compensation for the inherent risk involved. Both projects C and P cost £10000 of initial capital and the net cash flow is as follows (the relevant discount factors at 12 per cent per annum being year 1 = 0.893, year 2 = 0.797 and year 3 = 0.712):

Year	Computer C (£)	Photocopier P (£)
1	3 000	6 000
2	5 000	4 000
3	6 000	2 000
	14 000	12 000

The net cash flows would be discounted as follows:
at 10 per cent discount rate

Year		C (£)		P (£)
1	£3000 × 0.909	2727	£6000 × 0.909	5454
2	£5000 × 0.826	4130	£4000 × 0.826	3304
3	£6000 × 0.751	4506	£2000 × 0.751	1502
		11363		10260
	less capital cost	10000	less capital cost	10000
		1363		260

at 12 per cent discount rate

Year		C (£)		P (£)
1	£3000 × 0.893	2679	£6000 × 0.893	5358
2	£5000 × 0.797	3985	£4000 × 0.797	3188
3	£6000 × 0.712	4272	£2000 × 0.712	1424
		10936		9970
	Less capital cost	10000	Less capital cost	10000
		936		(30)

It can be seen that both projects achieve a return in excess of the cost of capital, but only project C is favourable when compared with the 12 per cent rate, and therefore is to be preferred to buying a photocopier (project P).

Obviously, here the £120 received at the end of the year is more than enough to meet the cost of £100 + £15 interest. The question is whether the investment would still be desirable if £130 were to be received in two years time. Therefore, here, one must calculate compound interest for two years, on £100 at 15 per cent, giving a figure of £132.25 to arrive at the conclusion that the cost exceeds the return and therefore the investment is unfavourable. Alternatively, since £132.25 is a terminal value, one could discount the future return of £130 at 15 per cent per annum for two years and compare this PV of the future return with the investment cost. The factor arrived at (from discount tables) is 0.756 and when applied to the £130 gives a figure of £98.28, and we can again conclude that as the PV of the return does not exceed the cost the investment is unfavourable. The layout used in the mini case example treats the capital cost as a deduction from the PV of the net cash flow. Another method would be to treat the capital investment as a cash outflow occurring immediately, cash outflows being designed as negative and cash inflows as positive.

The Internal Rate of Return (IRR)

This is the rate of interest at which the NPV of a project is zero (that is, the PVs of the cash outflows and inflows are equal). The use of the yield method, therefore, applies principles similar to the NPV method by calculating the rate of discount which when applied to future net cash flows reduces them to a PV equal to the cost of the project. Effectively, the yield is the rate of interest which when paid allows the project to break even. This rate may be found from appropriate tables in some cases or it may be found by trial and error; that is, selecting an interest rate, discounting the project using the factors for this rate and, if the NPV does not come to zero, continuing to select rates until the rate of interest is arrived at which will reduce the NPV to zero. To determine the yield, the cash flow of the project must be tabulated as before; the step-by-step procedure will then be as follows:

1 Estimate a rate of return for the project.

2 Using this rate, calculate the present value as before. If this results in a total inflow which is greater than the total outflow, the estimated rate of interest is too low. Similarly, if the total outflow is greater than the total inflow, the rate is too high.

3 Choose another rate of interest. The result obtained in step 2 above will show whether this needs to be higher or lower, and the size of the difference will give an indication of how much higher or lower it needs to be.

4 Once two rates have been established, one which is too low, and one which is too high, the actual rate of interest is found by interpolation. This simply means that the rate is calculated according to the relative size of the net totals obtained for each percentage.

The following example illustrates the procedure suggested above:

Year	0	1	2	3	4	5
Cash flows (£)	(1000)	200	200	300	300	400

Table 7.3   Calculating the Internal Rate of Return (IRR)

Year (1)	Cash flows in (out) (£) (2)	10% index (3)	Present values (£) (4)	12% index (5)	Present values (£) (6)
0	(1000)	1.00	(1000)	1.00	(1000)
1	200	0.91	182	0.89	178
2	200	0.83	166	0.80	160
3	300	0.75	225	0.71	213
4	300	0.68	204	0.64	192
5	400	0.62	248	0.57	228
Total (Outflow)			(1000)		(1000)
Inflow			1025		971

1 For convenience, the discount factors are only taken to two decimal places in Table 7.3.

2 The rate of interest is estimated at 10 per cent.

3 The present values (PV) are calculated in columns (3) and (4) in Table 7.3. It can be seen that the total inflow is greater than the total outflow, so the rate is too low.

4 A higher rate of interest is required. Since the excess of inflows over outflows is only £25, it is not necessary to go much higher. A rate of 12 per cent is chosen and the present values calculated – columns (5) and (6). It can be seen that for this rate of interest the outflows exceed inflows by £29. Obviously the true rate lies somewhere between 10 per cent and 12 per cent.

5 Since the differences between the two rates are 2 per cent, a proportion of this difference is calculated and added to the lower figure of 10 per cent.

The proportion of the percentage is related to the differences in the total present values. Hence the rate of return is found by interpolation as:

$$10\% + \frac{1025 - 1000}{1025 - 1000 + 1000 - 971} \times 2\% = 11\% \text{ approximately}$$

A careful consideration here will reveal the logic of the calculation. At the 10 per cent rate there is an excess of inflow over outflow of £25. At the 12 per cent rate there is an excess of outflow over inflow of £29. Hence the total difference in the present values between 10 per cent and 12 per cent is £54. In other words, 2 per cent is equal to £54. Now the lower rate, that is 10 per cent, needs to be raised to a point where the excess of £25 is eliminated. The addition therefore is 25/54 of 2 per cent, that is the rate of return is:

$$10\% + \frac{25}{54} \times 2\% = 10.9\%, \text{ round-up to } 11\%$$

In this case it has been possible to find two rates of interest which are fairly close together, but in many cases one is not so fortunate owing to the difficulty of estimating percentages. The smaller the difference between the two percentages, the more precise the result will be, but generally it is not necessary to be very precise. It is often sufficient to use percentages of 5 per cent, 10 per cent, 15 per cent and so on, and to interpolate within a 5 per cent difference.

SOURCES OF FINANCE

The main external sources of capital for established retailers are banks, and for public companies, shareholders; private investors and venture capitalists have a role too, demonstrated in the acquisition of BhS by Philip Green and his financial backers. For many independent retailers the owner's savings and family support provide an important sources of finance. An internally generated source of capital for investment is retained profit, effectively 'ploughed' back into reserves for future use. In a public company retained profit remains after costs, dividends, interest on loans, and tax have been paid. However, high levels of retained profits held as reserves do not necessarily guarantee sufficient cash to undertake investment projects, because of the difference in accounting terms between profit and cash balances.

Shareholders

In considering the issue of shares and debentures as possible sources of finance, it must be remembered that the Companies' Act 1985 permits only a public limited company (plc) to offer its shares and debentures for sale to the general public in the United Kingdom. Students are advised to refer to regulations concerning the issue of shares in standard accounting or legal texts. A public limited company (plc) may issue either ordinary shares and/or preferential shares to its shareholders in order to obtain sufficient capital for investment.

Ordinary shareholders are effectively the owners of a limited company, being entitled to vote at company meetings and to share in the distribution of assets should the company be wound up. They can also be called on to raise more capital, typically to finance a new development or acquire another buisness. The procedure for retailers wishing to raise funds in this way is to make a 'rights issue', whereby existing shareholders have a right to buy the issuing new shares (see Upchurch, 1998). The new shares would be offered to existing shareholders in proportion to their present shareholding; for example, a retailer making a 'one-for-three' rights issue would issue one new share for each three existing shares. If current shareholders do not wish to take up their new shares, then the 'rights' may be sold either to other current shareholders or to new purchasers.

By issuing ordinary shares, the total amount of ordinary dividends paid out is likely to increase, even if the same rate of dividend is maintained. Thus if the retailer's profits do not match the operating profit expectations, the retailer may have difficulty in meeting a higher amount of dividend.

The retailer could issue debentures to pay for a capital investment programme. A debenture is the term applied to a loan made to a limited company under the company's seal and would normally be raised from investors other than banks. Debentures are often subdivided into 'stock' units, for example 15 per cent debentures with a total face value of £500 000 could be subdivided into 5000 units of 15 per cent debenture stock, each with a face value of £100. For retailers, debentures could be attractive because their issue does not affect the balance of voting power, and the interest rate is generally fixed for the life of the loan and the interest payments qualify as a tax-deductible expense. The drawback of this facility is that the company could become highly-geared if it issued more long-term debts. This might cause a problem if profits begin to decline and the company is committed to paying out a high proportion of its earnings in the form of debenture interest.

The retailer could also issue preference shares, which carry the right to preferential payment of dividends compared to ordinary shares. This means that preference shareholders will be paid first out of available profit. From the retailer's point of view, preference shares have the advantage of paying a fixed dividend and of conferring no voting rights on their holders. Preference shares are based on the share's norminal value, so a 15 per cent preference share with a £1 norminal value will pay a fixed annual dividend of £0.15.

Bank Loans

Bank loans are made over a term – a fixed period of time – sometimes at a fixed rate of interest, sometimes at a rate that fluctuates in line with changes in the market rate of interest. Again the level of risk in the retail business can influence the rate of interest negotiated by the bank. Banks are a readily accessible source of finance and, although interest must be paid, issue costs are minimal and interest payments qualify as a tax-debuctible expense. Despite these advantages, during the early 1990s the popularity of bank borrowing declined as a source of finance among retailers (Ghosh, 1994). This may have been due to a combination of factors:

- a tightening of banks' lending criteria;
- imposition of greater restrictions on the use of borrowed funds;
- interest-rate movements; and
- a decline in the general economic situation in the UK and Europe as a whole.

In spite of its importance as a potential source of funding, especially for small and medium-sized retailers, bank borrowing by UK retailers has largely been confined to short and medium-term loans. In contrast (Upchurch, 1998), bank borrowing is predominantly long-term in countries such as Germany and Japan, with bank representation at board level being common.

COST OF FINANCE

As mentioned earlier in this chapter, the cost of capital is central to discounted cash-flow calculations. The sources of finance we have discussed above can be divided into two general categories for cost of capital calculations: ordinary shares and preference shares and debentures. In this section, however, our focus is on calculating the cost of ordinary shares using the capital asset pricing model (CAPM), and the weighted average cost of capital (WACC).

Dividend-based Approach

Investors purchase shares in retail organisations in the expectation of earning a return, comprising dividends plus capital growth – an increase in the market value of their shares. It is therefore possible to argue that the current market value of shares is based on investors' expectations about future returns and that, in order to render its shares attractive to investors, retail organisations must offer returns which are at least equal to these expectations. Investors' minimum returns thus represent the cost of this source of capital to the retailer. In order to determine the cost of ordinary shares, it is necessary to make assumptions that investors discount expected future returns at a personal discount rate; and shares are not redeemed by the retailer, so that future returns are effectively received in perpetuity.

In general, the present value of a perpetual future cash flow is the annual cash flow divided by the discount rate. Amending this so that it relates to the current market value of a share and its anticipated future dividend stream, we get:

$$P_0 = \frac{d}{r}$$

where P_0 is the share's current market price; d is the expected future annual dividend; and r is shareholders' required rate of return.

This formula assumes a constant rate of future dividend, but could be manipulated to reflect other desired results and outcomes. For details of how the formula is constructed and assumptions inherent in its determination students are referred to standard Management Accounting texts.

Weighted Average Cost of Capital (WACC)

The concept of opportunity cost is an important consideration in determining the cost of capital, as capital can be used for a variety of purposes and to choose one means giving up any profit that may have arisen from another. The profit from the best of the alternative uses represents the opportunity cost of the capital.

Various ways are available to arrive at the cost of capital; for instance each project could be identified with a source of capital with which the project will be financed. But this is too arbitrary a guide, so a better method is to weight the proportions of different capital and calculate an average cost of capital from the weighted costs of

Exhibit 7.3   Sources of finance for projects of Ogenmar Ltd

The finance for proposed projects of Ogenmar Ltd is to be provided from equity £200 000; 6 per cent debentures £120000; and a bank overdraft of £80000. The return on equity is 10 per cent and the bank overdraft interest is 8 per cent. The weighted average cost of capital is calculated as follows:

	£	Weighting	Rate (%)	WACC (%)
Equity	200 000	0.5	10	5.0
Debentures	120 000	0.3	6	1.8
Bank	80 000	0.2	8	1.6
Total	400 000	1.0		8.4

$$\text{WACC} = 200\,000/400\,000 = 0.5 \times 10\% = 0.50 \times 100 = 5.0\% \text{ for equity}$$
$$= 120\,000/400\,000 = 0.3 \times 6\% = 0.018 \times 100 = 1.8\% \text{ for debentures}$$
$$= 80\,000/400\,000 = 0.2 \times 8\% = 0.016 \times 100 = 1.6\% \text{ for bank.}$$

the different sources of capital, this rate then being used to discount cash flows to obtain a net present value or for comparison with the yield. This cost of capital will then be the level of return below which no project will be accepted as Exhibit 7.3 demonstrates.

The average cost of capital of 8.4 per cent can be used as the measurement for capital investment appraisal in general; although a certain amount of common sense is required and it is possible that certain types of investment may have to be made by virtue of the nature of the enterprise even if the anticipated return is less than 8.4 per cent. Ogenmar Ltd may feel it is essential to invest in items of research equipment, although the expected return is small, say, in comparison with an item of electronic retailing equipment, where its products are increasingly becoming obsolete due to advances in such areas as retail technology and retail design.

Furthermore, other rates at variance with the average may be used where a project carries certain advantageous financing opportunities. Where Ogenmar, for example, undertakes certain activities even if they are bound to lose money, NPV cannot then be used as a decision rule, but can be used as a measure of what Ogenmar is prepared to lose. It is imperative that the overall position of the company is considered and all relevant factors taken into account when considering an individual project. To this end, Ogenmar will have an overall capital expenditure budget allowing for a disparity in rates in certain cases provided that the total overall capital expenditure programme meets a minimum return figure.

When it is proposed to invest in a capital project this must be checked with the capital expenditure budget to confirm that the proposal is in order as regards the overall position of Ogenmar's budget plans; and it meets the company's requirements as regards individual measures of investment criteria, after considering anything which may imply the proposal should be treated differently from the norm.

The use of the weighted average cost of capital (WACC) to discount the cash flows associated with specific capital investment proposals may be supported or questioned, depending on the specific circumstances. If a project is to be funded from sources already existing within the retail organisation, then it may be reasonable to use the WACC on the basis that the exact origin of these funds is no longer traceable, thereby precluding determination of a more precise cost of capital. On the other hand, there are arguments against the use of the WACC within retail organisations. If a proposal, for example, is to be funded from an identifiable source, then it could be said that the proposal's first priority should be to satisfy the required return of the investors who are funding it. Taking this sort of approach to the cost of capital may create difficulties of its own if the particular types of funding fluctuate over time.

The Capital Asset Pricing Model (CAPM)

The current financial approach to the capital asset pricing model (CAPM) has developed from traditional capital budgeting based on discounting methods (Wensley, 1981), and the use of discount rates related to the systematic risk of the project (its beta, β). The CAPM is based on the risk–return relationship hypothesis, that is the higher the perceived risk of an investment the higher will be the investor's required return; and the lower the perceived risk, the lower the required return. This seems to be a sensible proposition whether it is viewed in the context of a stockmarket or individual capital investment proposal.

The basic principles underlying the CAPM approach, which is the means to apply Markowitz' portfolio theory to resource allocation decisions both at the level of the individual investor (Mossin, 1966) and of the firm (Rubinstein, 1973), will prove to be fairly robust to most of these issues. The CAPM approach is concerned with the selection of the appropriate discount rate to apply to the cost and benefit stream for any particular project. The approach rejects the use of the same discount rate for all projects, and recommends a project-specific rate related to the systematic risk of the project. The systematic risk (unavoidable risk) is not the total risk but only that portion of total risk that is non-diversifiable from the point of view of the portfolio investor.

The level of systematic risk is characterised by its 'beta' which is strictly the covariance between the asset returns and returns from a fully diversified market portfolio. The higher the beta of any particular project, the higher the required return for that project. In using the CAPM, it is important to bear in mind that investment risk cannot be completely removed, we can only attempt to minimise it by careful investment decisions. The availability of computers and advanced statistical software has helped to make the application of this model easier to use and understand. Regression analysis could be used in combination with factor analysis to compare and evaluate returns on two or more securities simultaneously for investors and retailers.

Limitations in the use of the CAPM are that since the model has been derived from finance theory, it has a high degree of internal consistency. There are, however, a number of problems in extending the model to resource allocation decisions on projects within the firm. An analysis of the project cash flows on the basis of the discount rate related to the project's beta gives reasonable answers. The problem is that the determinants of the correct Beta in this case (Wensley, 1981) are complicated and relate to such factors as the link between cash-flow forecast errors and the forecast errors of market returns as well as asset life, the growth trend in the cash flows, and the pattern of expected cash flows over time.

Finally, it has been recognised that the existence of a positive NPV against the appropriate risk-adjusted discount rate cannot be taken as the automatic indicator of acceptance. A large NPV must reflect anticipated scarcity or competitive advantage. Retail management must, therefore, decide how much effort should be expended on the basic application of the CAPM compared with a strategic analysis of competitive advantage in any resource allocation decision.

BUDGETING AND FINANCIAL CONTROL OF RESOURCES

A budget is a short-term financial plan that relates a retailer's expenditure to its objectives within a given time period. Each budget requires a formal, quantitative approach that targets the achievement of one or more objectives. It aids the coordination and control of the retailer's acquisition and utilisation of resources at the appropriate time. It is a function of the coordination of data and opinions of a number of managers in the organisation based on:

■ Future expectations regarding the retail environment

■ Past retail management experience which can be used to shape projections of likely retail performance

■ Expected retail management influences on future activity that is necessary to direct future operations.

The number and level of managers involved in budgetary planning depends on the retailer's approach of financial decision-making. If it operates 'top down', it is senior management driven whilst 'bottom up', uses middle managers' contributions to the development of the budget. But in order to be successful it must coordinate its expenditure between different functions and levels, and control it through analysis of variances between expected and actual business performance.

In practice a number of budgets are prepared at different levels and for different functions and elements within the retailer that include:

■ Property: stores, warehouses and office accommodation; fixtures and fittings
■ Equipment: computers, and other equipment
■ Staff costs: number and type of management and employees
■ Personnel: training, benefits
■ Central administration: payroll, cash and credit management, audit, legal compliance.
■ Sales Promotion and Advertising
■ Store operations: utilities, cleaning and maintenance, security
■ Stock holding (inventory)

Some of these will involve capital expenditure costs for large, long-term investments including stores, distribution centres, and new equipment. Others will be operating expenses incurred in the day-to-day running of the business. The individual budgets are combined into an overall budget for the retail business known as a master budget, comprising profit and loss, balance sheet and cash flow. Once prepared, the master budget can be closely examined to see whether all the parts of the plan can be accommodated. For example, if the sales budget increases substantially this may require changes in the stock and staff costs budgets.

The preparation of individual budgets can be a useful exercise even if nothing further is then done about them, since the exercise forces retail management to look ahead. It is a natural human tendency to be always looking back, but past experience is not always a guide for the future. If retail managers are asked to produce a budget, at least it does encourage them to examine what they have done in relation to what they could do. The full benefits of a budgeting system are only realised when it is also used for control purposes. This is done by the constant comparison of actual results with the budgeted results, and then taking any necessary corrective action. This leads us to consider in more detail the areas of internal budgetary control.

Internal Budget Controls

In a typical retail organisation, budgetary control has several important features:

- retail management responsibilities have to be clearly defined;
- individual budgets lay down a detailed plan of action for a particular sphere of responsibility;
- retail managers have a responsibility to adhere to their budgets once the budgets have been approved;
- the actual performance is constantly monitored and compared with the budgeted results;
- corrective action is taken if the actual results differ from the budget;
- departures from budgets are only permitted if they have been approved by senior retail management; and
- variances (differences) that are unaccounted for will be subjected to individual investigation.

Any variance that does occur should be carefully investigated, and if it is considered necessary then the current actual performance will be immediately brought back into line with the budget. In some instances the budget itself will be changed if there is an unexpected increase in sales. Such changes may have an effect on other budgets, so changes cannot be undertaken in isolation: the sequences in the budgeting cycle are shown in Figure 7.5.

Uses of Budgets

One of the key uses of budgets in retailing is the measurement of sales and expenditure and their impact on profitability and cash flow. Sales planning is problematic due to the many business environment and competitor factors that are beyond the

Figure 7.5   *The Budgeting Cycle*

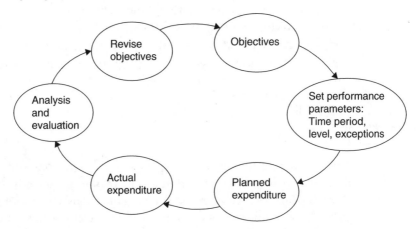

Exhibit 7.4   5 year sales plan for an e-retailer start-up

	2000 plan	2000 actual	2001 plan	2002 plan	2003 plan	2004 plan
Sales units	82000	6000	209875	419750	839500	1679000
Gross sales (£)	153300	12000	419750	839500	1679000	3358000
Costs of sales	61320	4800	167900	335800	671600	1343200
Gross profit	91980	7200	251850	503700	1007400	2014800
Depreciation	(1000)	(1000)	(60000)	(62000)	(62000)	(62000)
Operating costs	(40000)	(4000)	(80000)	(90000)	(100000)	(120000)
Marketing	(200000)	(5000)	(350000)	(500000)	(700000)	(800000)
Website development	(20000)	(8000)	(75000)	(50000)	(50000)	(100000)
Interest income/(expense)	20000	20000	5000	2000	5000	25000
Profit/(Loss)	(149020)	9200	(308140)	(196300)	100400	957800

retailer's control. Nevertheless, the importance of an accurate sales forecast must be emphasised. It should be realistic because over-optimism about the future may lead to increased capital expenditure, which may not be recoverable at a later date. It may disguise a deteriorating sales position and fail to create a high enough level of cost savings to produce a satisfactory profit. On the other hand, unduly pessimistic sales forecasts may lead to an under-investment in new projects, or merchandise, and lead to missed sales opportunities.

Exhibit 7.4 illustrates the sales plan for a small scale e-retailer start-up, its expenditure for five years, and the actual performance achieved in 2000. During the year, the managers dramatically reduced expenditure on marketing, operating and website development costs. In the light of much lower than expected sales in 2000, expenditure budgets were subsequently reviewed downwards for 2001–4. Without a severe round of cost cutting, weak sales and inadequate cash generation to pay for its expenses will lead the company to 'burn' its existing cash and ultimately fail.

SUMMARY

This chapter has identified that financial planning is one of the key areas that supports retail management operation in all its forms. Retailers are likely to be concerned about the financial well-being of their organisations, since their operations are geared to profit generating strategies. Thus, the chapter demonstrates how retailers make their capital investment decisions, how financial planning and control affect retail management, and how the availability of funds tends to shape the direction of investments. In this way, retailers constantly investigate their performance using both marketing and financial tools.

The chapter started with brief reviews of how and for whom financial information is relevant and how regulators require retailers to collect a great deal of information. Such information is used for both internal and external operations; in addition, capital investment decisions are made based upon this information. Capital investment decisions encompass two aspects of the long-range profit plan; estimating the future net increases in cash inflows or net savings in cash outlays which will result from an investment, and calculating the total cash outlays required to carry out an investment. There are several techniques for appraising investment proposals from a financial point of view, and three well-known techniques are:

1 the payback method, which emphasises the length of time required to recoup the investment outlay;

2 the accounting rate of return, which seeks to express the average estimated yearly net inflows as a percentage of the net investment outlays for the purpose of assessing the profitability of a proposed investment; and

3 discounted cash-flow methods, which attempt to evaluate an investment proposal by comparing the present value of the net cash inflows accruing over the life of the investment with the present value of the funds to be invested.

The chapter has highlighted the fact that the amount of money required by retailers for capital investment projects is considerable because capital is required for stock, equipment, premises and running expenses. In general, the sources of such capital may include retailer profit, shareholders, banks, investors and venture capital. In assessing the cost of capital, two measurement instruments have been reviewed – the capital asset pricing model and the weighted average cost of capital. The weighted average cost of capital is based on the concept of opportunity cost, while the capital asset pricing model is developed from traditional capital budgeting based on discounting methods. The use of discount rates is related to the systematic risk of the project (its beta value).

The final section of the chapter has discussed budgeting and financial control within retail organisations, defining the budget as a quantitative plan for estimating the future income and expenditure of the organisation.

Case Study

Financial Growth and Profitability of the UK Food and Drinks Industry

Financial growth and profit margins in the UK food and drink industry strengthened significantly in 1997, but these profit levels are not likely to be sustainable unless companies can drive top-line sales revenue growth. According to OC&C Strategy Consultants, the profitability of the UK food and drink industry is improving but at the expense of revenue growth. In their analysis of the 1998 Corporate Index (see *The Grocer*, 5 December 1999) they hinted that the growth in profitability of the UK food and drink industry improved during 1998. This growth showed operating margins up by 0.5 per cent to 7.0 per cent and the average return on capital employed (ROCE) up by 0.4 per cent to 20.0 per cent. In many cases this has been achieved at the expense of revenue growth. They predicted that 'the real long-term winners will be those who can drive future profit improvements by growing the top line'.

Table 7.4 shows profitability comparisons for large and small companies over the previous two years. For both sets profitability has improved (with about 70 per cent of companies showing increased margins year on year) while the differential in profitability remains, with the larger companies enjoying a 2.0 per cent margin advantage. Unusually, average revenues have declined across the index for both large and small firms in 1998 (see Table 7.5). This may result from the effect of the ongoing process of rationalisation and focus through disposals of non-core activities within the industry. In the 1997 Index, OC&C argued that management had become 'distracted from their long-term aim of creating new customer value and hence new shareholder value rather than simply unlocking the wasted shareholder value hidden in inefficient operations and broken business processes'. 1999 figures suggest this assessment was an accurate one.

Table 7.4

Profitability and Performance Variations

Company sales	No of companies in index	Revenue growth (%)	Profit margin (%)		Return on capital (%)		Increasing profit margin this year '99 (%)
			'96/'97	'97/'98	'96/'97	'97/'98	
>£100m	86	(1.7)	6.6	7.1	20.0	20.4	70.9
<£100m	66	(2.1)	4.4	5.1	13.8	14.2	68.2
Total	152	(1.7)	6.5	7.0	19.6	20.0	69.7

Source: *The Grocer*, 5 December 1998.

(Continued)

Table 7.5

Trends in Revenue Growth (%)

Year	'93/'94	'94/'95	'95/'96	'96/'97	'97/'98
All companies	3.8	4.4	4.1	5.7	−1.7
Companies > £100m	3.8	4.4	4.1	5.6	−1.7
Companies < £100m	3.6	5.8	3.5	9.3	−2.1

Source: *The Grocer*, 5 December 1998.

OC&C argues there is a limit to how far one can go in terms of cost-cutting and rationalising the business portfolio.

In the face of relentless margin pressure from the ever-more powerful retail trade, companies must exploit all opportunities for profit growth by:

■ building business systems which ensure ongoing, institutionalised cost and process efficiency;

■ continuously challenging the contribution of every business unit and making ruthless decisions as to which businesses are value-creating versus those where value can best be created under alternative ownership;

■ participating in any value-creating sector restructuring, seizing a share of the value to be created through capacity consolidation and rationalisation; and

■ demonstrating the vision and focus of effort required to develop profitable, organic revenue growth.

OC&C's analysis shows that the companies with the highest profit margins are those with large and strong brands including, Walkers, Nutricia, Cadbury Schweppes, Weetabix, Coca Cola Schweppes Beverages, Kraft Jacobs Suchard, and Bestfoods. They continue consistently to deliver superior margins improving year on year in nearly all cases. Among the smaller companies, alongside the familiar niche-branded competitors are Lofthouse of Fleetwood (the Fisherman's Friend brand), which heads the list in its first year of inclusion in the Index. Other new entrants that make it into the top 10 are Basildon Dairy Foods, Betty's & Taylors of Harrogate (Tea) and Dunhills (sugar confectionery, including the Haribo brand).

This list demonstrates that a company does not have to be one of the large, dominant brands to be a strong competitor in the UK food and drink industry (but it certainly helps!). The successful companies include smaller niche (predominantly branded) competitors and those in lower profile 'upstream' businesses (Devro, for example, is global leader in the supply of cellulose and collagen-based skins and casings to the meat processing industry.

OC&C believe that long-term, sustainable profitable growth opportunities are available to all companies but that to seize these opportunities often requires a major mindset shift for management who have spent recent years focused on rationalisation and cost-cutting. Their key finding was that many companies that have spent the last few years driving costs out of their businesses and struggling with the strategic challenge of refocusing effort and investing for growth are now successful. They suggested that those who identify strategically robust growth opportunities and, at this point in the cycle, demonstrate the courage to invest appropriate resources against them will be the long-term winners.

SEMINAR QUESTIONS FOR DISCUSSION

1 From reading the case study, what do you consider to be the key requirements for successful profit growth in the UK food and drinks industry?

2 Would you say small companies are in any way disadvantaged in terms of competition within this industry?

References

Dyson, J.R. (1997) *Accounting for Non-Accounting Students*, 4th edn (London: Financial Times/Pitman Publishing).

Ghosh, A. (1994) *Retail Management*, 2nd edn (New York: The Dryden Press).

Glautier, M.W. and Underdown, B. (1997) *Accounting Theory and Practice*, 6th edn (London: Pitman Publishing).

The Grocer, 'Shrinkage: A Costly Game', 26 May, p. 37.

McGoldrick, P.J. (1990) *Retail Marketing* (Maidenhead: McGraw-Hill).

Mossin, J. (1966) 'Equilibrium in a Capital Asset Market', *Econometrics*, vol. 34 October, pp. 768–83.

Omar, O.E. (1999) *Retail Marketing* (London: Financial Times/Pitmans).

The European Retail Theft Barometer (2001) Centre for Retail Research, Nottingham.

Rubinstein, M. (1973) 'A Mean-Variance Synthesis of Corporate Finance Theory', *Journal of Finance*, vol. 28, March, pp. 167–81.

Upchurch, A. (1998). *Management Accounting: Principles and Practice* (London: Financial Times/Pitman Publishing).

Wensley, R. (1981) 'Strategic Marketing: Betas, Boxes, or Basics', *Journal of Marketing*, Summer, pp. 173–83.

Retail Location Strategy

INTRODUCTION

This chapter introduces the retail location process and its strategic implications, through an assessment of the characteristics and availability of different locations. It moves on to review the decision-making process starting with the general search and the identification of a geographical area in which to trade. The final section summarises the practical issues arising from the selection of a site, its acquisition and related costs.

LOCATION STRATEGY

Store location is one of the most important determinants of retailer success. The cost of property development, rents and other operating charges represent a major financial element for retailers. The relative inflexibility of investment in property, particularly arising from leases in the UK, leads to location being amongst the most long-term decisions to be undertaken by retailers. As such it finds a central place in the company's strategy, both as a resource and in its function as the final point of distribution that provides consumers with access to products and services. More specifically, stores will be designed and located to meet consumer needs, through the retailer's market segmentation strategy, to gain competitive advantage. Location strategy will determine other property decisions extending back into the supply chain through the siting of distribution centres and warehouses.

At the strategic level, store decisions are made around issues of size to accommodate the product offer and market positioning. In turn, size will largely determine policy towards urban or out-of-town locations, although other constraints such as availability of sites and government planning restrictions can oblige companies to turn to new or different types of location. The number of new sites or relocations depends on the desired rate of growth or consolidation. Demand for property is in part sectoral, food multiple retailers, for example, demonstrate a consistent demand for new sites; but partly too it reflects the strength of individual retail brands and their property portfolios. In the UK, growth strategies of companies such as Matalan and IKEA seek to extend their geographical reach; Next, on the other hand, seeks not only to expand the number of stores but also to trade from larger stores.

During the 1990s, the deflationary effect of static sales and downwards price pressure from consumers was experienced across much of the retail industry, leaving retailers with property as their main upward cost. Rents that might have been negotiated downwards in this situation were maintained at least in prime locations by competitive pressure from new domestic and international entrants seeking strategic locations; the demand for flagship stores against limited supply in London's Oxford Street is a typical driver of rent increases. Many retailers in the UK have 25-year property leases with upward-only rent reviews at five-year intervals. In these circumstances they have been faced with the need to re-examine their property portfolio. Caught between growing aspirational brands and discounters, mature clothing retailers including Marks and Spencer, Arcadia and Littlewoods have re-organised their portfolios, reducing the number of stores they trade from, and in the case of C&A, withdrawing from the UK market completely. However, rationalisation itself has long-term implications, and may not be cost-effective or even feasible within a short time frame (Guy, 1999). The nature of retail site selection is changing too, as 'the easy sites go first' in a competitive environment. As competition has become more intense, so experience has become a less reliable guide to the future and led retailers to evaluate locational implications in increasing detail (Clarke *et al.*, 1997).

Strategic decisions are ultimately implemented at store level. However, to achieve this degree of detailed planning the decision-making process must work through three levels. Clarke *et al.* (1997) propose that:

■ The strategic or macro level to plan the retailer's locational objectives

■ Operational management level, to which strategic goals of sales and profit are directed

■ Individual store level where tactical and immediate decisions are implemented through local marketing policies.

This structure of decision-making can be extended further into an assessment of the external environment which is then interpreted internally within the organisation and culminates in the creation and maintenance of the property portfolio (Hernandez and Bennison, 2000).

The strategic aim of the retailer will concern the individual performance of each store, which must be located to maximise its return on investment. The market char-

Figure 8.1 *Levels of Decision-Making in Location Strategy*

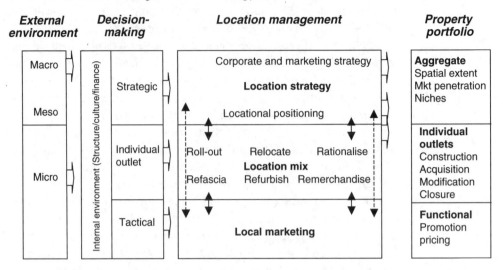

Source: Hernandez and Bennison (2000).

acteristics of its catchment area, size and geographical proximity, and competition will determine store profitability. The types of decision available to retailers at store level depend on the expansive or defensive nature of corporate strategies, and the costs and risks associated with them, are shown in Figure 8.1.

TYPES OF LOCATION

Store location is fundamentally concerned with the distribution of the population, and shopping locations that arise from a wide variety of stores and outlets. The UK has many distinctive shopping areas, from urban high streets to regional out-of-town centres, the characteristics of each affording retailers different strategic opportunities. Urban locations constrain the size of a store by creating barriers to large store development, but also create opportunities for smaller-scale discount food retailers, and specialised formats such as Tesco Metro, and Sainsbury's Local. Out-of-town locations, on the other hand, favour large-scale retail developments and afford greater accessibility and convenience by car, but provide limited opportunities for independent retailers and small-scale enterprises.

The Urban Environment

The complexity of urban areas has attracted particular attention and offers a diversity of opportunities. Different types of shopping area define urban retailing with town and city centres providing the core area through their wide choice of stores and merchandise. Further out, the development of suburban shopping accompanied housing development in the 1920s and 1930s, and the appearance of small suburban centres consisting of between 4 and 10 shops to serve residents of the local estates (Dawson, 1983). Other urban locations include inner suburban and district centres which

> **Exhibit 8.1   The definition of types of urban shopping centre**
>
> **Town centre**. City, town and traditional suburban centres providing a broad range of facilities and services that act as a focus for the community and public transport. In large cities the main shopping centres usually perform the role of town centres and are supported by district centres.
>
> **District centre**. Groups of shops separate from the town centre, usually containing at least one food supermarket or superstore, and non-retail services such as banks, building societies and restaurants.
>
> **Local centre**. A small grouping usually comprising a newsagent, a general grocery store, a sub-post office and occasionally a pharmacy, a hairdresser and other small shops of a local nature.
>
> Source: PPG6 Annex A.

provide fewer facilities and less choice, but offer accessibility and convenience in compensation. Even smaller centres fit within the hierarchy of retail provision, comprising neighbourhood and, lastly, local centres from which limited ranges of goods can be accessed most conveniently.

The spatial dimensions of retail locations can be understood not only from a retailing perspective, where goods are exchanged, but also in a *social* context as the 'locale' in which people socialise and interact with each other (Clarke, 1999). In this sense shopping areas in general can be seen as places of social activity, and centres valued in terms of public and social life. They are complex, socially constructed arenas of consumption of retail goods as well as places of leisure and entertainment, an environment for the interplay between retailer and consumer directed by social and economic factors (Lowe and Wrigley, 1996).

Town centres can be understood, too, from the perspective of *institutional analysis* of power and influence. The physical evolution of town centres reflects the change of relations between the main agents including property owners, investors and developers (Evans, 1997). The practical implications for location strategy lie in the retailer's analysis of urban spaces, and the ways in which it will fit into the urban location to enhance its overall attractiveness as a destination.

Public policy has shaped retail location both within and outside the town centre. The Town and Country Planning Act of 1947 introduced a planning control system in which local authorities have assessed planning applications against their development plans. However, regulation did not bring a consistent approach to post-war town centre development which has gone through a number of stages (Table 8.1). Compulsory purchasing in the 1960s and 1970s led to comprehensive restructuring. During the 1980s a more disengaged approach by the government led to a weakening in town centre monopolies. The decentralisation of retailing that had begun with the development of suburbs through the 1930s–1950s now took on different forms; out-of-town development not only of retail parks but also larger regional centres, business parks and leisure complexes (Figure 8.2).

The city centre must be an unrivalled location in the conurbation as a whole and perceived as such by the public. At a regional level, comparisons between the major European cities of Bristol, Hanover and Bordeaux show that retail quality and loca-

Table 8.1   *Town-Centre Development since 1950*

Since 1945, five phases of town centre physical restructuring have been found in the UK:

■ 1950s postwar reconstruction
■ 1960s comprehensive development
■ 1970s large-scale, better quality shopping centres, such as Eldon Square in Newcastle
■ 1980s speciality centres; infilling in context leading to small-scale specialist shops, and some leisure facilities
■ Late 1980s refurbishment of earlier schemes, adding food courts and leisure facilities and leading to the concept of town-centre management

Source: DoE (1992).

Figure 8.2   *Locational Positioning*

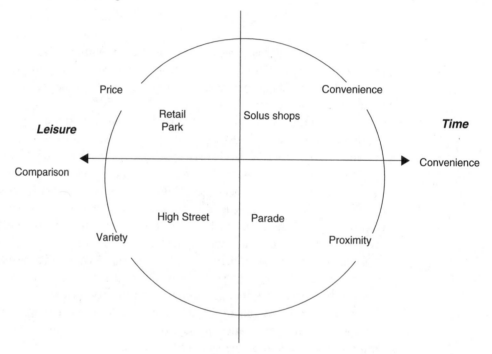

Source: Davies and Clarke (1994).

tional strength remain the most important measures of town-centre attractiveness (NRPF, 1996). Smaller towns and suburban centres are the losers in the evolving scenario of polarisation between the larger urban and regional locations offering strong comparison shopping opportunities, and local ones based on convenience and proximity. Smaller town centres that lack the scale to offer a full range of stores for comparison shopping, but are not small enough to provide convenience and speed, will struggle to maintain their appeal.

The impact of out-of-town development on town centres is variable, in some cases such as Dudley causing major decline, in other larger city centres such as Sheffield contributing to visible deterioration in the quality of shopping and the street environment. The effect of the retail development at Bluewater Park on other centres has highlighted the role of town-centre management to support the coordination and control of wide-ranging activities and the support of programmes to improve the urban environment.

The impact has been felt across all retail sectors. There is evidence that large food-stores in edge-of-town centres and out-of-centre locations reduce the market share of the principal food retailers in market towns and district centres by between 13–50 per cent. In 1994, Safeway announced the closure of 17 town-centre stores in the light of declining profitability. The Boots Company announced a strategic review of its £800 m. property portfolio brought about by the threat of e-commerce as well as a continuing drift of customers to edge-of-town shopping with a view to creating value from its town-centre sites (*Property Week*, 2000). However, restrictions on new large-scale developments and the diminished level of competition in food retailing in urban centres has led to the reappearance of supermarket facias in central locations. Discount foodstores such as Aldi and Lidl moved into urban areas in the absence of strong competition in the 1990s, and more recently larger food retailers including Sainsbury and Tesco have expanded their Local and Metro formats.

Shopping Malls

Urban shopping centres (Table 8.2) possess a distinctive identity and provide convenience shopping through their many individual store units typically offering a broad selection of comparison goods. But central locations also bring problems: the right sized location may not be available, and may attract major retailers already represented in the town centre. The shopping centre must be seen as part of the wider, central shopping area that integrates into the town centre as a whole (Guy, 1994). Shopping malls in general are characterised by their space utilisation; the first stage of the development will require an anchor tenant, a major retailer such as a department store. The aim will be to provide a strong branded destination store around which to group an appropriate retailer mix. The second phase of development will be directed to attracting other tenants, usually to offer a wide range of retail goods. There will be some discouragement to competition between tenants and multiples are preferred to independent retailers for their reliability and brand strengths.

Table 8.2   *UK Major Urban Shopping Centre Developments (1999)*

Centre	GLA (square metres)
Manchester Arndale	116 250
Milton Keynes The centre: mk	111 000
Nottingham Victoria Centre	92 900
Croydon The Whitgift	88 236
Newcastle-upon-Tyne Eldon Square	78 965
Watford The Harlequin	78 965
Peterborough Queensgate Centre	74 320
Luton Arndale	69 675
Reading The Oracle	65 000

Source: Retail Week/Healey and Baker 1999.

By 1999 there were around 900 in-town shopping centres occupying over 11.5 million square metres of retail space in the UK (Mintel, 2000). The average size of UK shopping centres is just under 14 000 square metres, although some very large schemes within major towns and city centres comprise more than 65 000 square metres. In-town schemes continue to be popular with around 300,000 additional square metres of new space added in 1999, and in some instances retailers have preferred in-town locations to out-of-town ones where existing trading might be adversely affected.

Out-of-town Shopping Malls

The growth of out-of-town retailing in the UK has been discussed in terms of three waves of retail decentralisation (Schiller, 1986):

1   1970s – the first wave of development took place in the form of food supermarkets and hypermarkets of over 2500 square metres trading space, with parking space which encouraged more infrequent bulk buying of food.

2   1980s – retail warehouses for furniture, carpets, electrical goods and DIY developed with leisure and fast-food restaurants. This type of development continued with the 1980s development of suburban retail parks, typically near existing food stores. From one park in 1980, 250 were in existence by 1992.

3   The development of regional shopping centres. In the 1980s between 35–50 were envisaged although only five were open by 1990 and a further six completed during the 1990s.

A fourth wave has been identified following the economic recession of the early 1990s, when out-of-town developments began to combine value for money with a more upmarket and quality image. This phase saw the arrival of the warehouse club and factory-outlet formats from the USA (Fernie, 1998).

The dynamics of changing locations lie in the drive for greater market share. Retailers have preferred out-of-town destinations (Table 8.3) as they are less costly and complex to enter than town-centre locations. They are found in areas of expanding demand due to their accessibility and decentralisation from urban centres. Customers express a preference for the quality of the environment in the centres, primarily

Table 8.3   *Measures of Out-of-Town Attractiveness*

Push out of town centre locations	Pull into out-of-town locations
■ Decline in the urban economy ■ Dispersal of population and jobs ■ Environmental problems ■ Transport problems, such as car parking, poor public transport ■ More mobile population ■ Failure of town centres to adapt to customer expectations	■ Attractiveness of the product offer: wide ranges of food influence the number of shops and product diversification ■ Cleaner, safer, more accessible and with more facilities ■ Retail of home-based leisure pursuits ■ Customers values have shifted

---

Exhibit 8.2 European shopping centre development

Ireland and Great Britain. Shopping centres are characterised by the absence of hypermarkets as shopping-centre anchors. Retail parks are also important in these countries.

France, Holland, Belgium. The hypermarket is the anchor of the shopping centre and also the promoter. In France, local authorities have had a big influence on the opening of new shopping centres. A large number of shopping centres are the result of town-planning considerations for expanding and articulating town centres.

Germany and Sweden. The shopping centres opened from the 1980s onwards are smaller than previous centres and lack a hypermarket. Germany is well below the European average in gross lettable area (GLA) per inhabitant, whilst in Sweden the rate of new openings has stabilised.

Greece, Portugal, Italy and Spain. This block of Mediterranean countries shows the greatest activity in European retail development. Apart from Spain the other countries in this group have quite a low concentration of shopping centres. Possible reasons include the preeminence of medium-sized shopping centres in Italy, and the failure of large retail areas to establish themselves; in Greece and Portugal the lower rate of economic growth has set back retail development.

Eastern European countries. This group of countries is seeing the start of a revolution in retailing that occurred in Spain in the late 1960s. Business opportunities will lie mainly in centres which include a hypermarket, given the greater demand for basic products in these countries, thereby benefiting French hypermarket retail companies.

Source: Molla and Frasquet (1997).

---

spaciousness and convenience; whilst the centres' accessibility by car has enabled consumers to take greater control over where they shop. This combination of favourable factors leads to increased expenditure: at the Meadowhall Shopping Centre near Sheffield it was found that an average customer spent £50 as opposed to £10–20 in existing centres (Reynolds and Howard, 1994).

The shortage of supply of new sites set against a continuing consumer demand for out-of-town shopping has maintained a strong property market for both occupancy of centres and investment in them by institutions.

Retail Parks

Retail parks formed the second wave of out-of-town development. Their origins were found in the retail discount warehouses of the 1970s, with large units attracting customers for bulky, low-value goods that could be accessed by car, typically in the DIY, electrical and furniture and carpet sectors. Most developments were proposed for industrial estates and out-of-centre development (Table 8.4).

As the development process became more formalised, retail parks took on specific characteristics, and from 1985 their image was made more respectable by dropping the reference to 'warehouse' (Thomas and Fernie, 1990). The parks, as they came to be known, consist of more than three single-storey retail units, each over 10 000 square

Table 8.4   *Types of Location*

Edge-of-centre for shopping purposes has been defined as a location within easy walking distance, 200–300 metres from the main shopping area, although in practice this distinction is not clearly made. Often parking spaces will be available to serve the centre as well as the store. For other usages, for example offices, the distance from the centre may be further away

Out-of-centre describes a location clearly separate from the town centre but not necessarily out of town

Out-of-town describes a development on a greenfield site or on land not currently within the urban boundary

---

Source: Annex A PPG6 (1996).

feet, let as a single retail entity and taking up more than 50000 square feet in total. Retail parks, however, could be far more substantial than this minimal definition suggests, with some almost as large as the smaller regional shopping centres, including purpose-built pedestrian areas as well as joint car-parking facilities (Guy, 1994). In the UK the number of sites had increased to 489 by January 1999, although extensions to existing sites account for the more recent developments. Their significance cannot be underrated, as some 245 sites comprising over 100000 sq ft of trading area let to five or more tenants account for two-thirds of total retail park space (Mintel, 1999). In all, retail parks occupy over three times as much trading space as out-of-town shopping centres.

Planning constraints have been particularly influential on the development of retail parks, and as the rate of completions exceeds the consent for new schemes so the development pipeline is drying up. Restrictions on occupancy have limited the use of many of the sites to the retail of 'bulky goods', for example, DIY materials that cannot be easily located in town centres, and the location and physical structures of the stores themselves restrict usage to this type of retailing. Where suitable retail parks have a non-food use, a recent trend for developers has been to reconfigure suitable locations for high street and comparison goods retailers. Fosse Park, Leicester, is the model for this type of scheme even though there are only half a dozen or so fashion-dominated retail parks in the whole of the UK.

Factory Outlets

During the 1990s, out-of-town development was further extended with the arrival of factory outlets and warehouse clubs, both successful US concepts. These were distinguished from previous developments by their specialised, and specifically value-driven formats (Fernie, 1996). Factory outlets resemble shopping centres in their size and controlled tenant mix, but their upmarket focus on clearance of branded merchandise, and their diverse and in many cases original design makes them stand apart. Warehouse clubs have been the less successful of the two. This format is based on membership and provides access to bulk, low-priced purchases, largely from home and electrical product ranges. Although Costco arrived in the UK in 1994, its impact has been limited apart from initial competitive responses in the food retailing and cash-and-carry wholesaling sectors.

Factory outlets attract customers through the breadth of their designer-brand assortment, and are predominantly occupied by fashion retailers at low prices. The concept provides a solution to manufacturers and brand leaders for their old stock; sale lines can be cleared well away from their retail customer base, and the locations of these outlets are evenly spread between urban centres, edge-of-town and out-of-town to provide some degree of protection for the brand. It also allows brand leaders to try out new products and measure the customer's response. Outlet centre leases often contain specific provisions – such as minimum discounts to be offered – and management teams have to adapt tenant mix, centre configuration, lease terms and rental levels to maximise turnover and investment value. The success of the concept is reflected in sales of £1.2bn. from 29 outlets trading in 1999, and opportunities for leisure and other ancillary facilities will extend their appeal in the future by widening the centres' catchment areas and lengthening visit times.

From the UK, the factory outlet concept has moved into Europe with some 800 000 square metres scheduled for completion by the end of 2000, more than doubling the amount of space across the continent in just two years. A measure of success for the format in France has been the number of visitors, over three million at the first French outlet at Troyes, to buy discounted leading designer brands such as Armani, Versace and Calvin Klein. However, tighter planning polices may limit the number of centres developed both in France and elsewhere in Europe where unfamiliarity with the concept may mean the number of outlet completions will remain relatively small.

Regional Centres

In the UK, major regional out-of-town shopping centres account for a majority of the space defined as out-of-town shopping locations. Regional centres are defined as enclosed free-standing centres of at least 50 000 square metres gross retail space built outside existing town centres (Guy, 1994; PPG6, 1996). Drawn from American and European developments, regional centre proposals proliferated during the 1980s in response to retail demand and relaxation of government planning restrictions. They now form the largest out-of-town locations, with an extensive choice of stores and an increasingly diverse range of facilities for eating out and entertainment (Table 8.5).

Although over 40 schemes were outlined by the late 1980s, many of these failed to materialise as economic recession and government attitude against out of town development hardened. Nevertheless by 1998 total space occupied by regional centres amounted to some 17 million square feet with a final 2.6 million added during 1999. Their popularity has been demonstrated by the size of their catchment area and is reflected in the rents demanded by their landlords; regional centre stores represent expensive operational costs. The most recent two in Table 8.5, Bluewater and Braehead, provide a combination of comparison shopping consisting of major High Street brands with leisure activities, including cinemas, cafes and restuarants. They are distinctively positioned, too, to appeal to the mobile and affluent consumer through the quality of their design and retail mix. However, despite their popularity with consumers there are unlikely to be any more centres on this scale unless planning restrictions on out-of-town development change.

Table 8.5   *Regional Centre Development, 1976–99*

Location	Opening	Number of outlets	GLA	Estimated number of annual visitors (millions)
Braehead Park, Glasgow	1999	100	600 000	20
Bluewater, Dartford, Kent	1999	315	149 574	30
Metro Centre, Tyne and Wear	1986	350	147 154	30
Merry Hill Centre, Dudley	1989	250	144 000	24
Trafford Centre, Manchester	1998	280	130 064	26
Lakeside, Thurrock, Essex	1990	311	126 430	25
Meadowhall, Sheffield	1990	270	124 490	31
Brent Cross, Hendon, London	1976	105	78 000	13
The Mall, Cribbs Causeway, Bristol	1998	130	67 354	14

Source: industry estimates.

SPATIAL PATTERNS OF RETAIL LOCATION

The theoretical explanation of locations concerning different types and sizes of stores, and where they are to be found, has been the subject of two main strands of study. Central place theory seeks to explain the roles of different centres for shopping and their hierarchy. However, the arrangement of shops within the centre can be explained by bid rent theory that takes accessibility to the central core as the determinant of the highest land values and, consequently, rents (Scott, 1970).

Central Place Theory

Christaller's (1966) central place theory arose from a study of the spatial distribution of retailers in Southern Germany in the 1930s. Starting with the assumption that urban centres of all sizes exist to provide goods and services for the surrounding area, it can be observed that people will travel into them to shop from the surrounding area. The provision of services defines central places, their centrality being located by the distance that shoppers will travel to obtain the good, creating a 'complementary region'. The larger the centre, the more extensive the market area and the greater the specialisation in service provision. A larger centre will have more establishments and business types, offer more goods and services and achieve greater volumes of business. The classification of goods offered at each level and the distance shoppers are prepared to travel for that type of good creates a hierarchy of centres and urban rankings, with lower orders of centre nested within the higher ones. The range of the centre depends on the farthest distance the population is prepared to travel in order to buy an item in that particular place. The limits are defined by competition among centres providing the same product or service. The centre will also be sustained by a minimum purchasing power to support the supply of each type of good.

Where central place theory has been put into practice, for example in Bavaria, essential supplies in all areas are met by neighbourhood stores, non-essentials and semi-luxury goods in medium centres, and specialist luxury goods are available in large centres (Davies, 1995).

The theory has been held to be generally valuable in establishing the relationship between the size of population of a centre, the threshold to support the number and different types of shop, and the farthest distance shoppers are prepared to travel to buy a good. The concept is observable in the UK in the spatial arrangement of shops in many towns and cities where the centre provides a core shopping area for comparison retailing, shopping for expensive and infrequently purchased goods. Convenience shopping districts surround the core, becoming more dispersed towards the edge of the urban area as the population densities decrease. The concept of a shopping centre hierarchy is also apparent in structure plans, drawn up by county councils from the 1980s to define land use for an area together with a policy to maintain it. The hierarchy extends from regional to local levels and the aim is to support existing centres and avoid creating over-supplies of floor space against projected demand. The theory has been criticised in its details though; the regularity of spatial patterns of location are not evident in the UK for historical reasons, and the theory assumes the spatial distribution of locations is static. More significantly, the theory has led to further studies into centre attractiveness using factors other than population alone. Central place theory explains the location of stores by place but does not contribute to the patterns of distribution within it; for these, land value theory and bid rents serve an explanatory purpose.

Land Value Theory and Bid Rent

The analysis of the arrangement of land use, in this context retail use, within urban centres can be explained by the bid rent curve. It proposes that the location of different firms will depend on competitive bidding for different sites. Retailers will bid for a site based on their estimated net returns on investment in the future but, crucially for this theory, its accessibility. The economic rent for a location is represented as the residual after non-rent costs, including return on capital, and net profit is deducted from the output (sales) achieved. As a result, competition for sites will lead to a systematic pattern of development determined by the maximum rents that specific types of retailer are able to pay for each site. Land use will depend on the payment of the highest rent for more central and accessible areas as opposed to secondary and marginal areas. Willingness to pay falls away the further from the centre of the town creating a 'rent gradient'. It has been shown that retailers at the core include jewellers who can pay the highest rents because they can exploit most fully those sites where the pedestrian flows are heaviest. Bids may also reflect benefits to specific retailers from particular sites, and the size of the space combined with its location. The theory has been criticised for its assumptions concerning accessibility, segregation of land use, a free market in property and an economics approach to utility maximisation, uninfluenced by non-economic forces (Clarkson *et al.*, 1996).

One consequence of retail concentration has been the polarisation of central sites into prime and secondary locations. Initially, independent retailers were driven out by high rents to secondary sites during the 1980s, to be joined and often replaced by financial and leisure services such as banks, travel agents and restaurants. In turn, escalating costs of location and competition from online information services have forced further economies, particularly on the financial service sector. As a consequence, the town centre is seeing a further change in its constituency, and with sites in the centre attracting specialist retailers.

SITE ASSESSMENT AND EVALUATION

The techniques used to decide on the location of a new store, or to assess stores within a property portfolio, will aim to evaluate their sales potential and the probability of the store's success or, for existing stores, their continuing viability. This is an information gathering process on potential sites and existing levels of demand and competition, combined with the organisation's own requirements for return on investment, trading policy and operational capabilities.

Initial location decisions concern the general assessment of geographical areas for potential store development, which lead on to detailed feasibility studies of specific sites and their relationship to store performance (McGoldrick, 1990). Three stages of assessment have been proposed in this process (Ghosh and McLafferty, 1987):

1 At the broadest level, market selection decisions are made about the general metropolitan region, town or city. At this level minimum information is required about population and income, and competitor factors including the number of stores, their sizes and their strengths and weaknesses.

2 'Areal analysis' is undertaken at a second level, within the selected market. This stage of assessment evaluates a division of the market through analysis of its physical structure. Barriers to accessibility, roads and transport networks influence residential patterns, and locations and shopping opportunities. There is a more detailed requirement for information on population At this stage size, demographic and socio-economic characteristics matched to the target store and sub-area competition. From this analysis it should be possible to rank trade areas.

3 Site evaluation relates location to existing retail structures in the region, and will require detailed assessment of the physical characteristics of the site, its accessibility, and traffic flow.

Defining the Trade Area: Sources of Information

Site evaluation techniques require information about what characterises the area and its population catchment, to enable accurate sales forecasts to be made for the proposed store. Information can be extracted from internal company resources and external sources.

Internal data

Such data will include customer and outlet information, and sales data by store and trading area, information which is relatively straightforward to acquire from company records. Large amounts of data are captured from customer transactions, omnibus surveys, product guarantees and warranties and promotions. (O'Malley et al., 1997)

Figure 8.3   *The 'Glam-Glum' UK Market Size/Positioning Matrix*

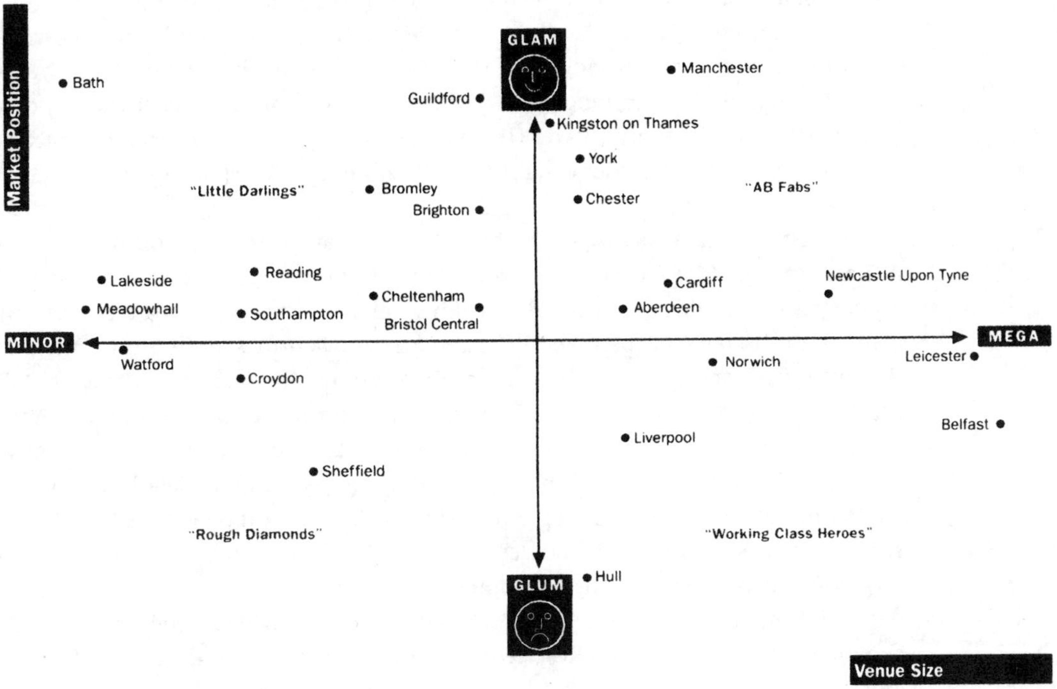

Source: Management Horizons Europe (1999), with permission.

that are used alongside external databases. Internal sources will also provide comparable measurments of property values, pedestrian flows, and sales densities from retail floor space.

External data

These data are derived from publicly or commercially available sources, and provide information for specific markets and locations:

- *Demographic and population data.* Censuses provide the basis for national statistical information on the location of the population and some social data. The 2001 census added dwelling type and lifestage of household structure information to support more sophisticated planning decisions.

- *Competition.* Competing centres must be identified, mapped and visited in the field (Davies and Rogers, 1984). This exercise should establish the number of key competitors, the distances from the proposed location, and the number of competing outlets within a given distance. A topic of current debate is the extent of competition between grocery retailers and market saturation. One definition of saturation at a local level assumes the local population is sufficiently well-served that it does not desire any more outlets, and where the entry of a new store impacts directly onto another major grocery store (Guy, 1996).

■ *Geographical information systems* (GIS) provide datasets from which to build up accessibility and attractiveness characteristics. GIS concerns the building of small-area census-based classification systems. These started with social and economic variations in individual cities but evolved in the 1970s into geodemographics, area typologies that discriminate consumer behaviour and act as aids to market analysis. The UK census in 1981 provided the first commercial opportunity to use geodemographic databases (O'Malley *et al.*, 1997).

The first systematic approach to the use of geographic information in the UK was A Classification of Residential Neighbourhoods (ACORN), which used ward and parish typologies to examine variation in consumer behaviour between area types, enabling comparisons to be made between different cities and counties. In its 1991 form it used six categories each reducing into 17 ACORN groups, or 54 types, through linked census-based geography to postcodes and on to address-based data. In the intervening years a number of competing products were launched including Pinpoint and MOSAIC. The latter developed the classification process in more detail by combining data from other sources including electoral rolls, and post office address files. Lifestyle surveys, too, have supplemented census data to provide yearly updates to postcode profiling of consumers. Future developments suggest a greater use of current data (real time) and the use of geodemographics developed for individual retailers, rather than generic systems and linking lifestyle databases to transactional data (O'Malley *et al.*, 1997).

A number of organisations provide detailed datasets based on geodemographic analysis. These include demographic reports for local areas, site information, estimation of local market size and catchments and competitor locations. Other suppliers provide data without analysis as a mapping service (Dugmore, 1998; see Figure 8.4).

Locational Planning Techniques

A number of techniques have been employed by retailers to decide on individual store locations. Hernandez and Bennison (2000) have identified six groups and the situations in which they might be used:

■ *Experience*. The simplest rule-of-thumb approach. This technique is sometimes described in terms of 'counting the chimney stacks', and relies on the quality of the retailer's instinct for a good site. For smaller retailers developing a number of sites or small multiples, this may be the most realistic as well as affordable solution to site evaluation. The process can be considerably influenced by the owner or founder of the business leading to subjective decision-making. A further weakness in this approach is that it can be very time consuming.

■ *Analogue and checklists*. These provide a more objective approach, by which new store sales forecasts are achieved by comparison with other stores in the company that possess similar physical, locational and trade-area characteristics. The process requires the compilation of historical trading information through checklists, and will be presented in tabulated data. The proposed store's turnover

Figure 8.4   *Store Catchment Areas*

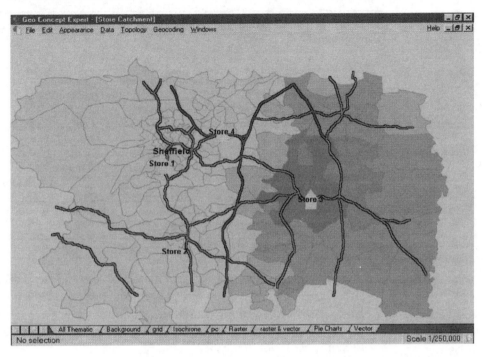

Source: Dugmore (1949), reproduced with permission.

and profitability is derived by analogy with the characteristics of the other stores. The method originally proposed 'customer spotting', the use of customer surveys to determine the geographical location of customers from each analogue store, as well as their demographic features and spending habits. However, as the data becomes more detailed and the relationships more complex, so analysis becomes more difficult and interpretation more subjective.

Alternatively, retailers could follow the behaviour of other, larger retailers and base their locations on their decisions in a 'parasitic approach'. This method requires a need to understand the way stores trade and the variance in performance of stores in similar geographical locations.

■ *Regression techniques.* These techniques rely on multiple regression using a dependent store's forecast turnover and its correlation to a set of independent or explanatory variables. The range of variables are typically drawn from its population, the socio-demographic features of the market area, size of the store, competition and accessibility, although the number of variables is not predetermined. Information is required from analogous stores, but unlike the analogue method multiple regression allows more complex relationships to be examined. Through these the most important sales forecasting variables are identified. However, the process requires a considerable amount of data complied

Table 8.6   *Checklist for New Store Attributes*

Local demographics	Traffic flow and accessibility	Retail structure	Site characteristics	Legal and cost factors
Population base of the local area Income potential in local area	Number of vehicles Number of pedestrians Public transport facilities Access to road system, congestion and quality of access	Number of competitors in area Number and types of stores in area Complementarity of neighbouring areas Proximity to commercial areas	Availability of parking spaces and distance from store Visibility of site Size and shape of site Condition of any existing buildings Quality of entrances/exits	Length of lease Restrictive clauses on usage Local taxes Operating and maintenance costs Local regulations

from other stores and the trade area itself. The regression approach has been criticised in a number of respects, for providing static information and failing to handle spatial interactions or customer flows adequately, as well as a tendency to assume the heterogeneity of sites whilst examining each one in isolation (Birkin *et al.*, 1996).

■ *Neural networks and expert systems.* Neural networks provide an alternative approach to regression analysis of location variables. The approach operates in parallel rather than sequentially within a layered structure, and uses computer software to creates a capacity to learn by being trained. It has the advantage of being relatively easy to use compared to regression analysis, although as yet it remains relatively untried in the retail industry (Coates *et al.*, 1995).

■ *Cluster and factor analysis.* At a more strategic level, analyses may be used to facilitate market segmentation by fascia within a portfolio. Stores are grouped by significant population and operational variables.

■ *Spatial interaction models.* These techniques are used to estimate the size of trade areas and to forecast the store's potential sales. They provide the basis for catchment definitions and allow the simultaneous consideration of significant factors such as distance, competition and store image.

The origins of the gravity modelling approach are generally attributed to Reilly (1929), who related shopping frequency to neighbouring cities to the population size of each and the distance for a shopper to travel. Shoppers are more likely to shop in a bigger town because of the agglomeration of shops and the assortment they offer, supported by the population; however, the attractiveness of a town or shopping centre decreases with the distance shoppers have to travel. The point of indifference between two towns arises where the gravitational pull of each trade area is equally attractive to shoppers from the intermediate area. More precisely, Reilly's law holds that two competing towns will attract shoppers from communities in the area between them, in direct proportion to the towns' populations and in inverse proportion to the square of distances from those towns to the communities between them.

Using the earlier law, trade area boundaries were defined by Converse's (1949) formula of 'break points' between one retail centre – which could be a store, shopping centre or town – and all competing retail centres.

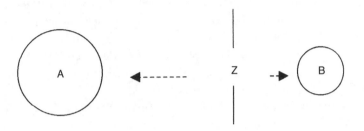

The break point between centre A and centre B

$$\text{Break point} = \frac{\text{Distance A to B}}{1+ \sqrt{\dfrac{\text{Population A (the larger centre)}}{\text{Population B (the smaller centre)}}}}$$

(distance from smaller centre)

For example: using population as a substitute for attractiveness, if town A has a population of 60 000 and B has 20 000, and the distance from A to B is 8 miles, then the break point will be:

$$\text{Break point} = \frac{8 \text{ miles}}{1+ \sqrt{\dfrac{60\,000}{20\,000}}}$$

Distance from small centre (B) =   2.93 miles

Reilly's law has attracted considerable attention. The main drawbacks, which its successors have attempted to address, concern assumptions relating to market attractiveness, size and gravitational pull. Huff's (1964) probability model identified the more complex nature of consumer decisions about choice of store or shopping centre. The attractiveness of the merchandise offer, its breadth and depth influences customer patronage and the distance they will travel to shop for different types of product. The travel time itself may vary depending on the shopper's perception of convenience or the value they place on the goods, for which they may go to great lengths to search out. The measure of a centre's attractiveness according to its population size has been replaced by measures of floor space of a centre and the assortment of different types of product. Distance in kilometres can be substituted more realistically by distance in travel time, recognising that time remains a more subjective measure. Shopping journeys reflect a more complex variety of decisions by the shopper, depending on the motivation to make a journey; a single journey can be contrasted with a journey requiring several or more stops.

Using Geographical Information Systems (GIS), retail location analysis could take place through a series of stages. The starting point might be to identify a neighbourhood type by its postcode or enumeration district. Using this unit of measurement, coverage by a GIS can show the spatial extent, population and neighbourhood type of the area. This can be overlaid with a set of retail locations, and basic GIS buffering techniques used to calculate the population within specified bands around each outlet, at 1 km, 2 km and more remote intervals.

However, straightline distances do not reflect geographical accessibility meaningfully, so drive-time bands are found to be more useful around an outlet or centre; CLN's 'Environ' package uses population aggregations within 15, 30 and 45 minutes' drive times. The weaknesses of geodemographic approaches relate partly to their reliance on dated census figures that provide a cross-section of the population at a point in time. They can only express limited characteristics and they may lead to statistical misinterpretation of the market opportunities within each cluster.

Spatial analysis techniques are often used with GIS packages that emphasise analysis routines associated with the overlays of different 'layers' of spatial data (Davies and Clarke, 1994). For example a town might be zoned by postal sector. For each sector, demand could be calculated based on small-area population census data from publications such as the UK Family Expenditure Survey to arrive at an average household expenditure pattern on a range of retail goods by household size and social class. Competitors' influences on sales need to be assessed. In calculating store revenues, a 'buffer and overlay' analysis will enable planners to make an assessment of how far consumers are willing to travel and therefore their travel time. The delimit around the store (the buffer) marks the time to travel to that location. Revenue estimations will arise from consumer spending overlaid with the area around the store. It is usually assumed that the closer people live to a store the more they will spend, but problems arise when overlapping buffers occur between different stores and require an allocation of revenues to each store (Benoit and Clarke, 1997).

GOVERNMENT INTERVENTION IN LOCATIONAL DEVELOPMENT

Government planning requirements determine the broader process of retail development. The patterns of development and consequently retail site availability have varied over time and country, the main trends being the degree to which governments, both central and local, have adopted more or less liberal attitudes to urban and particularly out-of-town shopping.

The pattern of retail development in the UK has been strongly influenced by the Department of the Environment, Transport and the Regions' (DETR's) *Parliamentary Planning Guidance 6* (PPG6). The first version of PPG6 appeared in 1988 and has been revised in 1993 and even more stringently in 1996. It provides guidance to regional and local planners on new out-of-town development in response to the growth of retail parks, the impact of regional centres and their impact on town centres and the countryside. Although amended in subsequent years, it has had the effect of restricting out-of-town development. New retail developments must benefit the community from competition between retailers, and must consider the impact on trading in town centres and seek sites there before looking to out-of-town locations; finally they must be accessible by a variety of means of transport (Fernie, 1996). Development plans over 20 000 square metres will be referred to the Secretary of State. Proposals must be evaluated using a sequential test as planners' first preference will be for town-centre sites, followed by edge-of-centre, district and local centre sites, and finally out-of-centre where a choice of transport renders the site accessible.

In addition, government ministers have generally opposed out-of-town development, requiring a planning 'need' to be identified for new development and creating a distinction in the sequential planning process between format and classes of goods that further restricts large-size retail formats. As a result, out-of-town development has become extremely difficult, with very few plans in the pipeline even as developments with planning consents are completed. Plans for an extension to one of the biggest centres, Metro Centre in Gateshead, were referred to the Secretary of State following a Public Enquiry, as was a major new urban scheme in White City, West London.

The regulatory environment has considerable significance for the internationalisation of the industry. Whilst out-of-town planning remains tightly controlled in the UK, elsewhere in Europe there is a diversity of attitudes to the planning of new sites, the size of stores and their location. Tighter controls have been applied in some countries; for example France's initial response to the development of hypermarkets (whose development began in the early 1960s) was the 1973 Royer Law that required a permit to open commercial space greater than 1000 square metres. Nevertheless, the development of large-scale retailing continued in France, from 200 hypermarkets in 1973 to 1000 20 years later. Retail planning policy was tightened up further with the Loi Raffarin of 1996 that required special authorisation for developments over 300 square metres, and retail growth has been further constrained by the bureaucratic process that has resulted in development applications being delayed by up to 12 months. Spain, too, has seen restrictions imposed on its relatively relaxed approach to planning, with the General Commerce Law requiring licencing for new store or centre development over 2500 square metres. Paradoxically, early studies indicated that small

---

Exhibit 8.3   A summary of planning guidance for large store development (PPG6)

There should be a three-fold sequential test for planning applications for large stores:

Whether they can be accommodated within existing centres;
Whether there are possibilities for edge-of-town sites;
Whether out-of-town centre sites can be reached by all forms of transport

Planning permission should not normally be given to proposals for out-of-centre regional shopping centres and factory outlet centres.

Local authorities should be mindful of imposing restrictions on changes of use for bulky-goods stores.

It is accepted that some bulky-goods stores cannot be accommodated within existing centres.

The concept of town-centre management is endorsed and supported.

In 2000, PPG11 qualified the government's approach to regional planning. In producing Regional Planning Guides, the regional planning bodies should assess the need for major new retail facilities or large-scale expansion of existing retail facilities of regional or sub-regional importance taking account of any forecasts of retail demand for the region. This should involve consideration of whether certain town centres should take the majority of this development. The Government's policy is to use retail development to regenerate existing town centres. There is unlikely to be scope for major additional out-of-town shopping facilities without adversely affecting the vitality and viability of existing centres and the environment more generally, including through unsustainable pressures on the road network. Similar considerations will apply to major entertainment facilities.

Source: DETR (2000).

---

retailers, the very retailers the law was designed to protect, and hypermarkets would lose ground to large supermarkets and discounters (Houssemaine, 1995).

The former Eastern bloc countries have continued to experience the legacy of communist planning. In the Czech Republic retailers need a planning permit to ensure that development is in line with the Master Plan. In addition, a building permit is required which may impose technical restrictions and recommendations. The permit process can be lengthy. Limits on the size of shopping centres are not prescribed but handled in each case through the planning permit. In Poland, planning requires completion of an environmental audit and infrastructure survey and building permit. Out-of-town development on agricultural land can be complicated and time-consuming.

On the other hand, some European countries currently experience a less regulated regime. In Italy the Retail Planning Act of 1998 addresses some of the problems that have held back retail-sector development to establish new retail outlets and modernise the fragmented retail market. Planning, otherwise, has been complex and strict, with out-of-town developments blocked in the wealthier northern regions. The new planning process will see decisions being taken at a single Conference of Services attended by representatives of both district and town councils, and 120-day time limits have been set for public authority responses to planning requests. Planning licence applications, however, have been made more straightforward, and restrictions on product ranges and opening times have been reduced (Carati, 1998).

SITE ACQUISITION

The final selection of the store location depends on the nature and degree of specialisation of each retail business. The availability of the site may be restricted, therefore cost/benefit analysis of the physical characteristics of the location is valuable. The area of the store and its frontage-to-depth ratio, with special attention to the shape and quality of the floor space to maximise customer flow, is important. Upper floors are avoided by electrical retailers but may be sought by clothing retailers separating men's and women's wear between two floors.

Costs of building a new store are substantial and clearly cannot be considered lightly; development costs can range up to £20 million for a new supermarket. In 1998 Sainsbury had 38 building contracts worth over £1 million each, in total over £322 million. Marks and Spencer at the same time had £184 millions' and Asda £164 millions' worth (*Retail Technology Directions*, 1999). Nevertheless, new development by retailers is viable for large store construction for supermarkets and superstores and tends to be restricted to this size, typically in out-of-town locations.

Many retailers' strategies do not require the construction of new stores; their location requirements will be directed to units on existing or new developments. As a result, the cost of occupancy will be determined by rent (O'Roathy *et al.*, 1997), although other local tax charges – in the UK the Uniform Business Rate, and in shopping centres the service charges – can contribute significantly to operational costs. As shoppers visit fewer centres, the majority of the population now shops for comparison goods in just 73 locations compared to 207 in 1971, so rental growth has been matched to the most popular places. In the period 1995–98, rents in the top 1000 shopping areas increased by 25 per cent, with major city centres recording 56 per cent increases; however, the less-attractive smaller locations only recorded around 16 per cent increases. Higher rents lead to higher operating costs and raise the 'hurdle' level of performance at which profits can be made and rents justified. Rental growth shows that the most successful locations attract retailers that can deliver high sales productivity and high gross margins. Those that cannot achieve these are obliged to find other types of site or distribution channels.

Shop units in the UK are generally valued for rental by a zoning method (Morgan and Walker, 1988). The front part of a shop, usually measured to a depth of 20 feet (6 metres) is referred to as zone A and attracts a quoted rental per square foot. This reflects the greater value of the front part of the shop, and the willingness of retailers to pay more rent for a wider shop frontage. Zone B comprises the next 15 feet. (4.5 m) and is valued at half of zone A; zone C is valued at one quarter of zone A and the remaining depth, at one-eighth. Shop rentals reflect supply and demand for property, and so move with the property market. For example, the most accessible and prestigious locations in London's Oxford Street attract zone A rentals of up to £600 per square foot, driven particularly by retailers' requirements for a London flagship store.

Leases

Property is seen as investment in the UK, with shopping centres typically owned by pension funds and insurance companies. As a result the owners look for stability in their investment through long-term leases, usually of 25 years with upwards reviews every five years. Lease terms have become more flexible depending on the property market, locations and relative negotiating power of the retailer; 10-year terms been shown to have a positive impact for footwear retailers, 15-year terms for both footwear and clothing retailers, but 20-year terms are preferred by department stores, in part due to the high cost of fitting out the store (O'Roarty, 1997).

However, both long leases and reviews can lead to profitability problems, where store turnover declines. These problems are illustrated by stores in the Lakeside shopping centre reporting declining sales of 20–40 per cent as a result of the opening of the nearby Bluewater Park centre. Nevertheless they faced substantial rent increases in their second five-year rent review, by as much as 108 per cent. The issue is increasingly reflected in national portfolio reviews as well as local ones. The Boots Company announced its intention in 2000 to seek more break clauses in its leases and to have the facility to exchange property in and out of its portfolio. However, in continental Europe rent reviews are more usually indexed to market value allowing the rent to move both downwards as well as up.

Financial incentives to retailers to take a site include inducements that are offered selectively from developers and property owners depending on the quality of the prospective retailer and their negotiating power. The types of inducement offered include rent-free periods, capital contributions to the costs of fittings and fixtures and rising rent schemes, which start with a low rent rising to a market rate over a period of time. The value of inducements has declined at the end of the 1990s, reflecting subdued demand for many types of retail property.

RENOVATION AND REDEVELOPMENT OF SITES

Town centres remain vulnerable to competition from other resurgent town centres as well as adapted retail parks. Those that can adapt to accommodate the changing structure of retailing will be the most successful. With shoppers demanding greater choice in the most convenient and pleasant surroundings, retailers are responding by increasing their space requirements to provide for and exploit this demand. If town centres are unable to offer appropriate accommodation retailers will move to another location. Many town centres suffer from old accommodation, with high barriers to new space – difficulties in location and configuration, space availability, multi-ownership and land costs. Urban centres that cannot overcome these problems will see a change in their role, serving smaller catchments with lower penetration levels and acting more as convenience centres.

In-town upgrades contribute to the decline of the bottom end of the retail property market, especially in secondary locations around the edge of town and city centres. This space can eventually, when redundant as retail space, become available subject to planning approvals for conversion to leisure or combined retail and leisure use. New formats, together with new products and niche marketing, will create more competition in town-centre retailing. In the future size will become increasingly attractive, and as shops become larger so the number of units may be reduced. Smaller grocery retailers and food specialists will be vulnerable to multiple retailers' product diversification; their opportunities may lie in further specialisation in attractive central shopping locations. Out of these areas, smaller stores will be able to compete on convenience and by their proximity to local neighbourhoods. One scenario envisages centres serving only a declining number of inner-city workers with top-up goods and specialised products, with limited ranges to match the income and consumer expenditure profiles.

Rationalisation will lead to the opening of new and different types of store offering mixed leisure and retail opportunities. Out-of-town will continue in competition with town centres, and new formats such as factory outlets will add to the competition, even though the planning constraints of PPG6 combined with government opposition effectively stop new large-scale development. Nevertheless there has been a trend towards 'out of town by stealth'. Many retail parks and food superstore sites on edge of town locations hold A1 open planning permission that provide redevelopment opportunities for new owners. A number of high street style retail parks have already appeared in the UK with others proposed (Management Horizons Europe, 1999). Other opportunities will have to be sought outside the centre including the evaluation of previously unattractive sites. Urban regeneration policies may enable retailers and local councils to avoid PPG6 altogether through the development of industrial land. Developments in south and south-west London shopping centres in response to the opening of Bluewater Park demonstrate a determination to increase the 'pull' through a range of development strategies. These approaches demonstrate the role of common interests and partnerships in the future of large-scale retail location planning.

SUMMARY

Location strategy is determined by the corporate objectives and detailed marketing positions of companies. It is one of the most important strategic growth opportunities: sales and profits growth depend on customer visits and their expenditure with each visit. Access and convenience, product choice and services are defined by the number of stores and their locations. Flexible use of location is important to enable retailers to reconfigure existing product offers, or add new ones. The store concept itself may change if the site and planning consent allows; existing space and new space is constantly being examined for its potential to generate additional sales.

The types of location possess different characteristics which enable retailers to match existing formats and develop new ones as opportunities arise. The urban environment offers a diversity of such opportunities, from central locations and in-town shopping centres, to district centres and brownfield sites. They bring with them a number of constraints and limitations too. Edge-of-town opportunities and the redevelopment of retail parks appear to offer viable alternatives for large-scale formats. Out-of-town development from individual sites to the largest of developments, regional centres, appear to present very limited opportunities for expansion due to the rigorous application of PPG6.

Location decision-making moves through a number of stages. An initial area evaluation followed by more detailed local assessments will define a site with an appropriate catchment area. Such an area will be a measurement of local population and its characteristics combined with accessibility to the proposed site, often expressed in drive times, which will guide the retailer to an optimum location. Individual sites will be evaluated for their sales potential, but all must generate a required level of profit. Rents are one of the most important factors in decision-making between alternative sites. A site's turnover less its rent and operational costs, including cost of goods, provides its net profit. However, lease terms, planning consent and developers' inducements to take on the site also contribute to the final decision.

QUESTIONS

1   To what extent will retailers be drawn back to town and city centres?

2   Explain the hierarchy of retail locations.

3   How will the location of shopping change in the next 10 years?

4   Evaluate location decision-making processes.

5   Justify the case for government regulation of retail development.

Case Study

Geodemographics at Safeway

Large grocery multiple retailers have used data supplied by geodemographics for a number of years. This information has been used not only for location analysis, but also for category management and targeted promotions using detailed knowledge of a store's catchment area. Geodemographic profiling provides retailers with an indication of the make-up of the local population, and data suppliers like CACI have cross-referencing of a demographic profile with other data, such as expenditure details, to identify market potential.

Retailers' loyalty schemes are used to acquire valuable information about customers.

The combination of loyalty data with geodemographic information has the potential to provide more customer-specific profiling. GIS enables the interaction between the consumer and an outlet to be examined using demographic data and drive times. Analysis of the datasets supports the relative importance of drive times analysis over loyalty when determining traffic flows. Within a retailer's portfolio, store formats or brands will require significantly different demographic data to establish not just who is living in the area, but also who works in it. For example, an urban location may be busy at lunchtimes and have a different market spread to an out-of-town store. Increasingly grocery retailers are combining GIS with lifestyle database information and product use to identify their target customers so that they can better understand shopping behaviour. Both product ranges and marketing programmes can be adapted to specific stores' catchment areas, enabling retailers to move towards smaller localised stores entirely tailored to specific customers needs.

Location analysis at Safeway begins with intensive quantitative analysis. Network analysis enables the company to identify customers and the distances they are prepared to travel so that travel times and catchment zones can be created. Locations throughout the UK have been studied to identify the types of customers who already shop at existing Safeway stores. This enables the company to identify locations where there is existing underprovision.

Gravity modelling allows Safeway to evaluate the attractiveness of a location. The resulting market analysis will include a sales forecast of the store, its attractiveness to the retail sector, and competitor stores and drive times. The company prioritises those systems over the whole of the UK, ranking sites as priorities one, two, three and marginal. Those priorities are given to development controllers who scour those locations and look for a site that fulfils the potential outlined. When the company has identified a site, it builds a matrix from the centre to look at the four adjoining one-kilometre squares and then an outer area 11 by 11 kilometres. In each of those squares Safeway will identify how much spend there is, how much is likely to be spent at a superstore and what the pulling power of the proposed store would be against any competition. The company's formula relates the available food expenditure multiplied by the proportion of available spend in the superstores multiplied by the attractiveness of Safeway multiplied by the travel time factor divided by the attractiveness and travel time factor of all the other stores. From that, Safeway can calculate how much to pay for any particular site and whether it is a good investment.

GIS assists Safeway in other business-planning activities including individual store analysis, tactical advertising and store expansion and refits. In effect it brings together geo-demographic and corporate data to model and analyse different types of outlet and location swiftly and effectively.

Sources: *Marketing Week*, 12 March 1998; *Marketing*, 1 May 1999; *European Retail Digest*, 17 March 1998.

SEMINAR QUESTION FOR DISCUSSION

Does the Safeway approach to locational planning have a long-term future?

References

Batey, P. and Brown, P. (1995) 'From Human Ecology to Customer Targeting: the Evolution of Geodemographics', in P. Longley and G. Clarke (eds), *GIS for Business and Planning* (London: GeoInformation International).

Birkin, M., Clarke, G., Clarke, M. and Wilson, A. (1996) *Intelligent GIS, Location Decisions and Strategic Planning* (London: GeoInformation International).

Benoit, D. and Clarke, G.P. (1997) 'Assessing GIS for Retail Location Planning', *Journal of Retail and Consumer Services*, vol. 4, no. 4, pp. 239–58.

Clarke, I. (1999) 'Retail Development and Store Choice in the UK Grocery Sector: Changing the Ability to Consume', Paper presented at the 10th International Conference on Research in the Distributive Trades, University of Stirling.

Clarke, I., Bennison, D. and Pal, J. (1997) 'Towards a Contemporary Perspective of Retail Location', *International Journal of Retail and Distribution Management*, vol. 25, no. 2, pp. 56–69.

Clarkson, R.M., Clarke-Hill, C.M. and Robinson, T. (1996) 'UK Supermarket Location Assessment', *International Journal of Retail and Distribution Management*, vol. 24, no. 6, pp. 22–33.

Coates, D., Doherty, N., French, A. and Kirkup, M. (1995) 'Neural Networks for Store Performance Forecasting: an Empirical Comparison with Regression Techniques', *International Review of Retail Distribution and Consumer Services*, vol. 5, no. 4, pp. 412–32.

Converse, P.D. (1949) 'New Laws of Retail Gravitation', *Journal of Marketing*, vol. 14, pp. 379–84.

Davies, M. and Clarke, I. 'A Framework for Network Planning', *International Journal of Retail and Distribution Management, Special Issue of 'Retail Location: a Strategic Perspective on Planning and Management'*, vol. 22, no. 6, pp. 6–10.

Davies, R. (ed.) (1995) *Location Planning Policies in Western Europe* (London: Routledge).

Davies, R.L. and Rogers, D.S. (eds) (1984) *Store Location and Store Assessment Research* (Chichester: John Wiley and Sons).

Dawson, J.A. (1983) *Topics in Applied Geography; Shopping Centre Development* (Harlow: Longman).

Department of the Environment, Transport and the Regions (2000) *Planning Policy Guidance Note 11: Regional Planning, Public consultation draft* (London: DETR).

Department of the Environment, Transport and the Regions (2000) *The Impact of Large Foodstores on Market Towns and District Centres* (London: DETR).

Dugmore, K. (1998) 'Opening and Closing: What Information is Available to Make the Best Locational Decisions?' *Journal of Targeting, Measurement and Analysis for Marketing*, vol. 6, no. 4, pp. 359–65.

Evans, R. (1997) *Regenerating Town Centres* (Manchester: Manchester University Press).

Fernie, J. (1998) 'The Breaking of the Fourth Wave: Recent Out of Town Developments in Britain', *International Review of Retail Distribution and Consumer Research*, vol. 8, no. 3, pp. 303–18.

Fernie, S. (1996) 'The Future for Factory Outlets in the UK: the Impact of Changes in Planning Policy Guidance on the Growth of a New Retail Format', *International Journal of Retail and Distribution Management*, vol. 24, no. 6, pp. 11–21.

Ghosh, A. and McLafferty, S.L. (1987) *Location Strategies for Retail and Service Firms* (Lexington MA: D.C. Heath).

Guy, C. (1999) 'Exit Strategies and Sunk Costs: the Implications for Multiple Retailers', *International Journal of Retail and Distribution Management*, vol. 27, no. 6, pp. 237–44.

Guy, C. (1994) *The Retail Development Process* (London: Routledge).

Hernandez, T. and Bennison, D. (2000) 'The Art and Science of Retail Location Decisions', *International Journal of Retail and Distribution Management*, vol. 28, no. 8, pp. 357–67.

Houssemaine, D.A.D. (1996) 'Retail in Spain: The Evolution of an Industry Winter', *European Retail Digest*, OXIRM pp. 8–12.

Huff, D.L. (1964) 'Defining and Estimating a Trading Area', *Journal of Marketing*, vol. 28, July, pp. 34–8.

Lowe, M. and Wrigley, N. (1996) *Retailing, Consumption and Capital* (Harlow: Longman).

Management Horizons Europe (1999) *UK Shopping Industry Report*.

McGoldrick, P.J. (1990) *Retail Marketing* (Maidenhead: McGraw Hill).

Mintel (2000) *Shopping Centres* (London: Mintel International Group).

Mintel (2000) *The High Street in 2000* (London: Mintel International Group).

Molla, A. and Frasquet, M. (1997) 'Shopping Centres in Spain: Some Conceptual Deliminations and an Exploratory Study of their Customers' Behaviour', Paper presented at the 9th International Conference on Research in The Distributive Trades, University of Leuven.

Morgan, P. and Walker, A. (1988) *Retail Development*, Estates Gazette.

The National Retail Planning Forum (1996) *A Tale of Three Cities What makes for a successful City Centre?* (London: National Retail Planning Forum).

O'Malley, L., Patterson, M. and Evans, M. (1997) 'Retailer Use of Geodemographic and Other Data Sources', *International Journal of Retail and distribution Management*, vol. 25, no. 6, pp. 188–96.

O'Rearty, McGreal, S. and Adair, A. (1997) 'The Impact of Retailers' Store Selection Criteria on the Estimation of Retail Rents *Journal of Property Valuation and Investment*, vol. 15, no. 2, pp. 119–31.

Property Week (2000) 17 March p. 1.

PPG 6 (1996) Parliamentary Planning Guidance 6 (London: Department of the Environment, Transport and the Regions).

Reilly, W.J. (1929) 'Method for the Study of Retail Relationships', *Research Monograph No. 4 University of Texas Bulletin no. 2944* (Austin: University of Texas Press).

Retail Week (1999) 'Shopping Centre Guide – Shopping Centre Leagues', 22 October.

Reynolds, J. and Howard, E. (1994) *The UK Regional Shopping Centre. . . .* OXIRM.

Retail Technology Directions (2000) *Arthur Andersen with Cornhill Publications*, Issue 2, pp. 36–7.

Scott, P. (1970) *Geography and Retailing* (London: Hutchinson).

Schiller, R. (1986). 'Retail Decentralisation – the Coming of the Third Wave', *The Planner*, vol. 72, no. 7, pp. 13–15.

Thomas, T. and Fernie, J. (1990) 'Retail Warehouse Operators – The Comet Case', in J. Fernie (ed.), *Retail Distribution Management* (London: Kogan Page).

Wrigley, N. (1988) *Store Choice, Store Location and Market Analysis* (London: Routledge).

CHAPTER NINE

Human Resource Management (HRM)

LEARNING OBJECTIVES

On completion of this chapter you will be able to:

- Explain the types of organisational structures in retailing and their implications for management.
- Understand issues in recruitment and retention in the industry.
- Analyse the effect of organisational culture on working practices.
- Explain differences in working practices and behaviour.

HUMAN RESOURCE STRATEGY

Human resources (HR) relate to the organisation's strategy through their ability to create competitive advantage. For many organisations this can be achieved through the use of different skills, the adaptability of the resource base, or the combined innovativeness of the workforce (Johnson and Scholes, 1999). A fundamental issue for retailers, within a people-oriented industry, is the management of customer relationships. The ways in which employees relate to customers create loyalty and retention to the retailer over the longer term (Walters and Hanrahan, 2000). Service standards should be aligned to the retail customer's needs and, more strategically still, may encompass internal customers as well.

A second strategic issue concerns the cost of people in the organisation to deliver the required level of service demanded by its strategy. People, Product and Property form the three most significant areas of cost to a retailer, and where property often represents a long-term investment, employees and inventories have to be managed more flexibly to meet short-term financial and operational objectives. The link between human resources and shareholder value is usually but not exclusively quantitative; however, human capital may also be evaluated intangibly through the quality of people's knowledge, skills and abilities.

The focus on both customer and employee satisfaction and the arising financial implications lead to strategic HR decisions concerning:

■ The structure of the organisation, which will influence both the ways in which strategy is created and implemented, and determine the number of people required and their skills needs.

■ Job design and control systems, both informal and formal, to ensure the right sort of people are available to undertake the right sort of jobs.

■ Organisational behaviour.

■ Managing the organisational culture to ensure the effective implementation of strategy throughout the business.

To achieve these objectives it is necessary to scan the retail environment for relevant social and demographic changes and implications for the business. In Chapter 2 a number of broad environmental themes were identified; these and a number of more specific trends in employment and retail markets have an influence on HRM strategy.

The pace and impact of change continues to play an important role by influencing the nature of the industry and the skills required (Dench *et al.*, 1997). Forces for change such as globalisation, low-cost telecommunications and the spread of computing have an impact on all businesses. Globalisation itself holds particular implications for HR policies in terms of employment of people in new store openings and their organisation and management, but together these have an impact on the development of new forms of working such as teleworking and the creation of call centres (Huws *et al.*, 1999). Some of the more specific influences on the nature of employment and jobs are detailed below:

■ Individualism and self-management in a number of aspects, including careers, learning and workload. The role of the workforce in shops is changing with the result that hierarchical management structures characteristic of traditional manufacturing companies and administrative organisations will be less evident (Hope-Hailey *et al.*, 1997).

■ Economic changes result in the displacement of employees from old to new forms of employment, and frequently lead to reduced employment status for those whose skills are obsolete and who are unable to adapt to new businesses.

■ New technology results in the automation of formerly labour-intensive processes, improved communication and information, and the growth of new kinds of organisations, occupations and jobs. This can result in deskilling of some jobs, but also creates new skills requirements at all levels in stock management, sales planning and logistics.

■ Changes in the business culture and changes in organisational practices such as refocusing around core business activities have raised awareness of the corporate culture as a source of strength, resourcefulness and flexibility.

■ Increasing demands from customers for improved services, products and delivery. Time resources are particularly pressing in customer service as, 'consumers looking to save time expect fast, efficient service, those looking to spend time want to enjoy themselves, to have a good experience and make the most of it. Fulfilling the needs of a consumer who is spending time rather than saving time requires a different skills set for retailers' (LSFU, 2000).

One result is an increasing polarisation between convenience shopping and destination shopping. On the one hand retailers have to satisfy consumer needs for '24/7/365' (hours/weeks/days in a year) accessibility and convenience, typically at supermarkets and garage forecourt outlets. Extended trading hours lead to changes in work patterns, increasing shift work and give rise to issues of responsibility and control. On the other hand, consumers are increasingly looking at retail as leisure; in this sense the retail theatre provides a diversity of different and pleasurable experiences and entertainment, and the opportunity at least to sustain social and human relationships. The pressure on retailers, then, is to relate and balance the contrasting needs of operating efficiency and innovation with customer care. From a sociological perspective, the dominance of the consumer has led to less 'ownership' of the store by staff. Sales skills have become more and more important at the expense of social ones, leading to more systematic attempts to embed them into the workforce (Miller, 1998).

■ Innovation will influence not only visible product and store activity but organisational structures too. Management will require skills that encourage and sustain employee creativity rather than ensure compliance. This means that more open organisational communication channels will be required, and 'low trust' cultures will need to be changed. The balance between the three areas will determine job roles and skills development across the industry (Scase, 1999).

These changes will have far-reaching consequences for organisations and individuals. The overall effect will be a widening diversity of career patterns and experiences in which many people will have more fragmented and mobile careers. As a result, perceptions of career insecurity are likely to continue to spread across the labour force (Jackson *et al.*, 1996). In particular, there will be more but different sorts of transition involving periods of retraining, self-employment, part-time employment and even unemployment that place greater emphasis on employability and 'portfolio' employment.

ORGANISATIONAL STRUCTURE

With the growth in multiple retailing, functions and structures have become more complex. Larger organisations demonstrate more tenuous communication links; divisions and departments reinforce people's identity at an organisational level rather than integrate to achieve overriding company objectives. Flexibility and adaptation to the changing environment become more difficult to achieve.

The retail industry is characterised by polarisation between large businesses, and many small micro businesses employing less than 10 people – typified by the independent retailer trading from one shop. Historically employment patterns in the retail industry have been typified by the independent grocery sector, with an owner and a few full-time shop assistants; it has been estimated that only 2 per cent of small shops employ more than two people (Freathy, 1997). Small, creative businesses' organisational structures and management styles are based on specialist and changing customer needs and tend to produce flexible work roles, duties and responsibilities. Features of these organisations are adaptiveness and job variety. In such simple organisations issues of responsibility are well-defined, communications informal, and strategy tends to be highly intuitive and non-analytical. They provide few formal promotion prospects, but rather psychological rewards through self-fulfilment and individual recognition.

With increasing complexity, HRM strategy needs to emphasise the design of the organisation, a task described as 'the division of work to be performed and the determination of an appropriate (efficient) basis for grouping the efforts of the resulting subunits' (Bedeian, 1984). In a wider sense, 'organisational design' also includes the culture of an organisation and the 'fit' or 'coherence' of structure and culture (Knez, 1999). In other words there is a strong relationship between *what* people do and *how* they do it.

Organisational structure concerns people and their work roles, and implicitly how best to coordinate the organisation through lines of responsibility and the span of control (Table 9.1). Mintzberg's (1985) definition of organisational structure as 'the sum total of the ways in which its labour is divided into distinct tasks and then co-ordination achieved among these tasks' emphasises these issues. He suggests that co-ordination is achieved in a number of different ways depending on the degree of standardisation of work processes and skills to integrate the organisation's different activities. The intertwining of formal and informal structures increases coordination, and structures that best achieve a trade-off between specialisation and coordination need to be both reliable and flexible.

Head Office functions provide direction and control, but the dynamics of retailing also require a high level of coordination with trading conditions in the stores. Peters and Waterman's (1982) proposals for successful structuring for the 1980s hold some relevance still for large retail organisations. The retail structure must be one that can respond to three prime needs: a need for efficiency in functional management, a need for continuous innovation, as well as responsiveness to major difficulties. As a result they suggest that any successful business structure must respond to those needs whilst retaining a simplicity of form and a minimum of headquarters staff.

For multiple retailers, structures are fundamentally distinguished by operational store management and their related distributive activities, and central functions which serve the entire organisation. Larger organisations began to centralise decision-making

Table 9.1   *Elements of Organisation*

- Allocation of tasks and responsibilities to individuals
- Designation of formal reporting relationships
- Grouping of individuals into sectors and divisions
- Design of communication and decision-making systems
- Delegation of authority

in Head Offices, as Figure 9.1 illustrates, with buyers, finance and personnel typically grouped into departments. Structural hierarchies created lines of management, with each level responsible to a line·manager above it. On the operations side, the geographical spread of the retailer determined the number of regional and area managers, with each of the latter controlling up to 20 stores.

However, centralisation of control led to new reporting channels that resulted in diminishing store-based responsibilities. The need for specialised knowledge had started to decline with the development of self-service and prepackaging. Price and assortment became more strictly controlled leaving managers locally to concentrate on maximising sales and the control of costs. But paradoxically, even though store managers' decision-making responsibilities have been more restricted, the position has increasingly required well-trained and professional personnel (Freathy, 1997).

During the 1990s the central structure, and particularly the reduction in hierarchical management, changed to emphasise the advisory roles of the support functions. Figure 9.2 demonstrates the changes to the structure caused by out-sourcing financial

Figure 9.1   *A Functional and Hierarchical Retail Organisational Chart*

Figure 9.2   *A Retail Organisation Focused on Core Activities*

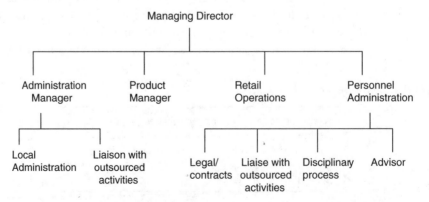

and personnel activities to other organisations, given the need to save costs of people and expensive Head Office space.

Divisionalisation

Business divisionalisation is characteristic of large retailers in order to realise specialised efficiencies and achieve specific goals. With multi-business retailers such as Arcadia and Kingfisher, functional structures are extended within each facia, or group of facias, and the Head Office takes on a corporate coordination role. This scale of business raises issues of direction and control from both strategic and financial perspectives:

1 Profit responsibility is passed onto divisional general managers; multi-divisional firms have units from which profits can be measured and transfers made. These businesses can identify and audit substandard performances, and the corporate level relies heavily on the division as a means of control.

2 The corporate HQ is concerned with strategic planning, appraisal and allocation of resources. The degree of decentralization of the resource allocation process must be specifically designed in view of the firm's diversity and size, and the structure must effectively exploit opportunities for resource-sharing, usually resulting in staff at corporate level influencing resource-based decisions and functional policies.

3 Corporate managers should be committed to the performance of the total organisation, not just the individual division. Incentives and rewards as well as controls need to reinforce this aim.

A multiplicity of markets requires an ability to continually refocus, which in turn demands organisational flexibility and decentralised decision-making. However, there is a balance to be maintained between centralised and decentralised decisions as investment in information and communications technology (ICT), warehousing and distribution require centralised planning to create an integrated approach to logistics, personnel and training needs (Segal Horn, 1987).

Control and Empowerment

Centralisation and control systems can lead to conflict with service quality. Goffee and Scase (1995) summarise the dilemma faced by many companies that

> under considerable financial pressures to sustain growth . . . [they] face the threat that greater scale will demand more systems, standards and controls. On the one hand this process of bureaucratisation may damage the delivery of a personal service; on the other, it can become increasingly difficult to nurture or sustain employee flexibility, involvement and innovation.

As a result retailers must decide on their organisational approach to service quality, whether they seek to standardise practices or devolve decision-making to local levels

> **Exhibit 9.1   Changes to the core retail structure at Marks and Spencer**
>
> Marks and Spencer stressed that the restructuring of the company at the end of 1999 was part of a long-term strategy: 'This is not a defensive move at all', said the group, 'It is the next stage of a lot of restructuring that has been going on for some time.'
>
> The M&S business was split into five areas – UK retail, overseas retail, financial services, property and new ventures. The latest changes will be made to the five-strong UK retail board, which reports to the main board. The group said it could not give details of the changes that were still subject to board discussions. However, it said the reforms were expected to affect about 45 people during the first phase and would then move down through the business to the shopfloor. 'These changes are about realigning us to our customers' needs quickly and simply' reorganising the retail management into 'customer business units' which is supposed to make us more customer-focused, devolving power to [...] people within an identified leadership.
>

of responsibility and commitment is particularly important in global retail management. Devolution of authority is part of what fuels the type of restructuring seen in Figure 9.2 and especially underpins greater deliverables from team-working and greater employee involvement. Empowerment and diversity lie at the root of this issue, and retailers are increasingly examining the ways in which responsibility and authority can be delegated at all levels, with firms becoming less hierarchical, moving from superior–subordinate relationships to one of peer control and 'not letting down the team' (Hope-Hailey *et al.*, 1997).

Similarly, downsizing of middle-management layers has been used to respond to customer needs for improved value or service. But the process of delayering, the reduction in levels of command within organisations, is unlikely to succeed using a simplistic formula, for example by applying a 'five-layers' approach. Sustained improvements will be most easily achieved in those organisations that follow the argument for organisational form, its structure, to follow function. Changing the way in which work is done and removing unnecessary tasks that fail to add any value is as important, if not more so, than simply changing the levels of managers doing it. Moreover, delayering is unlikely to bring sustainable cost advantages on its own; team-working, cross-functional working and a high-involvement management style will all need greater emphasis.

There is no one best way to implement a flatter structure. What makes the most effective change process depends largely upon the prevailing culture and values. Involving employees and winning their commitment increases the odds of success. Line managers are both the object of delayering and related HRM inspired initiatives, as well as the designers and deliverers of their repercussions. As such, they will require additional support to deliver their people-management responsibilities effectively during a period of change.

Exhibit 9.2   The John Lewis partnership goes beyond the purely commercial

Some 70 years ago the founder of the John Lewis Partnership launched a unique experiment in business ownership by handing over the company to a trust for its employees. For many, this retailer is a model employer sharing the fruits of its success with its 35 000 staff, or 'partners', and giving them a say in how the group is run. For others it is weighed down by bureaucracy, that stifles individualism and entrepreneurship.

Partnership works in a variety of ways. One of the main aims is to hold managers accountable to staff through an elaborate network of councils and the weekly staff *Gazette*. Branch councils scrutinise management decisions at store level while a 135-strong central council acts as a group-wide forum. More informally, employees writing to the *Gazette* – anonymously, if they so wish – are entitled to a written response from a relevant manager. Another element of the concept is what the company calls the 'best profit-sharing scheme in the country'.

Partnership is not just about pay and perks. For one employee it is about 'not letting the side down'. For another it is about 'decency and honesty' – meaning you wouldn't use your store discount card to buy goods for your sister. It aims to benefit everyone it comes into contact with, ensuring suppliers are paid promptly and the shop is 'never knowingly undersold'. But critics say the bureaucratic council system smacks more of the Soviet era than the modern one, while the paternalism is reminiscent of Japanese corporate culture. The rigidities are certainly not to everybody's taste: 'People discover fairly quickly whether they like it or not, and if they don't they leave', says one employee.

It also carries costs that many other groups would consider an extravagance. These include the councils, registrars (a discreet breed of advisers to partners and local managers), private country clubs and the cost of funding a raft of other benefits. The group clearly believes these ultimately pay for themselves in terms of employee motivation.

David Young, deputy Chairman, says the group's structure has resulted in lower levels of staff turnover and staff theft. The stability extends from the shopfloor to the boardroom. No big company has gone anything like as far as John Lewis in the array of benefits or degree of employee involvement.

Source: adapted from *Financial Times*, 6 November 1996.

CULTURE AND HUMAN RESOURCES

Organisations are designed, in the context of their particular business, to achieve strategic objectives through the distribution of work. Employees may be told what to do in the store, or are trained to do a job in a certain way, or provided with a rule book, but consistent and acceptable behaviour is learnt through the organisation's culture. In order to implement its strategy, management must support a culture that is consistent with the organisation's business purpose. An organisation's culture is reflected in the dominant beliefs about the ways in which work should be organised, authority exercised and people treated; in short 'the ways in which things are done around here' (Drennan, 1992). Retailing is characterised by large investments in human assets, with the consequence that organisational culture has a significant role in sustaining the strategic aims of the company.

Culture has a number of roles that affect human resources and their management. It is generally held to be valuable in promoting social cohesion in the organisation,

---

Exhibit 9.3   Cultural proximity at Wal-Mart and Asda

Corporate culture between Walmart and Asda is very close, largely because by Asda's own admission it has spent years stealing Walmart's ideas. These include everyday low pricing, as well as a management culture that discourages management culture: Asda does not have 78 000 employees, it has that number of 'colleagues', inspired by Walmart's associates. Customer service, too, has been copied by Asda. The US people-greeters and 'Ten-Foot Attitude' for associates to look customers in the eye, greet them and ask if they need help. The Asda 'Happy to help' badge echoes the Wal-Mart chant 'Who's number one? The customer'.

Source: *Financial Times*, 15 July 1999.

---

to enable groups and teams to function effectively. Culture is often referred to as a 'glue' by acting as a force to hold the organisation together. It reduces both conflict and uncertainty, as common purposes and ways of working are learned through interaction and observation of other experienced colleagues. New employees learn what is important, how to go about the work and behave (Brown, 1995). Retailers frequently use visual images in uniforms and name badges for sales staff that reflect the company colours and logo to reinforce the sense of identity. The extent to which the use of names and style of communication are more or less formal can be indicative of closeness or distance in working relationships. Informal transmission of stories and myths about the company circulate in staff rooms and around the coffee machine. The success of Marks and Spencer over many years has owed much to the ability of organisational routines to extract high levels of performance from its staff.

The expression of strongly held values within the culture can provide mechanisms for control and coordination; Body Shop's Anita Roddick set in place ethical and social values that help to direct and guide decision-making by which some courses of action can be simply and unequivocally rejected. Culture can be motivational through its promotion of loyalty and sense of worth, and in its transmission of stories, ceremonies and rites that create a sense of belonging, and human resource management has a significant role in encouraging and maintaining these cultural elements. Actions and behaviours can be maintained by the organisation's culture and at the same time culture is also a result of these same dimensions. The human resource management function will be closely involved in supporting cultural change through the planning and implementation of organisational structuring with departmental and line managers. The RAEW matrix can be a valuable analytical tool to evaluate jobs and their fit within the organisation and its culture. It requires an assessment of:

■ *Responsibility*   the function of the line or team in achieving tasks.

■ *Authority*   a position may not necessarily have responsibility for carrying out tasks.

■ *Expertise*   the ability to a fulfil a role may identify training needs or job transfer.

■ *Work*   the level and scope of work required in a job.

Behavioural changes can be made through staff appraisal procedures and recruitment, revised job specifications and analysis of training needs and processes.

Organisational cultures are unique, but nevertheless share some characteristics through their stages of development, the historical evolution of the business, and the values and ethos of its founder and leaders. *Young companies* need a strong, clear culture to find themselves a source of identity and strength in overcoming threats and resistance from competitors and the environment. *Mid-life companies* have strong cultures within the larger company culture, which can be shaped by systematically allocating resources and power to the sub-cultures that best fit the organisation's long-term strategy. *Declining organisations* recognise that basic assumptions may be dysfunctional because of environmental changes and that long-held beliefs may have to be thrown out. In this phase cultural changes may be required to address issues of decline, to develop positive motivational techniques and reestablish appropriate attitudes (McKiernan, 1992). However, a strongly held culture may lead to lengthy battles within the organisation and hold back the process of change.

Interpretations of culture can create undesirable ambiguities. Employees from other companies bring their own cultural heritage with them; stores may reflect the behaviour of their managers rather than company-initiated behaviour; and maintaining a coherent culture across many sites requires strong coordinating actions. Culture can also depend on hierarchy – the views of senior management can be quite different to those of employees further down the organisation. There is evidence in food retailing, at least, to suggest there are significant problems in the relationship between strategy, culture and people. The interconnections between these three areas makes them difficult to control with the attitudes of senior managers tending to focus on strategy and discount the value of either culture or human resource management (Ogbonna and Whipp, 1999). At shopfloor level, the very people who are most in contact with the customer have the most fragmented perspective of the organisation's culture. The issue is whether they will adopt values that are consistent with their companies espoused values (Harris and Ogbonna, 1998). To achieve this aim, companies increasingly engage with their staff, for example through staff satisfaction surveys, to assess employee response to major cultural change.

Leadership

Business leadership and the ways in which power in the organisation is exercised have a major impact on the formulation and delivery of human resource policies in terms of change management and strategic direction. Views on the modern chief executive suggest the need for a range of skills to be able to manage increasing organisational complexity. Effective leadership should:

- Inspire. Among the most important leadership skills is the ability to capture the audience in competition with many other people, and to achieve this leaders will have to be 'emotionally efficient'.

- Establish integrity and ethics.

- Communicate sensitively; leaders need to build and develop people.

Exhibit 9.4 Keys to success at Nordstrom

The Nordstrom culture sets employees free. The company believes that people will work hard when they are given the freedom to do their job the way they think it should be done, and when they treat customers the way they like to be treated. Nordstrom believes that too many rules, regulations and strict channels of communication erode employee incentive. Without those shackles, Nordstrom people can operate like entrepreneurial shopkeepers. The company is:

- Informally organised.
- Empowers shopfloor people to accept returned merchandise.
- Salespeople are free to sell merchandise to their customers in any department.
- Department managers begin their career as salespeople.
- Managers are encouraged to have a feeling of ownership about their department: responsible for hiring, training, coaching, nurturing and evaluating their sales team.
- Buying is decentralised to regions.
- Empowerment for getting the right merchandise in the store begins on the floor.
- Employee compensation is based on sales commission.
- Goal-setting is essential to the culture.
- Employees have access to sales figures.
- Outstanding sales performances are rewarded with prizes.
- Top sales people are encouraged to help others with sales techniques and building a customer base.

Source: Spector and McCarthy (1995).

- Establish organisational values and culture; variation and experimentation will need to be encouraged.

In many respects it is easier to be seen as a leader in crisis situations where results are produced from weakness and successes can outweigh mistakes. Successful leadership is also about the ability to bring about sustained culture change and it is clear that many retail leaders have an important role to play in changing the ways in which organisations work. Declining sales and profitability at previously successful businesses have resulted in new leaders at Marks and Spencer and Sainsbury to turn the companies around.

A characteristic of senior retail management is their direct involvement in the business; at Wal-Mart Sam Walton talked about the importance of 'getting into the field', and Lord Seiff at Marks and Spencer likewise explained the importance of contact with the stores themselves and their response to customer needs (Seiff, 1987). This hands-on chraracteristic can be observed through a diversity of leadership styles from visionary leaders such as Richard Branson, to the more strategic style of Archie

> **Exhibit 9.5   Leadership and management**
>
> What sort of leadership characteristics should we look for in the 21st century? Increasingly, businesses need new ideas and products to encourage enterprise and creativity. The standard models of leadership, especially command and control models, do not appear to be appropriate. Some argue that a more inclusive style of leadership is needed. People learn from each other because their collective knowledge and skills, the ability to solve problems, is best found in groups. In the view of Walter Bennis, 'none of us is as smart as all of us. The Lone Ranger is dead.' Creative leaders have to nurture a style that suits the group, to act decisively but also consistently, to respect the individual space of other members of their group. In short, they have to 'devise an atmosphere in which others can put a dent in the universe' (Bennis, 1998).
>
> Others argue that individuals, the innovators who build businesses from nothing but the strength of their ideas, are the people to provide solutions to today's problems and sow the seeds for the future. These successful achievers possess a lifelong curiosity, as well as creativity. Power and control are present in their personalities, but not obsessively so; rather the urge to express themselves seems an important motivation. For people like Richard Branson, the 'world is a bundle of possibilities waiting to be explored' (Handy, 1999).

Norman and Allan Leighton at Asda, each demonstrating a commitment to employees and customers.

The need for *leadership*, in contrast to *management*, is suggested by the development of teams and the decline in hierarchies. Individuals will find themselves belonging to several teams and therefore will be increasingly offering their contribution rather than having it demanded of them (Weightman, 1999). Team-leadership skills will be increasingly demanded as global businesses find themselves focusing on teamwork to increase productivity. Indeed, teamwork has been shown to be an important activity as managers report spending between 50–90 per cent of their time in team activities and facilitation (Lussier, 1999). At all levels, managers can reduce complexity for their colleagues by clarifying role definitions, allowing individuals more freedom to pursue a different style to the norm, judging performance by outcomes, and giving time to produce results.

HUMAN RESOURCE MANAGEMENT

The main objectives of human resource managers themselves have been discussed in terms of 'quality, customer orientation, flexibility, commitment, involvement, leadership, team working and continuous learning' (Torrington and Hall, 1998). Their focus is on obtaining, training and maintaining an efficient workforce to achieve financial and marketing objectives (Davidson *et al.*, 1988). The need for effective retail personnel management is due to increasing costs of payroll and the consequent need to increase productivity: through self-service and automation, improved store design and improvements in performance management.

Figure 9.3   *Types of Personnel Management*

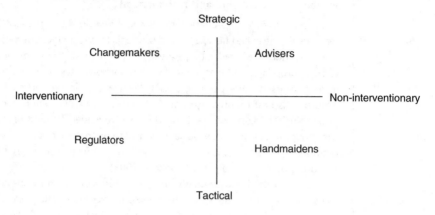

Source: Storey (1992).

However, the role and function of human resource managers has changed over the past 20 years. Personnel management of the 1970s was largely concerned with industrial relations, although these have not been particularly confrontational in retailing, and an administrative role. In the 1980s, human resource management defined a flexible function broadly defined by two approaches: best practice/outcome or contingency/strategic (Hope-Hailey *et al.*, 1997). Storey identifies four types based on the intervention and strategic position of managers (Figure 9.3).

■ Advisers provide an internal consultancy.

■ Handmaidens are reactive too, but more customer-led in the services they offer.

■ Regulators are more interventionary, with a role defined by formulated, monitored observence of rules, the traditional paradigm of industrial relations.

■ Changemakers have higher ambitions, seeking to put relations with employees on a new footing. Some have a distinctive human resource perspective, other possess the new business style of the senior team. They use a more quantitative, business-strategy approach to manage people, as in a headcount and in as rational a way as any other resource. This might be described as a hard-face compared with soft-face, to do with unique human resource qualities; for example close regard to motivational techniques, two-way communications, development and leadership (Storey, 1992).

The personal preferences, motivation and experience of senior management have often dominated organisations. As a result it has been argued that the human resource function must position itself to minimise the negative effects of ill-planned change. It should establish the systems and culture that will support the necessary adjustments to skills and relationships. Its ability to do this is countered by a declining influence in the boardroom, and as a result behavioural change tends to be achieved through performance management rather than attention to large-scale organisational development.

The retail industry has been shown to have some unique aspects of the retail personnel function that require both planning and operational management skills:

- Seasonal and irregular demand and extensive use of part-time employment.
- Inexperience of employees, with many young people employed in the industry.
- Consumer time preferences for store hours leading to longer hours of opening.
- Importance of employee personality and appearance (Davidson *et al.*, 1988).

As strategic HRM and personnel services are separated out, with the traditional HR welfare role in counselling, discipline and assessment transferred to line management, the HR specialist's role changes to one of internal consultant. Other managers will develop an increasing awareness of these issues so HR management skills will be required by many more line managers. Performance, output, accountability and measurement will be typically emphasised, but through a diversity of practices and determined by complex contextual factors.

THE PEOPLE FACTOR

Recruitment

Recruitment is the process by which an organisation secures its labour requirements. To recruit it is necessary to determine what the job consists of and the key aspects that specify the type of person required to undertake the job. Identifying vacancies will require a knowledge of the sort of person required for the longer-term aspects of the job, the type of work they need to undertake and the job description – such as the purpose of the job, tasks and scope (Weightman, 1999). Job analysis, description and specification involves detailed and specific knowledge of duties involved, and the characteristics of applicants necessary to match the job (Davison *et al.*, 1988).

The sheer size of the retail sector in the UK, with around 2.76 million employees, and its emphasis on youth has the potential to create a positive image. The appeal of working for an aspirational brand succeeds in attracting employees. However, skills training opportunities and at least some well-paid and exciting career opportunities are balanced by long hours, low status and, for many employees, low pay. Progression though the organisation to supervisory and managerial positions has become less obvious too. The image of sales work is viewed as something that restricts the ability of employers to attract the highest calibre recruits. Therefore recruitment materials are particularly important in presenting the retailer in the most positive light.

The process of recruitment consists of four stages beginning with a search of the labour market to attract sufficient numbers of employees of the required type. Secondly, applicants will have to be assessed, then jobs allocated through induction to work tasks and 'placement', and finally evaluation of performance against criteria established for the job (Thomason, 1990). A clear structure in the recruitment process provides opportunities to explain the job and its purpose so that new employees can clearly align their expectations with those of the company. Recruitment is often a two-way process in which the recruiter and applicant assess whether the job will meet the needs and expectations of both sides, and for more senior positions may require

Table 9.2   *Recruitment Methods*

Newspapers, national and local	Universities, colleges and schools
	Trade press (for example *Retail Week, The Grocer, Drapers Record*)
Local radio	Recruitment consultants
Internal advertising	Headhunters
Job centres	Word of mouth

several meetings of varying degrees of formality. The induction programme that follows recruitment can continue this process by grounding the starter in the company's culture and behaviour, and at the very least informing the recruit of basic health and safety requirements and working practices.

Retail recruiters operating in tight labour markets in which the supply of employees is limited are faced with particular problems. Recruiters must recognise current trends and issues in order to fill shortages from new labour pools such as students, single mothers, retired people and the long-term unemployed on government retraining schemes (Table 9.2). There is evidence that recruiters often express a desirability for experience over qualifications, and are reluctant to draw from the unemployed. However, there is an increasingly strict legal framework surrounding discrimination in employment. Laws against racial, sexual and disability discrimination have been supplemented more recently by the Employment Relations Act (1999) which provides even more specific rights for women not to be discriminated against on the grounds of pregnancy, maternity or childbirth. In many respects, it is desirable to recruit people from a wide background and demonstrate a commitment to equal opportunities.

Gender

Women account for around 65 per cent of all retail employees, rising to 68 per cent of sales assistants and 77 per cent of check-out employees, compared to the 50 per cent industrial average (DNTO, 2001). One problem arising from the increasing proportion of women in low-paid jobs is the unequal opportunity for personal development between the genders. Women's position in the labour market impacts directly on their access to training, with those most disadvantaged having the least access to job-related training. The lack of training and qualifications prevents these women from moving up the occupational hierarchy into better and more highly-paid jobs, while inhibiting the participation of others (Callender and Metcalf, 1997).

Age

Retail employment is heavily weighted towards younger age groups for both men and women, and there is evidence that most young people were recruited for lower skilled or routine positions. However, whilst the number of women in the older age groups decline relatively slowly, the number of men in this type of employment declines significantly beyond their mid-20s (Table 9.3). Employers appear to vary markedly in the formality of their approach to training young people. Employers providing trainee-

Table 9.3   *Sales Assistants by Age and Gender, London*

Age	Male	%	Female	%
16–24	33 000	23	36 000	26
25–34	15 000	10	16 000	11
35–44	9 000	6	16 000	11
45+	N/A		15 000	10
Total	57 000	44	83 000	59

Source: Labour Force Survey (1999).

ships tend to adopt a more 'programmatic' approach to training, although it may still be fairly informal. One problem widely found in employment of younger people is that few employers provide for their long-term development apart from those with fairly detailed training programmes. The skills developed by young people appear to fall into one of three categories: generally transferable skills, occupationally or sectorally transferable skills, and organisation or job-specific skills (Hillage *et al.*, 1998).

However, by 2011, 35 per cent of the population in the UK will be aged over 55, a demographic trend that suggests retailers should be more active in recruiting older age groups. It has been shown that older workers can have desirable attitudes to work; they are likely to demonstrate a high degree of commitment to their job, and to provide higher levels of stability, knowledge and customer service than younger employees. Nearly three-fifths of those aged 50 and over 'do the best they can' with respect to their job, 'even if interferes with the rest of their life'. This compares to less than two-fifths of those aged 18 to 24 (British Social Attitudes Survey, 1996). B&Q, Sainsbury and Tesco all have policies in place to employ older people, and anecdotal evidence also suggests that there is no difference in productivity between older and younger workers.

It therefore seems logical that if there are fewer younger people available in the labour market and more older people who want to continue in work, employers will need to consider how to attract and accommodate an older workforce. Opportunities may include open learning and flexible learning opportunities, as well as making training 'older friendly', for example by filling skills gaps, confidence building and tailoring training to older workers' preferred learning methods and experience (Kodz *et al.*, 1999).

Full and part-time working

Part-time working in the retail industry is increasing and now accounts for around 58 per cent of employees. There is some evidence that geographical location may determine the mix of full-time and part-time working. In London the two types are evenly balanced in inner city areas, which include the main shopping districts, whilst in the suburbs a higher percentage of employees, around 68 per cent, work part-time. By gender, men tend to hold more full-time jobs, whilst for women part-time working dominates with 77 per cent working part-time in the suburbs. The challenge for recruiters will be to provide accessible and flexible opportunities for part-time workers, especially women, to develop new as well as existing skills.

Staff retention

Staff retention has important implications for company image, service and perfor-mance. Rates of staff turnover can vary by retail sector; in fast-food retailing it can be consistently over 200 per cent, whereas 75 per cent down to 25 per cent represents a scale from satisfactory to excellent in the clothing and footwear sector. In part, reten-tion is related to perceptions of retailing itself, but more importantly to the individ-ual retailer's culture as well as regional and local employment levels. Changes in attitudes to work also contribute to retention problems; 'generation X' has been used to define an age group whose personal goals are shaped by variety, choice and per-sonal achievement within or outside the workplace, and these may not be satisfied by the retailer's style of working.

The main causes of staff turnover (Table 9.4) have been identified as low pay, low morale or unhappiness in the job, as well as limited personal career prospects (*Retail Week*, 1997), so retention policies will focus on:

■ *Recruitment and selection*, which involves making the right choice of employee.

■ *Motivation*; practical incentives at store level can be achieved by creating a fun element to work, or comfortable and well-equipped staffrooms. Financial rewards such as bonuses may have a limited long-term effect. Succession planning that enables employees to move between jobs or take on secondments can substitute for the loss of career progression routes in delayered organisational structures.

■ *Benefits* can include vouchers, commission payments and travel cards, but do not work for everyone.

■ *Managers*; personal management styles and coaching lack of skills can often cause a breakdown in employee relationships.

There is evidence that early experience of the retailer can support longer-term reten-tion and the survival rate for the first six months is a good indicator of how long the employee will stay in the business.

Table 9.4   *Retail Staff Turnover, 1999*

	Retail (%)	All industries (%)
Working for the same firm	75	81
Working for a different firm, but same occupation	2	3
Working for a different firm, different occupation	8	7
Unemployed	3	2
Student	8	4
Sick	0	1
Other	4	3

Source: DNTO (2001).

Retail Employment: Operational Roles

By far the largest group of employees work in sales occupations. With the downsizing of supervisory and middle management positions in many retail organisations, sales assistants have become not only the largest group of retail employees, but also one which faces the most challenges in the front line of customer service. The range of sales assistant roles is particularly diverse. Department stores may place great importance on communication skills, whilst discount food retailers or specialist electrical stores may have quite different priorities. The role is evolving, too, with the high level of customer service offered through personal shoppers at an increasing number of department stores and other upmarket clothing retailers including Marks and Spencer.

Sales assistant jobs have traditionally been regarded as requiring little real ability or skill (Dench *et al.*, 1997). However, there is evidence that this may not be the case as, increasingly, sales staff are expected to cover a wider range of tasks and to have a greater depth of knowledge. The *Retail Week*/MTI (1997) survey, identified skills gaps for junior trainee and shopfloor positions in eight areas, with leadership skills, office/business skills and presentation the weakest. Many aspects of customer service and selling involve some understanding of human behaviour and psychology, and in particular there is a growing need for people to work more smartly, more efficiently and flexibly. Part of this trend may see the disappearance of checkout and till-based staff to work on the shopfloor. Table 9.5 lists some areas for skills development.

Recruiters must attract staff to a range of other positions, broadly classified as either operational or Head Office functions. In addition to sales and check-out staff, operational roles include store supervision and management in stockrooms, warehouses, distribution and logistics. Logistics includes specific transport and distribution jobs, but also a wide variety of roles in the supply chain from operations management to logistics planning, project work and strategic development. These require distinct personal qualities and competencies in two areas: technology skills and people skills. In the first area, PC literacy and the ability to work with information systems in the automated or 'smart warehouse' is critical. On the people side, skills and abilities are more widely shared with other managerial positions to include problem-solving, leadership, communication, team-building and sound decision-making.

These jobs are important for their role in delivering customer satisfaction through timely and cost-effective stock control. The ways in which merchandise are displayed

Table 9.5   *An Agenda for Skills Development*

- Customer service and communication
- Changing methods of stock control
- Addressing changing customer demands, including the extension of opening hours, and keeping up with, or ahead or, the competition
- Display and product presentation skills
- Greater commercial awareness and business sense
- The continuing importance of people skills, and how these can be enhanced
- New technology: computerisation and other forms of automation
- Increased responsibility and widened functional roles

Source: Based on Dench *et al.* (1997).

to create an attractive selling environment is primarily the function of the Display and Visual Merchandising team; the importance of these functions tends to be underestimated. Retailers may use a specialist in both fields or in each, with display focused on shop-window presentation and visual merchandising on instore layout and presentation. However, many creative people do not enter the retail industry in preference to other forms of design and art, because, additionally, in the retail environment they need to be articulate, numerate and to have presentation and team-management skills.

Head Office Occupations

Head Offices offer a wide range of employment opportunities, although numbers are considerably fewer than for front-line sales staff. London alone has over 75 retail Head Offices across all sectors with functions ranging from small-scale administrative 'addresses' to large, centralised functions for multiple businesses.

From an early stage of organisational development a retailer will create a specialised buying function to select and control wider and more complex product ranges. The exact responsibilities vary from one sector to another; clothing buyers will be expected to have a strong design background and creative flair to interpret new fashion trends. Food buyers, on the other hand, will be expected to have well-developed commercial skills to negotiate strongly on price. The buyers may work as a team with assistant buyers and buying clerks taking on some buying and most supplier administration functions. Increasingly, retailers are recruiting graduates to these positions, with a design degree being quoted as an essential requirement for clothing buying by recruitment agencies. As the retailer extends its activities it requires more complex stock management systems. The merchandiser or stock controller usually works alongside the buyer and other specialists to plan and control the levels of stock in the business. The merchandiser may also be responsible for an assistant and stock allocators as part of their team. These positions require numeracy and analytical skills as well as strong communication and team skills.

Marketing staff tend to have more prominent roles in the food, electrical and toiletries and cosmetics sectors rather than in clothing. In these sectors category management teams bring together buyers, stock managers and marketing staff to work in cross-functional groups. A recent report identified skills gaps in the ability to create and express a business vision, flair to identify new opportunities, influencing skills, and analytical and project management skills. Roles within sales and marketing are changing, demanding higher-level skills rather than new ones. Retaining marketing and sales people with these skills is critical, since effective sales and marketing is a major lever for competitiveness. Moreover, as employers recognise the need to develop a marketing culture within organisations, customer service and selling skills are becoming a requirement for many employees, not just for those employed directly in sales and marketing. Head Offices provide employment, too, for smaller groups of professionals working in product technology, property management, design services, information systems, finance and accounting, and human resource functions. However, returning to Figure 9.2, it is clear that numbers of specialist staff are likely to decline as line managers take on further responsibilities and more specialised functions are contracted out of the business.

EFFECTIVE WORKING PRACTICES

This section examines the ways in which people work, their skills and adaptability to new working conditions that may be encountered in the retail industry. Working practices are defined by a retailer within the appropriate legislative and industrial frameworks. The rights and responsibilities of employees are primarily laid out in contracts of employment that specify the term and type of employment relationship, whether it is permanent or temporary, full or part-time, or offers term time or zero hours conditions. Government legislation has become increasingly concerned with both employers' and employees' responsibilities, specially in Health and Safety and Discrimination procedures. Compliance with these and other regulations will be the responsibility of the company's Directors, who must create legally binding working practices at the highest level of planning.

Training and employee development forms an important part of ensuring that the retailer's working policies are put into action. The provision of training by

Figure 9.4   *Elements of the Employment Contract*

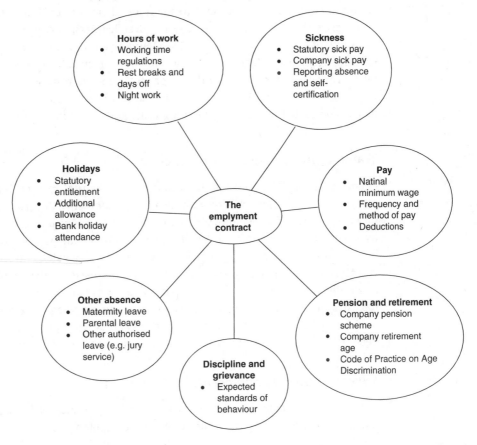

employers is a mixture of pragmatism and implicit or occasionally explicit strategy. Few organisations plan their business strategy all the way down to staff training, even if clear links between the two are evident. Those retailers committed to meeting quality standards and competing at the higher end of their markets tend to be the firms with a more formal approach to training, through written training plans, assessment processes and so on. At the other end of the scale, organisations com-peting in terms of price and speed of delivery tend to have a fairly systematised organisation of work, in which employment 'slots' are filled by young people. Here, the tasks tend to be fairly narrow and defined, and the training limited to ensure employees have the skills to carry them out efficiently and effectively (Hillage *et al.*, 1998).

As suggested earlier in this chapter, the more strategic of these two approaches finds retailers increasingly looking to combine customer care with efficient operational management. In general terms this means that staff training and development needs to engage with:

■ Broader responsibilities and multi-skilling;
■ Delegated responsibilities from managers;
■ Greater flexibility in the performance of diverse tasks; and
■ Skills development, training and qualification programmes will be based on these trends.

Continuous learning is needed to achieve these aims, to equip people to deal with environmental uncertainties and to maintain their employability. Lifelong learning emphasises the individual and can empower learners, providing more choice and flexibility of opportunity. However, the changing employment context creates its own training problems in leaner organisations, as in practice it becomes more difficult to take busy sales staff away from their work to attend training sessions where there are few or no replacements to cover their absence. These pressures can lead to courses being fragmented into smaller learning units and poor attendance.

Training and Development Practice

Retailers typically see 'people' in various ways as central to their business, which is reflected in their approaches to training and development. Most training and develop-ment is customer-focused, but also arises from the recognition that common capabil-ity needs should stimulate movement across internal company boundaries to create a more flexible workforce. Alternatively the company may value and strongly believe in employee education and learning in itself. Training-needs analysis will align corporate and individual needs with the organisation's aims as part of a formal process of inter-nal assessment and benchmarking against other employment practices (Figure 9.5).

Training in specific activities and functions and development, providing for broader personal needs, tends to follow one of two approaches or discussed below.

Structured training approaches

This approach is competency-based. Increasingly the industry has adopted a compe-tence approach to employee development, competent being a 'standard required

Figure 9.5   *Elements of Employee Performance Measurement*

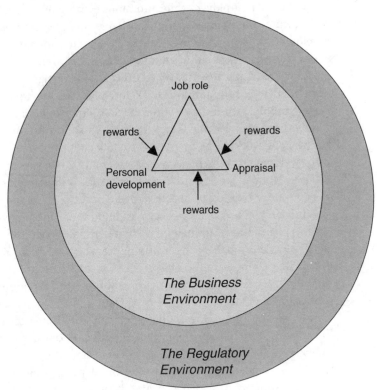

successfully to perform an activity or function' (Jessop, 1991). The concept has broadened to include meta competences at graduate level and in management training. New recruits work through a series of training modules which may last from one week to three months. Workplace-based coaches act as assessors, and appraisal identifies further training needs.

National Vocational Qualifications (NVQs) provide a national standard for learners to demonstrate their competence in the workplace. These are more often used for employee development in retail operations, and run from levels 1 to an A-level equivalent at level 3. An employee meets performance criteria over a number of units, with evidence gathered over a minimum of three months.

Longer-serving staff use higher-level training units or develop specialist skills. Assessment and appraisal identify training needs and measure changes in ability to perform a task or activity, such as customer service.

Flexible training and development approaches

Personal development plans are linked to appraisal and managers identify individual needs. Some retailers enable employees to take responsibility for managing their own learning and skill development; for example at Body Shop where staff are empowered to set their own learning objectives rather than take formal courses (Prickett, 1997).

Learning centres at Head Office and in larger stores are staffed by the training team, and individual employees call in for advice and guidance.

A feature of employee training in large retailing organisations is a preference to develop their own in-house learning materials, including videos, workbooks and books, although external learning materials and trainers are also used. In small and medium sized Enterprises (SME) retailing it is clear that verbal instruction and demonstration in the shop are almost exclusively used for updating product knowledge. Underlying the face-to-face approach for interpersonal development is the creation of an environment for behavioural learning, 'team skills require one on one, and small groups'. The workplace can be used to 'talk about interpersonal skills, team meetings, and development though managers' presentations on success' (Kent and Hawkisworth, 2000). Facilitated workshops can be used for a variety of training purposes including a wider understanding of business for managers.

Motivating employees to learn is important. Interactive media reaches out to otherwise unmotivated new employees in a recognisable and acceptable form; 'generation X is looking for continuing learning which requires a whole different way of thinking about training. This generation sticks around so long as it is satisfying to them. We need to appeal too to generation Y for variety and challenge' (Kent and Hawksworth, 2000). Often classroom training takes place at the pace of the slowest learner, so the more able trainees became bored and distracted. Emphasis on the individual's development plan and self-directed development encourages employee interaction.

There is some evidence for an evolution in learning media starting with paper-based materials supported by video, universally used by these retailers, and some audio materials. The creation of CD ROMs form another step in the development of learning materials prompted by the need to incorporate a more graphical style. The final stage is the development of multimedia materials for the Intranet. In short, at this stage interactivity enables the trainer to check the trainee's understanding of the learning material.

Evaluation

Evaluation concerns the obtaining of information on the effects of a training programme and the assessment of the value of training as a consequence. Different levels of evaluation can be determined using Kirkpatrick's (1982) model:

- *Reaction level*   assess the trainee's views on the training session.
- *Learning level*   what the trainee learned.
- *Behaviour level*   how the training changed the individual's behaviour and their application of learning.
- *Organisational level*   the impact of training and the difference it has made to the organisation.

Annual or more frequent appraisals are the most common form of assessment, but certification is also an important issue for some retailers partly as a measure of

Table 9.6	*Key Skills*	
■ Communication	■ Improving own learning and performance	
■ Working with others	■ Information technology	
■ Application of number	■ Problem-solving	

learning effectiveness and employee development and partly of productivity effectiveness. With retail outlets spread over wide geographical areas, costs and control become significant issues; one US store group estimated that $10 000–15 000 savings per store could be achieved using computer-based training for large groups of employees.

Skills

Retail skills are often distinguished as basic skills and technical skills. Basic or key skills provide an individual with a personal resource that is transferable across functions and industries. Key skills, as such, have been embedded into the national qualification system for 16–18-years-olds and continue into higher education as a central element of government and education policy (Table 9.6). They have been shown to be important in improving the employability of young people, to provide them with the skills required by employers and to equip them as effective learners.

Key skills are viewed as an important part of the self-employed mindset increasingly required by many jobs. Within increasingly uncertain labour markets, most employers recognise the importance of an appropriately skilled workforce that can adapt to changing circumstances and ensure business success. However, the relevance of key skills to an occupational area is not always clear and some concerns have been raised about key skills development for adults (Kodz, 1998). Communication skills mean different things to different retailers; for example, they could include listening skills, writing skills and, in a generic sense, soft skills. There is a sense, too, that these skills are more appropriate for management or trainee management. Both customer service and IT skills are frequently identified both through the media and in company reports as playing a critical role in the implementation of the service dimension of retail strategies. In terms of technical skills, product knowledge, customer service, communications skills, and point of sale training are key developmental areas for employees in operational roles, although further specialised training and development will be required by buyers and professional support staff.

MOTIVATION AND REWARDS

Employee motivation has become an important point of measurement, as customer and employee satisfaction are shown to be closely related. There is a case to argue that employees should be viewed as business assets rather than costs, and that increasing employee commitment has measurable business implications, as an increase in employee commitment independently increases sales (Barber *et al.*, 1999). In terms of financial value, it has been shown that a one percentage point increase in employee satisfaction can lead to an increase in sales of £200000 per store per month (Carrington, 1999).

Since more motivated employees tend to lead to higher levels of performance, an understanding of the relationship between motivation and behaviour is required. Motivation theories fall into three fields:

- *Context motivation theories*: identify people's needs in order to understand what motivates them. These include Maslow's Hierarchy of Needs, and Herzberg's Two-Factor, hygiene and satisfier, theory.

- *Process motivation theories*: how and why people are motivated, an approach which focuses on behaviour rather than needs.

- *Reinforcement theories*: view motivation as control of behaviour through rewards, getting people to do what you want them to do (Lussier, 1999).

In practice, approaches to motivation are determined by the organisation's culture, with some retailers favouring control where others focus on behaviour. Many retailers use money as the prime motivating force with rewards related to pay; common types of compensation plans include salary and commission-based schemes. Straight salary has the advantage of providing staff with a definite income, and so employees are not penalised for time in non-selling activities and job flexibility is easier to implement. Straight commission, on the other hand, rewards employees exclusively for their own endeavours, providing no or very low guaranteed salaries. Whilst this approach provides an effective incentive, reduces excess sales people and relates staff costs more closely to turnover, it is only achievable in appropriate organisational cultures. However, it can also create a negative effect as unrewarded jobs such as administration or stock control are neglected in favour of selling.

Time-based systems that include other benefits reflect a hierarchy of needs approach (Marchington and Wilkinson, 1996). Typically retailers supplement a straight salary scheme with bonuses based on a profit-related formula. The range of benefits in these systems include payments based on results, merit, performance and profit, and extend to share-ownership schemes. Other benefits include pensions, sick pay and insurance provision. Job enrichment and job design can also motivate by providing more variety, autonomy and responsibility in a job; work and task configurations can also be rewarding (Weightman, 1999).

The overall aim of performance management is to establish a culture in which individuals and groups take responsibility for continuous improvement of business processes and their own skills and contributions. The purpose of an effective performance management system is to align individual performance with the organisation's mission, vision and objectives. In practice, retail employees' performance is measured through sales productivity appraisals usually held annually, and regular evaluations. But these measures can conflict. Where emphasis is placed on sales, and performance is driven by quantitative financial measures, other important strategic measures such as service may be diminished.

Performance-related pay has become more popular since the 1980s with around 43 per cent of UK businesses using it in some form and increasingly evaluating managers

Table 9.7   *Rewards Through Pay: Sample Pay and Bonus Rates*

Adult weekly pay rats (April 2000–1)	
Job	**£ (range)**
Packer	161.46
Checkout assistant	165–174.33
Kiosk assistant	187.30

Sample of bonus schemes:
- At Asda all employees can add up to £250 on their basic pay, base on their store's profit
- John Lewis partners awarded 15% of salary (2000), equivalent to 8 weeks' pay

Source: IRS Employment Trend (2000).

on the results of annual group rather than individual performance. Three reasons have been proposed for performance-related pay; it motivates people to perform better or to develop their skills; it puts across a message that performance and competence are important; and it is fair and justifiable to reward people for their performance (Armstrong and Baron, 1998).

The definition of performance measurement is caught between different and conflicting interests. Achievement of financial targets, marketing objectives and operational efficiencies may not be compatible, with one – usually financial performance – predominating. However, performance measures can be designed to align employee behaviour more coherently with corporate objectives. From a customer perspective, customer priorities can be translated into strategic priorities that in turn form a plan for what should be measured, and against which results of improvements can actually be measured. An alternative method is to adopt the balanced scorecard approach, that starts with the premise that 'what you measure is what you get' (Kaplan and Norton, 1992). The aim is for managers to use a balanced presentation of financial and operational measures, where strategy and vision are valued alongside centralised control mechanisms.

SUMMARY

Human resource management has a strategic function in its ability to create customer satisfaction though the ways in which the organisation is structured, roles created and people motivated in line with strategic objectives. The organisational structure provides a framework within which the retailer will assign roles and responsibilities. Creating and managing the organisational culture will have a profound effect on the ways in which these are undertaken to achieve corporate objectives.

Changes in the labour market and the demands of retailing are providing new challenges to the HR function. The role of HR itself varies between companies and over time; it can have a more strategic involvement in shaping the organisation, but this has tended to fall and HR has been less well-represented at the highest levels of decision-making. At the other extreme, the role has never evolved beyond a reactive focus on personnel and implementation of support activities. With the delayering of the management structure, line managers are becoming more involved in traditional personnel activities.

A distinction has been made between operational and Head Office roles; in retailing, shop staff account for a high proportion of the total headcount and this group presents specific recruitment and employment challenges through distinctive age and gender profiles and patterns of part and full-time working. Skills analysis and development is both necessary and important for all employees to achieve efficient working practices that meet company objectives. Employees can be motivated to these ends through a supportive organisational culture in which performance is rewarded through financial and non-financial incentives.

QUESTIONS

1   Assess the role of HRM in creating strategic value.

2   Compare the impact of 'delayering' in the department store sector and the multiple grocery sector.

3   How will changing skills needs affect retail organisations in the next 10 years?

4   To what extent is organisational culture a source of competitive advantage?

5   What are the solutions to the retail industry's recruitment problems.

Case Study

Richer Sounds

Julian Richer is an entrepreneur in the style of Richard Branson and Anita Roddick, who built up Richer Sounds from one shop in 1979 into a highly successful hi-fi retailing chain. Leaving school at 18 with poor exam results, he opened his first small Richer Sounds shop at London Bridge, specialising initially in end-of-line hi-fi equipment. Later, this store entered the Guinness Book of Records, with a world record for the highest sales density achieving £17 533 of sales per square foot. The concept of the company was to buy cheaply directly from the factory and to sell at low prices, but also to

provide the best customer service that could be offered. Although the company no longer deals in end-of-line products, the fundamental basis of the business has not changed.

Richer has built himself a reputation for unusual but effective management ideas that have been taken up by other organisations. Firstly, his appearance is casual and, as a person, he is strikingly friendly. He places great emphasis on establishing a rapport with every new member of staff. Many of the Richer Sounds staff have been recruited from among customers, using advertisements placed in the regularly updated product catalogue. A recruitment page also appears at the company's website. Shop staff are also chosen for their friendliness and enthusiasm for hi-fi, rather than their selling experience. As an introduction to Richer Sounds, employees spent their first three days at his home in York where they undergo intensive training in a purpose-built annexe. The emphasis is on working hard and playing hard. They have a choice of tennis, badminton, snooker or they can take to the swimming pool, cinema or discotheque. Having fun and developing a club 'feel', in a non-intimidating atmosphere for the customer is a deliberate and important part of the business culture.

This difference is extended to the details in the store environment. Browsing is encouraged, and every shop has a dispenser serving free coffee and a machine that dishes out mints. Pets are welcome and if it is raining when someone buys some hi-fi they get an umbrella thrown in. There is a mirror which says 'you are looking at the most important person in this shop', and a little bell that customers can ring if they think they have been well-served. The company will always change items that a customer is not absolutely happy with. The company is highly customer-focused, their opinions are carefully monitored, and ultimately decide a sizeable proportion of staff pay since bonuses are geared to customer satisfaction, not sales.

The company puts its people first and is committed to providing the best possible service through job satisfaction and development of its employees. It gives staff the skills and knowledge they need to do their jobs well. Richer adopts a stick and carrot approach to staff motivation. This approach regards staff satisfaction as crucial to its success and uses some novel approaches to improve performance. Employees are given £5 each once a month to go off to the pub and talk about ideas. The company suggestion scheme is an essential element of the organisation, generating many of the new ideas that have been instigated.

Monthly team rewards for shops providing the best customer service include winners having the use of the company Jaguar and Bentley for a month. Importantly for staff morale, Richer recognises that not all employees can win awards, so lunch at the Savoy and a short holiday is the norm for everyone who has worked at Richer Sounds for five years. There are also five holiday homes which employees can book free of charge. One effect of this involvement is that absenteeism is between 1 per cent and 2 per cent, less than half the national average. The stick comes out for those who are dishonest. Any kind of theft results in instant dismissal, and stock loss is half the rate experienced by many other shops.

The methods of achieving the results have evolved. Richer is a disciple of the Japanese idea of *kaizen*, continuous improvement. Richer may seem relaxed but he runs a tightly controlled operation, and has an almost fanatical attention to detail, working from a cardboard work sheet that lists his tasks in minute handwriting; 'I have never had a computer in my life', he says. He has a policy of slow growth, arising from past mistakes when he tried to overreach himself. Like Branson, he has started building separate businesses. He had nine in 1997, including the consultancy, and expects to have between 20 and 30 in the next two or three years.

Richer has no plans to take his business public. 'I have spoken to others about that, like Anita Roddick, and I know they think it has been a mistake', he says. His plan is to keep on building: 'I love it. By lunchtime on Monday if I was on the beach in the south of France I would be bored out of my mind ringing people up. I always reckon I will die at my desk and I wouldn't have it any other way.'

Source: adapted from 'How to hit the right note', the *Financial Times*, 27 March 1997.

SEMINAR QUESTIONS FOR DISCUSSION

1 How transferable is the Richer Sounds approach to other retailers?

2 What does the case study tell us about leadership style?

References

Adair, J. (1982) *Action Centred Leadership* (Aldershot: Gower).

Armstrong, A. and Baron, M. (1998) *Performance Management, The New Realities* (London: IPD).

Barber, L., Hayday, S. and Bevan, S. (1999) 'From People to Profits', *Institute of Employment Studies Report 355*, University of Sussex.

Bedeian, A.G. (1984) *Organizations: Theory and Analysis* (New York: The Dryden Press).

Bennis, W. and Biederman, P. (1992) *Organizing Genius: The Secrets of Creative Collaboration* (Reading, Mass.: Addison-Wesley).

Brown, A. (1995) *Organisational Culture* (London: Pitman).

Callender, C. and Metcalf, H. (1997) 'Women and Training', *Research Report No 35* (London: DfEE).

Cappelli, P. and Crocker-Hefter, A. (1996) 'Distinctive Human Resources are Firms' Core Competencies', *Organizational Dynamics*, Winter pp. 7–23.

Carrington, L. (1999) 'Motivation Secured', *Human Resources*, July/August, pp. 13–14.

Child, J. (1984) *Organisation: A Guide To Problems and Practice* (New York: Harper & Row).

Davidson, W.R., Sweeney, D.J. and Stampfel, R.W. (1988) *Retailing Management*, 6th edn (New York: John Wiley).

Dench, S., Perryman, S. and Kodz, J. (1997) 'Trading Skills for Sales Assistants', *Institute of Employment Studies Report 323*, University of Sussex.

DNTO (2001) *Labour Market and Skills Issues in the Distributive Industry: A Skills Foresight Report* (Harpenden: Distributive National Training Organisation).

Drennan, D. (1992) *Transforming Company Culture* (Maidenhead: McGraw Hill).

Edwards, R., Raggatt, P., Harrison, R., McCollum, A. and Calder, J. (1998) 'Recent Thinking in Lifelong Learning: A Review of the Literature', *Report no. 80* (London: Department for Education and Employment Research).

Freathy, P. (1993) 'Developments in the Superstore Labour Market', *Service Industries Journal*, vol. 13, no. 1, pp. 65–79.

Freathy, P. (1997) 'Employment Theory and The Wheel of Retailing: Segmenting the Circle', *Service Industries Journal*, vol. 17, no. 3, pp. 413–31.

Goddard, J. (1997) 'The Architecture of Core Competence', *Business Strategy Review* (UK), Spring, vol. 8, no. 1, pp. 43–53.

Goffee, R. and Scase, R. (1995) *Corporate Realities: The Dynamics of Large and Small Organisations* (London: Routledge).

Goleman, D. (1996) *Emotional Intelligence* (London: Bloomsbury).

Harris, L.C. and Ogbonna, E. (1998) 'A Three Perspective Approach to Understanding Culture in Retail', *Personnel Review*, vol. 27, no. 2, pp. 104–24.

Hart, C., Harrington, A., Arnold, J. and Loan-Clarke, J. (1997) 'Retailer and Student Perceptions of Competence Development', *International Journal of Retail and Distribution Management*, vol. 27, no. 9, pp. 362–73.

Hillage, J., Atkinson, J., Kersley, B. and Bates, P. (1998) 'Employers' Training of Young People', *Research Report 76*, August (London: DfEE).

Hope-Hailey, V., Gratton, L., McGovern, P., Stiles, P. and Truss, C. (1997) 'A Chameleon Function? HRM in the 90s', *Human Resource* Management *Journal*, vol. 7, no. 3, pp. 5–19.

Huws, U., Jagger, N. and O'Regan, S. (1999) 'Teleworking and Globalisation', *Institute of Employment Studies Report 358*, University of Sussex.

Jackson, C., Arnold, J., Nicholson, N. and Watts, A.G. (1996) 'Managing Careers in 2000 and Beyond', *Institute of Employment Studies Report 305*, University of Sussex.

Jessop, G. (1991) *Outcomes – NVQ and the Emerging Model of Education and Training* (Brighton: Falmer Press).

Johnson, G. and Scholes, K. (1999) *Exploring Corporate Strategy*, 5th edn (Hemel Hempstead: Prentice Hall Europe).

Kaplan, R.S. and Norton, D.P. (1992) 'The Balanced Scorecard-Measures that Drive Performance', *Harvard Business Review*, Jan.–Feb., pp. 71–9.

Kent, A. and Hawksworth, A. (2000) *The Role of Computer Based Training in the Retail Industry* Paper presented at the EAERCD Conference on Retail Innovation, ESADE Barcelona.

Kettley, P. (1995) 'Is Flatter Better? Delayering the Management Hierarchy', *Institute of Employment Studies Report 290*, University of Sussex.

Kirkpatrick, D.L. (1982) *How to Improve Performance Through Appraisal and Coaching* (New York: Amacom Book Division).

Knez, M.J. (1999) 'Trade offs in Organisational Design', Mastering Strategy 8, November 15, Financial Times.

Kodz, J., Kersley, B. and Bates, P. (1999) *The Fifties Revival*, Institute of Employment Studies Report 359, University of Sussex.

Kodz, J., Dench, S., Pollard, E. and Evans, C. (1998) 'Developing the Key Skills of Young People', *Institute of Employment Studies Report 350*, University of Sussex.

LSFU (2000) *Skills for Tomorrow's High Street*, London Skills Forecasting Unit. The London TEC.

Lussier, R.N. (1999) *Human Relations in Organisations, Applications and Skill Building*, 4th edn (Maidenhead: McGraw Hill).

Mabey, C., Salaman, G. and Storey, J., 2nd edn. (1998) *Human Resource Management: A Strategic Introduction* (Blackwell: Oxford).

Marchington, M. and Wilkinson, A. (1996) *Core Personnel and Development* (London: Institute of Personnel and Development).

Miller, D., Jackson, P., Thrift, N., Holbrook, B. and Rowlands, M. (1998) *Shopping Place and Identity* (London: Routledge).

Mintzberg, H. (1985) *Structure in Fives* (Englewood Cliffs, NJ: PrenticeHall).

Morgan, G. (1986) *Images of the Organisation* (London: Sage).

Ogbonna, E. and Whipp, R. (1999) 'Strategy, Culture and HRM: Evidence from the UK Food Retailing Sector', *Human Resource Management Journal*, vol. 9, no, 4, pp. 75–91.

Peters, T.J. and Waterman, R.H. (1982) *In Search Of Excellence* (New York: Harper & Row).

Prickett, R. (1997) 'Essential Toils', *People Management* no. 6, pp. 43–4.

Retail Week/MTI Survey (1997) *Retail Employment in the UK* and *Trading Skills for Sales Assistants*.

Scase, R. (1999) *Britain Towards 2010 The Changing Business Environment* (London: Economic and Social Research Council).

Segal Horn, S. (1987) 'The Retail Environment in the UK', in J. McGee (ed.), *Retail Strategies* (Chichester: John Wiley and Sons).

Seiff, M. (1987) *Don't Ask the Price: The Memoirs of the President of Marks and Spencer* (London: Weidenfeld & Nicolson).

Spector, R. and McCarthy, P.D. (1995) *The Nordstrom Way The Inside Story of America's Number 1 Customer Service Company* (New York: John Wiley).

Storey, J. (1992) *Developments in the Management of Human Resources* (Oxford: Blackwell).

Thomason, G.A. (1990) *Textbook of Human Resource Management* (London: Institute of Personnel Management).

Thompson, J.L. (1993) *Strategic Management: Awareness and Change,* 3rd edn (London: Chapman Hall).

Torrington, D. and Hall, L. (1998) *Human Resource Management,* 4th edn (Hemel Hempstead: Prentice Hall Europe).

Walters, D.W. and Hanrahan, J. (2000) *Retail Strategy: Planning and Control* (Basingstoke: Macmillan).

Weightman, J. (1999) *Managing People* (London: Institute of Personnel and Development).

PART THREE

Merchandise Management

The following four chapters develop the theme of merchandise management. Their sequence follows the buying process from product selection and sales planning in Chapter 10, to subsequent issues surrounding supplier sourcing and management of the supply chain in Chapter 11. Ordering and allocation of merchandise, deliveries to the retailers and internal goods handling complete the decision-making sequence into store (Chapter 12). To simplify the organisation of this section, it concludes with a detailed discussion of merchandise pricing issues in Chapter 13.

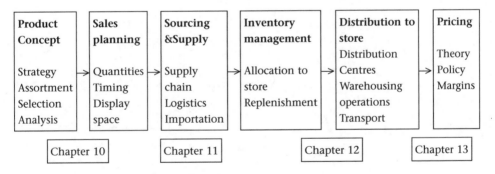

Product Concept	**Sales planning**	**Sourcing &Supply**	**Inventory management**	**Distribution to store**	**Pricing**
				Distribution	Theory
Strategy	Quantities	Supply	Allocation to	Centres	Policy
Assortment	Timing	chain	store	Warehousing	Margins
Selection	Display	Logistics	Replenishment	operations	
Analysis	space	Importation		Transport	

Chapter 10	Chapter 11	Chapter 12	Chapter 13

Product Planning and Selection

LEARNING OBJECTIVES

After studying this chapter the reader will be able to:

- Introduce the organisation of buying.
- Examine product planning and control decisions.
- Demonstrate how buyers create distinctive product assortments and how they manage them.
- Explain the impact of buying department organisation on product management.
- Evaluate product assortment (range) planning and control methods.

THE BUYING FUNCTION

The buying function depends on the size and stage of development of the organisation, as well as its business sector. Independent retailers run as a single outlet by an owner manager may only have the resources and needs for the manager to undertake the merchandise selection, negotiation with suppliers and stock control. As the organisation becomes more complex, through expansion into multiple site retailing and product range extensions, the buying activities become more complex too. At some point a specialised buyer and later teams of buyers with specialised responsibilities are required to maintain a detailed knowledge of product market developments and suppliers.

Clearly products could be bought with varying levels of sophistication. A buyer could take decisions based on their own understanding of the type of business the company is in, and interpretation of what customers want. The selection process could be a simple as a visit to the cash and carry or from the local wholesaler, the buyer chooses from the available stock whatever is required at that time. Costs and selling prices would be relatively straightforward to manage, as would delivery from a single source; it could even be that the buyer loads up the goods in the back of his car.

However, the very simplicity of this approach raises a number of questions about buying decisions. To answer these, multiple retailers have created central buying functions in a Head Office location, the advantages of which are:

■ Better prices and terms through bulk buying.

■ Specialisation of full-time buyers in particular product categories.

■ Increase in buying efficiency (no travelling costs to suppliers, merchandise transfer from store to store to match demand, buying costs spread over higher turnover).

■ Market trends anticipated and buying opportunities created more easily.

■ More consistent quality control within the organisation.

■ Store managers become more specialised sales managers (McGoldrick, 1990).

The disadvantages of centralisation are that local needs may be ignored as the buyer manages a larger operation and is more distanced from the customer than in the store. This may cause sales staff morale to decline too as their role in delivering customer satisfaction is diminished. From a financial perspective, additional costs are incurred from centralised warehousing and distribution, as retailers specify deliveries to warehouses for breakdown into branch deliveries.

The Buying Department

Roles within a buying department change as organisations become more complex, and this is partly a result of buying for multiple retail outlets. Clearly no two retail outlets will sell exactly the same merchandise however they are measured, whether by type of product, price, individual or pack size, fashion or brand. Although outlets share some sales characteristics and can be grouped together for planning purposes, the larger the number of stores the more complex decision-making becomes. Critical activities include planning the lines of merchandise and their allocation to each outlet, followed by the management of replacement stock.

The buying function can be split between buyers and their administrative assistants, who take on the responsibility of stock management and liaison with suppliers. However, with increasing specialisation, sales planning and stock control is managed by a merchandiser and merchandise allocators leaving the buyer to concentrate on product selection and supplier negotiations (Figure 10.1). Large retailers can reflect the complexity and dynamics of their business sector by undertaking further reorganisation to increase their responsiveness and flexibility to market conditions. Product management teams may be formed to include technologists, marketing specialists and distributors. In food retailing the development of category management has led to teams being formed typically between buying, marketing, distribution and operations management to manage every aspect of a product group sharing similar characteristics, the key to successful category management is cross-functionalism, that reflects a customer-led rather than supplier-led approach. Where previously buying decisions were driven by suppliers' product-led initiations, selection is now driven by customer demand and research.

The role of buyers varies by retail sector as well as size of the organisation. Selecting a clothing range will require a degree of individual design flair. Buying in other

Figure 10.1   *A Buying and Merchandising Structure*

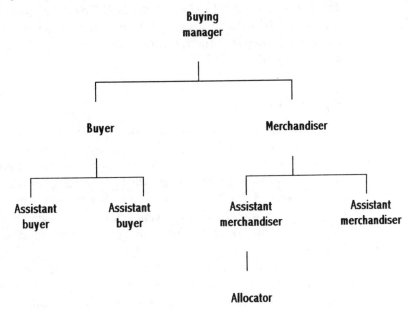

sectors or categories may be limited to a small number of brands which require a higher level of market analysis and detailed planning and with specialisation, buyer knowledge has become an important element of competitive advantage. Personal and commercial abilities expected of the clothing and footwear buyer will be reflected in knowledge of sizing and product construction, and global sources to secure production. Product technology and market testing, environmental auditing and health and safety assessments may be important considerations for other buyers.

Negotation

All buyers will be involved in negotiation, and negotiating positions are determined by the objectives of the supplier and retailer and their relative strength. In the past 20 years, power has tended to move to the multiple retailer as industry concentration increases retailer size. This is particularly evident in the food retail sector in many Western European countries, and has formed an element of the UK Competition Commission's investigation in 2000 into supermarket pricing. The aim of the buyer will be to secure profit targets for specified quantities of merchandise to achieve sales during an agreed period of time. These might be gained by single or multiple deliveries, and can include negotiation over single or multiple products, promotions and returns.

Areas for negotiation primarily reflect the need to achieve gross profit margin targets through quantity discounts, special discounts for promotions and shelf allocation, and retrospective discounts for achievement of agreed levels of turnover. Settlement terms establish the time in which the supplier will be paid, ranging from payment with order, through 30 days or monthly credit to 60 and 90 days credit. Successful negotiation of settlement terms are desirable because they can have a signifi-cant effect on cash flows and working capital. Terms are agreed for a period, from each individual order to annual reviews where business is conducted on an ongoing basis. For overseas orders, transport, insurance and freight handling will also be negotiated into the cost price.

Buying Strategy

The starting point for buying decisions lies within the organisation's strategy. This defines long-term profitability objectives, return on investment being particularly important, and the application of its resources to achieve these ends. Following the overall company objectives there will be a series of plans, descending to opera-tional statements for different functions, departments, areas or sections. The mar-keting plan will help define viable customer groups, product ranges, pricing and promotional policy, and from this point a more detailed buying plan can be drawn up.

We can see this most easily at the extremes of retailing; for example, the buying strategy for an exclusive department store like Harrods will be quite different to a dis-count retailer, such as Aldi. The strategy of the former, will position it as an exclusive, desirable brand in itself and a place to acquire other branded products that support its image. At Aldi, on the other hand, the strategy will concern low cost, value for money food lines for a target market that values low prices above brands, service and selection. Resource issues for a retailer aiming to be a leader in exclusivity would include expenditure not only on high quality interior design and visual merchandis-ing, but also high levels of customer service and product availability. There may be a need to carry wide assortments to create the appropriate choice for their customers, with correspondingly high levels of stock investment. For the low-cost retailer, invest-ment will limited by its smaller assortment and lower levels of stock holding.

Own-Buy Decisions

Before any merchandise can be bought, decisions need to be taken about the product ranges and how they are to be supplied. These reflect the retailer's strategic position on branded and own-brand merchandise, and the number and type of supplier relationships.

Retail brands in the UK have built a very significant position for themselves in the UK. European grocery retailers on the other hand have only recently begun to develop their own brands, and in the USA, too, the scale of development has been limited. The abolition of Resale Price Maintenance in 1964 had a profound impact on the balance of power between retailers and manufacturers in the UK. Manufacturers were no longer able to dictate the selling price of their goods, which enabled grocery retailers in particular to decide on branded product price points and introduce lower priced own brand merchandise. Key factors in UK own-brand development subse-quently included the source and use of retail power, centralisation of management decisions, retail image, and the crucial role of the trade name (Burt, 2000).

Buyers of manufacturers' brands are essentially managing the opportunity to use inherent product qualities, brand names and the promotional activity of their suppliers to meet their customers' preferences. Other retailers will be competing with the same products, so market share considerations, price negotiation and promotional opportunities will form an important part of the evaluation and selection process. Branded merchandise carries the advantage of higher levels of consumer awareness and influence in the consumer decision-making process. Also as brands have become more important so differentiation between them has relied on the superiority of particular aspects of each brand (de Chernatony and Dall'Olmo Riley, 1998). But branding creates selection problems, too, for retail buyers when many competitors carry similar lines and provide opportunities for consumers to easily make price comparisons.

Retailer-led product design and packaging overcome the problems of differentiation and pricing arising from branded merchandise. This process has attracted a range of definitions including own-brand and own-label, store brand and, more commonly in the United States, private label. Retailer own-brands enable the company to create a wide range of product attributes with the store, where own-label products may not contain any supplier or retail fascia branding.

Wileman and Jary (1997) identify five stages in retail brand development (Figure 10.2) that generally align with the development of the retailer itself:

■ Stage one, *generic products* provide a basic function at a low price, and require little investment in product or packaging.

■ Stage two, *cheap* retail branded products share similarities with branded packaging but at lower prices and with minimal investment in the product.

■ Stage three, *re-engineered products* are distinguished by a higher level of management and investment. This level is typified by the European hard discounters such as Aldi and Netto, who source from third-tier brands or

Figure 10.2   *Stages of Store Brand Development*

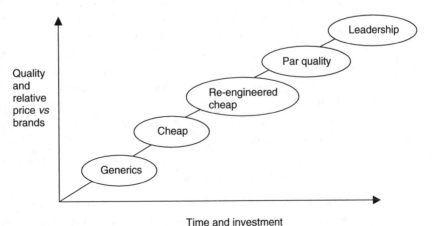

Source: A. Wileman and M. Jary (1997), *Retail Power Plays*, published by Macmillan Press Ltd, reproduced with the permission of Palgrave Macmillan.

suppliers with excess production capacity to develop products to sell on a marginal basis. Netto, for example, are prepared to work with 1 per cent operating profit margins, by comparison with 6–7 per cent at Sainsbury or Tesco (Burt and Sparks, 1997). The task for the buying team is to negotiate low costs to achieve the lowest prices in the market, but at a distinctive quality level by working with their suppliers. The policy of stocking only a limited number of lines in a discount food store, typically around 800–1000, means that the supply base is necessarily limited.

■ *Par quality* products sell typically at 10–25 per cent lower prices than the branded equivalent, but at the same quality.

■ *Leadership* brands enable retailers to develop price premiums through product innovation and repositioning. For example, Marks and Spencer have traded under the St Michael and more recently Marks and Spencer brands to build a strongly differentiated market position. Quality of ingredients and preparation in their food ranges, together with originality in new menus of chilled and frozen foods, have enabled the company to create distinctive, high-profit margin lines.

These stages of development do not exclude retailers from managing different levels of own-label products simultaneously, to create a comprehensive offer. In the UK, grocery mu... own-label positioning is increasingly ... lent at three levels – economy, a... premium are ad... either side of the standard product level. And although th... growth of own-brand in this sector is slowing, the balance of own-label to manufac... brands has now reached around 40–2 per cent, and as high as 50 per cent in Marks & ... (Mintel, 2000). In the cl... sector, multiple retailers use own-br... labels either exclusively such as ... as Gap and Next, or more comm... ... a ... mix of ... solutions ... ccessfully adopted by Debenhams ... investment will vary depending on the type of products and th... ... required ...

The deve... ... of own-brand merchandise requires different buying skills and organisation ... to buying finished products ... the buyer will change requiring a ... working relationship in a longer term ... bach to product development, qu... ... ... of products, technical developmen... ... ... quality that ... ... production process lie in the hand ... ... : investment has been made in m... ... ... involvement of selectors, techn... ... ... product. Many large retailers have the buying power to dominate or at least work demandingly with suppliers to achieve their specifications.

New Product Development

The development of new products carries different implications according to the characteristics of the retail sector. Primarily functional products with predictable demand create a requirement to minimise costs. Alternatively products may be primarily innovative, requiring the retailer to accurately interpret early sales and act quickly during a short lifecycle (Fisher, 1997). In either case, new product decisions, concerning

Table 10.1   *UK Grocery Multiples' Own Labels*

Retailer	Economy label	Premium label
Tesco	Value	Finest
Sainsbury	Economy	Fresh Creations
		Be Good to Yourself
Safeway	Savers	
Asda	Smart Price (replacing Farm Stores)	Sam's Choice

Exhibit 10.1   Own brands and product development at Debenhams

In 2000, Debenhams initiated two product branding developments. 'MEA', was positioned as a premium make-up and skincare brand, that the company claims is the first skincare range to be developed by a UK department store. The second new development was the Media and Entertainment department to meet demand for electronic products. Its focus is 'must-have' lines, that fit with the company's brand strategy to combine international brands such as Sony, Panasonic and Philips with its own-brand Lecson.

The company's intention is to expand the ranges of its existing designer clothing brands currently numbering over 26, including Jasper Conran, Maria Grachvogel and Lulu Guinness, as well as to introduce new ones. New designer brands exclusive to Debenhams are targeted at womenswear for sizes 12–16, lingerie, nightwear and childrenswear. These ranges offer aspirational products at affordable prices, and occupy a high profile within the company.

A further area for development to which the brand strategy has been applied, is the gifts and boards games area. Once again, international brands, designer brands and the own brand, Equipment, will support substantial forecast growth in the company's drive to become the destination for Christmas gift shopping. Home and cosmetics gift offers will be expanded and the company intends to introduce other new product areas during the Autumn/Winter season. In total the company has over 500 international brands and its brand strategy aims to provide customers with an unrivalled 'one-stop' choice.

---

acceptance or rejection and the retention of existing selections as rebuys, or for deletion, are fundamental to retail buying (McGoldrick, 1990).

The rate of new product development can be defined in terms of demand characteristics. Amongst the highest fashion businesses, for example the French fashion houses, exclusivity lies in the ability of the designer to create new products consistently. In the mass-market clothing business, buyers will demonstrate an ability to adapt and modify designs from fashion shows and leading fashion stores to create own-brand clothing that satisfies the demands of their target market. New product development is nearly continuous as seasonal and inter-seasonal ranges are introduced. Success is measured by the ability of the retailer to provide the appropriate degree of product innovation within the marketing mix.

Innovation carries greater opportunities to create a distinctive position but also greater risk (Berman and Evans, 1998). High-growth sectors create driving forces that repay the costs of product development; for example personal computer and mobile phone retailers exploit the latest technological developments to create differential advantage. On the other hand, retailers in more mature sectors such as food and household find less opportunity for new product development. For market entrants, business concepts are often based on innovative approaches to products. Over the years some of these, such as Body Shop, have maintained their innovative approach; others, such as Laura Ashley, have found their initial distinctiveness difficult to sustain in the face of changing market conditions.

Target Markets

The potential customers within the population, the market segments, which the retailer has identified in its marketing plan should determine product planning and selection. Planning the dimensions of the merchandise range form one of the most complex and managerially difficult areas for retail buyers.

There may be number of broadly-based attitudinal trends amongst their targeted customers which influence product selection. These could include price/image trade-offs, product quality, and convenience (Lucas *et al.*, 1994). These may be more important to some consumer segments than others, but over time they will broadly affect product design, promotion and decision-making.

In more detail still for clothing retailers, customers' fashion attitudes are important, determined by a number of factors. Lifestyle and lifestage based on age, values, income, occupation and interests combine to provide a profile of the typical customer. The target market can be identified through market research, and given substance by customer profiling. For example, research undertaken by Laura Ashley using focus groups from their target market, provided very similar 'storyboards' from each group detailing their view of the company, and the importance of retaining the relaxed, English-country feel of the brand and its products. The retail buyer will want to know where the customer shops and what they wear – the contents of their wardrobe – the frequency of their clothes shopping, and how much they spend as more precise indicators to shape their plans for the product range.

SUPPLIER SELECTION AND EVALUATION

The aim of supplier evaluation should be to assess the supplier's compatibility with the retailer's strategic and tactical objectives. The dimensions of the evaluation in undertaking this task include the use of primary and secondary data. Companies such as Dun and Bradstreet provide risk summaries based on financial checks using sales, supplier payment profiles, legal judgements, financial strength and operational management. Objective and subjective appraisals can likewise be provided by both external and internal sources. Technical and quality audits can include both performance and conformance to specifications, on-time delivery, flexibility and responsiveness. Increasingly, a range of issues summarised under the heading of ethical appraisal can be important, including supplier policies and adherence to social and environmentally responsible behaviour. For companies like Body Shop, environmental responsibility is a critical element of strategy to be shared by its suppliers.

Table 10.2 *Supplier Selection Checklist*

Quality	Design	Sourcing	Administration	Financial position	Ethics
■ Quality control department and its efficiency ■ Control standards in place, including national standards	■ Flexibility to meet retailer's requirements ■ Product innovation record ■ In-house design team ■ Creativity ■ Commercialism	■ Sourcing flexibility ■ Head Office location ■ Lead times ■ Length of relationship with their factories/ suppliers ■ Pricing structure	■ Accuracy ■ Competence ■ IT systems, internal and external compatibility ■ Location of warehouses/ distributiion centres ■ Delivery methods and performance	■ Ability to meet margin requirements ■ Payment terms ■ Fund mark-downs and promotions ■ Financial strength and stability ■ Reliance on particular customers	■ Evidence of integrity/ trust ■ Compliance with laws ■ Social and ethical policies in place ■ Audit procedures

The purpose of evaluation is to enable decisions to be taken in a number of areas. The creation of alliances or partnerships between the retailer and suppliers will be based on careful evaluation of supplier capabilities and compatibility with the retailer's operations. Supplier reduction has been a common trend in the past decade achieved through the evaluation of suppliers against strategic objectives of the retailer. Decisions are based on performance monitoring of supplies using measurement criteria for quality, quantity and identity; for example correct labelling, conformity, packaging, and chronology (Lamey, 1997). The focus is often to reduce the cost base of trading with a large group of suppliers: concentration on fewer suppliers should lead to improved profit margins and a reduction in administrative costs. The evaluation may be focused on profitability alone, and the ability of the supplier to deliver desired quality at the right cost. It may include a need to use suppliers with a global capacity or capability for world-class development, and in some situations supplier certification may be required (Table 10.2).

PRODUCT SELECTION

A product range, or assortment, consists of related merchandise lines selected by buyers to optimise selling opportunities to a target market, and will be determined by a number of dimensions:

■ *Market positioning.* The selection decisions will be based on an appropriate selection of price points, product qualities and characteristics and the ways in which parts of the range complement each other. Clothing ranges may be coordinated about colour themes to encourage multiple purchases of a particular fashion colour. Brand mix may be an important part of the range assortment too: the brand leader may support the inclusion of a number of other products around its best-selling lines. Other brands may be necessary to build up a convincing assortment, create interest or add novelty – 'something different' –

to the customer even if they have a lower market share or brand awareness. For food retailers it may be particularly important to understand how products are purchased together, or how many lines were sold in a store between certain dates and times of day.

■ *Timescale.* Product ranges will be selected for a period of time. Clothing retailers have traditionally planned ranges for spring/summer and autumn/winter for obvious reasons. In theory, July and January sales clear out old-season stock leaving the rails free for the new season's merchandise. In practice this has to happen, even if it means lightweight clothing in spring colours appears in the shops in February, and coats are displayed in August: these end of season months leave too little time to continue the current seasons' range and then clear out any lingering stock before the onset of the new season.

Increasingly, though, buying departments are developing separate inter-season packages for early Spring or Autumn, and even 'winter-cruise' summer merchandise for sale at Christmas and New Year. These range sub-divisions enable retailers to manage seasonal clothing more accurately to meet customer demand and to reduce the problems of end of season overstocks. As a result the historic two-season buying plan is disappearing as retailers want to purchase smaller quantities, more frequently. For clothing retailers this may mean deliveries every six–eight weeks supplemented by core line replenishment on a five-day cycle. Jaeger have developed their products within a capsule collection that takes only 13 weeks from design to store, compared to nine months for the core collection (Lea-Greenwood, 1997). Other industry commentators have proposed an even shorter turnround time of just three weeks from order specification to delivery.

In food retailing, time horizons tend to be much shorter, but even within the sector buying requirements will vary. Fresh foods have distinctively different shelf lives over 1–2 days, compared to ambient foods with a number of weeks' stockholding. The wine buying process takes place over a longer timescale but compared to chilled foods is relatively straightforward in terms of development time.

■ *Range width.* Depth and width of the range provide further criteria for range planning. The retailer may have a strategic or marketing objective to maintain a strong presence in a product category. Deep ranges will offer customers considerable choice of stock in the selection of colour, sizing or specification. This provides a high level of service at the cost of a large number of stockkeeping units (SKUs) (Figure 10.3).

Shallow ranges, on the other hand, will provide a limited choice of product options within a category, typified by the offer from mixed goods retailers or food discounters. Some retailers hold wide assortments in varying depths; in the case of Clarks Shoes, children's sizes and widths are held to exceptional depth, but less so for fashion shoes. The implications of these decisions are felt both in the marketing position of the retailer and its financial management; one of the problems for in-depth shoe retailers is the volume of stock required to support potentially modest sales. However, micro-merchandising techniques will

Figure 10.3   *Specialisation of Major Retail Formats*

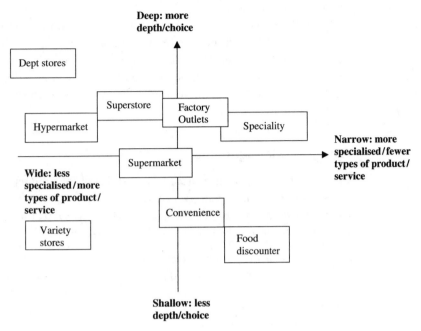

increasingly utilise customer information derived from loyalty cards to create store personalities and more accurately define product ranges for each store (Logistics and Transport Focus, 2000)

- *Price structure.* The life of the product in the assortment depends on its sales and profitability, and its position in the marketing mix. Low or declining sales trends may be balanced out by above-average profit margins. The product's centrality to the range or category, whether by brand, fashion statement or utility, will contribute to its continuation and appropriate replenishment. Some retailers will designate products as 'core' to be continued or slightly modified over a longer period of time than peripheral lines (see Chapter 13 for more details on pricing).

- *Number of options.* Assortments or ranges are structured to offer a balanced range of products at each individual outlet (shop, concession) level. Therefore they add up in two different ways: to provide a total stock and buying requirement for each SKU, and secondly, the total range dimensions for each branch. As retailers have become more involved with the details of stock management, so branch-level activity has become more critical (figure 10.4).

Typically, the range plan is used to create a model stock plan for each branch from which is made an initial stock allocation. Branches with higher turnover characteristics such as size, location in respect of higher spending consumer markets or passing trade (for example airport shops), will receive larger quantities of merchandise than other, lower turnover sites. The ranges need to be modelled to local needs as far as possible though; some parts of the range may sell very well in otherwise weaker stores;

some stores may have a strong local competitive position or a loyal customer following for certain products.

The differing characteristics of each store in a multiple store group will lead to a grading plan. Although every store should be ideally modelled for its stock to meet its specific requirements, this can be difficult to achieve in practice with a very large number of stores. Stores will be grouped by turnover, and if possible other relevant characteristics, with the largest stores occupying the highest grades and the smaller the lowest ones.

Category Management

Category management is a more recent approach to product management that provides a coherent and integrative solution. It arose as a development from the Efficient Consumer Response (ECR) approach in the early 1980s for suppliers to service the retail industry more efficiently. The function requires.

> a customer orientated methodology which brings together all the organisational, strategic and operational management required to develop, plan, distribute and sell on the range of products, so that sales and profits are optimised and maximum customer values is delivered.

As such it fundamentally concerns the relationship and ways of working between retailers, distributors and manufacturers as trading partners.

A category itself is defined by the American ECR board as 'a distinct, manageable group of products/services that consumers believe to be interrelated/or substitutable in meeting a consumer need.' Its origins were based on the need for brand rationalisation by manufacturers', in which central management could exert greater control over diffused brand management responsibilities. In other words, brand responsibility is coordinated more closely by economic management of groups of brands. Retailer

Figure 10.4   *Breakdown of a Product Range Plan*

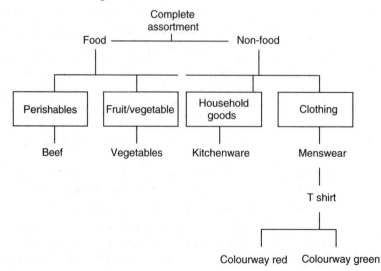

category management evolved from this approach and involves the management of suppliers as well as brands. In Europe the process tends to be driven by retailers, whereas in North America suppliers tend to drive the process. For retailers, too, the focus is at the SKU management level, with each SKU being managed as an economic entity with its own profit and loss (Mintel, 1997).

Different types of categories can fulfil different functions; for example, creating destinations within the store, or for cash flow, or margin enhancement. One critical measure is the use of stockturn to match stock levels to consumer demand. Category management aims to bring together the right mix of products, the most profitable brands and to minimise the selection of underperforming items; slow-moving lines are replaced with faster turning ones. The process is consumer and product-oriented, rather than supplier and margin-focused.

Category Management increases the value of functions that previously may have been outside the main cost focus of the organisation. Visual merchandising, marketing and promotion, customer research, and customer loyalty initiatives are drawn into the management process in this way (Table 10.3). For the function to succeed, information technology is essential. EPOS (electronic processing at point of sale) should provide information from a number of areas that can be integrated for planning, store space management and marketing. The types of performance measures that need to be calculated include market share, space productivity, return on investment (ROI), stockturn, supplier performance and customer satisfaction.

The benefits of category management are found in improved performance measurements; Supply-chain efficiencies should increase as the sales rate of each product is more effectively analysed and understood, and ordering and replenishment is more accurately defined. There should be an improvement in the use of assets in terms of reduced investment in stocks. Improved knowledge of the business will enable retailers and their partners to identify strengths and weaknesses more effectively and develop new products. The integration of different functions should result in improved communication, and more rapid response to changes in customer demand.

Category management is most developed in the grocery sector. Types of category can include groups such as alcoholic beverages, hot and cold beverages, main meal, or breakfast. The category team responsibilities as a result have a broad remit. The team will typically comprise the category manager, assistant manager or merchandiser,

Table 10.3   *Category Management*

Category management characteristics	Traditional product management characteristics
■ Customer Satisfaction ■ Flexible responses to market trends ■ Combines control with entreprise ■ High and consistent standards ■ Managers learn from current trading ■ Manageable sales and profit growth ■ Efficient team-based organisation	■ Focus on internal operations ■ Rely on historical information ■ Unclear lines of responsibility for customer satisfaction ■ Variable standards ■ Aggressive relationship with suppliers ■ Functional and hierarchical organisation

---

Exhibit 10.2 Category management in action

La Rinascente in Italy has 400 stores including supermarkets and hypermarkets. It undertook a study into category management in the mature market of home surface cleaners. One significant result was the development of new category segmentation leading to new shelf layouts:

Large surfaces	Small surfaces	Windows	Special cleaners	Basic Liquids
Generic	Powders	Trigger	Kitchen	Bleach
Disinfectants	Creams	Refills	Wood	Ammonia
Perfuming	Liquids	Glasses	Metal	Alcohol
Protectives			Bathroom	
Waxes			Plunger	

Drogerie Markt a retailer in south-central Germany assessed their large category of skin care products, which consisted of 438 SKUs. Category management identified some key areas for management attention:

■ Over and underpopulation of different segments
■ Reduced number of items by 10%
■ Repositioned some lines and added a few to fill gaps
■ Shelf layout changed from brand structure to skin-care application structure

Source: by kind permission of Roland Berger Strategy Consultants.

---

buyer and an assistant. They will undertake the buying, assortment planning, pricing, promotion, shelf presentation and product supply.

The concept provides ideas for review and range planning. It can create focal points and assist in the segmentation of departments. It provides the basis for coordination of products and the integration of some departments, and it assists in the creation of visual identities for selling space in the store.

SALES PLANNING AND FORECASTING

Retailers' decisions about the product range plan have to be completely integrated with the financial sales plan. This will be derived from the financial objectives of the retailer. However, detailed buying plans will also require a high level of information from current as well as historical and forecasted future trends. The dynamics of the market increasingly demand more real-time responsiveness to sales recorded at line-level. These factors combined, enable the retailer to decide on how much product to buy and when to buy it.

There are two dimensions to the sales planning process:

■ *Analysis of past performance from the previous year's, month's, or week's sales.* By using a comparable past period to the planned period, or by analysing historical trends over a number of periods, it is possible to forecast future sales. However,

Figure 10.5   *Sales Planning Sequence*

- *Outline sales plan.* Produce line-level expected sales as a starting point for the planning process using sales history, seasonality, smoothing, and allowing for new products and new stores.
- *Plan sales.* Adds human judgement and real-world factors taking account of promotional effect; price changes; stock availability; market trends; and other external factors.
- *Calculate intake.* The sales plan drives deliveries. Assign appropriate distribution centre. Allocate weeks' cover by product type or distribution centre. Plans generated for short to long-term requirement. (See Chapter 12)
- *Ordering.* Review suggested intake figures. Raise orders as easily as possible. Define delivery location. (See Chapter 12)

the level of accuracy depends on the predictability of sales for different types of product and the dynamics of the market; grocery commodities sales patterns are more consistent than teenage fashions; washing machines more than personal computers (Figure 10.5).

As retailers attempt to respond more accurately to customer demand, so the time horizon for historical analysis is reduced: a week is becoming a long time for the retail industry. But there is an issue of 'analysis paralysis' from excessive data and it is important for the company to decide on the levels at which it will analyse its past sales performance and the quantity of information it can manage, and this may be as much to do with organisational culture as with capability. Analysis can be undertaken at the individual line level, at the product group level, the category level or ultimately for a whole department, to determine how quickly products will sell and in what quantities.

■ *Future trends.* New products or fashions form an increasingly large part of the retail assortment, and decisions in respect of these are based on information derived from a number of sources.

☐ *Trade exhibitions or fairs.* Every retail sector brings buyers and sellers together at national and international trade fairs to meet the buyers' timetables. These provide opportunities to confirm market trends, research new sources of supply and analyse current assortments, in one location. Buyers can visit suppliers, or simply absorb the visual impact created by the exhibition stands, to compare products and build up their selection criteria for their own retail market.

☐ *Trade journals.* As industries specialise, so one or more trade newspapers or journals are published on a regular basis to report on that sector's activities. In the UK, *Retail Week, Drapers Record, The Grocer, Greetings Weekly* and *Retail Automation* provide a sample of the available media. Their use is for general market information, competitive activity and suppliers' news, which can help to shape product selection criteria.

☐ *Suppliers' representatives.* Contacts take place at single and multiple levels, in teams and individually. A senior manager, such as a national account

---

Exhibit 10.3 Examples of Annual trade fairs in the retail industry

Trade fairs are organised for each sector of the industry, and buyers have a choice of a number of national and international fairs. Many retail support activities are represented at Trade Fairs too.

■ The Toy Fair is held in January at the new ExCel Exhibiton Centre in London.

■ The National Gift Fair in the UK is held at the National Exhibition Centre in March so that buyers can assess current and new merchandise offered from a wide range of suppliers for Christmas.

■ The Prêt á Porter clothing exhibition is held in Paris each spring to help clothing buyers to make their selection for the following autumn season.

■ The ISPO International Sports Trade Fair for sports equipment and fashion is held in August for buyers to select the next season's ranges for delivery in December onwards.

■ Retail Solutions is a trade fair to bring together suppliers of retail information systems and other retail technology.

---

manager or sales manager will provide information about their product in order to sell it. Consequently the buyer has to be aware of the inherent bias in the information, and that details about product characteristics, promotional support, availability and pricing will be used to condition the buyer as part of the negotiating process. The supplier may use an agent to undertake the sales and marketing function in smaller markets. Membership of a Buying Group can take over much of the retailer's sourcing and product development role, and centralise information gathering.

☐ *Sales literature*. Catalogues, leaflets, newsletters and price lists can provide information about new developments in the market from potential suppliers or updates from existing suppliers.

☐ *Market research reports*. Market research can be commissioned exclusively by a retailer, or bought from a research organisation or consultancy such as Verdict, Mintel or Management Horizons. The information is more usually analysed by a marketing specialist and used to brief the buyer, but may be accessed by buyers directly to assess consumer and competitive trends.

☐ *Competitive shopping*. Other retailers may have access to new products or present them in an innovative way to the market. This might be achieved through an exclusive deal with a supplier, own-brand development, as an early mover to a new fashion trend, or through strategic repositioning. Awareness of current activity, and if necessary acquisition of key products from competitors, widens the lateral base for range planning.

Research and analysis of past trends and future directions can be considered in two dimensions: quantitative and qualitative. The sources of information concerning new developments, described above, tend to be qualitative, relating as they do to the market, products and suppliers. The quantitative framework on the other hand is derived from historical data, supported by feedback on merchandise from customers, shop and operational management reports and managerial perceptions.

Analysis of previous sales is measured both in physical units and value (see Table 10.4 for analysis by price) to estimate the quantity of stock required to achieve the sales plan, the amount to be ordered, the timing of orders and, for seasonal merchandise, to minimise the stock left over at the end of the period. Two further factors to be considered are:

■ *Sales density.* The objective is to plan the range to achieve a targeted level of sales per square metre, the sales density. Merchandise will be planned for a specific period within the range or category to meet space and sales requirements in store and also at the distribution centre, as it is not always possible to maintain adequate stock levels of each product in the shop itself. In the sales plan, assumptions will have to be made about the rate of sale, replenishment strategy and the life-cycle of each product.

■ *Rate of sale.* Rate of sale refers to the speed at which each product will sell, and equates to the other planning definitions of week's cover and stockturn. Subjective decisions will be made about sales for the product groups and

Table 10.4   *Analysis of Clothing Line Sales Performance by Price*

Price points (£)	Autumn/Winter 20xx/20yy actual sales		Autumn/Winter 20xx/20yy actual sales		Number of units bought		sold %
	units	%	Value (£'000s)	%	units	%	
£2.50	329	0.3	0.7	0.1	439	0.2	74.9
£2.99	1946	1.6	4.9	1.0	3887	1.6	50.1
£3.50	65090	52.4	194.5	41.2	126939	52.3	51.3
£3.99	1001	0.8	3.5	0.7	2008	0.8	49.9
£4.50	18558	14.9	74.0	15.7	38485	15.8	48.2
£4.99	19615	15.8	83.8	17.7	39736	16.4	49.4
£5.50	0	0	0	0	0	0	0
£5.99	15854	12.8	95	20.1	26906	11.1	58.9
£6.99	139	0.1	1	0.2	239	0.1	58.2
£7.99	0	0	0	0	0	0	0
£8.99	1435	1.2	12.9	2.7	3775	1.6	38.0
£9.99	198	0.2	2	0.4	404	0.2	49.0
£11.99	0	0	0	0	0	0	0
TOTAL	124165	100.0	472.3	100.0	242818	100.0	51.1

The table is laid out for a typical analysis of a range of products, in this case for a previous Autumn/Winter season's sales (6 months), although the period could be reduced to meet the company's requirements. The sales history is presented by price points (column 1), numbers of units sold and their value (columns 2–4), as well as the number of units bought for that season (column 5–6). The final column indicates the percentage of sales to stock bought for the season (column 2 divided by column 6 × 100).

individual lines based on sales histories for similar products and predictions of forward demand. Fashion trends, competition, marketing strategy and financial constraints will also contribute to the assessment of the selling characteristics. A stock pattern can be created for clothing lines, which creates a sizing ratio and required stockholding. Combining these elements enables the buyer to estimate how much stock should be bought for an initial delivery and the amount and timing for later deliveries.

Using the Sales Plan

The sales plan provides the means for detailed financial control over the product ranges, from top-level summaries to category or line level. It can be effectively adjusted by using a forecasting system at the category and department level once the selling season has begun. As sales rarely proceed according to plan, it would be unwise simply to leave the plan alone if the actual performance begins to show a significant variance. Entering new forecasts enables the buying and merchandising teams to replan the remaining balance of the season's sales on the basis of current trading conditions.

Sales are monitored in detail at periodic intervals; if the sales trend is higher than planned, the forecast for future sales could be adjusted in line with the percentage uplift trend to that date, and stock requirements adjusted upwards in line with expected weekly sales. In this way a key merchandising aim, to maintain stock on order and in the business with anticipated demand, is satisfied. Similarly, if the sales trend is below plan, a forecast in line with the trend will allow the management team to reduce future order commitments and to consider action to promote, markdown or return slow selling lines to the supplier. The monthly sales profile for the new planning period will be based on previous periods' achieved sales trends, so that the plan follows the same profile through the year.

A system will be required to monitor stock levels and to generate purchase order proposals for the buyers, and both centralised and decentralised buying departments must work with appropriate systems. The merchandise planner will need to calculate requirements where stock levels have changed, to optimise quantities ordered, to schedule delivery dates and create purchase orders. With perishable goods, planning intervals are likely to be very short, with planning and ordering taking place every day. Where predictions of sales of goods are difficult to forecast owing to their seasonal nature, then replenishment planning is useful. In these instances reorder points are created and when stock levels reach the minimum threshold, including a safety stock level, then replenishments are triggered (see Chapter 12).

BRANCH PLANS AND SPACE MANAGEMENT

The planning and layout of products to fit the space within a store is critical to at a number of levels (see Figure 10.6). Space management includes the overall location of merchandise within the store, the placement of the category or product group within

Figure 10.6   *Dimensions of Range Plan Analysis*

SALES PLANNING	Sales plan £	Comparative sales last year (LY) £	Margin %	Profit £	Average selling price £

STOCK/ SPACE BY VALUE	Space allocation (display units)	Sales per standard display fixture £	Profit per standard display fixture £	Average stock £	Stockturn

STOCK/ SPACE BY UNITS	Units sold last year	Unit sales per standard display fixture	Average stock units per fixture	Average stock holding total

the store and the detailed merchandise plan. The challenge facing the merchandise team and operational management is to provide enough space in each shop to display the right quantity of each product. The right quantity will be enough to satisfy demand each day, and to maintain an appropriate visual identity, without running out or carrying excess stock. These requirements will be determined by:

- Size of shop
- Types of fixture and fitting
- Diversity of ranges
- Image and aesthetic requirements
- Practicality
- Variable rates of sale between different products

A clear plan and numerical assessment of the shop selling space is required in square feet or metres, so that performance measurements can be accurately recorded. The retailers' aim is to determine how much merchandise sales' units can hold, and to create a standard measurement of selling space in the store, a figure that will be exclude any stock room space. Square metreage, or footage, is used for measuring and comparing productivity of selling space. Product groups can be zoned into areas within the store and the sales of each zone divided by their square footage/metrage provides a guide to how profitably the space in the store is being used. However, it does not enable the planners to plan merchandise into the store in detail because products sit on shelves, or hang off selling arms on wall units or other display equipment, rather than fit conveniently into 'square footage' boxes.

One solution to this problem is to calculate the display space available in the sales area using a linear measure. This is a measure of actual selling space, along the length of a shelf or on a hanging arm or table, surfaces whose length could be measured and on which products can be presented for sale. Standardisation is valuable, both of fixtures and fittings and products: boxed and packed items with defined areas can be more accurately calculated in terms of shelving space than soft goods like clothing. The planning team will have to agree how many units of each product can fit into a linear metre or foot. These may have to be averaged out if they come in a variety of sizes. Some products can be displayed fairly flexibly, such as books, whilst others such as postcards or loose stock will require special racks or dispensers which will require separate space calculations. Some types of fixture and stock densities for a sports shop are given in Table 10.5. Products with more predictable sales trends rather than variable seasonal or fashion merchandise will also present more straightforward planning solutions. A wall panel in a clothing department could be configured with a number of different hanging arms or brackets to carry a very large number of socks or small number of ski jackets so initial space modelling is required.

The merchandising plan or planogram provides a detailed map of where each product will fit in a store, to allocate space efficiently. The total amount of space in each area will vary, but should be maintained in proportion to each product group or category segment. Within each of these, brands should be arranged according to their relative importance with the larger and more prominent presentation devoted to leading brands. Each segment should lead into the next with brands that display many of the characteristics of both groups situated on the edge of the segment. Finally, space should be allocated to reflect market share.

This approach is typical in grocery or toiletries and cosmetics retailing where category management is used. With Van Den Burgh's yellow fats products, a hierarchy of sales was identified with the aim of getting the consumer to trade up from more basic low-cost products, classified as the 'kitchen sector', to the 'health' and 'taste' added-value sectors. Retailers selling larger products such as electrical goods may provide a simpler layout guide. The buying department of each type of retailer will be required to construct its ranges to maximise the sales opportunity in each store as well as provide a tight stock control. Devoting more space to the most important sectors reduces shopper confusion and adds value to the category.

In planning the layout of the shop further parameters may need to be considered: the product ranges to be featured for an agreed period of time, the number of lines and quantity of each, and the location of the features and the space these will take up. The promotions timetable will require display guidelines so that the category or product group is clearly and coherently displayed together. The displays will have to create interest, so that changes to the store space allocations need to be planned to retain the attention of repeat customers and to attract new ones. Spaces should also be created for marked-down stock so that it is cleared effectively and does not detract from the main message of the retailer.

Layout themes may be planned in a number of ways:

Table 10.5   *Space and Stock Planning for a Sports Clothing Department*

Fixture	Linear metres	Densities of stock per linear metre			
Free standing clothing rail	3.6	T shirts	20	Sweat tops	18
Wall panel (unit)	2.4	Skiwear	6	Tennis shirts	18
Gondola	2.4	Swimwear	15	Tennis shorts	18
Sock stand	1.8	Socks	20		
Exercise equipment stand	1.2	Tracksuits	7		

■ *Range adjacencies*. Products that have been bought as range or group and share common design or product features have a more powerful appeal if they are displayed together.

■ *Promotions*. Promotional lines in particular have been bought to support other activity and close attention should be paid to the promotional area as a prime selling space. Some lines may sell well or sell through early in the promotion, whilst others may underperform or worst of all arrive late into the promotion. Both situations should be managed so that the promotional display retains its integrity.

■ *Core products*. Consistent sellers, these lines should always be in stock and feature prominently within their range grouping. The most critical lines will be high sales/high margin lines.

■ *Slow sellers*. These lines should not be given prime space in an attempt to speed up sales, but may not justify deletion from the range. The merchandise manager may have to keep moving the stock around in order to create new and interesting adjacencies.

■ *Stockouts*. If the store runs out of stock, the space should never be left empty. If necessary, merchandise should be regrouped to increase displays of core products or near substitutes.

For grocery retailers, the layout of products on shelves reflects consumer shopping behaviour and category strategies. Space allocation is the amount of space allocated to categories including section length and linear footage. Space can be allocated in uniform or cluster displays, and decision criteria are based on the target consumer:

■ The *presentation* should be logical or shoppable, based on the needs or wants of target consumers and how they make purchase decisions in the category.

■ *Competitive positioning*. The shelf presentation should help highlight key points of competitive differentiation sought by the retailer.

■ *Marketing strategy*. The desired variety image should be communicated and reinforced by the shelf strategy.

■ *Category role and strategies*. Decisions need to be taken on the consistency of the shelf presentation with the category role and strategies (Figure 10.7).

The costs and benefits of various shelf presentation options should also be considered in terms of operational issues, for example shelf-stocking costs, and the impact a particular location within the store may have on category sales and profits. In more qualitative terms, the shelf presentation should help the retailer implement its customer service strategy at store level.

The complexity of space planning is resource-intensive, and is leading to more integrated computerised packages. Halfords, for example, a retailer trading from over 400 automotive and cycle stores, plans seasonally using two-dimensional CAD draw-

Figure 10.7   *Product Sales and Space Performance*

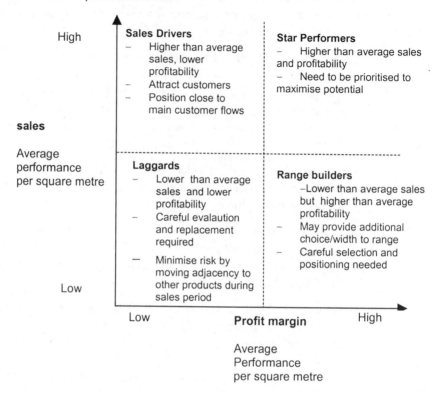

Figure 10.8   *Shelf Presentation Tactics Guidelines and Planogram*

Shelf sets should direct consumer attention to higher priced SKUs Manager to consider blending higher priced SKUs throughout the set to increase consumer exposure and purchase

High profile location and competitive category shelf space allocation. Overall shelf should be attractive and invite consumers to return to the store. Highlight loyalty SKU segments.

The planogram should direct attention to higher margin SKUs. Capitalise on impulse lines. Locate higher margin categories in high traffic areas.

Maximise visibility of private label and high profit SKUs/segments.

The planogram highlights new/high profile SKUs/segments. Adequate space to get consumer attention.

Source: by kind permission of Roland Berger Strategy Consultants.

ings featuring only basic fixture locations within each store layout. The company works on two seasons together with a promotional plan; for each seasonal change 24 area planners, each responsible for 20–25 stores, work for three weeks intensively on the new season's plan.

Space planning systems, such as retail FOCUS, enable head office managers to

Figure 10.9   *Shelf Presentation Tactics and Planogram*

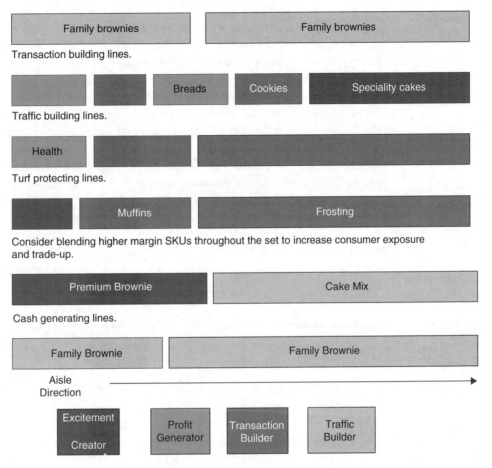

Source: ECR Europe Category Management Best Practices Report, by kind permission
of the Partnering Group and Roland Berger & Partners.

instantly access space utilisation and performance data. The six-week reporting cycle the company previously adopted has become instantaneous, and promotions can be more accurately targeted and presented using detailed store-specific information on products and gondola availability.

SUMMARY

The buying function has become more complex and specialised under the influence of a sharper marketing focus and intense industrial competition. As a result multiple retailers have developed centralised buying departments staffed by teams of buyers, merchandise managers and, in some organisations, marketing and distribution managers. Buyers take responsibility for the external sourcing activities, primarily stock selection and negotiation, whilst merchandisers plan and control the stock. However, retail size and structure will determine the exact range of roles and responsibilities. Category management provides an opportunity to integrate the centralised buying functions with store planning and distribution to respond quickly and efficiently to consumer demand.

Product planning begins with marketing-led activity, by targeting and defining market segments that fit with the company's strategic objectives. Customer profiles enable the buying team to identify key attitudes and behaviours that determine the scope of the product assortment. The planning process moves from broadly defined product categories to detailed ranges and lines of individual products, down to stock-keeping units (SKUs), the lowest level of control. The structure of product plans depends on the industry sector; the fundamental distinction between the approaches lies the rate of change in product acceptability to the consumer. Clothing retailers will manage at least two seasonal ranges with many adding interseasonal and other specialist collections during the year. Other retailers' range plans will be more stable, changing as new brands and products are introduced.

Product range width and depth should satisfy the purchasing needs of customers, and at the same time meet both financial and store-space planning requirements. The retailer's sales plan will determine the ranges' sales units and value, which are broken down by store to create individual store plans. Each range needs to be planned to an allocated space to maximise sales and stock efficiency.

QUESTIONS

1   Evaluate the roles and responsibilities of buyers in the food and clothing retail sectors.

2   To what extent does category management meet merchandise planning needs?

3   In what ways is range planning 'only as good as yesterday's sales'?

4   How scientific is store space planning?

Case Study

Miss Selfridge

Miss Selfridge's market position presents some important range-planning issues. Its primary target market is 15–25-year-old women with the average customer aged 18. The brand is aimed at all socio-economic groups, with 57 per cent of its customers drawn from the ABC1 categories. The store has always been at the forefront of young fashion clothing and in 1998 an internal fashion development team was set up to absorb ideas from around the world that would enable its buyers to focus even more clearly on the latest fashion trends. These have to be rapidly interpreted to meet affordable price points for the Miss Selfridge customer, and ordered within exacting timescales; up to ten ranges, or range extensions may be planned through the year.

The product assortment has been successfully extended, too, and in recent years the company has introduced new ranges of toiletries and cosmetics, footwear and swimwear for teenagers and younger girls, to create a lifestyle offer and one-stop fashion shop. As a result, it not only holds a strong position in clubwear and other fashion outerwear categories, but also fashion and novelty accessories to which it devotes 14 per cent of its space. Research into the target market showed that core product ranges were being overlooked as well; in 1997 the company realised that sales opportunities in jeans had been overlooked and subsequently introduced the Falmer, Levi and Pepe brands.

In the UK, Miss Selfridge trades from 96 stores and 18 concessions, and its high-fashion image is vital in main city centres. However, in suburban and smaller town sites the extreme look has to be moderated, and these contrasting requirements place planning constraints on the merchandise teams. Young clothing fashion trends can be short-lived and there has been an understandable temptation for merchandisers to allocate limited supplies of the latest styles to the best-selling stores. This means that in some areas Miss Selfridge's merchandise has not been as consistently fashionable as it should have been.

As a result of a planning review in the mid-1990s, Miss Selfridge developed a 'range diamond' model defining each store as needing particular mixes of merchandise, from 'leading edge' to 'basic' to ensure that all stores maintain the right image. A new merchandise management system was installed to rationalise stock planning and control across the womenswear businesses. The most important features enable merchandisers to check up on the other former Sears Womenswear companies' dealings with suppliers, for example, to assess their geographic commitments in sourcing or cloth analysis. The merchandise and planning databases are held separately so that each can be modelled independently. Planning is undertaken at a category level, although users can mine data as far down as line level. Branch performance, too, can be monitored easily on a seasonal basis to assess local demand and forecasts amended to take account of emerging trends. Manufacturing support applications can be added in, providing the potential for production information on demand, and enabling the company to respond more rapidly to changing sales activity.

SEMINAR QUESTIONS FOR DISCUSSION

1 Discuss the range selection and distribution problems facing Miss Selfridge

2 What systems would you recommend for a high fashion retailer?

References

Berman, B. and Evans, J.R. (1998) *Retail Management: A Strategic Approach* (Englewood Cliffs, NJ: Prentice Hall).

Burt, S. and Sparks, L. (1997) 'A Cross National Consideration and Comparison of Retail Margins', *British Journal of Management*, vol. 8, pp. 133–50.

Burt, S. (2000) 'The Strategic Role of Retail Brands in British Grocery Retailing', *European Journal of Marketing*, vol. 34, no. 8, pp. 875–90.

De Chernatony, L. and Dall'Olmo Riley, F. (1998) 'Marketing the Components of the Brand', *European Journal of Marketing*, vol. 32, no. 11–12, pp. 1074–90.

Dussart, C. (1998) 'Category Management: Strengths, Limits and Developments', *European Management Journal*, vol. 16, no. 1, pp. 50–62.

ECR (1999) *European Category Management Best Practices Report*, Roland Berger and Associates (London).

Fisher, M.L. (1997) 'What is the Right Supply Chain for your Product?', *Harvard Business Review*, March April, pp. 105–106.

Harris, D. and Walters, D.W. (1992) *Retail Operations Management* (Hempstead: Prentice Hall Europe).

Jayaraman, V., Srivastava, R. and Benton, W.C. (1999) 'Supplier Selection and Order Quantity Allocation: A Comprehensive Model', *The Journal of Supply Chain Management*, Spring, 1999, pp. 50–8.

Lamey, J. (1997) *Supply Chain Management* (London: Financial Times Publications).

Lea-Greenwood, G. (1997) 'Case Study: Jaeger', *Journal of Fashion Marketing and Management*, vol. 1, no. 2, pp. 150–3.

Logistics and Transport Focus (2000) 'Startling Results of Smart Merchandising', *Logistics and Transport Focus*, vol. 2, no. 1, January-February, pp. 36–7.

Lucas, G.H., Bush, R.P. and Gresham, L.G. (1994) *Retailing* (Boston: Houghton Mifflin).

McGoldrick, P.J. (1990) *Retail Marketing* (Maidenhead: McGraw Hill).

Mintel (1997) *Efficient Consumer Response* (London: Mintel International Group).

Petroni, A. and Braglia, M. (2000) 'Vendor Selection Using Principal Component Analysis', *The Journal of Supply Chain Management*, Spring, 2000, pp. 63–72.

Visual-technology (2000) *Retail FOCUS Testimonials for Store Planning – Halfords Case Study*, www. visual-technology.co.uk.

Walters, D.W. (1988) *Strategic Retail Marketing: a Case Study Approach* (Hemel Hempstead: Prentice Hall Europe).

Wileman, A. and Jary, M. (1997) *Retail Power Plays: From Trading to Brand Leadership* (Basingstoke: Macmillan).

Supply Chain Management

INTRODUCTION

Decisions about product assortments and sales planning were introduced in Chapter ten and this chapter continues the theme of merchandise management into its next phase: the sourcing of products and their delivery from suppliers to the retailer. The term 'supply chain management' originated in the early 1980s, and is used to define these inbound processes and the management of a network of interconnected businesses involved in delivering goods and services to the ultimate customer (Harland, 1996). The aim of this chapter is to expand the boundaries of supply-chain management, starting with issues of how and why products are sourced from suppliers. Chapter 12 will complete the cycle by following the merchandise into the retailer and analysing the internal processes of inventory management.

SOURCING

The retailer is the final organisational point in the supply chain, providing services and products to the consumer. To evaluate how customer demand pulls supplies through the chain of intermediaries; it is important to analyse how retailers take decisions about products and then apply them to the process of sourcing, how they relate to their suppliers, and achieve deliveries into their domestic market.

In recent years the retail industry has become more involved in the evaluation of existing sources of supply, and especially the network of suppliers and efficient distribution systems. The awareness of new products by consumers has developed in the past 30 years as populations become better educated and more affluent. More accessible and wide-ranging communications and sophisticated media create and sustain an increasingly diverse range of interests. At the same time, suppliers have developed an increasingly international base for manufacturing and distribution. Global brands such as Nestlé or Sony enable consumers to have an awareness of, and retailers to have access to, new products beyond their own country. To develop these opportunities retailers need to have experience in three areas, identification of sources and products, the reliability of warehousing and delivery, and on-going contact with suppliers or intermediaries.

Sourcing and Competitive Advantage

Supplier and product sourcing is a key element in retail strategy, and the process of delivering the product to the consumer has become an important point of competitive advantage. The dimensions of strategic sourcing can be identified around their importance to the business and their financial impact on the organisation. Their significance is illustrated in Figure 11.1, where buying decisions extend from automatic processing, on which as little time as possible should be spent on buying, to strategic partnering, where considerable attention should be given to formal partnerships or alliances.

Strategy will determine how resources and the retailer's business opportunities are used to guide the marketing plans of the organisation. Buying decisions on product and price as well as promotion will influence and be influenced by issues such as availability, cost and brand position, supported by the manufacturer's promotional activ-

Figure 11.1   *Strategic Sourcing and Supplier Relationships*

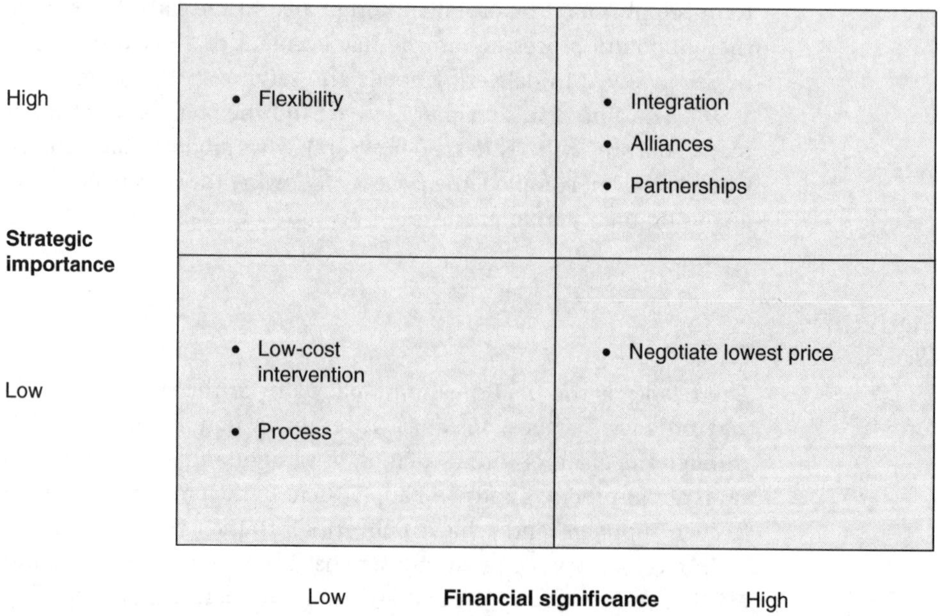

Exhibit 11.1 Using product sources for competitive advantage: Lands End catalogue

The following statements were made by Land's End in their Mail Order clothing catalogue, to demonstrate the quality of their individual clothing lines through close attention to materials and manufacturing processes in the supply chain.

- Trousers: Corduroy: worked with fabric mill for 84% cotton 16% polyester blend rich
- fibre reactive dyes
- Polo shirt: Peruvian cotton (extra long staple had picked three times each season)
- Shirts: pure combed pima cotton creates a fine yarn
- Turtle neck shirt: uses cashmere from inner Mongolian cashmere goats
- Pullover: Australian wool and British finishing
- Shetland woollens: New Zealand wool, spun in Scotland
- Outdoor jackets: Polartec fleece from Malden Mills, USA

Lands End Direct Merchants.

---

ity. In addition [...] y should not only aim for lower c[...] oduct and service characteristics ([...])

The abil[...] by stages of organisational grow[...] the scale of operation is the devel[...] tion to or as a substitute for proc[...] brands, as it [...] ntiation. The decision to develop [...] brand produc[...] and strategic investment in supp[...] require relatively low levels of inve[...] ds, however, involve a shift from c[...] brands to an approach based on quality and in[...] (Exhibit 11.1). At these levels retailers will be obliged to invest in design and product development, quality management and long-term supplier relationships (Wileman and Jary, 1997). In the UK, Marks and Spencer's market positioning has demanded more complex garments, more innovative fibres and higher standards of tailoring in its menswear, and so its suppliers are required to invest in new machinery, skills and management.

Sourcing Policies

Retailers have to decide on a sourcing policy which not only includes domestic suppliers but also increasingly turns to international and global sources. Some factors will push the sourcing out of the domestic country and others may pull the retailer into new markets. Some developing markets may have little or no domestic supply base. As a unique home furnishings store concept, THE One in Abu Dhabi has virtually no local suppliers and has needed to originate its supply base. Consequently it anticipates ordering 6000 products from 163 suppliers, with the aim of buying competitively from wherever a product can be sourced, including the USA, Europe and Asia.

Sourcing from the Domestic Market

Sourcing by retailers has been undertaken traditionally within their domestic market, from local suppliers and wholesalers. Even where products have originated in other countries, the retailer has relied on intermediaries to supply the goods. With industrialisation, manufactured goods became more diverse and competition increased supplies to retailers and their customers. However, this manufacturer-led process of selling goods to retailers has been reappraised in recent years. Where suppliers formerly 'pushed' their goods into markets, supply chains are increasingly being seen in terms of consumer demand 'pulling' goods through retailers and other distributors back into the supply chain.

As retailers are exerting their power in the relationship with suppliers to source products more widely and directly in order to exploit competitive advantages, so selling price structures, product assortment and quality of design, technology and taste will be determined by supplier selection and values within the chain of suppliers. As suppliers become more concentrated in domestic markets, retailers need to balance the contraction in product availability assortment by increasing the scope of their sourcing activity (Pache, 1998). Nevertheless, sourcing from domestic suppliers offers a number of adv

- Problems of   s are avoided, and the commu   nost developed countries.

- Delivery sc   ed overland, whereas so   is of transport and stages betv   cs management enables th   s in less-developed economie

- For simil   able in the domestic market a

Internatic

One of the   ircing is the high level of domestic production costs.   the retailer to achieve higher margins or lower selling prices. This drove Marks and Spencer to fundamentally change its sourcing policy when it decided to increase the number of garments sourced outside the UK from around 20 per cent of the range to over 50 per cent. Changes in sourcing policy also created opportunities and problems for its suppliers; one leading supplier had to turn over the entire production at its Sri Lankan factory to meet the retailer's needs.

Limited production capacity and lack of product innovation in the domestic market provide further impetus for change (McGoldrick and Davis, 1995). As a function of post-industrial development, the UK has expanded its service industries, but in many markets now sustains a manufacturing base too small to offer a wide choice of products. Although this trend is acutely observed in the UK, the relationship between service industry growth and manufacturing is found in many other Western countries. The growth in global branding, and the rationalisation of production and distribution to supply regions rather than countries adds to the need for retailers to take a broader view of their sourcing. Availability and diversity of products become increasingly important; consistency of service and higher-quality specifications pull retailers to source outside the domestic market.

Distinguishing the clothing sector is the need to create a strong visual identity and consistent fashion awareness in a retailers' target markets. These features can be combined with low-cost sourcing to support low–moderate fashion positions, but also to create distinctive higher fashion positions by sourcing from more expensive or exclusive suppliers. Retailer brands may need to be supported by investment in more complex fashion supply chains, as they take on greater responsibility for the design to delivery specifications.

Sourcing patterns are constantly changing for clothing retailers as buyers look for garment suppliers in new markets to provide ideas, better quality and improved value for money. In the past 10 years these criteria have become more critical as the clothing retail sector becomes increasingly concentrated, competition is heightened and customers more sophisticated in their individuality. Retail buyers typically cite better margins and quality as key reasons to buy from the Far East, an important source for UK buyers as Table 11.1 demonstrates. At the same time, improved communications

Table 11.1   *Sources of Supply for UK Clothing Retail Buyers*

Principal sources used	No. of retailers	Retailers buying in each country (%)	Average % bought in each country
UK	31	100	32
China	22	79	13
Hong Kong	20	71	16
Korea	19	68	4
India	19	68	12
E. Europe	19	68	8
Italy	18	64	11
Indonesia	13	46	6
Taiwan	11	39	4
France	8	29	3
Japan	5	18	5
Spain	3	11	8
USA	2	7	15
Other Europe	16	57	14
Other Far East	16	57	10
Rest of World	6	21	6

Source: Pretious (1996).

and reduced lead times to delivery have reduced the risk of sourcing from these markets (Pretious, 1996). Increasingly the same needs are being felt in other fashion-related retail categories, such as home furnishing and household goods.

In other sectors, prestige, quality and superior or innovative technology may enable retailers to offer higher specifications and value in their products from non-national sources. Consumer electronics provide good examples of retail sourcing through the use of own-brands, new product development and branded promotions to compete successfully.

ASSESSMENT OF GLOBAL SOURCES OF SUPPLY

The assessment of international sources of supply should enable the retailer to evaluate the risks of investment in overseas manufacturers, the effect on the supply chain, and to assess the likelihood of interruption to supplies (Garten, 1997; see also Table 11.2). Marketing environment audits are valuable for assessing potential opportunities and risks for international sourcing. Assessment of the political environment takes on a greater significance than in the domestic market to clarify issues of political stability, the democratic process and government attitudes to market intervention. Social, demographic and cultural analysis should identify factors which impact on the availability and capabilities of the workforce (Dibb, 1996).

Table 11.2   *Product/Service Evaluation for Global Sources of Clothing*

Product type	Service requirements	Source requirements	Location
Commodity, low fashion	Continuous supply	Low labour cost, materials availability and high volume capability	Developing economies, e.g. Asia, India, Africa
Seasonal low fashion, regular colour/style change	On-time delivery and responsiveness to colour/style requirements	Low labour cost, technical ability, materials availability, volume flexibility and communications/ logistics links	European rim/more developed Asian sources
Seasonal medium/high fashion	On-time delivery and responsiveness to in-season selling patterns	Technical ability, communications/logistics links, volume flexibility, short-run capability, materials availability and low labour costs	European rim/domestic
High fashion	On-time delivery and immediate response to trends	Short-run capability and lead time, communications/logistics links, and material availability	Domestic

Source: Shepheard-Walwyn (1997).

Identifying potential countries for supply can be understood through the process of national development. Porter (1990) proposes four stages of development in the creation of national trading competitiveness. In the earliest stage, factors such as availability of raw materials or a large potential labour force can lead to rapid economic development in specific sectors. These in turn create clusters of competitive strong industries from which the economy can broaden. The economic development plans for Korea show how heavy industrial development was a priority in the early years; however, this sector experienced a low level of international competitive advantage whereas light industrial products such as clothing, footwear, textiles and luggage were highly successful, providing a major source of supply to rapidly growing consumer markets.

Since the 1980s there has been a move towards economic deregulation in many developed Western countries that has stimulated greater efficiency and responsiveness to consumer demand. In Eastern Europe, the former communist states have begun the transition from centralised command to market-led economies, creating accessibility to their markets and sourcing opportunities. Poland, Hungary and the Czech Republic are in the forefront of market reforms, whilst Slovakia, Bulgaria and Romania have moved more slowly. Russia faces more fundamental structural political and economic barriers to development. Among the practical problems encountered in these and other developing economies are the lack of managerial skills. In one example of the early post-communist period, the management of a Czech shoe factory was unable to supply any details about its suppliers, product costings and selling prices or even the floor space of its factory.

Clothing retailers in developed countries will particularly look for low-cost workforces with existing or easily developed skills. At the earliest stage of development manufacturers will tend to be limited to large production runs of relatively straightforward designs such as T-shirts or canvas shoes, where a limited number of materials and components can be sourced domestically or imported. This simplifies local import practices and distribution as well as enabling the manufacturer to become more productive through a shorter learning curve. Consequently more buyers are buying is turning to third-world countries; some of these are familiar, such as Bangladesh, but others such as Vietnam, Laos, Kenya, Tanzania and Nepal are comparatively new trading partners in manufactured goods. It appears that their competitiveness over developed countries' production can only increase as they gain experience in using higher quality fabrics and more advanced production techniques.

Patterns of sourcing will be determined not only by resources but also by local and national communications infrastructures. The absence of good quality road and rail systems and underdeveloped port and airport facilities will restrict shipment dates and lengthen transportation to the retailer. Since political relations with Vietnam have been normalised, the country offers opportunities to source low-cost textile and footwear products; however, it faces a range of infrastructural difficulties which inhibit its development including the lack of deepwater ports and poor road and trucking networks (Cooke, 1997). By contrast, the continuing strength of Singapore as a major regional distribution point reflects the slow development of facilities in neighbouring countries. Its position is further enhanced as a leading trading centre by its advanced communications systems, and strong financial community.

The emergence of strong, locally-based businesses and technologies will drive the economies forward through investment and innovation-driven stages of development. Hence, Korea and Taiwan have progressed on to strong international positions in high value electronics industries (amongst others), but in the process of wealth creation they have begun to lose the labour cost advantages they previously held in lower technology industries. Information, communication and technological industries in particular will increasingly extend beyond narrow national boundaries to create global networks of supply.

Managing Sources of Supply

Retailers can select and manage their supplier sourcing through a variety of channels depending on the industry structure, the size and complexity of the product ranges and the stage of development achieved by the organisation itself. Small and medium-sized (SME) retailers in most sectors will be limited by their size to low complexity sourcing, using domestic manufacturers and wholesalers both for domestic and internationally sourced products.

As the retailer increases its turnover through expansion of its outlets or through home shopping media, the organisation will gain more experience of its product market and support more functional specialisation. The combination of greater confidence in its product selection, industry knowledge and other stakeholder interests, such as increasing gross margin needs, will drive the retailer to explore new sourcing opportunities.

Agents provide local expertise and contacts with a range of local manufacturers. The size and scope of the agency can vary widely from large multi-divisional groups with representative offices in many countries to individual agents supported by a small local team of quality controllers and clerks working in a single country or area. The agent provides local knowledge of types of production and capacity, cost price ranges and quota availability if necessary. The company can overcome operational problems of locating suppliers and organising meetings as well as translating and providing communications support to overseas buyers. When buyers' schedules are tight, an efficient and well-organised agent can maximise business opportunities and reduce non-productive time spent on research and administration.

Larger retail organisations may establish their own buying offices. Experience of international markets and volumes of imported merchandise will be high enough to support an office in key trading locations, such as Hong Kong. However, it is important to maintain expert knowledge of local customs and culture in order to maximise negotiating positions. In this respect the selection and recruitment of local staff to research and manage suppliers will continue to be a priority. Ultimately direct import channels enable retailers to exercise more control over their supply chains at the cost of investment in personnel and information and communication technology.

Regulating the International Trading Framework

International trading agreements and regulations will influence retailers' decision-making about the location and quantity of imported products. A number of restrictions on trade have been noted. The more visible restrictions include quotas, tariffs, exchange controls, subsidies and qualitative controls (Worthington and Britton, 1997).

Quotas are set by governments to regulate the import of types of merchandise as a means of protecting the domestic market. Not all products attract a quota, but typically quotas are given an annual limit beyond which products will not be admitted to the importing country or will be seized for disposal by the customs department. Other goods may continue to be imported at a higher tariff rate once the limit has been exceeded.

The Generalised System of Preferences (GSP) allows tariff-free imports from selected developing nations, provided that the products have been made in those countries and not merely re-exported. Even this system has seen changes in emphasis; since 1995 two major changes have taken place, the elimination of tariff quotas and ceilings, together with the introduction of a nil rate of preference, and secondly the imposition of four categories of preference on products based on the sensitivity of industries in developed countries (Wilson, 1996).

There may be other less obvious methods of control including government pressure on manufacturers and suppliers:

- Countries needing Western currency, for example China, will encourage suppliers to sell on a delivered to customer basis using their own national shipping and marine services (Johnson and Wood, 1996).

- The specification of employment practices as a condition for trade could be used by developed countries to protect domestic industries from low-cost competition.

- By regulating amine-based Azo dyes in textiles, Germany was interpreted as creating a hidden trade barrier by India, where many clothes are made from textilies dyed in this way. Access to foreign markets was reported to be the single greatest limit on the growth of India's textiles industry.

However, international purchasing and global sourcing have become more widely used as international trade barriers become less restrictive through international treaties. The promotion as of free trade is undertaken by a number of regional and global organisations and initiatives. Since January 1995, the World Trade Organisation (WTO) has provided a forum for continuing negotiations and provides an effective court for international trade disputes. The EU for example, plans to bring competition issues to the WTO in instances where national policies keep out imports and reduce competition (Exhibit 11.2).

THE SUPPLY CHAIN

Decisions about product sourcing increasingly involve analysis of the supply chain and the identification of opportunities to create cost savings and to deliver higher standards of service through closer supplier relationships. The supply chain can be understood from a number of perspectives, primarily concerning the management of

---

Exhibit 11.2 Trade regulation

The World Trade Organization (WTO) is the only global international organization dealing with the rules of trade between nations. At its heart are the WTO agreements, negotiated and signed by the bulk of the world's trading nations and ratified in their parliaments. The goal is to help producers of goods and services, exporters, and importers conduct their business (www.wto.org).

One of its activities is to oversee the withdrawal of the protective quota scheme, the Multi-Fibre Agreement (MFA), which was designed to protect the textile industries of developed countries from low-cost imports. The EU will choose which quotas it removes at each stage, starting with more basic products from 1995 but later moving on to more technologically complex ones. However, the EU is coming under pressure from regions which rely on clothing and textiles industries; Southern Europe in particular is looking to protect these sectors which form an important part of its economy.

Figure 11.2   *The Supply Chain*

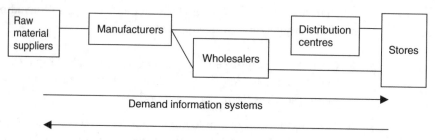

raw materials to delivery of the final product to the consumer. This has been described as a flow rather than a series of processes (Lamey, 1997), and as a complex network of links and nodes involved in the conversion of materials (de Wilt and Krishnan, 1995). Cost-driven reorganisations resulting in business outsourcing, downsizing and delayering have contributed to this network structure (Harland, 1996); as a result, supply chains rely very much on the coordinated initiatives of individual companies and the responsiveness of market sensitive business units in larger companies (Christopher, 1998).

Ultimately changes have been driven by the external demands of customers for higher service levels, and the focus to this activity lies in satisfying customer requirements by retailers, manufacturers and suppliers (Saunders, 1994). The structure of the supply chain (Figure 11.2) for an organisation will enable it to identify and manage processes and activities that add value to its products and services. Many of these exist outside its internal boundaries to embrace both suppliers and customers in collaborative relationships and partnerships. Cost reductions are an important outcome from fully collaborative relationships; in Italy and Germany total cost reductions for ambient products delivered through regional distribution centres amounted to 2.5 per cent of retail sales, and 1.5 per cent in the UK. An attainable target might be 7.5 per cent depending on the country and the company supply chain costs (Walker, 1994). In addition, the supply chain needs to work in an international environment, moving away from country-based models to reduce costs and improve efficiency and provide a more responsive service.

Shorter lifecycles, and the increasing globalisation of industries combined with the need for local customisation and organisational integration push both retailers and manufacturers towards closer collaboration. This is essential to supply-chain management, and the working relationship should aim to optimise resources and reduce duplications, inefficiencies and delays, of time as well as materials. Within Europe alone stock held in supply chains varies between an average of 28 days in the UK to 42 and 50 days in France, Germany Italy and Spain (Warburg, 1996). The need for greater efficiencies to reduce stock levels will inevitably lead to increased retail concentration and the decline of smaller businesses.

Discounters in Europe, such as Aldi and Netto in the food sector, seem likely to increase their market share forcing established retailers to develop cost-saving strategies. The selection of delivery channels will play an important role in the configuration of the supply chain and, increasingly, retailers must deliver more for less in order to survive and compete. Jointly created business plans by retailers and suppliers can eliminate wasteful practices through the supply chain. In this way, Procter and Gamble saved its US retail customers $65 m in 18 months through efficient logistics management alone (Cottrill, 1997).

The characteristics of the supply chain will depend on the retail sector, too, as cost structures vary. Costs of storage, transport and administration need to be carefully assessed by product category and if necessary at line level. Rates of replenishment will also affect the configuration and management of the supply chain: groceries may need to be delivered in multiple daily deliveries, whereas clothing deliveries may be made twice per week, and other merchandise on a 'ms-off' basis.

Key factors in successful supply-chain management include:

- The selection and consolidation of the number of suppliers used by the retailer, enabling the retailer to focus on the development of the business and create administrative efficiencies. These efficiencies are replicated elsewhere in the supply chain; in one case Xerox reduced its supplier base from 5000 to 300. Industries with many suppliers, such as the automative industry, have begun to adopt a tiered strategy to its supplier strategy. Similarly for suppliers there is a need to reduce or consolidate the customer base, through the selection of companies to be traded with directly and the smaller ones which can buy through wholesalers or distributors.

- The coordination of prices and inventory policies to avoid short-term demand created by promotional and trade deals; in the USA, Procter and Gamble was able to reduce its price lists by cancelling 27 sales promotions. Stock management by suppliers is easier with consistent demand, rather than the over- and understocking cycles caused by promotional activity with retailers. Through the supply chain there are a number of trade-offs which have to negotiated to maximise efficiencies and service levels. The balance between cost of stock and service levels is one of the most difficult to achieve, as retailers seek to reduce stock holdings and improve the availability of stock at the same time. Within

---

Exhibit 11.3   Shell Select

Shell Select was launched in 1990, and by 1998 traded from nearly 1000 stores. It is now the largest company-owned convenience store chain.

It reorganised its supply chain to give it greater control. Whereas previously Shell used up to 20 different suppliers and wholesalers, it now places its ordering and distribution in the hands of one logistics company, Hays. Shell's category management team retain responsibility for negotiation directly with suppliers, but Hays select the product range, monitor sales patterns and place up to 150 replenishment orders each day to maintain agreed service standards. The major suppliers use EDI. This is all achieved from one national, multi-temperature distribution centre, five regional centres and by using 100 Select branded vehicles.

Source: *Retail Week*, 12 March 1998.

---

the chain, suppliers and retailers will have to agree on order quantities and stockholding, manufacturer capacity and stock levels, and warehousing and transport (Management Horizons Europe, 1998).

■ The need to share information between partners in the chain. At their simplest, information flows are necessary to avoid stock imbalances and to minimise out-of-date stock. The transfer of information between different parts of the supply chain is dependent on the development of appropriate technology, and this can lead to more sophisticated stock management. Electronic data interchange (EDI) and, increasingly, Internet-based systems enable companies to communicate with each other for ordering, invoicing and payment. The main uses are to minimise stocks of high volume, and bulky or capital intensive products. Low-cost items or products that are not space-intensive do not appear to be high priorities for EDI, especially as there may be barriers to using this type of communication. Smaller suppliers may not have the skills and equipment to enter into EDI and there remain problems with non-standard messaging systems (see Exhibit 11.5).

More confident and sustained use of EDI enables retailers and suppliers to reduce delivery times and stock levels, and to develop processes such as warehouse cross-docking. As the partners become more integrated, sharing of information has reduced the barriers between supplier and retailer still further, with vendor-managed inventory (VMI) techniques in which inventories are managed at the customer's location through highly automated electronic information systems. The closer working relationships can lead to more effective product development too by bringing in suppliers at an earlier stage than might be possible with a more distanced relationship.

Partnerships

Successful supply-chain management requires joint problem-solving, and partnerships must involve joint decision-making, planning and operations (Figure 11.3). In these relationships there is a need for open and honest communication and greater transparency in the transfer of information. This may require an extensive appraisal of each

Figure 11.3   *Role of partnerships*

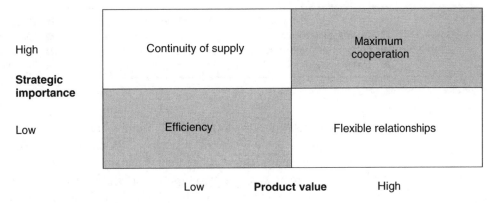

organisation, so that every member in the relationship recognises the need for mutually adaptive corporate cultures. Each partner should know the roles and rules of the relationship and clearly understood the mechanism for ending it (Tate, 1996). Supply-chain management must rest on a foundation of trust, which if it is to contribute significantly to the long-term stability of the organisation will require a willingness to forego opportunistic behaviour (Nooteboom *et al.*, 1997).

The traditional view of supply-chain management is for retailers to leverage the supply chain to achieve the lowest initial purchase prices whilst assuring supply. Typical characteristics include multiple partners, partner evaluations based on purchase price, arms-length negotiations, formal short-term contacts and centralised purchasing. The fundamental assumption in this relationship is that trading partners are interchangeable and that they will take advantage of the retailer if they become too powerful. In the new paradigm supply-chain management is redefined as a process for designing, developing, optimising and managing the internal and external components of the supply system consistent with overall objectives and strategies (Spekman *et al.*, 1998).

Valsmakis and Groves (1996) found that partnerships contribute to better quality of supplies and of the final product due to higher conformance to specification and lower returns from customers. Improvements in delivery performance were matched by a new product development process, measured by a greater number of new launches and shorter product development times. Non-financial performance measures can be considered as drivers of financial performance, so partnerships lead to better financial performance in lower overhead costs, greater labour efficiency and greater stock-turn, reduced overhead costs and greater fixed asset efficiency.

In practice, openness may be difficult to achieve. Supply-chain performance in the USA has been disappointing, with costs actually rising in some cases due to competitive relationships and dislocational promotional pricing. In the British grocery industry there is little evidence of sharing of sensitive cost-related information (*The Grocer*, 1998). Competition remains an important issue, as retailers are unwilling to share marketing plans with suppliers where their ranges might compete. It is less likely, too, that suppliers will work with competitors to coordinate deliveries. Lack of trust, the relative strength of the companies undertaking the partnership and their use of

Table 11.3   *Customer service standards in supply-chain management*

■ Order size constraints	■ Ordering convenience	■ Documentation quality
■ Ordering convenience	■ Frequency of delivery	■ Claim procedures
■ Order status information	■ Delivery reliability	■ Order completeness
■ Order cycle time	■ Stock availability	■ Technical support

Source: Based on Christopher (1998).

strength in the relationship form the most common barriers to successful partnerships. It is significant that one of the most powerful US retailers, Wal-Mart has moved to take control of its supply chain, rather than share ownership (Blatherwick, 1998). Problems with partnerships can be seen in terms of criticality and value or unit cost, and work best where the investment of the customer's and supplier's time is best spent.

Poor performance may lie outside partnership relationships. The design of the supply chain itself may have dysfunctional consequences, and the requirements of the supply chain will vary depending on the functional and innovative characteristics of products. Predictable demand and lowest cost supply will define physically efficient supply processes for functional products such as core grocery items, whilst market responsive processes are needed for unpredictable demand, typically found with fashion goods (Fisher, 1997). Therefore retailers and suppliers need to closely analyse the nature of their product and supply strategies to create the anticipated efficiencies.

A customer-driven supply chain must identify the priorities set by the customer in each stage of the chain. There is a need then to identify service standards so that customer expectations are met. The priority placed on standards will vary with customers, but must at least include a wide range of dimensions as defined in Table 11.3.

The management of service standards will require the internal management of the supply chain members to organise themselves across functional boundaries, modifying the traditional management of supply practices which have involved purchasing, production, sales and marketing, and distribution functions operating exclusively of each other in meeting customer requirements, too often running against the needs of effective supply-chain management.

Supply-Chain Management in Food Retailing

The process known as Efficient Consumer Response (ECR) has been a significant development in the distribution of grocery products. The retailer-led initiative was first publicised in the USA in 1993 following innovative work by Wal-Mart with its suppliers in the early 1990s, and was adopted several years later by a European working party of suppliers and retailers. ECR focuses on the efficiency of the entire grocery supply chain rather than its individual components, reducing costs and improving consumer choice of grocery products. By creating closer relationships between suppliers and retailers, customer needs can be more closely met. More specifically it involves the flow of information and products from both sides working together in joint planning and demand forecasting. As a consequence, fundamental changes may have to take place in an organisation:

Exhibit 11.4 Guiding principles established by the ECR Europe group

■ Consistent focus on providing better value to the grocery consumer.

■ Driven by committed leaders committed to changing their working practices to business alliances.

■ The provision of accurate and timely information.

■ Creation of product flows with a maximisation of value-adding processes to ensure the right product is available at the right time.

■ Common and consistent performance measurement.

Source: Lamey (1996).

Both sides might take on functions traditionally handled by the other if they can do it better and at a total lower cost. It will drive changes in business processes, organisation structure and information systems. (Lamey, 1996)

In the early development of ECR, four interdependent components were identified as central to its operation:

■ Continuous Replenishment (CRP)
■ Efficient Promotional Practices (EPA)
■ Efficient Assortment (EA)
■ Efficient New Product Activities (ENA)

Of these, continuous replenishment practice was identified as the most important area. The aim of CRP is to reduce stock in the retailer's business, on the shop shelves, stores and warehousing largely through cross-docking. However, the process is highly dependent on consistency through the supply chain with the use of universal bar coding to identify products, and retailer IT resources to facilitate transfer of information and transfer of EPOS data to the supplier. Moreover, ECR requires the suspension of manufacturer – retailer trade deals which encourage forward buying by the retailer at a promotional price, and causes a temporary build up of stock in the supply chain.

The main elements of ECR are focused on the customer partnerships and integration creating benefits in the form of cost reductions by reducing labour and administration. It has been estimated that if ECR were to be fully implemented across Europe's grocery industry, the supply-side cost savings alone would amount to a 5.7 per cent reduction in final consumer prices arising mostly from lower operating costs and lower stock levels, a saving of some $33 billion (Castle, 1999).

The achievement of ECR in Europe varies widely. The Netherlands and the UK have been shown to be leading the development of operational efficiencies through the use of ECR, but in many other countries it is restricted to order placing and invoicing. In addition, market reports in the early 1990s suggest these two countries were more broadly attempting to form partnerships in logistics, sales and own-brand product development, whereas businesses in France and Spain remained with confrontational retailer–supplier relationships (de Wilt and Krishnan, 1995).

The lack of openness and sharing of information between retailers and suppliers has led to a further strategic initiative from the USA, Collaborative Planning, Forecasting and Replenishment (CPFR). CPFR is designed to bring networks of trading partners together with the aim of exchanging information, to synchronise activities and deliveries to meet consumer demand. Partners will use CPFR to more clearly identify excess stocks in the supply chain and consequently provide a higher quality service at lower cost.

Supply-Chain Management and Clothing Retailing

In the clothing sector, supply-chain management has focused on the Quick Response concept. Clothing retailing is characterised by short life cycles, volatility, and unpredictability in demand arising from a wide range of factors, and high levels of impulse purchasing (Christopher and Peck, 1998). Planning and replenishment problems diminish with sourcing through local production facilities, although as production has come to be located in low-cost countries, remote from the retail locations it frequently requires long lead times for delivery. Moreover, delays are more likely to be encountered at both the supplier and retail ends of the chain due to import and export procedures (Fernie, 1999).

In 1985 it was estimated that some $25 billion was lost annually in soft goods (clothing) merchandise due to excess inventory and long lead times by Kurt Salmon Associates. As a consequence a three stage quick-response approach was devised to improve supply chain efficiency:

■ Implementation of integrating technologies;

■ Redesign of internal processes; and

■ Collaboration in joint forecasting, product development and category management.

The Development of Logistics

The logistics function has developed from the need for suppliers and their customers to work together more efficiently and responsively in their supply chains. Distribution of products from suppliers to retailers has typically taken place through functionally independent activities: from production, to warehousing for onward delivery to the wholesaler, or direct to retailers' shops or warehouses. In the 1960s the process of physical distribution management developed in response to cost-reduction needs, through lower stockholdings and by the development of more reliable transportation (Davies, 1993). Logistics continues this process, with a focus on the coordinated movement of materials and information flows that extend from the end consumer through the pipeline from the retailer to distributors and successions of manufacturers, producers or processors.

The rationale for logistics expands on the added value benefits of integration, and the need to manage increasingly global trading through the exchange of information a and cultural reorientation towards customer service (Fernie, 1994). Where these features are in place, logistics has the potential to determine business strategy, requiring a careful segmentation of a customers and their needs and delivery of a customised logistics service (Fuller, 1993).

The essential elements of the logistics function lie in the integrated management of inventory, information, warehousing and materials handling and transport (Christopher, 1986; Bowersox, 1996). The practice of just-in-time (JIT) delivery introduced by Japanese manufacturers provided a focus for retailers on the need to reduce time taken in delivery cycles. Unilever in Holland reported that the country's leading grocery group, Albert Heijn, is demanding more frequent deliveries and smaller quantities in each drop. Where deliveries were made in 72 hours, the requirement is now for an 18-hour turnaround on orders. Speed of delivery and reliability are seen as critical elements of logistics performance (EIU, 1995).

Although a strategic approach to logistics is important there remains a need to consider retail logistics as having its core in physical distribution. As manufacturers see the world market as a single entity, trading-off costs of production against transport and delivery lead times so inventories and information become more centralised. In Europe, national distribution is being replaced by pan-European distribution centres and warehousing, particularly for relatively standardised products, such as branded electronic goods, white goods, and household products. Typically logistics managers' responses are to consolidate their warehousing, develop central logistics departments, classify priority products and introduce information systems to regulate fluctuations in demand. Information systems need to be designed around requirements to deliver the required level of customer service, to enable organisations to plan and control their operations and to coordinate flows through the system. Customer service is then based on communicating loading and delivery information to the retailer, allowing the retailer to interrogate the supplier on order and delivery status. Planning and control requires anticipation of retailers' needs and control systems to monitor these. Coordination by suppliers' systems must link production with purchasing and distribution to optimise delivery schedules to meet customers' needs. Developments in information systems and computer technology in communications including satellite tracking has enabled major advances to take place in the delivery of stock, and automated replenishment systems.

The Internet and Supply-Chain Management

The Internet has created a new communications resource for supply-chain management and e-commerce. Rapid communication of the most important details between the organisation and its suppliers on a continuous basis is central to supply and replenishment. The more demanding and varied the factors determining the success of the organisation, the more complex the need for communication between the organisation and its suppliers (Labram, 2000). For larger organisations CPFR represents one of the initiatives linked by the Internet at this level. However, the Internet also enables communications to take place with small and medium-sized businesses at lower costs that conventional EDI, and more efficiently than telephone-based communications.

The medium provides new opportunities for electronic sourcing and purchasing, as online trading hubs and auctions enable buyers to access suppliers and products more

---

Exhibit 11.5 Logistics at the Boots the Chemist

The company has worked with around 3500 suppliers, of which Boots Contract Manufacturing is the largest with 14% of total supplies. When the company first started out with an Efficient Conumer Response (ECR) programme with its suppliers, it did not share the detailed information acquired from its Electronic Point of Sale (EpoS). However the company was working with a category management system and one of its strategic objectives with suppliers has been to recreate the relationship that exists in product marketing in the logistics function. The main issues concern quality of suppliers, measuring their performance and evaluation. With third parties, these issues concern specifying what services the company wants, how the third parties are managed and how they can be monitored. Even the environmental impact of the supply chain is monitored to ensure that appropriate levels of environmental performance are achieved. Questionnaires are used to assess the environmental credentials of all new suppliers and a risk assessment process is used to determine whether a more detailed quality audit is warranted.

Boots has worked with many contractors for a long period, in some cases 20–30 years, and the levels of trust it has built up are reflected in the absence of contracts. On the contractor's side Boots is a reliable, large-scale business that is prepared to maintain long term relationships against demanding requirements. Where contractors are taken over, the business is placed out to tender rather than automatically continued with the new company. Any company tendering for business without a business record with Boots must demonstrate the professionalism of its management and ability to deliver.

Sources: Lamey 1997; The Boots Company plc.

---

quickly and efficiently. A trading hub is a form of online catalogue where suppliers provide products and information to customers. These can take two forms:

■ A horizontal hub that offers access to a wide range of diverse suppliers who can service a range of products and service requests across industries.

■ A vertical hub for a narrower or more specific supplier community to serve a particular industry (McKie, 2001).

Hubs often provide business-to-business (B2B) auctions, that are driven by suppliers seeking to sell discontinued product lines, surplus inventory, and spare capacity to the highest bidder. Reverse auctions start with a customer's request for products or services that are subsequently selected from the bids submitted by suppliers. Benefits to retailers include:

■ A catalogue facility for easy access to new suppliers;

■ An extensive network of suppliers;

■ Lower product costs through reverse auctioning amongst preselected suppliers;

■ A single quote when the retailer has international requirements across different countries;

■ Negotiable volume discounts;

Exhibit 11.6 Supply-chain information: issues facing a department store

Department stores have a number of supplier problems to manage. Their suppliers are measured in thousands rather than hundreds, buying power is low compared to supermarkets, and they can handle over 33 000 SKUs compared to around 40 000 in a large supermarket.

Electronic Data Interchange (EDI) is one response to the need to reduce the cost of bringing goods to the market. But by 2000 only 10% of UK businesses used EDI and these were nearly all larger ones. As a supplier may have to use a different system for each retailer, the process can become complicated and expensive. A small supplier or retailer may not have internal access to experts, but rely on a small management team and many standards of flavours of standards to implement. Consequently, errors in the supply chain become difficult to identify and mismatches occur. In practical terms, matching the advice note to an order is a difficult manual process. Retailers typically create a computer based product file that holds the latest cost and selling prices, so that products can be easily and quickly identified. Bar codes, using the Electronic Article Numbering Universal Product Code (EAN UPC) system can be used to standardise product descriptions between supplier and retailer, but this comes at a cost that many small suppliers cannot afford.

However, the Internet provides a lower cost alternative for smaller suppliers to transmit information. Where an EDI trial can cost around £10 000 to set up (excluding the cost of messages), the Internet is both less expensive to set and run, is intuitive, and lacks unnecessary complexity. IT specialists can package these qualities with ease of use and flexibility to reduce disruption to business procedures.

For one department store, the results from an Internet-based trial have been impressive: some 50 new suppliers signed up, with 35 of them trading actively. As a result e-information has given rise to only 12 errors on 2000 items from the product catalogue, and so measurably contributes to a more accurate and efficient business. But *simplicity* is the key: a trial with another, more *complex* – and expensive – EDI system over 18 months resulted in just three messages.

■ The reduction of costs in the supply chain: for example in an industry exchange, members such as M&S, Kingfisher and Tesco use the same ships to cut costs

In the retail industry, B2B collaborative industry exchanges have been built around GlobalNet Xchange (GNX) and WorldWide Retail Exchange (WWRE). Established by rival retail memberships during 2000, they facilitate auctions, e-procurement, supply-chain management, as well as CPFR techniques. For GNX, basic auction activity has formed a starting point from which to develop new collaborative applications, which include a product catalogue, marketplace negotiation facilities, and a B2B hub to enable interactions between different exchanges (see also Table 11.4).

However, a number of issues have emerged about the future scale and scope of large-scale online exchanges:

■ *Timespan.* The development of online sourcing and buying may take a number of years to establish itself, with 5–7 years to set up the processes.

■ *Industry-led versus private exchanges.* Industry-led exchanges can demonstrate experienced management, access to customers and credible plans for expansion,

Table 11.4   *Electronic Sourcing and Buying: Stages of Development*

Sourcing and Buying Processes	Information processes
Retailer to supplier	telephone, fax, written communications
■ Ordering ■ Processing ■ Invoicing	
Private exchanges	EDI
■ Retailer and suppliers develop a collaborative system to enable suppliers to access retail sales data to improve their forecasting and replenishment	
Trading hub/exchange	Internet/Worldwideweb
■ Online 'catalogue' with many suppliers ■ Retailers act collectively to request bids from suppliers ■ Auction/reverse auction ■ Auction: sellers request for an offer and sell to the highest bidder ■ Reverse auction: suppliers reply to a request from the buyer who will select best offer based on price, terms, quality and delivery.	
Extended collaborative facilities	Internet/Worldwideweb using sophisticated interactive software
■ Supply-chain management ■ Product design ■ Human resource management	

but appear to act too slowly and at the lowest possible levels. Some companies such as Dell Computers take a mixed approach to improve their exchange effectiveness, using their own 'private' exchange to connect to suppliers as well as public ones.

■ *Funding.* Collaborative planning services require more complex systems that need funding. Turnover will be essential to fuel future growth, and future revenues will come from transaction tariffs and subscriptions. How much 'liquidity' also remains to be seen. Auctions now seem to be only appropriate for a limited range of commodity goods and typically not for sales to customers.

IMPORTATION

International supply chains and logistics inevitably require retail buyers and distribution managers to administer efficiently the process of ordering and supply. The stages in managing the stages from point of purchase to domestic warehousing are considered briefly in this section.

Delivery Schedule

The time taken to deliver is a critical issue for all retailers in calculating their inventory requirements. For food retailers competing on quality and freshness of fruit and vegetables and wider ranges of prepared and chilled products, lead time to delivery and stockholding is necessarily very short. Other canned and packed foods may be prepared to allow considerably longer shelf lives.

For fashion retailers the question will be whether the product has a seasonal or short-term demand or what the market wants by the time it arrives with the retailer. International sourcing necessarily requires an understanding of the trade-off between immediacy and cost and availability from international suppliers. As retailers seek to become more responsive to consumer demand, so lead times are reducing. External observers suggest that from order detail to delivery, retailers should be working to a benchmark of no more than 3 weeks.

Freight Shipment Selection

The mode of shipment for supplies will vary considerably according to distance and type of transport. Sea freight from Hong Kong and Singapore will take four weeks to a European port, and five weeks from Korea, whilst airfreight will take less than a day to travel the same distances. In the USA, trucks or land trains can travel from west to east coast in 24 hours, and with increasingly open borders within the EU the same types of rapid overland delivery can be achieved.

Clearly there are trade-offs between the cost of shipping and airfreight; and these have to be made between lower gross margins and net margins. In setting the selling price of products the product management team will need some estimate of the total cost of buying and shipping goods. For example, if a fashion shirt has a first priced lifespan of 6–8 weeks before markdown of up to 30 per cent, the cost could be 10 times that of airfreighting. By taking decisions later, markdowns can be reduced and only a 10 per cent increase in sales at first price may mean that air freighting becomes worthwhile. However, with basic products such as jeans, the cost of airfreighting may not be viable because these tend to have a more predictable sales rate throughout the year, and also margins may be lower (*Retail Week*, 1994). Whichever method of transport is selected there are a number of procedural details to follow, and to be included as shipment advice to the retailer:

- Appointment of a freight forwarding service to coordinate, consolidate and ship goods from the manufacturer. A number of critical timing issues occur in the freighting process, and even though goods may be despatched from an overseas factory on time, shipments may have to be held back to satisfy consolidation and sailing requirements at the port of origin

---

Exhibit 11.7 The global supply chain at Donna Karan

The design facility for Donna Karan is based in New York, which together with Milan, act as the sales offices for the brand's clothing, shoes and accessories. However, orders are despatched to all European retail customers from a completely new distribution centre in The Netherlands.

However, distribution to all European retail customers is undertaken from a completely new distribution centre in the Netherlands. Donna Karan does not work with collections for just the two spring/summer and autumn/winter seasons, but has a separate collection for each of the four seasons. The time between the placing and delivery of an order is therefore relatively short, about 8 to 12 weeks. That leads to a constant flow of goods amounting to between 40 000 and 60 000 articles per week. peaking during the summer months in time for the autumn, the highest sales period.

Due to the short lead-time from design to delivery, some 90% of imports are air-freighted to nearby Amsterdam and Twente airports from the Far East and the USA. These amount to around five air-freight containers packed with hanging clothes every week, in addition to the flow of packed goods from European suppliers by road.

Source: Twente Tracks.

■ Negotiation of the freight route. Shipments by sea carry with them a Bill of Lading (the airwaybill is the equivalent for air freight) in effect the 'ticket' for the goods which includes their description and freight details.

■ On arrival in the destination country the goods will have to be handled by appointed agents to clear customs and despatched on to the retailer's warehouse.

Terms and Conditions

Negotiations for goods bought in another country will establish payment terms. Goods may be paid for in the currency of either the importing country or the exporting country, or in US dollars. US dollars may be favoured in many Far East countries where currency restrictions may apply and where dollars are more transferable (Diamond and Pintel, 1995).

Where the order has been negotiated in another currency, the buyer will have to arrange the purchase of currency with their domestic bank for the time the contract is due for completion by the supplier. Therefore the buyer must either buy currency 'forward' for a future date at a price quoted by the bank, or take a risk that the exchange rate will not have fluctuated unfavourably by the time the payment date arrives, and buy the currency at the prevailing 'spot' price. Since it can be extremely difficult to determine the rate of exchange in say six months, and a deteriorating rate could fundamentally affect the profitability of an order, most buyers will agree with their bank to buy the required currency at a known rate.

Typically payment is made by Letter of Credit where payment cannot be avoided, provided there is evidence of the loading of the goods for shipment, or by cash against documents to the exporter, although a number of options are available which provide greater control and flexibility to one or other party with a trade-off of greater risk of non-payment. Open Account trading is encouraged within the EU to enable European partners to offer the same terms and conditions to other member states as they do to their own domestic businesses.

Costs of Importing Goods

With non-domestic sources, the mode of shipment, and costs of insurance and delivery from the supplier's factory form the main additional costs to be calculated into the price of the delivered products. Domestic suppliers' costs are negotiated from the factory or the supplier's warehouse, or at a point specified by the retailer, typically their warehouse. With externally sourced products costings will depend on the agreed point for the transfer of the consignment from the supplier's responsibility to the buyer's. INCOTERMS, an internationally agreed form trading terms and conditions provides a full schedule of the possibilities available between buyer and supplier.

SUMMARY

This chapter has examined the framework in which decisions about product and supplier sourcing are taken and related them to the supply chain and logistics of delivery. Retail buying is increasingly moving beyond issues of product selection and negotiation. It draws on wider considerations of supplier location to achieve strategic and marketing objectives. Competitive pricing, quality and product differentiation can be achieved through identifying sources of supply which are consistent with the organisation's values, and the process of transporting merchandise from supplier to retailer offers an opportunity to create distinctive competitive advantages. Retailing in many Western European countries and North America is becoming more concentrated. Pressure is intensifying to anticipate and meet consumer demand and, simultaneously, stock levels are tightly scrutinised. The change in product emphasis from manufacturer-push to customer-pull will be an important arena for competitive initiatives and responses for an expanding number of retailers and markets.

QUESTIONS

1   Analyse the ways in which product sourcing creates competitive advantage.

2   What problems may arise out of moving supplies from the retailer's domestic country to foreign ones?

3   Explain the benefits of supply-chain management to retailers and suppliers.

4   To what extent is logistics central to supply-chain management?

5   In what ways do import practices influence retailer responsiveness?

Case Study

Sourcing from Mauritius

Textiles are the main export of Mauritius, an island in the Indian Ocean that has built up a large trade with developed countries; some 83 per cent of exports from the Export Product Zones are from this sector. Hong Kong, the source of 22 per cent of all foreign investment, is the largest foreign investor in the textile sector, with important representations from France, Britain and Germany. Two foreign firms, Socota and Woventex, dominate the textile industry, and as long ago as 1991 the government recognised this overdependence on one sector and urged diversification into non-clothing industries such as electronics.

The pattern of trade was stimulated by preferential treatment in the European Community under the Lomé Convention. The first Lomé Convention was signed in 1975 in the Togolese capital of Lomé between the then European Community and 71 former European colonies of Africa, the Caribbean and the Pacific (ACP). The agreement set out in that convention provided non-reciprocal trade preferences – goods from the ACP countries were allowed to enter European markets without tariffs but without a corresponding treatment. However, the current convention expires in January 2001, and EU countries are pressing for greater economic liberalisation in the ACP countries as well as extending conditions for preferential trade into political reform. Another problem lies with the WTO, that defines such a trade arrangement as an unfair trading practice because of its discrimination against trading partners outside the ACP–EU trading bloc.

As opportunities in the EU become more fraught, so the United States may offer exporters more relief. Debate of the Africa Growth and Opportunity Bill by the American government provides a new opportunity for African exporters. Draft legislation has yet to be agreed on the exact range of duty-free and quota-free access to the US market. At its least restrictive a wide range of manufactured goods, including clothing and textiles, may be allowed in duty free whilst a less generous proposal would limit duty-free access to manufactures of clothing and textiles made from US yarns.

Despite the price war with Asian exporters, and an average import duty of 18 per cent as well as quotas, Mauritian sales to the USA have almost doubled since 1996 to around $259 million in 1998. Mauritius accounts for 43 per cent of sub-Saharan clothing and textile exports to the USA, though a mere 0.86 per cent of clothing imports, reflecting the very small African market share. Mauritian exporters are building a good reputation with US buyers for quality, innovation, reliability and flexibility. At the same time, US buyers are establishing new marketing links with Mauritius.

Nevertheless, Mauritius is still finding it difficult to compete in the US market. The chief problems are costs and logistics; transport times are as long as 45 days and until 1999 there was no direct shipping line. Air freight costs are high, 30 per cent more than on exports to the EU, while US customers are more demanding than their European counterparts who take 70 per cent of the zone's output. Quota-free entry will enable Mauritian companies to expand clothing exports in the lines where they are most competitive – T-shirts, shorts, pullovers and trousers – while duty-free entry will provide the same cost advantages as in the EU market under the present Lomé system of preferences. This is a huge opportunity since, without quotas and duty, the American market will become as reachable as the EU.

The timing of the American decision is significant in another respect too. Under the

Uruguay Round trade agreement, the Multi-Fibre Arrangement (MFA) which imposes quotas on clothing and textile exports will end in 2005. As a result, high-volume, low-cost exporters – especially China, but also India, Pakistan, Bangladesh and Indonesia – will become direct competitors to Mauritius. African exporters such as Mauritius will still have an edge from duty-free entry, but on current trends they will be seriously disadvantaged because of the combination of lower production costs in the mass-production Asian economies and higher levels of worker productivity. Mauritian labour costs in the textile sector of $1.41 an hour are substantially above those of its Asian competitors. The comparative figure in Indonesia was only 24 cents, in Madagascar 41 cents and in India and China 60 cents and 62 cents.

SEMINAR QUESTIONS FOR DISCUSSION

1 As a buyer for a European clothing retailer, evaluate the opportunities for sourcing from Mauritius.

2 Should the textile trade be regulated?

References

Blatherwick, A. (1998) 'Vendor Managed Inventory: Fashion Fad or Supply Chain Strategy', *Supply Chain Management*, vol. 3, no. 1, pp. 10–11.

Bowersox, D.J. and Closs, D.J. (1996) *Logisitical Management: The Integrated Supply Chain Process* (Maidenhead: McGraw Hill).

Castle, D. (1999) *Category Management: Winning Competitive Advantage Through a Team Approach* (London: FT Retail and Consumer Publications).

Cooke, M. (1997) Emergence Of A Market For Western Clothing In Vietnam', *Fashion Marketing and Management*, vol. 1, no. 2, February, pp. 174–180.

Christopher, M. (1986) *The Strategy of Distribution Management*, (Oxford: Butterworth Heinemann).

Christopher, M. (1998) *Logistics and Supply Chain Management: Strategies for Reducing Costs and Improving Services*, 2nd edn (Hemel Hempstead: Prentice Hall).

Christopher, M. and Juttner, U. (1998) 'Developing Strategic Partnerships in the Supply Chain', Paper Presented at the 2nd Worldwide Research Symposium on Purchasing and Supply Chain Management, London.

Christopher, M. and Peck, H. (1998) *Fashion Logistics*, in J. Fernie and L. Sparks (eds), *Logistics and Retail Management: Insights into Current Practice from Leading Experts* (London: Kogan Page).

Cottrill, K. (1997) 'Reforging the Supply Chain', *Journal of Business Strategy*, vol. 18, November–December, pp. 35–40.

Davies, G. (1993) *Trade Marketing Strategy* (London: Paul Chapman).

Diamond, A. and Pintel, J. (1995) *Retail Buying* (Englewood Cliffs, NJ: Prentice Hall).

Dibb, S. (1996) 'The Impact of the Changing Market Environment on the Pacific Rim', *International Journal of Retail and Distribution Management*, vol. 24, no. 11.

The Economist (1998) July, p. 164.

The Economist Intelligence Unit (1995) *Supply Chain Management* (London: The Economist).

Fernie, J. (1994) 'Retail Logistics', in 'Logistics and Distribution Planning, Strategies', for management, 2nd edn J. Cooper (ed.) (London: Kogan Page).

Fernie, J. (1999) Retail Logistics in Walters, D. (ed.) *Global Logistics and Distribution Planning: Strategies for Management* 3rd edn (London: Kogan Page).

Fuller, J.B., O'Connor, J. and Rawlinsm, R. (1993) 'Tailored Logistics: The Next Advantage', pp. 87–98. *Harvard Business Review* May/June.

Garten, J.E. (1997) 'Troubles Ahead In Emerging Markets', *Harvard Business Review*, May–June, pp. 38–50.

Harland, C. (1996) 'Supply Chain Management; Relationships, Chains and Networks', *British Journal of Management, Special Issue S63–S80*, vol. 7, March.

Johnson, J.C. and Wood, D.F. (1996) *Contemporary Logistics* (Hemel Hempstead: Prentice Hall Europe).

The Federation of Korean Industries (1987) *Korean Economic Policies 1945–1985* (Seoul: The Federation of Korean Industries).

Labram, J. (2000) *Why Internet Supply Chain Management Makes Sense* http://www.charteris.com.

Lamey, S. (1997) *Supply Chain Management*, Financial Times Publications.

Management Horizons Europe (1998) *Proceedings of the Supply Chain Integration Seminar*, London.

McGoldrick, P.J., Betts, E.J. and Keeling, K.A. (2000) 'High-Low Pricing: Audit Evidence and Consumer Preferences', *Journal of Product and Brand Management*, vol. 9, no. 5, pp. 316–24.

McGoldrick, P.J. and Davies, G. (1995) *International Retailing* (London: Pitman).

McKie, S. (2001) *E-Business Best Practices: Leveraging Technology for Business Advantage* (Chichester: John Wiley).

Nooteboom, B., Berger, B. and Noorrdemaven, M. (1997) 'Effects of Trust and Governance on Relational Risks', *Academy of Management Journal*, vol. 40, no. 2.

Owen, G., Vidal, O., Toole, R. and Favre, R. (1998) 'Strategic Sourcing, Aligning Procurement Needs With Your Business Goals', in J. Gattorna (ed.), *Strategic Supply Chain Alignment*, (Aldershot: Gower).

Pache, G. (1998) 'A Transactional Approach to Global Sourcing', *International Journal of Retail and Distribution Management*, vol. 26, no. 2.

Porter, M. (1990) *The Competitive Advantage of Nations* (London: Macmillan).

Pretious, M. (1995) Paper presented at the Marketing Education Group Conference University of Strathclyde.

Saunders, M. (1994) *Strategic Supply Chain Management* (London: Pitman)

SBC Warburg (1996) *The Supply Chain Revolution – Driving Forecast Profit Upgrades*, (London).

Shepheard-Walwyn, S. (1997) 'A Vision Of Sourcing For A Global Market Fashion', *Marketing and Management*, vol. 1, no. 3, May, pp. 251–9.

Sislian, E. and Satir, A. (2000) 'Strategic Sourcing: A Framework and a Case Study', in *The Journal of Supply Chain Management: A Global Review of Purchasing and Supply*, vol. 36, no. 3, Summer, pp. 4–16.

Spekman, R., Kamauff, J. and Myhr, N. (1998) 'An Empirical Investigation into Supply Chain Management – A Perspective in Partnerships', *International Journal of Physical Distribution and Logistics Management*, vol. 28, no. 8, pp. 630–50.

Tate, K. (1996) 'The Elements of a Successful Logistics Partnership', *International Journal of Physical Distribution and Logistics Management*, vol. 26, March, pp. 7–14.

Valsmakis, V. and Groves, G. (1996) 'Supplier-Customer Relationships: do Partnerships Perform Better?', *Journal of Fashion and Marketing Management*, vol. 1, no. 1, pp. 9–25.

Walker, M. (1994) 'Supplier–Retailer Collaboration in European Grocery Distribution', *Logistics Information Management*, vol. 7, no. 6. pp. 23–7.

Wileman, A. and Jary, M. (1997) *Retail Power Plays* (Basingstoke: Macmillan).

Wilson, J.R. (1996) *Getting Started in Importing: A Practical Guide* (London: Kogan Page).

Wilt, G.J. de and Krishnan, T.V. (1995) 'Supply Chain Management', *European Retail Digest*, Spring, pp. 34–49.

Worthington, I. and Britton, G. (1997) *The Business Environment*, 2nd edn (London: Pitman).

Inventory Management and Control

PLANNING AND CONTROLLING STOCK LEVELS

The sales plan drives the stock, or inventory, requirement to achieve the required level of sales. However, retailers can achieve this objective by adopting a number of different approaches to the amount of stock needed at any specific time. Large inventories would enable them to minimise lost sales, to manage their stock easily with lower levels of management intervention, but will be very costly. Low inventories, on the other hand, require detailed stock management and ordering systems, and efficient supply chains that are more costly in terms of management time and skills. However, the stockholding costs (Table 12.1) will be considerably lower, and it is towards this position that retailers aspire.

Whilst the cost of inventory has been well-understood for many years, in practice retailers are able to manage reduced stock levels more effectively with developments in supply-chain management and information systems. These have taken place in parallel with supplier inventory-reduction programmes, although the initiative has varied between supplier and retailer in the past 10 years. Stock-management requirements of retailers are distinctive from those of manufacturers. Wider merchandise assortments,

Table 12.1   *Costs of Stockholding*

■ Storage costs
■ Rent/depreciation
■ Labour
■ Overheads, including heating, lighting, security
■ Financial investment, including loss of interest, opportunity cost
■ Clearance costs of old stock
■ Stock deterioration, for example fresh foods
■ Management costs
■ Transport costs
■ Handling costs

consumer interaction with the products, changing patterns of consumer demand and highly visible and competitive markets distinguish the industry's ordering and replenishment needs.

The development of supply-chain management has implications for stock management, with the trend away from supplier-push towards consumer-pull. Retailers can adopt either push or pull approaches for both automated and manual stock-planning methods. In some instances, it may be desirable to push merchandise through to stores to meet requirements for one-off events or for initial allocations of new lines. In normal trading activity, stores will pull merchandise through the supply chain based on actual sales data captured at the point of sale. In this way, buying requirements are ultimately driven by sales reported from stores, and stock monitored both in the store and distribution centre.

There are a number of information requirements to analyse, as well as physical handling issues, to manage stock levels within retailers' budgets and resources. Stock levels can be controlled by physical unit, by value using financial parameters, and by a combination of the two methods (Bohdanowicz and Clamp, 1994). The value of physical stock levels is normally recorded at retail price, and where records relate to individual lines, information systems allow them to be valued at cost as well. Consequently, inventory management by physical unit must be integrated with financial accounting data.

The ordering and replenishment activities to meet these requirements are described in Figure 12.1. The key elements to be integrated will include:

■ Planning and sales forecasting (see Chapter 10).

■ Inventory management – deciding the right quantities of stock to have at each location.

■ Ordering – deciding order quantities, placing orders on suppliers and communicating with suppliers.

■ Stock control – that is, tracking the movement and storage of products.

■ Stock movement – receiving, checking, storing, picking and dispatching goods. This may include the ticketing or coding of products.

Figure 12.1   *Dimensions of Stock Management*

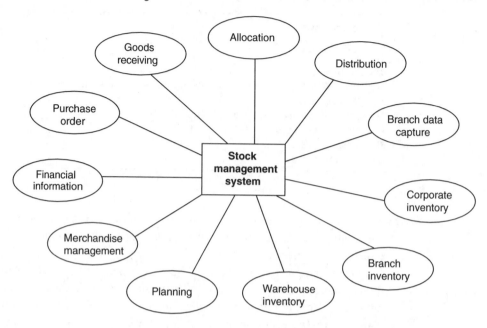

■ Distribution operations – planning and managing the operation of warehouses and transport fleets.

Planning and controlling stock in stores and in the branch distribution system is necessary for several reasons. Firstly, the role of merchandise management is to keep an optimum amount of stock in the business; with too little stock there will be a danger of lost sales caused by products being out of stock in store. With too much stock, the retailer's return on investment will be reduced through the cost of stock and potentially from lower achieved margins as surplus merchandise has to be cleared. The efficiencies achieved through managing stock ordering and replenishment quickly lead to significant cost savings. In a study of six European companies undertaking efficient replenishment trials, inventory levels fell by 65 per cent, category profits rose by 30 per cent, warehousing costs fell by 45 per cent, and overall distribution efficiency rose by 200 per cent (Mintel, 1997).

The financial cost of stockholding has a major impact on company performance. For many retailers it will be one of the most important controllable costs, alongside the cost of employees, rents and local property taxes which are often much more difficult to manage over short periods of time. Stocks have to be financed by capital, in practice from bank loans, shareholder equity or retained profit. The higher the stock levels in the business, the higher the cost of capital either in terms of loan interest payments, dividends or diversion of retained profits from other potentially more valuable activities. The aim is to manage stock levels so that they meet customer demand over a defined period. In a sense there is a balancing act to be performed between the rival demands of financial officers seeking to minimise the costs of stock, and the marketeers seeking to optimise customer service by providing continuous in-stock levels across the product range.

Figure 12.2   *Stockholding Requirements*

Stockholding

Shorter term

Food retailers' fresh foods
Will have a shelf life of only a day or few days at most before they cease to fulfil their marketing function, for freshness, variety or other point of competitive advantage. Planning and replenishment cycles for these categories are very short, and are normally ordered daily. The seasonality of fresh foods, too, may cause problems with forecasting accuracy

Longer term

Footwear retailing
Each style of shoe has to cover many size options; for men at least six sizes must be carried in stock. There may be two width fittings for each size, and the shoe may be available in two or more colours. To satisfy customers' needs, each style must be stocked across the SKU options. As the retailer must stock a number of styles to create an appropriate product offer, and depending on the retailer's market position and predictability of sales, shelf life stretches over weeks if not months

Forecasting sales of core lines may be relatively accurate, but an increase in the seasonality and fashionability in the product offer will tend to result in less reliable forecasts. These concepts apply across all retail sectors.

The number of days or weeks of stock held in the branch and in warehouses and stockrooms will depend on the retail sector, and the quality of both management and information systems. At the two extremes, food retailers with rapid turnover requirements for their stock will require significantly less merchandise to meet future demand than those facing slower demand, for example selling footwear (Figure 12.2). The rate of sale and product characteristics will determine how much stock is needed and when it is required.

Secondly, stockholding will affect the management of space in the store; the space requirement of a greater depth of stock held in the store will physically restrict the retailer's ability to display a wider product range. In a clothing store a line can be stocked in its sizing pattern in depth, with many units displayed for each size. Alternatively the merchandiser may have planned for a limited size stockholding and in the same space choose to display other complementary products. The product width is expanded at the expense of depth, and whilst it risks being out of stock it creates more selling opportunities. The same principles apply to other retail sectors. Food retailers will use branded market share as a determinant for space; in this way many categories have experienced rationalisation or repositioning. In UK foodstores, products will be typically stocked by brand leader, own-brand premium line and value line, and the development of 'power brands' will further drive the consolidation of shelf space.

Stock planning and control in each case enables the retailer to create space to meet its marketing objectives and maximise its profitability. The initial allocation of stock will arise from product range reviews, and an assessment of the sales potential of each category and product line. Decisions will be taken about the sales period and contributions each category and line makes to the total sales and profit mix. The aim will be to provide each branch with enough SKUs to meet forecasted demand, and to plan refills to the line for the duration of the plan. The management system will determine which lines can be ordered and replenished from a predefined product list, and planning itself can be automated or manually controlled according to the situation.

ORDERING, ALLOCATION AND REPLENISHMENT

The ordering process results in new products to create an initial allocation to each store and, as they sell through, to ensure that they are replenished. Replenishment basically concerns the continuity of stock in store to meet customer demand, and with continuing or 'core' product ranges this process may continue for many years. Responsiveness and cost-effective stock levels are two key requirements, and these can be achieved through a number of methods from visual inspection of merchandise on the shelf or hanging rail to automated processes.

Consumption-based Planning

These techniques can be undertaken using reorder forecasting, costing and time-phasing:

■ Reorder point forecasting is most usually expressed in the EOQ (economic order quantity) method. The aim is to determine the value of Q, the order quantity, in order to minimise the total annual cost of stockholding and the annual order cost. However, this method requires a number of assumptions about the nature of the stock, that there is single-item stock management where demand is uniform and deterministic, and where there is no lead-time requirement and delivery quantities are not constrained. As the retail environment becomes more dynamic, these conditions become more difficult to establish for many products.

■ Sales planning and forecasting methods of inventory management typically operate around estimates of the number of weeks' stockholding desired to meet forecast sales, or relate inventory to beginning and end-of-month targets. The weeks' cover method concerns exactly how many weeks stock the retailer wants to hold in each trading week. It is determined by the retailer and can be changed to suit different trading circumstances, such as financial constraints on stock investment or the need to reduce end-of-season stock. As a result this method is often used by clothing retailers to manage fluctuating seasonal demands, generally following the rule that the shorter the fashion season, the lower the number of weeks' cover requirements.

A different approach is used with beginning-of-month (BOM) and end-of-month (EOM) stock calculations in which inventory is apportioned to each month using various measures of annual sales. For example, the basic stock method for a month allows for a level of safety stock against unforecasted variations in sales, and would be appropriate for retailers with low stockturns (Lucas *et al.*, 1994). To achieve this objective the stock requirement for the beginning of the month is calculated as:

BOM stock = planned monthly sales + average monthly stock
                    − average monthly sales

If the planned monthly sales are £1 100 000, average monthly sales are £1 500 000 and average monthly stock is £1 800 000, then:

BOM stock = £1 100 000 + £1 800 000 − £1 500 000 = £1 400 000

In other situations, the number of weeks' supply can be managed in direct proportion to sales planned for the year (Berman and Evans, 1998).

■ Time-phased planning can be used if suppliers deliver consistently on the same day of the week. The requirement will be calculated by average daily sales multiplied by (planning cycle + delivery time + processing time) + safety stock. Stocks are planned using the same time phase, but moving forward by the time it takes the vendor to deliver.

Weekly Sales, Stock and Intake Method

In fashion retailing this approach, abbreviated to WSSI, provides an alternative sales planning and stock-management system. The main difference between it and the BOM/EOM method is the decision to hold stock for an agreed number of future weeks' sales. These vary according to the type of business: higher fashion businesses will need to move their stock through quickly in response to emerging fashion trends, and will therefore require fewer weeks' stock cover against their sales. The relationship between stock and sales, in terms of cover and stockturn, is expressed as:

Stock cover required = the sum of planned sales for n number of weeks

$$\text{Stockturn} = \frac{\text{Sales for a period}}{\text{Average stock in the same period}}$$

In the example of Table 12.2, at week 1 a cover of 10 weeks' sales includes sales planned from weeks 1–10 and is £226 000. Maintaining the same 10 weeks' cover from week 2–11 is £234 000 as the stock requirement moves forward one week. The steps in managing this method involve:

Table 12.2   *Sales Planning by Weeks' Cover*

Week 1	Planned weekly sales	Planned stock level	Weeks' cover
1	20 000	226 000	10 (weeks 1–10)
2	18 000	234 000	10 (weeks 2–11)
3	16 000	240 000	10 (weeks 3–12)
4	25 000		
5	22 000		
6	20 000		
7	30 000		
8	27 000		
9	25 000		
10	23 000		
11	28 000		
12	24 000		

Table 12.3   *Sales, Stock and Intake Planning*

| | Step 3 | Step 4 | | | | Step 1 | | Step 2 | |

Week	Opening stock	Deliveries (intake)	Markup	Markdown	Actual sales	Planned weekly sales	Actual closing stock	Planned forward requirement (closing stock)	Weeks cover
1	210 000	30 000	0	0	*19 000*	20 000	*221 000*	234 000	10 (weeks 1–10)
2	221 000	50 000		25 000	*22 000*	18 000	*224 000*	240 000	10 (weeks 2–11)
3	224 000								

1 Sales planning decisions on a weekly sales over a sales period.

2 Definition of future stock requirements by the number of future weeks' sales to be held in stock at any one time (number of weeks' cover). This value will depend on the financial and marketing position of the retailer.

3 Opening stock and weekly delivered orders (intake).

4 Markups and markdowns that affect the value of stock.

The sales, deliveries, markdowns and markups need to be recorded as planned or forecasted, and also as they actually occur. Subsequently the opening and closing stock levels each week can be calculated. The relationship between the functions is shown in Table 12.3, where:

opening stock + deliveries + markup – markdown – sales = closing stock

which then becomes the opening stock figure in the next week. With this method, an Open-to-Buy is created when the opening stock and orders due are less than the forward stock requirement.

Initial Allocation

Centralised buying enables retailers to plan, control and monitor the allocation of merchandise. Initial allocations will be made to fit the store density and layout planning policy; alternatively there may be other sets of predefined rules that allocate a new line to a particular assortment. The parameters might include the merchandise category, assortment grade, characteristic values and layout to match articles to assortments. Manual allocation of a line to an assortment will enable the merchandise manager to group articles for a particular purpose, such as a promotion. The system can replenish the exact quantity of merchandise sold, or scale replenishments to take account of faster or slower rates of sale. Quantities can be adjusted to meet logistical requirements such as minimum order quantities or the need for full pallet loads. Reorder points can be used for merchandise replenishment which takes place only when the order points have been reached.

Assortments need to be communicated to stores so that layouts, staffing and operational planning can be managed. Information on availability, presentation, selling price and features such as promotions will be required, and new lines and discontinuations need to be highlighted too.

Replenishment

Stock replenishment can take place using either manual or automatic techniques. The quantities depend on the amount of initial allocation, and the rate of sales achieved, whilst the replenishment cycle depends both on rate of sale and the retailer's store delivery capability. Manual techniques include visual inspection; with a manual planning and replenishment system shop staff will require information on lines to be reordered, and quantities. Useful information will include details of the last order, the vendor used, order units and quantity restrictions. Manual shelf checking requires staff to count stock items on the shelf and record the data centrally. The processes involved in this procedure are time consuming, expensive in terms of labour resource and liable to manual errors. The product reordering process can be delayed if staff are interrupted in their task or reassigned to other duties. As a result, inadequate stock replenishment, lost sales and reduced customer satisfaction with the store's product selection and availability can occur.

Manual ordering, too, can lead to overstocking because of the slowness and delays within the reordering process. As a consequence, the store must carry the cost of both excess stock and wastage if goods exceed their sell-by date. Some stores have introduced handheld scanners to make shelf-checking more accurate and faster, but handheld scanning is liable to either underordering or overordering. Because it is undertaken periodically it can be vulnerable to sudden bulk purchases, and inaccurate as items can be missed or replaced mistakenly by customers.

With automatic replenishment, replacement stock is requested or reported by the store through EPOS sales data which is used by the buying office. Clothing retailers typically use automatic replenishment in one of two ways:

- Pattern replenishment, which fills up the initial stock allocation by replacing each sold item to maintain the initial stockholding.

- Sales reactive replenishment, which takes place where the system attempts to match replenishment to future demand.

In both cases, though, a certain degree of human intervention is required to interpret sales trends and control the distribution process more intuitively.

With grocery-based approaches such as Efficient Consumer Response (ECR), ordering can take place automatically from the store to the distribution centre (DC) and on to suppliers. As a purchase is made at the checkout, EPOS captures the scanned data and transmits it into the store database. This data is then processed by a computerised ordering system, which then passes on orders to the distribution centre, typi-

Figure 12.3   *Ordering and Replenishment Sequences*

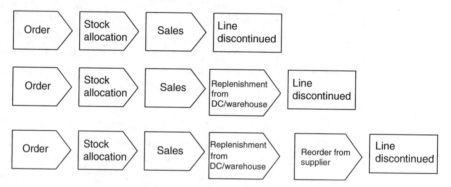

cally via internal e-mail or file transfer (Mintel, 1997). Replenishment takes place with orders being generated via EDI and increasingly the Internet to external suppliers (Figure 12.3). Automated ordering eliminates manual data collection but also levels of centralised intervention in the replenishment process. Using a range of inventory management parameters the stock can be managed to an optimal level for each store.

Integrated computer-based ordering systems assist in providing useful information to other ECR functions. The ability to monitor and forecast demand for a wide range of differently performing goods, including slow movers, special promotions and seasonal goods, provides information that is key to a wide range of category management areas (Mintel, 1997).

Managing Obsolecent Stock

At some point retailers will require a markdown facility to reduce the sales value of merchandise. The timescale may be measured in terms of days for fresh foods, weeks for high-fashion merchandise, or seasons for many clothing lines. And nearly every retail sector in the UK uses January and June–July as a clearance period for old stock. In each case the fundamental reason for a markdown is to increase sales by exploiting elasticity of demand in the expectation that sales will increase in response to the lower price.

A markdown is undertaken either to clear stock at the end of its sell-by date or as a promotion to accelerate the rate of sale to meet retailers' sales and profit targets. The reasons for slower than planned sales, and the accumulation of stock include:

■ Retail buyers' misinterpretation of market trends leading to overbuys. In fashion retailing it is often difficult to predict sales of new seasonal colours and designs.

■ Unseasonal weather conditions slowing down sales of seasonal merchandise: this affects a wide range of seasonal products from ice creams to winter coats.

■ New product introductions.

■ Competitor activity.

Markdowns have both financial and physical impacts on the business. The effect on gross margins are discussed in Chapter 13, but the lower value of stock has an impact on sales and stock-planning methods. If the company is overstocked reducing the value of the slower selling lines is clearly a desirable outcome; however, it may also create shortages against future weeks' sales plans. Returning to the stock-management example in Table 12.3, in week 2 the stock and orders less sales would have met the planned forward requirement defined in the closing stock column. However, the markdown of £25000 has reduced the actual closing stock to below the planned level to £224000. Depending on outstanding orders the shortfall may require new orders to be placed to return the stock levels to plan.

The physical effect of the markdown is to clear sales and storage space so that other lines can be introduced, and this is evident in clothing retailing at the end of a summer or winter season. There needs to be a function too, to enable merchandise to be discontinued, either by supplier or by line within a range or through selected stores or companywide. This will enable the stock to be phased out throughout the supply chain systematically and prevent inadvertent reordering of the product (Figure 12.3).

Some merchandise will need to be returned to the supplier, for example at the end of a promotion or with discontinued lines. Returned deliveries and returns can be distinguished; returned deliveries take place as a reversal of the delivery process, and returns take place some time later. Since returns was originate at the distribution centre, store or direct from customers the stock management system will need appropriate facilities.

Inventory Management

Inventory levels can be managed both in a number of storage locations and across the company. It may be important to distinguish stock that is available for use, from stock that is being inspected, or is in transit from one location to another. Some stock may need to be managed by the supplier so that any special packaging can be returned.

Merchandise may be difficult to manage at the SKU or individual article level, in which case grouping products, for example within fruit and vegetables, should be undertaken. Where an exact article is not recorded, the inventory may be managed only on a value basis; cost and retail prices may be known but information on precise quantities will not be available. Stock that may not be required or even sellable due to damage or seasonality must be written down to a level that reflects its value. Depending on accounting policy, stock can be valued on a LIFO (last in, first out) basis in which it is assumed that the most recently delivered stock is used first. This method ensures that rising prices do not result in older stock being overvalued. In a FIFO (first in, first out) valuation, in the other hard, the valuation of stock is based on the goods received most recently.

Stock should be counted regularly, at least once every year by law in the UK and more frequently if a tighter control is required. The aim is to correct any discrepancies between stock recorded on the system, book stock, and the actual physical quantities. Where are there are discrepancies a recount may be required. Stocktaking can be managed in three ways:

- *Periodic stock counts.* All stock is counted in preparation of an annual balance sheet, and no movements of goods are allowed during this period, effectively creating a standstill so that each product can be counted and double counting or omissions are avoided. Some faster-moving lines may be counted at more frequent intervals.

- *Perpetual inventory.* This method provides greater flexibility as stock is counted at least once through the year.

- *Inventory sampling.* Stock is counted in random samples and, based on the accuracy of the physical sample against the book records, assumptions can be made about the validity of the balance of the stock. As only some stocks are counted, this method saves time and costs.

Stock counts take place wherever merchandise is stored, so shops must be able to undertake local counts and transfer information back to a central point, usually Head Office, using EDI. Physical inventory documents, can be sent to store either electronically or as documents, and returned in the same way after the count.

Vendor-Managed Inventory (VMI)

VMI involves the manufacturer replenishing a customer's usual inventory. With VMI the retailer no longer places orders, but provides the supplier with maximum and minimum stock levels to be maintained. The retailer will help the supplier to plan production and the customer only pays for the goods when used. This task is accomplished by the customer sending daily activity updates to the manufacturer. The manufacturer then uses replenishment software in coordination with agreed service levels and desired stockturn requirements to generate replenishment orders for the customer. This process enables the customer to spend more time on other 'value-added' purchasing activities, as well as the potential to negotiate improved margins with chosen suppliers.

For the supplier, the benefits lie in the exclusive supply of products that block-out competitors and offer the potential for cost savings through closer alignment of production and supply scheduling with demand. The aim for the supplier will be to reduce inventory levels while maintaining or increasing service levels for their customers. In practice, contractual problems can arise out of the cost of maintaining inventory at the retailer's location and the need to understand the critical elements of the customer's operation. VMI moves suppliers beyond sales activity or more basic supply-chain relationships into the more complex area of joint stock management with demanding and often powerful retailers.

WAREHOUSING AND DISTRIBUTION CENTRES

Although the development of the logistics function has already been introduced, it is useful to distinguish logistics from the more practical activities in distribution management. Both terms are applied to the processes that move goods through the supply chain, and are sometimes used interchangeably. However, the fundamental difference lies in the strategic focus of logistics management on the movement and storage of materials and products from suppliers, through the firm's distribution systems, to retail outlets and customers. By contrast, physical distribution management includes planning for capacity loads in warehouses, for labour, transport and fleet management.

Distribution is capital-intensive, and the main external costs in logistics alone in the UK add up to over £10bn each year (Buchanan, 2000). Cost structures are variable, too, according to the industry sector; with high storage and transport costs in the food, drink and tobacco sectors, whereas consumer goods have more significant administration costs (Lamey, 1997). Analysis of retailers' margins shows that distribution systems have significant opportunities to add percentage points to the bottom line and improve net profit margins. Sainsbury, for example, attribute 'efficient logistics and distribution' as providing 1 per cent of their net margin with scope for a further 0.5 per cent. With annual profits of £700 million, they believe in excess of £100 million is directly attributable to these efficiencies (Mintel, 1997).

The practice of physical distribution is based on the efficient management of contracts, people and transport (Figure 12.4). At a strategic level retailers need to decide on whether to maintain their own in-house distribution operation or to contract it out to another party, and there have been strong pressures on retailers to contract-out since it provides financial advantages through opportunity cost and off-balance-sheet financing (see also Chapter 3). The management focus changed, too, through the 1980s as organisations turned to the management of their core businesses, leading to the disposal or contracting-out of peripheral operations. Increased specialisation in information systems and operational planning requires skills that are more easily developed by large contractors rather than individual retailers, and competitive pressures to develop national distribution networks within short timeframes have provided the incentive for some retailers to use contractors' managerial and planning resources (see also Table 12.4). The advantages of contracted-out services include:

Figure 12.4   *Elements of Physical Distribution Management*

Contracts	Human resource management	Transport
Third party	Motivation	Running costs
Equipment purchasing	Training	Depreciation
Information systems	Organisation	Routing

Table 12.4   *Advantages and Disadvantages of Third-Party Logistics*

Advantages	Disadvantages
■ Capital cost advantages: no need to buy vehicles ■ Day-to-day operating cost savings; economies of scale exist where accounts are too small to run properly enabling retailers to focus on areas of expertise ■ Retailers' operations become more flexible and efficient ■ Usually fixed-rate charges give access to specialist expertise with core skills in logistics/distribution management	■ Changeover costs of moving from own account to third party, including sunk costs in vehicles ■ Use of third party may lead to loss of control over delivery ■ Third-party managerial skills may be weaker than the retailers' ■ Third party lacks experience of retailers' products/markets ■ Problems may arise from coordination of delivery service with the retailers' requirements ■ Loss of confidentiality

Source: Ruston and Oxley (1997).

■ Flexibility in the range of services, from exclusively transport to a total distribution service.

■ Adaptability to the range and variety of information systems used by suppliers.

■ Financial management: a contractor may be required to plan, build and manage a regional distribution centre (RDC) at a cost of between £15 and £20m.

■ Contractual management: contractors can offer a range of terms from a management fee for managing the assets of the client, to acquisition of the retailer's entire distribution operation. Many contracts are dedicated to one customer, so that facilities, employees and management are exclusively used for only one customer.

Most contracts are undertaken on an 'open-book' basis, in which contractor and client recognise capital commitment costs of facilities, equipment, establishment and overheads. Services are provided within an agreed timespan, with notice periods and non-performance clauses. Capital depreciation and servicing capital items are included in the costings to which are added a management fee relating to the final cost. The aim is to create transparency in the cost structure of the contract and encourage a more open style of partnership.

Warehouse Management

Retail warehousing has been a typical element of the push supply-chain mechanism in which the product is manufactured, stored and processed through the supply chain in phases, each with definite linkages. At each stage, the product is stored until it can be pushed further down the supply chain towards the retail store. However, the need to replenish merchandise more efficiently has led to changes in the use of warehousing and distribution.

As retailing has become increasingly concentrated with fewer, larger companies so their logistics strategies have featured the development of centralised warehousing, replacing a number of smaller locations. Centralised distribution has the dual effect of raising customer service levels, whilst reducing inventory levels (Walters, 1999). Centralised distribution centres can usually operate more efficiently, and have more resources (Ruston and Oxley, 1997).

The purpose of the warehouse is determined by the needs of the organisation, and retailer strategy will determine the role of the distribution function. Inventories may be kept out of stores to maximise selling space and minimise costs in distribution centres, and distribution centres themselves will be increasingly determined by out-of-town locations where more suitable sites are available and rents are lower, as well as providing greater accessibility to stores. Where a retail group owns a number of brands, each sharing many suppliers and with store locations in the same towns, distribution may be integrated to provide a more efficient service.

Historically, the physical nature of the operation has emphasised the degree of its labour-intensiveness, calling for a high level of man-management and control. However, the introduction of technology into the warehouse in the form of radio communication and better handling and storage systems has changed the emphasis to being system-driven, offering the opportunity for increased effectiveness. The basic aim of warehouse management is to achieve a balance between the cost of the operation and the desired level of service to stores. Warehouse costs are a major part of the overall distribution cost, and in a cost survey conducted by the Institute of Logistics and Distribution Management (ILDM), on average 24 per cent of the distribution costs related to the warehouse. Within the warehouse, distribution costs are generally split into three categories, labour, space and equipment, with labour taking 48 per cent, space 42 per cent and equipment 10 per cent (Mintel, 1997). The level of service provided will be determined through effective practices and procedures to receive, store, retrieve and despatch goods. This is usually measured by testing the accuracy of the pick, against the desired quantity. As the product mix for grocery retailers has become less centred on packaged goods with long shelf lives, to become more diverse emphasising fresh foods with shorter sell-by dates, so the reduction in time the product spends in storage becomes significant.

The dominant objective of depot location is the minimisation of the total distribution cost, and location will affect the ability to generate sales in an area. Modelling systems in logistics are typically used to manage tactical and operational distribution problems. Sainsbury uses logistics modelling to perform strategic analyses of their distribution network, which has enabled them to select intermediate warehouse locations and find opportunities to improve their primary distribution network. Modelling techniques include:

- *Optimisation* – based on assumptions about constraints and costs.

- *Simulation* – utilising mathematical and logical relationships to replicate a given system, enabling a more realistic representation of system costs to be made.

- *Heuristics* – rules of thumb that enable near-optimal solutions to be found quickly.

- *Hybrid models* – combining simulation and optimising algorithms into unique modelling approaches.

Discrete methods have three stages in the decision-making process: preselection of possible locations, evaluation of locations and a search for optimal and near optimal locations. A further dimension is provided by dynamic location models to show how stock should be relocated through time. The continuous approach involves finding a point that minimises the total radial distance to a small number of given locations. In this case the aim is to find the pattern of depot location or relocation to maximise profits or return-on-assets (ROA) over a specified planning period (McKinnon, 1989).

To maximise efficient distribution into the retail network, central requirements include locational and merchandise-specific features:

- Location of stores, other distribution centres and proximity to markets. Warehouses can be accessed in different ways; they can be rented, defined as public warehousing, or leased or owned – as such, private warehousing (Lambert and Stock, 1993). Availability of premises is an important factor – warehousing and storage can be user-ready or purpose-built. User-ready includes older multistorey premises and modern single-storey units on modern industrial estates (McKinnon, 1989). Units on a single floor bring benefits in terms of organisational and handling efficiencies, and are generally sited in more accessible locations.

- The number of stores to be serviced from a centre will contribute to determining its size, transport access and loading areas in particular.

- The characteristics of merchandise to be stored, such as perishable foods, ambient goods or hanging clothing. Special areas might have to be allocated for preparing different types of goods for sale. Merchandise should be considered in terms of its spatial dimensions, height and width, as well as the maximum merchandise weight to meet shelving and other storage requirements.

- The quantity of merchandise to be stored.

- The storage system the merchandise might require, which could include pallet racks, shelves, bins, refrigerated or secure areas, or combinations of these.

- The methods of transporting goods to and from the warehouse and types of access to the warehouse required. Road connections, nodal interchanges between different types of transport, and choice of contractor will be significant determinants.

- Unloading and loading factors governed by numbers of vehicles each day.

- Staff requirements, numbers and skills. Labour availability is not usually a factor in location as many activities require a relatively low skills base.

- Opportunities for future development and expansion.

In determining a new site for a distribution centre, these conditions need to be assessed together with additional requirements that include land availability, planning regulations, access to distribution networks, and proximity to existing and proposed stores. Planning for a new location may be difficult as warehousing has low employment densities and therefore is not as attractive as other forms of development in stimulating local economic activity. However, area-specific grants and tax reliefs may be available as commercial incentives. Construction costs should be managed to meet budgetary requirements per metre. Costs of new site development form one of the most critical aspect of the distribution function, and are handled through project-management techniques. The transfer from a manual to automated warehouse will also require the identification of time, costs and benefits of the change.

Actual patterns of location tend to demonstrate clustering around strategic requirements. This problem was encountered in France by the Intermarche cooperative which had developed a network of large distribution centres, in part to handle its high volume forward-buying commitments With a revised strategy in the 1990s, the company focused on reducing its stockholdings in response to retailer and consumer demand. Arguably the company now finds itself with too many distribution centres, of the wrong size and location (Pache, 1999).

The design of a warehouse should logically take account of workflows, normally with receipts at one end and issues at the other. Internal organisation should be designed to avoid backtracking to save time and money. The type and quantities of materials to be stored will often determine the storage facilities required and handling equipment needed. The internal layout will be influenced by the equipment needed, influencing factors such as gangway size, headroom and turning space for vehicles.

Efficient storage of materials will require storage facilities that will not cause products to be damaged or deteriorate but at the same time enable maximum space utilisation. The type of materials used will determine whether open storage, pallets, bins or racks are used. Modern materials handling equipment permits greater used of space through high stacking, movable binning or racking running on rails where only one gangway is required for several racks. The amount of time goods spend within the storage facility should also be considered with regard to where and how goods are to be stored. For example, fast-moving and slow-moving items will have different requirements. The final layout must facilitate supervision, checking and stocktaking, and if the process involves storing and returning empties this should be incorporated into the design stage.

Storage equipment is available in many forms to suit different types of operation:

- Storage bays – single unit adjustable shelving, single or double sided.
- Stacks – several bays joined together.
- Compartments – space between two adjacent shelves.
- Bins –storage space in a compartment with a front lip.
- Shelving – may be open or closed, with options for locking, fitting out with trays or other necessary storage items.
- Pallets.
- Cages.

Shelving and bins may be mobile, or slide on rails or rollers to make more efficient use of space through access from one gangway rather than two. Pallets are wooden platforms designed to fit forklift trucks, on which typically merchandise is shrink-wrapped or boxed for convenient storage or transport. Cages are tall, mesh-sided containers on wheels that are frequently used to transport mixed goods, including flat-packed clothing into individual stores. Hanging rails are used to transport clothing such as dresses and suits that cannot easily be folded or packaged without creasing the garments.

Planning warehouse-handling equipment will require an assessment of quantities of goods to be moved, and their handling characteristics such as size and weight. Investment in this area will take the form of conveyors, belts, chains and rollers, and industrial trucks to move goods around, as well as into and out of the storage area.

Workforce management

A significant problem in physical distribution has been staff motivation. Traditional working patterns have tended to lead to stable working hours around a 40-hour week with premiums being paid outside these hours, for example weekend working. However, longer store opening hours and Sunday trading for many retailers in the UK have led to flexitime working, contractual overtime, and normal patterns of working extended to Saturdays and Sunday. Hours of work can be flexed at 24 hours' notice from between five to 12 hours to be more responsive to workloads. In some centres quality is pursued through team-empowering programmes, and more decision-making is being made at operator team level to create a more motivated workforce. Communication becomes more important too, achieved through the use of regular team briefs, in-house magazines and multi-disciplined quality teams.

Cross-docking

The rationale of cross-docking is that the product is 'pulled' through the supply chain so there is no reason to warehouse the product, but instead simply ship it on to the stores directly (Figure 12.5). Two methods of handling this requirement are that ship-

Figure 12.5   *A Comparison of Conventional and Cross-Docking Techniques*

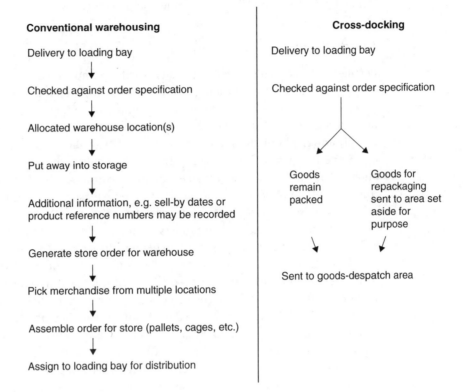

ping units are not repacked between being received at the distribution centre and, that those lines that have to be repacked are transferred to a special area before being taken to a goods-outwards area. In this context, warehouses in reality become distribution centres, rather than storage centres.

The benefits can be measured by far greater efficiency in the distribution centre's operations, and greatly increased product shelf lives. The rate of turnround increases and reduces the chance of spoilage of perishable goods in particular. The costs of prepacking and ticketing merchandise can be allocated to the supplier. Although its rationale is straightforward, cross-docking is not simple in operation; it demands a major effort in the coordination of transport, especially where the manufacturer and retailer use different shipping companies. Effective communications channels have to be constructed to link a number of companies across the supply chain, including the supplier, the distribution centre, shipping firms and the retailer.

There are different levels of cross-docking, and each has its own set of advantages and operating features. Within the ECR framework, three main levels of cross-docking are identified: cross-docking of full pallets; cross-docking of cases; and cross-docking of presorted pallets. Pre-sorted pallets is where the manufacturer assembles and ships pallets which are 'store ready'; this is the closest to the original vision of ECR, but is also the rarest in practice. Manufacturer costs rise with cross-docking presorted pallets, but retailers enjoy considerably lower costs with overall lower supply-chain costs:

an instance of where increased cost within one upstream activity implies greater efficiency throughout the rest of the value chain (Mintel, 1997).

Goods Receipt

Retailers with centralised delivery systems will attempt to control costs and inward delivery efficiency by allocating delivery times to suppliers. Each carrier will be allocated a precise delivery time for a consignment, and failure to deliver at the designated time will result in the carrier being turned away from the distribution centre. Usually another booking, at another time and date, will have to be made for the delivery. Some integrated information systems will enable delivery bays and doors to be allocated at the time of booking deliveries to maximise the efficient use of the goods-inward area. Supplier delivery reliability can be maintained at this point.

Merchandise has to be booked into stock from the supplier through a goods receipt. This is matched against purchase orders or shipping notification held in the retailer's system, and any discrepancies can be checked through it. Clothing orders with size details in each delivery can be more easily controlled through a matrix-type receipt form to enable all the details to be recorded. With physical shipments to stores, information about the delivery needs to be recorded at this point so that discrepancies can be corrected. Direct delivery to store from the supplier also needs to be recorded through a goods receipt system. Additional functions may include bonded storage, ticketing and repressing for clothing and textiles, as well as other preretailing activities. In an automated warehouse, all products will have a barcoded SKU. The storage locations in which the merchandise is put away are identified, too, with computer references or barcode labels so that they can be easily retrieved for distribution to stores.

Merchandise allocations to stores are transmitted to the warehouse or distribution centre and 'pickers' assigned to move between locations to assemble the branch delivery. In a large central warehouse a typical daily pick can be of the order of 400000 cases. The scale of picking together with pressure for next-day or same-day delivery has stimulated error reduction programmes. Incorrectly labelled or packaged products, replenishment and storage working practices, the picking process and subsequent sorting can give rise to inaccuracies that may be difficult and costly to correct further down the line (Coffey, 1999).

As a labour-intensive activity, too, this area has attracted a number of computer-based initiatives to reduce the time taken to locate and record picking, and to assembling and packaging activities. Radio frequency (RF) identification throughout the supply chain is becoming more prevalent, and within the warehouse RF terminals can be used to prioritise orders and produce efficient warehouse operations (Exhibit 12.2).

Distribution to Branches

The view that warehousing was carried out in by 'men in brown coats' servicing shops and stores reinforced the lack of role specialisation in the distribution industry. However advances in transport qualifications, with 'O' operating licences, certificates of professional competence and harmonisation of European legislation has resulted in an increasingly professional approach.

Exhibit 12.2   The use of RF in warehouse management

Picking lists can be transferred to a radio data terminal (RDT) to assign a single order at a time, and using an RF device present the next order to be picked.

■ The picker is directed to the first bin location and prompted with a quantity to pick. To ensure that the correct SKU has been picked, the picker can be required to either scan the SKU on each unit being picked or to bulk-scan the SKU. The picker is only allowed to bulk-scan a SKU if a carton, case or pallet quantity is being picked from the appropriate bin.

■ At the end of this phase the picker is notified that there are no remaining items to pick and is prompted to proceed to a packing station. When batch has been assigned to the RF device the pick records are accessed by warehouse location, bin location and SKU. The picker is first prompted to scan the cart they are using to gather the required items.

■ The picker is prompted to proceed to the first bin location where the following information is displayed. The picker scans the bin identifier on the shelving to verify the correct bin, then scans the SKU.

■ When the picker is finished at the current bin the system sends them to the next bin. Once all goods have been picked the system directs the picker to proceed to a packing station where he scans the station ID to pass the batch to the packer. After the pick cycle has been completed the picker is prompted to proceed to a packing station where they scan the station ID to pass the goods to the packer.

■ Physical picking in warehouses can be organised around fixed locations or from randomly-located stock. Picking lists are printed either for each delivery or combined for several deliveries at a time, which makes the pickers task easier as each bin only requires one visit.

Transport requires established tactical skills as well as strategic ones to ensure that all deliveries are made in as cost-effective manner to support the logistics function. The range of issues affecting the transport area include energy saving from environmentally designed vehicles, to the range of vehicles available. Distribution may require rigid trailers through to wagon and dray combinations, and more specific vehicles are being introduced to meet industry requirements. These require evaluation through a transport specialist who will need to take decisions about the correct vehicles, purchases or leases to meet the needs of the business.

Contracts for transport can form a significant cost with key issues forming around length of contract and service level. The method of purchasing vehicle fleets and mechanical handling equipment (MHE) equally require close attention, resulting in around 75 per cent of contracts being successfully negotiated and fulfilled.

Distribution, depending on the nature of the company and the product, can account for up to 30 per cent of costs, within which transport would typically account for 45 per cent of distribution spending (Mintel, 1999). Eibl (1996) quotes an earlier survey that suggests that transport costs can account for up to 52 per cent of a firms distribution expenditure. The rate of increase in road transport costs in the 1990s, forecasted at 50–80 per cent, impress the need for close analysis and management of transport costs (McKinnon, 1989); as a result, distribution and transport in particular have gained a greater prominence in business thinking in recent years.

The transport planning process will involve the movement of goods from the distribution centre or warehouse or store. The origin and destination of goods must be known together with the quantities, sizes, weights and frequencies of distribution. In transporting merchandise, the selection of the most suitable method to satisfy the retailer's needs at least cost is required, whilst delivering the goods at the right time at the right quality and in the right quantity (see also Exhibit 12.3). Most retailers and their suppliers will use road transport for their domestic operations or for international operations within a geographical land mass. Some retailers will use railways for bulk shipment; Benetton's central warehouse in Italy, for example, is connected to the rail network, but rail is less suited to individual store deliveries. For overseas retail operations, air and sea freighting will have to be used for merchandise that cannot be sourced locally.

The advantages of road transport include relative speed of delivery, avoidance of transhipment, and higher levels of security than other systems where transhipment is involved, for example rail to road. The costs of capital investment in the movement of goods are lower than for other forms of transport. Critically, road transport offers distribution flexibility since almost any landbound destination can be accessed, routes changed, and vehicles organised to carry a diverse range of products. Road transport operations can be managed to undertake three functions; consolidation, the collection from many locations; trunk haulage from point to point; and distribution, the disaggregation of goods (McKinnon, 1989). Increasingly retailers backhaul with their transport; at the end of a delivery run to stores the empty truck will pick up goods from suppliers for return to the retailers distribution centre.

Exhibit 12.3 How the right data can keep shoppers happy and loyal

The infomediary need not be quite so independent. Adopting a similar approach is logistics company Exel, which has just formed a joint venture with former rivals Tibbett & Britten to create Joint Retail Logistics which is now handling all non-food deliveries for Marks & Spencer.

The operation is based on Exel's Managed Transport Services development which uses the Internet to link the entire supply chain – from raw materials to home delivery – tracking trucks, products and orders electronically. 'Suppliers have ERP (enterprise resource planning) systems to monitor what goes on in the factory', says Exel's MTS project director, Carol Drury, 'but once the goods got to the truck, they just vanished from the system. Now, we can use the electronic ordering details as a glue to keep all the information about the consignment within the system.' Instead of simply performing as a conventional 'third party logistics contractor', MTS adds intelligent modelling and extended enterprise IT to the equation to assess when goods will be ready for collection and where they need be delivered with little need for manual intervention from the retailer.

Source: Adapted from *Financial Times*, 6 October 1999.

With road transport, retailers must decide on the ownership of distribution vehicles. Typically this decision depends on whether to invest in its own fleet of vehicles, or to contract-out to a third party. Other alternatives for smaller businesses could include hiring on a spot basis, with each contract treated separately. Decisions can be defined around three key factors relating to cost, organisation and physical factors. Vehicle characteristics and requirements will consider differences in products and product ranges and their requriements of vehicle size, body quality, equipment and unit load specifications.

Routing

Vehicle routing concerns the planning of the delivery of goods, and in some instances their collection, using one or more road vehicles. A scheduling element is added to create a vehicle routing and scheduling (VRS) function, when time constraints are incorporated (Eibl, 1996, and Figure 12.6). Planning multiple drop deliveries basically concerns establishing the shortest route around a series of points. An early view imposed two constraints on route formation; the maximum distance a vehicle can travel on a single route, together with the maximum load that the vehicle can carry. The algorithms include simultaneous methods, generally minimising the distance travelled without regard to the loading of vehicles and subsequently number of vehicles required. An alternative has been the sequential approach, which takes more account of vehicle utilisation and fleet size (McKinnon, 1989). Computerised route planning has been available since the 1970s, and in its evolution now provides routing, warehousing and discrete event simulations (DES). These simulations enable managers to model operations and facilities with different operating strategies and scenarios to evaluate alternative solutions and financial benefits through changes in transport, warehouse and distribution usage.

Although considerable work has gone into vehicle routing algorithms, many managers continue to use intuitive or rule-of-thumb methods of planning, as the mathematical complexity of these models can be daunting (McKinnon, 1989). Regular scheduled routes to stores or other distribution centres can be automatically scheduled by an integrated information system. A schedule can be set up on a weekly basis with one or more deliveries on one or more days. Groups of deliveries from the centre can be planned at the same time each week enabling picking and shipping to be planned efficiently. Product tracking by satellite enables both suppliers and retailers to accurately follow the progress of deliveries.

Increasing constraints on movement of delivery vehicles include timing and duration of access and restrictions in towns, especially the reduction of delivery hours during the night in residential areas or during the day in busy town centres. The use of delivery windows by retailers in allocating times for delivery, and nominated day delivery schemes, further restrict operational planning (McKinnon, 1989). Issues surrounding out-of-town deliveries and the return to town centres again creates logistics problems (Lamey, 1997).

Figure 12.6 *Time-Based Dimensions of Vehicle Routing and Scheduling*

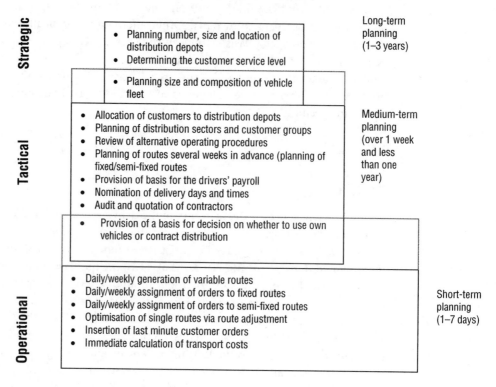

Source: Eibl (1996), with permission.

To add to the complexity of vehicle routing, environmental issues are becoming increasingly important and require integration into transport and routing policy. In particular, there will be a need to provide environmental awareness programmes as well as to take practical steps to reduce vehicle emissions, increase energy efficiency and work to reduce consumption of non-renewable resources.

SUMMARY

Inventory management is a process that should integrate a number of functions. It is financially driven by the need to minimise the cost of carrying stocks throughout the business, and to maximise the return on investment. This will require marketing-led decisions about pricing and the delivery of customer satisfaction, with the aim of ensuring company profitability as well as the continuing availability of product assortments. The buying and merchandising function, depending on the type of organisation, will have responsibility for ensuring that orders are placed to meet demand in response to sales. As actual sales are recorded, so forecasts of future sales can be adjusted to maintain future stock levels as accurately as possible. The value and physical quantities of stock both need to be managed, and any systematic method of managing stock must account for the effect of markdowns and promotions on its valuation.

The process of managing inventory concerns both these centralised functions, but in terms of handling the physical flows of merchandise, it also concerns decentralised operations. Stock management will be influenced by distribution policy and the quality of the distribution systems from warehousing and distribution centres through to store stockrooms.

QUESTIONS

1 Analyse the information flows in stock allocation and replenishment.

2 Evaluate the sales planning process.

3 To what extent is inventory management a Head Office function?

4 Assess the contribution of stock handling and storage practices to a retailer's service objectives.

5 Distribution to multiple outlets will become a major issue in the next 10 years. Discuss.

6 In what ways could cross-docking techniques evolve to further improve inventory management?

Case Study

Cross-Docking

Cross-docking is not a new phenomenon, parcel delivery companies have used the technique for at least 15 years. However, it was not until the mid-1990s that retailers became interested in the process, described by Michael Johnson of TNT Logistics as

> an operational technique for receiving, allocating, sorting and despatching product, while it remains on the dock of a distribution centre and therefore does not rely upon withdrawing stock from storage . . . in most cases it would be undertaken over a single shift.

The movement of goods must respond to the strategic needs of retailers which have focused on the reduction of operating costs, increased throughput, reduced inventory levels and increased sales space within stores. Retailers' initial caution in the process was finally overcome by developments in IT and supply-chain integration. Successful cross-docking may require major changes in company relationships so that retailers and suppliers work more closely together within a teamwork culture. Information must be shared on a much more extensive scale than before, through automatically transmitted online sales and

(Continued)

future demand forecasts from the retailer. Supply chains must be highly responsive, using EPOS, barcoding and stock-tracking technology so that delivery schedules and volumes meet branch requriements. Not only do exact times need to be agreed and coordinated across the supply chain, but also pallet numbers, quantities, product numbers and locations. Retailers must have confidence in suppliers' reliability to manage on-time deliveries as well as achieving consistent order quality across consignments so that time-consuming inspections are avoided. Cost analysis of warehousing and packaging activities will enable retailers to identify those that could be contracted-out to suppliers, such as labelling and packing floor-ready garments. This relieves retail staff from having to check goods in, remove goods from cartons, mark, repack or hang and so allows garments to move through a cross-docking area faster.

In many distribution centres, cross-docking works best when there is a despatch bay for each individual outlet fed by the distribution centre, or a 'door per store'. Usually, more than 70 per cent of goods should be conveyable to allow use of cost-cutting automatic systems, although one company has developed a system that allows high sortation of common goods without the need for costly sortation conveyors. The number of daily throughputs to justify cross-docking are hard to define, but equipment suppliers suggest a minimum of 2000 cartons a day. Typical automated systems, however, may need at least 3000 cartons/hr based on an even receipt rate. Businesses looking to adopt cross-docking must beware of relying on unrealistically low budgets. Typical errors include failure to allow for awkward packages and the peaks and troughs of real situations. Overlooking the fragile nature of goods with respect to pres-

sures and accelerations of fast sortation is another mistake. Pitfalls are often linked to costly capital spending without thinking of function flexibility. Sorting machines and robots are far from being the only answer, which if not used fully could be wasteful.

Among the leading proponents of cross-docking in the UK are the major supermarket chains. Time is particularly important to them because of the time-sensitive nature of frozen, chilled and fresh foods. Tesco's installation of an automated cross-docking system to handle fresh meat, poultry, fish and some chilled produce at +1°C moves 12000 items per hour through two high-speed sortation conveyors. The benefits include less than half the recorded damage for an equivalent manual system, more efficient store shelf-filling and better handling of fluctuations in demand. Asda achieved a 77 per cent reduction in inventory in its 213 stores in a trial that included space-intensive 'high cube', low-weight products from Kimberley Clark. Both companies claimed additional beneifts, too, from weekly meetings to open-book cost accounting, with the result that improvements were recorded in product availability and space utilisation.

Any technique which cuts distribution time prolongs product shelf life and therefore cuts losses from waste, but it is the need for reduced inventory and accurate picking that will lead to cross-docking's more widespread acceptance in other industries. Suitable products for cross-docking include high-volume goods, seasonal and time-sensitive items. Fortunately, the latest generation of materials-handling hardware can handle a much wider range of products, so system usage can be raised sharply and the investment payback time reduced.

Sources: *Distribution*, August 1998; *Asian Review of Business and Technology*, 22 March 2000.

References

Berman, B. and Evans, J.R. (1998) *Retail management: A Strategic Approach* (Englewood Cliffs, New Jersey: Prentice Hall).

Bohdanowicz, J. and Clamp, L. (1994) *Fashion Marketing*, Routledge.

Brockman, B.K. and Morgan, R.M. (1999) 'Managerial innovations in distribution: what prospects for ECR?', *International Journal of Retail and Distribution Management*, vol. 27, no. 10, pp. 397–408.

Buchanan, M. (2000) 'Purchasing in the Logistics Sector', *Logistics and Transport Focus*, vol. 2, no. 1, Jan–Feb. pp. 26–30.

Coffey, D. (1999) 'Zero in on Picking', *Logistics and Transport Focus*, vol. 1, no. 4, October pp. 22–23.

Eibl, P.G. (1996) *Computerised Vehicle Routing and Scheduling and Road Transport* (Aldershot: Avebury).

Fernie, J. and Sparks, L., eds. (1998) *Logistics and Retail Management: Insights into Current Practice from Leading Experts* (London: Kogan Page).

Financial Times (1999) *Contractors go continental: Third-party logistics companies are aiding integration in the pan-European supply chain*, Jun 17 (1999).

Lambert, D.M. and Stock, J.R. (1993) *Strategic Logistics Management*, 3edn (Homewood Ill.: Irwin).

Lamey, J. (1997) *Supply Chain Management* Financial Times Management.

Lucas, C.H., Bush, R.P. and Gresham, L.G. (1994) Retailing (Boston: Houghton Mifflin).

McKinnon, A.C. (1989) *Physical Distribution Systems* (London: Routledge).

Mintel, (1997) *Efficient Consumer Response* (London: Mintel International Group).

Pache, G. (1999) 'When Logistics Threaten to become a Source of Competitive Disadvantage: The Intermarche Co-operative Case', in M. Dupuis and J. Dawson (eds), *European Cases in Retailing* (Oxford: Blackwell).

Retail Week (1994) 25 March.

Ruston, A. and Oxley, J. (1997) *Handbook of Logistics and Strategic Management* (London: Kogan Page).

Walters, D., ed. (1999) *Global Logistics and Distribution Planning: Strategies for Management*, 3rd edn (London: Kogan Page).

Retail Pricing: Policies and Practice

INTRODUCTION

At its simplest, a retail-selling price is easily observed on a product or shelf edge. Collectively, prices are an indicator of whether the store appears to be expensive, reasonably priced or inexpensive. Price enables the consumer to make judgements about value, and from a financial perspective it provides a convenient measure of profitability.

Indeed, one of the most important aspects of pricing (Harris and Mills, 1982) is that the price of a product or service will determine how consumers perceive it. Pricing will reflect on brand positioning, influence the choice of the marketing channel, affect how the item is promoted and have an impact on the level of customer service expected by target customers. Figure 13.1 shows the range of factors that may influence a retailer's pricing decisions and those affected by the price the retailer sets.

A number of actions taken by a retailer can be explained in terms of long-term strategy rather than short-term tactics; so too with pricing, and a retailer's pricing

Figure 13.1   *Influences and Influencing Factors in Retail Pricing Decisions*

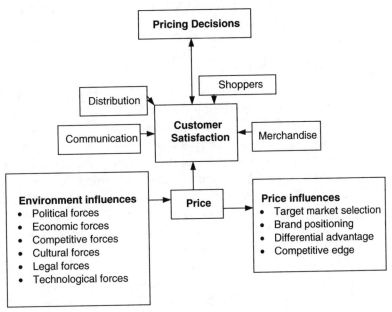

strategy is of crucial importance to the organisation since it has a direct effect on profitability both in the short and long term. At the same time, the price strategy may be subordinate to other long-term objectives such as price leadership, maximising profits, inhibiting entry of competitors and/or new entrants to the industry.

Apart from strategic pricing policies in a multi-product organisation, price decisions are influenced by a number of other factors. These include the marketing strategy for the product, the values that consumers set on the product, general business conditions, consumer and competitive responses to price and price changes, and supply and financial considerations. In any retail marketing situation, the retailer has some degree of price discretion largely determined by the extent to which the customer is concerned with price and the degree of product differentiation (Langrehr and Langrehr, 1983). Setting prices requires a comprehensive information system reporting current and likely future values for these numerous factors (Kotler, 1997). Conceptually, prices should be established independently of costs, as these are important only in determining relative profitability. In practice, this distinction is seldom followed; retail pricing decisions are characterised by a large element of intuition.

THE THEORY AND CONCEPT OF PRICING

Prices can be explained through economic theory as serving two general functions. Prices ration existing supplies of goods so that scarce supplies are directed to those who place most value on them and secondly, 'act as a signal to direct productive resources among the different sectors of the economy' (Frank, 1997). As a result, excess demand allows prices to increase, higher profits draw new resources into the industry and losses drive out resources into other industries. Consumer demand in the developed world has, over time, led to steadily increasing prices and ultimately contributed to the attractiveness of the retail industry.

Demand and supply

Markets, including the retail market, consist of buyers and sellers of a good or service. In economics, demand is defined as the quantity of the good, which buyers wish to purchase at each conceivable price. Demand will be different at each price that might possibly be chosen, and demand is normally, but not always, assumed to fall as price increases. For convenience, the demand curve in Figure 13.2 (with demand increasing as price falls) is shown here as a straight line, but it could follow other paths; indeed, it is most often shown as a smooth curve which is concave towards the origin, reflecting a constant price elasticity of demand (described below) – this is because demand is normally expected to be inversely proportional to price, that is the higher the price the less the demand.

Figure 13.2 illustrates the effect of one variable – price – on the quantity demanded. The classic demand curve D_1 is a graph of the quantity of products expected to be sold at various prices, if other factors remain constant (Simon, 1992). It illustrates that, as price falls, the quantity demanded usually rises. Demand, however, depends on other factors in the retailing mix, including shoppers' behaviour, product quality, retail communication and distribution. An improvement in any of these factors may cause a shift to, say, demand curve D_2. In such a case an increased quantity Q_2 will be sold at the same price P. It is important for students to understand that there are many types of demand, and not all conform to the classic demand curve shown in Figure 13.2. For example, prestige products such as selected perfumes, jewellery and cars, can sell in larger quantities at higher prices than at low ones.

Again, in economics, supply is defined as the quantity of goods which sellers wish to sell at each conceivable price. Supply is expected to increase as price increases (the reverse of demand), and the supply line is conventionally assumed to be straight.

Figure 13.2 *Demand Curve Illustrating the Price–Quantity Relationship*

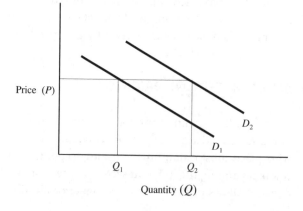

Price (P)

Q_1 Q_2

Quantity (Q)

The problem posed by this traditional 'economic' approach is that the 'demand function' is usually almost impossible to determine. It is difficult to find an actual demand relationship in practice. These problems are, to a large extent, a consequence of the very peculiarity of the demand function concept itself – the fact that it represents the answers to a set of purely hypothetical questions and that information is taken to pertain simultaneously to the same moment of time.

Price Elasticity of Demand

The change in shoppers' needs, variations in the effect of other retailing mix elements, the presence of substitute merchandise, and dynamic environmental factors can influence demand for products and services. Food retailers, for example, can experience large fluctuations in demand for some items of groceries daily, as well as over the longer term (see Exhibit 13.1).

The relationship between demand and changes in price is called the price elasticity of demand; this recognises that some products or services are more sensitive to price than others. Typically, economy or basic volume product lines are relatively undifferentiated from each other, except by price. The demand is said to be elastic if the percentage change in demand is greater than the percentage change in price. Clearly if retailers can determine the price elasticity of demand, it will enable them to set a price or a price range more accurately:

$$\text{Price elasticity of demand} = \frac{\% \text{ change in quantity demanded}}{\% \text{ change in price}}$$

On the other hand, where demand for a product is relatively unaffected by changes in price, it is said to be inelastic. By analysing total revenue, price multiplied by quantity, as prices change retailers can determine a product's price elasticity. If demand is elastic, a change in price causes an opposite change in total revenue, that is an increase in price will decrease total revenue and a decrease in price will increase total revenue. Inelastic demand results in a change in line with total revenue – an increase in price will increase total revenue, and a decrease in price will decrease total revenue.

Exhibit 13.1 Genetically modified (GM) foods lose their charms

The relationship between consumer demand and price can be difficult to predict. The arrival of foods containing genetically modified ingredients on supermarket shelves appeared to have an insignificant effect on demand. Genetic modification to crops increases their yields and potentially reduces the cost of produce enabling farmers and others in the supply chain to benefit from higher margins or lower prices. However, as a result of various public debates conducted in the media, people have walked away from buying groceries with 'genetically modified' on the label. In this case, a change in social attitudes towards the untested long-term consequences of using GM in food resulted in supermarkets rejecting GM ingredients to avoid the loss of loyal customers.

Exhibit 13.2   Demand elasticity

Unique or highly differentiated products and services can enable a company to set almost whatever prices it wants, within limits. As the percentage change in price is matched by a similar change in demand, it can be referred to as 'inelastic'. In retailing, intense competition, and in many sectors low barriers to market entry, have created a business environment where demand is generally sensitive to changes in price. Many retailers operate with rapidly changing product ranges, and so it is difficult to analyse consistent patterns of consumer behaviour in relation to pricing changes. In the case of PC hardware, software and peripherals, as competing products have entered the market and eroded the monopoly of the early entrants so demand has become more elastic. In effect, demand is now more sensitive to price changes than it used to be.

Cross Elasticity of Demand

If the price of one good is raised too high, some of its buyers will switch to an alternative good though this is not a perfect substitute. This is called the cross price elasticity of demand: the cross price elasticity of demand for good i with respect to changes in the price of good j is the percentage change in the quantity of good i divided by the corresponding change in the price of good j. The point to note here is that a 'good' in this context is a product in one market or segment i. The 'good' j is a product in another segment j.

There are limitations to the application of this theory as it assumes all consumers and suppliers come equipped with perfect knowledge of all the prices available for comparable products (a perfect market). In addition, it is assumed that all the demand is exactly matched by supply, and supply by demand, situations that are rarely found in retail markets. Indeed, it is almost impossible, by definition, for a marketeer to have any effect in a 'perfect market'. Even so, an understanding of the basic theories of supply and demand does offer the retailer a useful insight into some of the key factors which may affect the prices that he or she is able to obtain. In particular, the concept of 'elasticity of demand' is one which is widely discussed and does have a role to play in pricing decisions.

Other Factors in Pricing

The economics theory of price tells us that profits are maximised when marginal costing is equated with marginal revenues. Conceptually this is a very helpful idea, but its actual use is beyond the capabilities of most retail organisations; a typical retailer is unaware of the true nature of his cost and demand functions, leading to more intuitive decisions (Baker, 1993).

In practice we may mean different things when we talk about 'price'. As Langrehr and Langrehr (1983) noted, the general price policies that retailers adopt will be influenced by the customers to whom they hope to appeal, and the character of the stores they operate which must also be related to the market. The nature of competition in both the market local to a store and the whole retail market are also influencing factors. Other factors such as brand reliability and services provided have a substantial influence on choice behaviour.

East (1997) shows that consumers have an acceptable price range with upper and lower limits within which the reference price is the price they expect to pay. Expectations are determined in several ways: by how much they would like to pay, the price they usually pay or what they consider to be a fair price to pay. Consumers can also use their knowledge of the product to set a price and with little product knowledge they use prices, amongst other cues, as a quality indicator.

As product differentiation increases the retailer will usually have more discretion over pricing. With an entirely new product, it is possible to create a high level of differentiation since consumers have no knowledge of it and therefore they will have difficulty in establishing a reasonable price. And with a standardised product unless some differentiation is possible between the all the competing products, very little price discretion exists.

Table 13.1   *The Meaning of Price to the Retailer and Shopper*

To the retailer	To the shopper
1 An element in the retail marketing mix, or the retail promotional mix, which can be manipulated within a defined range, to achieve corporate objectives dependent upon the corporate needs and the market situation; e.g. to promote sales, to create an image, to forestall competition	A measure of the value of the total bundle of satisfactions they are offered, with the corollary that the significance of price may vary within the decision making process
2 Part of a relationship which, when taken in conjunction with the sales volume, yields a revenue fund from which costs can be met and a profit obtained	A cost; it may be important for the shopper to achieve a formal or informal budget
3 A measure of the risks to the retailer involved in the sale, and/or an insurance premium against the maturing of these risks	A measure of the alternatives foregone; either directly, i.e. directly competitive products or substitutes, or indirectly, i.e. alternative uses for the money to be spent
4 Part of an overall bundle of factors including discounts, settlement terms, and credit terms which can be used to affect both the 'willingness' and the 'ability' of shoppers to buy	A measure of quality. More difficult to measure in times of inflation, but gives rise to sayings such as 'You only get what you pay for' etc.
5 A signature of quality and value which is used as a positioning strategy and for self-differentiation from other similar retailers in the product market. It is also used as a basis for market segmentation within the retailer's market sector	Part of a conglomeration of things which shoppers often take into account (such as guarantees) which may affect their willingness or ability to buy.

Source: Omar (1999), *Retail Marketing*, p. 232.

Pricing Policies and Objectives

Retailer pricing policies fall within three main categories of pricing decision:

- *Demand–oriented pricing* relates to sales and market-share objectives, with pricing determined by what the consumer will pay. So the retailer may select any price range appropriate to its target market and strategy: prices could be consistently very low for a discount retailer, through to very high for a designer fashion business. Marketing literature places price skimming, typically to set high initial price points for new products for short periods and market penetration objectives, within this approach.

- *Cost-oriented pricing* is a policy where selling prices are derived from the product cost, with a selling price marked up from it. The markup covers operating expenses including staffing, rents and administration, and allows for a targeted profit level. Sound pricing decisions are therefore essential since retailers depend upon the prices they charge to cover the cost of their merchandise, to pay their expenses and to provide their profit. In practice, although a number of methods are used by retailers for establishing prices, costs play a central role.

- *Competitive pricing*. The most basic pricing decision retailers make concern the relationship between their prices and those of competitors (Sethuraman and Tellis, 1991), and, as one might expect, most retailers tend to set their prices close to those of their major competitors. But this statement needs two qualifications:

  (1) most retailers tend to think of other retailers of the same type as their major competitors; and

  (2) retailers such as supermarket operators who sell wide assortments of convenience goods will usually not try to match their competitors' prices item for item. They expect to be higher on some items, lower on others, and are more concerned with the general price image or impression that their store reflects.

Nevertheless, Welch and Massey (1988) observed that many retailers pay strict attention to item-by-item price comparisons. In order to maintain current information about rival stores, large retailers frequently employ comparison shoppers who check their store's prices, merchandise and service levels against competitors' prices (Russo, 1977). Garland (1992) asserts that multiple retail organisations have more options for meeting competition needs than small retailers. However, an astute small retailer can still adapt a number of pricing techniques to remain competitive.

The concentration of retail industry in the UK has meant that a small number of large retail organisations now dominate every sector (see Exhibit 13.3). As a result the focus on price competition has become intense. In dealing with competition, both large and small retailers usually assess competitors' prices and services; price their product and/or services to meet the competition; and use own-labels as a differentiating competitive strategy. Such detailed knowledge of competitors' prices enables the retailer to set realistic prices.

Exhibit 13.3   Pricing strategies in food retailing

In the UK each leading retail grocery multiple has its own strategy on price:

■ Asda uses a different approach from category to category, with longer-term promotions, while stressing supplier relationships.

■ Tesco takes the high ground on price cuts, and has returned to promotions on some staple categories, with local pricing and flyers.

■ Sainsbury concentrates on promotions, especially the multibuy, while focusing on quality.

■ Safeway concentrates on deep-cut price promotions, especially local ones.

Source: *The Grocer*, 2000.

A retailer's control over prices depends on the nature of the retail operation, and has much to do with its degree of freedom in setting prices. Department stores usually offer a range of services that are not available elsewhere, whilst other specialist stores attract shoppers who are more interested in assortment, services, or convenience than in price. Consequently, these stores can maintain higher prices and still be competitive.

Pricing objectives are defined by the corporate and marketing strategies of the retailer. Every retailer must price its goods and services in a manner that achieves profitability for the organisation and satisfies shoppers, while adapting to a variety of constraints. Pricing is a crucial strategic variable for a retailer because of its direct relationship with the business objectives and its interaction with other retail marketing-mix elements. Types of pricing objectives can include:

■ a desired sales volume;

■ a target return on investment;

■ a market position;

■ competitive edge;

■ price stability or margin stability; and/or

■ temporarily disrupting markets, introducing uncertainties to competitors' strategies (McGoldrick, 1990).

Other pricing objectives can be determined by the need for prestige in the community or social responsibility, found for example in the Co-operative movement.

Sales volumes have been, and remain, an important objective for many retailers throughout the world (Omar, 1999, see also Litvack *et al.*, 1985). Volumes can be measured in income and units, and high sales levels may need to be maintained by low prices, typically when a retailer follows a market penetration strategy (Berman and

Evans, 1998). Unique or strongly differentiated retail formats or products can also generate high sales, although these may be difficult to sustain.

Return on investment relates prices to profits and cost of investment in the retailer. The objective is to set prices that provide profit that exceeds the cost of investment at a level that is attractive to shareholders. Price cutting can contribute to a reduction in return to investors by squeezing profits, unless it is accompanied by a reduction in costs.

The retailer will aim to achieve consistency between the pricing strategy and overall marketing, profit and return-on-investment objectives. For instance, a retailer interested in an early recovery of a cash investment, because of an expansion plan, might enact a mass retail marketing strategy. Such an approach uses low prices to achieve its business objective calling for two types of price decisions:

1 The general price policy – the retailer has to decide on a general price level in relationship to competition; whether or not to follow a 'one-price' policy, and to organise prices into 'price-lines'.

2 Individual item pricing – the retailer must price individual items in conformation with these general policies.

Profits are a function of the interrelationships among prices, merchandise costs, store operating expenses, and the level of sales volumes. As such, prices must be attractive enough to the consumer to provide for a sufficient volume of sales, and yet be adequate to cover merchandise costs and operating expenses, as well as generate profits themselves. Considerable judgement is required on the part of the retailer to integrate pricing into a total merchandising strategy and in making pricing decisions, the aim should always be to further the long-term objectives of the retailer.

Market position concerns the shoppers' perceptions of a store's prices, whether they consider the store to be expensive or inexpensive, which will help determine whether they patronise the store or shop elsewhere. Consumers' awareness of, and interest in, price will vary with education, occupation, age, type of goods involved and demographic factors. Retailers should therefore identify how potential and/or present customers respond to various pricing and service practices in their stores. Some consumers are much more price-conscious than others. Whilst low-income consumers might be expected to be more sensitive to price than high-income ones, this is not always the case: they may be more interested in the availability of credit or other services rather than price.

Effective merchandising management may require that retail marketing objectives be achieved only in the aggregate. Not all goods need to be priced for profit so long as the aggregate prices charged on all merchandise yields adequate profits (Clodfelter, 1997). While merchandise costs are known for each item, most operating expenses can usually be related to individual items only in a general way, through an allocation process that can vary from company to company. When a price is changed, the sales volume of the item may change favourably or unfavourably; there may be a gain or loss offset by changes in the unit sales volume of other similar products in the retailer's store, or change in the unit volume of the category of which the item is a part. Even when this can be determined, it may be equally difficult to ascertain whether the change was due to the price or to other factors such as those concerning display or advertising, changes in competitors' prices and/or sales promotional activities, or even the effect of adverse weather.

Competitive edge. Sometimes the supplier seeks to establish the lowest retail price for a product, as is the case with some national brands, and in such cases the retailer can only decide whether or not to handle the item at the specified price. At other times, it may be necessary to sell certain items at a loss in order to meet competition or develop a merchandising strategy appropriate to a given situation (Bartholomew, 1992). This action is referred to as 'predatory pricing', involving 'loss leaders' when products are sold below cost, and is used competitively by multiple food retailers to attract customers and place pressure on financially weaker competitors. However, as Folkes and Wheat (1995) observed, it might be a mistake to think of 'high prices' as necessary to achieve high profits. With food retailers, the volume of own-label sales on certain commodity food lines can provide substantial profits though the percentage margin may be low.

Price and margin stability and disruption. Price stability provides a useful platform to maintain a satisfactory level of profitability. By contrast, a price war may develop when a number of competitors try to sell below each other's price ranges and keep reducing their prices, often drastically, in efforts to attract each other's customers. The war will often be confined to a few fast-moving items that may be reduced to one-half or one-third their normal price, before the battle is over.

Price wars end in various ways. All of the competitors may simply withdraw from the struggle when they find that their rivals quickly match their price reductions. In other cases, the retailers or their suppliers may have to take some form of joint action before prices move upwards. In other cases suppliers have used various methods to stop such retail price-cutting; for example major oil companies have terminated some local petrol price wars by supplying their petrol to service stations on consignment, thus retaining the right to fix final selling prices.

It does not follow that retailers have to adopt a single pricing objective (Smith and Sinha, 2000), but rather they may follow a number of objectives. Based on these, price calculations are typically aimed at maximising profit. The retailer's interest in price as a decision variable can be influenced by the product's contribution ratio. If this is low, small changes in price will result in large changes in profit. If the contribution ratio is high, then while the product makes a valuable contribution to fixed costs, profits are less sensitive to changes in price.

RETAIL PRICING CALCULATIONS

The markup and margin calculation plays an important role in the retailer's thinking, both in deciding on general price policies and in setting prices for specific items. Simple formulas are often used to compute prices, and to help determine whether prices will cover operating costs.

Markups and Margins

The retailer conducts a cost analysis and sets pricing goals as the next step in the pricing process. The difference between cost and selling price is referred to as the *markup* or *margin* (gross margin) and is important:

> Markup is the gross profit (selling price less cost price) price; expressed as a percentage of the cost price. This method of price determination is closely related to 'cost-plus' pricing, when a fixed percentage is added on to a total unit cost. (Baker, 1993)

Many smaller retailers set prices of individual merchandise items based on a markup percentage on cost, and this is advantageous because the calculation is easy to apply to a large number of items. Retailers, though, are faced with a problem in determining the appropriate markup to reach the required level of profitability, and different merchandise categories may require different markup levels since one percentage is seldom appropriate for all items.

Gross margin is the same difference between the cost price and retail price, but is expressed as a percentage of the retail price (Exhibit 13.4). A large number of retailers prefer to use the gross margin measure as a percentage of retail prices for comparability. Since retailers typically express financial data relating to net and gross profit margins and returns on sales as percentages of sales revenue, it is helpful for buyers and merchandisers to calculate in the same way. The discussion of cost here is for illustrative purposes only, showing the mathematical relationship between the respective measures.

Since the difference between selling price and merchandise cost determines the gross profit of the product, the retailer has to first compute the full cost before determining the price. The retailer includes in the merchandise cost the cost of the item from the supplier, any transportation charges paid by the retailer, and other direct charges such as excise duties, customs fees and quotas (for imported merchandise), *less* any trade, quantity or promotional discounts. The retailer groups other operating expenses such as payroll, rent, utilities, advertising and so forth under selling and administrative expenses.

The cost can be reduced further by the settlement period, an agreed time form the receipt of goods at which the retailer pays the supplier. Early payment of the supplier's invoice typically commands a discount for the retailer, in the region of 5–7 per cent for

---

Exhibit 13.4   Calculating markup and margin

When a store sells a child's coat it bought at £30 for £45, its markup is (£45 − £30) = £15. The markup percentage on cost is:

$15/30 \times 100 = 50\%$

In the same example its gross margin percentage on retail selling price is:

retail price less cost (£45 − £30) = £15,
divided by retail price $(15/45) \times 100 = 33\%$

payment within 7–10 days of receipt of goods. A commonly agreed settlement period is 30 days; in exchange for later payment the retailer forgoes a discount, and terms are 'net'. However, practices vary though from country to country, with 60 or even 90 day settlement periods negotiated by some retailers in Europe. The advantages of reducing costs through early payment discounts have to be balanced against the benefits from later settlement that result in improved financial liquidity and cash flow.

Initial and Maintained Margins

The initial margin relates to the price at which the retailer first offers an item for sale. However, since retailers frequently sell some amounts of merchandise below the original price due to a markdown in the price, at the end of a period a maintained margin is recorded (Exhibit 13.5).

In addition to settlement payments to suppliers for prompt payment, maintained margins may also be revised upwards by including retrospective discounts on achieving purchasing targets agreed with the supplier and other forms of adjustment to the initial margin (Elliott and Rider, 2000).

Price Adjustments Through Markdowns

Prices are constantly on trial (see Clodfelter, 1997), and must often be adjusted to meet changing conditions. Most price changes are decreases, referred to as markdowns. When prices are reduced and/or changed, shoppers must be informed and action taken by the retailer to prevent the shopper being overcharged for the reduced items on the shelves. Prices displayed on the shelves must be those charged at the checkout.

Markdowns have the effect of increasing sales because more shoppers are willing to buy at lower prices. However, retailers must carefully plan and implement markdown policies since a markdown reduces sales values without reducing cost, effectively lowering profits. For some product lines, the amount of reduction in monetary value can even exceed their total gross margins.

Exhibit 13.5   Initial retail and maintained retail prices

At the start of a season, a clothing store put a £25 selling price on a T-shirt, which cost £12 and gave an initial margin of £13. The retailer purchased 300 shirts but after selling 200 of them within the first month still had another 100 in stock. In order to sell the remaining stock faster, the store reduced the price to £19.99 and sold the entire lot in the next two weeks.

The cumulative original retail value for the entire stock of 300 T-shirts was £7500 (£25 × 300), and the margin £3900. But the actual retail sales for the stock reached only £6999 (2000 shirts × £25 and 100 shirts × £19.99). The maintained margin or the difference between the actual revenue and the cost for the consignment was £3399:

> Maintained margin = sales retail (net sales) − merchandise cost
> = £6999 − £3600
> = £3399

Table 13.2   *Markdowns in a Department Store*

	Markdowns as per cent of sales		Initial margin	
	1998	**1990**	**1998**	**1990**
Women's clothing	38.5	30.8	53.2	53.3
Infants and children's clothing	31.4	26.4	52.1	52.4
Men's and boys' wear	30.3	25.7	53.5	53.2
Footwear	31.9	23.3	51.0	52.0
Leisure and home electronics	19.3	13.5	45.9	47.3
Home furnishings	20.5	16.7	48.4	47.0

Source: arbitrary data compiled for the purpose of text explanation.

Table 13.2 shows typical markdowns for different categories of merchandise carried by department stores. But as retailers in other sectors have relied more and more on price as a competitive weapon, so they have used more markdowns.

Markdown calculations

Retailers can calculate markdowns both in terms of monetary value and as percentages. For the purpose of planning markdowns and evaluating merchandise performance, retailers express markdowns as percentages of net sales:

$$\text{Markdown percentage (of net sales)} = \frac{\text{Amount of net markdown} \times 100}{\text{net sales}}$$

Causes of markdowns

Markdowns fall into two categories, clearance and promotional. Initial prices are really only estimates of what customers will pay for the merchandise, and if experience proves that the original estimate is too high markdowns are necessary. A markdown does not necessarily indicate that the original asking price was wrong, or that the store buyer was at fault. It may be that:

- The cost prices have declined, so competitors who bought later have lower costs for the merchandise and are charging lower prices.

- Newer, more stylish or more acceptable products have come on the market since the goods being marked down were purchased.

- The goods have become worn out.

- The product is reduced in price to provide attractive promotional or sale appeal.

Retailers of seasonal goods often find that they must mark down the stocks of those goods remaining at or near the end of the season.

Exhibit 13.6   Markdown calculation

Suppose a store bought 100 T-shirts at the beginning of a season and sold 80 per cent of the stock at its original price of £50 each. The store then reduced the prices of the remaining T-shirts to £30 and sold them all. The problem is how the retailer will calculate the markdown percentage. Since it sold 80 T-shirts at £50 each and 20 at £30 each, its net sales revenue is £4600. The markdown amount is £400, since it marked 20 T-shirts down by £20 each. Thus:

Markdown percentage = (£400 ÷ £4600) × 100 = 8.69%

Markdown per cent per T shirt (off original retail price)

$$= \frac{\text{Price reduction per unit} \times 100}{\text{Original price/unit}}$$

= (£20 ÷ £50) × 100 = 40%

For advertising purposes retailers will compute markdowns based on original retail prices: the store's advertisement will announce a 40 per cent price reduction on the T-shirt, where it was sold and the length of time it was sold at the higher price. This is how much customers actually save compared with the original price.

Promotional markdowns result from a policy of deliberately purchasing more items than the store expects to sell at full price in order to have a good assortment on hand throughout the selling season. Often the retailer is not sure which particular items in a shipment of fashion goods will sell well, and consequently may decide to place a high margin on the products, possibly with the suppliers' assistance with a low cost to avoid reducing the maintained margin, and later use a markdown to clear out those that remain. Promotional markdowns are undertaken to draw shopper traffic, and are a normal competitive device, particularly for stores that follow a policy of trying to operate below the market average price.

Of course retailers must also avoid taking more markdowns than needed to accomplish merchandising and competitive objectives. A survey of men's clothing stores (Davies and Brooks, 1989) found that the most profitable stores had only an average initial markup, but suffered less than average markdowns.

Timing of markdowns

Retailers disagree as to the best time to make markdowns: some will delay them in the hope of additional sales at the original prices. Others only make markdowns during the three large sale events during the summer, Easter and Christmas/New Year periods. These yearly clearance sales become established in the minds of money-conscious shoppers and serve to unload shelves of the least desirable products. Exclusive stores, for instance Selfridges or Harrods, may delay markdowns to preserve the store image.

The advantages of early-season markdowns (Exhibit 13.7) are to:

■ make room for a steady flow of new products to the store and to keep stocks fresh;

> **Exhibit 13.7   Early markdown policy**
>
> This policy can be found in the basement store of African Textile Limited in Manchester, where all merchandise that remains unsold after six selling months is repriced at 60 per cent of its original price; and after 12 selling months at 40 per cent. At United African Company (UAC), the main UK supplier of African textiles, fabrics that could not be sold within six months of production are exported to Africa and Asia at considerably reduced prices. This policy has given the UAC a large, loyal following among African fabric retailers. Other stores that have tried similar methods have not pursued them vigorously and have not been as successful. In general, UK retailers want more flexibility than the automatic markdown plan provides.

- reduce the size of the markdowns needed to move the merchandise, since some products will lose more of their appeal as time goes on; and

- avoid the cost of special sales promotion.

Aggressive retailers may disagree about markdown policies for seasonal merchandise of a staple nature: toys not sold this Christmas may be sold next year, or computer games not moving this spring may find buyers next spring. Holding the products may be profitable if the retailer has available space. However, this practice (see Grewal *et al.*, 1996):

- ties up capital;
- involves storage costs;
- involves employees spending time packing the goods away; and
- is likely to cause some breakages.

In view of these disadvantages, it is often better to sell the goods out if this can be accomplished by means of a moderate reduction.

Size of markdowns

It is obvious that markdowns vary widely from one product line to another. To be effective, a markdown must be large enough to induce shoppers to buy the product, and the retail tradition that 'the first markdown is the least costly' is still true. The retailer must take into account not only tangible factors, such as quantity of merchandise on hand and rate of sale, but also such intangibles as how competitors will respond to a price cut and how shoppers who bought at the higher price will react. The retailer and the selling effort made by sales staff also relate the size of the markdown necessary to sell the merchandise involved to the scale of promotional activity.

PRICING STRATEGIES

The pricing policies established by the retail organisation must be integrated into the retailer's marketing position. Pricing should be consistent with the other parts of the retailer's marketing mix, including its merchandise, advertising and services. If image and price are not coordinated shoppers are likely to be confused, leading to lost sales. Inconsistency in pricing and store image may cause shoppers to doubt that the retailer is following a low-price policy, even if it actually charges less than the competition. Similarly, if it also differs from competing stores by providing more services, having more modern fixtures and giving discounts. A retailer who plans to charge relatively high prices will have to offer the atmosphere, merchandise, convenience and services that will make those prices acceptable to potential customers. This requires a decision about which services will be subject to extra charge and which ones will be included in the price of the merchandise.

Strategically, the retailer should create prices that are aligned with longer-term company decisions and that are concerned with competing through fundamental cost and differentiation positions. Exclusive stores and stores clearly differentiated from their competitors will be more able to sell at higher prices than those that have failed to create a sustained distinctiveness. At the other extreme, retailers may compete on low or lowest price strategies, and a retailer may plan to sell at very low prices for the first few months upon commencing a business in order to build up trade. Short-term earnings will suffer as a result of this policy, but as a *tactic* it may attract enough shoppers and build deficient repeat business to maximise profits in the long term.

Pricing Below Competitors and Discounting

Some retailers go beyond simply meeting competitors' prices and aim to price below them. Many supermarkets and discount retailers, among others, believe in seeking their profits through the use of relatively low prices to attract a large volume of sales. Low-price retailers usually have certain characteristics defined as:

1 They are 'hard' buyers, since they must acquire their merchandise at low cost to permit the profitable use of low prices.

2 They often operate with relatively low-cost physical facilities and they may dispense with many services that other stores offer.

3 They frequently limit their stocks to fast-moving items; they often use self-service or semi-self-service techniques; and credit and delivery services may be either curtailed or eliminated (Clodfelter, 1998).

Retailers who adopt a low-price policy must use consistent policies in the other aspects of their business. Those who do not will soon find themselves out of business or may drive away their customers to other competing stores. Some of these firms are now 'trading up' and offering more elaborate facilities and services, but others have been able to keep their operating costs at relatively low levels.

Discount stores that set prices consistently below competitors are normally limited in the variety of goods they can carry and services they offer. In the food sector, retailers including Lidl, Netto and Aldi are often strong advocates of own-label brands whose prices cannot be directly compared with competitors' offerings; and they generally devote their advertising to announcing price specials. In the clothing sector discounters buy surplus production stock and clearance lines that can include branded merchandise at very low cost to sell in volume. Consequently discount stores can cover their expenses on operating margins as low as 1% and prices that range from 5–15 per cent lower than many of their competitors.

Pricing above Competitors

Other retailers regularly sell some or all of their merchandise at prices above their competitors, an approach usually adopted by prestige and luxury stores such as Harrods and Selfridges. Retailers who follow this policy recognize that many non-price considerations, such as those outlined below, may attract customers to their stores. These retailers can often operate their businesses successfully in spite of charging higher prices, providing they offer a range of additional features, and experiences such as satisfactory services, prestige, convenient location, extended store hours, and exclusive merchandise and products of such a prestigious nature that are not generally stocked anywhere else.

Shoppers will pay a premium, too, to be able to shop at a convenient location and at accessible times through extended opening hours (see also Exhibit 13.8). Local grocery, CTNs, chemist and domestic equipment stores tend to have higher prices than more distant superstores and discount stores. A chemist or gift-shop in an airport terminal, a fast-food stall at a football stadium, or a store in an isolated community may have a virtually captive market because of its location, and thus be able to charge unusually high prices.

Brands and Own-Brand Pricing Policies

Since manufacturer's brands usually cost more than own-labels because of the extensive advertising and other marketing expenses borne by manufacturers, retailers can sell own-labels for less. The savings are passed along to shoppers in the form of lower prices, with the retailer still making the desired profit. Most retailers in their effort to give shoppers a variety of choice stock both national and own-label brands.

Retailers gain a certain amount of freedom from direct competition by offering own-label brands instead of manufacturers' 'national' brands. In the United Kingdom,

---

Exhibit 13.8 Premium pricing

Some department stores such as Harrods and Selfridges offer a higher level of customer services than other department stores appealing to a broader market such as Debenhams and House of Fraser. Consequently, Harrods and Selfridges can charge higher prices without losing too much custom to lower-priced retailers. Similarly, Omar (1997) suggested that small retail stores are more likely to build profitable trade with such service elements as speed of service, satisfaction of customer complaints, management's and employees' knowledge about their merchandise, and a helpful and friendly attitude of employees towards shoppers than by offering low prices.

Marks & Spencer is a typical example of a retailer selling only own-label brands in preference to manufacturers' national brands. Shoppers cannot compare the values of two different own-label brands sold by two different retailers with anywhere near the precision that is possible in comparing the same two retailers' prices for a specific national brand product. Marks & Spencer's prestige stores are able to command high prices for own-label brands, particularly through a policy of product innovation and added value.

In general, [...] ic appliances, clothing, and simi [...] comparable national
brands. With [...] d authenticates the
product so th [...] mer and the price is
unlikely to b [...] 97). Moreover, larger
brands have [...] tend to move in line
with change [...] en competing brands
are very sim [...]

Low price [...] competitors outlets,
help build s [...] chandise usually costs
retailers sut [...] nd consequently they
often receiv [...] n spite of their lower
selling pric [...] s own brand of paper
towels (No [...] arable national brands.
In doing tl [...] kup compared to 10 or
12 per cent on national [...]

Everyday Low Pricing (EDLP)

An EDLP strategy requires retailers to aim for low prices all the time. The objective is to assure buyers that they need not wait for a sale or promotion to achieve an attractive price across the range of products they want to buy. With this strategy retailers assume that consumers are attracted by their focus on low priced products, rather than marketing initiatives. Major branded suppliers such as Proctor and Gamble have also followed this strategy, which to a certain extent resembles the no-frills pricing policies adopted by food retailers in response to discounters. Asda, for example, set itself a target of price reductions on 10 000 products during 2000 as part of its Rollback price cuts and EDLP campaign (Mintel, 2000).

McGoldrick argues that few retailers actually conduct EDLP, that factors such as competitor activity, consumer confidence and not least the weather create unpredictable factors in stock clearance (McGoldrick *et al.*, 2000, and Table 13.3). Moreover, only low-cost retailers can maintain low and stable prices, a strategy affordable only by a few. Pricing strategies are not necessarily followed consistently, and there is evidence of retailers customising their pricing strategies and tactics to suit market conditions, categories and brands rather than taking a single position on EDLP/high–low pricing. Price consistency has been shown to form just one decision alongside promotion intensity, price/promotion coordination and relative brand pricing within a category.

Table 13.3   *Relative Merits of EDLP and high–low pricing*

EDLP advantages	High–low advantages
■ Reduce price wars ■ Reduced promotional advertising ■ More efficient use of store personnel ■ Improved inventory management ■ Increased profit margins ■ The retailer can concentrate on being a seller rather than a deal buyer ■ More consumer appeal: price perceived as more honest ■ Less buyer time spent managing 'sale' events and more time merchandising the entire line	■ Price discrimination: merchandise appeals to multiple market segments ■ Creates excitement ■ All merchandise can be sold eventually ■ Price confusion reduces awareness of prices ■ High initial prices guide customers' judgements of product and store quality ■ EDLP can be very difficult to maintain

Source: McGoldrick *et al.* (2000).

High–Low Pricing

A High–low pricing strategy gives an opportunity to improve profit margins by selling to non-price-sensitive consumers at higher margins and also enabling high margins to be maintained on less significant lines. Low prices are appropriate on lines that are known to be price sensitive or which are easy to compare, for example promotions, 'real' bargains and comparison prices on easy-to-compare lines. High–low policies are also necessary for stores to develop own-label products, they provide more flexibility to compete across the country and are more compatible with a higher quality perception (Corstjens and Corstjens, 1995).

E-Retail Pricing

E-commerce has the potential to create a perfect competitive market through low search costs, strong price reactions, low margins and weak market power (Tang and Xing, 2001). Pricing efficiency should result from trading online, and studies of the early development of online retailing have shown that e-retailers tend to consistently price below conventional retailers. However, multi-channel retailers using both the Internet and physical outlets need to manage consistency between pricing online and through their physical stores. If these retailers, rather than 'pure' e-tailers come to dominate web-based retailing, their pricing policies, reflecting their costs and promotional programmes, could erode the web's price advantage (*ibid.*).

A One-Price Policy

Most British retailers follow a one-price policy, that is, to charge the same price to everyone who buys the same item in comparable quantities under similar conditions. Of course, a one-price policy does not stop a store from having clearance sales or special sales promotions, but it is important to note that major multiple retailers and retailers with multiple brand chains may well price differently in towns across the UK where circumstances dictate this necessity or across different store brand names within the group as a whole.

Multiple food retailers are a good example of differential pricing of a similar good across different store brands. This policy builds up customer confidence, helps to set up a sales routine for every transaction, and therefore facilitates large-scale operations; however, with the implementation of powerful information systems by multiple retailers the opportunity to match pricing to local conditions is enhanced.

Variable Pricing

Some stores allow discounts to their employees on the merchandise they buy. Occasionally, a retailer may set up a special discount arrangement for a particular group, such as members of a sports club or workers in a nearby factory, in the expectation of obtaining a large share of their purchases. Such systematic discounts affect only a very small portion of all retail sales. Individual bargaining over 'trade-in allowances', a very common practice in the sale of cars for example, is a more important deviation from the one-price system. Bargaining and haggling often occur in the sale of durable goods, particularly in the marketing of cars and domestic/office furniture. Some small to medium-sized retailers dealing in other non-convenience goods will also occasionally lower or cut prices or give the customer a discount in order to close a difficult sale.

Price Ranges

Another policy decision, closely related to merchandising decisions, concerns the range of prices in the store. The width of the price range will be determined by the retail sector and market position, but attempts to cover too extensive a range, a 'something for everyone' approach from relatively inexpensive merchandise to luxury high-priced products, will result in a confused store image. As a result, most retailers will tend to concentrate on a limited price/quality policy.

Exhibit 13.9 Price level and profit maximization

A UK electrical retailer followed a high-price policy and consequently only attracted those customers who found his location or merchandise especially appealing. His total annual volume was £400 000, merchandise costs £280 000, operating expenses £104 000, leaving £16 000 as net profit. But the retailer decided to experiment with lower prices, which attracted trade and gradually increased sales to £600 000 a year. Since the store received greater discounts on its larger purchases, merchandise costs expanded at a somewhat lower rate than sales, becoming £390 000 and leaving a gross margin of £210 000. Although some expenses also increased as a result of the added sales, others such as rent, heat, light and power remained relatively unchanged. The present employees handled part of the additional work, so wages increased at a lower rate than sales. Consequently, operating expenses only rose to £150 000. Thus in spite of selling at lower prices, the retailer's profit increased from £16 000 to £60 000.

The narrowest possible price range is called a single-price policy. Under this policy a store sells all of its merchandise of a given type at the same price. This approach is usually only suitable for stores with inexpensive merchandise.

Price Lining

Price lining consists of selecting certain prices and carrying assortments of merchandise only at those prices, except when markdowns are taken into consideration. For example, men's ties may be carried at £2.99, £3.99 and £5.00; and women's dresses at £22.99, £29.99 and £39.99. The reasons for price lining may be given as the desire by shoppers for a wide assortment when buying goods (to which price lining is especially applicable), but their becoming confused by small price differences among the various items. Confining the assortments to certain specific points reduces the confusion. Having only few price points helps salespeople become well-acquainted with their prices and reduces mistakes. This facilitates selling and improves customer goodwill. Price lining may:

■ reduce the size of the store's inventory,

■ increase turnover,

■ decrease markdowns,

■ simplify stock control

■ reduce interest and storage costs, and

■ enables the store's buyer to concentrate on items that can be sold profitably at the preset price level.

Price lines are usually established through a careful analysis of past sales, picking out those prices at which the bulk of the sales were made. In some cases, however, past sales are disregarded; the retailer simply selects new price lines which the sales staff are then expected to 'push'. Although the number of price lines needed will vary in different situations, a retailer will usually want at least one below and one above the basic medium-price lines. Next, a popular-priced woman's-wear chain, however, has used four price lines. Other large stores may find that they need six or more price lines for such merchandise as hosiery to satisfy customers' requirements.

Some of the advantages of price lining are lost if the price lines are not far enough apart to indicate definite differences in quality, otherwise the customer will still be confused with several goods selling at fairly comparable prices. The retailer should have full assortments at each price line to serve shoppers attracted by that line. Retailers frequently check competitors' price lines to make sure that they have not found ones with greater customer appeal. The chief executive of Asda has expressed the need for constant reappraisal of price lines noting that the price-line picture can seldom be considered static; testing and checking are always helpful – above and below and in-between the established price lines.

Limitations of Price Lining

Price lining does reduce the buyer's range of alternatives in selecting goods for the store; the buyer must secure merchandise that will provide a profit when sold at the store's established price lines. This requirement can increase the difficulty of obtaining adequate assortments and more than offset whatever advantages result from only having to consider those items that fit the store's price lines. Price lining also limits the store's ability to meet competitive prices. Some other disadvantages include:

- The danger that the price lines selected will not be suited to the preferences of customers and prospective customers;

- The difficulty, already noted, of maintaining price lines and uniform quality during periods of change in price levels;

- The likelihood that price lines will multiply over a period of time; and

- The tendency to focus attention on price lining's advantages has resulted in widespread use of the practice in selling apparel and other shopping goods.

It is not as useful, however, in selling staples such as foods and toiletries, where shoppers generally do not want to compare an assortment of styles, colours or sizes at one price.

Odd Pricing

Retail prices are set just below a rounded selling price, typically ending in 9; for example £1.99 rather than £2.00. One view on the origins of this practice was operational; that each sale obliged the sales assistant to provide change from the till, which was recordable, rather than divert the money into their own pocket (Berman and Evans, 1998). However, there is a clear psychological element, too, by creating the perception of a lower price. Stiving and Winer (1997) summarise why price thresholds might exist, in a classification of the effects of price endings:

- Price Level effects: consumers underestimate prices.
- Consumers round prices down.
- Consumers compare prices from left to right.
- Consumers have limited memory capacity.
- Image effects: consumers infer meaning from the last digit of a price.
- Price-image effect: consumers view 9-ending prices as a signal of a price discount.
- Quality-image effect: consumers view 9-ending prices as a signal of inferior quality.

Studies based on actual purchases have been inconclusive. While prices ending in 9 cause a sharp increase in sales in some cases, they do not in others, with results differing within and across product categories. However, price endings have important implications for European retailers with the introduction of the euro. Retailers should continue to assume that price thresholds exist at small intervals unless they expect strong quality–image problems with price endings (Gedenk and Sattler, 1999).

Table 13.4   *Conditions Determining Price-level Strategies*

	Retailer pricing strategy		
	Below competitors	**Market level**	**Above competitors**
Low competition			
High-level product importance	−	+	+
Urgent needs	−	+	+
Easy to satisfy wants	−	+	+
Reasonable prices	−	+	−
Weak economy	−	+	−
High competition			
Low-level product importance	+	+	−
Not urgent needs	+	+	−
Wants not easy to satisfy	+	−	−
Prices too high	+	−	−
Strong economy	+	−	−

Effects of General Price-Level Changes

As shown in Table 13.4, the conditions dictating price-level strategies show that retailers face difficult problems in maintaining price lines when prices in general are changing markedly. Normally prices rise during periods of prosperity when most shoppers are willing to accept new and higher price lines if the retailer cannot secure satisfactory merchandise to sell at the old price levels. However, during depressed periods, or under intense competition when customers want to 'trade down' to lower price points, suppliers will come under pressure to reduce costs or retailers will switch to alternative sources.

SUMMARY

Pricing remains a critical element in a retail marketing mix; and is especially challenging to retailers in markets characterised by intensive competition. In setting the price of a product and/or service, the retailer follows a staged procedure:

1 The establishment of retail marketing objectives;

2 The determination of demand, which shows the purchase level per period at various price levels;

3 The estimate of costs;

4 The estimate of competitors' prices as a base for positioning own price;

5 The selection of suitable pricing methods; and

6 The eventual selection of a final price for the product.

Retailers normally adapt their price to varying economic conditions in the marketplace. These factors may include geographical pricing – where retailers price the product to suit distinct market segments; price discounts and allowances; promotional pricing; and discriminating pricing. When a retailer considers initiating a price change, he must carefully consider customers' and competitors' reactions to the changes in price. Shoppers' reactions are normally influenced by the meaning they see in the price change. Competitors' reactions flow from either a set reaction policy or a fresh appeal of each situation. A retailer considering changing his price must also anticipate the probable reaction of suppliers, and the government. If a retailer could help it, price changes should be minimal, as shoppers are usually confused when prices are changed very frequently.

Finally, the process of adjusting prices involves constant attempts to forecast results and such predictions are often inaccurate. Amongst other things, the retailer must estimate the effect on turnover of a certain price reduction, the effect on cost if sales increase, and how markdowns will be affected by a higher or lower initial markup. All of these forecasts are subject to correction when the price change is actually implemented. In other words, trial-and-error adjustments are necessary. If a certain reduction in gross margin does not bring the expected increase in sales, the retailer should try some other reduction; correct retail pricing involves a willingness to experiment. The retailer who tries to simplify pricing by the mechanistic use of a single markup will usually lose out to more aggressive retailers.

QUESTIONS

1 The best way to price a product is to add a fixed markup to the cost of the good. Comment on this statement.

2 Explain the meaning of price from the point of view of both the retailer and the shopper.

3 Explain whether or not it is possible to undertake practical pricing upon the basis and analysis of supply and demand.

4 Explain the term price elasticity. By how much will the demand for an item change when its price falls by 10 per cent, if its price elasticity is 1.8?

5 Explain what is meant by the terms 'initial mark-up' and 'maintained mark-up'.

6 What are the advantages and disadvantages of taking a markdown early in the season?

7 Justify the situation where major food retailers may cut prices or set low food prices to discourage competitors.

8 Discuss why there may be differences in price between own-label brands and national brands.

9 Why must the pricing policy appeals to shoppers?

10 When prices are reduced, shoppers must be informed appropriately. Why do you think this is a necessity?

Case Study

Supermarkets put 160 per cent Premiums on 'Green' Groceries

Supermarkets are charging premiums of up to 169 per cent for organic foods while more and more consumers are looking for chemical-free produce in the wake of the health scare about salmonella, bovine spongiform encephalopathy (BSE, commonly known as mad-cow disease) and genetically-modified food. Organic farmers fear they will suffer if prices are fixed by grocery retailers at an unreasonable level. Farmers argue that an average premium of 30 per cent is justifiable because it reflects the true increased cost of production.

Supermarkets deny cashing in on the food safety scare, but several have reported that demand for 'natural', chemical-free food doubled in the wake of adverse publicity about genetically modified foods. The *Observer* survey of food on sale (March 1999) at four leading supermarkets including Tesco, Sainsbury, Safeway and Waitrose showed a huge difference in the premiums they charge (see Table 13.5). Sainsbury and Waitrose, which have the most extensive range of organic foods, have the lowest mark-ups with the overall difference between their organic and conventional baskets 37 per cent and 41 per cent lower than

their competitors respectively. But within these averages were some very high premiums with price differences of 72 per cent on sugar, 91 per cent on milk and 86 per cent on apples. Organic carrots were twice the price of non-organic, and an organic chicken had a markup of 169 per cent.

Several supermarkets' agronomists have observed that the high premiums on milk are because non-organic milk has become much cheaper, but they admitted that many consumers would be 'put off by the prices'. On the other hand, they have argued that there was 'a huge shortage' of organic milk and other fresh produce and that growing consumer demand drove prices up. The marketing and production policies to encourage organic farmers that are already in place are expected to increase volumes.

The Soil Association, and the farmers who supply the leading supermarkets, accepted that shortages were a serious concern for the embryonic organic-food industry, but they recognised that the premiums on supermarket bread were not justified. Organic bread at Safeway was more than double an almost

Table 13.5

The Organic Premium

	Organic (£)	Non-organic (£)	Difference (£)
Carrots (per kg)	1.67	0.93	0.74
Apples (per kg)	2.60	1.47	1.13
Bread (loaf, own brand, 800 g)	1.08	0.65	0.43
Milk (pint of full-cream)	0.41	0.25	0.16
Oats (500 g)	0.62	0.43	0.19
Yoghurt (fruit, 450 g)	1.09	0.89	0.20

Note: Prices averaged from four supermarkets using directly comparable products.

Source: based on the *Observer*, 28 March 1998.

identical conventional variety. At Sainsbury the markup was 61 per cent. According to the farmers, the raw ingredients account for only 10 per cent of the loaf on the shelf. If it is the case that supermarkets are making excessive profits, then they should be exposed. But their retail business activities regarding the retailing of organic foods need to be carefully examined for proper retail price adjustment. The retail market information source revealed that Tesco, the market leader, in particular denied that it was ripping off farmers at one end of the chain and consumers at the other. Tesco was quoted as saying that its buyers usually pay 200 per cent more for organic carrots than for conventional ones, so the premium of 100 per cent on the shelf is not extreme.

The head of the Organic Farm Foods Co-op in the Welsh Borders, who supplies apples to several British supermarkets, was reported as being 'flabbergasted' by the prices being charged by these supermarkets, especially the £2.83 per kilo at Waitrose. A retail market analyst suggested that there was little justification for huge differentials on dairy, beef or lamb products. The price gaps on organic and non-organic baskets at Safeway and Tesco were similarly high at 87 per cent and 83 per cent respectively. The Consumers' Association said the Monopolies and Mergers Commission should include organic food prices in the investigation of the supermarket sector recommended in February 1999 by the Office of Fair Trading.

SEMINAR QUESTIONS FOR DISCUSSION

1 Express your opinion on whether or not a premium price on organic food is justified.

2 Write an essay justifying the intervention of the Office of Fair Trading (OFT) in adjusting retail prices for organic food products in supermarkets. Why do you think the OFT should get involved?

References

Baker, M.J. (1993) *The Marketing Book*, 2nd edn (Oxford: CIM/Butterworth-Heinemann).

Berman, B. and Evans, J.R. (1998) *Retail Management: A Strategic Approach* (Englewood Cliffs, NJ: Prentice Hall).

Bartholomew, D. (1992) 'The Price Wrong', *Information Week*, 14 September, pp. 26–36.

Clodfelter, G.R. (1998) 'Pricing Accuracy at Grocery Stores and Other Retail Stores Using Scanners', *International Journal of Retail & Distribution Management*, vol. 26, no. 11, 412–20.

Clodfelter, R. (1997) 'Pricing Accuracy at Non-Food Retail Stores Using UPC Scanners: a Preliminary Study', in R.L. King (ed.), *Retailing: End of a Century and a Look to the Future*, vol. 8 (Richmond: Academy of Marketing Sciences).

Corstjens, J. and Corstjens, M. (1995) *Store Wars: the Battle for Mindspace* (Chichester: John Wiley & Sons).

Davies, G. and Brooks, J.M. (1989) *Positioning Strategy in Retailing* (London: Paul Chapman).

Dickson, P.R. and Sawyer, A.G. (1990) 'The Price Knowledge and Search of Supermarket Shoppers', *Journal of Marketing*, vol. 54, July, pp. 42–53.

East, R. (1997) *Consumer Behaviour: Advances and Applications in Marketing* (London: Prentice Hall).

Ehrenberg, A.S.C. (1988) *Repeat-Buying: Facts, Theory and Applications* (London: Charles Griffin).

Elliott, F. and Rider, J. (2000) *Retail Buying Techniques* (London: Management Books).

Folkes, V. and Wheat, R.D. (1995) 'Consumers' Price Perceptions of Promoted Products', *Journal of Retailing*, vol. 3, no. 71, pp. 317–28.

Garland, R. (1992) 'Pricing Errors in the Supermarket: Who Pays?', *International Journal of Retail & Distribution Management*, no. 20, vol. 1, pp. 25–30.

Garry, M. (1993) 'Scanners: Error Control', *Progressive Grocer*, June, 105–8.

Gedenk, K. and Sattler, H. (1999) 'The Impact of Price Thresholds on Profit Contribution – Should Retailers Set 9-Ending Prices?', *Journal of Retailing*, Spring vol. 75, no. 2, p. 33.

Ghosh, A. (1994) *Retail Management*, 2nd edn (New York: The Dryden Press).

Gourville, J.T. (1998) 'Pennies-a-Day: the Effect of Temporal Reframing on Transaction Evaluation', *Journal of Consumer Research*, vol. 24, March, pp. 395–408.

Grewal, D., Mamonstein, H. and Sharma, A. (1996) 'Communicating Price Information Through Semantic Cues: The Moderating Effects of Situation and Discount Size', *Journal of Consumer*, vol. 23, September, pp. 148–55.

Harris, B.F. and Mills, M.K. (1982) 'The Impact of Item Price Removal in Scanner Suppermarkets', *Journal of Consumer Affairs*, vol. 16, no. 2, pp. 362–83.

Inman, J.J., Peter, A.C. and Raghubir, P. (1997) 'Framing the Deal: the Role of Restrictions in Accentuating Deal Value', *Journal of Consumer Research*, vol. 24 no. 1, pp. 68–79.

Kotler, P. (1997) *Marketing Management: Analysis, Planning, Implementation, and Control*, 9th edn (Englewood Cliffs, NJ: Prentice-Hall).

Langrehr, F.W. and Langrehr, V.B. (1983) 'Consumer Acceptance of Item Price Removal: a Survey Study of Milwaukee Shoppers', *Journal of Consumer Affairs*, vol. 17, Summer, pp. 149–71.

Litvack, D.S., Calantone, R.J. and Warshaw, P.R. (1985) 'An Examination of Short-Term Retail Grocery Price Effects', *Journal of Retailing*, vol. 61, no. 3, pp. 9–25.

McGoldrick, P.J., Betts, E.J. and Keeling, K.A. (1990) *Retail Marketing* (Maidenhead: McGraw-Hill).

Omar, O.E. (1997) '*Target Pricing: a Marketing Management Tool for Pricing New Cars*', *Pricing Strategy & Practice*, vol. 5, no. 2, pp. 61–9.

Omar, O. (1999) *Retail Marketing* (London: Financial Times/Pitman Publishing).

Russo, J.E. (1977) 'The Value of Unit Price Information', *Journal of Marketing Research*, vol. 14 May, pp. 193–201.

Sethuraman, R. and Tellis, G.J. (1991) 'An Analysis of the Tradeoff Between Advertising and Price Discounting', *Journal of Marketing Research*, vol. 28 May, pp. 160–74.

Simon, H. (1992) 'Pricing Opportunities – and How to Exploit Them', Sloan Management Review, vol. 33, no. 2, pp. 55–65.

Smith, M.F. and Sinha I. (2000) 'The Impact of Price and Extra Product Promotions on Store Preference', *International Journal of Retail & Distribution Management*, vol. 28, no. 2, pp. 83–92.

Stiving, M. and Winer, R.S. (1997) 'An Empirical Analysis of Price Endings Using Scanner Data', *Journal of Consumer Research*, vol. 24, pp. 57–67.

Tang, F.-F. and Xing, X. (2001) 'Will the Growth of Multi-Channel Retailing Diminish the Pricing Efficiency of the Web?' *Journal of Retailing* Fall vol. 73, no. 3, pp. 319–34.

Welch, J.L. and Massey, T.K. (1988) 'Consumer Cost Implications of Reducing Item Omission Errors in Retail Optical Scanner Environments', *Akron Business and Economic Review*, vol. 19, Summer, pp. 97–105.

PART FOUR

Operational Management

This part moves into the area of operational activities focused on the store itself. Chapter 14 introduces retail design from a number of perspectives, both managerial and design-led, to place the process of design and the store environment in context. The practical elements of display and visual merchandising form the second and more detailed part of this chapter. Chapter 15 examines the role of retail communications and the use of advertising and promotion through different media including store-based activities. The final chapter in this section, Chapter 16, develops the theme of customer service and the ways in which retailers understand and use service to attract and retain customers.

Store Design

INTRODUCTION

Retail design is concerned with the environments in which people shop: 'design is a means of communicating a message to people, and "good design" . . . must be a comprehensive and co-ordinated approach to everything the shopper sees' (Michell, 1986). It should add value to retail strategy by improving the quality of the shopping environment and by influencing consumer decision-making and loyalty. The visual identity of the retailer, its image and distinctive branding is fundamentally created by design. Design should be practical, too, in searching for and providing solutions to practical consumer needs, and it has an important role in profit maximisation through the efficient use of materials and space.

DEVELOPMENT OF STORE DESIGN

The appearance of today's stores owes much to the past application of design solutions to the needs of retailers as they arose; from department stores to self-service supermarkets and lifestyle clothing retailers. The retail designer draws from both historical contexts and contemporary sources, for inspiration and materials, to create innovative store concepts. In the nineteenth century new types of store architecture, the development of advertising, and improvements in window display stimulated competition and transformed the street scene. Improvements in glass manufacture led to uninterrupted windows, and the provision of gas and electricity as well as new display techniques brought a modern appearance to the main shopping streets. Electric lights extended the use of interior space, enabling every corner of the store to be used for the first time. In the 1920s the application of neon lighting created new levels of visibility for signage which we take for granted today.

The opportunity to create more interesting and attractive windows was enhanced by the development of display materials and equipment; from the 1880s onwards, for example, mannequins became available to display women's clothing. The importance of being modern and progressive led to an emphasis on the appearance of the premises. Shopfronts were designed to allow the maximum display of goods to act as 'silent salesmen'. Grocery stores created more organised displays, and butchers turned their attention to more hygienic storage and presentation, even if there was still a tendency for new shopkeepers to pack their displays with as much stock as possible. The arrival of sales advertising in the 1890s added a new graphics-led dimension to store branding, enabling retailers to create demand through newspaper advertisements (Adburgham, 1964).

Department Stores

Department stores have been a source for creative design for well over a century. Many originated as drapers and retained a strong bias to clothing; others such as Harrods started out as grocery businesses. Scarcity and the expense of city land obliged retailers to expand upwards, which led to the provision of lifts, elevators, modern lighting and heating as well as an opportunity for elaborately designed frontages. Barker of Kensington created a 'splendid new shop', with plate glass front, and three floors of rooms together with a lofty basement in 1870. Nearby, Derrys had 200 living-in assistants supplied with their own library. Seaman, Little and Co. introduced refinements such as lavatories, dressmaking rooms employing 90 people, and a kitchen on the top floor for the staff dining room. The store itself was handsome, with 'two broad solid oak staircases . . . a magnificent saloon, 200 feet by 40 feet, richly carpeted, ebonized and having walls lined with large glass showcases, relieved at intervals by glittering plate glass mirrors.' It also produced twice-yearly catalogues (Winstanley, 1983).

Later developments in the nineteenth century found retail design at its most formative. The 'aesthetic movement' created a new style at Libertys, in turn leading to an oriental craze in clothing and home furnishings so much so that Cavendish House,

---

Exhibit 14.1 The opening of Selfridges department store, London

Selfridges department store opened in 1909, with £100000 of stock and 1800 staff. It was unique in its design, having 21 windows in its facade which featured pictorial fashion tableaux. Gordon Selfridge had taken his ideas from Marshall Field in the USA, creating a palatial interior complete with a hidden string orchestra, banks of flowers in what was described as a 'final effect of opulence'. It provided unprecedented facilities, such as a Post Office and its own first-aid room. The overall aim was to make the shopper feel like a guest rather than a customer (Pound, 1960).

a department store in Cheltenham, had its own 'Liberty Department', an early example of a shop-in-shop concession.

Multiple Retailers

The extravagant experience of a department store visit was soon accompanied by the more modest experience of the multiple retailer. Developments in housing, transport and telephone communication enabled multiples in the UK such as Boots and Woolworths to substantially expand their businesses between 1918 and 1939. The main shopping streets in the UK came to be dominated by chains of shops (Evans, 1997). The variety in appearance of shopping areas was reduced, and a commonality of style asserted, through the combining of ownership and the conscious imagery of the expanding retail companies.

Modernity in architectural design led to simpler outlines and minimised motifs (Pevsner, 1974). The 'feeling for the pure cube', with facades of glass supported by minimal structures allowed more light and air to pass into the interior, but combined with the use of mass construction techniques created ever-more standardised approaches to the store design. Inside the store, design increasingly took on a functional role that extended well into the 1960s; its express purpose to create sales-driven environments. Many instore fixtures were sent from manufacturers expressly to promote their products (Offenhertz, 1968) and point of purchase displays were directly related to selling rather than complementing the store environment.

Design in the Grocery Sector

The arrival of self-service, first trialled in the UK by Sainsbury's in 1952, held fundamental implications for the interior design of stores. The disposition of space changed. Where the counter had formed a barrier behind which shop staff assisted customers in taking their orders, finding and retrieving the products, self-service required an altogether different approach. The design and layout had to facilitate customers in their search for goods, and sales checkouts had to be positioned near the exits. As supermarkets developed, aisles became wider and shelves lower. Frozen goods cabinets and chilled units were introduced in response to rising living standards, and an increase in the ownership of fridges and freezers. Following the abolition of resale price maintenance in 1964, UK grocery retailers led by Sainsbury's and Tesco accelerated the development of own-brand goods. The overall number of product lines increased from around 500 in 1950 to over 10 000 by 1990. This led to design initiatives in branding, packaging and presentation, as the need for product segmentation became more urgent.

Price had formed the mainstay of food retailer competition in the 1970s. However, with changes in lifestyle and distribution, price in the UK became less important than quality as a marketing objective. During the 1980s food retailers undertook a change in strategy to differentiate themselves through quality and service. Fresh food, particularly in fruit and vegetables, provided opportunities for changes in presentation and store layout. Delicatessen sectors were introduced in Sainsbury's in 1970 (Seth and Randall, 1999), and increasingly the larger grocery stores added instore bakeries, and recreated butchers and counters to add more personalisation to their service and create more enticing environments.

Lifestyle Retail Design

Elswewhere on the High Street, Conran's first Habitat shop in 1964 typified a new approach to store design, and with it a capacity to create a design-led, competitive advantage. The distinctive look of the store attracted customers by reflecting their personal aspirations towards a lifestyle. During the 1960s, clothing retailers in particular began targeting the 20–30-year-old age groups through fashionable boutiques, and the arrival of Laura Ashley added a new dimension of individualism to multiple retailing. By the 1980s store design was an integral part of successful multiple clothing retailers' strategies, leading the High Street towards both creative interiors and exteriors. Even W.H. Smith, a relatively conservative retailer, agreed that the future of 'the High Street is entertainment, [it's] fun, and retailers have to realise this. That's what the whole design thing is about' (Kay, 1987).

Design has enabled retailers to differentiate their brands and achieve distinctive market positioning; for some multiple retailers shops become the product itself, central to consumer communications. Where it is most fully embraced, retail design is an all encompassing style for the organisation and its customers (Harris and Walters, 1992). For some designers there is a sense of mission, a wider purpose in which the retail offer, both shop and products, can shape people's tastes, and good taste in Terence Conran's view at least could be acquired.

However, design has not been a central to all retail marketing strategies. It has been more significant among retailers competing for customers' wants rather than needs, where visual appearances matter as much as functionality. Whilst clothing stores and shopping centres attracted the most design attention, the other creations of the 1980s such as the retail warehouse and, collectively, retail parks were largely immune from these design trends. DIY, carpeting and electrical out-of-town retailing competed on cost, width of product range and accessibility to car-borne customers rather than lifestyle and image.

The Social Function of Retail Spaces

A traditional marketing-led approach will direct designers towards the functionality of shops, drawing on the theme of *selling* space, with its aim of creating profits and accumulating capital. As a result space is planned appropriately to maximise the opportunity using measurements of sales per square metre, merchandise department or product line. The concept of retail space as serving a more abstract *social* need has already been introduced in Chapter 7 in terms of retail locations. Here the concern is with the use and design of retail spaces in the store itself, and their extension into the wider shopping environment, typically the street, mall or centre. Such spaces are used for the consumption of products and services for different purposes. Shopping can be understood as a social activity in which consumption is for play or enjoyment. In this sense it is an important medium both for communication and interaction, and the synthesis of leisure and consumption.

Exhibit 14.2 The experience of Bluewater shopping centre

The Bluewater regional shopping mall in Kent opened in 1999 to critical acclaim. It stands out in a number of ways; at 139 530 square metres of retail space it is one of the largest out-of-town malls in the UK. It offers the widest range of catering in over 40 restaurants, bars and food halls, as well as entertainment from the 12 cinema screens. Parking should not be a problem either: there are 13 000 spaces in the car park.

The centre's innovative design is triangular with a department store at each corner. Each of the three malls has a different theme and associated leisure village. The south village has a media theme, the west village a civic square and the east village a winter garden, complete with children's grotto. The careful research which went into its design is evident in its real concern for its customers. It devotes very large spaces for movement and provides a welcome hall off each of three malls complete with hotel style information desks and seating.

In addition to its facilities, critics have appreciated the architecture, rooted in a vision of civic values, social beliefs, and customs. Arguably it is this approach which has raised shopping centre design to new standards. The three malls were given names that emphasise the Englishness of the place; The Rose Gallery, Guildhall and the Thames Walk represent the landscape, civic society and the position of Bluewater by the Thames estuary. Each mall is easily identified through its decoration; for example, the Thames Walk has a map of the Thames set in the floor. The walls are engraved with poetry from some of England's finest poets including Shakespeare and Kipling. Even the lettering is inspired by one of the foremost Renaissance architects, Alberti.

The design of the roof allows natural light and fresh air to enter the building and from the outside its angular shapes draw from the local tradition of oast house chimneys. Around 1 million shrubs and trees have been planted around the building and even in the car park, to create the effect of an orchard. Bluewater's designer, Eric Kuhne says it's all about 'restoring the pageantry of cities, aesthetically, but also in a deeper sense. For us architecture is narrative, a way a culture represents its belief in itself'.

Sources: *Guardian* 28/12/1998; Estates Gazette 27/2/1999; *Financial Times* 6/3/1999.

The influence of different products and information communicated to consumers may be profound; in food stores acceptance of exotic food varieties and organic foods reflect and perhaps even encourage social change. Gender, ideology and modern consumer culture too have their place in the creation of shopping space (Lowe and Wrigley, 1996). From another perspective, retail space can be understood as the location of a power struggle between its managers and consumers. On the one hand the confident shopper will be clearly aware of the temptations of the Shopping Mall to induce consumption, and is well-practiced in avoiding them by window shopping rather than purchasing. On the other hand, this view of the sovereign consumer contrasts with the view of the consumer as victim, in which retail space is organised by architects to persuade consumers to indulge in 'dwell time'.

The shopping environment itself reflects a diversity of forms. Different geographies of retailing, shopping malls, department stores and supermarkets offer different kinds of shopping experience and demand different kinds of knowledge. Miller (1998) has observed how the past 15 years in particular have seen new retail developments exploiting captured markets at airports and petrol station forecourts, taking consumption to the consumer through targeted shopping catalogues, as well as appealing to the 'leisured consumer' in Disney and Warner stores, and at football-club shops. In these ways, the designer is confronted by retail space in constant tension between producers, retailers and consumers.

The Experience of Retail Space

The consumer experience of shopping is a recent arrival in both economic and marketing literature, and marks a stage in the progression beyond the 'features and benefits' stage in the marketing of goods and services (Pine and Gilmour, 1998). Revolutions in information, branding and communication place customer experiences and consumption as central to the solution of marketing problems (Schmitt, 1999). Memorable sensory experiences engage customers and tie them in with the positioning of the company and its products and services. These perspectives impact on the use of retail space. Changes in lifestyle, consumption and retail structures have led to the emergence of the role of entertainment and leisure in retailing, in which the concepts of retail as entertainment and 'retail theatre', will become more prevalent as retailers compete to attract shoppers into their stores in the face of new ways to shop and alternative uses for shopping time.

Increasingly people want to enjoy the *experience* over the *transaction* of shopping, and in many new shopping malls such as the Bluewater Park shopping centre the experience is one of leisure as much as retailing. It recurs as a deliberate theme for some stores, and is essential to concepts such as the Rainforest Café. In order to be interactive and fun, retail space becomes a stage; the show draws in customers and allows the retailer to charge a premium price for what may be commodity products or services. Visual merchandising is fundamental to the store's operation. In this type of environment the designer must create customer 'clues' to draw the customer into a more fulfilling experience (Carbone, 1999). Other influences may be found beyond

---

Exhibit 14.3   The Mall of America

The Mall of America is a national tourism destination, achieving over 100 million visits in its first three years. In part, this is due to its location next to the international airport and 10 minutes drive from the centre of downtown Minneapolis and St Paul. However, as the largest shopping centre in the USA, it offers a unique blend of entertainment, food and retail, progressively updated by the addition of new attractions. Built on three levels, the Mall forms a huge square with the world's largest indoor amusement park in the centre. Each side creates a unique street measuring half a mile with a department store anchoring the corners. On this scale – there are over 400 stores – an important design consideration has been the provision of comfortable places to sit, places to take care of children, and other areas in which to enjoy the activities. Apart from shopping, the Mall offers entertainment in nine nightclubs, a wide variety of restaurants, and cinemas. Visitors can play virtual games, or spend time at the aquarium; it is even possible to get married there. The Mall of America consciously markets itself for business and social purposes by providing conference and banquet facilities that can accommodate groups from 10 up to 4000.

the physical environment. The impact of Internet shopping, and the increasing influence of interactive games design on web sites may encourage 'bricks and mortar' retailers to change the design of their stores to increase the leisure elements of the shopping experience.

Store Atmosphere

Quality of service in retail outlets encompasses both tangible and intangible elements. Understanding what they are and measuring their relative importance to the retailer is a significant element in customer satisfaction and creating loyalty. The transitory and subjective nature of concepts such as store ambience – how the shop feels to customers – are not easy to define, despite their importance. Consumer expectations of the shopping experience influence the levels of pleasure experienced (McGoldrick and Pieros, 1998). The psychological impact of 'the store's atmosphere creates a retail image in the shopper's mind', with the atmosphere influencing consumer behaviour in three ways, by creating attention, through messages and through an emotional, affective response (McGoldrick, 1990). This view draws on environmental psychology in which an individual's perceptions and behaviours are stimulated by an environment. Emotional responses, of pleasure and arousal, will lead to approach or avoidance behaviour to a store environment (Baker *et al.*, 1992).

The use of different senses in retail design contributes to distinctive selling environments. A characteristic of larger retail spaces, such as department stores and shopping malls, is the promotion of vision as the key sense. Colour is used to stimulate this sense and change the emotional state of the customer; warm colours such as reds and orange shades are used to excite, where more subdued shades have a calming effect. Levels of lighting have been shown to influence individual behaviour, with softer lighting creating more relaxed, pleasant moods than brighter lighting. Images are seen by the eye in many forms, as posters, in point-of-sale materials, in displays of products and their packaging, and signage. One consequence is that the consumer can become detached from the real world of real things. Spaces and places can take on their own properties rather than acting as a background to the products themselves. Stores that were originally designed to have some lasting qualities increasingly demonstrate a diminished sense of permanence. The visual environment substitutes for the physical presence and the preeminence of the physical world of products is supplemented or replaced with information (Miller, 1998).

This detachment of the visual experience from reality has led to a reappraisal of the need to use other senses; in self-service environments, to touch and taste foods, to listen in music stores, to try on clothes. Touching products, trying them or tasting them by engaging one's senses means that presentation becomes an important part of understanding the shop environment. Where the product itself is largely or exclusively concerned with information, such as mobile phone stores, information itself drives the experience.

Sensory psychologists can help to create a feeling of 'being at home' for shoppers. Sounds and smells can perform important, if not fully understood roles in this respect. An experiment carried out in two New York supermarkets, the one with lemon and spearmint-scented air and the other without, resulted in customers reporting that the

---

Exhibit 14.4 Redesign for Levi stores

The latest design for Levi's store in London's Regent Street has created a distinctively different selling environment as part of the repositioning of the brand. The previous store design reflected the company's heritage of tough, functional clothing from the American West. The use of natural wood, against which tightly packed and folded denim merchandise was displayed from floor to ceiling, contributed to the sense of enclosed space, and the pre-eminence of the product.

The new store is deliberately spacious. The layout allows plenty of room for customers to circulate and look at the merchandise on the new display fixtures that feature clothes draped over steel bars. The windows give a clear line of vision into the store and onto a few strategically displayed products. A spiral steel staircase leads to two booths, equipped for two DJs; and downstairs is a chill-out room with sofa, two Apple computers providing internet access and a screen featuring a programme of short films. At the back of the store is an area set aside to customise the cut and fit of clothing purchases to individual requirements.

---

first store was friendlier, higher-class and better managed than the second. (*Retail Technology Decisions*, 1999). Sephora, a leading perfume retailer in France, has recognised this need to provide sensory experiences on several levels, by creating a 'Temple of Perfumes' in its Champs Élysée, Paris store. Essentially the store has been designed to create a dreamy atmosphere, but one which is also international and technologically advanced by incorporating instore information points and access to the company's website (Dupuis, 1998).

Music, too, has been shown to influence behaviour, with background music used to create a pleasurable atmosphere. It can be used to manipulate customer behaviour in more direct ways too, as customer traffic flow is slower with slow music and so encourages browsing, than with faster music which can be used to increase the rate of flow. Customers may respond to more specific types of music; French accordion music has been shown to increase sales of French wine, and likewise 'typical' German music has significantly increased sales of German wine in the same supermarket:

> Not only can music be used as a marketing tool to attract customers to localities, but it can measurably influence the time consumers will remain in a location, their loyalty to a brand, their willingness to spend more and even the types of merchandise they will purchase.

COMMUNICATION THROUGH DESIGN

Design and Retail Branding

Design plays a significant role in the development of a brand. This is evident from the visual elements within a successful brand, its name, symbol, design or combination of all three (Doyle, 1993). Retail design has an important role in turning retailers into brand names that simplify shopping, guarantee a specific level of quality and allow degrees of self-expression. Branding will reassure consumers, and even cost-driven discounters can still offer, in their own way, order, simplicity and reassurance to their consumers (Uncles, 1993). The retail brand is highly visible and carries with it a strong image of the retailer to consumers; it can also prove difficult to change, taking some 10 years for Tesco to change consumer perceptions of the organisation.

The ways in which design contributes to branding are implicit in Pickton and Broderick's (2000) explanation of corporate branding in three separate but overlapping concepts:

- *Personality*: the essential expression of values and culture, and the raw material of identity.

- *Identity*: the means by which the corporate personality is projected, transmitted or communicated. Identity is conveyed by 'cues' or features understood by outsiders.

- *Image*: is created by the identity , the perception of the retailer by its audiences, what is felt or thought about it.

The function of design in creating identities has taken on greater significance as the values determining brand identity have shifted from reputations based on product or store functionality to those of symbolic images. The identity of the retailer is given expression through visualisation. Design has a dual purpose to communicate brand values but also to display merchandise effectively, using visual images to instil trust, consistency and quality in the consumer's mind.

Identity may be the only way of distinguishing companies when differences in actual products and services are minimal (Figure 14.1). Monolithic identity programmes are easily characterised by their association with an organisation. The Gap and FCUK maintain brand integrity through standardised international design approaches. In the case of Warehouse, the womenswear retailer, standardisation has been carried through by using exactly the same shop fittings and fixtures in its US stores as those in the UK. It is unusual to find a company causing unnecessary duplication, confusion and expense by maintaining two or more identities; Marks and Spencer, was untypical in retaining its St. Michael identity into the 1990s (Olins, 1990). However, highly developed retail markets put great pressure on the expression of retailer identity, where fresher, more desirable and more spectacular visual images are often demanded to enhance the value of the products.

Image became increasingly important during the 1980s and 1990s, across both domestic and global boundaries (Goldman and Papson, 1996). A key issue for the designer is to create a shopping environment that creates appropriate perceptions with the retailer's targeted customers. These can be found in a wide variety of approaches in fashion retailing from the traditional look of Ralph Lauren to the minimalist use of colour at Jil Sander (Conran, 1986). The design of the store will relate consumer behavioural needs to functionality and branding. For instance, the essential values of the Woolworth's brand are a warm and friendly environment, family products, good value and trouble-free shopping. These values can be applied to product

Figure **14.1**   *Elements of Retailer Identity*

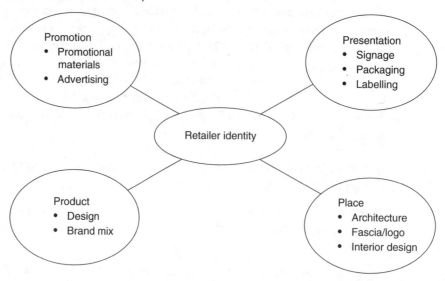

Source: Adapted from Schmitt (1999).

Exhibit 14.5   A design solution to Sainsbury's competitive positioning

Sainsbury's strategy has for a long time been based on quality and choice, but these differentiators have become increasingly submerged by customer perceptions as low-price marketing strategies have been implemented. In a return to an emphasis on quality the company has changed its logo to a 'living' orange colour that symbolises its focus on the customer; in effect design is used to change customers' perceptions. In this instance the sign communicates a new message through colour.

---

categories, too, provided that they set out to reinforce the brand authority in time (Bell, 1999).

Signs

Signs add value, and give the brand meaning. As they are used to identify the company and products signs form an important element in the development of the brand image. In this sense retailers need to evaluate the meanings of their brand transmitted through the design of their name and logo on shopfront fascias, and their internal signage transmitted both through visual images and text. Nor is this a static process, there is a continuing search for new signifying materials and allusions to previous advertising and promotional campaigns and a fashioning of new material out of the parts.

For a retailer, logo and fascia design will be the primary expression of corporate identity, the signal that customers remember and call to mind every time they think of the brand. Retailer name and logo carried on the fascia form the logical route into retail interior design and so it is essential that these capture and summarise all the retailer's brand values. The store interior can then develop those messages and add depth to the perceptions encapsulated in the logo. Designing the logo is critical, especially where the company is seeking to reestablish its identity or create a new identity, rather than a new brand. When fascias are redesigned it is important not to lose the continuity of customer recognition or to sacrifice positive brand attributes while introducing new or updated messages.

However, the design impact of fascias on the wider shopping environment must be considered too. British town centres have often had a limited visual appeal and cultural value due to the range of conflicting commercial and aesthetic interests. The variety of the streetscape has been reduced through the standardisation of logos and fascias to support corporate identities. These features, combined with the mass production of shopfronts, often sit uneasily in the local architectural context.

Graphics

As the retail environment becomes increasingly complex, so the appearance of the interior becomes more important. A consistent brand message is required throughout the customer experience, from walking into the store for either a brief or extended visit. Part of this experience will be in the brand or shopping 'post-visit' experience. Consequently the entire retail environment must be included in brand design to accommodate an increasingly demanding consumer.

Within the store, graphics are a key design resource in communicating the brand identity to the customer (Fitch and Knobel, 1990). Consistency in approach is important and internal signage typically draws from the corporate identity using the same colour signals and typefaces to create a coherent image. Not only signage but store information, displays, packaging, carrier bags and ticketing must all relate to the store's identity and market positioning.

As stores have grown in size, so the purchase support role of internal signage has grown too, and retail designers have struggled with the communication of directions to customers without cluttering the store with signposts, boards and help points.

Exhibit 14.6   Redesign at John Lewis

The John Lewis Partnership has taken a reflective look at itself and the ways it presents its department stores to the outside world, to make them appear more attractive and relevant to its customers. More particularly, it wants to understand what the customer sees in terms of graphics and how the design elements fit together. In updating John Lewis's corporate identity, the design consultancy group Pentagram will look at its 'onwards and upwards logo', its signs, packaging, carrier bags and stationery. The designers may even revise the basic green colour scheme that gives the store a very strong identity. However, the company insists that any changes will take place gradually to avoid losing sight of the basic aspects of the brand; the stores will remain recognisable and comfortable, and offer the same value and service to customers as they have always done.

The type and appearance of the signage materials supplement the visual impact of graphics, for example through the widespread use of clear and translucent acrylics (Mintel, 1999).

Materials

Materials create their own language in the store design and should be selected on the basis of their contribution to communicating the store's image, as well as their cost and practicality (Din, 2000). Floorings have a permanent durable function but also provide important visual cues to the defining of spaces and circulation routes. Colour and texture contribute to the store's image, for example where room sets might require rugs and matting. Recent trends have been towards the use of natural materials including hardwood, tile or marble, but there has also been an increase in the availability of decorative finishes including melamines that can be finished for hard wear or for more decorative uses in quieter areas of the shop. Special paint finishes can be used to provide marble and glitter effects, as well as textured and metallic finishes (*Retail Interiors*, 2000).

THE DESIGN PROCESS

Resolving these issues about how retail space is used requires a range of skills. It should now be apparent that retail design has to be multifaceted by linking together art, instinct and business in a problem-solving and planning process. Above all it must be creative to find or invent new environments in which space, cost and flexibility are matched to the effective communication of the retailer's brand values and the stimulation of consumer purchasing activity (Din, 2000). The holistic design tradition seeks to explore and understand a problem before creating a solution; it encompasses industries of all sizes from the craftsman to the global enterprise, and is itself an industry.

In some countries the design tradition is more distinct from the managerial one, and the integration of design into business strategies and organisational thinking is consequently more problematic. In Anglo-Saxon countries, in particular, the managerial approach is often one of focus and analysis, of justification through rational and often quantitative evaluation. In these environments design tends to be overlooked in strategic concepts used by managers, and is seen as a 'soft' activity by predominantly verbal, linear and analytical managers. Nevertheless, definitions of technology, innovation, design and marketing are very similar; in each case it is the focus that changes. For the full impact of design to be realised, the design function must be drawn into managerial decision-making.

Lorenz (1994) explains the ways in which design contributes to an organisation's success in terms of the transformation of specifications into reality, of actualising the organisation's vision. Design determines characteristics whilst the marketing focus is on the saleable outcome to meet customers' needs. More specifically, design may influence the development and performance of products in different ways and at different levels:

- *Product.* The design of quality goods and services can improve the company's image.

- *Process.* Designer interpretations can reduce the time taken to bring the product to market.

- *Production.* Often in conjunction with the use of technology, the designer can reduce the number of product parts and save on materials.

- *Strategy.* Brand-building through to the building of a corporate design culture, to use design to innovate (Trueman and Jobber, 1998).

A hierarchy of design dimensions can be identified, starting at the highest level with value, and working down through image, process and production, with the emphasis at each level depending on the industrial sector (Trueman, 1996). In retailing, the market positioning of the retailer will determine the exact emphasis on each dimension. The role of design in the department stores lies at an extreme from that in a hard-discount food retailer or DIY superstore, and value in low-cost operations may be best realised with minimal design input.

In the retail sector there are a number of design functions. The *architect* is typically involved with the building structure; a *store designer* with the interiors; and *visual merchandisers* with the selling environment. In some cases *project managers* may undertake new sales fixture design, and *layout planners* will optimise the store's merchandise lineage. The role of all or some of these functions, too, needs to be planned and strategically integrated. Decision-making will depend on the retailer strategy and centrality of design to differentiating itself from its competitors; the fashion clothing retailer, New Look, even found it could standardise its fittings and fixtures through its architects, reducing its costs by dispensing with interior design teams altogether.

Definitions of the design process, have been undertaken to determine the sequential nature of design activities. The RIBA's *Architectural Practice and Management Handbook* provided one of the earliest guides, and although many models have been produced the consensus on the external process lies in a four stage process (Cooper and Press, 1995):

- *Concept* Developing concepts that fulfil objectives.
- *Embodiment* Structural development of the most suitable concept.
- *Detail* Confirming precise specifications and production processes.
- *Production* Manufacturing the product or providing the service.

A linear solution to problems is unrealistic given organisational and environmental uncertainties implicit in the design process, and increasingly models of 'fit' with other activities throughout development, rather than 'sequence', are applied (Lawson, 1997). The process is a cyclical one (Figure 14.2) that is both multidisciplinary and iterative, proceeding from the project brief, leading through design proposal and product launch stages to market testing and research.

The *design brief* is the specific point of involvement of the designer with the retailer; it defines the problem and starts the conceptual development of the first stage. The

Figure 14.2   *A Design Process*

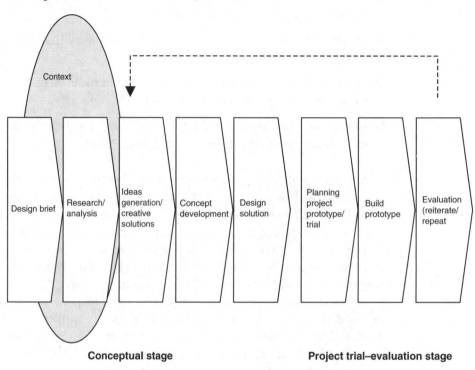

retailer's brief can vary from a concise summary of cost, concept and schedule, to detailing every aspect of the proposed work. The retailer must recognise the importance of the dimensions of design, how those dimensions are seen and interpreted by customers and influence their perception and experience of the retailer, and use these to shape their strategy (Doyle and Broadbridge, 1998).

Increasingly the project brief should be accompanied by market research so that the retailer's strategies, including design strategy, are focused on the same consumer target. Market research needs to establish and define in detail the customer profile by age, sex, income group and location so that the final design reaches the targeted customer, together with appropriate products and merchandise assortments (Fitch and Knobel, 1990). For Conran, too, market research underpins design policy and the development of a product range, 'everything that is made is designed, so why not make it good design backed by market research and with a degree of aesthetics' (Kay, 1987).

The research phase extends beyond an understanding of the selling environment into an appreciation of the dynamics of the shopping experience itself. One example of this broader approach is evident in House of Fraser's design programme 'to get clarity in our product offer, in our visual communications, our presentation in the store', to overcome branding confusion and interior design problems (*Design Week*, 1998).

Exhibit 14. 7   The relationship between designer and retail client

Retailers are becoming more demanding in their use of design to realise their marketing objectives. The marketing dimensions of size and scale, with low-cost to luxury positions require a consistent design approach. The ways in which design is handled depends on these but also on the retailer's organisational culture and the level of direction and control it expects to exert over the design process. At fashion retailer Karen Millen, the company has a long-term relationship with its designer allowing him a high level of independence over each store design. Relationships are widely preferred in the industry, and changing design teams is an indication of a new marketing direction or need for a creative, design-led approach.

Marks and Spencer, on the other hand, expects its designers 'to fulfil seven criteria by being: team players; global players; youthful but with maturity and integrity; big enough to handle the job; have a suitable track record; have the ability to understand business image and branding; and the ability to design concepts that can be rolled out throughout the chain.' For many retailers innovative design is an important requirement that has to be balanced with the practicalities of the store. For others, though, such as EasyEverything, a High Street access provider to the Internet, design must fit in with their simple low cost strategy.

Source: *Design Week*, 19 November 1999.

STORE LAYOUT AND CUSTOMER FLOW

Types of Store and Layout Requirements

Store layout has a number of purposes. A strategically designed layout combines the effective use of merchandise and aisles to draw customers through the store to maximise their exposure to the store's offerings (Donellan, 1996). The plan should have a 'transparency that allows the store to work well, guiding and helping the shopper through the space naturally without confusion' (Fitch and Knobel, 1990).

The primary purpose of the layout plan is to encourage circulation, allowing customers to see the retailer's merchandise. In addition to encouraging customers to visit all parts of the store, it should allow for promotional areas. Underhill (1999) emphasises that 'amenability and profitability are totally and inextricably linked', so layouts enable product ranges or categories to be located in a way that is easily recognised and understood by customers and also enable incompatible groups to be distanced.

The layout can facilitate sensory and tactile interaction between the customer and the product. For clothing retailers, in particular, layouts need to offer flexibility for seasonal changes or more fundamental remerchandising (Harris and Walters, 1992). In more stable sectors such as food retailing, greater emphasis will be placed on the organisation of gondolas and aisles and on creating sufficient space for checkouts. Warehouse retail outlets may have been located with a view to expansion, so the interior plan should reflect this requirement too.

However visitors to stores are unpredictable; they do not necessarily move through a store in ways anticipated by the retailer. Peripheral areas of vision are often underused, suggesting that planning of underperforming areas needs to be well-thought-out with well-placed visual messages (*Retail Interiors*, March 2000). The most obvious assumptions need to be tested; for example, it has been observed that customers have a poor awareness of advertising and information at the front of the store, compared to about three metres inside where fliers and baskets are rapidly taken up (Underhill, 1999).

The size, shape and type of store will influence the type of proposed layout. Simplicity, to counteract the complexity of the merchandise presentation and departmentalisation, and accessibility by designing wide-enough aisles to enable customers to see merchandise without causing congestion are required. Space allocation and layouts will be differentiated by the number of floors in the store, placing cafes and services on higher levels to draw customers through the store. Some product groups will habitually be located in ground-floor locations, such as perfumery and cosmetic counters at the front of the department store where their high value and low stock density and brand strengths provide an attractive and profitable entrance to the store.

Basic lay-outs can be considered as four types, according to Fitch and Nobel (1990):

1 The straight plan. This is a basic plan providing the visitor with direct access from the front of the store to the back. It encourages customer flow to the back of the store, and the circulation can be changed by altering the wall and floor units layout, both of which are used for stock.

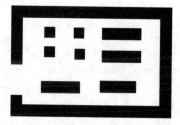

2 The racetrack walkway or pathway plan, used in department and other large stores where a distinct pathway is created by spaces between units or by different floorings.

3 Diagonal plan. This creates movement through a store by using diagonal converging lines to a focal point, such as cash till or special display.

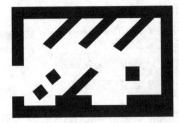

4 Curved plan. Curved walls 'suggest more movement than straight ones', and so encourage circulation; however, they are more expensive to construct than straight ones.

Layout plans are interdependent with product range and category management; there may be potential conflicts between space utilisation, sales and profit planning and presentation. To maximise space efficiency planograms are used as a means for deciding product layout on the shelf. Research is required to decide on the ideal layout, or it may be calculated from seasonal sales figures or preconceptions based on sales forecasts, when and in what quantities.

Analysis of sales data will also provide managers with information about the relative size and importance of each of the market segments and of the products within each segment. The total amount of space in each area will vary, but should be maintained in proportion to each segment. Within each segment brands should be arranged according to their relative importance with the larger and more prominent locations devoted to leading brands. Each segment should lead into the next with brands that display many of the characteristics of both groups situated on the edge of the segment, and ultimately sales space should be allocated to reflect market share (*European Supermarkets*, 1999; and Figure 14.3).

Layouts and displays should fulfill an additional function to deter theft and reduce stock shrinkage. Clear sight lines from the tills and service points and the minimisation of 'blindspots' in the sales areas, contribute to store security. Visibility of the shop floor can be supplemented by the use of mirrors, closed circuit TV (CCTV) and hidden cameras. In addition, the location of security barriers at store entrances may need to be planned into the store layout.

WINDOW DISPLAY AND VISUAL MERCHANDISING TECHNIQUES

Display and visual merchandising integrate with each other and to the store design in various ways. Until the 1980s display was limited to two largely uncoordinated

Figure 14.3   *Sainsbury's Supermarket Layout, Greenwich, London*

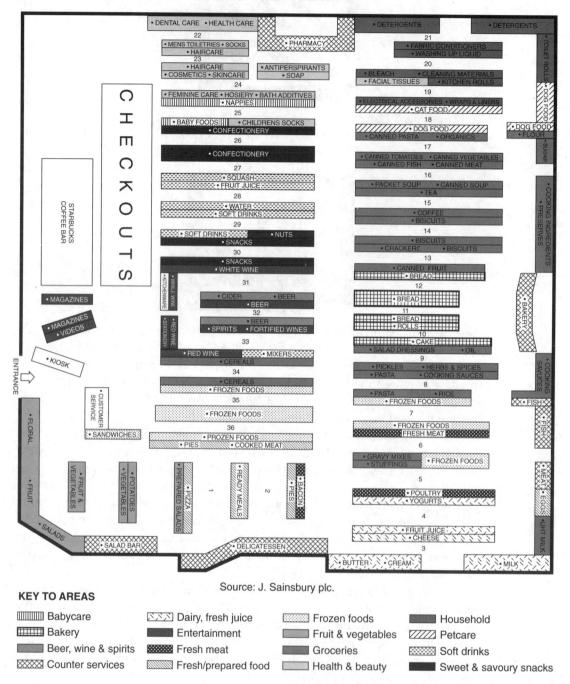

Source: J. Sainsbury plc.

KEY TO AREAS

Babycare	Dairy, fresh juice	Frozen foods	Household
Bakery	Entertainment	Fruit & vegetables	Petcare
Beer, wine & spirits	Fresh meat	Groceries	Soft drinks
Counter services	Fresh/prepared food	Health & beauty	Sweet & savoury snacks

activities, window dressing and the interior product presentation. Window displays had an important external perspective by linking shopfronts, including fascias, shop windows and upper floors and interiors to the environment of the shopping street (Mitchell, 1986). The display manager was required to be creative in much the same terms as today; even in the 1950s a sense of theatrical production was recommended, although this quality rarely extended to the shop interior.

However, the development of visual merchandising in the USA expanded the display function beyond window display to include floor layouts and the standardisation of merchandise presentation and signage. As a consequence it has come to integrate communications by reinforcing the market position of the company, creating interest and encouraging comparisons as well as stimulating purchase decision-making (Harris and Walters, 1992). Visual merchandising contributes to the total impact of display, marketing advertising and publicity activities for retail businesses to succeed in a particular community (White and White, 1996). It has a close relationship with product selection too, as a coordinating activity between effective merchandise selection and effective merchandise display (Walters, 1988).

A more functional role for visual merchandising is to enhance sales by creating visually appealing shopping environments (Donellan, 1996). The aim is to bring into view, show, put in plain light, exhibit, demonstrate and present merchandise and services to customers in a retail setting. It is a thinking process that involves the retailer doing the thinking for the customer, making product selection easy and enabling the retailer to combine a range of components to enhance the product and increase sales. In short, it concerns the ability of customers to find products and relate them to each other and 'effective interior product displays help customers to locate merchandise and can illustrate how the merchandise is used or worn' (Rabolt and Miler, 1997).

To achieve these objectives, product presentation can be planned in three stages. Firstly, store design provides the venue of surround colours, textures, materials, decoratives and lights; secondly, visual merchandising concerns the arrangement and presentation of products; and, finally, display adds the attention-getting techniques that create excitement, enhance the product and inspire lifestyle settings (Pegler, 1999). Pegler observes a distinction in New York between minimalism at one extreme of retail design and the need to be surrounded by more of 'everything' at the other. Somewhere in the middle, retailers use contemporary settings and a mix of materials to suggest richness and refinement. This finds an echo in the UK with House of Fraser's new department store in Nottingham positioned in the upper mid-market, and designed to be aspirational without being intimidating. This aim is translated in the design into the use of 'friendly' materials such as limestone, pale timber, cherry wood and steel, combined with glass and natural light (*Design Week*, 1998).

The process may require minute attention to detail. At Dixons it involves attending to lines of vision, signs and price tickets clearly printed and positioned; light, heat and noise at the right levels; and goods packed in to create excitement and make full use of the space. For Conran 'design is part of retail power . . . whoever said retail is detail is absolutely right. . . . the moment something jars the effect is lost' (Kay, 1987). Conran's 1986 critical redesign of BhS introduced a new logo, and the so-called 'Exclamations' pillars set out to achieve this objective. The pillars signposted different departments with illustrated merchandise alongside mood boards with photographs of the goods to stimulate impulse buying, creating a livelier and more attractive environment for the younger target market.

Use of Materials and Display Techniques

There are a number of elements to display and visual merchandising found in a typical store layout and these are listed in Table 14.1.

Table 14.1   *Elements of Display and Visual Merchandising*

■ Storefront windows	■ High and low glass display showcases
■ Promotions area	in department stores
■ Aisle merchandisers, gondola ends	■ Product blocking
■ Focal points; columns, shelves and ledges	■ Departmentalisation
usually used for branding, graphics and	■ Complete outfits / personal wardrobes
mirrors	■ Coordination
■ POS/cash wrap and information desk	■ Pause points
■ Merchandising through graphics	■ Fixture configuration

Windows

The purpose of windows is to engage people passing by the shop and to encourage potential customers to enter. They should be integrated with the brand image and marketing strategies of the company, as they provide a statement of the market position in terms of its product ranges, prices and services. Window uses can be broadly defined by the store's location, its size and the market sector within which it operates. Marketing and branding policies will determine the appearance of the windows, and the frequency with which they change. Clothing retailers will typically use a promotional calendar featuring seasonal product ranges and sales activity.

Primary and secondary themes may be identified, or the windows may be built around product brands sold in the store. Individual lines will have been selected for their strength in attracting customers from the core target market through techniques such as 'bullseye' branding that groups core merchandise and moves outwards in the presentation to secondary and other supporting lines.

Windows may have either open or closed backs into the shop selling space, enabling customers to see through into the store. Open backs create a more unified appearance and less formal atmosphere, but may be less effective as the store interior competes with the window display (Rabolt and Miler, 1997). The closed back provides greater surface area on the back wall for the creation of a powerful window theme, and provides a greater sense of theatre and entertainment for the window shopper; typically these are found at department stores. Posters can be used instore or in a window, usually to announce a product or promotion, and are likely to have a 'flashy, attention-getting style'.

The starting point for implementing a window display is the development of a creative idea or theme. Some elements are fundamental; the use of patterns in the display material whether vertical, horizontal or diagonal will create effects of height, width or impact respectively. Grouping is crucial to bring together related or unrelated items in an interesting eye-catching way (Wheeler, 1986). Colours and patterns need to be grouped, with some items selected as focal points. Shape and proportion frequently mean triangular groupings are most successful, although long, low groups or diagonal ones can be effective. Symmetrical displays provide a classical format for a more serious and formal window in which the predictability of the organised space is acceptable. Asymmetrical displays create an unbalanced effect but one that is more dramatic, and often simply looks right. Repeats of display merchandise and all-over grid effects working across the window are commonly used alternatives.

Store interiors

Visual merchandising within the store will have as a minimum objective the support and clarification of the message achieved in the windows about what business the store is in and what it is selling. The marketing plan and type of store will determine exactly how products are merchandised and, consequently, 'display equipment should be attractive and complementary to the merchandise it displays, without overpowering the goods it is designed to sell . . . The image of the store can be altered with relatively simple changes' (*Retail Interiors*, March 2000). The visual merchandiser's role is to create ways to display, present and encourage the sale of products whilst working with commercial need to deal with stock densities, equipment and merchandise organisation (Fitch and Knobel, 1990). Ultimately a good quality and appropriate display of the merchandise is vital for effective sales generation.

Some retailers retain an attachment to linear store design and layout. But as architecture in the 1990s moved away from the linearity of modernism and embraced sweeping curves and the use of circles, so display systems have had to match the image of the retail environment. The presentation of merchandise is the most important criteria for fixturing. Fixtures can be:

■ Uniquely designed, to support a distinctive and difficult-to-copy style for the retailer. Some new products, such as hi-fi and IT, may require specifically designed equipment (Din, 2000).

■ Customised systems to create more efficient displays and affirm the store's identity whilst using a standard display system.

■ Modular, standardised systems from suppliers may be more cost-effective for a multiple retailer and provide greater flexibility.

Fixtures are used to present merchandise, or to store it, and the retail industry has developed a number of forms and units to handle different types of selling spaces (Table 14.2). Common to both flour and wall areas in clothing stores will be appropriately designed garment hangers, mannequins and display models, all needing to be integrated into the design.

Fittings and fixtures can be considered in terms of permanence. Promotional displays, primarily for advertising and selling branded products, have a short life expectancy and as a result will be made from lower-cost materials such as cardboard. The designer in this instance is concerned with the marketing objectives of the materials. In their simplest form they may be formed out of the shipping cases of goods, particularly in discount food or warehouse outlets (Offenhartz, 1968). In these cases strong typography and colours are used to project the message clearly. Metal dump bins and mobiles have the same promotional function. Permanent displays from injec-

Table 14.2   *Types of Instore Merchandising Fixtures*

Floor	Wall
■ Free-standing floor units. These include gondolas – long, rectangular-shaped units typically found in grocery retailing, tables, clothing rails and shelving units ■ Cabinets are used to show smaller-sized merchandise and to minimise theft since article are not available for self-selection ■ Top-of-the-counter fixtures to display goods where merchandise can be touched and self-selected ■ Bins and baskets: often used for promotional and sale lines ■ Storage fixtures used to store fill-in or backroom stock ■ Specialist fixtures, e.g. carousels and literature displays ■ Plinth and dais areas ■ Room sets	■ Wall or ledge display shelving to utilise dead or unused space to show merchandise. Use of full floor to ceiling height can create powerful visual effects through: 　□ Slatwalls, commonly used over the past 20 years for both wall and freestanding floor units; however they tend to have poor durability and lack identity 　□ Ladder-racking systems that provide flexibility and a greater variety of design approaches. Shelves and brackets can be interchanged and spaces created for graphics

Sources: Din (2000); Donellan (1996); Rabolt and Miler (1997) and Mintel (1999).

tion moulded plastic, for example, or in the form of freezer units for branded ice cream are better made to last longer.

Whatever the plans for internal fixtures and fittings, the materials have to meet legal requirements through risk assessment and fitness for purpose tests. The equipment supplier can undertake these leaving the retailer with only limited legal responsibility. Health and safety needs should be considered, such as fire risks and weight loadings, especially where the display might be climbed on by children or leaned against.

Lighting

An early but important requirement of shop window lighting was to offset reflections in the window so that merchandise displays could be more easily seen. Internally the main effect of lighting is to create atmosphere, which can be designed in one of two ways. Stores such as supermarkets are ambient-lit for a standard level of illumination and to ensure good visibility of all products. The other method, typically found in clothing shops, involves accent lighting to create interesting or dramatic environments. In both cases the lighting must be designed to show off the merchandise, to make it brighter than its surroundings, and both light and shade need to be handled artistically.

Light sources need to be thoroughly costed from a wide variety of types, for their initial purchase cost, and also their replacement and maintenance costs (Fitch and Knobel, 1990). Overhead lighting in fluorescent strips will offer a harsh light that can add to a low price image needed in certain outlets such as discount warehouses. Their longevity, too, makes them suitable for inaccessible areas. Some lights offer poor colour definition but may provide warmth to an area; others such as low voltage tungsten-halogen lights create a hard but accurate colour rendition, generate little heat and are reasonably long-lived. These may be more useful in defining merchandise displays.

SUMMARY

The design of the interior spaces and external image of the store has a strategic significance in creating and sustaining the retailer's brand identity. The use of space has a practical physical function, and also social ones that must be considered in the design project. The process by which designers solve design problems comes from a distinctly different tradition to that of management, being more holistic in its approach rather than rational and sequential. Much of what the consumer sees has been shaped by the earlier use of space in the built environment, the oldest elements are visible in department stores and stand-alone solus sites, typically independent stores. The introduction of self-service supermarkets and superstores with increasingly large single-floor sales areas and lower levels of service and interior design have changed the landscape of retailing and introduced a more standardised approach to design.

Within the store the retailer's marketing position is supported by the use of design in communicating to the consumer, from the use of the fascia and logo design, through to coordinated instore signage, packaging and layout. Colour schemes, window displays and visual merchandising programmes provide an environment and ambience that creates customer satisfaction.

QUESTIONS

1 Explain the influence of the historical context on retail design.

2 Analyse the differences between design and management approaches to the store environment.

3 Evaluate the contribution of design to the customer's experience of the retail store.

4 In what ways does visual merchandising communicate the retail brand?

Re-Design at Selfridges

Selfridges department store in London commenced a complete refit starting in 1993 with the aim of renovating the entire store, and subsequently went about reinventing itself completely when it demerged from Sears in 1998. The £93 million store development completely changed its concept of the department store. Traditional coat, skirt and trouser departments have long since disappeared to be replaced by areas dedicated to brands, and Selfridges has become a 'house of brands', limiting the own-brand label to a limited range of foods primarily for tourists.

In reviewing its position, a number of strengths as well as weaknesses were identified. Amongst the strengths it can number the largest façade in Europe, dating back nearly one hundred years, and a large retail area with six acres of selling space accommodating 100 different departments. It has a history of dramatic marketing exploits, and inspires a great sentimentality amongst its customers. These qualities had to be set beside weaknesses mostly relating to its antiquated infrastructure. In the entire store there were only two small escalators and four lifts, and many departments appeared outdated in a rambling, dirty environment.

In terms of customer services, initial research established how and why people shop and buy, in order to create an environment speaking to the needs of the contemporary customer. As a broad aim, the store was expected to exceed customers' expectations with a range of services on offer; to appeal to the aspirations of its customers and 'inspire desire'. The design had to anticipate future requirements and, not least, bring customers through the design and renovation process without alienating them.

The new store design reflected a view of shopping as entertainment, a provider of plea-surable experiences for even the smallest purchases. One objective was to increase circulation throughout the store, opening it up vertically through a dramatic central escalator. This will improve the credibility of the product assortment through the impact of the merchandising, and by its design features and signage provide clear visual direction to the new sales areas. The store had to be logical and easy to shop. A simple circulation plan was developed for each floor, with wide clearly marked aisles, unobstructed sitelines and open vistas so that, customers would know where they were. The new design established general design criteria for branding, colours, décor and fixture design including tills. Visual communication was created through the use of ceiling height, the placement of aisles and internal walls, fixture systems and by highlighting design and wall treatments.

The shop windows, too, formed a significant element of the store's marketing programme. Not only are they a key motivating factor to draw customers into the store, but they also enable Selfridges to present a design statement. Window displays are understood as modern works of art, so that even the concept of traditional Christmas 'lights' is pushed to the boundaries through futuristic fibre-optic lit messages.

Every floor of the store is divided into 'worlds' of related merchandise, and dedicated areas within the worlds must be immediately recognisable. For example, womenswear has contemporary, classic and designerwear, as well as designer and concession-branded shsop-in-shop. The ground floor attracts the teenage market through concessions including Kookai, Oasis, Miss Selfridge and Ted Baker, in a location that provides easy access for impulse fashion purchases. Opportunities for visual excitement must be created within each world, requiring a graphics programme to be integrated into the overall design. In practice, the store decides which brands it wants to include leaving the brand management itself to decide on the product assortment and marketing. The percentage of own-brand and concession stock influences the store plan to ensure that each concession brand is ideally sited. Around 45% of the 2800 brands are concessions, although the store concept ensures that the distinction is imperceptible. In Chief Executive Radice's words 'there is one receipt, one dialogue, one service, one packaging; there's one environment, there's one door: it's called Selfridges'.

SEMINAR QUESTIONS FOR DISCUSSION

1 Assess the key elements in the redesign of Selfridges.

2 In what ways is Radice's 'house of brands' a design or marketing-led concept?

References

Adburgham, A. (1964) *Shops and Shopping 1800–1914* (London: Allen and Unwin).

Baker, J., Levy, M. and Grewal, D. (1992) 'An Experimental Approach to Making Retail Store Environmental Decisions', *Journal of Retailing*, vol. 68, no. 4, Winter, pp. 445–63.

Bell, D. (1999) 'Creating a Global Retail Brand: Interview with Sir Geoffrey Mulcahy, Group Chief Executive, Kingfisher plc.', *European Retail Review*, Issue 21, OXIRM pp. 14–18.

Carbone, L.P. (1999) 'Leveraging Customer Experience in the Twenty-first Century', *Arthur Andersen Retailing Issues Letter*, vol. 11, no. 3, May, Texas A&M University.

Conran, T. (1996) *Conran on Retail Design* (London: Conran Octopus).

Cooper, R. and Press, M. (1995) *The Design Agenda: a Guide to Successful Design Management* (Chichester: John Wiley and Sons).

Darlow, J. (1972) *Enclosed Shopping Centres* (London: Architectural Press).

Design Week (1998) '. . . In the House' 6 March, pp. 18–21.

Design Week (1999) 3 September, p. 17.

Din, R. (2000) *New Retail*, (London: Conran Octopus).

Donellan, J. (1996) *Merchandise Buying and Management* (New York: Fairchild).

Doyle, S.A. and Broadbridge, A. (1998) 'Differentiation by Design', *International Journal of Retail & Distribution Management*, vol. 27, no. 2 pp. 72–82.

Europe Category Management Best Practices Report (1999) (London: Roland Berger Strategy Consultants).

Dupuis, M. (1998) 'New Concepts in Speciality Retailing', *European Retail Review*, Issue 19, pp. 9–13.

European Supermarkets (1999) March/April, p. 36.

Evans, R. (1997) *Regenerating Town Centres* (Manchester: Manchester University Press).

Fitch, R. and Knobel, L. (1990) *Fitch on Retail Design* (London: Phaidon).

Goldman, R. and Papson, S. (1996) *Sign Wars: The Cluttered Landscape of Advertising* (New York: Guilford Publications Inc.).

The Grocer's Window Book (1922) 'The Nest', unknown publisher.

Harris, D. and Walters, D.W. (1992) *Retail Operations Management* (Englewood Cliffs, NJ: Prentice Hall).

Kay, W. (1987) *The Battle for the High Street* (London: Piatkus).

Kroll, N. (1954) *Window Display* (London: The Studio).

Lawson, B. (1997) *How Designers Think: The Design Process Demystified*, 3rd edn (London: Architectural Press).

Lorenz, C. (1994) 'Harnessing Design as a Strategic Resource', *Long Range Planning*, vol. 27, no. 5, pp. 73–84.

Lowe, M. and Wrigley, N. (1996) *Retailing, Consumption and Capital* (Harlow: Longman).

McGoldrick, P.J. and Pieros, C.P. (1998) 'Atmospherics, Pleasure and Arousal: the Influence of Response Moderators', *Journal of Marketing Management*, vol. 14, no. 1, pp. 172–97.

Michell, G. (1986) *Design in the High Street* (London: The Architectural Press).

Miller, D., Jackson, P., Thrift, N., Holbrook, B. and Rowlands, M. (1998) *Shopping Place and Identity* (London: Routledge).

Mintel, (1999) *Retail Store Design* (London: Mintel International Group).

Offenhartz, H. (1968) *Point of Purchase Design* (New York: Reinhold).

Olins, W. (1990) *Corporate Identity: Making Business Strategy Visible Through Design* (London: Thames & Hudson).

Pevsner, N. (1974) *Pioneers of Modern Design from William Morris to Walter Gropius* (London: Penguin).

Pickton, D. and Broderick, A. 'Integrated Marketing Communications (Harlow: Financial Times/Prentice Hall).

Pine, B.J. and Gilmore, J.H. (1998) 'Welcome to the Experience Economy', *Harvard Business Review*, July/August, pp. 97–105.

Pound, R. (1960) *Selfridge* (Oxford: Butterworth-Heinemann).

Rabolt, N. and Miler, J.K. (1997) *Concepts and Cases in Retail and Merchandise Management* (New York: Fairchild).

Retail Technology Decisions issue 2 (2000) (London: Cornhill Publications).

Seth, A. and Randall, G. (1999) *The Grocers: the Rise and Rise of the Supermarket Chains* (London: Kogan Page).

Shmitt, B. (1999) 'Experiential Marketing: A New Framework of Design and Communications', *Design Management Journal*, Spring pp. 10–16.

Trueman, M. (1996) 'Global Perspectives of Design', Paper presented at the Elmwood Innovation Conference Pilot Survey, Leeds.

Trueman, M. and Jobber, D. (1998) 'Competing through Design', *Long Range Planning*, vol. 31, no. 4, pp. 594–605.

Underhill, P. (1999) *Why we Buy, the Science of Shopping* (London: Orion Business).

Visual Merchandising (1997) (London: ST Publications).

Walters, D.W. (1988) *Strategic Retailing Management A Case Study Approach* (Hemel Hempstead: Prentice Hall Europe).

Wheeler, A. (1986) *Display by Design* (London: Cornwall Books).

White, K. and White, F. (1996) *Display and Visual Merchandising* (Westwood, NJ: St Francis Press).

Winstanley, M.J. (1983) *The Shopkeeper's World 1830–1914* (Manchester: Manchester University Press).

Window and Interior Display: the Principles of Visual Merchandising (1952) (Scranton: Laurel Publishers).

Retail Communications

INTRODUCTION

The discussion of the competitive retail environment in Chapter 4 showed that success in current conditions calls for more than just choosing the right location, merchandise and price. To attract shoppers, a retailer must inform them of the store's location, the types of merchandise it carries, and the services it provides. It must also persuade consumers that the store can fulfil their shopping expectations and provide them with superior value relative to its competitors. In doing so, retailers must design effective communication programmes to provide information to customers and persuade them to shop at their stores.

Retail communication activities take place both inside and outside the store. This chapter presents a framework for developing a retail communications strategy and discusses implementation in each component area. The concept of retail promotion is discussed first, leading to retail communications through advertising, sales promotion and public relations, and ends with the discussion of some important legal issues relating to retail communications in the UK. The overall objective of the chapter is to provide an appreciation of the role of each component in retail communication programme and the issues related to designing effective communication with the customer.

RETAIL PROMOTION

A commonly accepted view of retail promotion is that it engages with activities and functions whose primary role is to invite, persuade and generally stimulate interest in and acceptance of the retailer and its policies. The most immediate targets will be potential and existing customers, by raising awareness and creating loyalty. But other publics need to be influenced too, including suppliers, politicians, news and pressure groups. Communication at this level will be at a corporate level, in which consistent and clear presentation of the brand is preferred by stakeholders, and success lies in the clarity of the mission as well as the personality and identity of the brand.

More specifically, retail promotion embraces all activities and devices that are designed to sell merchandise directly or indirectly to customers (Tellis, 1998). Accordingly, there is a potential promotional aspect to every phase of retail marketing, from buying and pricing, to store layout. The retail promotion programme can consist of many aspects that are difficult to separate from one another and from store operations. Promotional activities could include advertising, visual merchandising, display, personal selling, sales promotion without mass media, and other associated activities such as special sales events, competitions, discounts and 'loyalty cards' (see also Exhibit 15.1). The relative importance and effectiveness of the different types of promotional effort vary considerably from store to store and from time to time. Success with these sales-building tools depends upon ability to organise and coordinate them into a unified programme. The late 1990s in particular saw a considerable growth in expenditure as retailers put more money, time and effort into promotional activity. As a result it has become increasingly necessary for retailers to plan promotions in line with general store character, and their market research.

The concept of the store character is that 'consumers form an overall impression of the store's character or personality as a result of all the store's activities to which they are exposed'. Among the factors contributing to the store's personality are location, layout, product lines, merchandise assortments, services and advertising. Omar (1999) suggested that in a well-managed retail organisation, planning decisions in each of these areas are likely to be consistent with one another. Therefore these support a planned concept of a store's image as it is perceived by actual and potential shoppers.

Exhibit 15.1 Sales promotion reference points

Since retailers offer consumers similar products, competition between stores hinges primarily on retail price. But offering lower prices than a rival can lead to a price war with serious losses for all retailers. Sales promotions are a means by which retailers can creatively offer better value or lower prices than their competitors. For example, grocery stores are usually locked in intense competition, and to differentiate their offerings from each other stores have to develop various price-related promotion strategies. Some stores may follow a strategy of high–low pricing, injecting some excitement with a strategy of random discounts and double coupons. Other retailers such as Warehouse clubs offer everyday-low prices to consumers who are willing to pay for membership and buy in bulk (see also Johnson, 1993).

Careful research and experimentation are needed coupled with personal good judgement. Through analyses of the store's market, the retailer learns just whom the store's customers are, where they live, and knowledge of their shopping habits.

Promotional Planning

In a general sense, planning is a logical sequence of activities leading to the setting of management objectives and the formulation of strategies for achieving them. Promotion planning includes the preparation of a detailed schedule of events, with emphasis on what is to be done, when, and how it should be done. In the case of storewide promotion in a large multiple organisation, these plans are elaborated and extended across participating branches. The programme is likely to list promotional events separately, along with the proposed date, basic theme and objective, length of the promotion, and the number of departments or product class involved.

Effective promotion is characterised by teamwork, and so coordinated planning is an important determinant for success. The total impact of the forces of visual presentation, window and interior display, and retail selling is much greater when they are combined. The impact of any type of retail promotion can be increased by effective coordination with other promotional activities in the channel of distribution. Branded suppliers develop programmed merchandising schedules, indicating the nature and timing of all their promotional activities, and the kind of point-of-sale and other promotional materials that are available for use by retailers. The retailer's and supplier's promotional activities are then mutually supportive.

Promotional Objectives

In common with the other elements in the retail management programme, it is essential to set precise objectives (the results retail management intends to achieve) for the promotional programme. Promotion works in relation to the retail marketing strategy, but in the short term it must be organised against specific aims, or problems or needs. Individual promotions will then be tailor-made to fit the specific objectives set for that operation. Thus, shopper-related objectives may be defined in order to help:

- obtain initial consumer awareness,
- build up consumer interest,
- to be at the front of the consumer's mind at the moment of purchase,
- gain immediate consumer visibility,
- overcome image weaknesses of the product, or to strengthen an existing image,
- develop repeat purchases and brand loyalty, and
- offset the appeal of other brands.

The particular type of promotion will be set against the particular objectives of the moment, as listed above. Promotion can only help the product to sell, it cannot usually bring about a continuous purchase by itself. It is part of the total retail marketing effort which leads to a purchase as a result of the total elements employed by retailers.

Promotional Strategies

At the outset, it is vital to agree to a clear strategy for each promotion in question. This will cover the following:

- the general sales situation;
- the detailed sales problem to be overcome;
- precise sales targets for the period;
- a promotional timetable; and
- setting the budget.

The goals of media campaigns are similar to the promotional campaign and are coordinated with them. Promotional goals include attracting attention by breaking through the competitive noise level, getting trial, expanding share, and promoting new uses. The promotional strategy sets out in precise terms what the concept is and how it works in detail.

Advertising and Sales Promotion

Advertising seeks to inform, interest, stimulate and persuade, whilst sales promotion offers the consumer an incentive or a physical benefit rather than a message of persuasion (see Table 15.1), its motivation being the immediacy and strength of the incentive or offer (Woodside and Soni, 1990). That is, it also offers the consumer something over and above the intrinsic value of the product itself. This is usually regarded as its strength, although it may sometimes be seen as a weakness.

Sales promotion works directly, and usually in the short term, and uses no medium but itself; it tends to concentrate on the 'here' and 'now', as for example if you buy

---

Exhibit 15.2 A loading strategy

The goal of loading is to encourage consumers to stock up for future needs. The loading concept is also used to remove customers from the market just as a competitor is about to introduce a new or improved product. It increases the usage rates for convenience products such as snacks. Most of us are familiar with premium promotions, which represent over £10 billion to industry (and a unique channel of distribution). These are the products that we may buy at reduced prices by sending a coupon with two or more labels from the sponsoring brand's package. Retailers use premiums mainly as incentives, and reposition products in matured markets. Consumer premiums generate excitement at the consumer level and enthusiasm among salespeople. Consumer premiums were used, for example, to reposition Canada Dry Ginger Ale in the soft drink market.

Table 15.1   *Components of Store Sales Promotion*

■ Retail promotion	■ Exhibitions
■ Leaflets	■ Packaging
■ Catalogues	■ In-store selling
■ Direct mail	■ Display
■ Showcards	■ Gifts
■ Signs	

now, you get this benefit. It deals in present offers and not so much future satisfactions. It offers present incentives to meet present sales targets; and because a large amount of promotional activity depends on selling selected merchandise, this can mean measurable and forecast quantities of product sold to shoppers.

Sales promotion is normally built around the product itself, or the product package, through the use of promotional packs, or of special displays of standard packs. As Meenaghan and Shipley (1999) have observed, a good store promotion sets out to do a job for the product by using the product in themed presentations and visual merchandising. Promotion may be used in several ways and as follow-on from advertising; it may take the theme of an advertising campaign and develop it by another means, in another way. In its effort to further the product image, store promotion may extend that image by using devices which arise from the identity of the product itself, thus creating demand and acting as a final reminder to shoppers. Shoppers may have been preconditioned to the product, but promotion acting at point of sale works to make the product front-of-mind, and arouse shoppers' previous knowledge of the product. It helps decision-making in the final purchases situation, especially where impulse purchases may be concerned.

Promotion and the Retail Brand

Traditionally brand management has been concerned with creating perceptions that assist in differentiating the product or service from the competition (Aaker, 1996), and the strength of the brand is determined by the 'extent to which these perceptions are consistent, positive and shared by consumers' (McDonald, de Chernatony and Harris, 2001). Advertising campaigns can support product features and benefits, and help to create positive images. But increasingly retail communications must deliver *experiences* that support sensory, affective and creative relations and lifestyles with the brand (Schmitt, 1999, and Exhibit 15.3). This implies the focus of advertising will move increasingly away from classical fast-moving consumer goods (FMCG) approaches to define an experiential image of the retailer and/or retail brand.

Promotion can be undertaken at the corporate level, to promote the retailer, and at brand or line level. The typical characteristics of retail promotion at line level are seen as emphasising immediacy. Individual lines are placed on sale and promoted during specific, short time periods when immediate purchases are sought. This style

---

Exhibit 15.3   Strategic experiential modules in television advertising

Sense   Dynamic and attention-getting. Fast paced, fast-cut images and music.
Feel   Slower build up drawing the viewer in, building emotion gradually.
Think   Slower moving still, begin with a voice over and then move to text on screen
           to be thought-provoking.
Act   Show behavioural outcomes or lifestyles.
Relate   A group that the customer is supposed to relate to.

Source: Schmitt (1999).

Exhibit 15.4   The use of price in brand promotion

A number of devices are used to convey a more general image of price, rather than presenting a list of claimed reductions. For instance, 'ASDA Price' and Sainsbury's series of 'Discount' campaigns sought to establish a longer-term belief in the stores' value for money. Various discount stores and department stores have used themes such as 'never knowingly undersold' or 'we will match any competitor's price'. In most cases, however, the message simply serves as a price reassurance, allowing attention to be shifted to other store attributes.

---

of advertising does little to enhance customer loyalty; and it may diminish loyalty by encouraging shopping around.

The attraction of price cuts could be described as the most indiscriminate of consumer motivations. Using similar combinations of products and prices within similar formats does not create distinctive identities. The problem may be expressed in relation to each store promoting price in the same way, as for example 'our personal computers are cheaper by-far'. As Exhibit 15.4 indicates, many retailers are reluctant to be seen moving away from price-based appeal (see Chapter 13), but recognise the need for a more individual identity in their advertising.

Although prices play a major role in retail promotion, in very few cases can they provide the basis of a viable major strategy for brand-building. Only the market leaders are able to enjoy the best available buying terms and retail cost structures, and those that do enjoy this position may well benefit more from placing emphasis upon factors other than price. One may conclude, therefore, that although price as a platform can only ever be used as a tactical weapon, it is not a suitable brand-building strategy.

In selecting goods to promote, the retailer should be guided by:

- past experience regarding proven best sellers;

- the merchandise that is selling well in other stores;

- pretesting goods to determine their probable rate of sale;

- the desire to promote private brands;

- the advice of salespeople; and

- considerations of timeliness, buying habits of the community, variety, frequency of purchase and contribution to store image.

New fashion items and prestige brands are often used for the latter purpose. Retailers should feature items and values that are attractive to many customers, that are purchased frequently and that will not absorb the customer's total purchasing power.

RETAIL ADVERTISING

Once a store has been properly equipped and well-balanced assortments of merchandise selected to meet the needs of prospective customers, measures must be adopted to attract those customers into the store and to induce them to make purchases. Such measures, to be really effective, should build goodwill for the store to ensure continuous patronage from satisfied customers. When this is done, sales volume will be maintained at a profitable level.

Retail advertising is any paid form of non-personal presentation and promotion of ideas, goods or services by an identified sponsor (Table 15.2). Retailers may use it to tell people what goods and services they have available, to stimulate desire for those items, to keep people interested in their stores between visits, and to develop goodwill. In other words, the main function and goal of retail advertising is to create a desirable image in the minds of shoppers.

Traditionally, advertising has not provided a generally accessible form of communication. Thus, McGoldrick (1990) recommends that small retailers should avoid advertising (other than window display) because of the difficulty of making a strong impression with a limited budget. Kotler (1997), on the other hand, believes that small businesses could successfully accomplished this by careful targeting their advertising budget. However, advertising has undergone a major change in recent years, especially with the arrival of the Internet, and the very cheap advertising options of the Internet and mobile media has enabled smaller companies to advertise, using 'guerilla' advertising techniques.

Table 15.2 *Components of Retail Advertising*

■ Retail advertising media	■ Cinema
■ National press	■ Television
■ Local press	■ Radio
■ Magazines	■ The Internet
■ Books	■ The World Wide Web
■ Outdoor	

Those retailers who recognise the limitations of their advertising programmes and plan their programmes accordingly will derive the greatest benefit from such efforts. They should keep in mind that advertising could not:

■ sell merchandise that people do not want to buy;

■ sell merchandise in profitable quantities without the backing of every other division of the store; and

■ succeed to the fullest extent unless it is used continuously.

This clear warning emphasises the fact that for long-term effectiveness, retail advertising must be believable, truthful and provide shoppers with helpful information.

Models of the Advertising Process

There is no fully-developed theory of advertising in existence which describes its structure, roles and how its relative importance is influenced by factors such as the nature of the product and its market. Difficulty is experienced in managing the advertising effort since, as a behavioural process, the effect of advertising on people is poorly understood. Advertising planning begins with the retailing objectives and strategies derived from the overall objectives of the retail organisation as shown in Figure 15.1. These retailing objectives and strategies are the basis for retail communications objectives and strategies. Effective research is an essential input for both retailing and advertising planning; the results of the research allow retail managements to make strategic decisions that are translated into tactical areas such as budgeting, copywriting, scheduling and media selection. Post-tests are used in measuring the effectiveness of advertising, and serve as the basis for feedback concerning possible needs for adjustment.

Figure 15.1   *Elements of Retail Advertising Planning*

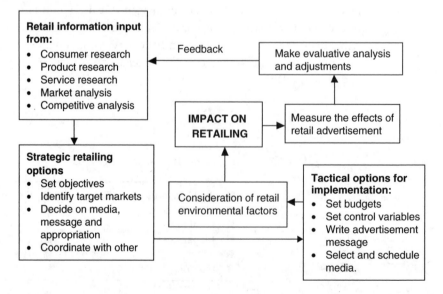

Table 15.3   *Models of the Advertising Process*

AIDA	DAGMAR	Hierarchy of Effects	ATR
Attention	Awareness	Awareness	Awareness
Interest	Comprehension	Knowledge	Trial
Desire	Conviction	Liking	Repeat buying
Action	Action	Preference	
		Conviction	
		Purchase	

Note: DAGMAR = Defining Advertising Goals for Measuring Advertising Results, and splits the process down to the four steps of awareness, comprehension, conviction and action.

The underlying basis for most advertising is that the behaviour of an actual or potential customer can be affected if he/she is presented with information on the existence of a product. Several models of the advertising process are shown in Table 15.3, each based on an understanding of the buying behaviour of consumers and how advertising may influence this.

The first three models in Table 15.3 assume that the consumer moves sequentially along a scale of commitment to the brand. As the consumer moves through each stage, it is assumed that his/her probability of purchasing the brand increases. Advertising can assist in this process by helping consumers to learn something or in converting non-buyers into buyers. In an analysis of these models, Rust (1986) could find no empirical evidence to support such a sequential type of model. Each of these three models prescribes a general pattern of awareness and attitude behaviour, which forms the conceptual basis for most advertising. However, empirical evidence to support the assertion that behaviour is caused by advertising has proved difficult to establish (Samli, 1989). The ATR model has been proposed by Ehrenberg (1976), based on his extensive studies of consumer brand-choice behaviour; advertising can be a valuable input at each stage of this process, but for mature brands the major determinant of success is the pattern of repeat buying, and here the role of advertising is likely to be defensive to reinforce the existing repeat buying habits of existing consumers.

Advertising planning

The care with which advertising plans are made will determine the results they produce. According to Ogilvy (1985), careful planning has many benefits:

1   It provides a definite concrete plan based on facts rather than indefinite, last-minute decisions based on opinions and guesswork.

2   It forces a review of past experience, thus focusing attention on past mistakes and successes.

3   It requires looking ahead – adopting a long-range perspective.

4   It considers and insures attention to all phases of the advertising programme including seasonal promotions, need for clearance sales, etc.

5 It provides balanced attention to the needs of each department and each branch in departmentalised and chain stores.

6 It schedules appropriate promotional activity to accompany planned developments, such as the addition of a major new merchandise line or a change in store and service policy.

7 It considers probable changes in competitors' policies and programmes.

8 It facilitates coordination between various types of advertising and between advertising merchandising, store management and control activities.

Advertising should be planned at every level of retailing, even in the small shop where the proprietor exercises direct supervision over all promotion. As in the promotional plan, the advertising plan should cover a period of several months and be subdivided into months, weeks or shorter special promotions. It should set forth programmes for various types of promotions, including selection of merchandise to be advertised and choice of advertising media. It should also provide for the coordination of advertising and special forms of sales promotions, as well as for adjustments to meet unforeseen conditions.

Types of Retail Advertising

Retail advertising may be divided into two main types: promotional or direct action; and institutional or indirect action. Most advertisements represent a blending of both types. The main purpose of direct action advertising is to bring customers into the store to purchase specific items of merchandise. Advertising with this emphasis constitutes the greater proportion of total retail advertising (Kotler, 1997), and may take one of three forms;

■ regular-price advertising, where the appeal is based on the desirability of the goods;

■ bargain advertising, which features price appeal in relation to value; and

■ clearance-sale advertising, whose main purpose is to close out slow-moving items, broken assortments and remnants at reduced prices.

Institutional or indirect action seeks to develop goodwill for the store and to create confidence in its merchandise and services; and thus to build permanent patronage (Abraham and Lodish, 1990). There are two main kinds: prestige advertising and services advertising. The former emphasises the store's or the department's character and leadership in style, merchandise quality or community responsibility. Often these characteristics are suggested by use of appropriate typefaces and illustrations rather than by flat statements in the advertisement. Service advertising seeks to attract patronage by stressing the various services and facilities offered by the store, which make it a desirable place in which to shop.

> **Exhibit 15.5 A legal trademark issue**
>
> After losing cellophane as a trademark in 1936, DuPont learned its lesson. Since then the company has been careful to protect its legal rights in Teflon and its annual investment of £4.8 million in advertising. It won a case against a Japanese firm for using the trademark 'Eflon' in what became a battle of opposing research. The DuPont survey established that 68 per cent of respondents identified 'Teflon' as a brand name and that only 31 per cent thought it was a generic term. DuPont has a trademark-protection programme that involves its legal department, its advertising department, and its advertising agency.

Trademarks

There is always the danger that an advertising campaign will become so successful that the trademark becomes the generic name for the product. Aspirin, nylon, cellophane and cola were proprietary trademarks at one time. The trademarks of Kodak, Kleenex and Xerox are generic names in the minds of some consumers, despite the companies' strong promotional efforts to the contrary (Davies and Brooks, 1989).

Cooperative Advertising

Usually, the retailer assumes complete responsibility for the preparation and cost of the store's advertising. At times, however, retailers engage in cooperative advertising, in which they share responsibility and cost with manufacturers or wholesalers. For instance, the product is advertised over the retailer's name with the supplier paying perhaps, 50 per cent of the media cost up to a maximum amount, such as 5 per cent of the retailer's purchases. It is estimated that £2 billion is spent each year by manufacturers in this way on cooperative advertising. The supplier gains from the added interest shown by the retailer in its product, from the retailer's prestige, from the extra space or time purchased by the retailer's contribution to the media cost, and from the fact that retailers usually buy newspaper space at lower 'local' rates than national advertisers are charged. Despite these advantages, many manufacturers dislike cooperative advertising. It is difficult to achieve a satisfactory return from the advertising allowance, and they often prefer to deal directly with the media (Ghosh, 1994).

To the retailer, cooperative advertising yields benefits such as assistance in preparing advertisements, tie-in posters and displays supplied for use in the store, and in the increase in the total space that can be afforded. The retailer should, however, be fully aware of the obligations involved and should be sure that the product has a suitable reputation. Moreover, retailers may be held responsible for the truthfulness of the claims made in cooperative advertisements that manufacturers have prepared. On balance, the retailer can profitably engage in cooperative advertising, but must be careful to select the best deals available.

Media Selection

The retailer should carefully evaluate the suitability of available advertising media. Each potential medium should be considered in terms of its coverage, suitability, its use by competitors, and its cost elements (see Stewart and Ward, 1994, and Table 15.4). The most important general categories of retail media are discussed below:

Newspaper

Media choices are changing today as retailers use increasing amounts of television and radio time. But newspaper advertising is still the main vehicle for large retailers and for many small stores whose trading area matches the circulation pattern of the local newspapers. These stores, and some other major chains, often use inserts (preprinted special sections) in addition to advertising in the regular newspapers to show large selections of price specials. Supermarkets also invest heavily in newspaper advertising of their prices lists. In contrast, newspaper advertising is usually too costly for small retailers – the corner grocer, for example, whose market is very limited. However, the growth of suburban and neighbourhood weekly and semi-weekly papers provides a useful medium for some small retailers. In addition, appliance and used-car dealers sometimes find classified advertising is worthwhile (see also Exhibit 15.6).

Table 15.4   *Leading Retail Advertisers in the UK (2000)*

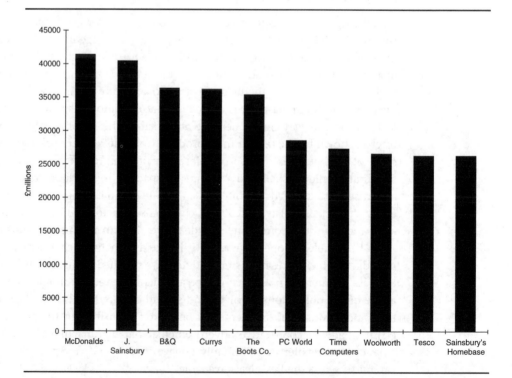

Source: *Advertising Statistics Yearbook* (2001).

> **Exhibit 15.6 Media communication usage**
>
> Arcadia plc invested around 76 per cent of its 1998 non-catalogue advertising budget in newspapers, 14 per cent in network and local television, 6 per cent in local radio, and 4 per cent in magazines. One trade source estimates that newspapers received about 48 per cent of retailers' media expenditures in 1997, radio about 14 per cent, television 12 per cent and all others 26 per cent. Discount department stores used newspapers even more intensively, spending about three-quarters of their advertising budget in that medium.

Many high-fashion retailers seek publicity on the women's pages of newspapers. Since the editors of those pages provide their readers with news of fashion developments, buyers who furnish such information have little difficulty in obtaining recognition for their stores. Retailers prefer newspapers because of their low cost per reader, market coverage, readership, quick response, quick check on results, availability for regular and frequent advertising, flexibility and speed, fewer size limits, and public acceptance. Despite these advantages, however, newspapers possess obvious limitations such as waste circulation in certain areas and among people who are not potential customers. There are limitations in their numerous editions with home coverage not proportionately large, and their short life. Other limitations lie in the large number of advertisements they contain, with keen competition for the reader's attention; and the difficulty of producing good illustrations on newsprint (Brassington and Pettitt, 1997).

Magazines

General-circulation national magazines do not generally fit into retailers' advertising plans, but magazines that are specialised either as to location or subject matter draw more retail advertising. *Girl About Town* and *Ms London* are examples of the growing number of inner-city magazines that, to a greater or lesser degree, appeal to residents and visitors in London and thus are suitable promotional media for stores in London (Omar, 1999). Retailers target special-interest magazines to match their readership profile to their market positioning. The most popular magazines in this category are those covering weekly womens' interest, home interest, gardening and computers (Mintel, 1999). In addition, the wide range of magazines enable retailers to identify precise market segments.

The major advantages of magazines are the ability to produce fine illustrations, specialised readership, their durability, and prestige among customers and employees. These are usually offset, for retailers, by the lack of flexibility because of long lead-times for preparation and publication; waste circulation; and, most importantly, high cost per reader.

Direct mail

Properly used, direct-mail advertising enables the retailer to select an audience and to make the message personal in nature; it obtains concentrated attention without distraction from competing advertisements; it permits a close check on results; and it provides a choice of several methods of conveying a message. But it also has definite limitations. Its effectiveness depends on a mailing list that may be costly to compile and maintain, specialised skills required to prepare the materials, and the cost per unit is high for materials, production, postage and preparation for mailing. Direct mail often gives very good results per monetary expenditure when sent to existing customers as part of loyalty or customer retention programmes. As more sophisticated information databases are introduced, so direct mailing and increasingly e-mail will more precisely target offers to consumers. However, the medium is often less efficient in reaching and selling to prospective patrons.

Broadcast media

Broadcast media (radio and television) have steadily gained popularity with retailers because of the number of people who primarily listen to or watch those sources rather than read print media. The rising cost of newspaper space, the development of relatively inexpensive television production techniques such as videotape, and the growing amount of experience retailers have in using television also contribute to the trend.

The retailer using radio or television may choose from a wide variety of programmes and vary appeals so as to reach all members of the family. The broadcast advertiser may reach customers at times when they are receptive to suggestions of merchandise suited to their needs, and may also make last-minute changes as they appear advisable. Merchandise can be shown in a convincing and effective way on television, and radio and television advertising lends prestige to some types of retailers and creates confidence and enthusiasm among employees. Broadcast commercials, however, are ephemeral; customers cannot always have the advertisements for reading at convenient times or for comparison-shopping. Also cost tends to restrict usage to large and medium-sized stores or to combinations of small stores, although relatively small retailers can afford spot announcements.

Internet advertising

The scope of advertising has changed with the arrival of the Internet and mobile media. Retailers of all sizes have developed web sites to provide information and services to support their physical operations. The medium has been slow to build a sales mass, which has held back the advertising spend on web-page space, for example banners, but retailers can increase their exposure through their selection of portals and hubs and at site level develop a hyperlink strategy through to other compatible sites. Increasingly, e-mail too is used to advertise products and services to targeted audiences.

Other media

Other media are used in specific, usually local campaigns but involve only a small portion of total retail advertising expenditures:

■ The shopping-news type of publication is a form of personal distribution typically owned cooperatively by advertisers, but some are non-retailer controlled. Usually published once or twice a week, each issue consists of retail advertisements plus some brief articles of interest to prospective customers. These papers are distributed free to households in the paper's area.

■ Handbills can be distributed instore or from house to house for local advertising and promotional activity.

■ Due to increased postal costs, many retailers now run their circulars as newspaper inserts or distribute them through house-to-house carriers. Even some large groups such as Mothercare and W.H. Smith make extensive use of circulars, which are especially useful for special sales events.

■ Billboards (outdoor posters), signs on or in buses and taxicabs, and other miscellaneous media are primarily forms of reminder advertising.

SALES PROMOTIONS

Specific techniques of sales promotion fall under the headings of *trade promotion* and *consumer promotion*. These are not, of course, completely separate categories since similar techniques may be used in each. In general it should be remembered that promotion equates with incentive, and that there are two basic types of incentives in terms of the things most likely to appeal to the customer – primarily monetary rewards, and product offers.

In order to motivate or obtain support, promotion tends to offer a gain or an extra benefit, in terms of money or in terms of free items of goods. The many individual techniques tend to be a variant on these two basic offers. The difference in technique lies in how these things are offered, and precisely how much of them is offered. Incentives appeal to what the trade or the consumer would like most, and we all generally appreciate cash or gifts in kind. Thus, the strength of the appeal is the strength of the sales promotion.

Trade Promotion

These are the incentives given by manufacturers to retailers or to other members of the distribution channels, sometimes called the 'middlemen' in the trade. Table 15.5 shows the leading techniques employed by manufacturers of national brands to persuade retailers to sell or stock their products:

Consumer Promotion

This is an incentive offered by the retailer to shoppers, or in the case of direct marketing the offer is made by the manufacturer to consumers. This type of incentive, addressed to the consumer, is generally based on a product offering or monetary

Table 15.5   *Trade Promotional Strategies and Applications*

Strategy	Application of the technique
1 Bonus as a standard offer	This usually comprises extra product against a basic order, shown in terms of cash value. It may be stated as a percentage, for example, '10 per cent bonus, worth £2.20 extra'. This can be offered on individual packs, but more usually on outer cases or ' statistical units' containing standard quantities of pack. Bonus would be given in relation to the amount of outer cases ordered, so the normal type of bonus would be offered along the following lines 'for every case ordered this month, you get a 10 per cent bonus, worth £x'
2 Discount	This is usually expressed as a percentage (for example, '10 per cent discount this month'), but can be expressed as a set amount of money (for example, '50p per case discount this month'). It is an alternative to a bonus, and it is another way of offering the trade a monetary advantage. In terms of discount offers, instead of money the recipient is offered discounts off a range of merchandise or services, producing a substantial cost saving. For example, each case ordered means £1 off the price of a continental holiday. Discount tokens may be used, each with a particular discount value, in which case the manufacturer makes an arrangement with a supplier or warehouse to provide goods at a saving
3 Coupons	These may be included within the outer cases, and exchanged for cash or goods. They will be redeemed by the manufacturer; for example, '10p voucher in each case', or '5p voucher off Shell petrol in each case'. The customer collects the coupons, and the more he buys the more he collects, with a worthwhile value at the end
4 Product offers	Instead of money, the recipient is offered goods. For example, with every two cases of product, a bottle of sherry, or for every case of product, a pair of overalls. That is to say, the merchandise may be related to the recipient's private use, or to business use within the retail outlet. This item may either be taken by the store manager, the buyer or the sales person
5 Gift catalogues	A catalogue may be offered showing a range of gifts, each obtainable with a particular number of cases. For example, 'buy six cases and get a hair dryer for only £3', 'buy ten cases and get a CD player for only £10', and so forth. Thus, this is a reduced price offer, alternatively, the gift may be given free. Here again, arrangements are made with a warehouse, and goods are made available at wholesale price
6 Trade competitions	Normally a limited number of major prizes is offered, either as money or merchandise. Free holidays are a popular variant. These competitions would probably be advertised in the trade press. The essence of them is that they should have a worthwhile prize, be easy to enter and appeal to the participants' sporting instinct. The participants generally are called on to show a knowledge of the product, and to list product features in order of importance. A panel of judges typically adjudges the entrants. There might be consolation prizes for the runners-up
7 Visits, tours, shows, parties	These may include the families of participants, and are on the lines of: a visit to a show; or a gala Christmas party at the best local hotel. These are therefore a form of corporate entertainment. Attendance is in relation to a required performance. These are usually very popular and sought after by trade participants, but require a great deal of planning and organisation on the part of the manufacturer. By bringing in families as well as buyers, they can prove very effective. Finally, in relation to trade incentives it should be said that head buyers of multiple-groups, department stores, etc., may also be offered incentives tailored to them personally, on an *ad hoc* basis. These would be large in size and cost as circumstances dictate

reward. A large number of consumer promotions and offers are variants of money incentives. Table 15.6 illustrates the incentives offered to consumers either by the retailer or the manufacturer for the purpose of selling the product or getting the shopper to trial a new brand.

Table 15.6   *Consumer Promotional Strategy and Application*

Strategy	Application of the Technique
1 Reduced price-pack	This is the basic, standard, and most direct method: e.g. 2p OFF now! It is related to the product itself, and is immediate. It is the clearest and simplest form of consumer price inducement. The price-reduction is shown on the pack itself. The reduction is generally paid for by the manufacturer, though occasionally the retailer may also contribute a proportion of the cost. Reductions will vary in size in relation to the normal selling price of the product. The bigger and more expensive the item, the more the reduction will need to be.
2 Banded packs	Several packs are banded together with a price cut, for example, 4 rolls soft white luxury bathroom tissue, 20p off. This may also be as a multi-pack, i.e. an outer wrapping containing several individual packs within it. That is to say, banded packs or multi-packs carry a price cut over a number of units of the product. Three for the price of two, and so forth. This is a variant on the above but is still a price offer. Free product, 'going with purchases' such as 'buy two, get one free', etc., is a price offer in disguise. The 'free' product is set off against the cost of the product actually paid for. 'Price-off-next purchase' – the most common version of this refers to the coupon on the pack, giving a reduction off the next pack bought. This is a way of ensuring several purchases of the product.
3 Cross-coupon, or cross price-cut	A coupon on product 'A' gives a price off product 'B'. Or, if you buy product 'A', you get 3p off product 'B' at once. This is a cross-promotion, spreading cost across several products, or using one product to gain sampling for another. An in-home coupon or a coupon dropped door-to-door, or mailed, provides money off when redeemed in the store. This can be done locally, regionally, or nationally. It is highly expensive, but it is usually very effective. The coupon can be of low value (for example, 20p) or high value (for example, £1.00) depending on the product. The cost to the retailer or manufacturer depends on the number of coupons redeemed, and the cost of in-home delivery. 'In-medium coupon' – in using this method, the coupon is carried in a newspaper or magazine advertisement. Again, it is redeemed at point of sale. This is cheaper to operate than a door-to-door coupon. The consumer cuts the coupon out of the newspaper, takes it to the store, where it goes towards a price cut. The essence of all coupons is the same, i.e. a price off a product. The method of delivery will vary. Coupons are attractive, easy and effective, but they are expensive
4 Self-liquidating premiums	Merchandise can be bought by the consumer at a concessionary price, usually by mail. The usual form is on the lines of: 'Normal price £10.99, yours for only £8.90p plus three packet tops'. This can provide the consumer with a very worthwhile saving, but it will not attract those consumers who do not want to buy the item being offered. Ideally, it should mean no cost on the part of the manufacturer, who deals in trade or wholesale prices to the consumer. This makes a strong display device, and is probably the cheapest promotion to run.
5 Gift coupons	Coupons go towards the acquisition of gifts from a gift catalogue, the gifts being in proportion to the number of coupons sent in. The best known exponents of this currently are the cigarette or petrol coupon operations. Gift coupons are very powerful, and very long-term. They are the ideal collection-device, but most costly to operate. Once a consumer has embarked on collection, then gift coupons can bring about high repeat-purchase.

In implementing a sales promotion campaign, all the characteristics of successful previous promotions from within the organisation or from other competitors should be explored. As far as implementation is concerned, sales promotions may be managed by the retailer's internal sales promotion department. Alternatively, the retailer may use the sales promotion facilities of its advertising agency, or use an independent specialist consultancy which may operate general promotional services or services of a specific kind around a promotional technique (McGoldrick, 1990).

PUBLIC RELATIONS AND PUBLICITY

The Public Relations Consultants Association defines public relations (PR) as

> the name given to the managed process of communication between one group and another. In its purest form it has nothing to do with marketing, advertising or 'commercialism'. It will, however, often promote one group's endeavours to persuade another group to its point of view and it will use a number of different methods, other than (although often alongside) advertising to achieve this aim.

The ways in which PR relates retailers with their various publics is shown in Figure 15.2. PR plays an increasingly important role in retail promotional strategy. It is generally seen as institutional advertising, which promotes the retailer rather than products; and public relations are used to either create an image, correct an image, or communicate a corporate philosophy.

Figure 15.2   *Retail Public Relations*

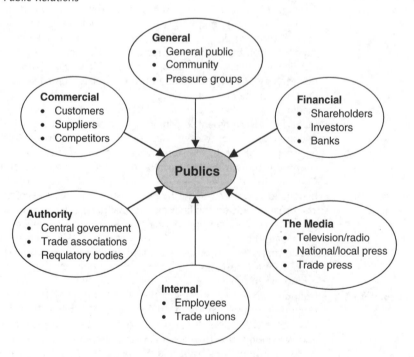

Source: Demolder (2000).

Table 15.7   *Consumer Promotion Expenditure by Types (12 weeks*
ending December 1999)

Types of promotion	Usage (%)
Store price reduction	37.2
Multibuy/Save	23.7
Manufacturers' reduction	12.4
Additional quantity in pack	9.2
Loyalty card	2.8
Free item	2.7
Coupon used	2.0
Banded pack	1.7
Send away offer	1.7
On-pack coupon	0.4
Any other offer type	6.2
Total	100%

Source: by permission of The World Advertising Research Centre, 2001.

The part of public relations that is most related to the retailer's products or services is publicity. Publicity may be defined as the non-personal stimulation of demand for a product, service or organisation by placing commercially significant news about it in a published medium or obtaining favourable presentation of it upon radio, television or stage that is not paid for by an identified sponsor (Kurtz and Boone, 1987). Since it is designed to familiarise the general public with the characteristics, services and advantages of a product, service or organisation, publicity is an information activity of public relations. While the costs associated with it are minimal in comparison to other forms of promotion; publicity is not entirely cost-free. Its expenses include marketing personnel assigned to creating and submitting publicity releases, printing and mailing costs, and other related items.

Some publicity is used to promote the retailer's image or viewpoint, but a significant amount provides information about products, particularly new ones. Since many consumers are likely to accept information in a news story more readily than they may accept it in an advertisement, publicity releases are often sent to media editors for possible inclusion in news stories. In some cases, the information in a publicity release about a new product or service provides valuable assistance to a newspaper or magazine writer, and information of this sort is eventually published. Publicity releases are sometimes used to fill voids in a publication, and at other times are used in regular features. In either case, publicity releases serve as a valuable supplement to advertising.

In recent years, public relations has to be considered an integral part of retail promotional strategy, though its basic objectives extend far beyond just attempting to influence the purchase of a particular brand. Public relations, and especially publicity, could be said to have made significant contributions to the achievement of retail promotional goals.

BUDGET STRATEGIES FOR RETAIL COMMUNICATIONS

The subjectivity and creativity of retail communication help to explain why it is so difficult to determine the level of budget for each component. Central to this budgeting decision is the difficulty of relating expenditures to profits on each element. Advertising, for example, is only one element in the retail communication mix which created a sale. Furthermore, the time lag between retail communication and sales revenue generation varies across products and market segments, which makes it difficult to link retail sales promotional efforts to profit. Using retail advertising campaigns as a typical example, there are two basic budget strategies: the breakdown, and the build-up methods:

- *The breakdown method* determines the size of the budget and then breaks it down into the copy and media strategies. The methods used include percentage of sales, a fixed amount per unit, competitive parity, returns on investment, and the marginal approach.

- *The build-up method* estimates the costs of executing all of the advertising strategies. These costs are added to build up to a total budget. Although it appears more logical than the breakdown method, it suffers from the costs and delays in establishing the costs to perform the tasks. Unless adequate research has been performed, the costs reduce to subjective estimates.

A fixed amount per unit is used in those industries in which the advertiser has considerable experience and therefore can estimate how much advertising will be required to sell a unit of the product. The packaged grocery trade and car manufacturers use this method when giving trade allowances for cooperative advertising. Using units rather than values makes the advertising effort independent of changes in price. Otherwise, a decision to change the price would automatically change the advertising budget in the same direction, which may be unrelated to the advertising task at hand.

Return-on-investment approaches view advertising strategies as investment portfolios. The strategy is sound, but the implementation is difficult except when advertising is the sole determinant of sales and when sales can be linked directly to advertising effort. Direct-mail marketing is one of the few situations that meet these two conditions; sales can be linked to a specific promotional piece or catalogue.

The marginal approach is based on the sound economic theory that advertising effort should be added in small increments until the costs of the additional units of advertising generated by this unit are equal. This economic concept states that profit will be maximised when the marginal cost equals the marginal revenue. The theory cannot be questioned, but the implementation is possible only in the case of a single-product firm that uses easily measured units of advertising effort. Few real-world advertising budgets meet these criteria.

Measuring the Effectiveness of Marketing Communications

For many retailers, communication with the customer represents a major expenditure, so it is important to determine whether a chosen campaign is accomplishing its promotional objectives. The determination of communication effectiveness is, however, one of the most difficult tasks undertaken in marketing. Although its measurement can be undertaken from several perspectives, this section discusses this difficult task from the two basic elements of pre-testing and post-testing.

Pretesting

This is the assessment of a communication's (advertisement's) effectiveness before it is actually used. It may include a variety of evaluative methods. To test magazine advertisement, for instance, one advertising agency may cut out an advertisement from advance copies of magazines, and then 'strip in' the advertisement it wants to test. Interviewers later check the impact of the advertisement on readers who receive free copies of the revised magazine. Another advertising agency may use a sales-conviction test to evaluate magazine advertisements. Interviewers ask heavy users of a particular item to pick which of two alternative advertisements would convince them to purchase it. Potential radio and television advertisements are often screened by consumers in a studio. In some instances, the proposed advertising copy is printed on a postcard that also offers a free product, and the number of cards returned is viewed as an indication of the copy's effectiveness. Blind product tests are also used in which consumers are asked to select unidentified products on the basis of available advertising copy.

Post-testing

This form of assessment of retail communication (advertising copy) measures advertisement after it has been used. Pre-testing is generally a more desirable testing method than post-testing, because of its potential cost savings. But post-testing can be helpful in planning future advertisements and in adjusting current communication programmes. A popular method of post-testing is where interviewers ask people who have read selected magazines whether they have read various advertisements in them. A copy of the magazine is used as an interviewing aid, and each interviewer starts at a different point in the magazine. For larger advertisements, respondents are also asked about specifics, such as headlines and copy. All such readership, or recognition tests assume that future sales are related to advertising readership.

Unaided recall tests are another method of post-testing advertisements. In this method, respondents are not given copies of the magazine but must recall the advertisements from memory. Respondents are required to prove they have read a magazine by recalling one or more of its feature articles. The people who remember particular articles are given cards with the names of products advertised in the issue and then list the advertisement they remember and explain what they remember about them. Finally, the respondents are asked about their potential purchase of the product. Some agents use telephone interviews the day after a commercial appears on television in order to test brand recognition and the effectiveness of the advertisement. Inquiry tests are another popular post-testing method. Regardless of the method used, retailers must realise that pretesting and post-testing are expensive, and they must therefore plan to use them as effectively as possible to arrive at a profitable conclusion.

LEGAL ISSUES IN RETAIL ADVERTISING

As advertising has become more sophisticated, so the dangers of misrepresentation have increased. Consumers complain about a range of perceived or real deceptions arising from visual, verbal and written statements; these include 'bait and switch' offers (Exhibit 15.7), unsubstantiated claims, 'free' offers that require a purchase, and exaggerated price claims. As a result, both legal restrictions and self-regulation of the industry through the British Codes of Advertising and Sales Promotion administered by the Advertising Standards Authority (ASA) protect the consumer. EU advertising legislation currently in force includes the Cross-Frontier Broadcasting Directive, and the Misleading Advertising Directive. Advertising legislation also exists for specific sectors such as tobacco, food claims and the phamaceutical industry.

Deceptive Advertising

An advertising message must represent facts and cannot mislead consumers. This principle guides the ASA, which can make cease-and-desist orders if it finds advertising false or misleading. The area of greatest concern is the accuracy of 'sale' prices or reductions announced in promotional advertisements. A retailer may announce price savings or reductions by comparing the promotional price to either the price at

---

Exhibit 15.7 Bait and switch

A retailer advertises a special sale on a Pentium II computer for £289 in the local newspaper. Attracted by this special price, a potential customer goes to the store to buy the computer. Once the customer enters the store, however, the salesperson claims that the model is sold out and is uncertain when a new shipment will arrive. The salesperson then talks down the advertised model and encourages the customer to buy a higher-priced one. Such a scene is enacted too often according to many consumer advocates and consumer magazines including WHICH. This store has engaged in *bait and switch*. It used the advertisement as bait to draw potential customers into the store and then tried to switch them from the advertised item to a higher-priced model. The primary purpose of the advertisement was not to sell the advertised item, but to attract into the store persons interested in buying Pentium II computers to try to persuade them, typically through high-pressure selling techniques, to purchase a higher-priced model. Bait-and-switch advertising is illegal because it is deceptive.

Many retailers have answered charges of running bait-and-switch advertising. It can be quite difficult, however, to differentiate between wilful bait and switch and legitimate trading up. In a trading up, a time-honoured and widely accepted retail selling practice, the retailer provides customers with information on models covering an entire price range and genuinely convinces them that a higher-priced model suits their needs better and provides better value. Honest trading up is a good sales technique because it matches a customer's needs with product features. The line between trading up and bait and switch is thin, however, with many retailers facing charges of bait and switch claiming that they were engaged in legal trading up.

which the retailer sold the item previously, or to the current price of identical merchandise at other stores.

When a retailer announces a 10 per cent price reduction, the promotional price should be at least 10 per cent less than the price at which the retailer sold the item immediately preceding the sale, on a regular basis, and for at least 30 consecutive days. Sometimes, retail advertisements compare prices to suggested retail prices to imply a saving. This is deceptive if representative major retailers in the market area did not actually sell the product at the suggested price prior to the sale. Under pressure from consumer groups, the ASA has been assessing retail advertising closely and requires stores to document their price claims. Policing of smaller retailers, however, is still lax, and some continue to make deceptive price claims in their advertisements.

Since their intentions may be difficult to judge, retailers should follow strict guidelines to avoid charges of deceptive advertising. They must not:

- refuse to demonstrate an advertised item;
- disparage an advertised item;
- refuse to ensure delivery within a reasonable period of time; or
- knowingly demonstrate a defective sample of an advertised model.

Regulatory scrutiny of retail advertising is increasing, especially for large retailers. In order to avoid legal problems, retailers must maintain adequate records to substantiate claims in their advertisements and stock adequate quantities of advertised items. Unfortunately, a few retailers mislead customers with false advertising. Such unethical practices, even if they are few or rare, hurt the entire retail industry by lowering the credibility of all retail advertisements.

SUMMARY

Advertising and promotion are the central elements in a retailer's communications strategy. These goals must be stated in terms of magnitude, time and concepts that are measurable. Communication models of the buying decision vary across products, but they reduce to the basic elements of awareness, attitudes and buying intentions. Retail communication seeks to create demand, to build a franchise for a product, and to establish a relationship between product and consumer. Advertising, for instance, may build acceptance but not necessarily instant sales; it may be long-term and slow working. Sales promotion is the implementary activity, operating over and above advertising, which seeks to bridge the gap between acceptance (as created by advertising) and actual selection. Advertising may build the ground for selection; sales promotion achieves the actual selection itself. It thus aims to resolve the element of trade and consumer uncertainty. This may be especially relevant at times of economic uncertainty, when the retailer needs more than ever some guarantee of sales to the distributive point.

Communication strategies include copy strategies (the selling message) and media strategies (the vehicles that will carry the message). Segmentation strategies apply to copy and media as well as to product strategies. Media strategies require decisions regarding reach (that is coverage) and frequency of message exposure to the target audience. Media timing strategies must consider the seasonally of demand, the consumers' purchase frequency, competitive reaction times, pulsing effects, and the need for frequency of exposure. Operations research methods are aiding the development of media strategies and execution, but they have not eliminated the need for creative input.

Sales promotional strategies (for example, money-off, coupons and premiums) may be directed toward the sales force or consumers. Promotional expenditures are about equal to media expenditures, but they have not received management's attention or the research that media strategies have received. The need to measure advertising effectiveness introduces many complex problems such as the psychological effect of advertising, the reliability of measuring instruments, experimental designs and sources of information. Budget strategies are a combination of the breakdown and the build-up methods. Although the breakdown method is easier to apply, it tends to ignore the communication opportunities and the cost to achieve advertising and promotional goals.

QUESTIONS

1   Define what you understand by the term retail communications, and explain briefly its major components.

2   What are the important matters that retailers must consider when planning a store's promotion?

3   How could the retail promotion be planned?

4   Define the term retail advertising, and explain briefly its main functions and goals.

5   People who understand retail advertising may know it is not capable of working in isolation from other store variables. Explain this statement.

6   Why do well-established retailers such as Tesco and Marks & Spencer need to advertise?

7   By what criteria would you judge the suitability of different media for a retail advertisement? Using these criteria, compare radio, newspapers and television as potential advertising vehicles for a regional supermarket chain.

8   Pay a visit to the local supermarket and note the types of in-store point-of-sale advertising there. Why do you think the use of in-store point-of-sale advertising is increasing?

9   It is illegal to wilfully mislead consumers with deceptive advertising. How could retailers avoid misleading consumers?

10 How could retailers measure the effectiveness of their advertising campaigns?

The Use of Advertising for Brand Image Building

Brand image may be defined as 'the set of beliefs held about a particular brand' or a set of associations usually organised in some meaningful way (see Meenaghan, 1995). The brand is often regarded as separate from the functional product, with the brand image being grafted on by advertising, thereby completing the transformational process from functional product to enduring brand. According to Kim (1990), a product is a physical thing; a brand has no tangible, physical or functional properties, and although it is just as real as the product, it simply exists like a myth in the imagination of the consumers. The product is seen as providing core functional benefits while the brand is responsible for creating the magnetic human-like aura around the actual product.

While it is quite common to regard advertising as a major factor in leveraging brand equity, it is worth noting that consumers are not passive recipients of image-laden advertising. Consumers usually take away from communications what they choose to, and indeed bring existing preconceptions to their choice. In reality, brand values are subjective; it is the consumers and their habit-forming tendencies that create branding. Branding is thus inseparable from the ability to choose. What advertising does is to help control the acquisition of value, and give it direction. If a retailer does not advertise, its service would still acquire a 'branding', but it might not be one that the retailer would like.

At all levels of retailing imagery, advertising is identified as one of the principal components of image building. The question of how advertising affects consumer behaviour represents one of the most complex and intriguing aspects of understanding in retailing. While it is convenient to describe two broad schools of advertising, affective and cognitive behavioural approaches to consumer decision-making, it is obvious that such a dichotomous view can hardly be expected to explain the diversity of consumer decision-making situations. The cognitive school views the consumer as a rational decision-maker working his/her way through a series of physical and mental steps towards the act of purchase. This school is represented by what might be termed the classical model of advertising effects. The second school, variously termed the brand image school or humanistic advertising, has at its core a more symbolic, intuitive and emotional view of products and advertising in the scheme of consumer decision-making. The function of advertising is to create the symbolism and imagery around the product that will result in a relationship between the brand and the consumer. The consumer is seen as active, knowledgeable, sophisticated and involved in the process of giving meaning to brands. Brand choice is based on emotional and intuitive feelings about brands, their images and meanings for consumers; and how these brands satisfy consumer needs and seem to fit into the consumer's relationship with his/her world.

Following from these two schools of consumer decision-making, two broad categories of advertising that bear a variety of labels in the retailing literature and have strong resonance to the rational or emotional motives debate can be identified. Putting it simply, advertising has two purposes: 'to excite and to inform'. In terms of building a personality for the product, advertising could be distinguished based on value-expressive (image) or symbolic appeals, and utilitarian (functional) appeals. The image strategy involves building a personality for the

(Continued)

product or creating an image of the product user. The utilitarian appeal involves informing consumers of the product benefits that are perceived to be highly functional and important to the consumer. Based on this classification there are two different routes to persuasion: self-congruity and functional congruity. The self-congruity route to persuasion can be viewed as a psychological process in which the audience focuses on source cues and matches these cues to their self-concept (see Omar, 1999). The greater the match of the source cues, the greater the probability of persuasion, and vice versa.

Functional congruity, on the other hand, can be defined as a match between the beliefs of product utilitarian attributes (performance-related) and the audience's referent attributes. A self-congruity route to persuasion can be viewed as a form of peripheral processing, whereas the functional congruity route is likely to be a form of central processing. In effect, the development of brand image is reliant on both the informational and the transformational abilities of advertising, with the brand image formed by the consumer being the composite of both functional and emotional components absorbed simultaneously.

SEMINAR QUESTIONS

1 The concept of branding is the relationship that the brand forms with the consumer. Discuss this statement in the light of the information provided in the case study.

2 The product is seen as providing core functional benefits while the brand is responsible for creating the magnetic human-like aura around the actual product. Basing your argument on the two schools of thought relating to advertising effectiveness as discussed in this case study, explain what you understand by this statement.

3 Discuss how you think advertising could be used to build brand image.

References

Aaker, D. (1996) *Building Strong Brands* (New York: Free Press).

Abraham, M. and Lodish, L.M. (1990) 'Getting the Most Out of Advertising and Promotion', *Harvard Business Review* (May/June).

Bonnal, F. (1990) 'Attitudes to Advertising in Six European Countries', Admap (December), pp. 19–23.

Brassington, F. and Pettitt, S. (1997) *Principles of Marketing* (London: Pitman).

Davies, G. and Brooks, M. (1989) *Positioning Strategy in Retailing* (London: Paul Chapman).

Ehrenberg, A.S.C. (1976) 'Learning about Promotion', *in the Contribution of Research to Decision Making on Promotions* (Amsterdam: ESOMAR) pp. 23–9.

Ghosh, A. (1994) *Retail Management*, 2nd edn (New York: The Dryden Press).

Johnson, B. (1993) 'Food Chains Stock Up On Promos: Recession Continues to Plague Southen California Supermarkets', Advertising Age (April), vol. 12, no. 26.

Kotler, P. (1997) *Marketing Management: Analysis, Planning, Implementation, and Control*, 9th edn (New Jersey: Prentice Hall International, Inc.).

Kurtz, D.L. and Boone, L.E. (1987) *Marketing*, 3rd edn (New York: The Dryden Press).

McGoldrick, P (1990) *Retail Marketing* (London: McGraw-Hill).

Meenaghan, T. and Shipley, D. (1999) 'Media Effect In Commercial Sponsorship', European Journal of Marketing, vol. 33, no. 3/4, pp. 328–47.

Mintel (1999) *Retail Advertising* (London: Mintel International Group).

Ogilvy, D. (1983) *Ogilvy on Advertising* (London: Pan Books).

Omar, O. (1999) *Retail Marketing* (London: Financial Times/Pitman).

Rust, R.T. (1986) *Adertising Media Models* (Lexington: D.C. Heath).

Samli, A.C. (1989) *Retail Marketing Strategy: Planning, Implementation and Control* (New York: Quorum Books).

Stewart, D.W. and Ward, S. (1994) 'Media effects on advertising', in J. Bryant and D. Zillmann, (eds), *Media Effects in Theory and Research* (Hillsdale, NJ: Lawrence Erlbaum & Associates).

Tellis, G.J. (1998) *Advertising and Sales Promotion Strategy* (Harlow, England: Addison Wesley).

Woodside, A.G. and Soni, P.K. (1990) 'Performance Analysis of Advertising in Competing Media Vehicles', Journal of Advertising Research, vol. 30 (February/March), pp. 53–66.

Customer Service

INTRODUCTION

Customer service is a highly significant element of retailing. In this chapter it is used to embrace the diversity of initiatives undertaken by individual retailers as well as more generalised customer-oriented programmes. Emphasis on the customer is not misplaced, because their role in retailing is a central one. They have both the spending power and discretion over where and how they will shop (Ghosh, 1994). Where retailers have competed largely on price, serving, caring for, or relating to customers offers an important alternative approach to business success (Shemwell *et al.*, 1994). However, in looking at the realities of British retailing customers might be forgiven for believing that retailers understand only lip service rather than customer service.

Customer service is all about *attracting*, *retaining* and *enhancing* customer relationships. There are in turn a number of ways of considering this. Customers could be attracted by the price offer of the store or in the services that are provided, such as a coffee shop or gift-wrapping; it is relatively easy to generate a list of such services that retailers may provide. One may argue that to attract certain customers to a store such services have to be provided as a 'qualifying' package of services to enter the customer's choice set. This qualifying service will vary by customer segment and be dependent on the target market of the retailer.

It is more difficult for retailers to obtain differential advantage in their market unless they offer unique products or services (Sivadas and Baker-Prewitt, 2000). In most sectors, however, retailers offer basically the same product assortments, provide similar services, and offer their assortments at similar price levels. Location still plays an important part in differentiation (see Chapter 8), as do differences in operating hours and conditions, though even these are not as important as they once were. There is less clarity among market participants as to who are competitors; the once clearly established definitions between supermarkets, chemists and variety stores are steadily eroding. The problem is further exacerbated by changes in lifestyle, income patterns and demographic factors.

Consequently customer service has taken on a critical function in influencing consumer demand. It represents one strategic element which can differentiate retailers from one another, and most importantly can be effectively used by retailers of almost any size.

This chapter is divided into two major sections. The first section discusses the importance and relevance of customer service in retailing, noting that while customer service is something that all retailers say that they are doing, few implement it in a systematic way. The second section of the chapter focuses on the unique characteristics of personal selling in retailing.

AIMS AND OBJECTIVES OF CUSTOMER SERVICE

Much of the attention in the service area has traditionally been paid to activities in four major areas (Bolton and Drew, 1994):

■ Support services such as credit, delivery, gift-wrapping and so forth;

■ Sales support services including telephone and mail-order activities (refer to Chapter 18);

■ Revenue services including leasing programmes, financial services and educational offerings; and

■ Courtesies primarily related to behaviour in respect of the sales transaction and post-transaction activities such as returns, maintenance and warranty matters.

Retail managers often confuse these four activities. They are viewed as services, not in the context of delivering consumer satisfaction but as a result of completing a transaction. Most retailers regard these services as extensions of the store's offerings rather than part of the total system of satisfying customers, and how well they are performed varies from one retail organisation to another. The main aim of customer service is to offer the customer the satisfaction he or she expects from the store as a result of patronising it.

Consumer choice brings with it problems. Customer service (see Exhibit 16.1) is based on the concept of the sovereign consumer, consumers who know what they want and who are confident in their ability to choose and switch between suppliers. A number of tensions can arise between the employee's service quality

---

Exhibit 16.1 Customer service at Gatwick airport

Airports are places for people, and everyone who walks through the doors automatically becomes a customer. This includes passengers, those coming to meet or send off passengers, and airport and/or airline employees. Recently, however, terrorist activities have had a predictable effect on the whole industry. Parking revenues dropped significantly at many airports including Gatwick, and concessions located past security typically lost more revenue than those in main terminal areas. Most passengers are usually nervous and only few people may actually like to fly. As a result of this anxiety, they are more demanding over services and goods than they would normally be, and they appreciate any effort made to help relieve their distress. Shops, cafés, bars and video games facilities are aimed at getting passengers' minds out of the sky and decrease their boredom.

In the early 1990s, British Airports Authority (BAA), the owner of Gatwick Airport, established the Airport Marketing Department specifically to determine a marketing strategy to deliver effective customer service at Gatwick. The main aims were to understand customers' needs; identify and build customer service based on the organisation's strengths; address weaknesses and develop innovative customer service offerings for the 1990s. The strategy worked very well and Gatwick Airport was repositioned as a customer-friendly international airport.

---

and relationship with the customer, and with managerial concerns over costs, sales and profits. Customer expectations of 'good' service are constantly being raised; employees' responses to customer service are often varied and complicated by the three-way relationship between themselves, the customer and their employer (Sturdy, 2001).

Every time a customer comes into contact with a store, its staff or merchandise, they experience a service encounter or 'a moment of truth'. Every moment of truth is an opportunity to attract, retain or enhance the relationship with the customer. Equally, every moment of truth is a potential disaster from a retailer's point of view, and one that could turn away a customer for life (Carlzon, 1987). The retailer, through its store staff, managers and ultimately its database, has a large number of moments of truth in which to impress or satisfy customers. Failure to satisfy customers, keep to promises or to remedy a situation, and a continued inability to see problems from customers' viewpoints can lead to the ultimate penalty of losing the customer's business in the future. One dissatisfied customer tells many other potential and actual customers, thereby compounding the failure.

According to Dabholkar *et al.* (1996), when customers enter a store they have expectations about what they will find and experience there. These expectations are based on received information and/or past experiences. If the expectations are not matched, then the customer may take his/her custom elsewhere. As Lacobucci *et al.* (1995) observed, continued dissatisfaction leads to loss of trade if there are competing opportunities. Retailers aim to meet these expectations and to keep their customers by binding them into a long-term relationship. To do this the retailer's offer must be positioned to meet the expectations of the target customer group matched by in-store and out-of-store activities.

CUSTOMER SERVICE ACTIVITIES

Customer service activities include what the retailer offers and how well the retailer does that, but also most importantly how well the retailer can coordinate channel activities. Customer service is embodied in the whole set of feelings of the customer during the progression of the transaction from the time the consumer comes into the store. These activities relate to the consummation of the transaction and the effects that are left if a transaction does not come about. In providing customer service, the retailer's key objective is transforming consumers into customers. The underlying proposition is that retailers must not simply differentiate themselves from their competitors, they must also be engaged in activities that bind their customers to them through the creation of a differential advantage (see Chapter 4).

A market that is characterised by generally low growth, extensive promotional activities and price competition is one that implies flux. It is a mature market and consumers move in reaction to shifts in the marketing programmes. In order not simply to survive through those shifts, retailers must undertake strategies that allow them to ensure customer loyalty. It must be remembered that the concept is customer not consumer. This is not simply a game of words, but an issue of emphasis, a difference in concepts that differentiates the store from others.

Customer Relationship Management

The concept of customer relationship management (CRM) focuses the organisation on the customer. It is as an enterprise approach to understanding and influencing customer behaviour through meaningful communications in order to improve customer acquisition, customer retention, customer loyalty and customer profitability (Sturdy, 2001). The goal is to increase sales opportunities by improving the process of communication with each customer with a targeted service, offer (product and price) and distribution channel whenever the customer wants it (see Table 16.1 and Figure 16.1).

The Integrated Customer Service Concept (ICSC)

The integrated customer service concept (ICSC) refers to the important function retailers play in the delivery of consumer satisfaction. Its central thesis is that in order to properly manage customer service, the retailer must not only pay attention

Table 16.1   *Critical Success Factors for Successful Customer Management*

■ Design the customer experience ■ Do not see the customer as 'outside' ■ Live by explicit values ■ Dare to be different: develop an innovative customer-centred culture that stands out from the competition	■ Learn from customers and let customers learn from each other ■ Treat work as 'serious fun' ■ Invert and flatten the organisational pyramid ■ Put customers second (or even third): satisfied customers follow on from satisfied suppliers and employees

Source: *Customer Relationship Management*, March 2001, pp. 29–32.

Figure 16.1   *A Model for the Development of Customer Relationships*

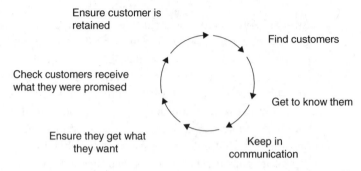

Ensure customer is retained

Find customers

Check customers receive what they were promised

Ensure they get what they want

Get to know them

Keep in communication

Source: based on Swift (2001).

to what consumers need but also to the quality of the customer services provided by their suppliers. They must also take responsibility for coordinating them in the context of the marketing channel. The implication is that retailers must really look over their shoulders at the input side of the operation in the development of their customer service programme as well as at the output side. Dwyer (1989) suggested that three distinct activities need to be coordinated by the retailer:

1   The retailer–customer component, which is the set of activities which allows the retailer to establish institutional loyalty, and to turn consumers into customers.

2   The intra-firm component, which is basically the coordinating function in which the retail management creates the organisational structures for coordinating customer service offerings of suppliers with the customer-service demands of consumers.

3   The inter-firm relations, that describe the point between what suppliers offer through their customer service programmes and the needs of the retailer.

The underlying premise of what retailers should do in affecting the design of inbound customer service system stems from fundamental characteristics of the retail function. Retailers perform an assorting function, namely: they bring together the product assortments most akin to consumer wants (Omar, 1999); retailing represents the point in the consumer marketing system in which the discrepancies of assortments are closed; and retail differentiation depends in part on the assembly of powerful inventory assortments that allow retailers to effectively serve the needs of their customers. When viewed in terms of the entire channel, retailers are active partici-pants in the development of these assortments. They deal with a wide variety of sup-pliers, and in general offer product assortments that are broader and deeper than from any one of these suppliers. The same argument can be extended to customer service.

Unlike products, which can be physically assembled, customer service must be coordinated so that it maximises the potency of the retail assortment. Simply, the retail offer is larger than the retail assortments; it incorporates all of those additional elements which facilitate transactions and meet the needs of customers.

Exhibit 16.2 The three rings of perceived value

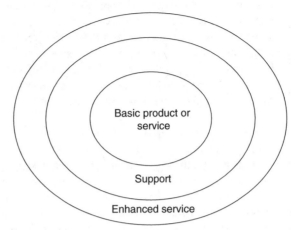

Basic product or service

Support

Enhanced service

In the UK, Whitbread has adapted Levitt's 'total product' model to its hotels and TGIF restaurant chain to ensure a consistent customer experience, with scope to meet individualised customer needs. The inner circle is the core product, the middle ring consists of management-led enhancements (e.g. training, CRM systems) and the outer circle is made up of low-cost individual touches, spontaneously delivered by staff, that supposedly result in the 'customer delight' (*Customer Relationship Management*, March 2001, p. 30).

Identifying Customer Needs

It is possible for a retailer to define its target market but fail to fully understand customers' needs. Although marketing is about meeting those needs profitably; understanding needs and wants is not always a simple task for most retailers. Some customers have needs of which they are not fully conscious, or they cannot articulate their needs precisely. Kotler (1997), distinguishes five types of customer needs as:

1 Stated needs – for example, the customer wants an inexpensive car.

2 Real needs – for example, the customer wants a car whose operating cost, not its initial price is low.

3 Unstated needs – for example, the customer expects good service from the car dealer.

4 Delight needs – for example, the customer buys the car and receives a complimentary road atlas.

5 Secret needs – for example, the customer wants to be seen by friends as a knowledgeable, value-oriented consumer.

Responding only to the customer's stated need may likely reduce the customer's actual total needs leading to a shortfall in satisfaction. Customer-oriented thinking requires

---

Exhibit 16.3   Customer service expectations in the UK and the USA

The contrast between grocery shopping at supermarkets in the UK and the USA is a typical example that could be used to explain how customer expectations could be depressed. In the UK, customers are expected to bag the groceries themselves and carry the goods to the car, possibly in the trolley. Their expectations of service are low. The last impression of the store the customer gets is often a long queue at the checkout, having to work themselves to pack their own purchases and then a trek to find the car and the resting place for the trolley. They may also have had to pay a returnable hire charge for the use of the trolley.

In the USA, by contrast, many stores offer a bagging service and carry the products to the car or have a drive-up collection point. The last impression of the store is of a sales associate placing their groceries in their car, thanking them for shopping at the store and wishing them a good day. The contrast is extreme, but the expectations are extreme as well. This is why in the USA retailers are at pains to dispel any 'I'm only a bag-boy' statements from such staff. They try instead to impress on such employees that their final contact with the customer can be the crucial contact in meeting the customer's expectations, as it is the last thing they experience and remember.

---

the retailer to define customer needs from the customer's point of view. Every shopping decision involves trade-offs, and retail management cannot know what these are without researching its customers.

It is, in some retailing situations, possible for customers' expectations to be depressed across an entire market (see Exhibit 16.3). To sell effectively, a salesperson must understand the customer (McGoldrick, 1990) and find the merchandise that best satisfies their need. Thus, the salesperson must learn as much as possible about the customer's budget as well as their motivation to purchase. Only then can the salesperson complete the exchange process by finding the merchandise that best matches what the customer wants. Since a variety of people shop at retail stores, determining customers' needs could be one of the most difficult steps in retail selling. Selling is an act of communication (Duncan and Hollander, 1977), and it is not always an easy matter to judge what a customer wants or needs in a product merely by observation.

For this reason retail sales staff must be expert listeners rather than just talkers. The basis for effective selling is listening to customers to ascertain their needs and identify the criteria by which they will select merchandise. Only then can sales staff find a product that will satisfy customers.

It is extremely important to satisfy customers because a retailer's sales come from two groups of customers: new customers and repeat customers. In retailing, attracting new customers is likely to cost the company five times as much as pleasing an existing customer. It may also cost a lot more to bring the new customer to the same level of profitability as the lost customer. Customer retention is thus more important than customer attraction, and the key to customer retention is customer satisfaction. A highly satisfied customer (Kotler, 1997):

■ Stays loyal longer.

■ Buys more as the retailer introduces new products and upgrades existing brads.

Exhibit 16.4   Customers' knowledge of their needs

Most consumer models assume that the majority of purchase decisions are not made on impulse but as a result of some rational, cognitive decision process; thus the choice of product would be determined before the purchase event takes place (see Garton, 1995). However, it is likely that there are a significant number of occasions when the actual item chosen is not decided on until the customer is in the retail outlet. Four factors may affect the outcome in these cases – the type of decision the consumer is making; the store's communications effectiveness; the preferred store choice; and the nature of the desired service.

In such instances, the retailer may need to assist the customer to make the service decision. Again, customers may not develop store consideration sets for each buying event, and may prefer to use store preferences they have evolved by experience. Retailers therefore need to create services that enhance good customer experience. Some customers may walk into a store with a clear idea of what product they need and even the brand they want; some, however, may know what product they want to buy, but not the brand, and yet others may want something, but not know precisely what. A person shopping for a gift for a friend's birthday or for a Christmas gift, for instance, may walk into a store without any clear idea of what to buy. The salesperson must first determine broadly the customer's need and decide what information will be relevant in helping the customer define the need more precisely.

- Talks favourably about the retailer and its merchandise.

- Pays less attention to competing brands and advertising and is less sensitive to price.

- Offers product/service ideas to the retailer.

- Costs less to serve than new customers.

Based on these criteria, it is important that the retailer measures customer satisfaction regularly.

Satisfying the Customer

Over the past few years, customer satisfaction has become one of the most important management issues around. An almost sudden and universal awareness of the importance and value of the customer in the retail success equation has created a number of significant challenges to retail management. The first and most fundamental challenge arises for senior management who have to decide whether customer satisfaction is the issue they should address and, if so, what should they do about it. The second challenge arises from middle managers and supervisors. If the retailer launches an initiative to improve levels of customer satisfaction, how will they manage the initial change of focus? More importantly, how will they measure the standards of performance in the areas for which they are responsible? The third challenge concerns staff. How do they manage their own behaviour in a way which improves the quality of service the customer receives?

Customer satisfaction is a broad-ranging issue, which to some degree touches every part of any retail organisation. It should be the long-term aim of any initiative. It is easier and more profitable in almost every business sector to do business with loyal, satisfied customers than it is to relentlessly chase new customers to replace dissatisfied customers lost through poor standards of service. Whilst customer service is what companies give, customer satisfaction is what customers receive, thus the level and degree of satisfaction is dependent upon the quality of service given. So customer satisfaction is a quality issue and has to be managed as such. The factors that affect customer satisfaction can be listed as:

- products – the quality, value and methods of marketing;
- premises – the environment created for the customer;
- procedures – the systems required to do business;
- people – the force that makes it happens (see Gagliano and Hathcote, 1994).

All these factors are important and no single area is sufficiently powerful to overcome major weaknesses in the other. Conversely, a relatively high interdependence strength may, in the customer's perception, provide greater satisfaction when compared to a company that may be excellent in one or two areas but poor in the others. A unique competitive advantage is therefore created from not just one, but from a combination of these factors. The relative weighting of each factor depends on the industry involved. The two areas of products and premises can be described as hardware, while procedures and people can be described as the software. The hardware usually takes time to change and often needs a consultant's intervention. The software is usually more flexible and can often be improved by a more rapid training-led intervention. However, improvements to quality of service also require a major change of culture (such as adjustment of employee attitudes and values) and the people element also takes time too. Whatever the change, it has to be managed by managers equipped to not only handle the short-term intervention, but also the ongoing activities.

THE CUSTOMER SERVICE PACKAGE

In providing a realistic customer service package, the retailer should remember that services are intended to contribute to the store's long-term profitability. An attempt to satisfy every possible customer would be both costly and futile, and also a few people will make demands that are impossible to fulfil. The important thing is to be certain that the store's merchandise and services will satisfy the great majority of its present and potential customers – the people who can provide the repeat business that is essential for ultimate success.

Emphasis needs to be placed in two main areas:

1 It is crucial that the retailer knows and understands the customer. Many retailers claim to do this and to know what customers want, but in fact it is debatable whether many retailers are truly proactive when it comes to changes in consumer demand, and research designed to meet customer requirements.

Figure 16.2   *A Customer-Care Model*

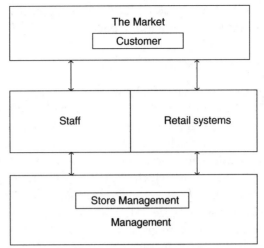

2 There has to be dedication to customer service, which in turn means a concentration on the service provided by sales employees to customers. The sales employee–customer relationship is crucial to the success of customer service policies, as this is the area with major potential for problems. An element of this is the emphasis to be placed on seeing the service a retailer provides in the customer's terms and on every occasion.

A customer-service focus on customer–employee relationships, however, does not mean that the systems and procedures of customer service can be forgotten; rather that the staff side of the provision of customer services is emphasised. This can be seen in Figure 16.2 which illustrates a customer-care model (Thomas, 1987). The model illustrates the number of instances where customer service is provided or supported. The four main components identified are customers, staff, management and retail systems. The interface between any of these has to be successful for effective and consistent customer service to be provided. The strength of this model is that it focuses attention not only on the systems (the physical service provision in most cases) but also on the people involved. It also emphasises that the systems and the staff have to have a shared direction or else they are pulling in opposite directions which will not result in a unique customer service package.

Elements in the Service Package and their Use in Retailing

The customer's image of the retailer is based on specific and measurable activities which the retailer undertakes to supply the appropriate customer service mix. The process of developing the correct customer service is based on three defined elements (Lalonde and Zinszer, 1976): pre-transaction elements, transaction elements, and post-transaction elements. The first of these in the context of the retailer has to do with the commitment of management to the development of written policies, the organisational structure to carry them out, and the means for evaluation. From the consumer's perspective this means that they are aware of the fact that there is a customer service policy, a policy which will be implemented by individuals in the store, and that ways of reacting to the policy exist.

Pre-transaction

The fact that customers know that there is a policy and that given service levels are expected is an important starting point for differentiation. However, it may be difficult to fully define such policies, unless they are based on the philosophy of 'the customer is always right'. Within this approach there may be expectations about the time that certain activities should take, the quality of the service offered by the employee, and the means by which evaluation can be made. While many retailers often state their policies about personal credit and returns, they often neglect to define those relating to special orders, delivery, and other such elements. Whether a retailer chooses to pursue such activities is less the issue than their lack of clarity in stating their availability and the level at which they are performed.

Customer service to be effective must take on the perspective of the customer. Therefore it may be necessary to determine customer viewpoints with regard to:

- additional elements that would be important if offered;
- the economic significance to customers in each segment; and
- ratings of competitors' service levels.

It may also be necessary to list questions that must be addressed to determine the most profitable service level for each major product line and each market. The determination of customer viewpoints, the stated importance of each element to the customer and an accurate and precise definition of customer service are the common elements in successful customer service programmes (Omar, 1999).

Transaction

A number of elements relate to the creation of satisfaction in the sales transaction. In a retailing context, these might include stock availability; the availability of substitutes; information availability; purchase convenience; the ability to place a special order; the ability to find stock in the system and to transfer it to the location of demand; and system accuracy in determining availability. The service environment, its design, signage and ambience will also contribute to transactional satisfaction.

Post-transaction

Post-transaction elements relate to follow-up activities to increase total satisfaction. These might include such services as the availability of installation; warranty support; alterations; repairs; parts' handling of customer problems; complaints; and claims. Other elements include tracking of products and providing follow-up information to customers as to recalls, product modifications and improvements. Another example might be the availability of temporary replacements for items requiring repairs or alterations.

Figure 16.3   *Conceptual Frameworks for Organising Integrated Customer Service*

Integrated Service Elements

An integrated customer service programme needs to combine four service dimensions:

- availability,
- convenience,
- support, and
- information.

A conceptual framework for the retailer in organising the customer service function is provided in Figure 16.3. In this contest, channel members other than the retailer could also use the concept with some changes. The figure shows the desires and expectations of the consumer at the centre of the integrated customer service concept. These expectations are surrounded by the four service dimensions, each of which is partially substitutable for the others. Availability is the primary element, as this is the service element which is most visible and of most immediate concern to the consumer. Although information, convenience and support are secondary they enhance the service provision.

Availability

Merchandise availability represents a series of management decisions starting from the selection of the product assortment, the location of inventories, and access to the assortment by the consumer, all of which represent physical availability. Each decision must be made within the context of satisfying consumer needs and must be integrated with the others. Each decision has the potential for affecting customer loyalty and the ways by which decisions are carried out are at the centre of customer service. While the choice of the product assortment itself should reflect consumer wants, it is really the second two that are more critical for the present discussion.

The location of the inventory both within the channel and within store affects the ease with which consumers make transactions. Location represents one part of the availability, as does consumer access; the first represents the spatial location and the latter the temporal. These may coincide, as when the product is at the normally expected location, or they may be separated when the product is available but not at the expected location. Under the second condition there is the normal concern for stockouts. Physical availability may often be defined as the percentage of time that an item is in stock and available for sale.

In other situations physical availability is the difference in time between when a purchase commitment is made and when the consumer actually possesses the goods. For retailers of consumer packaged goods, availability may mean having goods that are on the shelf and ready for selection and purchase by the consumer; while for retailers of consumer durable goods such as cars, appliances, carpeting and so forth, the consumer might expect, or at least accept, a time lag between commitment and possession.

Conceptually, stockout is failure to meet consumer expectations of availability. A stockout occurs when either the good is not immediately available, or when consumer expectations of time from commitment to possession cannot be met. Stockouts have several possible outcomes which may result in costs to the retailer and/or the supplier, not all of which are readily apparent. When faced with a stockout, the consumer may buy a different product variant such as a different size, style or colour; may switch brands; wait for the item to become available; or switch stores temporarily or permanently. Each of these potentially creates a cost for the retailer and/or supplier.

While the first three result in a sale for the retailer, several costs may be incurred. The contribution from the item sold may be less than for the item sought, or additional costs for special efforts to satisfy the consumer may be incurred. In the longer run, damage to customer loyalty and an incentive for the consumer to change future behaviour may result. One study found that customers who encounter a stockout left the store with a lower image of the store, less satisfaction, and reduced purchase intentions (Zinszer and Lesser, 1980). The cost to the retailer is greatest for a customer who switches stores. This may result in not just the loss of the contribution on the item which was out of stock, but also the loss of the contribution from other items which would have been purchased now or in the future.

The retailer can implement several policies to reduce the effects of stockouts. One is a policy of substituting a product of larger size or better quality at the same price as the one that is out of stock. While this could reduce the contribution on the item sold, other effects could more than offset this reduction. The customer's image of the store might be maintained or even improved, which may result in higher future contribution streams. Current sales of other items, which may have been lost due to the stockout, will be maintained. The negative side is a reduced contribution from the product that was substituted. However, reductions in current contributions from substitutions may be more effective in developing loyal customers and future contribution streams of such customers than attempting to build customer loyalty through price reductions.

Convenience

Convenience provides savings to the consumer in terms of the investment of time in the buying process and is related to many factors. Some of these, such as location of facilities, are not easily changed in the short run. Others, such as hours of operation, location of items in the store and the number of and methods of checking out and paying for goods are more easily changed. Convenience can also be considered relative to the availability of goods and services; one aspect is how easy particular items are to find in a given facility.

Convenience can also be provided through access to information about the available offerings, and on the status of goods which are out of stock. Information could be provided for other locations in the store where the item is in stock, expected future availability of the item, available substitutes, or even the identification of nearby stores where the item may be available. If convenience is viewed as a saving in time, then convenience and availability are highly related. If the items sought by the consumer are readily available then the expenditure of time by the consumer has been minimised. The cost of a stockout from the point of view of the consumer includes not just the loss of potential satisfaction from the product, but also the loss of time in attempting to achieve that satisfaction.

Support

Support is in part the willingness of the retailer to stand behind those goods which are part of the firm's assortment. Some common support components relate to return policies, installation, adjustment and repairs, as well as the provision of information. While the manufacturer or supplier may provide some of these, or assist the retailer, the ultimate responsibility lies with the retailer. Support and availability are also related in several ways; ensuring the availability of items such as lubricants, parts that wear out regularly, or repair parts. Support is also making a full line of items available, such as all size combinations, not just 'A' items. Information about changes in the product, changes in availability of parts or supplies – especially for older products, new options, or product problems and recalls are also important support components.

Individual initiatives can also help retain customers (Jones and Sasser, 1995). These include placing special orders for goods which are out of stock or for goods which are not normally carried. It also includes searching the firm, including branch stores, for the items and arranging transfers as needed for the items found. While additional costs may result, the present value of improved future contribution streams resulting from stronger customer loyalty may more than offset these costs. These procedures create a problem which must be addressed by top management – they create a trade-off between reduced current contributions in the expectation of increased future contributions. To reinforce desired employee behaviour, the retailer must recognise and reward employees for implementing these procedures. Three difficulties with implementation exist:

1 Determination of the estimated future value of these procedures upon which rewards should be based.

2 Measurement of the actual effects of these procedures to provide an estimate of future values used to compute rewards. While it is expected that these procedures will improve future sales, the measurement of the actual effects is confounded by other factors which influence sales. Nonetheless, efforts must be made to make estimates so that reward policy to encourage the desired behaviour can be implemented.

3 The identification of when one of the procedures is used and the recording of relevant information for both analytic and management purposes.

Information

Information serves both to tie the various service elements together and to provide customer service directly, and can prevent or reduce the effects of availability failures. Timely information on changes in demand can prevent stockouts by indicating when changes in ordering policies are needed. Information enhances convenience by indicating what is available, or unavailable, when it will be available, and where it can be found. Obtaining relevant information is becoming faster and easier. Within the firm the use of the barcode and optical character recognition systems provide accurate and timely information on inventories and sales. Between firms, the capability for efficient information transfer is improving through the development of electronic data interchange (EDI) and Internet-based systems.

MEASUREMENTS OF SERVICE QUALITY

The literature relating to retail management has seen a growing concern with the issues of customer service and particularly over how to provide good quality customer service. Tom Peters' (1988) work on business excellence as a whole has been influential in causing managers and researchers to focus on the customer, and service quality. While his work contains elements on the management of service quality, there are other more specialist texts on the subject. A more detailed study of service quality was undertaken (Zeithaml *et al.*, 1990) building on previous research into the dimensions of service quality, known as SERVQUAL (Parasuraman *et al.*, 1985). Parasuraman *et al.* demonstrated the way in which customers' expectations are often not met by companies in terms of service and how they might remedy the situation. Their analysis focused on the 'Gaps' model illustrated in Figure 16.4, which concentrates management effort on the identification of gaps in their service quality. What becomes apparent from the model is that gaps can develop from the mismatching of customers, management, staff and systems and that good service providers should aim to close them.

The model indentifies five gaps that cause unsuccessful service delivery:

1 The gap between consumer expectation, and management perception – retail management does not always correctly perceive what customers want.

2 The gap between management perception and service quality specifications – retail management might correctly perceive customers' wants but not set a specified performance standard.

3 The gap between service quality specifications and service delivery – the personnel might be poorly trained or incapable of or unwilling to meet the standard. On the other hand, they may be held to conflicting standards, such as taking time to listen to customers and serving them quality.

4 The gap between service delivery and external communications – statements made by retailer's representatives and advertisements affect consumer expectations.

Figure 16.4   *The Gaps Model*

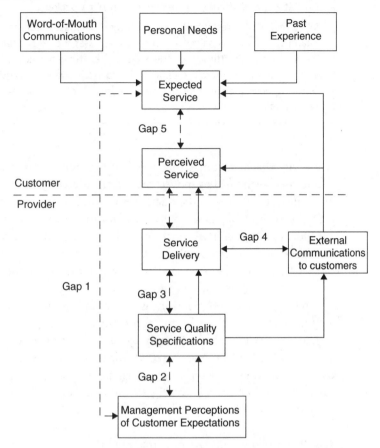

Source: Valarie A. Zeithaml, A. Parasuraman and Leonard L. Berry, *Delivering Quality Service: Balancing Customer Perceptions and Expectations*. New York: The Free Press, 1990.

5 The gap between perceived service and expected service – this gap occurs when the consumer misperceives the service quality.

The aim now is to show how aspects of customer service in retailing have been further developed.

Defining 'Quality' Service

Consumer perceptions of quality and value for money (price) are considered pivotal determinants of shopping behaviour and brand choice. Service quality and the definition of service quality has recently been a matter of some lively debate in service operations. It might be argued that the traditional manufacturing definition of quality as 'conformance to specification' is equally applicable to services, but formal service specifications are not always as readily available in service organisations as product specifications in manufacturing businesses largely due to the fact that the service deliverable is often intangible (Exhibit 16.5).

A further difficulty with the definition of quality as conformance to specification

> **Exhibit 16.5 Difficulty in specifying a service package**
>
> In an expensive restaurant, the customer purchases not only food but a range of intangible elements against which she/he assesses the service, including the presentation of the food, the attitude of the waiter, the ambience and so on. Specification of a service package is therefore difficult, being both qualitative and subjective in nature. If service specification is difficult, then measuring conformance to specification is clearly problematic.

is the fact that it assumes that the specification is what the customer wants. Total quality management has moved manufacturing away from the traditional definition of quality, towards a more market-orientated emphasis. A fundamental problem limiting work in this area involves the measurement of concepts. Quality and value are indistinct and elusive constructs that are often mistaken for imprecise adjectives like 'goodness, luxury, shininess or weight' (Zeithaml, 1988). Quality and value are not well-differentiated from each other or from similar constructs such as perceived worth and utility. As a result of such difficulties in definition, researchers often depend on unidimensional self-report measures to capture the concepts. They therefore must assume shared meanings among consumers.

Quality can be defined broadly as superiority or excellence (Parasuraman *et al.*, 1985). Similarly, Ganesh *et al.* (2000) suggested that, by extension, perceived quality can be defined as the consumer's judgement about a product's overall excellence or superiority. But, more specifically, Parasuraman *et al.* (*ibid.*) defined perceived quality as being:

- different from objective or actual quality;
- a higher-level abstraction rather than a specific attribute of a product;
- a global assessment that in some cases resembles attitude; and
- a judgement usually made within a consumer's evoked set.

One may distinguish between mechanistic and humanistic quality. While 'mechanistic quality involves an objective aspect or feature of a thing or event, humanistic quality involves the subjective response of people to objects and is therefore a highly relative phenomenon that differs between judges. Similarly, a distinction could be made between objective quality and perceived quality. Objective quality is the term used in the literature to describe the actual technical superiority or excellence of products, and refers to measurable and verifiable superiority on some predetermined ideal standard or standards.

The term objective quality is closely related to, but not the same as, other concepts used to describe the technical superiority of a product. Again, a distinction could be made between product-based quality and manufacturing-based quality. Product-based quality refers to amounts of specific attributes or ingredients of a product, whilst manufacturing-based quality involves conformance to manufacturing specifications or service standards. Conformance to requirements and incidence of internal and external failures are other definitions that illustrate manufacturing-oriented notions of quality. It is the understanding of the precise definition of 'quality' that will enable the appropriate choice of measurement instruments.

Measurements in Use

Based on the arguments developed in this chapter and the definition of quality as conformance to the customer's requirements, achieving quality is not merely a matter of adhering to specification – it is mostly about satisfying the requirements of customers. This customer-orientated approach towards understanding quality has also permeated the service-marketing literature. Lash (1989), for example, defines service quality as 'the degree of excellence intended and the control of variability in achieving that excellence, in meeting customers' requirements.

In terms of measurement, service quality is best evaluated in terms of achieving customer satisfaction, which is the match between customers' expectations of the service and their perceptions of the service they actually receive. Parasuraman *et al.* (1988) developed this idea into a service model which identified five ways in which a mismatch or 'gap' can arise between customers' expectations and their perceptions of service, as already shown in Figure 16.4. Customer satisfaction, *CS*, is described by the relation:

$$CS = \sum_{\chi=1}^{\eta} \omega\chi * SF\chi$$

where *CS* is the sum of satisfaction with various service quality factors *SF*, weighted according to customers' feelings, ω, for all χ factors.

Apart from the 'gap' analysis, Parasuraman *et al.* also identified five determinants of service quality, which, presented in order of their importance as rated by customers are:

1 *Reliability* – the ability of the retailer to perform the promised service dependably and accurately.

2 *Responsiveness* – the willingness of the retailer to help customers and to provide prompt service.

3 *Assurance* – the knowledge and courtesy of employees and their ability to convey trust and confidence.

4 *Empathy* – the provision of caring, individualised attention to customers.

5 *Tangibles* – the appearance of physical facilities, equipment, personnel and communication materials.

Other studies have also shown that retailers who offer excellently managed service share the following common practices: a strategic concept, a history of top-management commitment to quality, high standards, systems for monitoring service performance, systems for satisfying customers' complaints, and an emphasis on employee and customer satisfaction.

THE PROCESS OF RETAIL SELLING

Selling combinesa number of activities, and in order to help understand the different actions and tasks involved the selling process is best viewed as a sequence of steps shown in Figure 16.5: approaching the customer, determining customer needs, presenting merchandise, closing the sale, and follow-up.

Approaching the Customer

One major difference between retail selling and other forms of selling is that retail salespeople do not have to search for their customers. They usually rely on the other elements of the retailer's marketing strategy to bring prospective customers into the store. If, for example, a courteous greeting makes the customer feel welcome, the selling process gets off to a good start, but neglecting customers may lose sales. The salesperson's opening remark when approaching the customer often critically affects the development of their interaction. The ideal approach allows the salesperson to initiate a conversation with the customer and discover his or her needs (Ghosh, 1994).

Determining Customer Need

The salesperson may approach a browsing customer by asking open-ended question such as: 'what are you looking for?', 'Have you seen these new styles?' Do you have something special in mind?' All these phrases offer assistance to the customer without the customer asking for it. At the same time, the answers help the salesperson get a better idea of the customer's needs and shopping expectations. The manner in which the salesperson approaches the customer is as important as the questions.

Presenting the Merchandise

With knowledge of the customer's needs, the salesperson can start presenting the merchandise to the customer according to the customer's needs. Presentation involves more than just physical demonstration of products, and Hummel and Savitt (1994) observe that three distinct tasks are involved:

Figure 16.5   *The Retail Selling Process and Steps*

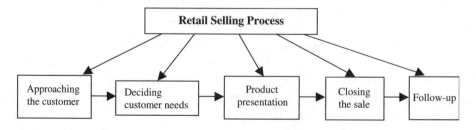

1 Provision of merchandise information – the salesperson must show the customer merchandise items and explain how they fit his or her needs.

2 Refine understanding of customer needs – while presenting merchandise the salesperson must pay close attention to how the customer responds to each item so that appropriate action may be taken to assist the customer.

3 The handling of customer objections – to make a sale the salesperson must overcome any customer objections to the merchandise being presented.

Closing the Sale

The sale is the ultimate objective of selling; once all customer objections have been handled, the salesperson must attempt to close the sale by asking for an order. According to a number of studies, sales personnel often find this difficult and commonly try to close a sale with an open question such as: 'Shall I wrap this up for you?' The question prompts the customer to a number of mutual closing techniques. The most important decision in closing is timing. The salesperson can lose the sale by attempting the close too quickly or too late: attempting to close too early may make the customer resentful of being pushed by the salesperson, but on the other hand stores often lose sales when they delay the close too long and the customer postpones the decision to buy.

In deciding when to close, the salesperson must consider each shopper individually; no single rule can cover all of them (see also Table 16.2). As mentioned earlier, some customers may walk into a store with a relatively clear idea of their needs, and they may well be ready to close early. Others may require more time to make their decision and would not like to be rushed to a close. The salesperson must judge a customer's position for themselves. They must bear in mind that each customer will

Table 16.2   *Approaches to Closing the Sale*

Approach	Procedures
The summary close	The salesperson summarises all the benefits of the product
The balance sheet close	The salesperson writes down the reasons for buying the product on a sheet of paper
The continuous yes close	The salesperson asks a series of questions, each worded in such a way that the customer will answer 'yes'. The final question requests the customer to buy
The assumptive close	The salesperson acts as if the customer has already agreed to buy. For instance, the salesperson can close by saying, 'I will write the order for you'
The standing-room-only close	The salesperson tries to get the customer to buy immediately instead of postponing, saying for instance, 'the sales ends today, you will to pay more if you wait until tomorrow'

provide verbal and non-verbal cues suggesting the best time for the salesperson to initiate a close.

The selling process does not stop with the closing of the sale; following up the sale, within the store and through communication programmes, should aim to ensure that customers are completely satisfied. Successful selling is dependent upon building a long-term relationship with the customer in which follow-up increases customer loyalty and provides an opportunity for new sales.

Suggestion Selling and Trading Up

The total sales that the store achieves at the end of any day depends on the average amount of money for each sales transaction and the number of transactions completed during the day. Total sales equals the average revenue per transaction multiplied by the number of transactions. In order to increase sales, therefore, the store must increase the number of transactions by attracting more customers or increasing the amount customers spend at the store. Suggestion-selling and trading-up are two ways in which salespeople try to increase the average transaction size:

- *Suggestion-selling* increases the transaction size by cross-selling related items to the same customer. In the time between closing a sale and ringing it up, a salesperson has the opportunity to suggest merchandise that is related to the article the customer has just bought. A salesperson may, for example, suggest a tie to go with a new suit, a Kodak film for a new Kodak camera. Unfortunately, many sales staff loses the opportunity for suggestion-selling because they neglect to ask, or make the suggestion improperly (Omar, 1999).

- *Trading-up* is another technique for increasing the sizes of transactions. In this process, the salesperson tries to sell a better-quality and higher-priced product than the one the customer originally intended to buy. After first showing items within the price range requested by the customer, a salesperson will also show higher-priced alternatives, explaining their relative advantages over the lower-priced brands. The customer then has the opportunity to consider the costs and benefits of all the alternatives and reassess his or her need. Often customers choose an item that costs more than they had originally contemplated spending once they become aware of its additional benefits.

Trading-up is a well-established sales technique for increasing the transaction size. It should, however, result from a genuine reevaluation of needs and expectations by the customer and not from aggressive or deceptive selling on the part of the salesperson.

STAFF TRAINING AND DEVELOPMENT

Like all other retailing functions the selling function, too, must be managed with diligence. Implementing a sales programme involves recruitment, training, motivating and directing the behaviour of sales personnel. The recruitment of good salespeople

Figure 16.6   *A Model of the Customer Service Chain*

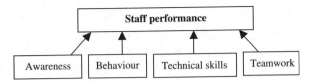

is the foundation of all effective sales programmes (see Chapter 9), and the manager must find salespeople and then train them in selling skills and product knowledge. He or she must also motivate them to perform effectively and create a working environment that encourages them to continue their employment with the firm. A number of important issues related to training, motivating and compensating retail sales personnel are discussed briefly in this section.

As they search for ways to improve their productivity and gain competitive advantage, many retailers are evaluating the effectiveness of sales training for their employees. Training in selling techniques can greatly enhance the effectiveness of retail sales staff, and, given the complexity of the retail environment, the need to improve service quality and the installation of complex automated transaction systems, the need for formal training has increased. Sales training may include both sessions in a classroom setting, and, increasingly, on-the-job training.

People are the most dynamic component in the customer satisfaction equation, and their performance depends on the development of a range of skills including awareness, teamwork, technical skills and behaviour (Figure 16.6).

This model not only establishes an initial means of performance diagnosis, it also provides a means by which standards of performance can be managed and measured over a sustained time scale thus providing middle management and supervisors with a means of 'making it happen'. Performance is affected by individuals' competence in the areas shown in Figure 16.6, and these performance variables are now each explained briefly.

Awareness

An awareness of properly researched customer needs and expectations is required whether customers are internal or external. This also calls for an understanding of how every individual's performance contributes to the customer service chain, the chain of events which leads from the individual, perhaps through internal customers to the external customer. The effectiveness of the customer service chain determines the quality of service received. Awareness is a skill which helps to seek out customer needs proactively.

Teamwork

In every organisation almost everyone is part of a formal team or an informal customer satisfaction chain. Working effectively with colleagues is the key to meeting customer satisfaction needs and continually resolving local customer satisfaction issues. Teamwork skills solve service issues.

Technical Skills

These skills deliver the basic competence a customer expects. They also translate the service philosophy into business results. Their relative importance varies according to the individual's role, but includes areas such as selling skills, product knowledge, telephone skills, communication skills, and the personal management of standards. Technical skills satisfy the customer's basic desire for professionalism.

Behavioural Style

When every individual member of staff understands the strengths and weaknesses of their own behavioural style and can adapt their own style to meet the behavioural needs of each individual customer, then behaviour becomes a powerful tool for stimulating individual customer loyalty.

The real skill, however, lies in the ability of individual staff members to blend these four ingredient skills to create a solution which meets the unique needs of each customer. This may be viewed in terms of an 'instant satisfaction test' (IST) at each customer interface. For this reason the process may be called creative customer satisfaction management.

Implementing the Customer Service Plan

The process for improvement is dependent upon the status of each individual retailer, and a typical seven-step process is shown in Figure 16.7. Such a process should always be tailored to meet the needs of each individual retailer; otherwise a unique competitive advantage cannot be created. This tailoring process takes longer, but is always that much stronger since it cannot be easily copied.

As Ganesh *et al.* (2000) put it, customer satisfaction is a management issue just like

Figure 16.7   *Process of Improvement*

profitability, cost control, productivity, and many others. It must therefore be relentlessly managed as such if permanent and consistent improvement is to be achieved and full revenue benefits enjoyed. Outside our work environment we are all customers and we recognise the quality of service we expect to obtain satisfaction. Retailers must strive, as customer service providers to make their organisations meet the expectations of their customer expectations. When this is achieved, customers will continue to give their custom, and the revenue and profitability that go with it. The customer *is* the retail business – there are no retail businesses that run without customers.

SUMMARY

This chapter has considered aspects of customer service in UK retailing. The fundamental belief identified is that it is essential to build a long-term relationship with customers and that customer service is one way of doing this. The service illustrations considered are to an extent exceptional in that they are interesting examples of service provision in the UK. It has to be remembered that not all British retailers practise good quality customer service, and that 'gaps' can be identified quite readily.

The provision of effective customer service is one method by which the retailer can achieve a differential advantage. In order to do this effectively the retailer must look at both the customer and the supplier. The customer service activities of the retailer must be based on the wants and needs of the customer, and the supplier's provision of service to the retailer makes it possible for the retailer to effectively satisfy the customer. The retailer must therefore direct the supplier as to the kinds of service that must be provided. To do this effectively requires that the members of the channel recognise their interdependence and be willing to cooperate with each other. The primary form of cooperation is the exchange of information, and the formation of agreements needed to realise retailer-defined customer service programmes. Achieving such cooperation is not a simple matter, it requires a realisation by all channel members that their individual success is ultimately based on customer satisfaction and that their efforts must be based on providing satisfaction.

The effective implementation of integrated customer service also requires that channel members take a long-run perspective on customer service as a means of differentiation. The effects of customer service activities may lag its provision, and the costs of providing service now may not be returned to the firm until much later. These future benefits may be hard to measure since they could take the form of either increased revenue, reduced costs of maintaining loyal customers, or some combination.

Regardless of how the customer service system evolves, it works only if there is a full commitment to seeing that it works. In greater part this means affecting employees through rewards, training and retraining to make certain it works. Customer service only happens when people make it happen, and even the best-designed and most comprehensive system only works as well as the people who are responsible. While the chapter has provided a discussion of what the integrated customer service concept should look like, we must not overlook this important point that its people who really make it happen, a point all too often ignored by many retailers in the UK.

QUESTIONS

1   Describe the information and guidelines that will help a fashion retailer decide on the nature of customer services to offer.

2   What are the likely factors that may encourage a supermarket to offer an additional customer service package?

3   Customer service is embodied in the set of feelings that the customer receives in the progression of the transaction from the time the customer comes into the store. Discuss this statement in the light of the food retailer's customer service provision objective.

4   What essential activities must the retailer coordinate in order to ensure the effectiveness of the integrated customer service concept?

5   In accordance with good retail management operation, customer-orientated thinking requires the retailer to define its customer needs from the customer's point of view. Discuss how this could be done.

6   With an aid of examples, explain what you understand by the term 'customer satisfaction' when shopping for groceries.

7   Customer service is all about attracting, retaining and enhancing the customer relationship. Expand on this statement.

8   The customer's image of the retailer is based on specific and measurable activities which the retailer undertakes to supply the appropriate customer service mix. What is a customer service mix in retailing?

9   People are the most dynamic component in the customer satisfaction equation. What skills do you think retailers need to enable them to provide customers with a satisfying service?

10 All the retailers have to do as customer service providers is make their organisations meet the standards of customer expectations. How could senior management ensure that standards are met?

Case Study

The 'Customer is King' Philosophy: Airport Customer Services

As many airports struggle with the financial instability of the airline industry, operators are looking for ways to generate more revenue. They have found that increasing food, beverage and merchandise sales is a lucrative way to accomplish their financial goals. This can only happen through the provision of better customer services at airports. Air travellers, often forced to wait an average of an hour or more for a flight, have little to do but eat and shop. Retailers have realised that travellers will spend more money if good food and appealing merchandise are backed by good customer service. This has led to revolutionary changes in airport retailing throughout the world, and has ensured that the customer is paramount. Airport operators are therefore introducing nationally known brands to airports, such as fast-food outlets like Burger King and Pizza Hut, and popular retailers like Body Shop and Tie Rack. This trend, called the 'branding concept', enables operators to increase retail traffic, profits and to offer a better customer service.

With the introduction of national brands, airports are beginning to resemble shopping centres with quality food and merchandise, quick, friendly service and at affordable prices. Although the average airport traveller has more money to spend than the average shopping-centre customer. It is not every airport customer that may want recognisable food outlets and shops. A frequent business traveller might prefer foods and beverages that are familiar, but a family going on holiday might want a taste of the local cuisine and culture. The food, beverage and merchandise mix needs to appeal to all customers to maximise sales. In order to accommodate everyone who visits the airport, retailers need to add local brands into the airport merchandise mix of national brands and provide a reliable customer service.

Also, more friends and families are coming to the airport to meet and greet travellers. Mintel research shows that 86 per cent of retail customers are in the midst of travelling, either arriving, departing or connecting flights, but the other 14 per cent, which includes people saying goodbye, meeters and greeters, cannot be ignored. Together these groups comprise a firm customer base for which good customer services could be provided. The BAA annual report shows that the UK domestic air traveller spends an average of 60 minutes in airports

before or in between flights. International travellers have up to 80 minutes on average. Passing time is the main reason travellers use retail stores: 53 per cent of lounge customers and 30 per cent of food customers say having time on their hands drove their decision to make a purchase. Money to spend combined with time to kill spells good news for food, beverage and merchandise sales. Add the restaurant and retail names that people want, equals increased revenue for airport consumers. Thus, the opportunity to increase retail sales exists if operators and retailers adopt one simple philosophy: 'the customer is king'.

In order to implement a customer-driven philosophy with the greatest positive impact on the bottom line, airport operators and retailers need to recognise that every airport situation is unique. The retail development plan, whether it is for a new terminal or a renovation of existing space, should be based on the airport's passenger needs and preferences, justified by research. The combination of airport rents, space needs and, most importantly, the available markets should help guide retail choices. But we must keep in mind that what works at, say, London Heathrow, one of the world's largest international airports, might not be possible at London Stansted airport. Customer satisfaction surveys and market research is an essential part of any retail development, and should be conducted regularly to identify customer needs within the airport retail environment. Through regular customer research, high-street retailers have learnt that the prime factor in customer satisfaction is quality, followed by an almost equal mix of service, price and location. In merchandising, location is the most important satisfaction driver, followed by layout and atmosphere. In airport shopping, it is friendly service first, followed by product price and speed of service. This type of information helps airport retailers implement improvements at

(Continued)

airports to increase customer satisfaction, including new pricing philosophies.

One benefit of being part of a local shopping centre is the marketing resources available. An airport is no different. Retailers can increase the traffic at restaurants and shops by marketing products and services as a package, just as they do in the high street. At London Gatwick airport, the British Airports Authority (BAA) is continually designing a marketing campaign to bring customers into the airport. Advertisements inside and outside the airport are aimed to draw attention to the customer services provided. The goals of such campaigns are to establish a brand identity in the customer's mind for the customer services provided at the airport. By listening to customers through market research, airport operators and retailers can create facilities that appeal to the wide range of airport users with a mix of merchandise. By implementing a comprehensive retail marketing campaign to draw attention to improvements, airport retailing is likely to be more rewarding.

SEMINAR QUESTION FOR DISCUSSION

Passing time is one of the main reasons why travellers use airport stores. Discuss how airport retailers could provide better customer services to enable travellers to enjoy their experience of the airport.

References

Bolton, R.N. and Drew, J.H. (1994) 'Linking Customer Satisfaction to Service Operations and Outcomes', in R.T. Rust and R.L. Oliver (eds), *Service Quality: New Directions in Theory and Practice*, pp. 173–200.

Carlzon, J. (1987) *Moments of Truth* (New York: Harper & Row).

Dabholkar, P.A., Thorpe, D.I. and Rentz, J.O. (1996) 'A Measure of Service Quality for Retail Stores: Scale Development and Validation', *Journal of the Academy of Marketing Science*, vol. 24, no. 1, pp. 3–16.

Duncan, D.J. and Hollander S.C. (1977) *Modern Retailing Management: Basic Concepts and Practices*, 9th edn (Homewood, Ill.: Richard Irwin).

Dwyer, F.R. (1989) 'Customer Lifetime Valuation To Support Marketing Decision Making', *Journal of Direct Marketing*, vol. 3, no. 4, pp. 8–15.

Gagliano, K.B. and Hathcote, J. (1994) 'Customer Expectations and Perceptions of Service Quality in Retail Apparel Specialty Stores', *Journal of Services Marketing*, vol. 8, no. 1, pp. 60–9.

Ganesh, J., Arnold, M.J. and Reynolds, K.E. (2000) 'Understanding the Customer Base of Service Providers: An Examination of the Differences Between Switchers and Stayers', *Journal of Marketing*, vol. 64, July, pp. 65–87.

Garton, P.A. (1995) 'Store Loyal? A View of Differential Congruence', *International Journal of Retail & Distribution Management*, vol. 23, no. 12, pp. 29–35.

Ghosh, A. (1994) *Retail Management*, 2nd edn (New York: The Dryden Press).

Grant, L. (1998) 'Your Customers Are Telling the Truth', *Fortune*, no. 16, February, pp. 164–6.

Hummel, J.W. and Savitt, R. (1994) 'Integrated Customer Service and Retail Strategy', *International Journal of Retailing*, vol. 3, no. 2, pp. 5–21.

Jones, T.O. and Sasser, W.E. (1995) 'Why Satisfied Customers Defect', *Harvard Business Review*, November–December, pp. 88–99.

Kotler, P. (1997) *Marketing Management: Analysis, Planning, Implementation, and Control* 9th edn (Englewood Cliffs, NJ: Prentice-Hall).

Lacobucci, D., Ostrom, A. and Grayson, K. (1995) 'Distinguishing Service Quality and Customer Satisfaction: the Voice of the Customer', *Journal of Consumer Psychology*, vol. 4, no. 3, pp. 277–303.

Lalonde, B.J. and Zinszer, P.H. (1976) 'Customer Service: Meaning and Measurement', (Chicago: The National Council of Physical Distribution Management).

Lash, L. (1989) *The Complete Guides to Customer Service* (New York: John Wiley & Sons).

Marketing Brief (1998) 'Bad Service Means Bad News For Retailers', *Marketing News*, vol. 31, no. 22, p. 2.

McGoldrick, P.J. (1990) *Retail Marketing* (Maidenhead: McGraw Hill).

Omar, O.E. (1999) *Retail Marketing* (London: Financial Times / Pitman Publishing).

Parasuraman, A., Zeithaml, V.A. and Berry, L.L. (1985) 'A Conceptual Model of Service Quality and Its Implications For Future Research', *Journal of Marketing*, vol. 49, no. 4, pp. 41–50.

Parasuraman, A., Zeithaml, V.A. and Berry, L.L. (1988) 'SERVQUAL: A Multiple-Item Scale for Measuring Customer Perception of Service Quality', *Journal of Retailing*, vol. 64. no. 1, pp. 12–40.

Peters, T. (1988) *Thriving on Chaos* (London: Macmillan).

Shemwell, D., Cronin, J. and Bullard, W. (1994) 'Relationship Exchanges in Services: An Empirical Investigation of On-Going Customer Service-Provider Relationships', *International Journal of Service Industry Management*, vol. 5, no. 3, pp. 57–68.

Sivadas, E. and Baker-Prewitt, J.L. (2000) 'An Examination of the Relationship between Service Quality, Customer Satisfaction, and Store Loyalty', *International Journal of Retail & Distribution Management*, vol. 28, no. 2, pp. 73–82.

Sparks, L. (1992) 'Customer Service In Retailing – the Next Leap Forward?', *The Service Industries Journal*, vol. 12, no. 2, April, pp. 165–84.

Sturdy, A. (2001) 'Serving Societies', in Sturdy, A., Grugulis, I. and Willmott, H. (eds), *Customer Service, Empowerment and Entrapment* (Basingstoke: Palgrave).

Swift, R.S. (2001) *Accelerated Customer Relationship Using CRM and Relationship Technologies* (Upper Saddle River, NJ: Prentice Hall).

Thomas, M. (1987) 'Customer Care: the Ultimate Marketing Tool', in Wesley, R. (ed.), *Reviewing Effective Research and Good Practice in Marketing Proceedings* (Warwick: MEG).

Zeithaml, V.A. (1988) 'Consumer Perceptions of Price, Quality, and Value: A Means-End Model and Synthesis of Evidence', *Journal of Marketing*, vol. 52, July, pp. 2–22.

Zeithaml, V.A., Parasuraman, A. and Berry, L.L. (1990) *Delivering Quality Service* (New York: Free Press).

Zinszer, P.H. and Lesser, J.A. (1980) 'An Empirical Evaluation of the Role of Stock-Out on Shopper Patronage Process', Paper presented at the Educators Conference Proceedings, American Marketing Association, Chicago, pp. 221–4.

PART FIVE

New Developments in Retailing

This fifth part concerns developments surrounding the use of technologies and store-based retailing. Chapter 17 examines the use of information technology in retailing and its potential to define the ways in which retailers manage their businesses. Chapter 18 provides an overview of non-store retailing, placing the Internet and other electronic forms of selling in a historical context beginning with mail order.

Information Technology in Retailing

INTRODUCTION

The relationship between technology and retailing is important to retailers because it concerns the direction of their resources and capabilities to satisfy consumer needs. Information technology provides the means to more fully meet these needs (Exhibit 17.1).

An understanding of the difficulty of dealing with technologies can be illustrated by the level of change in the retail industry. As the retail environment becomes more

---

Exhibit 17.1 Technology in retailing

Every purchase recorded by a checkout or other pay point represents a piece of information about a product, a price, a method of payment, a checkout operator and a time of day. The value of that information depends entirely on the extent to which the checkout, the store and the retail organisation use computer technology. For those retailers capable of exploiting this information to the full, the benefits are immense and can be felt through the entire retail organisation from the individual checkout to the boardroom. This is what differentiates retailers and provide competitive advantage.

---

complex, so information is used to manage, develop and initiate responses. A *system* will be required by a retailer to provide routine and recurrent information, but which also has the flexibility to upgrade for future information needs. An information system provides the necessary ingredients for management to make strategic and operational decisions. It must also coordinate the total information-gathering efforts of the retailer to enable relevant and timely information to be captured, organised and delivered when needed. This chapter presents a general model of information technology in retailing in an effort to clarify its conceptual basis. Thus, it seeks to identify information sources, types of information, the information flow process, and the components of information technology management, with an emphasis on in-store IT systems.

THE DEVELOPMENT AND USE OF IT IN RETAILING

During the 1980s when scanning systems and electronic point of sale (EPoS) were introduced, retailers' use of information technology tended to focus on counting 'things' such as goods sold, money taken, or items left on the shelf. Since then, the technological emphasis has shifted and is now concerned with people – tracking shoppers as they enter the store, monitoring customers' purchasing patterns or giving them the technology to record their own transactions (Figure 17.1). The retail market leaders talk of 'customer-facing' systems or 'efficient consumer response', while 'point-of-service' is replacing 'point-of-sale'. Similarly, 'supply chain' is giving way to 'demand chain' in the retail vocabulary.

As competition increases (see Chapter 2), many retailers are turning to more sophisticated marketing tools, and in order to differentiate themselves they have to use information technology to their advantage. Retailers compete on value, not solely on price, because value is the 'total experience' which can be enhanced by an assortment of leading-edge technologies. These range from the use of radio systems for interrogating office computers and solving shoppers' queries on the shopfloor, to the sophisticated use of interactive media (in-store or in the home) to encourage repeat store visits and purchases (see Exhibit 17.2). The following sections trace the developments and uses of information technology in retailing both in the UK and elsewhere in Europe.

Exhibit 17.2 The use of self-scanning in supermarkets

In supermarkets in the USA, self-scanning, in which shoppers scan their own purchases rather than waiting for a checkout operator to do so, is seen not so much as a means of reducing staff numbers, as an improved customer service. In such stores, the use of hand-held scanners from Symbol Technologies, originally developed with the Dutch chain Albert Heijn (part of the Ahold group), is now widespread. The system is said to have considerable appeal to young families for whom time is at a premium. In the UK, Safeway have led the way in the introduction of similar customer-operated systems.

Figure 17.1   *Trends in the Development of Information Technology in the Retail Industry*

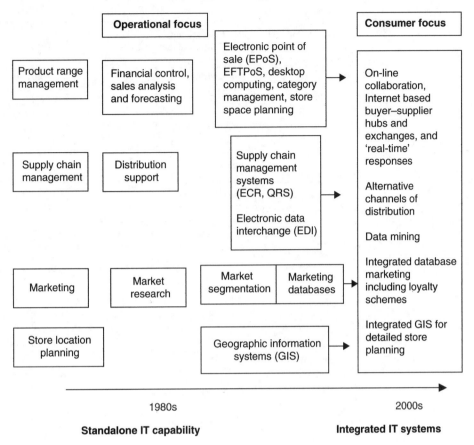

The Retailing Information System

Information technology is defined as the gathering, processing, storage, retrieval, display and communication of information or data by means of computers. It forms an increasingly important function of retailing management at both the strategic and operational levels. Since successful retailing starts with the possession and proper use of business information, many retailers have developed and implemented a retailing information system (RIS).

An RIS is an interacting organisation of people, machines and methods necessary for the retailer's problem-solving and decision-making activities (Figure 17.2). It has to be tailored to the needs of a particular retail organisation and should provide a planned and sequential flow of information for it to be effective. The RIS should support four functions which are to locate, gather, process and utilise pertinent retailing information. However, its fundamental purpose is to provide a framework for gathering information from both the retailer's external and internal environments so that the retailer can develop the best possible type of output in the form of correct decisions.

Figure 17.2   *The Holistic Retail Information System*

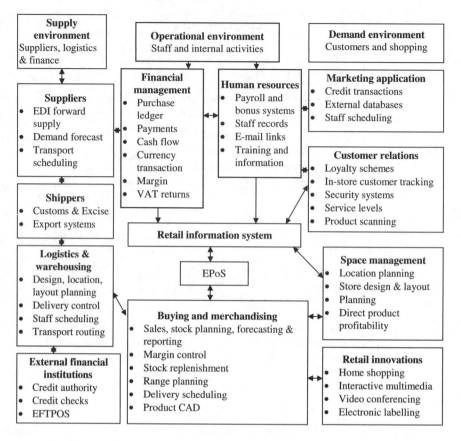

The retailer seeks and extracts information from a variety of sources to cater for its decision-making needs. It is necessary, however, for validating purposes of the data and for understanding some of the functions of the RIS to distinguish between two main types of information:

■ *Secondary information*, which has been collected for a different purpose and then published might not fit the retailer's precise needs, but a major function of the RIS is to convert this information into a reservoir of useful knowledge.

■ *Primary information* is collected by the retailer for a specific purpose tailored to its needs. The kinds of information in which the retailer should be interested are those that can make problem-solving and decision-making as effective as possible.

The RIS constitutes the retailer's operational backbone, and provides assistance to retailers to make decisions about customer purchase factors including:

■ in-store price promotions,
■ consumer expendable income,

- seasonal influences,
- in-store personal selling,
- retail advertising and promotion,
- number of brands and of shoppers,
- display space and brand positioning, and
- availability of goods.

For retailers to operate successfully, recognition should be made at a high level in the organisation that information data is an important asset and should be managed accordingly. If data is perceived as a strategic asset, retailers must take account of future information requirements. Increasingly it is recognised that the need for RIS in the future may be markedly different from today's needs. The data management approach must therefore be closely aligned with the system and information planning processes. O'Connor and Galvin (1997) strongly advocate this view, and recommend a flexibility analysis for the purpose of identifying where future changes are likely to occur in the retailing environment. In this way, planning can be oriented towards introducing flexibility in the systems at those areas of possible change.

IT Uses in Retailing

Pressure on retailers to use information technologies comes from a number of directions; from the marketing needs of an increasingly competitive and fragmented marketplace, to the information demands of a more responsive supply chain. Internally, retail information systems increasingly include many subsidiary support systems for micro-planning in detail, such as space planning, store modelling and staff scheduling.

As consumers have become more affluent and discerning, it has become possible to segment them into small, highly targeted, lifestyle-specific and possibly geographically specific market segments, each requiring highly targeted new products and/or services. So the need to keep in contact with customer demand has never been more critical. In such a fluid and competitive marketplace, most retailers may have to diversify into new products, develop internationally into new markets, or acquire market share from competitors.

It is in making such decisions that retail IT can play a significant role. Since stock, staff and space are the three most important resources for retailers, and their complete and accurate control is vital to maintaining a competitive edge, the gathering and use of information in these three key areas must be at the heart of any modern retail information system. Figure 17.3 shows how information from the transaction starts the process and which is then used to co-ordinate operational resources.

Historically retailers have always been more interested in what sales they have taken rather than in the sales they have missed. To analyse sales trends, a combination of computer software systems may act as a multiple toolkit for merchandise planning, product range planning, stock allocation and replenishment. Using industry standard databases, such systems help to plan, control and support decision-making for the complex stock flows experienced by retailers. However, they may encourage a dependence upon forecasting at a time when forecasting may no longer be so important,

Figure 17.3 *The Use of Technology in Retail Operations*

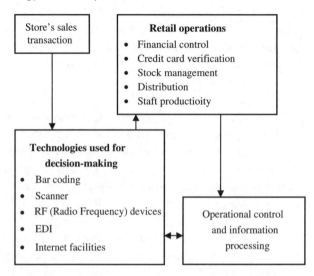

Source: adapted from Omar (1999), p. 416.

and 'real time' analysis is required. In addition, these systems may create massive amounts of data – often too much for managerial staff to absorb, process and adequately act upon. To enable customer service to be a reality, retail IT systems must be 'manageable' within each retailer's management structure.

Integrating Business with Technology

There is a need to encourage retailers to use technology in more innovative ways, to move from identifying processes that can be automated to creating a new organisational structure fully integrated with any new technology. This is particularly important in a climate when, so often, new retail systems fail to deliver as a result of a poor implementation process and a failure of management to break down historical organisational barriers and preconceptions. The complexity of retail marketing decision-making processes may be the root cause of the problem.

At the conventional 'front end' of retailing, technology can radically improve customer service. Supermarket checkout queues are much shorter as a result of store traffic monitoring systems; stores are adequately staffed at key times as a result of staff-scheduling information systems; and transaction speeds are getting faster. Levels of stock availability are improving, and the specific targeting of marketing communications to the right customers is becoming more precise. More powerful computers are used in parallel processing, data mining and the extensive use of data warehousing to enable retailers to understand their customers' individual shopping habits. This information can be applied to more accurate product selection and stock availability for targeted markets, but also to create more convenient and accessible store layouts (see also Exhibit 17.3).

> **Exhibit 17.3 The strategic use of information at Whittard of Chelsea**
>
> In 2000, Whittard launched a multichannel retail strategy to enable its customers to buy its upmarket tea and coffee products in its 103 UK stores, eight overseas locations, by mail order or online at whittard.co.uk and bestofbritish.com. This initiative enables the company to achieve two of its objectives; to introduce its luxury product lines into bestofbritish.com and expand its premier brand globally through whittard.co.uk.
>
> The combining of JDA's Merchandise Management System and Retail IDEAS data warehouse package has enabled the company to adopt its new retail model efficiently and focus on improving each channel's profitability. A number of specific business benefits have been achieved. Replacing manual data processing with the combined system results in a 20% time saving, equivalent to one day each week of the Merchandise Manager's time. Decision-making timeframes are shortened as the Retail IDEAS capability provides quick access to current data such as sales, margins and inventory. Improved operational efficiencies arise from greater visibility of product performance and in-season trading across departments and retail channels. This has enabled Whittard to centralise their buying and create greater economies of scale. Finally, customer service has improved as the result of better information sharing and improved buying decisions about core and newly-introduced product lines.
>
> Source: *Retail Technology*, April 2001, p. 20.

IT AND PRODUCT MANAGEMENT

One of the commonest reasons for retailers opting for an IT solution is to improve stock control. For more accurate stock control, the retailer needs better sales information and that means item-level data recording and electronic point of sale (EpoS) technologies. A computerised system, however, provides more than just automated stock records. The basic data can be modelled to highlight slow-selling lines or star performers, and it provides immediate reports on outstanding orders. Sales and/or stock information may similarly be produced, which can be linked through to conventional financial and accounting packages for transfer to purchase or nominal ledgers.

For many retailers, off-the-shelf software is perfectly adequate while many of the specialist retail software houses catering for the market can economically tailor standard systems to meet individual needs. Many retailers see installing a central merchandise system as part of a 'hasten slowly' approach to eventual full EPoS installation. Alternatively, hand-held units can collect the sales data in the store and these can be downloaded to a central computer on a daily or weekly basis. The use of EPoS systems for stock control is limited usually to large supermarkets that are able to pay for the system. A small local shop owner has no access to the sort of financial or merchandise analyses EPoS systems can provide.

Effective control of stock requires a merchandise information system that provides up-to-date information on sales of different brands, styles, colours and so on. Retailers are increasingly using software packages that analyse information gathered by electronic point-of-sale terminals to improve their management of stock. Such systems of stock control highlight the sales performance of an entire store in terms of both unit sales and revenues from sales. They show the store's week-to-date sales, sales during the previous weeks, stock in hand, and stock on order. They break down the information on total sales into three categories based on price status:

- regular priced merchandise,
- promotional priced merchandise (items with temporarily reduced prices), and
- permanently marked-down merchandise.

Stock control using such a method gives stores invaluable retailing tools for managing merchandise sales. It provides the information necessary to balance inventory with sales and determine which item to mark down and which to reorder. The highly competitive and continuously changing retail environment makes computerised merchandise information systems essential for controlling stock. As stores handle larger numbers of merchandise items, their needs for proper information systems increase. At one time only large stores could afford computerised information systems, but many systems now run on personal computers and costs are more reasonable. Retailers who invest in these systems can reduce their inventory investment by 15 to 30 per cent and control their markdowns much more effectively (Omar, 1999).

Capturing Data with Bar Codes

Widespread adoption of electronic data interchange between retailers and suppliers hinges on the development of a uniform and standard numbering system similar to the American Universal Product Code (UPC) system. This facility is provided by Electronic Article Numbering (EAN). EAN International, a European based association, specifies several different barcode types although EAN-13 is the main 13 digit scheme used in Europe for retail article numbering. The numbers are assigned by each country's association and use a numeric only coding scheme, enabling products to be tracked throughout the supply chain. The EAN-UCC system has been widely adopted by more than 800 000 companies world-wide enabling products to be managed through unique codes printed or attached to their packaging. Optical scanners can read the codes, speeding up the checkout process and allowing computers to maintain inventory records automatically.

More importantly, retailers can precisely identify the brands and sizes of items they wish to order with the appropriate bar code. At present, the product code system has been more widely accepted for supermarket products. However, a consortium of British retailers, suppliers and computer firms is actively supporting the development of a commonly accepted product code system in order to promote its use.

Product Analysis

Much of product planning depends, of course, upon access to relevant information. General and task environment information is broadly available in a conventional form

---

Exhibit 17.4   Klick Photopoint's new EPoS system

Klick Photopoint are the country's largest specialist photo processing chain operating from 451 retail outlets throughout the UK. Since photographs are very personal items, customer service is a vital element of the company's business and the PoS systems play a vital role in delivering that high level of service.

In 1999, following a merger, Klick decided to invest over £1 million in new millenium compliant tills to provide greater functionality and incorporating a new compatible PoS system within the new organisation. During 1999 the new systems were to rolled out to 280 stores at a rate of 30–40 per week at the peak of the project.

The tills provide a number of important features. The interface is very intuitive, guiding staff through the interaction and with key usage shown on the screen. Promotions are handled by the software too, so that for example 'Four films for £5' promotions are automatically discounted without staff intervention. At Head Office the new system also delivers up-to-date management information. Each night the central PowerCentre software polls each of the PoS terminals to upload their daily sales information. By 12.00 the next day, Head Office managers can have a complete picture of the previous day's business.

The company was attracted to a system running on standard Microsoft technology Windows NT and the Access database. They see this as providing flexibility for future development and some degree of 'future proofing' against software obsolescence.

Source: *Retail Technology*, May 2001, p. 29.

---

to all retailers. IT, however, allows individual retailers to process their own market research data much more cheaply and quickly, and through reading EPoS bar-coded information to gather and analyse data on sales and profit performance. Such analysis allows retailers to know not only how much of an individual product line is bought over a period of time, but also how often it is bought, at what time of the day or week and in what size of pack, as part of how large a single transaction or 'till', along with what other items, and, in injunction with EFTPoS, by whom or at least what type of customer.

The use of information systems by retailers to increase their power over suppliers became evident in the Direct Product Profitability (DPP) approach to managing product costs during the 1980s and early 1990s (see Figure 17.4). DPP permits the retailer to attribute to each product, or product category, the direct warehouse, transport and in-store costs associated with it. Allowance can also be made for direct revenues such as special manufacturer deals, and prompt payment discounts. The retailer can thus arrive at an accurate refined margin or direct product profit. This influences merchandise decisions as well as directing the search for increased efficiency of store operations. In terms of differentiating the product range, IT and EPoS data in particular allow retailers to tailor individual store merchandise ranges to local markets. While a 'core' of merchandise may be dictated for each store within a group by head office, 'micro marketing' provides for particular additions to individual branches on the basis of local differences in socio-economic and competitive variables (Exhibit 17.5).

Figure 17.4   *The Institute of Grocery Distribution (IGD's) Model for DPP*

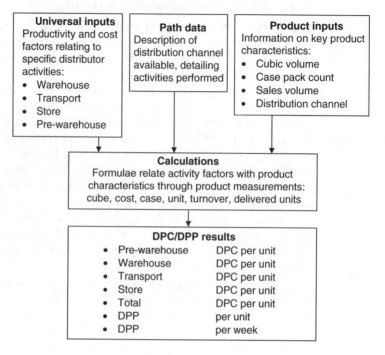

New IT Developments in Stock Management

Retail information systems have been commonplace for over two decades, and the flexibility of the latest developments combined with increasing computer literacy on the part of retail managers create new applications. From being largely an operational tool, IT is seen as a strategic resource in retailing, especially with the development of relational databases and electronic marketing systems to aid decision-making. The growing use of open systems and relational databases also means that there will be more opportunities for linking separate data sources to give even better management information.

A key resource in this respect is the Internet, which has created opportunities to manage information more directly to a wide range of organisational stakeholders. For business-to-business transactions (B2B), the Internet has already proved its applicability to the exchange of information to develop relationships and alliances with suppliers. Specifically within the delivery infrastructure, sales forecasting and product

> **Exhibit 17.6   IT incorporated into product and/or service**
>
> Car manufacturers employ IT to control many functions that in the past were tradition-
> ally operated by mechanical means, including ignition control, central locking, breaking
> systems, air conditioning and automatic drive. Similarly, many household items contain
> computer chips which operate and control their functions. By 2000, developments in
> IT and the Internet enabled Electrolux to introduce the Screenfridge, which includes
> an IP-capable flat-screen computer on its door. Amongst other functions, the 'kitchen
> manager' will detect when certain foods are approaching their expiry date and make
> recipe suggestions based on refrigerator content. It can also perform Internet-based
> commerce activities such as ordering food items when needed, exchanging e-mail and
> paying bills.

tracking through the supply chain are possible at increasing levels of detail. The Internet creates the opportunity for greater transparency and responsiveness; for example
in the management of promotions in food retailing, many suppliers will access rates
of sale and current inventory levels on a daily basis. Greater price transparency and
cost removal will become increasingly applicable in product management.

The use of information technology creates greater efficiencies in the design
and manufacture of products and services, ones in which IT is incorporated into the
products themselves. In this way, more direct contact will be created with the
consumer at the end of the supply chain (see Exhibit 17.6).

IT AND FINANCIAL MANAGEMENT

During the later part of the 1980s, the electronic funds transfer at point of sale
(EFTPoS) system was introduced. EFTPoS is an electronic payment system available to
customers buying goods and services from a retailer. The two systems that were first
introduced were those developed by Barclays, known as Connect, and CardPoint
developed by Lloyds. Banks and building societies have cooperated to developing a
nationwide EFTPoS service which incorporates a structural EFTPoS terminal capable
of accepting all major cards, including debit, credit and charge cards (Figure 17.5).

The benefits of using this system are as follows:

■ Authorisation must be given for every transaction, thus a stolen card will be
immediately identified.

■ Funds are guaranteed, overcoming a disadvantage of the current £50 limit with
cheque payment. If the customer has insufficient funds in their account the
transaction will not be authorised.

■ The system is fast to use and there is little paperwork.

For the customer the advantages are less obvious but offer another means of cashless
payment, and procedures at the point of sale should be quicker and more efficient. It
should be noted that, as with credit payment schemes, the retailer is required to pay
a transaction fee to the organisation providing the service.

Figure 17.5 *The Debit Card Process from Point of Sale*

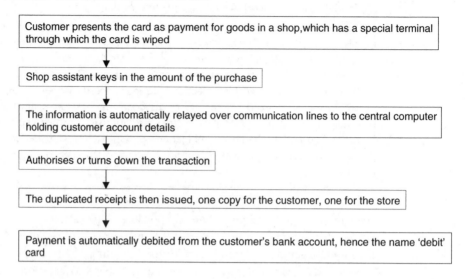

Customer presents the card as payment for goods in a shop,which has a special terminal through which the card is wiped

Shop assistant keys in the amount of the purchase

The information is automatically relayed over communication lines to the central computer holding customer account details

Authorises or turns down the transaction

The duplicated receipt is then issued, one copy for the customer, one for the store

Payment is automatically debited from the customer's bank account, hence the name 'debit' card

Electronic Data Interchange (EDI)

The entry of computers into retail stores and advances in communication technologies are profoundly affecting retailers' management of ordering and supplier payment. Multiple retailers can link all their stores with regional and national headquarters and to central warehouses through satellite communication systems. Although smaller chains are not able to afford their own satellite channels, individual stores can send information to warehouses over high-speed data transmission lines. Direct communication links between stores and warehouses speed up ordering and improve accuracy. Store personnel can type an order into a computer and instantaneously transmit it either to the chain's warehouse or to a supplier. In some sophisticated and automated systems, special computer programs automatically check a store's inventory records, determine if inventory on hand is below the reorder point, and then electronically place an order if necessary.

Direct electronic communication links between retailers and suppliers promises to be one of the most important breakthroughs in inventory management. Direct links with suppliers will reduce lead times and therefore stock needs at the store. Electronic transmission speeds up the ordering process and can save significantly on labour costs for large chains that place millions of orders every year (Figure 17.6). The store can also program computer software to check for inaccuracies in orders and verify delivery dates. If it finds that the supplier is out of stock, the retailer can modify or cancel an order on the spot.

Electronic Payment Systems

Technological advances have allowed retailers to improve the services they offer customers and to increase their productivity for a better competitive edge. Electronic

Figure 17.6   *Electronic Procurement*

Order	Order transmission	Order tracking	Receipt processing	Payment processing	System update
Supplier Online hub Online catalogue	Automatic approval Electronic submission	www. URL email	Web browser Real time 24/7	Electronic transmission after matching invoice to receipt	Database(s): supplier accounts inventory buying

Information flow

Source: based on Mckie (2001).

commerce is the term used for a variety of different methods of conducting business electronically, and the term covers a wide variety of different concepts and payment mechanisms. In terms of payment, the three broad categories are electronic funds transfer (EFT), electronic data interchange (EDI), and electronic money. The first two have already been discussed and this section therefore concerns itself with electronic money.

The benefits claimed for electronic money include greater efficiency, as hard currency and cheques are not required, and greater security, as no cash is handled. Given that cash accounts for 80 per cent of all payments made in the UK (O'Connor and Galvin, 1997), its displacement by electronic means is likely to be a slow process. Although there is some evidence of this happening, Flohr (1996) has cited four main areas of concern:

1 *Authentication* – so that buyers and sellers can verify that the electronic money is real and suitable for making payments for items purchased.

2 *Security* – to ensure that online transactions, transferring funds and creating electronic money are universally secure.

3 *Divisibility* – so that electronic money comes in small (penny or smaller) denominations that can make high-volume, small-value transactions practical.

4 *Anonymity* – to assure consumers and retailers that the transactions remain confidential.

In spite of these problems, many of which are yet to be resolved, several electronic money initiatives have been started. In the UK, a number of organisations have come together to develop the Mondex card, while in France VISA cards have carried micro-chips since the 1980s. Europay, MasterCard and VISA cards have created the EMV standard for electronic payments involving smart cards. In Sweden, the two banks that control 70 per cent of the credit banking market, Sparbanken Sverigeand Nordbanken, have also launched an electronic purse scheme based on the EMV standards. In Japan,

Toshiba and VISA have collaborated on a project to promote electronic commerce and smart cards which can be used in PCs to purchase goods over the Internet. There are also several other electronic payment systems in operation around the world During the 1990s development began on specialist Internet payment services to provide a cost-effective way of paying for small items of information or products. The aim is to find a more viable way to pay than by credit card where charges become prohibitively expensive for low-price purchases.

ELECTRONIC DATA AND MARKETING

The impact of information technology on marketing has been dramatic. As O'Connor and Galvin (1997) have identified, customer segmentation is moving into a new information-rich era based on behaviour rather than traditional demographic methods. Sales promotions are becoming more targeted as a result of more, and better, information. Distribution channels are multiplying and intermediaries are coming under increasing threat as manufacturers market their products directly to customers using the Internet. These changes are taking place within retail marketing as a result of improved system of retail information.

An increasingly important aspect of retail information systems is the comparatively new technique of customer-relationship management. This essentially involves retailers in combining information from sales, merchandise files, EFTPoS transactions, customer surveys and external sources such as geodemographic databases or drive-time information in order to selectively target consumer groups or aid store location-planning. Identifying individuals and targeting sales to them is seen as a priority for many retailers (Exhibit 17.7).

Exhibit 17.7 Customised marketing

Systems Market Link has been responsible for the development of the Rover Group's *Catalyst* magazine that is mailed to named Rover car customers. The customer completes a detailed questionnaire about his/her car and likely replacement needs and also selects personalised segments for the magazine. By matching the needs of customers to their tastes gives the magazine a more individualised quality. Having built up a detailed data-base of individuals the supplier can contact customers when their cars are due for replacement with details of new models and special offers. It is a technique which is proving far more effective than universal mailings to target customers.

Exactly the same techniques can be used by grocery retailers, with money-off coupons tailored to individual preferences or frequent-shopper promotions for regular customers. The mechanisms for doing this already exist and are continually being extended by the Internet to provide online coupons and promotions to build customer relationships. Retail managers need to be highly selective in their marketing strategy, and to relate to individuals and product customisation rather than anonymous groups of target customers.

Database Management

The advance of hardware and software computer technology creates the opportunity to deal with large amounts of information at a reduced cost to retailers, regardless of their size: even a personal computer (PC) can maintain a database that some years ago would have needed an expensive mainframe computer. Furthermore, relational database software makes it easier to process, analyse and have access to information held in different files. Present technologies allow personalisation not only of the messages, but also the promotional incentives based on past purchases.

Databases (Figure 17.7) are not new to the retail industry; they have been used for credit and inventory management for many years. Harvey (2000) has argued that developments in UK supermarket practice will continue to demand better systems of information. He observed that the major source of information for a retailing database is the account-receivable file of the retailer's own credit card. Loyalty cards provide the same function and customer information is also gathered through frequency programmes and point of sale (PoS) systems that allow name and address input.

The transaction data are best sourced directly from audited PoS sales files, and matched to name and address information using account numbers or unique customer numbers. Demographic information such as age or presence of children can be sourced from the credit application or purchased. A typical retailer in the USA and Europe will have 60 to 85 per cent of its annual sales volume matched to a customer or household on its marketing database (Harvey, 2000).

The impetus for integrated database management has stemmed from information highways and audiovisual interactive systems (Sallick, 1994) which have made possible, in a short time, an advanced communications environment. Database management reflects the increasing complexity of the industry, characterised by:

Figure 17.7   *Database Structure*

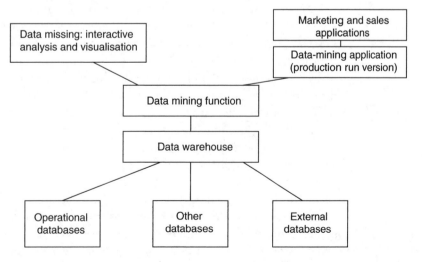

Source: from CRM/IT Interface in Stone and Foss (2001) *Successful Customer Relationship Marketing.*

■ Increasing competitive pressure, especially in mature markets, where to gain even a little market share is becoming more expensive.

■ Consumers who are better informed and more demanding. They know in depth the characteristics of products and services offered to them and are aware of the similarities between alternative brands. They are therefore more sceptical and less loyal to brands or retailers.

■ Distribution channels that are more concentrated and powerful. Producers are losing control of the relationship with the customer and are more dependent on large retailers. This market situation means more pressure on prices, reductions in operating margins and a subordination of promotional activities to the interests of distribution.

■ Fragmentation and saturation in mass media, especially in TV communications, with the consequent decrease in the effectiveness of general advertising activities.

■ Rising costs of commercial activities, especially those related to the salesforce.

Consequently, interest of all kinds of retailers in database management is not surprising. Using it as a power system to engage direct and relationship retailing strategies, retailers are increasing their contact with the market, increasing consumer loyalty, reducing their dependence on supply channels and optimising their retailing efforts. Retailers following this process will continually need to redefine the way they market and promote their products and services, and it seems reasonable to think that future retailing will be based on new rules, different paradigms and dominated by the use of information technology.

Loyalty Cards

Many major retailers are putting more marketing emphasis on customer loyalty schemes following Tesco's success in the UK grocery sector (see Conneran and Lawlor, 1997). Long-term loyalty is one of the hardest qualities to build among customers yet is critical to the success of any business. Customer loyalty schemes (Omar, 1999) are now accepted as one of the marketing phenomena of the past decade, and the recent focus on this area stems from a recognition of the benefits loyalty has to offer. Loyal customers, for example, buy more, pay premium prices and bring in new customers through referals (Reichheld and Sasser, 1990). Loyalty schemes are appropriate in mature, concentrated industries where differentiation is difficult to achieve and switching costs are low (Hawkes, 1996).

In the past, plastic cards were usually associated with getting money in and out of the bank. Today they include 'Reward' (that is, spend and save) or 'Club' cards issued by retailers. In theory, loyalty cards are designed to help retailers get closer to their customers and produce a shopper database for direct marketing. Retailers are therefore able to match their offers to the individual. In practice, database maintenance is expensive and most retailers avoid making mail shots too personal. The fear of

---

Exhibit 17.8   Putting loyalty to the test

For Boots the Chemist the introduction of its Advantage card loyalty scheme has been a great success. With nearly 11 million card holders and around 12 million customer visits to its 1400+ stores each week the company needs to understand customer behaviour in order to tailor the customer proposition.

The Advantage card provides three key benefits: insights into customer behaviour, immediate loyalty and targeted marketing offers. Insights into customer behaviour were revealed by the monitoring of buying patterns with the help of sophisticated data management tools. A complete data warehouse solution with support from appropriate business intelligence tools was provided by IBM.

The architecture of the data warehouse, the Customer Data Analysis System (CDAS) had to be right from the start. The key requirement was a system that provided maximum flexibility. The MicroStrategy business intelligence tool was designed in such as way that it would support complex queries on vast amounts of data. The types of report supported by the system include demographic profiling, basket analysis and direct marketing questionnaires. The basket analysis data provides insights into product purchasing repertoires of different groups of customers.

In analysing promotions, too, the new system enables an activity that took four hours of intensive data manipulation to be reduced to five minutes of data input and report that is run off within minutes. The information is automatically passed onto the Direct Marketing application, so that 'all the management of promotions, such as ensuring the appropriate people are mailed, is handled automatically'.

Boots' long term customer relationship management (CRM) strategy brings together the ability to segment the market based on life-stage, repertoire and value, differentiating the ways in which they communicate with customers. Advantage Point kiosks in stores deliver a range of personalised offers to customers, and future developments include communicating through mobile phone, digital TV, the Internet, kiosks, in-store, mailing and telephone. 'It is the company's view that the consumer will select the way they want to contact the brand. We must ensure that we have a single view of the customer so that however they contact Boots, the brand and their personalised proposition is the same.'

Source: *Retail Technology*, January/February 2001, pp. 34–5.

---

committing some highly publicised error by misinterpreting an individual's history of purchases or using out-of-date information is a potent deterrent. As a result, all cardholders tend to be given the same rewards and promotional mail shots.

In spite of UK retailers' initiatives, the use of loyalty cards is more widespread in the USA than in Europe. US retailers have realised that shoppers need to be rewarded differently, with high spenders encouraged to buy even more (Fraser *et al.*, 2000). The US experience suggests that the highest-spending 30 per cent can contribute 75 per cent to sales volumes, while the lowest 20 per cent will account for less than 15 per cent of profits as they hand-pick the product assortment for special cut-price offers. As Uncles (1994) proposed, retailers need to have a different price and benefits package for different customers and this should be based on an estimate of their economic worth to the organisation. Similarly, O'Malley and Evans (1996) observed that loyalty is really about economics and there is a real need to de-average customers and focus on economic value.

Exhibit 17.9   How Icom taps the power of data

One company that is thriving on the information explosion is Icom Information and Communications, based in Canada. Serving clients such as Procter & Gamble, Johnson & Johnson, Nestlé, and Unilever, Icom epitomises target marketing in the information age.

The company aims to find innovative and cost-effective ways to target individual consumers and has become one of the fastest-growing database marketing companies in North America. It collects detailed product usage and purchase profiles from more than 20 million households through proprietary census surveys and houses the resulting mass of individual consumer information in a specialised database using advanced data scanning, interpretation and computer storage technologies. This information is then used to construct a range of data and communications products for marketers. The company also provides database design services.

To help marketers 'narrowcast' a range of messages, samples and coupons to relevant segments of the database, Icom has automated the process of syndicated mailings, where the contents of each mailing are tailored to the habits of each target household. Information technology has allowed Icom to create the economies of scale associated with traditional mass marketing while achieving the persuasiveness of one-to-one selling. But individualised mailing is only one of the possibilities created by the explosion in information-based marketing. Accordingly, Icom is working in a number of new areas. Its statisticians and programmers have developed a program that can track brand usage among consumer segments with specific media habits. The company is also developing a series of new information products that link consumer purchase habits to retailer-specific shopping behaviour. The initial response to these products, says Levine, indicates that there is a substantial market.

Source: Financial Times, *Mastering Marketing*, Part 8.

It is for this reason that customer-specific marketing is the key, and technology an enabler to identify the most profitable customers and calculate the 'direct customer profitability'. Captured information can be used to identify how frequently customers shop in a store and monitor how recently they have made purchases to focus attention on the regular customers. But other companies may use the explosion of information technology for other marketing reasons as the case of Icom of Canada suggests (Exhibit 17.9).

Managing the millions of records from a scheme such as Clubcard demands significant IT investment, and for retail IT suppliers it is seen as a huge growth area. As well as IBM's Electronic Relationship Marketing application selected by Safeway, ICL and Amdahl have developed comparable Precision Retailing systems. These systems are based on analysis of a shopper's purchases or shopping basket, giving retailers insights into customers' preferences and lifestyles. Critics of 'points-for-prizes' loyalty projects suggest that tools like these can make generic customer targeting just as effective at increasing sales as current card schemes.

Customer Tracking

The harnessing of the data storage capacity of computers enables retail marketers, to know more about their customers, to understand more accurately what they want and

Table 17.1   *Online Households via PC in Europe, 1998 and 2003*

Country	PC ownership 1998	PC ownership 2003*	Expected increase (%)
Germany	4557	12170	22
UK	2019	8651	34
France	982	5669	42
Sweden	924	1724	45
Netherlands	884	2532	47
Italy	605	4214	13
Switzerland	467	1116	23
Finland	443	877	36
Spain	397	2515	17
Denmark	351	770	15
Norway	334	730	29
Austria	252	914	19
Belgium	240	1119	17
Greece	20	379	81
Total	12475	43379	28

Note: Figures stated in thousands; *denates estimates based on forecasted trends.

Source: Datamonitor (1998).

when they want it. By building up customer files, which focus on the lifetime value of the customer, retailers can create a more valuable source of competitive advantage than short-term sales gains. A longer-term focus enables new products to be developed to meet evolving customer needs (Dawes and Worthington, 1996). Decision Support Systems (DSS) can be used to gain an overview of the business or target specific data such as tracking frequent customers and combined with decision support applications they make existing information presentable, to allow predictive analysis to be undertaken.

In practice, consumers must be encouraged to reveal information about themselves. Consequently, retailers and consumer goods manufactures have to make initial contact with purchasers. Customers can manually fill out a card at point of sale or from a direct mail shot so that they can be informed of future retail promotional and sales activity. In this way, stores build up a substantial mailing list. Information on the customer's address, telephone numbers, annual income, residential areas and monthly consumption of products can then be collected and stored for tracking. In many cases, however, such a method produces limited results, possibly nothing more than an address and a telephone number. Retail tracking is more efficient when done with the store's magnetic stripe credit and loyalty cards that automatically register purchases in a computer program. As personal computer (PC) ownership increases per household in Europe (see Table 17.1), companies can access this information to maintain contact with their customers and gain competitive advantage within their market sectors.

Whilst Loyalty cards help to boost 'frequency of shopping' especially in the food sector, in-store technology comes into play long before any purchases are made by measuring customer traffic using infra-red or video-tracking systems to monitor shoppers' movements, identifying 'cold spots' in the store and helping to ensure adequate staffing levels in service-critical areas. Information technology systems sort out customer activity helping to classify shoppers by type of purchase and promote goods that will appeal to them by product juxtapositions or related discount offers. In using these tracking techniques, retailers are less concerned about the personal details of t he shopper but rather the flow of shoppers in the store. The customer-focused retail environment is thus one of data warehousing, shopping basket analysis and seamless systems integration to enable managers to access information from any of their stores.

STRATEGIC IMPLICATIONS OF IT DEVELOPMENT

Both European and American retailers have put forward a number of reasons for investing in retail information technology. The most common (Gilbert, 1999) include the need to sustain and improve competitive position; increase sales income; reduce retail costs; and improve operating flexibility. O'Connor and Galvin (1997) observe that the use of information technology has become increasingly strategic in retailing for several reasons including:

■ A significant increase in the choice of operating options available to retailers;

■ Its affect on the process of retailing strategy development by providing more information to retail managers;

■ Its potential to integrate different parts of a retail organisation; and

■ Its affect on the retail organisation's interface with the external environment.

Leadership in customer focused IT solutions can create significant competitive advantage over others in the industry. Thus, in fashion retailing, for instance, Arcadia invested heavily in IT in the 1970s and 1980s to gain a strong market position in the clothing sector. More recently, the UK fashion sector continues to perform well despite an uncertain economic environment. Retailers such as Oasis, New Look, Next and River Island have increased their market share through the efficient use of information technology.

The ever-increasing impact of information and communications technology, but also the costs of implementation, demand proportionate management attention. Market analyst, Mintel, forecasts an increase in information technology spending by retailers, with a rise in the number of EPoS terminals both in the UK and in other European countries. Table 17.2 shows the estimated expenditure on IT by top UK companies in 1998 demonstrating the scale of retail investment. The cost and rate of change in the industry have led to fundamental strategic decisions concerning the *location* of IT provision, as an in-house or outsourced function. Specialist suppliers providing IT consultancy are often able to provide a higher level of service more consistently to retail clients.

In broad terms, information technology (IT) can be used to improve both the strategic and the operational dimensions of an organisation as shown in Table 17.2. More specifically with regard to retailing, IT adds value to the operations of retail organisa-

Table 17.2   *Estimated IT Spend of Top UK Companies, 1998*

Sector	Annual turnover (£m)	IT spend (£m)	Percentage (%)
Retail (12 companies)	67189	2986	4.44
Others (38 companies)	366989	6485	1.77
Total	434175	9471	2.18

Source: *Corporate IT Strategy*, May 1999.

Table 17.3   *Strategic and Operational Opportunities for Information Technology*

Strategic opportunities	Operational opportunities
■ Build barriers to entry	■ Cost reductions and efficiency increases
■ Build in switching costs	■ Elimination/reduction of clerical effort
■ Change the basis of competition	■ More timely information
■ Change the balance of power in supplier relationships	■ Greater flexibility
	■ New opportunities for practice
■ Generate new products	■ New integrated systems
■ Change organisational objectives	■ Less idiosyncratic judgements
	■ Reduction of coordination problems

tions and allows retailers to implement their chosen strategy and merchandise policy in the most efficient manner.

Strategic IT Developments

As information technologies converge they will be used as a source of innovation in external relationships with suppliers, competitors and consumers. In particular, by taking advantage of the Internet, retailers will carry out more immediate and accurate supplier evaluation in terms of rate of sale, margins, comparative prices and delivery performance and trade credit (see also Table 17.3).

By developing their own e-commerce platforms, retailers are able to facilitate direct trade and create advantageous non-tariff barriers to suppliers and potential suppliers. Wholesalers may seek to dominate suppliers by tying voluntary group retailer customers to their computer-based ordering system, thus increasing the 'switching' costs of the former. In effect, value-adding services from IT can make a strategic contribution to retailing by changing the competitive structure of the market, and the value contained in information itself will enable retailers to realign their strategies (Dawson, 2001).

Information has affected the competitive structure of the retailing sector by increasing the incidence of scale economies arising from IT investment, and also by creating large initial capital and knowledge requirements for entry into the sector. Both of these phenomena are likely to operate to the disadvantage of the smaller retailer, and also increase the emphasis in retailing upon sales growth and absolute size against which to write off the investment and overhead costs of IT. However, the lower cost

> **Exhibit 17.10   Retail planning**
>
> The use of IT allows retailers to develop 'models' of their operation for planning purposes. These may relate to consumer behaviour or cash flows, and may be easily manipulated to ask 'What if?' questions in respect of changes in overall consumer spending patterns or interest rates in the economy. W. H. Smith, for example, spent £250 000 on a system combining EPoS and CAD (computer-aided design), which allows it to model on a computer screen the interior of any one of its 365 UK stores. This involves, in part, modelling consumer behaviour in a store (distinguishing, for example, between adults and children), and seeks to maximise the net profit per square foot by changing the store layout on the screen – 'What if?' – to arrive at the optimally-designed store.

and accessible alternative of the Internet introduces new strategic opportunities to outflank retail competitors using more complex and less flexible systems. Large retail organisations must balance the power of 'exclusive' information with an evaluation of strategic opportunities arising from the exchange of information, with suppliers but also other retailers. Online hubs and exchanges such as GlobalnetXchange (GNX) provide information services by and for retail members to develop best supply-chain practices.

The retailer's power of possession of information over suppliers in the market chain arises from a number of factors. A physical advantage in trading terms, and psychological or sociological adjacency to the customer; easier and less costly access to information on consumer behaviour; and because the activities of gathering, processing and analysing the relevant information have decreased in cost in real terms as a result of the applications of IT. Development of information technologies will enable retailers to change their relationship with consumers in another dimension; by increasing convenience and personalisation of services (see also Exhibit 17.10). Phototronic devices will increase the amount of data that can be stored, whilst more powerful audio systems will enable targeted messages to be made to small instore spaces and way include the use of voice recognition. Smart cards using micro-processors will be able to carry detailed personal information to provide retailer and product information as well as basic payment services. Investment in present Internet technology provides a platform for the evolution of real time, 24/7 access to a communication network that may bypass stores or require a reevaluation of the store as a place to shop. Instead, the home may become a network gateway from which consumers will manage a range of services and activities (Coca-Cola Services, 2001).

Operational IT Developments

It is in the area of operations that the most obvious advantages of IT development become apparent. Retail distribution is, after all, an information-intensive operation. A food superstore will stock around 36 000 lines, with Sainsbury customers buying well over 100 million items each week. Large retail organisations buy from a large number of suppliers (each of whom is being monitored by the retailer), and sell to millions of individual customers each year. Each customer expects products to be accurately priced on the shelves and passed quickly through the check-out, and to be provided with an accurate bill for the shopping basket of goods (Knox and Denison, 2000).

Developments in handheld devices linked to electronic shelf labelling and central information databases will enable fewer staff to work more accurately on stock management. Electronic shelf-edge labelling can be through liquid crystal displays (LCD) instead of plastic labels. Individual units of merchandise are no longer priced (thus reducing store labour costs), and the content of the individual LCD is controlled centrally in the store, or even the group, with the facility to change prices rapidly and at very low cost in response, for example, to the pattern of sales. Further advances in IT may enable stores to communicate directly to customers in store, with personalised messaging about pricing and promotions.

However, retail management also has to confront certain organisational issues arising from the introduction of IT. The adoption of IT systems centralises decision-making over which there was previously greater discretion further down the organisation. Check-out operators and even store managers may experience a considerable erosion of responsibility and interest in their jobs as the tasks of the former become increasingly automated, and the merchandise, pricing and display decisions of the latter are made centrally in the store organisation on the basis of computer-controlled information and models. There is evidence that store operations management has already become disillusioned (and possibly has been so for some time) as an increasing amount of responsibility (and job satisfaction) has been transferred into a centralised organisation structure. These organisational and staff motivation issues will have to be overcome if retail management is to obtain the maximum advantage from the adoption of retail information technology.

SUMMARY

Retailers invest decisively in information technology to gain competitive advantage. Competitive advantage is a relative and transitive state, and is based on access to information that creates customer value through marketing and operational efficiencies. From the beginnings of EDI and EPoS in the UK, the pioneering retailers in these fields gained a better and faster access to their suppliers, therefore reducing costs, as well as being able to analyse and forecast sales more efficiently. At that time, retailers were able to have competitive advantage over their rivals because the benefits from the mentioned applications where clearly identifiable.

These transitive and relative characteristics inherent to the concept of competitive advantage help explain the constant quest for differentiation relentlessly sought by retailers. Retailers seek differentiation by gathering the types of information and creating those systems reviewed throughout this chapter. They want to provide better differentiation in their prices, in the location of their stores, in the merchandise, in the promptness of their services, in the efficiency of their staff. To do this they need to understand the whole of the environment in which they operate, their suppliers, their personnel, their customers, even the weather.

In terms of integrated systems, when systems are tackled in isolation, huge investments in hardware and software will often, as in the past, fail to achieve an acceptable rate of return. The payback from any particular system can be substantial, but only if this system is integrated into the entire retail organisation. While EDI and Internet-based systems can help improve inventory management, other leverage factors such as distribution, management of assortments and promotional strategies are able to boost returns on investment disproportionately to the capital required by improving inventory turnover. Therefore, these levers should be integrated into the whole of the retailing system.

In conclusion, retailers pursue information and processing systems to gain competitive advantage in the marketplace, and in order to effectively gain this advantage they have to carefully integrate their systems. However, people play a preponderant role. If retailers have been successful in the last three years, for example in using technology, it is because retailers have begun to learn that the benefits of technology come not from the concept, nor from its introduction, but from its acceptance and use by those it impacts upon each day.

QUESTIONS

1 The relationship between technology and retailing is important to retailers because retail management is concerned with the means retailers use to direct their resources and capabilities to satisfy consumer needs. Discuss.

2 Define what you understand by the term, 'retail information systems'.

3 The use of information technology in retailing is to enable the decision-making process to be carried out effectively by controlling stock and finances effectively. Discuss this statement with the aid of a diagram.

4 Discuss how you think the role of information technology has changed the way retailers now operate their businesses.

5 To what extent do you think retailers have now embraced the use of information technology?

6 Explain how retailers could use information technology to differentiate their services from their rivals.

7 What is the major impact of information technology on retailing?

8 Electronic funds transfer at point of sale (EFTPoS) is an electronic payment system. What do you consider to be the benefits of this system?

9 Databases are not new in retailing, they have been used for credit and inventory management for many years. Discuss the role of databases in developing loyalty cards.

10 Discuss the strategic implication of IT development in retailing.

The Use of Information Technology to Improve the Grocery Supply Chain

In the UK grocery sector, information technology (IT) is not just revolutionising every stage of the supply chain, it is also defining and creating new markets (*The Grocer*, 18 July 1998). Over the past 10 years, IT in the food industry has reached out in both directions from the first checkout EPoS systems. It has moved forward to the customer and the whole home shopping area (direct to consumers), and back from the store via head office to the supply chain. In the UK, at least, the strategy of command and control to boost profits and improve distribution among retailers has been highly successful. It has all become information-based – how much of which product the store is selling to different customer groups, and of course how much the store is taking from the supplier.

These developments pose their own particular problems when, as in the case of Tesco, the onus switches from the UK to overseas expansion. Tesco, whose property holding includes more than 80 stores in Central Europe and 13 hypermarkets in Thailand, is currently rolling out different systems for different areas of operation. In certain areas such as scanning, the same system is implemented in all stores from the UK. However, in other areas Tesco has to work with whatever system is available, the priority being that it is able to provide the correct information to the group as a whole.

The industry's seemingly insatiable need for information is just one reason why information technology is now at the heart of every retail organisation's strategic decision-making. In a complex, multi-channel marketplace, decisions about what business to be in, let alone what products to sell, have come to rely on the message behind the data. At the start, EPoS did much to get the ball rolling, at least from a retail perspective. It was not only that retailers knew what they were selling, but they also started to understand product margins and product profitability in more detail. It is not surprising, therefore, that IT has suddenly become the focal point in retailing. If point of sale technologies could track products and profits, then why not customers who might ultimately be persuaded to buy and return to the store not only out of habit but because of what was on offer. The data warehouse and the whole concept of customer loyalty followed these aspects.

A significant challenge for retailers and suppliers has been the use of IT to extend customer relationships. In simple terms, customer knowledge has to be consolidated so that it can support every layer of a business. In a saturated food retailing market where the customer is spoilt for choice, the whole process has taken on a new significance. All the major retailers know that taking market share and growing margins have become important elements of competitive strategy and a new focus in retailing. The challenge brought by IT has been to help retailers operate their stores with improved information flows, tightening up the supply chain and ultimately helping to deliver those higher margins. Give customers more of what they want and persuade them to spend more on added value is a dictum made for modern food industry information technologists, whether they are talking about the traditional Friday night battle through the checkouts or digital out-of-store alternatives.

In this context, one may talk about food retailers and suppliers needing to become 'value innovators', whether that means having a chef dispensing recipe ideas in the super-

(Continued)

market or getting products direct to the consumer via the Internet. In both cases, IT can play its part by helping to identify consumers' preferences and boosting marketing to what could be described as 'the moment of value', and providing the key to success – and probably even survival – in the future. Value, of course, is not only what the consumer wants but also where he/she wants it. Tesco has built on its staggeringly successful data warehouse backed Clubcard service with 11 stores now participating in the Tesco Direct home shopping alternative. Tesco's stance is to run the store network as the home shopping base. At its store in Romford, for example, customers are able to place an order on the Internet which will be picked in the store, actually pointing the trolley to the right aisles.

This, for the moment at least, is customer-facing technology at the margins, but for some Tesco customers it is starting to take the drudgery out of shopping. It is customer demand rather than anything else which is driving this type of IT development. This is only true to a point, since predictions just a few years back that 30 per cent of consumers would be involved in some sort of IT-based home shopping still look wildly awry. In the store-based arena of scanning, Safeway has led the way at the checkout. This began at the beginning of the 1990s when Safeway was the first UK food retailer to introduce EPoS scanners, and more recently has moved to self-scanning systems which are now available to high-spending ABC customers in around 160 of the company's stores. At first glance, Shop & Go, as Safeway has called it, would appear to be a neat 'win–win' for the company. It is not only that it tackles congestion at the checkout, it also singles out high-spending customers and allows them to do their own scanning. The only possible drawback is that the thought of a quick dash through the checkout may encourage a shopper to leave the store too quickly.

According to successive surveys by consultant KPMG on the use of IT in European food retailing, paying is something the industry knows all about. Despite IT expenditure rising significantly as a proportion of sales since the first study in 1989, the latest report points out that IT management departments are struggling to keep up with the fast-changing demands of the business. This results in overspending and missing dates. The report, undertaken for CIES, draws the distinction between the largest companies who have reached an advanced level of IT development, and their smaller competitors who are tending to lag behind. Predictably, perhaps, the report predicts a continuing rise in the role and importance of information technology in retailing. The prime need for all those involved is to see IT at both the retail and the technology level. Retailers have to understand how it works and how it can be integrated; the integration of technology with the different sections of the retail organisation is the key point. The retailer needs to deploy people into the different business units, but at the same time bring them together. The real challenge for an information technologist in the food industry is to take up his/her position at the management level. As technology becomes not merely driven by retail strategy, but becomes an actual driver of the different components, then the information technologist must be prepared to step up to partner the managing director.

SEMINAR QUESTION FOR DISCUSSION

Suggest ways in which you believe food retailers could improve the development of information technology in their organisations.

References

Conneran, E. and Lawlor, K. (1997) 'Consumer Perceptions of the Superclub Loyalty Scheme and Its Influence on the Store Choice Decision', *Journal of Targeting, Measurement and Analysis for Marketing*, vol. 5, no. 3, pp. 210–20.

Coca-Cola Services, S.A. (2001) 'The Store of the Future, Consumer Relationship Strategies and Evolving Formats', Coca-Cola Retailing Research Group Europe.

Dawes, J. and Worthington, S. (1996) 'Information Systems and Competitive Advantage: A Case Study of a Top Ten Building Society', *International Journal of Bank Marketing*, vol. 14, no. 4, pp. 36–44.

Dawson J. (2001) 'Is there a New Commerce in Europe?', *International Review of Distribution and Consumer Research*, vol. 11, no. 3, July, pp. 287–99.

Financial Times (n.d.) *Mastering Marketing*, Part 8.

Flohr, U. (1996) 'Electronic Money', *Byte*, June, pp. 18–20.

Fraser, J., Fraser, N. and McDonald, F. (2000), 'The Strategic Challenge of Electronic Commerce', *Supply Chain Management, An International Journal*, vol. 5, no. 1, pp. 7–14.

Gilbert, D. (1999) *Retail Marketing Management* (Harlow: *Financial Times*/Prentice Hall).

Hawkes, P. (1996) 'The Customer Loyalty Challenge', *Admap*, January, pp. 47–8.

Harvey, M. (2000) 'Innovation and Competition in UK Supermarkets', *Supply Chain Management: An International Journal*, vol. 5, no. 1, pp. 15–21.

Knox, S.D. and Denison, T.J. (2000), 'Store Loyalty: Its Impact on Retail Revenue. An Empirical Study of Purchasing Behaviour in the UK', *Journal of Retailing and Consumer Services*, vol. 7, pp. 33–45.

Kotler, P. (1997) *Marketing Management: Analysis, Planning, Implementation, and Contro*, 9th edn (London: Prentice Hall International).

O'Connor, J. and Galvin, E. (1997) *Marketing and Information Technology: The Strategy, Application and Implementation of IT in Marketing* (London: Pitman).

Ody, P. (1990) *Information Technology for Retailers: A Review of Applications and Developments*, (Harlow: Longman).

O'Malley, L. and Evans, M. (1996) 'Retail Loyalty Schemes: Intrusive Cocaine Snorting For Cats and Dogs?', Paper presented to the Marketing Education Group Conference, University of Strathclyde.

McKie S. (2001) *E-business Best Practices: Leveraging Technology for Business Advantage* (New York: J. Wiley & Sons).

Omar, O.E. (1999) *Retail Marketing* (London: *Financial Times*/Pitman).

Reichheld, F. and Sasser, W.E. (1990) 'Zero Defections: Quality Comes to Services', *Harvard Business Review*, vol. 68, no. 5, September/October, p. 107.

Sallick, K.H. (1994) 'Retail Database Marketing: Strategies Beyond Direct Mail,' *The Journal of Database Marketing*, vol. 2, no. 2, pp. 112–21.

Samli, A.C. (1989) *Retail Marketing Strategy: Planning, Implementation and Control* (New York: Quorum Books).

Stone, M. and Foss, B. (2001) 'Successful Customer Relationship Marketing' (London: Kogan Page).

Uncles, M. (1994), 'Do You Or Your Customers Need A Loyalty Scheme', *Journal of Targeting, Measurement and Analysis for Marketing*, vol. 2, no. 4, pp. 335–50.

Non-Store and Internet Retailing

INTRODUCTION

Non-store retailing is the selling of goods or services outside the confines of a physical retail facility. This form of retailing accounts for an increasing percentage of consumer purchases (Exhibit 18.1) and includes personal sales methods such as in-home retailing and teleshopping, and non-personal sales methods such as automatic vending and mail-order retailing, including catalogue retailing. Certain non-store retailing methods fall into the category of direct marketing such as the use of non-personal media or telesales to introduce products to consumers, who then purchase the products by mail or telephone.

Many consumers consider shopping through mail, telephone or interactive devices to be risky and to lack confidentiality (Ghosh, 1998), which creates resistance to buying merchandise from non-store retailers. One reason for this reluctance is the consumer's inability to physically examine the quality of the products offered by non-store retailers, in contrast to retail stores where consumers can touch and feel the product and make immediate purchases.

The limited merchandise selection offered by non-store retailers is also a drawback since it restricts the potential for comparison-shopping. Moreover, as McGoldrick

> **Exhibit 18.1   Growth of non-store retailing**
>
> Non-store retailing in Europe is expanding rapidly with the mail-order sector estimated to be worth over £45.8 billion (Mintel, July 1999); most of the growth comes from increases in sales through home shopping. Developments in technology and the pursuit of economies of scale in Mail Order have been squeezing smaller competitors out of the market. As a result the four main competitors in Europe, including Otto Versand and Quelle from Germany, La Redoute from France and Great Universal Stores from the UK, are building their share from the current level of 47 per cent of the European market (see *The Economist*, 1999).
>
> With most companies facing limited expansion opportunities in their domestic markets, these large operators are looking to expand in underdeveloped markets such as southern Europe. Quelle is planning expansion in Portugal and is moving into central and Eastern Europe. Spain and Portugal are showing good growth for Otto Versand. Although still in its infancy in Europe, development of electronic shopping based on a non-store retailing philosophy could lead to an increased market share for mail order. On-line, interactive and television shopping, plus catalogue distribution through CD-ROM, are among media that will enhance the growth of non-store retailing.

(1990) has explained, many British shoppers value retail stores as an important part of the social and cultural landscape and consider shopping an important form of entertainment. The future of non-store and, especially, electronic retailing is still unfolding, and while it will grow in importance with time the dynamics of technological development increase its unpredictability.

This chapter reviews the growth of electronic commerce, specifically via the Internet. It considers the variations in European opportunities, which Internet connectivity affords, before reviewing progress in on-line retailing. However, the chapter starts with the developments in mail order, shopping by television, kiosks and CD-ROM. It draws to a conclusion by reviewing the fundamental changes in the way business is being conducted due to the arrival of the Internet.

DEVELOPMENTS IN MAIL ORDER

Mail order includes direct response and direct selling activities, together referred to as the home shopping sector. The origins of mail order are distinguished from retailing by several features. Notably companies started by selling to their customers through a network of agents, and secondly they offered credit terms, often to populations that were otherwise unable to afford goods. Products were offered through catalogues, and orders and deliveries were made by agents working in their nearby neighbourhood. The agent collected and administered weekly payment schedules too. Consequently mail-order companies developed expertise in the fulfilment of individual orders, and product design and marketing lagged behind.

During the past 20 years, more attention has been paid to these functions as companies focus on attractive lifestyle market segments, and the creation of 'specialogues'. Increasingly sophisticated segmentation and targeting techniques enable these shorter

> **Exhibit 18.2   Catalogue retailing in the USA and the UK**
>
> In the USA, General Foods created Thomas Garroway Ltd, a mail-order service supplying gourmet cheese, coffee and similar items. Other leading packaged-goods manufacturers involved in catalogue retailing include Hanes, Nestlé, Lipton, Sunkist and Whiteman Chocolates. These catalogue retailers are able to reach many two-income families who have more money and less time for special shopping.
>
> In the UK, manufacturers and grocery retail groups tend not to be involved with catalogue or home shopping, although department stores and clothing retail groups sell through a variety of different printed media. The UK mail-order market is dominated by specialist catalogues achieving sales worth over £5.4 billion, which has grown by 113 per cent since 1982 (Mintel, 1999). However, in recent years growth has levelled off and the sector is looking to develop by exploiting the changing leisure habits of consumers and through new technologies.

but more specific catalogues to be mailed out to selected customers. Fashion and sports retailing, for example, have seen an increasing interest in specialised mail order in the UK. Accompanying this development has been a trend away from agency mail order to direct mail order. The Next Directory was a major departure in this field. Launched in 1987, it specifically targeted new catalogue users, dispensing with agents in favour of more convenient phone and credit card-based ordering and sales. Although the company acquired a chain of newsagents with some intention to use the shops as collection points, deliveries were made direct to the respondent's home. The use of technology and higher quality products resulted in a transformation of image for the mail-order sector.

The advantages of mail-order retailing include efficiency and convenience. Mail-order houses such as Freemans, Grattan and Littlewoods can be located in low-cost areas and avoid the expense of store operations. Eliminating personal selling efforts and store operations may result in savings that can be passed on to consumers in the form of lower prices. On the other hand, mail order provides limited services and lacks immediacy. Table 18.1 shows the comparative strengths of retail store and mail order (non-store).

A further sector of Mail Order is Direct Response, although it is almost completely distinct from catalogue home selling. About a quarter of Direct Response expenditure is accounted for by companies marketing limited edition plates, prints, collectables and gifts.

Electronic Mail Order

It might be expected that UK non-store or mail order companies would be early adopters of electronic media who seek to extend their "paper formats into the electronic world of cyber-commerce" (Jones and Biasiotto, 1999). Furthermore, their customer information and logistics systems are already configured for direct distribution. Similarly, their financial structures favour further investment in non-store systems.

An additional strength of many mail-order houses rests in their increasingly international presence (Table 18.2) which positions them well to take advantage of the

Table 18.1 *Comparative Strengths of Store versus Mail-Order Retailing*

Advantages of store over mail order	Advantages of mail order over store
■ Customers can see, inspect, touch and feel the goods before deciding	■ Delayed payment
■ Customers can try on for best fit or test goods for quality and safety	■ Ability to choose product at leisure
■ No delay in acquiring purchases	■ Choose goods at own convenience
■ Easy to return goods	■ Easy to return goods without penalty if undamaged
■ Easy to compare prices	■ Saves time and hassle
■ Shopping is enjoyable for some consumers	■ No pestering or store intimidation
■ Customers can be given in-store advice on brand usage etc.	■ Shopping is a bother to some people
■ Some customers see in-store shopping as cheaper	■ Purchased items are delivered to the buyer's home

Table 18.2 *Selected Leading Non-US Mail-Order Houses*

Global rank	Company	Mail order sales, 1998 ($m)	Home country
1	Otto Versand / Grattan	16500	Germany
2	Quelle	8040	Germany
11	Great Universal Stores	3199	UK
13	La Redoute / Empire (UK)	2647	France
15	Neckermann	2259	Germany
20	Cecile	1885	Japan
21	Littlewoods	1764	UK
22	Senshukai	1745	Japan

Sources: national mail associations; *Direct Marketing* (1999).

global nature of the Internet. However, mail-order operators may still fail if the target markets addressed by the new technology are not natural extensions of their established markets (see Exhibit 18.3). The growth contribution from Internet sales to the performance of US mail-order houses has been minimal, although nearly all the major retailers in the established mail-order sector have developed an online presence (Benjamin and Wigand, 1995). International operations by mail-order houses, whether via the Internet or not, are of course necessarily more complex and standards may have to vary, at least in the early stages. Otto's immediate delivery in Germany, for example, becomes eight days by regular post in its newly-established Shanghai Cheer-Otto business in China. However, an increasing number of catalogue firms are generating international sales from their web sites and have to respond to increasingly diverse demands (Fraser *et al.*, 2000). In another example of internationalisation, Lloyd and Boyle (1998), cited the US computer retailer Cyberian Outpost offering a currency converter for 200 different currencies and online catalogues in 10 languages, including Japanese (which alone accounts for over 10 per cent of the company's orders).

Exhibit 18.3   The development of websites by mail-order retailers

Quelle (http://www.quelle.de) sees its website as the natural development of an involvement with online dating back to 1979 and the German Bildschirm text videotex service. But this is part of a broader strategy. The company is quoted as saying that it would like to be reachable wherever its customers look for it. Customers may look through the catalogue, the PC or even by means of television. The company aims to be available in every household (*European Retail Digest,* June 1998). Global market leader Otto Versand claims sales via new media to be running at over $200 million (180 million) in 1996 (although this includes CD-ROM and kiosk sales). The company's website was begun in late 1995 and offers the entire product portfolio. This is nothing exceptional, but what sets the site apart from the competition is the scale of the support operation. Otto's own distribution company within Germany, Hermes Versand, offers 24 to 48-hour and even immediate delivery (for goods ordered before noon). Deliveries can take place up to 9 p.m. on weekdays and on Saturday mornings.

In the USA, the pioneer amongst conventional mail-order houses using the Internet has been Lands' End, although the company used the site primarily as a communications tool rather than as a direct selling medium in the early days. Established US companies have also been slow in building back-office links from web software to ordering and fulfilment systems (see KPMG Electronic Reports, 1999). As *PC Dealer* (1999) stated, personalised websites for individual consumers, which deliver genuine one-to-one marketing along the lines of CNN's *Custom News* or *Hot-Wired* magazine, are still a remote prospect for mainstream catalogue retailers.

The continuing preoccupation with the 'catalogue' has led to the growth of a number of meta-sites offering a buyer's guide to mail-order catalogues. Buyer's Index (http://www.buyersindex.com) is a bespoke search engine offering access to over 8000 listed mail-order companies and over 19 million products. Its object is to help mail-order buyers find the best suppliers on or off the Net. The Catalogue Site (http://www.catalogsite.com) is a competing but more broadly based service for mail-order enthusiasts, which includes a monthly newsletter. Cleverly, the site provides links to the catalogues listed but retains its own frame around the destination site.

TV SHOPPING, KIOSKS AND CD-ROM

Electronic retailing can take the form of one-way media programmed by the retailer, such as television shopping and two-way media interactively used by the customer. Television shopping started in the USA in 1982 with the Home Shopping Club set up on a local cable network. Sales reached $11 million in two years, and in 1985 the concept was launched nationally. The format was based on creating a sense of urgency through the speed and price-cutting techniques used in each show. The common theme of TV shopping has been this element of 'hard sell', typically of jewellery, collectibles and clothing. QVC Network joined HSN in competition in the USA, and in 1995 extended its brand of selling to the UK with some success (Cope, 1996).

Interactive television has developed this narrow sales-driven base with the aim of enabling viewers to access products and services presented on TV. By using a modem or other connective device, viewers are able to view, acquire information and take purchasing decisions from online suppliers. Television remote control units enable the process to take place without users needing to move from their chairs. Credit-card payment or withdrawals from an online bank enable the financial transaction to take place using the same hardware. Unlike the PC, interaction takes place through the familiar and accessible television set.

The first trials took place in the USA in 1993, with the trial launch of the Sega channel on a cable network. Whilst a number of other trials have taken place, with an excellent response reported by Carphone Warehouse selling a limited range of products during 1999–2000, the vision has been constrained by the need for further technological development. Other interactive media have been used; during the 1980s in France Minitel enabled telephone subscribers to access information and services through computer key pads attached to their phones. However this project has been largely overtaken by the greater flexibility offered by the Internet.

The Grocer (1998) commented that home shopping or TV shopping may not be a threat to store-based retailers, rather that retailers could run TV shopping (see Exhibit 18.4) alongside their existing store businesses. The main problem with developments in this area is not the capability of the technology, but the willingness of consumers to participate, and much depends on the number of homes connected to either satellite or cables systems, with wide variances across Europe as Table 18.3 shows.

Table 18.3   *Cable and Satellite Penetration in Europe, 1997*

Percentage of households owning television

Country	Cable	Satellite
Austria	28.6	12.8
Belgium	87.5	5.3
Denmark	65.3	15.6
Finland	41.8	14.9
France	10.9	8.4
Germany	49.7	20.2
Greece	19.5	1.5
Ireland	49.8	22.5
Italy	58.3	5.9
Luxembourg	65.6	0.6
Netherlands	88.4	32.1
Portugal	18.9	15.8
Spain	15.3	29.3
Sweden	59.9	38.7
United Kingdom	28.9	65.8

Source: *European Retail Digest*, June 1998.

> **Exhibit 18.4   Digital television (Open)**
>
> 'Open-all-hours TV shopping' is an electronic shopping mall conducted through digital television. Open is partly owned by BSKYB, along with BT, HSBC and Japan's Matsushita Corporation. No special equipment is required apart from the digital set-top box and Satellite dish (a digital TV package) and a telephone link. Unlike the Net, the telephone cost does not start until viewers go online to buy or interact. The service is quick and consumers may select and order all the items they need within minutes. The retailer is able to deliver the selected items to the customer within 48 hours after the goods have been selected and ordered. For the average consumer who simply wants to shop, bank or order tickets, Open is a useful system and seems faster and more streamlined than the Net.
>
> Unlike Web traders, retailers on the 'open-all-hours system' must agree to abide by UK consumer legislation, offer full refund and/or replacement services and delivery within 48 hours. 1.2 million consumers had signed up to SKY Digital by 2000, which gives them automatic access to Open and it is assumed that this figure will rise to 5 million by 2003.

Electronic Kiosks

A transactional kiosk is 'an electronic service station that allows customers to access information, order merchandise or secure services by using a credit card or personal identification number' (Lucas *et al.*, 1994). An early development of this facility was the automatic teller machine (ATM) that has now been in operation since the 1970s, and services to provide information and some products since the 1980s. For retailers, the Interactive Multimedia Kiosk (IMK) serves a number of purposes when integrated into a marketing strategy. Its primary role is to improve customer service by providing product information and facilitating sales. Typically kiosks enable interaction through a relatively limited sequence of touch screens that guide the customer through their search. Some kiosks take credit and debit card payments and are provided with printers to print tickets or receipts; for example for train tickets at railway stations. Increasingly they facilitate use through visual presentation and multimedia rather than the textual interfaces found in the earlier machines.

In addition kiosks enable expansion of the customer base, reduce labour costs and increase potential revenues by multiplying the points of contact. In 1998 the IMK market in Europe was worth over US$150.8 million and has been projected to grow to over US$726 million by 2005 when used in conjunction with other distribution channel technologies (*Retail Technology Directions*, 1999). The medium has proved particularly suitable for intangible service elements such as holiday or hotel information, as well as ticketing. It is also expanding by increasing the number of Internet-based kiosks and convergence of Point of Information (PoI) with Point of Sale (PoS). Research shows that these would be widely accepted by technology-literate consumers, serving the dual purpose of dispensing promotional material or advertising brands (Mintel, 1999). Whilst banking and financial services form the largest European market, retailers continue to experiment with these new delivery channels to reduce costs and reach a wider customer base. The leading supermarket chains are considering linking them to loyalty cards, so that customised money-off vouchers can be dispensed to customers in exchange for loyalty points. However, kiosks have been criticised for being user-unfriendly, which has inhibited their widespread adoption (Mintel, 1997).

Despite this problem, a number of retailers have used kiosks for sell or promote their products and services. In 1996 the Iceland grocery store carried out a successful store-based pilot to help with selling white goods. Customers communicated via sound and video with professionally trained staff at the company's headquarters. This acted as a far more informative and personal means of selling than its catalogue system. Other companies have undertaken trials, primarily to extend their markets into specialised product ranges. Sainsbury's Bank was launched in 1997 with services available in 244 of the retailer's supermarkets, and Savacentres. The instore 'bank' is no more than a kiosk displaying brochures about financial products with an ATM machine and a nearby telephone for customers to call the 'direct' bank which is open 24 hours a day; tests are extending to further financial services and food in the longer term.

Compact Disk (CD)

Less flexible than the Internet, the CD provides a comparatively simple way to enhance customer service. However, a disadvantage of this technology is a limitation in the currency of the recorded data, and although Tesco have used a monthly disk that housed their virtual shopping programmes, development of fully online services appear to provide greater flexibility and timeliness.

THE INTERNET

If the 1990s were considered the era of database-driven customer management, the next decade presents a more 'integrated approach to retailing' (Mulhern, 1997) through interactive customer management. Potentially, the Internet offers the means to target and interactively communicate with consumers individually, through to the final purchase transaction of the product (Reynolds, 1998). Moreover the World Wide Web (Web) unlike other Internet options like e-mail, provides sophisticated graphics, digitised pictures and audio and visual files, with the ease of point-and-click access (Reynolds, 2000). It is here that many retailers have set up sites which give a visual display and options to scroll through listings, graphical representations of merchandise and preset payment forms.

Considerable attention has been focused on the Internet as a medium for its commercial potential for retailers in both business-to-business (B2B) and business-to-consumer (B2C) roles. However, in focusing on B2C activities, two key areas of concern have emerged; the first relates to the role the Internet plays in retailing. For some (Van Tassel and Weitz, 1997; Hart *et al.*, 2000) the Internet will provide a new retail format, usurping the traditional dominance of fixed location stores. Less comprehensively, Hazel (1996) sees the Internet performing a supporting role for existing marketing activity. Alternatively, both roles may be adopted and whichever succeeds will determine consumer demand for online shopping and thus the development of e-retailing.

According to Hart *et al.* (2000), this raises a second concern regarding the size, growth or future potential of the e-retail market, but also the extent to which retailers are online and using the Internet strategically or tactically for short-term marketing gains. This distinction is critical for retailers developing Internet retailing strategies, and may help identify the sectors or variables that hold most potential for online retailing. Conversely, it could also expose any retailer weaknesses or threats to existing retail formats.

So far, the Internet has been used in five main ways to facilitate retailing (Ghosh, 1998):

1 It is a means of communicating information about the retail organisation, its products and services (Bruno, 1997).

2 It is used as a more proactive marketing tool, inviting consumers to interactively access the website to gain more product information to facilitate their buying decision-making process (Hazel, 1996), at the same time providing valuable consumer data for retailers to enable greater targeting.

3 It is a communication tool for attracting new customers, penetrating new markets, promoting the company's brand and improving customer retention (Ernst and Young, 1999).

4 It allows retailers to physically sell products online through transactions with consumers (Hoffman and Novak, 1996).

5 It is an additional channel to an existing store-based or mail-order operation.

If the Internet channel proves successful, it could replace at least some fixed-location stores with a new electronic retail format (Van Tassel and Weitz, 1997). The implications are considerable; ultimately the Internet could fundamentally alter the ways that consumers shop and thus transform the retail environment, through the creation of a global shopping space.

Market Size

A continuing difficulty for retailers in evaluating the opportunities and risks of the Internet is its intangibility, and a key task is to enumerate the size, scope and characteristics of the market within which they seek to operate. There are a wide range of methodologies which retailers may use in seeking to develop an understanding of the Internet. Each method seeks to set the rules of engagement and has contributed to some of the confusion about the medium (Reynolds, 1998). The number of end-users or potential online customers has been difficult to define, as techniques for measuring the online market evolved from 'an inexact' art form (Nua Ltd, 1997) and have been only be indicative of a growing market of end-users. Until more reliable data are forthcoming, only vague predictions are available to speculate about the Internet's commercial potential (Whinston, 1997).

Accurate figures regarding the use of the Internet and the Web have varied widely depending upon their source. Estimates of the top 15 countries ranked by Internet usage at the end of 1998 are reproduced in Table 18.4. Information compiled by Nua Ltd (1997) reveal that at the end of 1996, for example, some 50 per cent of US

Table 18.4   *Most 'Wired' Countries in 1998*

Rank	Country	Weekly Internet users (millions)	Population 1998	Internet penetration (%)
1	Finland	1570000	5158372	30.43
2	Norway	1340000	4438547	30.19
3	Sweden	2580000	8911296	28.95
4	US	76500000	272639608	28.05
5	Australia	4360000	18783551	23.21
6	Canada	6490000	31006347	20.93
7	UK	8100000	58113439	13.93
8	Netherlands	1960000	15807641	12.39
9	Germany	7140000	82087361	8.69
10	Japan	9750000	126182077	7.72
11	Taiwan	1650000	22113250	7.46
12	Spain	1980000	39167744	5.05
13	France	2790000	58978172	4.73
14	Italy	2140000	56735130	3.77
15	China	1580000	1246871951	0.12

Sources: *Computer Industry Almanac* (1999); US Bureau of the Census, *International Data Base* (1999).

households owned a personal computer, whilst Dataquest estimated some 28 per cent of American consumers to be online, compared to 20 per cent and 13 per cent respectively in the UK (Dataquest, 1999).

However, global penetration of the Internet is very mixed. From examination of usage rates with reference to the population (Table 18.4), the US possesses the highest penetration per capita for Internet usage. Internet penetration within Europe remains unevenly distributed with the three small Nordic countries dominating the rankings. The penetration figures for Europe's three largest markets – the UK, Germany and France – languish between 25 and 15 percentage points behind US levels. It is this 'lag' to which retailers have historically alluded when deemphasising the importance of alternative channels on their strategic agendas, and which so concerns market analysts. However, Internet connectivity in Europe is growing at an annual rate of 47 per cent and is expected to reach 11 million households by 2003 (Gilbert, 1999). Strong growth comes mainly from smaller European markets such as Norway and Belgium, although some large markets such the UK and Germany also show significant development (see Figure 18.1). There is some evidence too of catching up from southern European countries such as Spain and Portugal.

However, as Reynolds (1998) anticipated, many retailers are still unable to make rational decisions in order to estimate or realise the online potential in their particular organisation and in their particular market. There are also far too many unsubstantiated assertions in the popular media which merely serve to confuse the issue. Although no-one can predict the future growth rate of the Web with certainty, few would argue that access to the Web will be one of the most significant media 'happenings' of the next decade. Clearly, a framework is needed to enable informed decisions to be made regarding the role of e-retailing by individual organisations (Hart *et al.*, 2000).

Figure 18.1   *Internet Penetration within Europe*

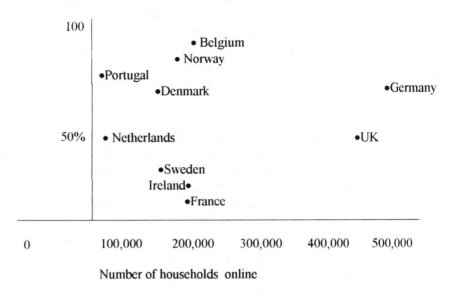

Market
Penetration %

Source: *European Retail Digest*, June 1999.

Exhibit 18.5   Shoppers are reluctant to shop via the Web

A mall on the Web, like an individual trader, has to struggle to make shoppers feel secure. Obviously, the threat of physical violence disappears when shopping from a keyboard, and a host of other annoyances from parking problems to bad weather also disappear, but it is clear that the vast majority of people are still very nervous about passing their credit card details over the Net. A study of UK Internet users by the Internet Research Company ⟨www.internetresearch.co.uk⟩ revealed that there is a strong reluctance to purchase online. However consumers will use the Net to gather information before going to the store to make the purchase. Women are generally more confident shoppers and, perhaps because they are more familiar with buying from catalogues than men, may be more likely to accept the idea of buying on the Net. This is particularly so for repeat purchases of goods of known brands and for low-cost items. On the other hand they tend to be less confident with the technology which increases their reluctance to shop.

Consumer demand for Internet access is a key factor that will ultimately drive widespread adoption of the Internet by retailers. Whether the consumer has access and how they use or perceive Internet shopping (see also Exhibit 18.5) will affect its success (Shirky, 1997). However, the Internet also places specific demands on end-users. Cognitive ability with the medium and its technology (Thurig *et al.*, 1995), as well as comprehension, information searching and sorting abilities (Alba *et al.*, 1997) may deter some consumer segments from switching to online shopping. An obvious parallel may be drawn between fixed and virtual stores, and various attempts have been made to apply store image theory (Spiller and Lohse, 1997) and retail patronage behaviour (Palmer, 1997). However, certain aspects of retailing theory do not transfer easily from a physical store to a virtual one. Hart *et al.* (2000) suggest that image and patronage dimensions that were once relevant to fixed-location stores may no longer be applicable to the virtual retail store. Thus a new set of image dimensions for the virtual store may need to be determined via future consumer research.

Physical barriers to consumers accessing e-commerce are found in its cost and technology. Access technology needs to be low-price, and create interfaces between software and hardware that are intuitive. High telephone costs remain a significant factor to mainstream adoption of the Internet. Speed of access will increase with the development of broadband services and the potential reappearance of subscription services. Broadband technologies are developing rapidly, and both mid- and broadband services will enable a wider range of content types to be adopted and provide access to high-quality streamed media. Integrated services digital network (ISDN) is already established, providing higher-speed access, and emerging delivery technology will see the appearance of XDSL, for high-speed data transfer over conventional lines and cable modems using cable TV networks as well. Cable modem technology should rapidly enable reasonable penetration levels in heavily cabled European markets such as the Benelux countries, France and Germany. In addition, asymmetric digital subscriber line (ADSL) technology, though expensive, is a competing development from telecom providers pushed by them in response to the offerings of the cable companies (Cornet, Milcent and Roussel, 2000).

The Internet as a New Retail Format

Consumer predispositions towards the new retail format created on the Internet may also constrain future growth. Within the UK, as elsewhere, growth of retail formats has been gradual as the physical infrastructure has been established, so providing the consumer time to adapt to the new methods of delivery. While Internet retailing could be interpreted to be at the innovation stage of the retail life-cycle (O'Keefe *et al.*, 1998), the rate of retailer penetration of the Internet as a new format may, in turn, affect the rate of adoption by consumers. This may signal the demise of other, older formats. As a consequence, those retailers with a strong and established brand presence, physical distribution relationships and capital investment in traditional formats may be less inclined towards rapid expansion into a non-store, electronic format (Ghosh, 1998).

New entrants to the retail sector may face fewer competitive barriers to entry and are thus better positioned adopt the new format. However, the opportunities and potential success factors for these new 'pure' e-retailers, and existing retailers extending into e-retailing, as 'bricks and clicks' operators continue to be questioned (Dawson, 2000). O'Keefe *et al.* (1998) suggested that smaller retail organisations are a category most likely to adopt the Internet due to their greater flexibility; limited resources and lack of scale, encouraging collective retailing via small business networks. Product and market differentiation or redefinition strategies can succeed for small businesses in highly specialised niches where higher investment and operating costs have caused cash-flow problems for less-focused online businesses.

While it appears that size of organisation may be a critical factor influencing retailer adoption of the Internet, initial US experience has indicated otherwise. A survey of top US retailers suggested that smaller companies were less likely to be online (Morganosky, 1997) than larger ones. This raises an issue of whether market concentration found in the physical retail environment may be replicated in the virtual market.

Shopping Activities on the Net

The type of shopping activity may further indicate the product groups most likely to succeed on the Internet. Early evidence from the US experience of Internet retailing demonstrated a preference for electronic and related products (Morganosky, 1997). Other surveys showed that in addition to PC peripherals, banking services, books and magazines accounted for 47 per cent of Internet sales in the USA (Pavitt, 1997), whereas grocery shopping was considered less compatible with Internet use. By 1998, personal computers (PCs), pornographic magazines, CDs and speciality products such as flowers made up over half of all online consumer revenues. Increasingly, convenience shopping and speciality goods as well as bargain hunting through auctions may offer varying attractions to online consumers.

Consumers seem to have an open mind about what they would buy on the Net. *The Economist's* (1999) survey shows that 75 per cent of people using the Internet who had not yet bought anything online would consider this medium, for making hotel reservations, paying for online subscriptions, and buying computer software, airline tickets, records, tapes, CDs and videos. Some key retail sectors are considered below:

Computers and Software

Some products find an excellent fit with online distribution: computer equipment, for example. Some large companies have been ordering PCs online for years using proprietary systems, but now the Internet has extended that convenience to the consumer market. Consequently, leading PC manufacturers such as Dell estimate their online sales approaching 10 per cent of their business (*The Economist*, 1999).

Books and Music

This market is no longer the exclusive preserve of Amazon.com now that America's two largest booksellers, Barnes & Noble and Borders, have gone online, along with such international competitors as Britain's Blackwells, BOL, and many other smaller companies (Reynolds, 2000). However, online sales in the music sector reached a mere £20 million in 1998, and industry-wide gross profits were just £200 000 (Gilbert, 1999). Music has been badly affected by downloading from free sites, which led to legal disputes over the copyright of the material. MCI, an American telephone company, closed its 1–800-Music-Now site after spending nearly £40 million promoting it in 1998 (Reynolds, 2000). Now legal protection for music copyright owners may contribute to the re-vitalisation of general music sites. However, as Firefly has shown with its Bignote site built around a thriving community of music fans, specialisation may provide longer-term opportunities.

Travel and Leisure

Travel agents are another group that has survived on exclusive access to information. By knowing their way around ticket prices, schedules and flight availability, they have been able to hold their own despite the airlines' efforts to sell straight to consumers and avoid paying the agents' 10 per cent commission. Evidence from *Verdict* (1999) shows that most travellers prefer using travel agents to calling every airline themselves or calculating how to work the flight booking services on commercial online services, especially since using an agent costs them no more.

However, by providing an easy-to-use direct link to consumers the Internet is giving the airlines an opportunity to erode the place of the middleman. They are doing this in two ways:

1 by selling seats on their own websites (see for example, EasyJet); and

2 by cutting the fees they pay to online travel agencies to 5 per cent on the ground that costs are far lower than in the physical world because customers find and book the flights themselves (see *The Economist*, 1999).

In spite of these opportunities for cost reduction, airlines may face an uphill struggle. Although top online travel sites such as Expedia sell more than $1 million of tickets a week, online sales still make up less than 1 per cent of total ticket sales (*Verdict*, 1999). The assumption is that the figure may gradually move upwards to about 1.5 per cent and future growth may depend on cost and convenience.

Emerging Areas: Car Retailing

The prospect of buying a car online seems unlikely but with online customers in the US reporting prices up to 10 per cent lower than in face to face negotiations at the dealers, the Internet presents an appealing opportunity (see Morganosky and Cude, 2000). The reason for the lower prices because it costs a dealer only a small amount of money to respond to a Net application, rather than hundreds of pounds to conventionally advertise and sell a car.

In 1998, for instance, two million of the approximately 15 million cars sold in America went to customers who set foot in the dealership only to pick up the car (*The Economist*, 1999). Chrysler, who put its Internet sales in 1998 at just 1.5 per cent of the total, reckons that in four years' time the figure will be 25 per cent (*Verdict*, 1999). Manufacturers in the UK and elsewhere in the world are likely to use this opportunity to bypass dealers to exert greater control over their distribution channels (Omar, 1998).

Some sectors seem to provide less immediate opportunities, and grocery retailers, for example, have only slowly expanded their online delivery services. However, high concentration and competition in the sector combined with static food sales and possible saturation of the market suggest that the major food multiples may perceive the Internet as an additional marketing channel.

However there is no point in selling online if the retailer only has ambitions to sell a few items and update the site once a year (*The Grocer*, 1998). The issue is whether this criticism applies to the retail industry in general or to more specific sectors of retailing. Given the flexibility of the Internet, at any one time retailers could be introducing websites and existing sites may be updated to develop a new offering. The dynamics of this medium thus cloud the true picture.

MARKETING AND COMMUNICATION ON THE INTERNET

In terms of communication, a website combines elements of direct selling and advertising. It can be designed to generate awareness, demonstrate the product and provide information without interactive involvement. It can play a cost-effective role in the communication mix (Exhibit 18.6). The site is also cost-effective in providing feedback on product and/or service performance. Nakayam (2000) has suggested that websites might typically be viewed by retailers as complementary to direct selling activities and as supplementary to retail advertising.

Marketing opportunities can be created in various ways, typically through sponsorship and advertising, including banner advertisements where premiums are paid for banners on other companies' websites. Other techniques include editorials and advertising, in which promotional spend can appear as an objective review. Distribution through a third-party site provides a further possibility. Publicity and promotion can be managed through search engines that have a major influence on directing people to a site, as well as via printed materials and multimedia advertising campaigns (Tiernan, 1999). The cost of advertising in 2000 has been estimated at $35.13 per 1000 eyeball rate for a banner (*ibid.*) and consequently the cost of 'eye-traffic' is emerging as a key issue in assessing the value of a site. Achieving brand awareness on the Internet and associated advertising expenditure by e-retailers has provided a significant contribution to their cash-flow problems.

It is likely that different retail organisations will have different retailing objectives for establishing and maintaining a Web presence. An organisation might wish to use the Web as a means of introducing itself and its new products to a potentially wide, international audience. Its objectives could be to create corporate and product aware-

---

Exhibit 18.6   Immediate advertising results from the Net

Internet advertising can be compared with a television advertisement which has to create such a strong impression that it has to be remembered days later when the consumer shops. Since online advertising offers the capacity for an immediate response, it challenges the observation that retailers know that only half of their advertising works, but not which half. On the Internet it is easy to know the half that worked. Indeed, in 1998 Procter & Gamble refused to pay for advertisements that people did not click on. Websites were outraged, but one way or another advertisers will demand more evidence of effectiveness in future.

According to KPMG (1999), total Internet advertising revenues in 1998 were just $267 million compared with $33 billion spent on television advertising in America alone, despite top Internet sites having television-sized audiences of a million viewers a day. America Online, with 8 million subscribers the biggest Internet service provider, has more viewers than any cable television network or newspaper, and all but the world's two most popular magazines.

ness, and inform the market. In this sense, the Web provides the retailer with the opportunity to expand the potential customer base at the global level at minimal expense. However, if the surfer knows of the retail organisation and its products, then an online dialogue can be used to propel this customer towards a purchase decision. Alternatively a retail organisation may be marketing well-known existing products, and its website objectives are to solicit feedback from current customers as well as informing new customers.

Thus websites can be used to move customers and prospects through successive phases of the buying process. They do this by first attracting visitors, making contact with interested visitors, qualifying/converting a portion of the interested contacts into interactive customers, and keeping these interactive customers engaged. Different tactical variables, both directly related to the website as well as to other elements of the promotional mix, will have a particular impact at different phases of this conversion process. Electronic links which link a particular site to and from other relevant and related sites, for example, may be critical in attracting visitors. However, once attracted, it may be the ease of interactivity on the site which will be critical to making these visitors continue towards a purchase.

In an era of network or relationship marketing and just-in-time (JIT) delivery, maintaining effective communications with customers (actual and potential), suppliers, agents and distributors is critically important to successful retailing. The Internet provides various tools for improving or supporting communications with different sections in the retailer's network – including e-mail, usenet and listserv groups, and video conferencing. As an increasing number of competitors form relationships with suppliers, partners, and agents supported by electronic communications, any retail organisation that is not connected faces being shut out of the network. Within a very short period of time a business card without an e-mail address has become as useful as one without a telephone number.

SITE LOCATION AND DESIGN

For many retailers with global marketing ambitions, a home page can provide an attractive low-cost method of sales promotion to global customers. The software available for designing good quality websites is becoming increasingly sophisticated to create eye-catching pages. The key to achieving the range of benefits illustrated in Figure 18.2 is a well-designed site, effectively marketed to ensure a large number of hits. This means that site location plays a highly strategic role in attracting customers. The most successful will be designed to encourage browsing, 'stickiness', the ability to extend the visit to the site and revisits.

Site Location

Web pages need to reside on a Web server, and a retailer has two options of either setting up its own Web server, or renting space on a commercial server. There are advantages and disadvantages to each approach other than costs, and the retail organisation has to choose the location of its server based on criteria such as the following:

Figure 18.2   *The Role of Website Design*

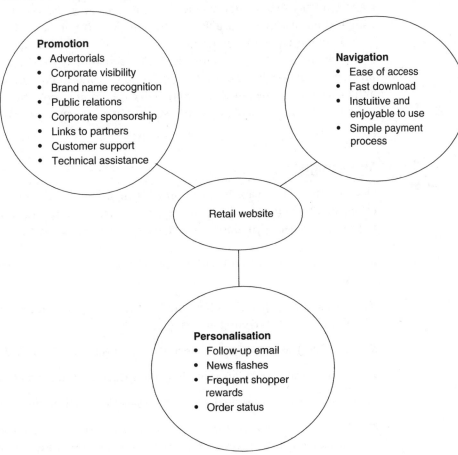

■ Bandwidth of the connection between the Net and the Web server;

■ Frequency and cost of updating – how frequently and at what cost can information be updated?

■ Usage statistics – what statistics on usage are provided by the specialist company?

■ Maintenance of ordering, feedback and e-mail forwarding services – does the specialist company maintain ordering, feedback and e-mail forwarding services for the subscribing company?

Individuals must have a starting point when clicking into the Internet, and such points are increasingly understood to be critical to competitive positioning. *Portals* provide a gateway for the online user into the Internet, and *hubs* are where many services and products are to be found. In effect there is a considerable degree of overlap between these locations as providers seek to gain market share to justify advertising revenues.

Yahoo is an example of a portal exploiting strong traffic flows by linking users to other sites. A further area of development in the consumer market, as it becomes more complex, has its origins in B2B activities. An Application Service Provider (ASP) can deliver online technical applications and back-up services that companies require, and saves them having to provide in house maintenance. In addition, e-brokers provide a search engine service for specific topics, and to find information, products and merchants. In the future, the contestable area for the consumer franchise between providers and suppliers of goods and services may become a key issue.

Site Design

Design of the home page is critical in creating interest – the equivalent of an interesting shopfront (Cope, 1996). In order to design and implement a successful retail website a number of common characteristics need to be considered:

- the site needs to be information-rich with regular updating to encourage repeat visits;

- clear navigation paths to allow smooth movement around services rather than just a place for marketing and sales;

- interactivity and responsiveness to user feedback must be provided;

- the site should be designed to allow the gathering of information about users;

- the site must be integrated with other marketing channels used by the company;

- the site should have its own budget and be supported by the whole organisation rather than being the responsibility of a small group of experts; and

- the site needs to be marketed properly in order to ensure high access.

Success may be achieved in various ways, including registering the site with all of the major online search engines; establishing reciprocal cross-linkages to other sites; and ensuring that the URL address is used in a retailer's correspondence.

PAYMENT AND DELIVERY SYSTEMS

McBride and Rogerson (1995) differentiate between two types of sales conducted on the Internet:

1 sales and distribution of information where the product being bought and sold can itself be transmitted over the Net; and

2 sales of products and services in which the Net provides the means of carrying out the transactions, while the products or services are delivered by other means.

A complete sales transaction can be processed automatically without human intervention and the sale can be charged to a customer's credit card or billing account.

Secure credit-card transactions are appropriate for higher value transactions, but for retailers of low-cost items such as magazines, online digital payments (ODP) will facilitate small-value micropayments through the Internet. Sales of information in particular will benefit from ODP systems where credit card costs to the online seller are prohibitively expensive. This will require IT companies and financial institutions to cooperate on standards for secure electronic transmissions (SET).

DigiCash, for example, has a software product that can be downloaded onto a user's machine. The software is free to users, and the company hopes to make money by licensing its banking software to financial institutions that want to offer banking on the Internet. To shop on the Net, consumers first draw digital e-cash from their Internet bank and then stores it on the hard disk. The cash is used when the seller's software prompts for payment. E-cash also has the advantage of being anonymous. Knorr (1999), for example, believes that the arrival of e-cash will have a significant impact on retail market activity. However, for it to be successful, there needs to be some clear ground rules about the standards associated with the implementation of e-cash; a universal protocol for electronic money is necessary.

While security remains an issue (Exhibit 18.7), some operators are still encouraging shoppers to place an order by electronic mail and then call a free-phone number to provide credit and shipping information to a personal shopper who creates the order. However, it is necessary to recognise that 'secure' is a relative term as cheques, cards and cash are regularly used in fraudulent ways in normal business transactions. Great variation also exists in the reliability and cost of packaging and delivery (Cornet *et al.*, 2000). Nevertheless in many markets, a large hurdle to the expansion of e-commerce is lack of confidence in online credit card transactions. Persistent financial

---

Exhibit 18.7 Security issues on the Net

Any computer-based system is vulnerable to external attack. As retailers move more of their core businesses and transactions to the net and become part of e-businesses, they become potentially vulnerable because the Net increases the number of entry points exponentially. Exposure may take a number of forms: apart from simple theft, financial documents may be altered and illicit transactions carried out in the retailer's name; the interception and abuse of credit card or banking information may compromise a customer; confidential documents may be made public or passed to competitors; copyrights and patents may be infringed; and above all incalculable damage may be done to the retailer's brand image and reputation.

Without adequate security technology, therefore, e-business rapidly becomes untenable. The first point of defence for most retailers is a gateway allowing safe external connections to internal applications. These gateways should stop outsiders without the right credentials from gaining unauthorised access. The other main ingredients of net security are 'encryption', and the 'authentication of identity' which uses a password to unlock the hash code in the form of a unique signature. These and the 'virtual private network' (VPNS) which offers a controlled pathway through the Net to other authorised users should help to increase confidence of retailers and consumers in using the Net.

fraud and e-commercial financial crises will discourage consumers from sending confidential information down a phone line.

Fulfilment

Internet retailing requires different order-entry and fulfilment systems from store-based retailing, and bears more similarity to mail order. Operational requirements include creating unique customer records for individual consumers, multiple shipping addresses, and splitting orders into multiple shipments to different recipients (Willmott, 2000). Online order parcel sizes are smaller but greater in number, and require many daily deliveries. The process of order fulfilment takes place from the time the order is placed through to its delivery to the customer. Many online retailers such as Amazon.com ship goods directly from their own warehouse, and as they seek to customise their service, offer individual delivery tracking options. Alternatively, retailers can use companies that operate warehousing systems and call centres, that deliver through carriers or the postal service or offer third-party logistics functions (see also Table 18.5).

Table 18.5   Fulfilment Options

Type of fulfilment	Method of distribution	Indicative products	Advantages	Disadvantages
Integrated	Use current retail distribution centre (DC)	Mail-order; clothing; big-ticket items	Lower cost of investment and faster implementation	Different methods required for store and online deliveries; inventory management systems
Dedicated	Dedicated DC	Books, CDs, electrical, food	Lower long-term costs; easier to manage; fast delivery	High initial investment; decreased flexibility and inventory management
Outsourced	Third-party DC	Start-up low volume; can work with other options	Lowest investment; minimises learning curve	Third-party selection; high operational costs; strategic risks
Supplier	Supplier/ manufacturer	Industrial products with longer lead times	Cost-effective if supplier can deliver in small quantities	Negotiating power shifts to supplier; quality and reliability control
Store	Retail store (pick from store stocks)	Some food retailers; electrical; useful option for returns	Investment and stock savings	Quality control and integration are barriers; store congestion
Flow-through	Current retail DC to retail store/pick up point	Electrical	Sell over Internet but customer picks up at store/other pick up point	Not yet proven

Source: adapted from Logistics Consulting Partners and the *Harvard Supply Chain Review.*

Other specialist fulfilment companies are developing a different model to compete on faster response through Internet searches for stock held by other parties, rather than holding stock in anticipation of demand.

The ability of online retailers to maintain these types of operations in the early years of operation has been questioned. Late deliveries reflect poor quality service by the e-retailer and reduce its reputation and undermine the loyalty of its customers. It is also a serious problem, since during 1999 it was reported that 20 per cent of online orders were delivered late. At the same time, customer delivery expectations are expected to rise; and with instant purchases now possible, customers expect increasingly rapid delivery of goods (see also Exhibit 18.8). BizRate.com reported that nearly 90 per cent of a sample of online buyers consider e-retailers' returns policies to be a determining factor in continuing to buy from that company.

In practice, a number of local administrative difficulties have been encountered

---

Exhibit 18.8   Ocado: a warehouse-based fulfilment system for online grocery sales

Ocado, an online supermarket shopping venture works in partnership with Waitrose on the product side, and Gist distribution for warehouse and picking operations. The company will supply Waitrose merchandise as its in-house own-label brand, plus other complementary goods. The company is 40% owned by the John Lewis Partnership who invested around £47 million in the project. This warehouse will initially be treated like any other Waitrose store: staff will forecast demand as orders increase, with most goods being delivered from Waitrose's Bracknell distribution centre (DC). Perishables will be supplied direct from manufacturers.

The company decided to launch its service from a temporary 6505 square metre site at Hemel Hempstead, some 30 miles north of London, in 2001 using the expertise of Gist, a well-established distribution company. This enabled them to learn about the market and adapt to it before launching into a large-scale, untried investment. The relationship is more than a simple third-party one, though, it is a joint development with staff from both companies working alongside each other. When a purpose-built distribution centre (DC) is completed at nearby Hatfield, both parties will continue the relationship. Later it's anticipated that more direct deliveries will be made to this site as a regional distribution centre. This DC will serve the south-east of England with a phased roll-out commencing with a localised marketing campaign in a targeted area. Waitrose did not want to invest in an expensive dedicated fulfilment centre until grocery home shopping proves viable. Working with Ocado provides a lower-risk route to new customers outside existing catchment areas. Waitrose has started out in its southern heartland partly due to expediency: the opportunities to develop large new DCs in the south is more difficult and time consuming than in the north, where the planning process can be faster. Future DCs will be developed to serve major centres of population, whilst smaller centres will be served by selection from Waitrose's own stores.

In terms of delivery to the customer, Ocado will retain control. The only physical point of contact for the customer with the company is the delivery; and this will be handled by customer service assistants rather than 'delivery men'.

Source: P. Ody (2001) 'E-fulfilment: Gearing up for Growth', *Retail Week Supplement*, November 2001, *New Technology in Retail*.

in European countries, such as a requirement for the sequential numbering of VAT receipts in Portugal and Greece. Compared to the USA, the growth rate of e-commerce may be constrained by the absence of a tax moratorium on e-commerce, and lack of integration in Europe leading to additional expense as cross-border shipping charges remain high and complex. The variety of cultures and languages in Europe is to some extent matched by the fragmentation of its e-commerce infrastructure.

THE FUTURE POTENTIAL OF THE INTERNET

Since businesses have started to use the Internet, both researchers and commentators have been active about its potential as a new retailing channel. According to Jones and Biasiotto (1999) the Internet's global connectivity opens up new avenues for business in a manner that traditional commercial channels cannot match. Yet concerns about lack of security, payment methods, access restrictions and various technological restrictions have limited the Internet's early succession over traditional marketing tools (see Hoffman and Novak, 1996). The early stages of development of e-retailing have posed questions about the identification of users and consumer groups, profitable products and services, consumer access and logistical support that require further attention from retailers (Dawson, 2000).

A number of academic studies including Reynolds (1998) and O'Keefe *et al.* (1998) have focused on the commercial adoption of the Internet, but they only provide limited contribution to the structure or scale of adoption. Moreover, previous research has tended to focus only on active websites or those sites having a high global/brand presence. Also, the majority of research has concentrated on the highest areas of activity in the USA, for example the top 100 US retailers (Morganosky, 1997), and there is as yet little evidence to suggest whether European or UK retailers as a sector will adopt the Internet to the same extent (KPMG, 1996). The studies may have identified that there are variations in how companies use the Internet for retailing, but ongoing research is required to identify the relationship between physical and virtual retail environments.

The rate of technological change cannot be overstated. Wireless application protocol (WAP) enables mobile phone users to access e-mail and Internet facilities, with the opportunity to create immediate personal access to information and services unconstrained by physical connectivity to phone lines, power cables, PCs or TV. As phones display a larger amount of information, and suppliers or retailers access satellite-based information to know where a customer is, marketing will be transformed to an even more personalised micro level offering a potential revolution of the next decade. Online retailers should seek to avoid overconcentration on the Internet and maintain a continuous environmental scan on technology to keep abreast of other technological platforms under development throughout the world.

Established store groups may not automatically adopt electronic commerce, and thus their approach to the new technology will impact on its future penetration. There is as much if not more to be learned from the brand leaders' take-up of the Internet, as there is to be learned from those currently involved.

SUMMARY

This chapter has defined non-store retailing as the selling of goods or services outside the confines of a retail facility. This form of retailing accounts for an increasing percentage of sales and includes personal sales methods such as in-home retailing and teleshopping, and non-personal sales methods such as automatic vending and mail-order retailing. Mail-order retailing also includes catalogue retailing aimed particularly at the poorer consumers in society. A growing form of non-store retailing is the use of the Internet to market and sell goods and services, and through this medium orders can be placed using a credit card via a home-based personal computer.

Overall, this chapter has argued that the Internet's low entry barriers permit retailers with limited capital to become efficient communicators at an early stage in their development. The consumer interface through site design and navigation will have to be balanced with the need to adapt to new technologies. The Internet is an efficient new medium for conducting retailing research, for example gaining feedback from customers, establishing online consumer panels, tracking individual customer behaviour and so forth.

The implications of selling tangible products over the Internet have been identified. The Internet, by connecting end-users and producers directly, will reduce the importance of traditional intermediaries such as agents and couriers in non-store retailing. To survive, intermediaries will need to begin offering a different range of services. Their value-added will no longer be principally in the physical distribution of goods but rather in the collection, collation, interpretation and dissemination of increasingly detailed retail information. The critical resource possessed by this new breed of 'cybermediary' will be information rather than inventory. The Net will become a powerful tool for supporting retailers' distribution networks, both internally and externally. A critical element in establishing confidence in online selling will be the need to critically evaluate appropriate fulfilment systems in the delivery of goods to the consumer.

Despite such developments, accurate figures regarding the use of the Internet and the World Wide Web are impossible to obtain. Estimates vary widely, largely depending on the method of measurement and different definitions of use. Although no-one can predict the future growth rate of the Web with certainty, few would argue that access to it will be one of the most significant media developments of the next decade. In the UK alone, digital television will widen potential access to the Web in every household. Consequently, a framework is needed to enable informed decisions to be made regarding the role of the Web in retailing within the individual retail organisations.

QUESTIONS

1   Retailing is conducted through a variety of outlets. Account for the rapid growth in non-store retailing in the UK.

2   Non-store retailing may involve personal selling, selling to the customer at home through television, computers and a variety of other methods. Evaluate and discuss the advantages and drawbacks of non-store retailing for confectionery retailers.

3   Mail-order retailing has a long history and traditionally consists of a printed catalogue from which customers select goods which are then delivered to the home either through the post or by couriers. Discuss how modern electronic retailing has changed mail-order retailing.

4   Briefly compare the strengths of mail-order retailing with store-based retailing. Which of these two methods of retailing would you recommend for a retailer selling computer software and why?

5   How has the arrival of digital television improved the operation of electronic home shopping?

6   What benefits are there for retailers selling their goods via electronic kiosks?

7   Define the term 'the Internet' and explain its competitive advantages for retailers using the Internet as a global communication tool.

8   Security issues on the Net are of concern to both retailers and consumers. Discuss what steps are being taken to eradicate Internet fraud.

9   What are the limitations of retailing via the Net?

10 The Internet is allowing every business to become part of a global network where all retailers are equally easy to reach. Comment on this statement citing current examples from the UK retail industry.

Case Study

Putting Tesco Online

Tesco describes itself as 'a world-class logistical, marketing and service enterprise that can respond to individual customer needs'. From its mission statement, it is clear that the company is one of the leading retailers in the UK food retailing market. With some 570 stores in the UK and a further 190 outlets in Europe, it is also a profitable retailer.

Tesco is a customer-oriented business that pushes the boundaries of supermarketing forwards. Amongst its marketing initiatives it became the first UK supermarket to make full use of loyalty cards to identify its customers more precisely. Indeed, its main competitor, after losing up to 10 per cent of its market share, was forced to catch-up in the loyalty-card business having previously rejected the concept. It is not surprising, that Tesco is just the kind of company to fully embrace the concepts of online and home shopping. The fact that Tesco is not part of any other online mall service is not a matter of arrogance, but because Tesco believes it can retail better than anyone else.

It was in 1996 that the first Tesco online store opened as a pilot scheme based on the catchment area of Osterley in West London. It grew to embrace five more stores around London and Leeds, and is still expanding.

Tesco began offering goods for home delivery from its Ealing supermarket in September 1996, just before the launch of the Internet store. The pilot allowed Clubcard members to use a traditional catalogue to prepare an order, which they then placed by phone or fax. This was rapidly expanded to include a CD. The installation of the CD on the shopper's computer allowed a shopping list to be prepared offline for submission to Tesco's Home Shopper service. Originally, the data link was achieved via CompuServe, but soon afterwards the power and accessibility of the Web was harnessed for the first Internet Superstore. Today, the two systems – the Internet Superstore and Tesco Home Shopper – run in parallel. Customers can either shop 'live' using the website, or draw up their shopping list offline and connect just to make the exchange of data. Either way, they can specify a timeslot and a day up to 28 days ahead when someone will be at home to receive the goods.

The deal for shoppers is about as reasonable as it could be. In order to gain access to the full 22 000 or so products in a live Internet Superstore, customers must live within a five-mile radius of the participating store. This restriction is an obvious matter of logistics; a fleet of refrigerated vans and transport timeslots mean that the service has to remain fairly local for efficient delivery. Wherever customers live, they can still browse through a representative Internet Superstore at ⟨www.tesco.co.uk⟩ where they will also find an online registration facility. If customers live in one of the postcode areas served by the superstores currently online, they will be able to sign up for the online shopping service and request a copy of the Tesco Home Shopper CD. Of course, anyone can shop online from anywhere in the world for a selection of gifts and special seasonal items such as Christmas Hampers that Tesco Direct can deliver to any mainland UK or Northern Ireland address. Customers do not have to be members of any Tesco shopping scheme offered at ⟨www.tesco.co.uk⟩. Unless consumers live in the catchment area of one of the participating stores, however, they would not be able to shop online or offline for a full range of Tesco stock items.

Online shopping, so far as Tesco is concerned, is just another route for customers to access the Tesco brand, but it also allows the company to use information that people volunteer and that they provide by actually shopping to personalise the experience. Online shopping is a logical extension to the Clubcard loyalty scheme, which helps an individual Tesco store to modify the range of items it stocks and the way it does business to reflect the requirements of the shoppers that use it. The data-gathering potential of customer loyalty cards (and in due course, the online customer-oriented database that will grow from online shopping habits) means that each store can adjust its range and approach to match the population it serves.

The Tesco philosophy is a move away from the 'one size fits all' approach to retailing. The Home Shopping and Internet Superstore concepts will, in due course, allow the company to try new ideas for physical stores online. By observing the ways that customers create, maintain and use shopping lists, Tesco may

(Continued)

gain insights into more effective ways to design physical and virtual stores. It is much cheaper and easier to amend a CD-ROM than it is to amend a store. Ideas can be tried out much more quickly online than they can be in a real superstore. Direct shopping is not yet big business for Tesco; tills in an average Tesco superstore can ring up around £1 million a week, whilst the entire Tesco Direct operation has yet to reach that turnover. Tesco is still learning about its customers and about the possibilities that online shopping could hold.

SEMINAR QUESTION FOR DISCUSSION

Shopping on the Internet described in the case study appears to be rudimentary. What do you think retailers like Tesco could do to improve the popularity of shopping on the Internet?

References

Alba, J., Lynch, J.C., Weitz, B., Janiszewski, C., Lutz, R., Sawyer, A. and Wood, S. (1997) 'Interactive Home Shopping Consumer, Retailer and Manufacturer Incentives to Participate in Electronic Marketplaces', *Journal of Marketing*, vol. 61, July, pp. 38–53.

Alexander, N. and Colgate, M. (2000) 'Retail Financial Services: Transaction to Relationship Marketing', *European Journal of Marketing*, vol. 34, no. 8, pp. 938–53.

Assadi, D. (1998) 'Internet Can Offer More Than a Quick Sale; Try Car-Shopping', *Marketing News*, vol. 32, no. 2, p. 9.

Benjamin, R. and Wigand, R. (1995) 'Electronic Market and Virtual Value Chains on the Information Superhighway', *Sloan Management Review*, vol. 36, no. 2, pp. 62–72.

Bruno, L. (1997) 'Working the Web', *Data Communications*, vol. 26, no. 5, pp. 7–9.

Cope, N. (1996) *Retail in the Digital Age* (London: Bowerdean).

Cornet, P., Milcent, P. and Roussel, P.-Y. (2000) From E-Commerce to Euro-commerce, *The McKinsey Quarterly*, Number 2: Europe, pp. 30–8.

Dataquest (1999) '*Gartner Group's Dataquest says 50 per cent of US households Have a Personal Computer*', http://garmer11.gartnerweb.com.

Dawson, J. (2000) 'Retailing at Century End: Some Challenges for Management and Research', *The International Review of Retail, Distribution and Consumer Research*, vol. 10, no. 2, pp. 119–48.

Economist (1999) 'Business and the Internet: the Net Imperative', *The Economist*, 26 June, pp. 5–44.

Dennahum, D. (1995) 'The Trouble with E-Cash', *Marketing Computer*, vol. 15, no. 4, pp. 25–7.

Ernst and Young (1999) *The Second Annual Ernst and Young Internet Shopping Study* (New York: Ernst & Young).

Fraser, J., Fraser, N. and McDonald, F. (2000) 'The Strategic Challenge of Electronic Commerce', *Supply Chain Management: An International Journal*, vol. 5, no. 1, pp. 7–14.

Ghosh, S. (1998) 'Making Business Sense of the Internet', *Harvard Business Review*, March–April, pp. 126–35.

Gilbert, D. (1999) *Retail Marketing Management* (Harlow: *Financial Times*/Prentice Hall).

Gray, M. (1995) 'Measuring the Growth of the Web', cited by R.F. Morgan in 'An Internet Marketing Framework for the Web', *Journal of Marketing Management*, vol. 12, pp. 757–75.

Hazel, D. (1996) 'Non Store Retail Comes Together with Chains', *Chain Store Age State of the Industry Supplement*, August, pp. 32A–3A.

Hamill, J. and Gregory, K. (1997) 'Internet Marketing in the Internationalisation of UK SMEs', *Journal of Marketing Management*, vol. 13, pp. 9–28.

Hart, C., Doherty, N. and Ellis-Chadwick, F. (2000) 'Retailer Adoption of the Internet: Implications For Retail Marketing', *European Journal of Marketing*, vol. 34, no. 8, pp. 954–74.

Hoffman, D.L. and Novak, T.P. (1996) 'Marketing in Hypermedia Computer-Mediated Environment: Conceptual Foundations', *Journal of Marketing*, July, pp. 26–39.

Jones, K. and Biasiotto, M. (1999) 'Internet Retailing: Current Hype or Future Reality?', *The International Journal of Retail Distribution & Consumer Research*, vol. 9, no. 1, pp. 69–79.

Knorr, E. (1999) 'Dawn of the Digital Market Place'. *Upside*, vol. 11, no. 11, pp. 124–37.

KPMG (1999) *Electronic Commerce*. Research Report (London: KPMG).

Lloyd, P. and Boyle, P. (1998) *Web-Weaving: Intranets, Extranets and Strategic Alliances*, (Oxford: Butterworth-Heinemann).

Lucas, G.H., Bush, R.P. and Gresham, L.G. (1994) *Retailing* (Boston, Mass.: Houghton Mifflin).

Matthews, V. (1997) *Companies Still Resist Electronic Age*, 13 October, *The Financial Times*. p. 17.

McBride, N. and Rogerson, S. (1995) 'The Effect of Global Information Systems On Business Vision and Values', Paper presented at the Bit '95, 5th Annual Conference, Manchester Metropolitan University.

McGoldrick, P.J. (1990) *Retail Marketing* (Maidenhead: McGraw-Hill).

Morgan, R.F. (1996), 'An Internet Marketing Framework for the World Wide Web', *Journal of Marketing*, vol. 12, pp. 757–75.

Mintel, Market Intelligence (1997) *Grocery Retail Marketing* (London: Mintel International Group).

Mintel (1999) *Online shopping* (London: Mintel International Group).

Morganosky, M.A. (1997) 'Retailing and the Internet: a Perspective on the Top 100 US Retailers', Research Note, *International Journal of Retail & Distribution Management*, vol. 25, no. 11, pp. 372–7.

Morganosky, M.A. and Cude, B.J. (2000) 'Consumer Response To Online Grocery Shopping', *International Journal of Retail & Distribution Management*, vol. 28, no. 1, pp. 17–26.

Mulhern, F.J. (1997) 'Retail Marketing: From Distribution To Integration', *International Journal of Research in Marketing*, vol. 14, pp. 103–24.

Nakayama, M. (2000) 'E-Commerce and Firm Bargaining Power Shift in Grocery Marketing Channels: A Case of Wholesalers' Structured Document Exchanges', *Journal of Information Technology*, vol. 15, pp. 195–210.

Nua Ltd. (1997) *How Many Online?* Nua Limited, vol. 1, no. 11, p. 4. http://www.nua.ie/surveys.

Ody, P. (2001) 'E-Fulfilment: Gearing up for Growth', *New Technology in Retail, Retail Week Supplement*, November.

O'Keefe, R.M., O'Connor, G. and Kung, H.J. (1998) 'Early Adopter of the Web as a Retail Medium: Small Company Winners and Losers', *European Journal of Marketing*, vol. 32, no. 7/8, pp. 629–43.

Omar, O.E. (1998) 'Franchising Agreements In New Car Retailing: An Empirical Investigation', *The Service Industries Journal*, vol. 18, no. 2, pp. 144–60.

Pavitt, D. (1997) 'Retailing and the Super Highway: the Future of the Electronic Home Shopping Industry', *International Journal of Retail & Distribution Management*, vol. 25, no.1, pp. 38–43.

Palmer, J.W. (1997) 'Electronic Commerce In Retailing: Differences Across Retail Formats', *The Information Society*, vol. 13, no. 1, pp. 75–91.

Dealer, P.C. (1999) 'To e or not to e', *PC Dealer*, 27 January.

Reynolds, J. (2000) 'Commerce: a Critical Review', *International Journal of Retail & Distribution Management*, vol. 28, no. 10, pp. 417–44.

Reynolds, J. (1998) 'Opportunities for Electronic Commerce: Electronic Retailing', *The European Retail Digest*, vol. 18, June, pp. 5–9.

Rowley, J. (1996) 'Retailing and Shopping On the Internet', *International Journal of Retail & Distribution Management*, vol. 24, no. 3, pp. 26–37.

Shirky, C. (1997) 'Attention Strategy Suggestion', *Communications of the ACM*, vol. 40, p. 24.

Spiller, P. and Lohse, G.L. (1997) 'A Classification of Internet Retail Stores', *International Journal of Electronic Commerce*, vol. 2, no. 2, pp. 29–56.

Tiernan, B. (1999) *E-tailing*, (Chicago: Dearborn Trade).

Thuring, M., Hannemann, J. and Haake, J.M. (1995) 'Hypermedia and Cognition: Designing For Comprehension', *Communications of the ACM*, vol. 38, 8 August.

Van Tassel, S. and Weitz, B.A. (1997) 'Interactive Home Shopping: All the Comforts of Home', *Direct Marketing*, vol. 59, no. 10, p. 40.

Verdict (1999) *Verdict on Electronic Shopping* (London: Verdict).

Whinston, A.B. (1997) 'Electronic Commerce: A Shift In Paradigm', *IEEE Internet Computing*, November/December, pp. 17–19.

Willmott, P. (2000) *Strategies for the Successful Business Practice, Financial Times* Retail and Consumer Special Report (London: *Financial Times*).

Index